The

Official®

DIRECTORY TO

U.S. FLEA MARKETS

The Official® DIRECTORY TO U.S. FLEA MARKETS

Edited by
Kitty Werner

SIXTH EDITION

House of Collectibles
The Ballantine Publishing Group • New York

Important Notice: The publisher assumes no responsibility for any losses incurred as a result of consulting this directory, or for any objects or services bought, sold, or traded at any flea market listed in this publication. All information relating to specific flea markets has been obtained from the owner, manager, or promoter to the best of the publisher's knowledge and is accepted in good faith.

Published by: House of Collectibles
The Ballantine Publishing Group
201 East 50th Street
New York, New York 10022

Distributed by The Ballantine Publishing Group, a division of Random House, Inc., New York, and simultaneously in Canada by Random House of Canada Limited, Toronto.

Cover design by Min Choi
Cover photo by George Kerrigan

Manufactured in the United States of America

ISSN: 1073-208X

ISBN: 0-676-60139-1

Sixth Edition: February 1998
10 9 8 7 6 5 4 3 2 1

CONTENTS

INTRODUCTION

When using the listing of markets at the end of each state keep in mind that I have not personally checked each of these markets and cannot guarantee that they exist after this book is printed. For the 1996 book, one market sent in their listing and closed within a month! If the market is new to you, please call first, just in case. Quite a few markets have closed—some burned down, others had their land bought from under them. And just as many have opened since the Fifth Edition.

I was in Spain for a winter week in January and there in gorgeous Segovia was a local flea market covering about two blocks in the old part of town—no doubt the same place vendors have been selling for centuries. My children and I traveled around Europe for two summers and found that even in tiny villages in Provence, France, the Saturday market in my grandfather's hometown was similiar to the markets in tiny villages in northern Germany, near my husband's hometown. So much of the new merchandise is exactly the same as that sold here in the States. What makes a market different are the people, the atmosphere and the local produce and crafts. When you find a market that suits you—frequent it. Get to know its dealers and learn about the old treasures. Most of the dealers I have met love to talk about their wares and the history behind them.

In writing this book, I have spoken to hundreds of strangers in as many cities and towns around this country. I learned a great deal about flea markets in general, and collected some terrific stories. In this edition, these stories have been added to their respective market's listing. If you have a market story to share, send it along to me; my address is in the back of this book.

What I have gleaned from many conversations with these markets are these two basic facts:

1. The majority of people running flea markets are working for the fun of it, for the "family" a really good market becomes, and because they are, quite simply, dedicated to antiques, collectibles, and the treasures that may show up.

2. Those markets opened up "just to make a buck" quickly fold. It takes a lot of work and dedication to make a market work and grow; and more important to the market's survival, a healthy, loyal following of customers and dealers.

In fact, some of these markets become so "family" to dealers and customers that weddings and other major events are planned around market days. In one case, an elderly gentleman who lived at "his other home" for twenty-some years of the market's existence, seated at a different dealer's booth each week, died just before the market re-opened in April. His funeral happened to fall on opening day. As a tribute, his funeral procession drove slowly through the market in a final salute.

Two dealers we heard about, again, both elderly, died at their booth spaces, one while laughing with his customers, the other, an 87-year-old who had vowed to die on "his space," did so after having driven completely around the market, pulling into his accustomed space, and getting out of his car.

Another market, newly opened, became "family" so fast, that when one dealer's husband required surgery, the other dealers kept her booth running for her so the family wouldn't go broke.

In a different vein, one market told me that one of their dealer spaces was lost/won (depending on your point of view) in a divorce settlement!

So, What Do You Sell?

When it came to asking about the merchandise sold, I asked the same question: What sort of things does your market sell? The answer is invariably the same: "You name it, we've got it!" Perhaps we should rename this book.

Occasionally I encountered a nagging question, "Was this market really a flea market?" Some markets are, of course, flea markets by any definition of the phrase. But still, what is the *real* definition of today's flea market? Do they sell only "old" items—a former qualification? Or is new merchandise fair game? Some markets have grown so large, they have turned themselves into "malls." Quite a few of the "really malls" were removed from the book. However, some one-person antique shops were included, kept or added, simply because I felt that if you are hunting for antiques and collectibles, and these places were highly recommended, then they should be here for you, the dealer, looking to buy treasures.

Recent changes in markets and what they sell stem from the simple fact that there are only a finite amount of antiques and collectibles available. Period. Chippendale only lived about 61 years and could only create a finite amount of furniture. The same goes for other "names" in the business. There were only so many baseball cards printed in any one year. That is what makes one card more valuable than another.

Trends make a difference too. Where sports cards were the rave several years ago, now it's something entirely different. Beany Babies are hot. Collectible Barbies are hot. Star Wars is hot. Cards aren't.

More Is Less, or Is It More?

As more markets open for business, the fewer dealers there are to go around. If there are, in fact, more dealers (as more go into the business), there is still a "finite" amount of goods to spread even more thinly.

As a result many markets have opened their stalls to "new merchandise." Still, the die-hards hold out and you can still find markets that only deal in antiques and collectibles. They are mentioned in the description of each market. But remember, to keep the market doors open, many markets that may have been more selective are now forced to sell the products the dealers have to sell—namely new merchandise.

Many markets proudly boast about their size—"we are the largest in northeast Whatchamacallit!" Or we are the "largest Wednesday and Thursday market anywhere!" Sometimes you have to take such claims with a grain of sand. I had one man tell me he had the largest market in the business—"125,000 square feet!" I'm afraid I shattered his ego when I told him about a market that opened in an abandoned Ford factory (since gone out of business). Using only two of the six floors, they owned close to 750,000 square feet altogether. In fact, there are many markets in the 100,000-square-foot category. And just as many smaller ones—they seem to have the richest stories to tell. Bigger isn't always better. It simply depends on what you are looking for: a good time, your "other" family, a specific object, just to waste a day, a carnival atmosphere, whatever.

Many of the markets listed have turned into semi-carnivals to attract buyers, or to provide a more interesting place to visit as a get-away with the family. One market owner bought the contents of a former amusement park and has all the gnomes and creatures scattered around his property, including a 30-foot totem pole and twin pink elephants. Colonial Valley in Pennsylvania had a 26-inch-tall steer named Clyde (who unfortunately died). Mt. Sterling, Kentucky, celebrates the Third Monday Court Days, started in 1870 when the circuit court judge would pass through the towns of Maysville, Flemingsburg, and then Mt. Sterling doing his business—including the sentencing of some offenders to hang! The entire town shuts down and celebrates for three days (with over 2,000 dealers). Maysville and Flemingsburg joined in the act around twenty years ago restarting their

"Court Days." Their markets start Sunday after church and continue until the dancing ends on Monday night.

This year I found the Texas Court Day markets and added most of them to my listings. Traditions die hard.

Educate Yourself

A neighbor of mine has found the greatest antique treasures in the local flea market, not noted for anything grand. She says you just have to look carefully and know what you are getting. Her house is furnished with numerous pieces of furniture, from chests and beds to baby highchairs, mostly culled from this one market. She has collected complete sets of china and silverware in five different patterns for each of her five children—all from flea markets.

A caution about being sure of what you want and knowing its value. There are numerous stories sprinkled throughout this book of surprise finds—the dealer who sold a frame for $75 only to hear later that the savvy buyer sold the old master in it for $250,000. And so on. Look carefully. You never know.

Do educate yourself if you are a serious buyer of antiques and collectibles. It obviously pays off.

FLEA MARKETS: THEN AND NOW

Look at the history and development of the phenomenon of flea markets as an alternative to *shopping*—that is, going to town and wandering from store to store. The term "flea market," a direct translation from the French phrase *marché aux puces*, has come to signify a specially designated occasion for the purpose of exchanging a wide variety of goods—anything from valuable antiques to backyard junk.

In France, where the term was coined, fleas were found to accompany old furniture and clothing drawn from attics or barns. Today, some flea markets in the United States maintain a curious tie to this tradition by demanding that all furniture be either fumigated or else banned from the sale area entirely.

The flea market in the United States, however, has taken on other European customs—customs found not only in France but throughout the Continent. One custom is Market Day, a regularly scheduled time when a portion of town, usually the main square, is closed off from traffic as farmers, itinerant tradesmen, butcher and bone-men, and other dealers sell their merchandise—anything from produce and clothing to fresh meats and kitchen appliances—to the people of the town and surrounding area. From early in the morning—6:00 AM, even earlier—to the middle of the afternoon, buyers and sellers get together in a particular place for the single purpose of striking bargains. In America, where so many ancestors came from rural Europe, small towns have since the first settlement conducted fairs, animal shows, and farmers' markets as means of distributing locally made products. For early farmers, tool makers, and other craftsmen, the local market could prove an effective gateway to the larger markets of other cities and large towns in the region, as buyers from nearby districts would frequently come looking for special deals. The flea market in the United States, then, is a bit of mongrel, with its Old World mixed parentage combined with that peculiarly American flair for the entrepreneurial. The giant flea markets like the Rose Bowl Flea Market in Pasadena, California, and the First Monday Trade Days in Canton, Texas, are cousins, and not very distant, to that of the antique shows and sales that keep popping up with increasing frequency throughout the country. The current popularity of flea markets large or small around urban centers as well as in the deep country, suggests that these events have become a welcome and permanent part of our day-to-day lives.

A flea market may range in size from just a few sellers standing on the side of a highway trying to clean out the unwanted contents of their homes to a complex, labyrinthine structure of dealers' booths sprawled out across acres of open space indoors or outdoors or both. In other words, a flea market is rather like beauty—it is all in the eye of the beholder.

Thinking another way, it is not so much a particular kind of event (whether it's a "swap meet" or an antique show and sale), but rather an alternative to shopping at the mall—a place where the individual buyer is on equal terms with the individual dealer, where no prices are fixed, and the fun comes in finding just what you want and buying or selling it for a price that feels right to *you*.

In this sixth edition, our directory has grown to include the listings for all the markets we could find in business directories. That should bring our total number of markets to thousands. Just be reminded that we didn't contact any of them listed in those sections. There simply isn't enough time and space to do so. We do include just about any conceivable flea market from the one-man market to the gigantic San Jose market in California. One of my criteria was courtesy and friendliness. I didn't find every market that exists. I've been told that between Kansas and Texas, there must be 4,000 flea markets alone! But I did find some obscure markets that are fund-raisers for churches, schools, and firehouses. According to the people who run these markets, you wouldn't believe the treasures that can be found there. One Texas market is simply the local residents' once-a-year garage sale. There is another market in Maryland doing the same thing.

There are some newer markets that have opened and grown tremendously since the fifth edition was published and we've added them too.

I think you'll find this a wonderful mix. There are plenty of places that cater to families, providing rides, perhaps video arcades, games, petting zoos, and whatever they can think of that children might enjoy.

You could plan a vacation around many of the markets listed here. Don't be shy. The people I have talked with represented a rich cross-section of America, doing this because they loved the people who came as dealers and those who came as visitors. They are having fun and they want to share it. It's up to you.

BUYING AND SELLING AT FLEA MARKETS

COMING PREPARED

When shopping at flea markets—and this is as true for the fine antique shows as for the markets that feature new merchandise—be sure to distinguish between the valuable and not so valuable articles offered for sale. Keep in mind that flea markets trade in all kinds of things, not only antiques and fine collectibles, but also brand new objects and some odds and ends that have ended up, somehow, in the dealer's hands. Notes promoter R. G. Canning of his early days organizing California's world-famous Pasadena Rose Bowl Flea Market and Swap Meet: "It was amazing to me that people would come to buy all that junk."

Of course, there is nothing wrong with your paying money for someone else's junk; it just depends on how much you value it. The flea market (in the most general sense of the term) is really not unlike a communal yard sale. It often provides the opportunity to sell things to other people who might be able to find a use for them—though they might be hard pressed to say what that is exactly at the moment of purchase.

But whether it is a fine antique show or something as manic as the Rose Bowl Swap Meet, it is advisable to subject *all* merchandise to careful scrutiny, and not just the antiques and collectibles, either. When shopping for "brand-name" items, be especially careful to check for fakes—some imitations are so masterful that they can fool a seasoned shopper. While imitations of brand-names appear to match the originals in craftsmanship and quality of materials, there have been many disappointed shoppers who have watched their "once-in-a-lifetime" bargains disintegrate in a matter of weeks or even days under normal use. Most flea markets monitor and insist that their dealers represent their goods honestly and use fair business practices. Several listed herein make known their policy of having their dealers not only stand behind their merchandise, but also offer refunds if the merchandise fails to please. This serves the double purpose of protecting both the buyer and the reputation of the market. Be sure to report any unfair or dishonest practices to the owner or operator of the market where this occurs. It is always best to be an alert and educated shopper.

KNOWING WHEN TO HAGGLE

At flea markets, as with just about any kind of trade, a deal is made when both the seller and the buyer think they are getting a bargain.

Put a value on an item as soon as you can and stick to it, as best you can. Changing your mind in the middle of a sale is a sign of weakness and uncertainty—one that a hardened seller will be quick to take advantage of. The more sure you are in your initial assessments, the easier and more pleasant your overall shopping will be. And when you encounter an object that is not marked with a price, don't suggest one, but rather prompt the seller to give you one. After all, it is the obligation of the seller to have a price to quote for any item he sells.

And don't forget that a main activity at the flea market isn't so much shopping as bargaining. In other words, don't automatically assume that the first price you hear is final, whether offered by voice or by a price tag. In fact, you have a right as a potential buyer to ask for a "last price" before you make up your mind on an item. (Remember, though, that you can only ask for a last price once.) You are not necessarily being rude by passing up an object after hearing the final offer, so long as you are polite in your refusal and thank the seller for his/her offer.

Don't ever let a seller use intimidation to force you to buy an object. You alone can know whether you want an object and, if so, how much it is worth to you.

Carry lots of cash, best of all in small denominations. As a general rule, always be working toward a deal in your negotiations with flea market salespeople. After all, their business is to sell, not to talk. Do not ask for a price on an item unless you are genuinely interested.

If you want to haggle, be careful how you do it. Part of the trick is in knowing real value, of course. Even if something is already priced low, a deft haggler takes the position that it can be driven down further. If he's going to make an offer he'll make a considerably lower one, representing maybe 50 percent of the asking price or even less, figuring that the end result is likely to be a compromise.

The wrong way to ask for a discount is by deriding the merchandise or the price, by suggesting that the dealer does not know his business, or by doing anything which could trigger a negative reaction. For example, never say "The shop down the street is selling one just like this for $20 less." Or, worse, "You don't really expect to get $75 for this, do you?"

Remember that the sellers have heard every possible pitch for discounts. They hear them every day, the same ones over and over. After just a short time in business they get thoroughly turned off by most types of discount-seeking approaches, and by most of the typical "I-want-a-discount" customers.

The majority of such customers act as if the dealer owes them a favor. You need to be a little original in trying to obtain a discount and, above all, courteous. Be inventive, use your imagination, and, most important, make a good impression. As they say in show biz, always leave 'em laughing. You may want to return some day, and you will want to be welcome next time.

SELLING AT FLEA MARKETS

First of all, decide which markets you want to participate in. There may be several nearby. A beginner is apt to make his choice based on the wrong considerations, thinking in terms of which show offers the best rate on space, or how he can save $1.50 on gas by selling close to home. It's really useless to give much thought to these points. The important thing is, at which flea market are you likely to do the most selling? Visit different markets as a browser; look at what is going on. How many dealers are present? Are nearly all the spaces taken, or are the grounds half empty? Unless the flea market is a new one, or in some cases the season is winding down, empty ground space indicates an unsuccessful market. What are the sellers offering? What percentage of the sellers are offering collectors' items? If you're interested in collectibles, for example, it is unwise to take a space at a show where collectibles are seldom sold.

After deciding on the flea market at which to sell, make arrangements for a space well in advance. Talk to the manager and find out about the rules and regulations. They are more or less the same from one show to another but there could be some differences. Every show has restrictions on what can and cannot be sold. With collectibles, you are not likely to run afoul of any taboos, except with firearms. Most flea markets do not permit the sale of firearms, antique or modern. Knives are almost always okay, except switchblades—some states have laws against them. Markets listed as "family" markets generally don't allow pornography either.

Mostly you'll want to find out what you will be getting for your rental money. Does the management provide a table? What is the exact size of the space you'll get? Will you be required to collect sales tax? Is this show held rain or shine? If the show is canceled because of bad weather, do you get a refund or a raincheck for the next show?

Put some thought into what you are going to take to the show. It's always better to have a variety of merchandise than to go heavy on just a few kinds of items. Large items such as furniture will cut down your exhibit space. If you are going to show small things of moderate or high value, such as jewelry or scarce coins, try to get a display box with a glass top and a lock. This will reduce the risk of theft. Clean up merchandise before packing it off to the show. This does not mean an indiscriminate scrubbing that could lessen the value and desirability of an antique, but dusting and (where appropriate) polishing. It does not enhance sales value when items have a just-out-of-the-dustbin appearance. Try to arrange everything in a way that will make browsing as easy as possible. If you are selling magazines, stand them upright in a carton. That way customers can flip through them with a minimum of fuss. This will also help to keep the covers from tearing, which is sure to happen if they are just piled together in a heap. When selling magazines of high value, or old comic books, slip them into protective Mylar bags. Scarce coins should be displayed in 2" × 2" holders. Some items are, of course, more of a headache to display than others: with glassware and china you run the risk of breakage not only as a result of clumsy browsers but strong gusts of wind. If you are displaying a lot of breakables, you can take the precaution of making certain that your table is well anchored. One way of anchoring a table is by sinking the leg tips two or three inches into the ground, if this is feasible. Another is to place heavy stones or bricks on top for ballast. In any event, keep breakables toward the center of the table if you can, where they are not as likely to be swept away by an errant arm or sleeve.

Figure out how much you want to get for each item before the show whether or not you are going to use price tags. Don't wait until somebody asks the price before you start thinking about it. Most flea market exhibitors mark prices on their merchandise, and this is probably the best course to follow, simply because many browsers just won't bother to ask the price, even if they are mildly interested. Of course the marked price need not necessarily be the actual sum for which you would sell the item; you can leave yourself some leeway for bargaining, and it is usually a good idea to do this. But don't set your marked prices too much higher than what you would be willing to accept.

PERIODICALS OF INTEREST

Following is a selective list of periodicals with good coverage of flea markets. The approximate geographical scope of each publication is listed in parentheses after its name. The publications listed are all produced in tabloid newspaper format. This list, though far from complete, should help the reader find the most up-to-date listings for some of the many flea markets that, due to space limitations or our own oversight, have regrettably been omitted from this guide.

Antique Review (Midwest). PO Box 538, Worthington OH 43085-0538. Tel: (614) 885-9757. Monthly. Subscriptions are $20 per year.

Antique Trader Weekly, The (Midwest). PO Box 1050, Dubuque IA 52004-1050. Tel: (319) 588-2073. Weekly. Subscriptions are $35 per year.

Antique Week (Two editions: Mid-Atlantic and Mid-Central). PO Box 90, Knightstown IN 46148-0090. Tel: (765) 345-5133. Weekly. Subscriptions are $25.45 per year Mid-Atlantic Edition; $28.45 per year Mid-Central Edition; and $51.20 for both; includes Antique Shop Guide issue.

Antiques & Auction News, Joel Sater's (Pennsylvania/Northeastern U.S.). PO Box 500, Mount Joy PA 17552-0500. Tel: (717) 653-9797. Weekly. Subscriptions are $17.50 per year, third class; $40 for 6 months or $70 per year, first class mail.

Antiques & Collectibles (New York City/Long Island, NY). PO Box 33, Westbury NY 11590-0033. Tel: (516) 334-9650. Monthly. Subscriptions are $18 per year.

Antiques & The Arts Weekly (basically New England/Northeastern U.S.). c/o The Newtown Bee, 5 Churchill Rd, Newtown CT 06470. Tel: (203) 426-8036. Weekly. Subscriptions are $52 per year.

Collector's Journal (Midwest). PO Box 601, Vinton IA 52349-0601. Tel: 1-800-472-4006. Weekly (except last two weeks in December and first week in January). Subscriptions are $26.95 per year. Email: antiquescj@aol.com.

Collectors Mart. 700 E State St, Iola WI 54990-0001. Tel: 1-800-258-0929. Bi-monthly. Subscriptions are $23.95 a year.

Collectors News (National). PO Box 156, Grundy Center IA 50638-0156. Tel: 1-800-352-8039. Monthly. Subscriptions are regularly $28 per year. Email: collectors@collectors-news.com. Web: http://collectors-news.com.

Hudson Valley Antiquer, The, and *Western CT/Western MA Antiquer*. (As the company is moving to a new town, we were asked to remove the address and phone number as they didn't know them as press time.) Distributed free at markets, antique shops and auctions. If you need the address, it will be in the newspaper.

Maine Antiques Digest (New England). PO Box 1429, Waldoboro ME 04572-1429. Tel: 1-800-752-8521. Monthly. Subscriptions are $37 per year, second class; $63 for two years, second class; $69 per year, first class.

Mid-Atlantic Antiques Magazine (Mid-Atlantic States). PO Box 908, Henderson NC 27536-0908. Tel: (919) 492-4001. Monthly. Subscriptions are $18 per year or $27 for two years.

New England Antiques Journal. 4 Church St, Ware MA 01082. Tel: (413) 967-3505. Monthly. Subscriptions are $12 per year or $20 for two years.

New York Antique Almanac, The (New York State). PO Box 2400, New York NY 10021-2400. Tel: (212) 988-2700. Published 9 times per year, including three bi-monthly issues. Subscriptions are $10 per year or $18 for two years.

New York–Pennsylvania Collector, The (Eastern U.S. and Canada). PO Drawer C, Fishers NY 14453. Tel: (716) 424-2880. Published 11 times per year. Subscriptions are $21 per year, $36 for two years, $48 for three years; US$31 for Canadian subscriptions for one year, US$54 for two years. Email: wolfepub@frontiernet.net.

Renninger's Antique Guide (Eastern U.S.). PO Box 495, Lafayette Hill PA 19444-0495. Tel: (610) 828-4614. Bi-weekly. Subscriptions are $15 a year for 25 issues or $28 for two years.

Today's Collector. 700 E State St, Iola WI 54990-0001. Tel: 1-800-258-0929. Monthly. Subscriptions are $21.95 a year.

Treasure Chest. PO Box 245, N Scituate RI 02857-0245. (401) 647-0050. Monthly. Subscriptions are $25 a year, first class.

The Upper Canadian. PO Box 653, Smiths Falls, Ontario Canada K7A 4T6. Tel: (613) 283-1168. Bi-monthly. Subscriptions are C$26 (US$27) for one year, C$46 (US$48) for two years.

HOW TO USE THIS BOOK

The flea markets listed in this book vary from those having fewer than 5 dealers to more than 2,000 dealers in some cases. The markets are listed alphabetically by state, and by town within each state. Each listing is broken down into the following subheadings:

DATES: Market days are listed here, including specific dates for 1998 where applicable. Rain dates are noted where applicable.

TIMES: Hours during which the flea markets are held are listed.

ADMISSION: If there is a cost to enter a market, the fee will be listed. Information about the availability and cost of parking is also presented.

LOCATION: A street address for the market is supplied where available; brief directions are provided for those traveling from out of town by car.

DESCRIPTION: This section discusses the size of the market, its age, the types of merchandise available, whether food is served on the premises, and any other interesting facts pertaining to its operation. All markets listed have toilet facilities on the premises or nearby, unless otherwise noted.

DEALER RATES: This section provides the most complete information available at press time regarding costs of selling space at the market, and whether advance reservations are required.

CONTACT: Complete mailing address and telephone number of the market operator are supplied wherever possible for dealer or shopper inquiries.

The Official Directory to U.S. Flea Markets has been designed to provide essential information about flea markets across the country selected for variety of merchandise, number of dealers attending, or other information of interest to the bargain hunter. The at-a-glance format previously outlined aids in making this guide the easiest as well as the most up-to-date reference available on the subject.

IMPORTANT NOTICE:

While the editors have made every effort to obtain the most exhaustive and accurate information available on a selection of flea markets from coast to coast in the continental United States, the reader is advised that in a work of this scope, inaccuracies may occur. House of Collectibles assumes no responsibility for any misprints or other errors found in this directory; all show dates, admission fees, dealer rates, etc. listed herein are subject to change at any time without notice. It is recommended that users of this directory call ahead or consult local sources whenever possible when planning a visit to a flea market.

FLEA MARKET LISTINGS

ALABAMA

ATTALLA

Mountain Top Flea Market

DATES: Every Sunday, year round. Rain or shine.
TIMES: 5:00 AM–dark.
ADMISSION: Free. Parking is free.
LOCATION: 11301 US Hwy 278 West, 6 miles west of Attalla. Hwy 278 W at 101 mile marker.
DESCRIPTION: Located on a mountain top on 96 acres, this mostly outdoor flea market first started in 1971 and currently consists of approximately 1,000 dealers selling everything from antiques and collectibles to new merchandise (jewelry, clothing, shoes, tools, furniture), from handcrafted items from three states to fresh produce from local farmers. They describe themselves as "Alabama's longest market with 2.6 miles of shopping." They average over 40,000 buyers every Sunday! Twelve snack bars are on the premises. Restrooms with handicap facilities are available.
DEALER RATES: $7 per 10' × 22' space outside per day, $10 for 10' × 10' booth inside (very limited inside space). Shed tops for rent at $4 per day. Call the toll-free number for the latest information. Overnight camping with showers and restrooms is available.
CONTACT: Janie Terrell, Mountain Top Flea Market, 11301 US Hwy 278 W, Attalla AL 35954. Tel: 1-800-535-2286.

BESSEMER

Bessemer Flea Market

DATES: Every Friday, Saturday, and Sunday, rain or shine.
TIMES: 8:00 AM–5:00 PM.
ADMISSION: Free. Parking is also free.
LOCATION: From Birmingham, take I-59 south to Bessemer Exit 112. Turn left under freeway, to Hwy 11, turn right and go 5 blocks to market on left.
DESCRIPTION: Started in 1980, this indoor/outdoor market accommodates approximately 600 dealers on 16 acres. There are as many as 10,000-15,000 people attending these shows. A variety of goods from antiques to new merchandise can be found. A snack bar serves a variety of concession food. Restrooms are available.

DEALER RATES: $6–$11 per day, depending on size. Weekend rates are $16–$33 per space. Prepayment is required to reserve indoor space, outside is always available. There are overnight parking and shower facilities for traveling dealers.
CONTACT: Bessemer Flea Market, 1013 8th Ave N, Bessemer AL 35020. Tel: (205) 425-8510.

BIRMINGHAM

The Birmingham Fairgrounds Flea Market

DATES: First weekend of every month, year round, plus the second and third weekends in December.
TIMES: Friday, 3:00 PM–9:00 PM. Saturday and Sundays, 9:00 AM–6:00 PM.
ADMISSION: Free. Parking is free.
LOCATION: Alabama State Fairgrounds. Exit 120 off I-20/59, follow the signs to the Alabama State Fair Complex.
DESCRIPTION: Operating under its current management for 10 years, this market has 600 dealer spaces, mostly indoors. Billed as "Alabama's Largest Indoor Flea Market." Antiques; collectibles; furniture; oriental rugs; gold, silver, vintage and costume jewelry; gems; sterling silverware; glassware; vintage clothing; new clothing and accessories; purses, prints and framed art; gifts; ceramics; fishing gear; electronic equipment; golf clubs and accessories; automotive accessories; dolls; plants; tools; leather; toys; crafts; phones; make-up; bedding; coins; sport cards; comics; knives; books; CD's; cassettes; records; lamps; jewelry repair; crystal restoration; flowers; and "you name it!" There are concession stands and restrooms on the premises, all handicapped accessible.
DEALER RATES: $45–$60 per 10' × 10' indoor booth, per weekend; $25 for a "two-parking-space" size area outdoors. The fairgrounds provide camping facilities for a fee.
CONTACT: Cindy, THE Flea Market, 621 Lorna Sq, Birmingham AL 35216. Tel: 1-800-3-MARKET (1-800-362-7538) or 205-822-3348.

Jefferson County Farmer's Market

DATES: Daily. Rain or shine.
TIMES: 8:00 AM–5:00 PM.
ADMISSION: Free. Parking is also free.
LOCATION: 342 Finley Ave West.

DESCRIPTION: This market is held in a 100' × 200' building and on an acre lot outside. There is an average of 50 to 150 "flea" dealers selling a variety of collectible items, including loads of fresh produce (from local farmers in season) and fresh chickens from their "chicken house." There are snacks and restrooms available on the premises.
DEALER RATES: $7 per space inside; $4.50 per space outside. Reservations are not required.
CONTACT: Jefferson County Farmer's Market, 342 Finley Ave W, Birmingham AL 35204. Tel: (205) 251-8737.

COLLINSVILLE

Collinsville Trade Day

DATES: Every Saturday. Rain or shine.
TIMES: 4:30 AM–2:30 PM.
ADMISSION: Free. $.50 for parking.
LOCATION: Hwy 11 South.
DESCRIPTION: Since 1955, this market averages about 1,000 vendors selling antiques, collectibles, books, jewelry, used and new clothing, tools, stamps, cookware, toys, fresh produce, and new merchandise. Up on Coon Dog Hill livestock is traded and sold. There are 15 concessions and snack bars to accommodate the hungry. Restrooms are available.
DEALER RATES: $8 for covered space, $5 for open space. Reservations are suggested.
CONTACT: Charles Cook, PO Box 256, Collinsville AL 35961-0256. Tel: (205) 524-2536.

CULLMAN

Cullman Flea Market

DATES: Every Saturday and Sunday.
TIMES: 8:00 AM–5:00 PM.
ADMISSION: Free. Parking is also free.
LOCATION: 415 Lincoln Ave Southwest. Next to I-65, on US Rt 278 at Exit 308.
DESCRIPTION: This market opened in May 1989. Located on 40 acres of land with nine acres just for parking, this market has 300 dealer spaces indoors and more space outdoors. Their dealers sell a variety of antiques, collectibles, handmade and craft items, tools, hardware, jewelry, woodwork, handbags, glassware, baseball cards, coins, fresh produce, cheese

and dairy products and new merchandise. Three concession stands with seating areas provide food to hungry shoppers. Clean restrooms with handicapped facilities are on the premises. They have added two antique buildings since 1994, open Thursday through Monday. Also on the premises is Country Village, a collection of speciality shops built of old barnboard, selling mostly antiques.
DEALER RATES: \$20 per 9' × 10' booth for two days; \$30 per 10' × 10' booth for two days. Reservations are required.
CONTACT: Frances Kilgo, Cullman Flea Market, PO Box 921, Cullman AL 35056. Tel: (205) 739-0910. Fax: (205) 739-5352.

DOTHAN

Sadie's Flea Market

DATES: Friday, Saturday and Sunday, year round.
TIMES: 8:00 AM–5:00 PM.
ADMISSION: Free. Parking is free.
LOCATION: On Rt 231 South, 5 miles south of Ross-Clark Circle in Dothan. From Rt 109, turn left on 231, market is a few hundred yards down the road.
DESCRIPTION: Open since May 1989, this market, located on 50 acres, has 300 booths with 60 permanent dealers, but many times is full to capacity. Dealers sell a large variety of everything including antiques, collectibles, crafts, produce, new and used merchandise—"real flea market stuff." A large Peanut Festival is held in the area in late October through early November. There are many antique car shows held in the area throughout the year. One large snack bar quells hunger, and two large handicapped-accessible restrooms are on the premises. There is a small RV park as part of the market.

A local ultralight plane club has frequent fly-ins attracting much local attention. Occasionally, a sponsored local gospel group or a country band will perform here.
DEALER RATES: Indoors: \$6 per day for a 10' × 10' booth; outside: \$3 per day for a 4' × 8' table. Reservations are preferred.
CONTACT: Sadie, Sadie's Flea Market, 7990 US 231 S, Dothan AL 36301. Tel: (334) 677-5138.

FOLEY

Foley Indoor Flea Market

DATES: Saturday and Sunday.
TIMES: 9:00 AM–5:00 PM.
ADMISSION: Free. Parking is free.
LOCATION: 14809 Hwy 59, 1½ miles south of Summerdale, 3 miles north of Hwy 98 on Hwy 59.
DESCRIPTION: This market opened in July 1997 and is quickly growing, filling its 197 indoor booths, and because the dealers wanted it, they added outdoor space for yard sales. The 45,000-square-foot air-conditioned/heated building sits on 16 acres. There are 10 dealers who specialize in antiques and collectibles. The rest sell plants, coffee, ceramics, wood crafts, collectibles, garage sale drag-ins, whatever comes along. TJ's offers food, including barbecue, during market hours.
DEALER RATES: $40 per weekend inside space, $10 and up per day for a table under awnings. Reservations are required. There are RV setups for the vendors.
CONTACT: Foley Flea Market, PO Box 838, Foley AL 36536. Tel: (334) 943-6349.

GUNTERSVILLE

All American Trade Day Flea Market

DATES: Every Saturday and Sunday, rain or shine.
TIMES: 8:00 AM–4:00 PM.
ADMISSION: Free. Parking is available and free.
LOCATION: 11190 US Hwy 431. Along Hwy 431 South, between Albertsville and Guntersville. Located just minutes from Boaz Outlets and Lake Guntersville.
DESCRIPTION: Established in 1989, this indoor/outdoor market on 30 prime acres is now under new management struggling to bring it back to its previous glory. There is an average of 150 dealers indoors and outdoors selling a variety of antiques and collectibles, "whatever you are looking for"—old, new, or used. As dealers and buyers see the job the new owners are doing, they are coming back. So much so that the owners have to keep adding space. Good job! Clean restrooms are available.
DEALER RATES: $8 per 8' × 10' space under roof perimeter daily; $5 per day for a 10' × 12' booth outside under sheds. There is 24-hour security, electric at all booths, and vendors can park at their space. Reservations are not required.

CONTACT: Margaret Parks, All American Trade Day, 11190 US Hwy 431, Guntersville AL 35976. Tel: (205) 891-2790.

HARPERSVILLE

Dixie Land Flea & Farmers Market

DATES: Friday, Saturday and Sunday, year round.
TIMES: 10:00 AM-4:00 PM.
ADMISSION: Free. Parking is also free.
LOCATION: I-280 East to Hwy 25 South, Exit at Harpersville about 4 miles south of Harpersville. On State Rd 25 between Harpersville and Wilsonville.
DESCRIPTION: Opened in 1986 on 70 acres of land, this market has 400 booths inside a 70,000-square-foot building and acres of outside booths selling antiques, furniture, arts and crafts, jewelry, baseball cards, toys, evening gowns, fruits and vegetables, and plenty of new and used merchandise. Friday is Garage Sale Day with special rates for outside booths. Three hundred of the dealers are permanent and the market advertises heavily in newspapers, on radio and television and hosts "live remotes" for on-air promotions. They have "everything and anything" in this country flea market. Huge deer and wild turkeys roam around this market "driving hunters crazy" during the appropriate seasons. This is a clean, well-run, friendly market. There is entertainment to keep the children busy. Plenty of food is available on the premises supplied by four restaurants, an ice cream parlor, and a barbeque pit. There are clean restrooms with handicapped facilities. When you pass through, say "Hi" to Jim for me! (Ask him about his special olive oil!)
DEALER RATES: $8 per day includes table, plus electricity. There are a few outside shed booths at $6 per day. Open outside space is $5 per day. Campers can camp and hookup for $3 per day. There is full-time security, showers for dealers, and special handicapped facilities. Each booth has its own entrance with parking behind it.
CONTACT: James Galantis, Dixie Land Flea Market, 3000 Hwy 25 S, Harpersville AL 35078. Tel: (205) 672-2022.

JASPER

Kelly's Flea Market

DATES: Wednesday, Saturday and Sunday, year round, and the occasional holiday Monday.

TIMES: Sunup on Saturday to sundown on Sunday, really. Wednesday 7:00 AM–1:00 PM.
ADMISSION: Free. Parking is free.
LOCATION: Hwy 78. Just 3 miles east of the city limits of Jasper, 6 miles from the city center or 5 NW of Birmingham on US 78.
DESCRIPTION: Opened in April 1978, this outdoor market has 40 booths outside and under sheds with dealers selling antiques, produce, farm and home needs—described as "yard sale heaven." It is a "very laid-back, friendly, popular, family market." The market started when June wanted to stay home with her small child, quit work and had a yard sale at Mom's. Mrs. Kelly was so friendly that soon others joined her. No problem, it still grew!
DEALER RATES: $4 in the shed with electric, $2 for a table. If you want to reserve, do so, but if you don't grab your spot by 7:00 AM, it will be gone! There are others waiting to use it.
CONTACT: Ray and June Fowler, 10016 Hwy 78, Jasper AL 35504. Tel: (205) 483-6045.

KILLEN

Uncle Charlie's Flea Market

DATES: Every Saturday and Sunday.
TIMES: 9:00 AM–5:00 PM.
ADMISSION: Free. Ample free parking is available.
LOCATION: On Hwy 72 West, 5 miles east of Florence, in the Killen area.
DESCRIPTION: This indoor market started in 1982 and accommodates approximately 400 dealers. They exhibit a wide variety of items including antiques, collectibles, arts and crafts, new merchandise and fresh produce. For your convenience, there are food and restrooms, with handicapped facilities, available on the premises.
DEALER RATES: $25 for 10' × 10' space per weekend. Reservations are required.
CONTACT: Tom Mabry, PO Box 190, Killen AL 35645. Day of show call or fax (205) 757-1771. Or call 1-800-542-2848.

MOBILE

Flea Market Mobile

DATES: Saturday and Sunday, year round. Rain or shine.

TIMES: 9:00 AM–5:00 PM.
ADMISSION: Free. Parking is free.
LOCATION: 401 Schillingers Rd N. Take I-10 to I-65, get off at Airport Blvd, about 8 miles west of I-65 take a right turn on Schillingers Rd. Follow the signs!
DESCRIPTION: Opened in 1988, this outdoor market is considered the largest in Alabama with 700 dealers selling under cover. The goods run the gamut: antiques, collectibles, jewelry, new merchandise—"everything." There are three full-size concession stands serving the hungry.
DEALER RATES: $20–$25 per weekend for 8' × 10' space or $30–$35 for a larger size.
CONTACT: Flea Market Mobile, 401 Schillingers Rd N, Mobile AL 33608. Tel: (334) 633-7533. Fax: (334) 639-0570.

SCOTTSBORO

First Monday Flea Market

DATES: First Monday and preceding Sunday of each month.
TIMES: 8:00 AM until dark.
ADMISSION: Free. Parking is also free.
LOCATION: Courthouse Square in the center of downtown Scottsboro.
DESCRIPTION: Said to be the second oldest market in the southeast, this is another classic 100-plus-year-old outdoor market started when the hanging judge showed up, held court and dispatched the bad guys. Which, of course, brought all the locals to watch the show—and, naturally, trade stuff. Although the court system has evolved somewhat, the market keeps going and going. From 250 dealers in winter to 500 dealers in the summer sell a variety of antiques, collectibles and secondhand items. For your convenience, food is served on the premises.
DEALER RATES: $15 per parking space. Availability of space is on a first come, first served basis.
CONTACT: Gayle Swafford, First Monday Flea Market, 409 S Broad St, Scottsboro AL 35768. Tel: (205) 574-4468.

SELMA

Selma Flea Market

DATES: Every Saturday, year round, rain or shine.

TIMES: 5:00 AM–until.

ADMISSION: Free. Parking is also free.

LOCATION: Selma By-Pass at River Road.

DESCRIPTION: This market opened in 1986 in beautiful historic Selma. It attracts from 170 to 200-plus dealers in sheltered spaces selling antiques, collectibles, handmade crafts, fresh produce and meats, new merchandise, garage sale and household items. There is food available on the premises, as well as overnight parking and an RV park on site.

DEALER RATES: $8 per 10' × 10' booth. Reservations are required.

CONTACT: Gary Maluda, 606 River Rd, Selma AL 36703. Tel: (334) 875-0500.

SUMMERDALE

Hwy 59 Flea Market

DATES: Saturday and Sunday, year round.

TIMES: 8:00 AM–4:00 PM.

ADMISSION: Free. Parking is also free.

LOCATION: On Hwy 59, between Foley and Robertdale, 13 miles north of Gulf Shores.

DESCRIPTION: This very busy market, "the best in this part of the country," has been in existence since the summer of 1985. Under new ownership since 1996, the market accommodates approximately 300 to 400 dealers outdoors but under cover, and 35 individual shops. They do not specialize in one particular area, instead they sell a wide variety of goods. Included are antiques, fine art, reproductions, and fresh produce, to name a few. The market is located on 33 acres which also includes a 10,000-square-foot antique mall. There is a snack shop on the premises as well as an RV park with reasonable rates ($150/month for vendors) and full hook-ups.

DEALER RATES: $10 for 10' × 10' space per day, per table. Reservations are not required.

CONTACT: Joyce, Hwy 59 Flea Market, PO Box 389, Summerdale AL 36580-0389. Tel: (334) 989-6642. Fax: (334) 989-6809.

OTHER FLEA MARKETS

We know or have heard about these markets, but have not personally contacted each one, as we have the markets with descriptions. If you plan to visit one of these markets listed below, *please call first* to make sure they are still open. Flea markets do come and go. While they were open when we went to press, they may not be later. We can't be responsible. *Call first!*

Abbeville: Lloyd & Bill's Flea Market, 103 Dothan Rd. Tel: 334-585-6954.

Alabaster: Buck Creek Flea Market, 1097 11th Ave SW. Tel: 205-664-0022.

Albertville: US Flea Market Mall, 5850 US Hwy 431. Tel: 205-891-3957.

Anniston: K & R Flea Market, 201 W 10th St. Tel: 205-238-9534.

Anniston: This & That Flea Market, 411 US Hwy 78 E. Tel: 205-835-2270.

Axis: Axis Flea Market, 406 Hwy 43. Tel: 334-675-6042.

Birmingham: Evans & Son Flea Market, 1818 Ave E. Tel: 205-780-8269.

Birmingham: North Birmingham Flea Market, 4650 Decatur Hwy. Tel: 205-841-8946.

Birmingham: Princeton Super Flea Market, 628 Tuscaloosa Ave SW. Tel: 205-787-4638.

Citronelle: Citronelle Flea Market, 19400 N 3rd St. Tel: 334-866-2811.

Cullman: Old Country Flea Market, Trimble Rd. Tel: 205-734-8230.

Cusseta: Dyke's Repair & Flea Market, 1040 County Rd 492. Tel: 334-749-9576.

Elmore: Bargain Place Flea Market, Rucker Rd. Tel: 334-567-7731.

Enterprise: Grime's Flea Market, Hwy 14. Tel: 334-393-4656.

Eufaula: Ole Mc Donald's Flea Farm, Hwy 431 S. Tel: 334-687-3706.

Eufaula: Rosa's Florals & Flea Market, RR 5. Tel: 334-687-2040.

Jasper: Uncle Bill's Flea Market, Hwy 5. Tel: 205-221-0772.

Killen: Greenhill Flea Market, 363 Hwy 43. Tel: 205-757-9247.

Lanett: The Korner Flea Market, 1008 County Rd 299. Tel: 334-576-6054.

Leighton: The Galaxy Flea Market, Hwy 184 & E 2nd. Tel: 205-446-5343.

Leighton: The Galaxy Flea Market, 1895 1st St. Tel: 205-446-5614.
Lillian: Best Little Flea Mkt. Tel: 334-962-4966.
Mobile: B & S Flea Market And Collectibles, 840 Blackburn Dr. Tel: 334-639-0323.
Mobile: Broadus Flea Market, 7790 Tanner Rd. Tel: 334-633-5060.
Mobile: Paul's Flea Market, 520 Houston St. Tel: 334-473-6722.
Mobile: Quality Furniture & Flea Market, 7313 Moffat Rd. Tel: 334-645-9815.
Mobile: Rollo's Flea Market, 1651 Schillinger Rd. Tel: 334-649-2620.
Mobile: Little Profit Flea Market, 2862 Brossett St. Tel: 334-473-6725.
Montgomery: Capitol Parkway Flea Market, 1747 Upper Wetumpka Rd. Tel: 334-264-7750.
Montgomery: Eastbrook Flea Market & Antique Mall Inc, 425 Coliseum Blvd. Tel: 334-277-4027.
Montgomery: Fantasy Land Flea Market, 3371 Atlanta Hwy. Tel: 334-272-8841.
Moulton: Treasure House Flea Market, 13533 Al Hwy 157. Tel: 205-974-3448.
Opelika: Huckeba Auction House & Flea Market, 829 S Railroad Ave. Tel: 334-745-5142.
Phenix City: Lynn's Bargains Flea Market, 3711 US Hwy 80 W. Tel: 334-297-5950.
Pinson: Pinson's Little Flea Market, 7385 Hwy 79. Tel: 205-681-1503.
Prattville: Prattville Flea Market, 1387 Hwy 72 W. Tel: 334-365-1031.
Prichard: Stoke's Flea Market, 236 S Wilson Ave. Tel: 334-457-8130.
Russellville: Davis Auction & Flea Market, 201 Coffee Ave. Tel: 205-332-3944.
Smiths: Lee County Flea Market Inc, Hwy 431 N. Tel: 334-291-7780.
Talladega: Boody's Furniture & Flea Market, 235 W Battle. Tel: 205-362-6699.
Theodore: Hwy 90 Flea Market, 7721 Hwy 90 W. Tel: 334-653-6589.
Tuscumbia: Gene's Grocery & Flea Market, Hwy 72. Tel: 205-381-3632.
Tuscumbia: Valdosta Trading Post/Seasons Flea Market, 1214 Old Lee Hwy. Tel: 205-383-4090.
Uniontown: Uniontown Flea Market, Water. Tel: 334-628-3042.
Vernon: Jim's Flea Market, Hwy 18 W. Tel: 205-695-8317.
Westover: 280 Flea Market, Hwy 442. Tel: 205-678-6729.

Wetumpka: Charlotte's Flea Market, 113 E Bridge St. Tel: 334-567-4166.
Wetumpka: Goolsby Farmers & Flea Market, Hwy 231. Tel: 334-567-5858.
Wetumpka: Hilltop Flea Market, Hwy 231. Tel: 334-567-5417.
Wetumpka: Lala's Flea Market, 120 Company St. Tel: 334-567-3962.
Wetumpka: Santuck Flea Market, Hwy 9. Tel: 334-567-7400.

ALASKA

SEWARD

American Legion Flea Market

DATES: Winter: Thursday through Saturday. April through September (when the cruise ships stop running): Tuesday through Saturday.
TIMES: 12:00 PM–4:00 PM.
ADMISSION: Free. Parking is free.
LOCATION: 402 5th Ave. In the American Legion's big gray building. Can't miss it!
DESCRIPTION: This 10-year-old market is a non-profit run by the American Legion to raise money for local charities, scholarships, help for anyone in need—and the famous "Santa-gifts-to-kiddies" scramble at Christmas (much like a similar stampede in Ross-On-Wye in Wales) the kids line up to collect their gift from visiting Santa, courtesy of the American Legion's donations. Everything is donated, period. However, the donations are incredible. Consider that anyone leaving Alaska tends to unload their worldly goods here so they don't have to transport it all down south. Therefore, antiques, collectibles, tons of clothes, dishes, furniture, winter sports gear, "the list in endless." People off cruise ships have been known to come in just for the buttons! Think of this as a huge garage sale in progress. This is the home of the famous Mt. Marathon foot races. Look for Gale "Windstorm" Colagross, she runs this place. Say "Hi" for me. She'll tell you all about the poor runners scrambling down that shale hillside during the downhill part of the race. Nasty!
DEALER RATES: Donations only.
CONTACT: Gale Colagross, American Legion Flea Market, 402 5th Ave, Seward AK 99664. Tel: (907) 224-2036.

ARIZONA

APACHE JUNCTION

American Park N Swap

DATES: Friday, Saturday and Sunday in winter. Friday and Saturday in summer. Rain or shine.
TIMES: Winter: Friday through Sunday 6:00 AM–3:00 PM. Summer: 4:00 PM–10:00 PM.
ADMISSION: $.50 per person walk-in.
LOCATION: 2551 West Apache Trail. US 60 to Signal Butte exit, north on Signal Butte to Apache Trail, turn east on Apache Trail. Park N Swap is on the south side of the road.
DESCRIPTION: This market, started in 1965, houses up to 500 dealers daily in winter and 100 daily in summer selling everything from desert gold and crystals, haircuts, Indian artifacts, golf clubs, redwood signs, silk plants, pet supplies, De Grazia, nuts, sandpaintings, kachinas, ironwood carvings, housewares, tools, books, produce, antiques, collectibles, crafts and handmade items, wind chimes, toys and bicycles—the list is endless! There is a huge barbecue pit in the center of the market and several smaller concessions are scattered conveniently around the selling floor. They are close to Superstition Mountain and recreational lakes.
DEALER RATES: $12 per 9' × 18' space Friday through Sunday. Reservations are suggested.
CONTACT: Mike Sleeseman, Manager, American Park N Swap, 2551 West Apache Trail, Apache Junction AZ 85220. Tel: (602) 832-3270.

BULLHEAD CITY

Bud's Hwy 95 Flea Market

DATES: Everyday but Monday.
TIMES: Summer 8:00 AM–2:30 PM. Winter 7:00 AM–5:00 PM.
ADMISSION: Free. Parking is free.
LOCATION: 5005 Hwy 95, 12 miles south of Laughlin, Nevada or 12 miles north of Needles, California.
DESCRIPTION: Started in 1987, this indoor/outdoor market has 150 dealers in winter and 30 dealers in summer selling antiques, collectibles, produce, coins, stamps, cards, garage sale goodies, crafts, furniture, toys, gift items, jewelry, flowers and new merchandise. There are 18 stores in six

buildings. A snack bar (open only in winter) and handicapped-accessible restrooms round out the facilities.
DEALER RATES: $10 per 12' × 24' space daily; $65 monthly; or $125 monthly for shed with a 12' × 24' space. Reservations are not required.
CONTACT: Jean or John, c/o Bud's Swap Meet, 5005 Hwy 95, Bullhead City AZ 86426. Tel: (520) 768-3103.

CASA GRANDE

Shoppers Barn and Swap Meet

DATES: Saturday and Sunday.
TIMES: 7:00 AM–4:00 PM.
LOCATION: Selma Rd and Hwy 84, between Tucson and Phoenix.
ADMISSION: Free. Parking is free.
DESCRIPTION: Open since 1983 under the same management, this outdoor market sells antiques, collectibles, new and used toys and merchandise, used auto parts, ceramics, and appliances. They are in town on a main road and next to many amenities. Restrooms are available.
DEALER RATES: $5 per day for center space, $7 per day for corner space, tables are $1 per day. First come, first served. There is security and the grounds are locked at night. Dealers can set up Friday night.
CONTACT: Bud Grey, PO Box 10250, Casa Grande AZ 85230. Tel: (520) 836-1934.

GLENDALE

Glendale 9 Swap Meet

DATES: Saturday and Sunday.
TIMES: 5:00 AM–until.
LOCATION: At 5650 N 55th Ave. South of Bethany Home Rd on 55th Ave. Northwest of Phoenix.
ADMISSION: $.50 per person, children 11 and under free.
DESCRIPTION: This outdoor market of 350–450 dealers sells about half new and half used merchandise including Indian crafts, antiques, collectibles and garage sale treasures. There is a snack bar, three concessions and some hot dog, soda and coffee carts roaming the market.
DEALER RATES: $10 for a 36' × 10' space. Reservations are available on a monthly or yearly basis. Vendors enter from 4:30 AM.
CONTACT: Dave Chapin, Glendale 9 Swap Meet, 5650 N 55th Ave, Glendale AZ 85301. Tel: (602) 931-0877.

PHOENIX

American Park N Swap

DATES: Every Wednesday, Friday, Saturday, and Sunday, rain or shine.
TIMES: Wednesday 4:00 PM–10:00 PM; Friday 6:00 AM–2:00 PM; Saturday and Sunday 6:00 AM–4:00 PM.
ADMISSION: Friday free, otherwise $1 per person, 12 and under free. Parking is free.
LOCATION: 3801 East Washington St at 40th and Washington. From Loop 202 go south on 40th St.
DESCRIPTION: This show first opened in 1961. It is both an indoor and an outdoor market that accommodates from 1,500 dealers in summer to 2,500 in winter. Billed as "the largest open air flea market in the southwest." Whatever you want, you will probably find at this market. There are dealers selling art, crystal, jewelry, musical instruments, toys, clothes, pictures, housewares, garage sale items, weight loss products, and tools. Even UPS has an outlet. There is also a printing service as well as a remodeling service in this enormous complex. Finally, when you grow hungry from shopping, hit one of the many food courts where there are many different types of foods available, from Mexican to Indian Fry Bread, to American burgers and fries. Handicapped-accessible restrooms abound.
DEALER RATES: $15 and up per 9' × 21' booth per day, Saturday and Sunday. $8 and up per booth per day Wednesday, $5 and up on Friday. Reservations are suggested.
CONTACT: Richard K Hogue, PO Box 61953, Phoenix AZ 85034-1953. Tel: (602) 273-1259. Day of show contact Monica Legliu or Susan Barrett.

Fairgrounds Antique Market

DATES: Third weekend of each month, except October (no show due to State Fair) and December when it is held on the second weekend.
TIMES: Saturday 9:00 AM–5:00 PM; Sunday 10:00 AM–4:00 PM.
ADMISSION: $1 for adults; children 14 and under free with parent.
LOCATION: 1826 West McDowell Rd, State Fairgrounds, at the intersection of Grand Ave, 19th Ave and McDowell Rd.
DESCRIPTION: This show started in June 1986. The indoor market currently draws over 200 dealers in summer and 500 in winter. Dealers set up to sell a variety of antiques and collectibles. Food is served on the premises and full overnight RV camping is available.

DEALER RATES: $65 for a 8' × 10½' space. Additional spaces cost $35. $70 for a corner 8' × 10½' space. Add on $20–$30 for electricity. Tables and free-standing pegboards are $9. Reservations are strongly advised.
CONTACT: Arthur or Linda Schwartz, Artlin Inc & Jack Black Enterprises, PO Box 61172, Phoenix AZ 85082-1172. Tel: (602) 943-1766 within AZ or 1-800-678-9987 nationwide.

Paradise Valley Swap Meet

DATES: Friday, Saturday and Sunday.
TIMES: Summer: 5:30 AM–1:30 PM. Winter: 5:30 AM–4:00 PM.
LOCATION: 2414 East Union Hills Dr. Go 1 mile north of Bell Rd and Cave Creek Rd. On the northeast corner of Cave Creek Rd and Union Hills Rd.
ADMISSION: Free. Parking is free.
DESCRIPTION: This market, in operation for over 18 years, has 132 spaces and hosts from 40 dealers in summer to capacity in winter. They sell everything from antiques and collectibles to soaps, tools, jewelry, boxed foods, produce, t-shirts, garage sale goodies, new merchandise and the occasional reptile. A hot dog cart provides food, and handicapped-accessible restrooms add to the amenities.
DEALER RATES: $10 per 10' × 10' or 10' × 29' space; corner space for $15; double space at $20 to $25 for 20' × 18' space; drop-off space at $10 for 10' × 10' or 10' × 15' space. Reservations are a must in the winter, not required in the summer. Office is open Thursday and Friday, 10:00 AM–1:00 PM.
CONTACT: Joseph Brudeau, Manager, Paradise Valley Swap Meet, 2414 E Union Hills Dr, Phoenix AZ 85024-3147. Tel: (602) 569-0052.

PRESCOTT

Peddler's Pass, Inc

DATES: Friday (except during January and February), Saturday, and Sunday, year round.
TIMES: Sunup to sundown.
ADMISSION: Free. Parking is also free.
LOCATION: Six miles east of Prescott on Hwy 69 in Prescott Valley.
DESCRIPTION: This growing market of 350 dealers in summer and 150 in winter started in 1987. The dealers feature a good mix of new and used merchandise and fresh produce with a strong market for antiques and col-

lectibles. They even sell used cars! When the heat is too much in valley markets, dealers head up to the cooler mountains of Peddler's Pass. They are the "largest market in Northern Arizona," aclean, neat and well-organized "no hassle" market. They have added a 3,000-square-foot building to house a farmer's market pavilion. Food is available on the premises. There are handicapped-accessible restrooms on site.

DEALER RATES: $5 per 12' × 22' space for used vehicle sales; $15 per 9' × 9' farmer's market space; $10 per 20' × 20' space; $12–$15 per 25' × 20' and $20 per 40' × 20' space. The largest space also comes with electric and water hook-ups. Reservations are suggested. Vendors can camp out on their site from Thursday noon until the market closes at 5:30 PM on Sunday.

CONTACT: Robert H Scott (Owner), 2201 Clubhouse Dr, Prescott AZ 86301. Tel: (520) 775-4117 Wednesday through Sunday.

QUARTZSITE

The Main Event

DATES: The Big Show is held annually the last full two weeks in January. 1998 dates are January 17 until February 1. The area is open every day of the year with 14 vendors in 7 shops.

TIMES: 8:00 AM–6:00 PM (essentially dawn to just before dark).

ADMISSION: Free. Parking is also free.

LOCATION: On I-10 (Business 10), Mile Post 17.

DESCRIPTION: This Annual Gemboree first began in 1982. It is held on 100 acres of land with over 1,000 dealers from all corners of the globe and is well known as one of the largest gem sales in the country, as well as one of the most exciting flea markets. Dealers set up to sell a virtually limitless range of antiques and collectibles including bottles, coins, hobby crafts, etc., along with lapidary equipment and thousands of specimens of gems and minerals from as far away as Brazil, Australia and Hong Kong. Food is served on the premises. Camping facilities for buyers as well as dealers are available with a fee for overnight parking.

DEALER RATES: $435 plus state sales tax for 18' × 32' space which includes electric, water and sewer hook-ups, and up, depending on space size. Reservations are advised.

CONTACT: The Main Event, PO Box 2801, Quartzsite AZ 85346-2801. Tel: (520) 927-5213.

TUCSON

MarketPlace USA

DATES: Friday, Saturday, and Sunday.

TIMES: Friday 12:00 PM–9:00 PM; Saturday 10:00 AM–9:00 PM; Sunday 10:00 AM–6:00 PM.

ADMISSION: Free. Parking is free.

LOCATION: 3750 East Irvington Rd. Off I-10 at Palo Verde North Exit, east on Irvington Rd approximately 2 blocks.

DESCRIPTION: Opened in November 1990 with 500 dealer spaces this growing market currently has dealers selling antiques, collectibles, crafts, produce and new merchandise. Housed in a 150,000-square-foot building, they offer everything from plants, electronics, and tools to chiropractors. Billed as "the largest indoor marketplace for independent retailers in the Southwest" this market has 505 spaces plus a 26,000-square-foot Exposition Center, 5 snack bars, 1 sports bar and a supervised arcade. Their Expo Center is attracting more shows yearly including Gem & Jewelry, Coin, and Corvette Shows, Bridge tournaments, Junior League Rummage Sales, and the like, all bringing in more shoppers.

DEALER RATES: $160–$360 for 4 weeks (12 selling days). Reservations are required.

CONTACT: Joanne Moebus, Manager, MarketPlace USA, 3750 E Irvington Rd, Tucson AZ 85714-1958. Tel: (520) 745-5000.

Tanque Verde Swap Meet

DATES: Thursday, Friday, Saturday and Sunday, year round, weather permitting.

TIMES: Thursday and Friday 3:00 PM–11:00 PM; Saturday and Sunday 2 sessions: 7:00 AM–3:00 PM and 3:00 PM–11:00 PM.

ADMISSION: Free. Parking is free.

LOCATION: 4100 South Palo Verde. Just south of Ajo Way. Or take I-10 to Palo Verde North, Exit 264B, go north 1 mile.

DESCRIPTION: This large outdoor family-owned market started in 1974 and is now considered a local tourist attraction as well as a city and county landmark. Its 800 dealers sell everything from antiques and collectibles to fresh produce; from unique southwestern items and handcrafted treasures to new and used merchandise. "Everything from toothpicks to houses, except processed food." There are 12 restaurants and snack bars. A well-equipped cafeteria, The Food Mercado, creates homemade Mexican dishes

and assorted specials every weekend, all at very reasonable prices. Live entertainment is scheduled periodically on a stage near the cafeteria.
DEALER RATES: $12 per 11' × 26' space; $14 per 11' × 35' space; $16 per corner space. Reservations are not required, unless for monthly reservations.
CONTACT: Tanque Verde Swap Meet, PO Box 19095, Tucson AZ 85731-9095. Tel: (520) 294-4252.

YUMA

Arizona Ave Swap Meet

DATES: Daily, October through May.
TIMES: 8:00 AM–5:00 PM.
ADMISSION: Free. Parking is also free.
LOCATION: 1749 Arizona Ave, 2 blocks south of 16th St on Arizona Ave.
DESCRIPTION: This outdoor show first began in 1976. Currently approximately 50 to 100 dealers sell a wide range of goods, including antiques and collectibles, fine art, arts and crafts, books, tools, chalk, new merchandise, and fresh produce, to name a few. Food is served on the premises.
DEALER RATES: $5 per 18' × 20' space per day; $25 per 18' × 20' space per week. Tables are available for $.50 per day.
CONTACT: Bob Butcher, 1749 Arizona Ave, Yuma AZ 85365. Tel: (520) 343-1837.

OTHER FLEA MARKETS

We know or have heard about these markets, but have not personally contacted each one, as we have the markets with descriptions. If you plan to visit one of these markets listed below, *please call first* to make sure they are still open. Flea markets do come and go. While they were open when we went to press, they may not be later. We can't be responsible. *Call first!*

Flagstaff: Big Tree Campground & Swap Meet, 6500 N US Hwy 89. Tel: 520-526-2583.
Lake Havasu City: London Bridge Swap Meet, London Bridge Shopping. Tel: 520-680-5685.
Mesa: Mesa Swap Meet, 10550 E Baseline Rd. Tel: 602-380-7467.
Nogales: Hilltop Swap Meet, 451 N Western Ave. Tel: 520-287-3903.
Peoria: Grand Ave Swap Meet, 7855 W Grand Ave. Tel: 602-979-0725.

Phoenix: The Great Southwestern Swap Meet, 1820 S 35th Ave. Tel: 602-352-1228.

Phoenix: Paradise Valley Swap Meet, 2414 E Union Hills Dr. Tel: 602-569-0052.

Quartzsite: Four Corners Swap Meet Inc. Tel: 520-927-5219.

Salome: Vicksburg Swap Meet. Tel: 520-859-4320.

Surprise: Surprise Swap Meet, 12912 W Santa Fe Dr. Tel: 602-583-1616.

Tucson: 6th Ave Swap Meet, 2310 S 6th Ave. Tel: 520-628-2000.

Tucson: The Arizona Flea Market, 3316 N 1st Ave. 520-292-3992.

ARKANSAS

ASHDOWN

Ashdown Flea Market

DATES: Friday, Saturday and Sunday.
TIMES: 8:00 AM–5:00 PM.
ADMISSION: Free. Parking is free.
LOCATION: 1540 Constitution, better known as Hwy 71 S. At the south end of Ashdown.
DESCRIPTION: This indoor/outdoor market, opened in 1996, even has seven steady dealers in winter with others still coming in, yet many more (up to 50 or so) in summer. One fellow brought in and sold reconditioned lawnmowers. Mostly, they sell clothes, garage sale finds, produce in season, antiques, pecans, peanuts and collectibles. There is a snack concession.
DEALER RATES: $5 per 8' × 8' booth, $15 per 8' × 12' booth for the weekend. In the building: $10 per day, or $20 for the weekend. Reservations are required for inside space, not for outside.
CONTACT: Ashdown Flea Market, 130 LR 68, Ashdown AR 71822. Tel: (870) 898-2377.

BATESVILLE

America's Flea Market

DATES: Every Friday, Saturday, and Sunday, year round, rain or shine.
TIMES: Friday 11:00 AM–6:00 PM, Saturday 8:30 AM–6:00 PM, Sunday 11:00 AM–6:00 PM.
ADMISSION: Free. Free parking is provided.
LOCATION: 310 West Main Street, at the low end of downtown Batesville. On the site of the historical Ringold home.
DESCRIPTION: This indoor/outdoor market first opened in 1980 and currently accommodates over 140 dealers. Everything from antiques and collectibles to new merchandise, from fine art to fresh produce can be bought here. It is located on the historic home site of one of the founders of Batesville. Food is served on the premises and handicapped-accessible restrooms round out the amenities.
DEALER RATES: Booth size is 10' × 10'; call for current rates. Advance reservations are required during winter months.

CONTACT: Farrell Hall, 310 W Main St, Batesville AR 72501. Tel: (870) 793-7508 or (870) 251-2813.

HOT SPRINGS

Higdon Ferry Flea Market

DATES: Daily.
TIMES: 10:00 AM–5:00 PM.
ADMISSION: Free. Parking is free.
LOCATION: 2138 Higdon Ferry Rd. Just off Rt 7 South. If you are coming from town, it's the first street on the right past and opposite the Hot Springs Mall and over the hill. If you are coming the other way, it's a left turn before the mall. Go behind the building, under the skating rink.
DESCRIPTION: Opened in 1986 on 11 acres, this market of over 70 dealers sells mostly antiques and collectibles, furniture, glassware, some reproductions and plenty of standard flea market fare.
DEALER RATES: $165 for a 12' × 24' single space per month. $60 a month for a 8' × 10' space with no walls. Reservations are requested. There are a few outdoor spaces for traveling dealers at $5 per day.
CONTACT: Higdon Ferry Flea Market, 2138 Higdon Ferry Rd, Hot Springs AR 71913. Tel: (501) 525-9927.

JUDSONIA

Thackerland Flea Market

DATES: Saturday and Sunday.
TIMES: 7:00 AM–5:00 PM.
ADMISSION: Free. Parking is free.
LOCATION: 666 Hwy 367. Only 50 miles north of Little Rock.
DESCRIPTION: Open for 10 years, this market is noted for its wonderful antiques collected and auctioned on the first and third Thursdays by the owner. Dealers set up indoors in two long buildings, outdoors and under sheds selling glassware, more antiques, collectibles, and more. This is a haunt for dealers looking to replenish their supplies. During the summer it's is more like a carnival with all the music and carryings on. A small restaurant is onsite and serves the vendors during non-market hours. On summer weekends there is entertainment and dancing for everyone. Gary is always adding to the market. They used to have dealers selling ostriches, pot-bellied pigs and other "exotic" animals during the appropriate fads which was entertaining in itself. However, as the fads have fazed, the market has

quietly enjoyed their newfound "peace and quiet." (There's still the awesome music!)
DEALER RATES: $12.50 inside space, $6 for outside space and it varies for the sheds depending on size. There is RV space with arrangements for vendors as well as bathing facilities. Reservations are suggested.
CONTACT: Gary Thacker, Thackerland Flea Market, PO Box 791, Judsonia AR 72081-0791. Tel: (501) 729-3063. Fax: (501) 729-3154.

PRAIRIE GROVE

Battlefield Flea Market

DATES: Daily, year round, except Thanksgiving, Christmas and New Year's Day.
TIMES: 9:00 AM–5:00 PM, Sunday 10:00 AM–5:00 PM.
ADMISSION: Free. Plenty of free parking.
LOCATION: 129 E Buchanan, on Hwy 62 W in Prairie Grove.
DESCRIPTION: Opened in 1990, this market is run by Mary for dealers who rent space by the month. Their 56 booths are loaded with lots of collectibles, some local crafts (including dried flowers and wooden crafts), and "dust collectibles." Restrooms are on site, and if you get hungry, there is a cafe a ½ block away or a fast-food place in the other direction a ½ block. An historical note: the Battle of Prairie Grove was fought here during the Civil War. There is a state park next door commemorating the battlefield site.
DEALER RATES: $1 a square foot a month for space. Reservations are required. There is a waiting list.
CONTACT: Steve and Martha Ritchie, Battlefield Flea Market, PO Box 688, Prairie Grove AR 72753-0688. Tel: (501) 846-1800.

SPRINGDALE

Discount Corner Flea Market Mall

DATES: Every day.
TIMES: 9:30 AM–5:30 PM.
ADMISSION: Free. Parking is also free.
LOCATION: 418 East Emma (downtown), approximately 3 blocks east of the railroad tracks.
DESCRIPTION: This indoor market started in 1987, and most of their 125 dealers have been with them since the beginning. These dealers sell antiques, collectibles, handmade and craft items, toys—both new and col-

lectible, tools and new merchandise. Other dealers from 19 states come shopping here. There are pleasant camper facilities nearby, as is the Shiloh Museum. A country music show is just down the street. Food is available on the premises.
DEALER RATES: No weekend space is currently available, however do call for information regarding monthly rates.
CONTACT: Frances Carpenter, Discount Corner Flea Market Mall, 418 E Emma, Springdale AR 72764. Tel: (501) 756-0764.

Oak Grove Flea Market

DATES: Saturday and Sunday, year round.
TIMES: 8:00 AM–4:30 PM.
ADMISSION: Free. Parking is also free.
LOCATION: Corner of Oak Grove and Elm Springs Rds.
DESCRIPTION: Considered one of largest and oldest of northwest Arkansas's flea markets, having opened in 1977, this indoor/outdoor market hosts between 60 to 100 dealers depending on the season. They sell antiques, collectibles, furniture, fresh produce, crafts and new merchandise. Two concessions serve American or Mexican food. Restrooms are available.
DEALER RATES: $6 per 12' × 14' space per day outside; $70 per month inside. Reservations are required for inside space; outside is first come, first served.
CONTACT: Ramona or Bob Wallis, 3 S Ethel Ave, Fayetteville AR 72701. Tel: (501) 756-0697 or (501) 521-5791.

SPRINGHILL

Springhill Flea Market

DATES: Daily.
TIMES: 8:00 AM–5:00 PM.
ADMISSION: Free. Parking is free.
LOCATION: 660 Hwy 65 North. Exactly 7 miles out of Conway going to Greenbrier, 5 miles from Pickle's Gap.
DESCRIPTION: This market averages 32 vendors selling "antiques to junctiques," including a vendor specializing in comics; one vendor with a collection of 30,000 books and "every variety of knife"; oil paintings, lamps and lampshades, clothing, antique tools. In warmer weather there are ven-

dors outside, but they tend to vanish in the cold weather (wonder why?). Sodas, coffee and restrooms are available on premises.
DEALER RATES: $90 per month for a 16' × 20' inside booth; $35 per month for outside space with electric, free outside setup otherwise; $3 per day for electric hook-up for dealers wishing to hang around awhile. Reservations are suggested, or at least a call, one week in advance for inside space; first come, first served for outside space.
CONTACT: Bill Wisler, Springhill Flea Market, 660 Hwy 65 N, Springhill AR 72058. Tel: (501) 679-9106.

WEST MEMPHIS

West Memphis Flea Market

DATES: Thursday through Sunday.
TIMES: 10:00 AM–6:00 PM.
ADMISSION: Free. Parking is free.
LOCATION: 512 East Broadway. Easy access from either I-40 or I-55 from Exit 7 (both interstates), go to Broadway, right, 2 blocks to market on your right.
DESCRIPTION: Located along the Mississippi River, this market of 45 permanent and up to a total of 75 dealers sells everything from antiques and collectibles to household goods, glassware, new and vintage clothing, jewelry, the latest fads, and new merchandise. Other dealers come here to shop because the deals and merchandise are so good. They are near a RV park, a dog track for the bold, and only 7 miles from Memphis.
DEALER RATES: Inside there is a waiting list, outside is $7 for a 12' × 20' space under canopy. Reservations for outside aren't really necessary.
CONTACT: Virginia McNeely, West Memphis Flea Market, 512 E Broadway, W Memphis AR 72301-3201. Tel: (501) 735-9332 or (501) 735-1644.

OTHER FLEA MARKETS

We know or have heard about these markets, but have not personally contacted each one, as we have the markets with descriptions. If you plan to visit one of these markets listed below, *please call first* to make sure they are still open. Flea markets do come and go. While they were open when we went to press, they may not be later. We can't be responsible. *Call first!*

Please note that some of the 501 area codes changed to 870. If you call and it doesn't work, try the 870 instead or check to see if there's another new area code.

Beebe: McDonald's Flea Market, 316 W Center St. Tel: 501-882-3119.
Benton: Benton Flea Market, 18325 Hwy I-30. Tel: 501-778-9011.
Benton: South Street Flea Market, 1229 W South St. Tel: 501-315-6185.
Bryant: Collector's Flea Market, 22430 Hwy I-30. Tel: 501-847-6899.
Clarksville: C & D Flea Market, 701 W Main St. Tel: 501-754-5262.
Conway: Ward's 64 East Flea Market, 348 Hwy 64 E. Tel: 501-730-0203.
Crossett: Helen's In Door Flea Mart, 1027 Hwy 133 N. Tel: 501-364-4383.
De Valls Bluff: Owen's Flea Market & Auction, Hwy 70 E. Tel: 501-998-2862.
El Dorado: Ginger's Flea Market, 1219 W Hillsboro St. Tel: 501-862-1935.
El Dorado: Herb's Cafe & Flea Market Park, 6633 Calion Hwy. Tel: 501-748-2408.
Eureka Springs: Old Town Flea Market, Hwy 23. Tel: 501-253-6557.
Fayetteville: All My Treasures Flea Market, 2932 Huntsville Rd. Tel: 501-575-0250.
Garfield: The Loop Flea Mart, 15708 Hwy 62. Tel: 501-359-3511.
Garfield: Martin's Flea Market, Hwy 62 & Oak. Tel: 501-359-3782.
Garfield: N & J Flea Market, Hwy 62 & Oak. Tel: 501-359-3089.
Gassville: Poor Girl's Flea Market, 135 E Main St. Tel: 501-435-6634.
Gould: Debby's Flea Market, Hwy 65. Tel: 501-263-4932.
Gravette: Gravette Flea Mart, 404 N 1st. Tel: 501-787-6162.
Green Forest: Hand's Flea Market. Tel: 501-438-5495.
Harrisburg: Downtown Flea Market, 404 E Jackson St. Tel: 501-578-5490.

Harrisburg: Harrisburg Flea Market, 8142 Hwy 163. Tel: 501-578-5216.

Harrison: Anita's Flea Market, Bear Creek Springs. Tel: 501-741-6455.

Harrison: Lake Harrison Flea Market, 112 W Stephenson Ave. Tel: 501-743-4287.

Hot Springs National: Central City Flea Mart, 3310 Central Ave. Tel: 501-623-4484.

Hot Springs National: Snow Springs Flea Market, 3628 Park Ave. Tel: 501-624-7469.

Huntsville: Little House Flea Market, RR 3. Tel: 501-738-2244.

Jacksonville: B & M Flea Market, 660 W Main St. Tel: 501-985-1788.

Jacksonville: Northside Flea Market, 18801 Hwy 107. Tel: 501-834-8060.

Jacksonville: P I Flea Market, 112 Marshall Rd. Tel: 501-982-0973.

Jacksonville: That Little Flea Market, 632 W Main St. Tel: 501-985-0694.

Jasper: Sloan Mtn Antiques & Flea Market, HC 31 Box 61. Tel: 501-446-5863.

Jonesboro: 49-1-2 South Flea Market, 3204 Southwest Dr. Tel: 501-932-7808.

Jonesboro: Forty Nine South Flea Market, 3202 Southwest Dr. Tel: 501-932-4538.

Jonesboro: Hwy 18 Flea Market, 6303 E Highland Dr. Tel: 501-931-9771.

Jonesboro: Nettleton Flea Market, 3339 E Nettleton Ave. Tel: 501-931-9307.

Judsonia: Exit 48 Flea Market, 359 CW Rd. Tel: 501-729-4769.

Knoxville: Hwy Sixty Four Flea Market, Hwy 64 W. Tel: 501-885-6104.

Lake City: Riverside Flea Market, 101 Cottonwood. Tel: 501-237-4883.

Lake Village: Dave's Flea Mart, Hwy 82. Tel: 501-265-2662.

Lincoln: The Treasure Chest Flea Market, 405 W Pridemore Ave. Tel: 501-824-3227.

Little Rock: Memphis Flea Market/Little Rock Show, 13000 Hwy I-30. Tel: 501-455-1001 or 501-455-0162.

Little Rock: Next to New Flea Market, 3302 Fair Park Blvd. Tel: 501-562-2826.

Malvern: Cotten's Flea Market, Hwy 270. Tel: 501-337-5772.

Mountain View: Mountain View Mini Storage & Flea Market, Hwy 66 W. Tel: 870-269-2656.

Mountain View: Rainbow Flea Market, Main St. Tel: 501-269-3261.

Mountain View: White House Historical Flea Market, E Main St. Tel: 870-269-2949.

North Little Rock: Beech Street Flea Market, 902 N Beech St. Tel: 501-372-7664.

North Little Rock: Granny's Flea Market, 9810 Mac Arthur Dr. Tel: 501-791-0991.

North Little Rock: This & That Flea Market, 100 E 13th St. Tel: 501-375-3638.

Paragould: Holland's Uptown Flea Market, 218 N Pruett St. Tel: 501-236-3474.

Paragould: Huffman's Flea Market, 207 N Pruett St. Tel: 501-239-9613.

Paragould: New and Like New Flea Market, 121 N 2nd St. Tel: 501-236-1278.

Paragould: Overpass Flea Market, 200 E Kingshighway. Tel: 501-239-4478.

Paragould: 7 Acres Flea Market, 2607 E Kingshighway. Tel: 501-236-1922.

Perryville: Hilltop Flea Market & Antiques. Tel: 501-889-5810.

Pine Bluff: Pine Crest Flea Market, Hwy 365 & Rhinehart Rd. Tel: 501-536-3532.

Pine Bluff: 270 & 65 Flea Market, 8112 Sheridan Rd. Tel: 501-247-9957.

Pleasant Plains: Pleasant Plains Flea Market, 6830 Batesville Blvd. Tel: 501-345-2720.

Pocahontas: D & D Flea Market, 1971 Hwy 67 N. Tel: 501-892-1562.

Pocahontas: J & R Auction & Flea Markets, 4603 Hwy 67 S. Tel: 501-892-7274.

Pocahontas: S & J Flea Market, 1971 Hwy 67 N. Tel: 501-892-7435.

Rogers: Pioneer Flea Market, 1018 N 2nd St. Tel: 501-631-6150.

Sherwood: Hidden Treasures Flea Market, 9107 Hwy 107. Tel: 501-833-0200.

Springdale: Best Yet Flea Market, 633 Sanders Ave.

Springdale: Historic Mercantile Flea Market, 136 W Henri De Tonti Blvd. Tel: 501-361-2003.

Springdale: Magnolia House Flea Market Inc, 312 S Thompson St. Tel: 501-751-1787.

Springdale: 71 Plaza Flea Market Mall, 1300 N Thompson St. Tel: 501-751-8222.

Strong: McStreet Flea Market & Antiques, 9537 Strong Hwy. Tel: 501-797-2620.

Stuttgart: L & D Flea Mart, 1802 S Park Ave. Tel: 501-673-4729.

Trumann: C & C Flea Market, 710 W Speedway St. Tel: 501-483-5622.

Trumann: Speedway Flea Market, 316 W Speedway St. Tel: 501-483-5881.

Walnut Ridge: Hidden Treasures Flea Market, 602 Hwy 67 N. Tel: 501-886-6034.

Walnut Ridge: Ma & Pa's Flea Market, 712 Hwy 67 N. Tel: 501-886-7737.

Walnut Ridge: Poor Boy's Flea Market, 502 SW Front St. Tel: 501-886-1513.

West Fork: Blue Barn Flea Market, 65 Mineral Springs Rd. Tel: 501-839-3261.

West Memphis: Eastern Arkansas Flea Market, 557 E Broadway St. Tel: 501-735-9055.

Wynne: Wynne Flea Market, 100 W Kennedy Ave. Tel: 501-238-8598.

CALIFORNIA

ANDERSON

Jolly Giant Flea Market

DATES: Saturday and Sunday, year round.

TIMES: 6:00 AM–4:00 PM.

ADMISSION: $1.35 for a family, $.50 general, 6 and under free.

LOCATION: 6719 Eastside Rd. Take I-5 to Anderson. At Junction 273, exit off I-5, the market is 4 miles north of Anderson. The cross street is Latona Rd.

DESCRIPTION: Started in 1979, this indoor/outdoor market has 90,000 square feet of merchandise for sale. As they describe it, "More fun than you can bargain for." Their 150-250 dealers sell antiques, produce, cards, coins, furniture, garage sale goodies, utility trailers, tools and new and used merchandise. When you wilt from hunger, try the bar, the snack bar, or one of three restaurants. When the need hits, there are handicapped-accessible restrooms too.

DEALER RATES: $6 for 10' × 10' space on Saturday; $8 on Sunday. Reservations are suggested.

CONTACT: Tim Roberts or Jim or Patti Smith, Jolly Giant Flea Market, 6719 Eastside Rd, Anderson CA 96007. Tel: (916) 365-6458 or fax: (916) 365-6450.

BAKERSFIELD

Bakersfield Fairground Swap Meet

DATES: Saturday and Sunday.

TIMES: 5:00 AM–3:00 PM.

ADMISSION: $1. Parking: $.50 on Saturday, $1 on Sunday.

LOCATION: At the Kern County Fairgrounds, at the intersection of Ming and Union, right on the corner.

DESCRIPTION: This outdoor market, open since 1986, attracts 300 to 400 dealers, year round, selling antiques, collectibles, crafts, produce, new merchandise, farm tools, cars, boats, motor homes, used merchandise and "everything under the sun." Loads of snack bars and handicapped-accessible restrooms add to the amenities.

DEALER RATES: $10–$15 for a 20' × 20' space. Reservations are not required.

CONTACT: Ed Murphy, Bakersfield Fairgrounds Swap Meet, 312 Stable, Bakersfield CA 93304. Tel: (805) 397-1504 or 833-1733.

Pacific Theater Swap-O-Rama

DATES: Sundays, rain or shine.
TIMES: 6:00 AM–4:00 PM.
ADMISSION: $.75, children under 12 free. Free parking is available.
LOCATION: 4501 Wible Rd. Take Freeway 99, Exit White Lane and Wible Rd, 2 blocks south.
DESCRIPTION: This show opened in 1971. It is an outdoor market that accommodates anywhere from 450 to 550 dealers. The dealers sell approximately 90% new merchandise, modern clothes, etc. for the mostly Hispanic shoppers. There is also an assortment of secondhand goods. For your convenience, there is Mexican food available on the premises, picnicking under the trees, carnival rides, plenty to keep the kids happy, and live music. Handicapped-accessible restrooms are on site.
DEALER RATES: $15 reserved space, $20 for non-reserved. Reservations are suggested. The office is open Friday for reservations from 9:00 AM–3:00 PM and Saturday 8:00 AM–6:00 PM.
CONTACT: Pacific Theater Swap-O-Rama, 4501 Wible Rd, Bakersfield CA 93313. Tel: (805) 831-9342.

BLOOMINGTON

Bel-Air Swap Meet

DATES: Wednesday, Friday, Saturday and Sunday.
TIMES: 6:00 AM–3:00 PM. Call for a rain check before 8:00 AM on iffy days.
ADMISSION: $.50. Parking is free.
LOCATION: 17565 Valley Blvd.
DESCRIPTION: Open since 1986 and moved down the road in June 1997, this outdoor market averages 475 dealers year round selling antiques, collectibles, crafts, produce, furniture, coins, stamps, cards, garage sale goodies, and new merchandise. A snack bar and restrooms are on site.
DEALER RATES: Vary by day of week, all reasonable rates for 18' × 25' space. Reservations are not required.
CONTACT: Bel-Air Swap Meet, 17565 Valley Blvd, Bloomington CA 82316. Tel: (909) 355-3000 or (213) 754-3000. Fax: (909) 355-3044.

CAMPBELL

Second Saturday Flea Market

DATES: Second Saturday of every month, weather permitting.
TIMES: 7:00 AM–dusk.
ADMISSION: Free. Parking is also free.
LOCATION: South from Santa Cruz on Hwy 17, turn west at Hamilton; then travel ½ mile to Winchester Blvd; then turn left and go ½ block to Campbell Center Shopping Center.
DESCRIPTION: This show started in 1971. The outdoor market accommodates 40–50 dealers. You can find almost anything here from antiques and collectibles to fine art and new merchandise—"whatever dealers bring that is legal to sell." Sometimes fresh produce is available. Although it originally started as only a mini-market it has grown to a full-fledged flea market. John, a record dealer, has been here since anyone can remember. He has found or sold "any record you can imagine." There are several restaurants in the shopping center. This market is noted for the friendliness of people. "It's like a family. When one gets sick, the others help out." Some of the vendors have been here every weekend since the market opened.
DEALER RATES: $10 for 10' × 10' space. Reservations are not accepted—first come, first served.
CONTACT: Second Saturday Flea Market, c/o Jersey's, 1781 S Winchester Blvd, Campbell CA 95008. Tel: (408) 374-1415.

COLTON

Maclin's Colton Open Air Market and Auction

DATES: Every Thursday and Saturday.
TIMES: 7:30 AM–3:00 PM. Antique auctions are held every Thursday at 10:00 AM.
ADMISSION: $.50, children 12 and under free. Parking is free.
LOCATION: 1902 W Valley Blvd. From points west, take 10 Freeway east to Riverside Ave, then north to Valley East. From points east, take Freeway 10 west to Pepper, then go north to Valley West.
DESCRIPTION: Maclin's has just celebrated its 50th anniversary. Over the years it has grown to accommodate 350 to 500 dealers and between 3,000 to 7,000 buyers daily. While the grounds are completely paved and the spaces are covered, it is considered an open-air outdoor market. Their furniture/antique/collectible auction, however, is held indoors. Their merchandise selection is huge. They sell antiques, fine art, collectibles, arts

and crafts, gold jewelry, clothing, home furnishings, and shoes, just to name a few!
DEALER RATES: $7–$30 depending on size and location. Walk-ins are welcome and advised to be there between 7:00–7:30 AM the morning of the market to get a good spot.
CONTACT: Maclin Markets Inc, 7407 Riverside Dr, Ontario CA 91761. Tel: (909) 877-3700 or toll-free in California 1-800-222-7467 for information about Colton.

CUPERTINO

DeAnza College Flea Market

DATES: First Saturday of every month, rain or shine.
TIMES: 8:00 AM–4:00 PM.
ADMISSION: Free. Parking is $2 on campus.
LOCATION: 21250 Stevens Creek Blvd. Take Hwy 280 north or south to Hwy 85 west, then to DeAnza College via Stevens Creek Blvd.
DESCRIPTION: This outdoor market began in 1972 and is operated by the student government and the student activities committee, with proceeds benefitting the student body. There are over 900 booths selling antiques, fine art, arts and crafts, collectibles, and new merchandise. From 10,000–15,000 people attend this event each day! Food is served on the premises.
DEALER RATES: $20 for two parking spaces approximately 18' × 20' as selling area; $40 for four spaces approximately 36' × 20'. Reservations must be made one month in advance.
CONTACT: DeAnza Flea Market, 21250 Stevens Creek Blvd, Cupertino CA 95014. Tel: (408) 864-8946.

DALY CITY

Geneva Swap Meet

DATES: Saturday and Sunday.
TIMES: 7:00 AM–4:00 PM.
ADMISSION: Saturday $.25, Sunday $.75. Parking is free.
LOCATION: 607 Carter, at the Geneva Drive-In next door to the Cow Palace.
DESCRIPTION: This outdoor market hosts 100 dealers selling about half new merchandise and half old or used—antiques and collectibles, produce, records, tapes, tools, sports cards, full-screen TVs and stereos, household

needs (laundry supplies, etc.), "everything you can think of." A snack bar and barbecue stand feed the famished. In 1997 they remodeled this market including making the restrooms handicapped-accessible. They do special holiday promotions, so watch for them.

DEALER RATES: $10 for a 11' × 18' space on Saturdays; $15 Sundays. Reservations are suggested for monthly or yearly. Additional reservation fee of $12.50 for the weekend.

CONTACT: Geneva Swap Meet, 607 Carter St, Daly City CA 94014. Tel: (650) 587-0515. (If the 650 area code doesn't work, then use the old 415.)

ESCONDIDO

Escondido Swap Meet

DATES: Wednesday through Sunday.

TIMES: Wednesday and Thursday 6:30 AM–4:00 PM; Friday 1:30 PM–9:30 PM; Saturday and Sunday 6:00 AM–4:00 PM.

ADMISSION: Wednesday $.50, Thursday $.35, Friday and Saturday $.75, Sunday $1.

LOCATION: 635 West Mission Ave. Take 78 east to Centre City Pkwy S, take next left at Mission Ave, left at Quince St. Market is on the right side.

DESCRIPTION: Since 1970, on the site of a drive-in movie theater, this indoor/outdoor market is generally fixed stands and set prices. There is mostly new merchandise with a heavy Mexican accent and some used goods. Some of the merchandise seen for sale: tools, loads of clothes, dishes and books. Eight concessions include Mexican, pizza, ice cream, fish and chips, barbeque, a standard snack bar, and a bakery. A farmers market sells inexpensive fresh produce, cheeses and dairy products and meats.

DEALER RATES: Per 18' × 20' booth: Wednesday $10, Thursday $8, Friday and Saturday $14, Sunday $18. Reservations are not required, first come, first served.

CONTACT: Lee Porter, Escondido Swap Meet, 635 W Mission Ave, Escondido CA 92025. Tel: (760) 745-3100.

FOLSOM

Annual Peddlers Faire and Antique Market

DATES: Antique Market (spring) is the third Sunday in April and Peddler's Antique and Collectible Faire (fall) is third Sunday in September. Rain date is the following Sunday. Harvest Festival is the last Saturday in October.

TIMES: 8:00 AM–5:00 PM.

ADMISSION: Free. Some parking is free, some paid.
LOCATION: On Sutter St in historic Folsom. From Hwy 50, take Folsom Blvd Exit, turn left, 2.9 miles to Sutter St.
DESCRIPTION: Started in 1966, this outdoor market in the Sierra foothills now accommodates 300 dealers that sell antiques and collectibles. No new merchandise is allowed. More than 20,000 people attend this semiannual fair. In the heart of "gold country" this fair is located in the middle of some fascinating history: the Folsom Powerhouse was the first commercial transporter of long-distance electricity; there are the logging and gold mining histories; Chinese diggings; special exhibits of early Indian life at the History Museum on Sutter St and more. Food is plentiful.
DEALER RATES: $80 for 10' × 10' space. Reservations are required; setup starts at 2:00 AM and dealers should take note that crowds may start appearing as early as 3:00 AM.
CONTACT: Attn: Maureen Gagliardi, Sutter St Merchants Association, PO Box 515, Folsom CA 95763-0515. Tel: (916) 985-7452 or Folsom Visitors Center at (916) 985-2698.

FRESNO

Cherry Ave Auction, Inc

DATES: Open every Tuesday and Saturday.
TIMES: 6:30 AM–5:00 PM.
ADMISSION: Free. Parking is $1 per car.
LOCATION: 4640 South Cherry Ave. Take Hwy 99 to Jensen Ave exit (Jensen is 2 miles south of downtown Fresno); then go west 1 block to Cherry; then go south to yard. Cherry Auction is on Cherry Ave between Central and American Aves.
DESCRIPTION: This show began over 60 years ago. Now there are over three acres of vendor spaces and walkways under sheds or canopy and 15 acres total vendor area. The 800-plus dealers who attend this market sell "1,000 + 1 items," from antiques and collectibles to new merchandise and fresh produce—it can all be bought. This is one of the oldest outdoor markets in the area. There is also a unique "Auction Line" where anything and everything is auctioned off. There is a variety of food available as well as clean restroom facilities on the premises.
DEALER RATES: Reservations are taken only by the month. The cost for dealer space is $10 per 10' × 20' space on Saturday; $8 per space on Tuesday (Tuesday is a 2 for 1 deal). Reservations are not required.

CONTACT: Cherry Ave Auction Inc, 4640 S Cherry Ave, Fresno CA 93706. Tel: (209) 266-9856 or fax: (209) 266-9439.

FULLERTON

Troubleshooters Antiques And Collectibles Round-Up

DATES: The first Sunday in May and October. Rain or shine.
TIMES: 9:00 AM–3:00 PM.
ADMISSION: $5, children under 12 free with adult. Parking is free. Dealers can get in early to buy for $10.
LOCATION: Cal State University just off the 57 Freeway at Nutwood Ave exit. Turn right on Nutwood at first light into the Cal State Fullerton campus and follow the signs.
DESCRIPTION: This outdoor show, started in 1962 and recently moved to this location, is sponsored by the Register Charities (*Orange County Register* newspaper) with all profits going to charity. The 800 dealers sell antiques and collectibles. It is the largest antique-related event in Orange County. Food is available on the premises.
DEALER RATES: $50 for 8' × 18' booth. Reservations are required.
CONTACT: RG Canning, PO Box 400, Maywood CA 90270-0400. Tel: (213) 560-7469 ext 15 or 560-SHOW (7469).

GALT

Galt Market

DATES: Every Tuesday and Wednesday, except Christmas Day.
TIMES: Tuesdays: wholesale hours: 6:00 AM, retail hours: 10:00 AM. Wednesdays: 6:00 AM until everyone packs up (usually around 3:00 PM).
ADMISSION: Free. Parking is free.
LOCATION: Approximately ½ hour south of downtown Sacramento. Take the Central Galt exit off Hwy 99. From the south, turn left across 99 and left onto Fairway. From the north, go straight across C St and the road becomes Fairway. Follow the green Galt Flea Market signs. The flea market is bounded by Meladee, Caroline and Chabolla with entrances off Caroline by the Galt Library, and off Chabolla across from the park.
DESCRIPTION: This is two distinct outdoor markets with the Tuesday market specializing in new merchandise, crafts, clothing, home decor items, jewelry, statuary, wood products, pictures/frames, dried flowers, awnings, oriental rugs, and loads more. The Wednesday market deals in antiques,

collectibles, crafts, garage sale goodies, and the like. The produce market is considered quite awesome with plenty of ethnic specialties. There are 860 dealer spaces on over 10 acres, with an average of 450 plus dealers. This market draws vendors from throughout California and the surrounding states as well as a number of foreign countries. Many of their vendors attend trade shows around the United States and some make regular buying trips to Europe, the Middle East and the Orient. Food vendors provide the eatables, and handicapped-accessible restrooms are available. Market advice: "Wear good walking shoes and shop until you drop!" Grab a market guide as you enter.

DEALER RATES: Tuesday: $30 for non-food vendors for a 10' × 30' space; food vendors pay $90 for a 20' × 30' space. They have a one-year waiting list for Tuesday spaces. Daily vendors are let in by lottery for whatever vacancies exist for that day. Wednesday: $17 for non-food vendors for a 10' × 30' space; food vendors pay $50 for a 20' × 30' space. Wednesday spaces are primarily on a first-come, first-served basis with the gates opening at 5:00 AM. Dealers must have a California Seller's Permit and a City of Galt Business License to sell.

CONTACT: Galt Flea Market, 890 Caroline Ave, Galt CA 95632. Tel: (209) 745-2437 for a tape message, or if you want a human when the tape starts touch "0" during office hours—Monday through Wednesday. Or call (209) 745-4695. Fax: (209) 745-9794.

GLENDALE

Glendale Community College Swap Meet

DATES: Every third Sunday of the month.

TIMES: 8:00 AM–3:00 PM.

ADMISSION: Free. Parking is free.

LOCATION: Glendale Community College, upper parking lot. Take the Glendale 2 Freeway north, exit on Mountain St, take a left, it is on the right side of the road just behind the bridge.

DESCRIPTION: There are approximately 150–200 spaces. From a reader who visited this market and was impressed: only antiques and collectibles are sold here, no new stuff. Goodies include: stamps, coins, books, crystal, dishes, glasses, knickknacks, some clothing and fabric. You can still make a deal. Snacks are available and there are restrooms.

DEALER RATES: $35 for a 3-parking-stall space per Sunday. You must park your vehicle in that space. If you are not considered an occasional seller, you must get a Seller's Permit from any local State of California Board of Equalization office. Reservations are an excellent idea, although if any spaces are empty, they are let on a first-come, first-serve basis. Gates open for vendors at 6:00 AM.

CONTACT: Jon Harris, GCC Swap Meet Office, 1122 E Garfield Ave, Glendale CA 91205. Tel: (818) 240-1000 × 5805, Monday through Thursday 8:00 AM–6:00 PM. Email: jharris@glendale.cc.ca.us.

GOLETA

Santa Barbara Swap Meet

DATES: Sunday.

TIMES: 7:00 AM–3:00 PM.

ADMISSION: $1. Parking is free.

LOCATION: 907 South Kellogg. Going south on Hwy 101, get off at Fairview, left on Hollister, right on Kellogg, stay on Kellogg until the end of the road. Going north on Hwy 101, get off on 217 Junction, right on Hollister, left on Kellogg, stay on until the end of the road.

DESCRIPTION: This outdoor market, open since 1967, has 200 dealers selling antiques, collectibles, crafts, furniture, garage sale goodies, cards and new merchandise. A snack bar feeds the famished. And handicapped-accessible restrooms are most welcome. If you wish to sell a vehicle, it costs $5 to do so!

DEALER RATES: $17 per 16' × 16' space. First come, first served.

CONTACT: Santa Barbara Swap Meet, 907 S Kellogg, Goleta CA 93117. Tel: (805) 964-9050. Fax: (805) 683-3601.

HUNTINGTON BEACH

Golden West College Swap Meet

DATES: Saturday and Sunday, year round. Rain or shine.

TIMES: 8:00 AM–3:00 PM.

ADMISSION: Free. Parking is free.

LOCATION: Golden West College Campus. Between Golden West St and Edinger Ave.

DESCRIPTION: This 15-year-old plus market operates to benefit the college programs and operations. The Saturday market is strictly old goods, antiques, collectibles and whatever. Sunday's market is old and new merchandise. Some of the 600–800 dealers sell fresh produce, records and

music memorabilia, as well as the usual flea market goodies. My market visitor was impressed with this market saying you can still get good deals.
DEALER RATES: $20 per space reserved. $25 for same day (i.e. grabbing space at the last minute). Cash only. To reserve space call the office at (714) 898-2BUY (2289) Wednesday between 8:30 AM–11:00 AM and 1:00 PM–4:00 PM.
CONTACT: Golden West College Swap Meet, 15744 Golden West St, Huntington Beach CA 92647-3197. Tel: (714) 898-SWAP (7927) for tape message, or (714) 895-8737 during office hours 8:00 AM–11:00 AM.

INDIO

Maclin's Indio Open Air Market

DATES: Every Wednesday and Saturday night.
TIMES: 5:00 PM–10:00 PM.
ADMISSION: $.50, children under 12 free. Saturday is free. Parking is free.
LOCATION: 46-350 Arabia St. From Hwy 111 take Monroe south, then east on Dr. Carreon to Arabia.
DESCRIPTION: Unlike any of their other markets, this Maclin's Market is open evenings. There is plenty of "locally-grown and nationally-famous" produce and baked goods, handcrafted arts and jewelry and just about anything and everything for your home, family, pets, or car.
DEALER RATES: Wednesday $17 per space, Saturday $15. Just show up the day of the market by 4:00 PM to get your space.
CONTACT: Maclin's, 7407 Riverside Dr, Ontario CA 91761. Tel: (909) 984-5131 or 1-800-222-7467 in California.

KING CITY

King City Rotary Flea Market

DATES: First Sunday in April, rain or shine.
TIMES: 7:00 AM–4:00 PM.
ADMISSION: $2 for adults. $1 for children age 12 and under. Parking is free.
LOCATION: Salinas Valley Fairgrounds. Take Hwy 101 to Canal St, then follow signs to Fairgrounds.
DESCRIPTION: This show began in 1969 and is both an indoor and outdoor market that accommodates approximately 150 dealers selling an-

tiques as well as new merchandise, crafts, collectibles, and fresh produce. There is also a variety of foods available, including American, Mexican, and Oriental. This market is a fundraiser for the local Rotary.
DEALER RATES: $15 for 10' × 15' space. $10 for each additional space. Reservations are required.
CONTACT: Chris Davis, King City Rotary, PO Box 611, King City CA 93930-0611. Tel: (408) 385-0414. Day of show call the fairgrounds at (408) 385-3243.

LANCASTER

Lancaster Chamber of Commerce Semi-Annual Flea Market

DATES: Third Sunday in May; first Sunday in October, rain or shine.
TIMES: 9:00 AM–4:00 PM.
ADMISSION: $3 per person, $2 seniors and military, $1 children 6–12, under 5 free. Parking fee is $2.
LOCATION: Antelope Valley Fairgrounds. 155 East Ave I. Take the 14 Freeway (Antelope Valley Freeway) to Ave I exit and head east exactly 2 miles to the fairgrounds at the corner of Ave I and Division St.
DESCRIPTION: This indoor/outdoor market has been operating since May 1966 as *the* fundraiser for local Chamber of Commerce. From 400 to 500 dealers from four states are attracted to this well-organized market selling antiques, arts and crafts, collectibles, quality art and jewelry, food, new merchandise, yardsale—whatever is legal. It is getting more upscale as the years pass. About a quarter of all the vendors sell food: Mexican, Thai, Oriental, Italian, barbeques, Greek—whatever your palate fancies. Handicapped-accessible restrooms are available.

When this market first opened, vendors would wait impatiently until the gates were thrown open, then race for whatever spot they could get. Now it is a finely-tuned event run by 300 volunteers.
DEALER RATES: $70 for 10' × 10' space inside; $25–$60 per 10' × 10' booth outside, depending on the location, first or second choice or yard sale location. Reservations are required on a first come/first served basis. Dealers must be set up and ready by 8:30 AM.
CONTACT: Special Event Coordinator, Lancaster Chamber of Commerce, 554 W Lancaster Blvd, Lancaster CA 93534-2534. Tel: (805) 948-4518 or fax: (805) 949-1212.

LODI

Lodi Street Faire

DATES: First Sunday in May and October. Rain or shine.

TIMES: 8:00 AM–4:00 PM.

ADMISSION: Free. Parking is free.

LOCATION: Downtown Lodi on School St, between Lodi Ave and Lockeford St.

DESCRIPTION: This semi-annual fundraiser attracts over 550 dealers selling antiques, collectibles, arts and crafts, and new merchandise. Food vendors sell a variety of treats in two Food Alleys. One parking lot is devoted to tables and chairs for those eating or resting. Over 40,000 attend this fair. There are volunteers roaming the fair in golf carts waiting to be flagged down by weary or overloaded shoppers looking for a lift. Roving entertainment is provided.

DEALER RATES: \$65 for 13' × 13' space, \$100 for 13' × 13' corner space. Reservations are required.

CONTACT: Lodi District Chamber of Commerce, 35 S School St, PO Box 386, Lodi CA 95241-0386. Tel: (209) 367-7840 or 1-800-304-5634. Day of show contact workers in on-site information booth.

LONG BEACH

Outdoor Antique and Collectible Market

DATES: Third Sunday of every month, rain or shine. Special Holiday show first Sunday in November.

TIMES: 8:00 AM–3:00 PM.

ADMISSION: \$4.50 for adults. No fee for children under 12. Free parking.

LOCATION: Veterans Stadium at Lakewood Blvd and Conant St. Take Lakewood Blvd North exit from Freeway 405, turn right onto Lakewood Blvd, go north approximately 2 miles, turn right on Conant St.

DESCRIPTION: This outdoor market opened in 1982 and is the largest regularly scheduled antique and collectible show in the west. It draws over 800 dealers. Please note that only antiques and collectibles may be sold here.

DEALER RATES: Booths measure 19' × 16' and range in cost from \$45 to \$55 to \$65 and \$80 for corners. Advance reservations are required.

CONTACT: Americana Enterprises Inc, PO Box 69219, Los Angeles CA 90069. Tel: (213) 655-5703.

MORGAN HILL

Morgan Hill Flea Market

DATES: Every Saturday and Sunday, year round.
TIMES: 7:30 AM–6:00 PM.
ADMISSION: Free. Parking is also free.
LOCATION: 140 East Main St in Morgan Hill, 25 miles south of San Jose.
DESCRIPTION: This show first began in 1964. The market is held outdoors and consists of over 200 dealers selling under shade trees. Shoppers may find antiques and collectibles, as well as new and used merchandise and fresh produce. Food is served on the premises.
DEALER RATES: $12 for 3' × 10' table on Saturdays and $15 on Sundays. Reservations are not required.
CONTACT: Morgan Hill Flea Market, 140 E Main St, Morgan Hill CA 95037. Tel: (408) 779-3809.

NILES

Niles Antique Faire

DATES: Last Sunday in August.
TIMES: 4:00 AM–4:00 PM. Flashlight shopping allowed!
ADMISSION: Free. Parking is $3 and is run as a Boy Scout fundraiser. Some free parking is available early.
LOCATION: In the Niles Business District. Take Hwy 680 to Mission Blvd north to Niles Blvd; or take Hwy 880 to Alvarado Blvd and Niles Blvd east.
DESCRIPTION: This one-day event has been a successful fund raiser for many local non-profit organizations since 1925. Most of Niles Blvd and side streets are closed as over 500 dealers turn Niles into antique heaven. Buyers may start arriving as early as 3:00 AM and continue to shop throughout the day. Antiques, arts and crafts, and a variety of collectibles can be found. Niles itself is an historic landmark, home of the former Essanay Studios (of Charlie Chaplin, Ben Turpin fame), Vallejo's Mill (the first flouring mill) and its Railroad Depot Museum with a large railroad layout. Non-profit organizations run the many food concessions as their fundraiser.
DEALER RATES: $125 for 10' × 12' space with early reservations, $135 for later reservations. Reservations are suggested. First come, first served.

CONTACT: Flea Market Committee, Niles Merchant Association, PO Box 2672, Niles District, Fremont CA 94536-2672. Tel: (510) 792-8023.

NORTHRIDGE

Northridge Antique Swap Meet

DATE: Every fourth and fifth Sundays (when there is one and there are four a year!) of every month.
TIME: 8:00 AM–3:00 PM.
ADMISSION: $5 before 8:00 AM, $3 after. Parking is free.
LOCATION: Cal State Northridge University. Take 5 or 405 to 118 Simi Valley West, exit Reseda Blvd, follow signs to California State University, Northridge. Located on the north parking lot.
DESCRIPTION: This open-air market is described by a reader as a "very nice antique market with only old stuff, collectibles, many garage sales and very positive dealing." The 150–330 dealers sell, among other things: post cards, stamps, coins, fishing equipment, dishes, crystals, toys and whatever. Food is available on site. The fifth Sunday market is huge and quite popular and as an added attraction includes a Hot Rods and Classic Car Show (and sale).
DEALER RATES: $50 per space. Reservations are suggested.
CONTACT: Daryll Fisher, Antique Attractions, 17041 Lakewood Blvd, Bellflower CA 90706. Tel: (562) 633-3836.

OAKHURST

Mountain Peddler's Show

DATES: The Saturdays and Sundays of Memorial Day and Labor Day weekends; rain or shine.
TIMES: From 9:00 AM Saturday through Sunday 4:00 PM.
ADMISSION: Free admission. Free parking.
LOCATION: State Hwy 41 and County Rd 426. Oakhurst is located in the Sierra Nevada foothills on California State Hwy 41, 36 miles north of Fresno, and 16 miles south of Yosemite National Park.
DESCRIPTION: Initiated as a revenue source for the Chamber of Commerce, the first flea market was held in 1979. There were 186 booths and a crowd of 10,000. Today, there are over 400 booths selling antiques, collector's items, high-quality antique furnishings, glassware, pottery, clocks, porcelain, vintage, estate and costume jewelry, arts and crafts, and food displays—everything from "tri-tip" sandwiches, pizza to beer and

iced tea are freshly prepared for the visitors. Live entertainment, free to the public, is provided.
DEALER RATES: $100–$110 per booth of various depths (8–12' or 14–18') with 20' frontage. Set up varies depending upon booth location. Some set up (tables, tents, tarps, but no merchandise) starting Friday at 7:00 PM. Remainder of set up Saturday 6:00 AM–9:00 AM.
CONTACT: Donna Cochran, Eastern Madera County Chamber of Commerce, 49074 Civic Cir, Oakhurst CA 93644. Tel: (209) 642-4244. Fax: (209) 683-0784.

OAKLAND

Coliseum Swap Meet

DATES: Tuesday through Sunday.
TIMES: 6:30 AM–whenever the dealers pack up.
ADMISSION: Tuesday and Thursday $.50, Friday $.75, Saturday and Sunday $1. Parking is free.
LOCATION: 5401 Coliseum Way. At I-880 and Coliseum Way, ½ mile south of the Oakland Coliseum.
DESCRIPTION: Next door to the Oakland "A's," this market averages 400 dealers selling "everything" including loads of antiques and collectibles, fruits, vegetables, used and new merchandise, and craft items during the holidays. This place is known for the antiques with many antique dealers prowling the place first thing everyday, just to nab the good stuff! (Get there early if you like antiques.) More antiques dealers are selling on weekends. Plenty of south-of-the-border fruits are sold here. Food is served on the premises.
DEALER RATES: $5 on Tuesday, $10 per 15' × 15' space Wednesday through Friday, $15 per space on weekends. They only handle monthly or yearly reservations. You must come in person to make your reservations.
CONTACT: Coliseum Swap Meet, 5401 Coliseum Way, Oakland CA 94601-5021. Tel: (510) 534-0325 for a recording or (510) 533-1601 to speak to someone.

OCEANSIDE

Oceanside Drive-In Swap Meet

DATES: Every Friday, Saturday, Sunday, and holiday Mondays. Rain or shine.
TIMES: 6:00 AM–3:00 PM.

ADMISSION: Mondays and Saturdays $.50 fee; Fridays $.35, Sundays $.75. Parking is free.
LOCATION: 3480 Mission Ave, 2 miles east of IF-5.
DESCRIPTION: This show started in 1971. There are now more than 1,000 dealers featured in this outdoor market. All types of new, used, and collectible merchandise are sold on approximately 40 acres of land, which includes places to purchase food.
DEALER RATES: Saturday $13; Sunday $17; Friday $6; Monday $8 for 18' × 24' space. Reservations are not required. Monthly reservations are available.
CONTACT: Greg Crowder, 635 W Mission Ave, Escondido CA 92025. Tel: (760) 745-3100. Day of show call Ben Gavin at (760) 757-5286, Saturday and Sunday.

ONTARIO

Maclin's Chino Open Air Market

DATES: Every Tuesday, Saturday and Sunday.
TIMES: 7:30 AM–3:00 PM.
ADMISSION: $.50, children under 12 free. Free on Saturdays. Parking is free.
LOCATION: 7407 Riverside Drive. From points west, take Fwy 60 east to Euclid south, then east on Riverside Dr. From points east, take Fwy 60 west to Grove south, then west on Riverside Dr.
DESCRIPTION: This unique place to sell and shop has been serving the public since 1936. It is a cross between a swap meet, a mall, a fish market and a country fair, with not just dealers but exotic foods and children's attractions. There is a genuine livestock auction on Tuesdays and a restaurant with a '40s beer and wine bar and a wide-screen TV. Between 350 to 500 dealers sell everything from antiques and collectibles to clothing and gold jewelry. Children's pony rides entertain the younger crowd.
DEALER RATES: Rates are from $15 to $25. They suggest dealers come between 7:00–7:30 AM to get a space.
CONTACT: Maclin's, 7407 Riverside Dr, Ontario CA 91761. Tel: (909) 984-5131. Or Toll-free in California 1-800-222-7467.

PALMDALE

Antelope Valley Swap Meet at Four Points

DATES: Saturday and Sunday, year round.

TIMES: Saturday 7:00 AM–4:00 PM; Sunday 6:00 AM–4:00 PM.
ADMISSION: Saturday $.50; Sunday $1; parking is free.
LOCATION: 5550 Pearblossom Hwy. Intersection of Hwy 138 and Pearblossom Hwy. Five miles east of Palmdale.
DESCRIPTION: "Everything under the sun!" describes this swap meet opened in 1977. About 350 dealers sell antiques, collectibles, crafts, garage sale goods, old and new merchandise, tools, fresh produce and "soup to nuts." Great food is easily found including homemade tamales and corn dogs, authentic Mexican food, and biscuits and gravy to mention a mouth-watering few. This market, with its country/western atmosphere, live entertainment and pony rides for the kids, seems to offer more than something for everyone. In 1997 they upgraded their facilities for the comfort of their patrons and dealers.
DEALER RATES: Saturday: $7 per 20' × 20' booth; Sunday $14 per booth. Storage sheds are available. Reservations are not required; first come, first served.
CONTACT: Joyce Bruce, Antelope Valley Swap Meet, PO Box 901807, Palmdale CA 93590. Tel: (805) 273-0456. Day of show call (805) 533-9102.

PANORAMA CITY

Valley Indoor Swap Meet

DATES: Wednesday through Monday.
TIMES: 10:00 AM–7:00 PM.
ADMISSION: Free. Parking is free.
LOCATION: 14650 Parthenia St. Take 101 Freeway to Van Nuys Blvd, go north 4 miles to Parthenia St.
DESCRIPTION: Started in 1986 and the only major retailing center to survive the Northridge earthquake, this indoor market of 250 dealers sells collectibles, crafts, furniture, and lots of clothing. Three snack bars and a bakery quell the munchies and handicapped-accessible restrooms are on site.
DEALER RATES: $500 monthly for a 9' × 13' space. Reservations are required.
CONTACT: Deanna McClintock, Valley Indoor Swap Meet, 14650 Parthenia St, Panorama City CA 91402. Tel: (818) 892-0183 or fax: (818) 894-5676.

PASADENA

Rose Bowl Flea Market and Swap Meet

DATES: Second Sunday of each month, rain or shine.
TIMES: 9:00 AM–3:00 PM.
ADMISSION: $5 per person, children under 12 free with an adult. Free parking, and VIP parking for a fee. Early admission for $10 from 7:30 AM–9:00 AM, and very early VIP admission is $15 from 6:00 AM–7:30 AM.
LOCATION: Pasadena Rose Bowl, at the corner of Rosemont Ave and Aroyo Blvd. Well marked. Close to the freeway junctions of 210 Foothill, 134 Ventura and 110 Pasadena Freeways.
DESCRIPTION: This monthly market ranks among the largest and best known in the country. It has operated outdoors on the grounds of the Rose Bowl Stadium since 1968 and currently hosts over 2,200 sellers and approximately 20,000 shoppers at each sale. Virtually anything under the sun can be found here, from antiques and collectibles to new merchandise and arts and crafts. Buyers often include Hollywood celebrities. Vendors may not sell food, animals, drug-related items or ammunition. Food and beverages and handicapped-accessible restrooms complete the amenities.
DEALER RATES: $40–$70 and up per 10' × 20' space per day depending upon location. Advance reservations strongly suggested.
CONTACT: RG Canning Enterprises, PO Box 400, Maywood CA 90270. Tel: (213) 560-7469 x11. Office hours Mondays and Wednesdays 10:00 AM–5:00 PM. Fax: (213) 560-5924. Email: rgc@rgcshows.com or website: www.rgcshows.com.

PASO ROBLES

Maclin's Paso Robles Open-Air Market

DATES: First weekend of every month, Saturday and Sunday.
TIMES: 6:00 AM–2:00 PM.
ADMISSION: Free. Parking is also free.
LOCATION: Mid-State Fairgrounds, 2198 Riverside Ave. Located off scenic Hwy 101 at the intersection of Hwy 46 and Riverside Ave.
DESCRIPTION: Many antiques, collectibles, clothing, produce, new and used merchandise are sold here. This is a new market for Maclin's.
DEALER RATES: $15 per day or $25 per weekend.
CONTACT: Maclin's, 7407 Riverside Dr, Ontario CA 91761. Tel: (909) 948-5131. Or Toll-free in California 1-800-222-7467.

POMONA

Valley Indoor Swap Meet

DATES: Friday through Sunday.
TIMES: 10:00 AM–6:00 PM.
ADMISSION: $1, parking is free.
LOCATION: 1600 East Holt Blvd. Take San Bernardino Freeway (10) to Indian Hill Blvd, go south 1 mile to Holt Blvd. Indian Hill ends at the swap meet.
DESCRIPTION: Started in 1985 this indoor market of 400 dealers sells crafts, furniture, new merchandise, and lots of clothing, shoes and accessories. This is considered the largest indoor swap meet in the Inland Empire with unique displays of Mexican and American merchandise. Four snack bars quell the munchies and handicapped-accessible restrooms are on site.
DEALER RATES: $330 monthly for a 10' × 10' space. Reservations are required.
CONTACT: Valley Indoor Swap Meet, 1600 E Holt Blvd, Pomona CA 91767. Tel: (909) 620-1449.

PORTERVILLE

Porterville College Swap Meet

DATES: Every Saturday, weather permitting.
TIMES: 5:00 AM–4:00 PM.
ADMISSION: $.50. Parking is also free.
LOCATION: From Bakersfield: Go north on Hwy 99 to Hwy 65. Then 50 miles to Hwy 190, then east 1 mile to college. From Fresno, go south on Hwy 99 to Hwy 190, then go east 17 miles to the college.
DESCRIPTION: Started in 1981, this market has an average of 300 dealers attending. There is always plenty of elegant junk available along with an ample supply of antiques, arts and crafts, collectibles, jewelry, and music tapes, along with new merchandise and fresh produce. This market is run for the benefit of the student scholarship fund and is a Foundation function. There is always plenty of food available on the premises.
DEALER RATES: $10 for 24' × 36' space (electricity costs an additional $1). Reservations are advised but not necessary.
CONTACT: Bill Goucher, Porterville College Swap Meet, 150 E College Ave, Porterville CA 93257-5901. Tel: (209) 791-2200 (college) or Mr. Goucher at (209) 784-9161.

REDDING

Epperson Brothers Auction and Flea Market

DATES: Saturday and Sunday, year round. Rain or shine.
TIMES: Sunup to sundown. Also, auctions are held at 6:30 PM every Wednesday and at 1:00 PM every Sunday.
ADMISSION: $1 per carload Sundays; Saturdays admission is free.
LOCATION: 5091 Fig Tree Lane, 1 mile south of Redding International Airport, off Airport Rd.
DESCRIPTION: The market, located on 20 acres of trees, first opened in 1962 and now consists of 100 to 150 dealers selling their goods both indoors and outdoors. Antiques, collectibles, arts and crafts, and new and used furniture can be purchased. Food, beer (had to mention that!), plenty of parking and handicapped-accessible restrooms are available on the premises.
DEALER RATES: $5 for 4' × 8' table (plus space for vehicle) on Saturday. $10 per space on Sunday.
CONTACT: Jack L Epperson, 5091 Fig Tree La, Redding CA 96002. Tel: (916) 365-7242 or Karen L Bloom at the same number.

ROSEVILLE

Denio's Roseville Farmer's Market and Auction, Inc.

DATES: Every Friday through Sunday, rain or shine.
TIMES: 7:00 AM–5:00 PM.
ADMISSION: $.50 or parking is $2 per car.
LOCATION: 1551 Vineyard Rd. Take I-80 to Roseville/Riverside exit, turn left on Cirby Way, right on Foothill Blvd to Vineyard, right on Vineyard Rd.
DESCRIPTION: Denio's is a family owned and operated business in the same location since 1947, serving northern California, southern Oregon, and western Nevada. It averages 1,500 to 2,000 dealers selling everything imaginable—antiques, collectibles, handmade/craft items, fresh produce and new merchandise. Delicious corn dogs and international foods are available on the premises.
DEALER RATES: Start at $15 per space. Reservations are not required.
CONTACT: Rental Office, 1551 Vineyard Rd, Roseville CA 95678. Tel: (916) 782-2704 seven days a week from 8:00 AM–5:00 PM.

SACRAMENTO

Auction City and Flea Market

DATES: Every Saturday and Sunday, rain or shine.
TIMES: 7:00 AM–5:00 PM.
ADMISSION: Free. Parking is free.
LOCATION: 8521 Folsom Blvd. Use Hwy 50 going to Lake Tahoe, take Watt Ave south to Folsom Blvd, turn right, go .8 miles to market on right.
DESCRIPTION: This show first opened in 1966. It accommodates 250–300 dealers in both an indoor and outdoor market. Four barns house fresh produce, antiques and collectibles in permanent space. This is said to be the longest-operating flea market within the city limits of Sacramento. Several restaurants operate on the premises.
DEALER RATES: $20 for one 4' × 8' table. $10 for each additional table. Reservations are accepted Wednesday through Friday 9:00 AM–5:00 PM.
CONTACT: Emil Magovac, Owner, Auction City and Flea Market, 8521 Folsom Blvd, Sacramento CA 95826. Tel: (916) 383-0880 or (916) 383-0950. Day of show call Harold Hennessey, Manager, at the above number.

Forty-Niner (49er) Drive-In Swap Meet

DATES: Thursday through Sunday.
TIMES: 7:00 AM–4:00 PM.
ADMISSION: $.25. Parking is free.
LOCATION: At the 49er Drive-In Theater. I-80 at Raley Blvd Exit, 2 miles west of McClellan Air Force Base.
DESCRIPTION: Now open about 10 years, this outdoor market draws from 100 dealers (except on Thursday to 250) selling garage- and attic-found treasures including old clothes, t-shirts, household cleaning supplies, some antiques and collectibles and "a little bit of everything." Because so much of the stuff coming in is from "Auntie's attic" there are a lot of great finds waiting to be discovered. A hot dog cart serves the starved.
DEALER RATES: Thursday $5, other days $8 per 15' × 15' space. However, if you come for Thursday, it's $5 for Thursday, then $4 for each consecutive day after, that weekend. Reservations are required for monthly; otherwise, first come, first served.
CONTACT: Bill Brancamp, 49er Swap Meet, 4450 Marysville Blvd, Sacramento CA 95838. Tel: (916) 920-3530.

SAN BERNADINO

San Bernadino Outdoor Market

DATES: Every Sunday, rain or shine.

TIMES: 6:00 AM–2:00 PM.

ADMISSION: $1, children under 13 are free with an adult. Free and paid parking is available.

LOCATION: National Orange Showgrounds. Directly off the 215 Freeway. Take the Orange Show Rd exit and follow the signs.

DESCRIPTION: There are almost 800 dealers attending this, the area's largest, weekly outdoor show. An enormous selection of merchandise can be found, about half new and half used. Antiques, collectibles, crafts and new merchandise are just some of the items to be ferreted out. Many sellers are "the average guy cleaning out his garage." From one reader: "Worth visiting every several months to keep in touch." For your convenience, food is also available on the premises.

DEALER RATES: $7 to $35 depending on location of space. Reservations are suggested. They claim to never turn anyone away. If you are more than a one-time seller, you need a Sales Tax Permit from the State Board of Equalization.

CONTACT: RG Canning, PO Box 400, Maywood CA 90270-0400. Tel: (909) 888-0394 Monday or Wednesday between 10:30 AM–4:30 PM. Email: rgc@rgcshows.com. Website: www.rgcshows.com.

SAN DIEGO

Kobey's Swap Meet at the San Diego Sports Arena

DATES: Thursday through Sunday and every day the week prior to Christmas.

TIMES: 7:00 AM–3:00 PM.

ADMISSION: Thursday and Friday $.50 per person, weekends $1, seniors $.75, children under 12 free. Parking is free.

LOCATION: Sports Arena at 3500 Sports Arena Blvd.

DESCRIPTION: Opened in 1976, this outdoor market of 1,000 spaces hosts 700 vendors selling antiques, collectibles, crafts, produce, coins, stamps, cards, garage sale finds, furniture and new merchandise. Food kiosks and restrooms are available.

DEALER RATES: Weekends $25 and up for a 16' × 18' space ($20 unreserved); $6–$8 for Thursday and Friday. Reservations are recommended during holiday or peak seasons. Reservations must be made in person

Wednesday through Sunday; Wednesday at the office, Thursday through Sunday at the main entrance, 3500 Sports Area Blvd.
CONTACT: Kobey Swap Meet, 3350 Sports Area Blvd #K, San Diego CA 92110. Tel: (619) 226-0650 (24-hour information) or (619) 523-2700 Monday through Friday from 9:00 AM–5:00 PM. Fax: (619) 523-2715.

SAN FRANCISCO

"America's Largest" Antique & Collectible Shows

DATES: 1998 dates: February 7–8; May 16–17; August 22–23, November 21–22. Call for 1999 dates.
TIMES: Saturday 8:00 AM–7:00 PM; Sunday 9:00 AM–5:00 PM.
ADMISSION: $5, $2.50 under 17, free under 12. Parking is $5 as of Fall '97.
LOCATION: Cow Palace. Cow Palace exit off Hwy 101, San Francisco.
DESCRIPTION: This indoor market opened in 1988 and attracts over 500 dealers selling antiques and collectibles only to over 8,000 shoppers. Food and restrooms are available on the premises.
DEALER RATES: $140 per 10' × 10' booth. Reservations are required.
CONTACT: Chuck or Christine Palmer, Palmer/Wirfs & Associates, 4001 NE Halsey Ste 5, Portland OR 97232. Tel: (503) 282-0877. Fax: (503) 282-2953.

The San Francisco Flea Market, Inc

DATES: Saturday and Sunday, year round.
TIMES: 6:00 AM–4:00 PM.
ADMISSION: $.50. Parking is free.
LOCATION: 140 South Van Ness. From 101, exit at Mission St, to the right. The market is located at the corner of Mission and South Van Ness.
DESCRIPTION: This popular market attracts over 100 dealers and thousands of shoppers. The dealers sell antiques, collectibles, new merchandise and garage sale goodies.
DEALER RATES: $25 per space for the weekend, first come, first served.
CONTACT: San Francisco Flea Market Inc, 140 S Van Ness, San Francisco CA 94103. Tel: (415) 646-0544.

SAN JOSE

Capitol Flea Market

DATES: Thursday through Sunday.
TIMES: 6:00 AM–5:30 PM.
LOCATION: Capitol Expressway at Monterey Hwy.
ADMISSION: $.50 on Thursday, Friday free, Saturday $1.25, Sunday $1.50. Children under 12 free. Parking is free.
DESCRIPTION: This outdoor market, in business since 1982, hosts from 500 to 900 dealers depending on the season. They sell mostly antiques, collectibles, and garage sale specials (self-billed as the "World's Largest Garage Sale"). Very little new merchandise is sold here. They describe themselves as an "old-fashioned" flea market in the best sense of the word. Covering 35 acres in a drive-in theater, they park from 4,000 to 12,000 cars a day! "We are crammed!" says their manager, Glen Norris. He advises you to "Come *early* for the bargains." They cater to families. There is a gigantic used car and truck sale every weekend selling vehicles at $12 a set of wheels! They've added a huge farmers market produce area (with 40–50 vendors here alone) featuring farm fresh fruits and vegetables at bargain prices. Live music and free raffles liven the weekends. There are restaurants and snack bars on site with a wide range of food available.
DEALER RATES: $14 on Thursday, $10 on Friday, $15 on Saturday, $20 on Sunday. Although spaces may vary, they all accommodate a car or truck and ample selling space. Reservations are not required. Monthly reservations are available.
CONTACT: Glen Norris, Capitol Flea Market, 3630 Hillcap Ave, San Jose CA 95136. Tel: (408) 225-5800.

The Flea Market, Inc

DATES: Wednesday through Sunday, year round.
TIMES: Dawn to dusk.
ADMISSION: Free. Parking is $3 Saturday and Sunday; $1 Wednesday through Friday.
LOCATION: 1590 Berryessa Rd between Hwys 680 and 101.
DESCRIPTION: This humongous market is billed as the "Original Flea Market" started in 1960 and is the world's largest covering 120 acres with well over 2,000 dealers selling everything! From antiques and collectibles, abused to garage sales. They have a ¼ mile long produce row, 25 snack

bars, clean, well-attended restrooms and an average of 80,000 visitors each weekend. Watch for their special events, the Salsa Festival including contest (you can eat yourself to death on the sauces and chips!), Octoberfest, Cinque de Mayo, Holiday Crafters Fair (just before Thanksgiving), Bicycle Fairs, whatever!

DEALER RATES: Per 17' × 20' space per day: Wednesday $15; Thursday and Friday $10; Saturday and Sunday $25. No reservations are necessary, but suggested if you have a preference for a space. For a garage sale special: $10 for the first Saturday of the month.

CONTACT: Reservations Manager, The Flea Market Inc, 1590 Berryessa Rd, San Jose CA 95133-1003. Tel: (408) 453-1110. Fax: (408) 437-9011.

SAN JUAN BAUTISTA

San Juan Bautista Annual Flea Market

DATES: First Sunday in August, rain or shine.

TIMES: 8:00 AM–5:00 PM.

ADMISSION: Free. Some parking lots nearby are free, some aren't.

LOCATION: In downtown San Juan Bautista, 30 miles south of San Jose on Hwy 101.

DESCRIPTION: This show first began in 1963, and nowadays over 500 vendors from nine states and 165 California cities come to participate in this event, all conducting their business outdoors on the main streets of the town. Antiques and collectibles, fine art, and craft items can be purchased. This market claims to be the oldest and largest one-day street show in California and has been named one of the top four flea markets in California by *Good Housekeeping* magazine. There are 12 restaurants and plenty of street vendors providing food.

DEALER RATES: $175 for 10' × 14' space. Reservations are required. Dealers start arriving as early as 4:00 AM.

CONTACT: Chamber of Commerce, PO Box 1037, San Juan Bautista CA 95045. Tel: (408) 623-2454. Fax: (408) 623-0674.

SANTA CLARITA (SAUGAS)

Saugus Swap Meet

DATES: Every Sunday, rain or shine.

TIMES: 7:00 AM–3:00 PM.

ADMISSION: $l for adults, children under 12 are admitted free. Parking is free.

LOCATION: 22500 Soledad Canyon Rd. From Los Angeles, take I-5 to Valencia Blvd exit, turn right on Valencia Blvd, then go 3¼ miles. Market is on the right.
DESCRIPTION: This show originally began in 1965. There are approximately 650 dealers conducting their business outdoors and selling everything from antiques and collectibles to new merchandise and fresh produce. The market is held on the grounds of movie star Hoot Gibson's former ranch. There is food available on the premises. From one reader: "...garage sales were good quality, good dealing available. About 60/40 percent new/collectibles. Many businesses come to advertise. There is art, pottery, carpets, home repair, remodeling; I guess everything is available with many food stands for food and drink."
DEALER RATES: $30 for 20' × 16' space. Assigned location space is available from $20–$60 a day. Reservations are not required. Park on space. Setup starts at 6:00 AM.
CONTACT: Saugus Swap Meet, Box 901, Santa Clarita CA 91380-9001. For information contact office Tuesday through Friday 8:00 AM–3:00 PM. Tel: (818) 716-6010 or (805) 259-3886.

SANTA FE SPRINGS

Santa Fe Springs Swap Meet

DATES: Every Wednesday, Thursday, Saturday, and Sunday. Friday nights April through October. Weather permitting.
TIMES: 5:30 AM–3:30 PM all four days. Night hours 5:00 PM–10:00 PM.
ADMISSION: $.50 on Wednesday; free on Thursday; $.75 on Friday, Saturday and Sunday. Parking is free.
LOCATION: 13963 Alondra Blvd. Take Valley View exit off I-5.
DESCRIPTION: This market first began in 1960 and is said to be the first swap meet in Southern California. Held at a drive-in theater, this market averages 700 dealers on weekends and 500 plus during the week selling arts and crafts, fine art, new merchandise, and fresh produce. There are kiddie rides and a video arcade to keep children busy. Food is served on the premises and there are handicapped-accessible restrooms.
DEALER RATES: $10 for approximately 15' × 20' space on Wednesday; free on Thursday; $25–$30 per space on Saturday and Sunday; $25 Friday nights. Reservations are required, although non-reserved space is available at the higher rate. Monthly rates are available. Advance shopping hours for dealers begins at 5:30 AM. They have a garage sale special: $5 on Saturday and $10 Friday night and Sunday, subject to available space.

CONTACT: Santa Fe Springs Swap Meet, 13963 Alondra Blvd, Santa Fe Springs CA 90670. Tel: (562) 921-4359 or (562) 921-9996 for tape message.

SANTEE

Santee Swap Meet

DATES: Saturday and Sunday, rain or shine.
TIMES: 6:30 AM–2:00 PM.
ADMISSION: $.50. Parking is free.
LOCATION: 10990 Woodside Ave N. Take 67 north to Riverford Rd exit. Turn left at exit, then left at Riverford Rd, left at Woodside Ave N. Market is on the right side at the Drive-In theater.
DESCRIPTION: Open since 1984, this outdoor market draws large crowds of buyers as well as sellers. Many a garage is cleaned out here as well as vendors selling new merchandise, antiques, collectibles, crafts and produce. This is a fast growing market which now holds special events on Saturdays. The second Saturday special event is strictly antiques and collectibles. It is held next to the main swap meet. A snack bar serves a wide variety of sandwiches, snacks and breakfasts.
DEALER RATES: Saturday $9 per 20' × 20' booth, Sunday $11 per 20' × 20' booth. Reservations are not required, it's a first-come-first-served market.
CONTACT: Joe Crowder, 635 W Mission Ave, Escondido CA 92025. Tel: (760) 745-3100. Day of show or tape information (619) 449-7927.

SEBASTOPOL

Midgley's Country Flea Market

DATES: Every Saturday and Sunday year round. Closed only when there is a "downpour."
TIMES: 6:30 AM–4:30 PM.
ADMISSION: Free. Parking is free.
LOCATION: Off Hwy 101 to Gravenstein Hwy or Hwy 116. Market is about 5 miles at 2200 Gravenstein Hwy South. Only 50 miles north of San Francisco.
DESCRIPTION: This outdoor market has been open since 1972. There are up to 500 dealers during the summer and anywhere from 300 to 400 dealers selling their goods during the winter months. There is a large variety of antiques, collectibles, crafts, new merchandise and even fresh pro-

duce available. Basically anything new or used is sold including clothes, books, pictures, jewelry, tires, and furniture, just to name a few. For your convenience there are two snack bars on the premises.
DEALER RATES: Start at $12 for 4' × 8' table and parking for one vehicle. Weekly, monthly and seasonal rates available. Reservations are not required.
CONTACT: Rosalie Midgley, Midgley's Country Flea Market, 2200 Gravenstein Hwy S, Sebastopol CA 95472. Tel: (707) 823-7874 or 1-800-800-FLEA in California.

STANTON

International Market Place (Indoor Swapmeet of Stanton)

DATES: Daily except Tuesday.
TIMES: Weekends 10:00 AM–6:00 PM; weekdays 10:00 AM–7:00 PM.
ADMISSION: Free. Parking is free.
LOCATION: 10401 Beach Blvd, 2 miles from Knott's Berry Farm.
DESCRIPTION: This two-story indoor market has 200 spaces with 70 vendors selling crafts, new merchandise, jewelry, perfumes, sportswear, athletic shoes, luggage, clothing, computer stuff, electronic appliances, gifts, nail and beauty salon, groceries, caps, embroidering, silk flowers and more. One snack bar, a restaurant, and handicapped-accessible restrooms are on-site.
DEALER RATES: $250–$600 for 4 weeks or 28 days, depending on the location, for a 8' × 12' space. Reservations are not required.
CONTACT: Manager (pick one: John, Avo, or Jila), Indoor Swapmeet of Stanton, 10401 Beach Blvd, Stanton CA 90680. Tel: (714) 527-1112 or (714) 527-1234. Fax: (714) 527-1595.

VALLEJO

Napa-Vallejo Flea Market & Auction

DATES: Every Sunday, rain or shine.
TIMES: 6:00 AM–5:00 PM.
ADMISSION: Free. $2 parking fee.
LOCATION: 303 Kelly Rd, off Hwy 29, halfway between Napa and Vallejo.
DESCRIPTION: This show began in 1947. It is both an indoor and outdoor market situated on 20 acres of land. The market accommodates approximately 600 dealers who sell antiques and collectibles, arts and crafts,

jewelry, books, sporting goods, and tools, to name a few. In addition, there is a produce market and several permanent businesses located here. There are four snack bar facilities on the premises which have been family owned and operated for 40 years including a Mexican food vendor and a barbecue.
DEALER RATES: $20 for 3' × 8' table, vehicle space is included. No reservations are accepted.
CONTACT: Nelson or Tom Harding, 303 Kelly Rd, Vallejo CA 94590. Tel: (707) 226-8862.

VENTURA

Ventura Flea Market

DATES: 1998: February 1, March 1, April 19, June 7, August 2, September 27, November 1. Check local papers for 1999 dates. They are advertised everywhere.
TIMES: 9:00 AM–2:00 PM. Although you can shop while the vendors pack up until 4:30 PM. Advice: come early for the best parking.
ADMISSION: $4, children under 12 are free with an adult. Parking is free. Early dealer and collector's hours start at 6:00 AM for an $8 admission.
LOCATION: Ventura County Fairgrounds, aka Seaside Park at 10 West Harbor in Ventura, just off the 101 Ventura Freeway at California St.
DESCRIPTION: There are over 800 dealers attending this outdoor show. Everything from antiques to collectibles to crafts and new merchandise to garage specials can be found here. It is one of California's most popular markets with 10,000 to 15,000 buyers. For your convenience, food and restrooms are available on the premises. As one shopper describes this market: "95% collectibles and garage sales, only 5% new stuff. Very good dealers who want to make a deal. Bargains can still be found here."
DEALER RATES: $20, $30, or $40 per 10' × 20' space. Reservations are suggested.
CONTACT: R G Canning, PO Box 400, Maywood CA 90270-0400. Tel: (213) 587-5100. Office hours are Monday and Wednesday 10:00 AM to 5:00 PM. Email: rgc@rgcshows.com or website: www.rgcshows.com.

VICTORVILLE

Maclin's Victorville Open-Air Market

DATES: Every Saturday and Sunday.
TIMES: 6:00 AM–2:00 PM.

ADMISSION: $1, children 12 and under free. Seniors $.75. Parking is free.
LOCATION: San Bernardino County Fairgrounds, 14800 Seventh St. Located off the 15 Fwy on Roy Rogers exit.
DESCRIPTION: Another new market from Maclin's with dealers selling household goods, clothing, new and used merchandise, collectible and specialty items. There is "great onsite" food service.
DEALER RATES: Saturday aisles $13, $15 corners; Sunday $10 for everything.
CONTACT: Maclin's, 7407 Riverside Dr, Ontario CA 91761. Tel: (909) 984-5131. Or Toll-free in California 1-800-222-7467.

VISALIA

Visalia Sales Yard, Inc

DATES: Thursday and Sunday, year round.
TIMES: 6:00 AM–3:00 PM.
ADMISSION: Free. Parking is also free.
LOCATION: 29660 RD 152, 1½ miles east of Visalia.
DESCRIPTION: This show began in 1948 and is currently an all-outdoor market that accommodates approximately 300 dealers. Among the items to be found here are antiques and collectibles, new merchandise, and fresh produce. Food is available on the premises.
DEALER RATES: $8 per 10' × 10' space.
CONTACT: Karen Green, Visalia Sales Yard Inc, 29660 Rd 152, Visalia CA 93291. Tel: (209) 734-9092.

WOODLAND HILLS

Valley Indoor Swap Meet

DATES: Friday through Sunday.
TIMES: 10:00 AM–6:00 PM.
ADMISSION: $1, seniors and children under 12 free. Parking is free.
LOCATION: 6701 Variel Ave. Take 101 Freeway to Desoto Ave, go north 1½ miles to Kittridge St, left 2 blocks.
DESCRIPTION: Opened in 1983, this is the first of three Valley Indoor Swap Meets in California. Housed in two buildings, their 500 dealers sell new merchandise and specialize in clothing and accessories. One of the buildings is open weekends only, the other from Friday through Sunday. Claimed to be "the most famous, well-known indoor swap meet in south-

ern California. Selling high-end merchandise. Many movie and TV celebrities can be seen attending on almost any weekend."
DEALER RATES: $360 in the 2-day building, $475 in the 3-day building, monthly for a 10' × 10' space. Reservations are required.
CONTACT: Jeff Kaplan, Valley Indoor Swap Meet, 6701 Variel Ave, Woodland Hills CA 91367. Tel: (818) 340-9120 or 340-9123. Fax: (818) 340-5413.

YUCCA VALLEY

Sky Drive-In Swap Meet

DATES: Saturday and Sunday, year round.
TIMES: 5:30 AM–2:00 PM.
ADMISSION: Free. Parking is free.
LOCATION: 7028 Theater Rd.
DESCRIPTION: This family-owned, still old-fashioned, "not overly commercialized" swap meet's 200 dealers sell a mix of antiques and collectibles, old tools, and new and used merchandise—described as from "junk to gems." As it is so easy to rent and set up here, many locals bring in tons of garage sale goodies. In fact, many items you might be looking for elsewhere and can't find, are probably here! The Sky Cafe serves homemade breakfast and lunch. Clean restrooms are on site.
DEALER RATES: $9 for a 20' space. Reservations are not required.
CONTACT: Bob and Elizabeth Carr, Sky Drive-In Swap Meet, 7028 Theater Rd, Yucca Valley CA 92284. Tel: (760) 365-2104.

OTHER FLEA MARKETS AND SWAP MEETS

We know or have heard about these markets, but have not personally contacted each one, as we have the markets with descriptions. If you plan to visit one of these markets listed below, *please call first* to make sure they are still open. Flea markets do come and go. While they were open when we went to press, they may not be later. We can't be responsible. *Call first!*

Alameda: Norcal Swap Meet, 1150 Ballena Blvd. Tel: 510-769-7266.
Anderson: Happy Valley Flea Mart, 17820 Strawberry Ln. Tel: 916-365-1466.
Anderson: Jolly Giant Flea Mart, 6719 Eastside Rd. Tel: 916-365-6458.
Arcata: Redwood Flea Market. Tel: 707-839-3049.

Aromas: Red Barn Flea Market, 1000 Hwy 101. Tel: 408-422-1271 or 408-726-3101.

Bakersfield: Fairground Swap Meet, S Union Ave. Tel: 805-397-1504.

Bell: Bell Swap Meet, 6515 Atlantic Ave. Tel: 213-562-2461.

Berkeley: Berkeley Flea Market, 1937 Ashby Ave. Tel: 510-644-0744.

Brentwood: Brentwood Flea Market, 6715 Brentwood Blvd. Tel: 510-634-3767.

Calexico: Santo Tomas Swap Meet, 1102 V V Williams. Tel: 760-357-9020.

Calexico: Santo Tomas Swap Meet, 1640 V V Williams. Tel: 760-357-3556.

Castroville: Castroville Flea Market & Indoor Swap Meet, 10900 Merritt St. Tel: 408-633-0369.

Ceres: Ceres Flea Market, 1651 Whitmore Ave. Tel: 209-537-3323.

Chatsworth: Winnetka Drive-In Swap Meet, 20210 Prairie St. Tel: 818-886-0108.

Chico: Cal's Flea Market, Silver Dollar Fair Grounds. Tel: 916-892-9205.

Chula Vista: South Bay Drive-In Swap Meet, 2170 Coronado Ave. Tel: 619-423-9676.

Clearlake: Clearlake Flea Market, 16080 Davis St. Tel: 707-995-2304.

Colton: Colton Indoor Swap Meet, 1157 N Mount Vernon Ave. Tel: 909-783-2031.

Compton: Compton Swap Meet, 2100 N Long Beach Blvd. Tel: 310-608-7000.

Corning: Corning Swap Meet, 1412 Solano St. Tel: 916-824-5886.

Corning: North State Flea & Produce Mart, 3015 Hwy 99 W. Tel: 916-824-1979.

Corning: North State Flea & Produce Mart, 7445 Hwy 99 W. Tel: 916-824-0602.

Corona: Everyday Swap Meet Price, 152 E 6th St. Tel: 909-340-9652.

Covina: Covina Indoor Swap Meet, 422 W Arrow Hwy. Tel: 818-967-1820.

Cypress: Cypress College Swap. Tel: 714-952-9355

El Cajon: Aero Drive-In Theatre & Swap Meet, 1470 Broadway. Tel: 619-444-8800.

Emeryville: San Pablo Flea Market II, 6100 San Pablo Ave. Tel: 510-420-1468.

Fontana: Bel Air Swap Meet Inc, 15895 Valley Blvd. Tel: 909-355-3000.

Fontana: Fontana Indoor Swap Meet Inc, 9773 Sierra Ave. Tel: 909-428-0818.

Fresno: Fresno Flea Market & Swap Meet, 1641 S Chance Ave. Tel: 209-268-3646.

Garden Grove: Calif Flea Market Info, 12421 Magnolia St. Tel: 714-539-9500.

Gardena: Vermont Swap Meet, 17737 S Vermont Ave. Tel: 310-324-0923.

Hanford: Marketa El Swap Meet, 8967 Lacey Blvd. Tel: 209-587-1179.

Huntington Park: Seville & Hill Mini Swap Meet, 7820 Seville Ave. Tel: 213-585-4545.

Indio: Sunair Swap Meet, 84245 Indio Springs Dr. Tel: 760-342-1113.

Irwindale: Irwindale Swap Meet, 13360 Live Oak Ave. Tel: 818-357-0104.

Jamestown: Jimtown Flea Market, PO Box 678. Tel: 209-984-0911.

Lake Elsinore: Grand Junktion Swap Meet, 18273 Grand Ave. Tel: 909-678-5095.

Lancaster: Linda's Mini Swap Meet, 1145 W Ave I. Tel: 805-723-9544.

Los Altos: Foothill College Flea Market, 12345 El Monte Ave. Tel: 415-948-6417.

Los Angeles: Alameda Swap Meet, 4501 S Alameda St. Tel: 213-233-2764.

Los Angeles: Bonito's Swap Meet, 620 S Alvarado St. Tel: 213-483-2554.

Los Angeles: Giant Swap Meet, 4433 S Alameda St. Tel: 213-234-6038.

Los Angeles: Gonzalez Indoor Swap Meet, 7925 S Central Ave. Tel: 213-588-0479.

Los Angeles: La Oferta Swap Meet, 1544 W 6th St. Tel: 213-483-7858.

Los Angeles: Pequeno Swap Meet, 3425 E 1st St. Tel: 213-269-7424.

Los Angeles: Shop & Save Inc Swap Meet, 4700 Whittier Blvd. Tel: 213-263-5900.

Los Angeles: Slauson Indoor Swap Meet, 1600 W Slauson Ave. Tel: 213-778-6055.

Los Angeles: Union Discount Swap Meet, 4632 Santa Monica Blvd. Tel: 213-661-5910.

Los Angeles: Ventura Flea Market. Tel: 213-588-2727.

Madera: Madera Drive-In Swap Meet, 201 E Lincoln Ave. Tel: 209-661-7927.

Mammoth Lakes: Eddie's Little Swap Meet, 94 Laurel Mountain Rd. Tel: 760-934-2570.

Marysville: Marysville Flea Market, 1468 Simpson Ln. Tel: 916-743-8713.

Merced: Country Boy Flea Market, 3140 Beachwood Dr. Tel: 209-722-4822 or 209-722-8711.

Modesto: Crow's Landing Flea Market, 3113 Crows Landing Rd. Tel: 209-538-3363.

Modesto: Modesto Furniture Auto Auction & Flea Market, 1119 S 7th St. Tel: 209-522-8463.

Modesto: Thompson's Indoor Flea Market, 1800 Prescott Rd. Tel: 209-579-2545.

Montclair: Mission Drive-In Theatre Indoor Swap Meet. Tel: 909-628-0019.

Napa: Napa Flea Market, 303 S Kelly Rd. Tel: 707-226-8862.

National City: National City Swap Meet, 3200 D Ave. 619-477-2203.

Newbury Park: Thousand Oaks Auto Swap Meet. Tel: 805-499-0782.

Nipomo: Nipomo Swap Meet, 263 N Frontage Rd. Tel: 805-929-7000.

North Hills: Van Nuys Swap Meet, 8345 Hayvenhurst Pl. 818-891-0983.

Norwalk: Norwalk Indoor Swap Meet, 11600 Alondra Blvd. Tel: 562-402-1007.

Orange: Orange Swap Meet, 291 N State College Blvd. Tel: 714-634-4259.

Oroville: Oro Dam Flea Market, 1141 Oro Dam Blvd W. Tel: 916-533-1324.

Pacoima: La Bahia Swap Meet Inc, 10551 San Fernando Rd. Tel: 818-896-5895.

Palm Desert: College of the Desert Swap Meet, 43500 Monterey Ave. Tel: 760-773-2567.

Paradise: Cal's Depot Flea Market, 5588 Black Olive Dr. Tel: 916-872-4943.**Paramount:** Paramount Swap Meet, 7900 All America City Way. Tel: 562-633-7041 or 562-634-7927.

Pomona: Indian Hill Mall Indoor Swap Meet, 1600 E Holt Ave. Tel: 909-620-4792 or 818-331-0173.

Red Bluff: Swap N Shop Flea Mart & Auction, 235 S Main St. Tel: 916-528-0522.

Reseda: Reseda Indoor Swap Meet, 18407 Sherman Way. Tel: 818-344-6194.

Riverside: Van Buren Drive-In & Swap Meet, 3035 Van Buren Blvd. Tel: 909-688-2829.

Rocklin: Rocklin Flea Market & Auction, 4500 Pacific St. Tel: 209-632-8853.

Salinas: Salinas Indoor Flea Market, 626 E Alisal St. Tel: 408-422-2228.

Salinas: Skyview Flea Market, 925 N Sanborn Rd. Tel: 408-757-3532.

San Bernardino: Mini Swap Meet, 1212 W 2nd St. Tel: 909-381-6184.

San Diego: 32nd St Flea Market, 3809-32D. Tel: 619-280-3444.

San Fernando: Ezasorerio's Valley Indoor Swap Meet, 14650 Parthenia. Tel: 818-894-3042.

San Fernando: San Fernando Swap Meet & Flea Market, 585 Glenoaks Blvd. Tel: 818-361-1431.

San Fernando: Valley Indoor Swap Meet, 14650 Parthenia. Tel: 818-892-0183.

San Francisco: Far East Flea Market, 729 Grant Ave. Tel: 415-989-8588.

San Francisco: San Francisco Missions Flea Market, 2260 Mission St. Tel: 415-552-7047.

San Francisco: Union St Flea Market, 1611 Jackson St. Tel: 415-771-2574.

San Ysidro: San Ysidro Swap Meet Shop, 2364 Via Segundo. Tel: 619-662-2433 or the office at 619-690-6756.

San Ysidro: Southern Calif Swap Meet, 2383 Via Segundo. Tel: 619-662-0502.

Santa Ana: Orange Coast College General Services Swap Meet, 2701 Fairview Rd. Tel: 714-432-5866.

Santa Ana: Santa Ana Indoor Swap Meet, 3412 Westminster Ave. Tel: 714-554-8989.

Santa Cruz: Skyview Flea Market, 2260 Soquel Dr. Tel: 408-462-4442.

Santa Maria: Hi Way Drive-In Theatre Swap Meet, 3085 Santa Maria Way. Tel: 805-937-9715.

Sausalito: Marin City Flea Market, 740 Drake Ave. Tel: 415-332-1441.

Selma: Selma Flea Market, 10951 E Mountain View Ave. Tel: 209-896-3243.

Shafter: Earlimart Swap Meet, 159 S Valente Rd. Tel: 805-849-2883.

Spring Valley: Spring Valley Swap Meet, 6377 Quarry Rd. Tel: 619-463-1194.

Stockton: The Fanci Flea, 925 N Yosemite St. Tel: 209-941-0707.

Stockton: San Joaquin Delta College Flea Market. Tel: 209-474-5485.

Stockton: Stockton Flea Market, 2542 S El Dorado St. Tel: 209-465-9933.

Tulare: Open Country Flea Market. Tel: 209-686-9588.

Turlock: Turlock Sales Yard Flea Market, East Ave & N Johnson Rd. Tel: 209-634-2120 or 209-667-4441.

Ukiah: Ukiah Flea Market. Tel: 707-468-4626.

Van Nuys: Mini Downtown Swap Meet, 6357 Van Nuys Blvd. Tel: 818-782-3161.

Van Nuys: Van Nuys Bazaar Swap Meet, 6477 Van Nuys Blvd. Tel: 818-785-1488.

Vernalis: Orchard Flea Market, 2553 E Hwy 132. Tel: 209-836-3148.

Watsonville: Watsonville Flea Market, 2605 E Lake Ave. Tel: 408-724-1068.

COLORADO

COLORADO SPRINGS

The Flea Market

DATES: Saturday and Sunday, year round.

TIMES: 7:00 AM–4:00 PM.

ADMISSION: $1, parking is free.

LOCATION: 5225 East Platte Ave. On Platte Ave 1 mile east of Academy Blvd.

DESCRIPTION: Started in 1965, this "super clean" outdoor market has 400 dealers in summer and 200 dealers in winter selling antiques, collectibles, crafts, produce, coins, stamps, cards, garage sale finds, furniture and new merchandise. There is a farmers market every Friday on this site and they have a great view of Pikes Peak to boot! Two snack bars, one restaurant and handicapped-accessible restrooms complete the amenities.

DEALER RATES: $15 per 20' × 20' space. Reservations are first come, first served.

CONTACT: Randy, The Flea Market, PO Box 7229, Colorado Springs CO 80933-7229. Tel: (719) 380-8599.

DENVER

Mile High Flea Market, Inc

DATES: Every Wednesday, Saturday and Sunday, year round.

TIMES: 7:00 AM–5:00 PM.

ADMISSION: $2 per person weekends, $1 per person Wednesdays, under 12 free.

LOCATION: I-76 and 88th Ave.

DESCRIPTION: This indoor/outdoor flea market started in 1977 and is currently America's third largest flea market and Colorado's largest flea market bringing over 1.5 million bargain hunters to 80 paved acres of brand name, close-out, garage sale and seasonal merchandise. It features from 1,800 dealers in summer to 1,500 in winter selling antiques, fine art, collectibles, new merchandise, sports shoes, socks and underwear, clothing, silk plants, crystals, sunglasses, tires, auto parts, tools, luggage, furniture, bicycles, fishing tackle, cowboy boots, baby clothes, army surplus, antique train bells, hog greasers, steamship whistles, one left mannequin leg, bowling balls, jackalopes, and seasonal merchandise including bedding plants,

Christmas trees, pumpkins and farm fresh produce. About 800 of the dealers are cleaning out their garages, and 700 to 1,000 vendors are regulars. A new family midway features rides for children and adults alike. This is billed as a family event with plenty of parking for motorhomes and tour buses. A restaurant, five food stands, two beer tents, corn roasters, outdoor grills and a fleet of 15 mobile food carts provide ample food and beverage. You can also rent shopping carts, wheelchairs and wagons.

DEALER RATES: $20 per 12' × 25' space per day for Saturday and Sundays; $10 per day on Wednesday. There is a $3 per space per day advanced reservations fee. Reservations taken all week beginning Monday afternoons for the following Wednesday and/or weekend (by phone with MasterCard or Visa). Monthly reservations are also available. Tables and storage containers are available for rental.

CONTACT: Jim Hurrell, Marketing Director, 7007 E 88 Ave, Henderson CO 80640. Tel: (303) 289-4656 or 1-800-861-9900. Fax: (303) 286-1922.

DENVER (NORTHGLENN)

Collector's Corner

DATES: Daily.

TIMES: Monday through Saturday 10:00 AM–6:00 PM, Sunday 12:00 PM–5:00 PM.

ADMISSION: Free. Parking is free.

LOCATION: 10615 Melody Dr. From Denver take I-25 north, go west on 104th 2 blocks, then 2 blocks north.

DESCRIPTION: This market, started in 1989, is housed in a relatively new, large building across from the Northglenn Shopping Mall. It has 130 dealers selling antiques, collectibles, primitives, furniture and breweriana. Restaurants and shops surround this market.

DEALER RATES: $120 per 8' × 10' space per month.

CONTACT: Gene or Pat Corwin, Collector's Corner, 10615 Melody Dr, Northglenn CO 80234. Tel: (303) 450-2875.

FORT COLLINS

Foothills Indoor Flea Market

DATES: Daily.

TIMES: 10:00 AM–6:00 PM.

ADMISSION: Free. Free parking is available.

LOCATION: Just off I-25, between Fort Collins and Loveland on Hwy 287. There are 2 markets here only 1 block apart at 6200 and 6300 S College.

DESCRIPTION: This market opened in 1982. It accommodates approximately 100 dealers each. Sold here are antiques, arts and crafts and collectibles. There is also a selection of new merchandise. There is no food available on the premises aside from popcorn. There are three more markets in this area, DJs, Itchy's, and Sidekick.
DEALER RATES: $140 plus a 7% fee per 100-square-foot space, per month. Reservations are required; monthly rates only are available.
CONTACT: Foothills Indoor Flea Market, 6300 S College, Fort Collins CO 80525-4044. Tel: (970) 223-9069.

Fort Collins Flea Market

DATES: Daily.
TIMES: 10:00 AM–6:00 PM.
ADMISSION: Free. Free parking is available.
LOCATION: Just off I-25, between Fort Collins and Loveland on Highway 287. These 2 markets are 1 block apart at 6200 and 6300 S College.
DESCRIPTION: This market opened in 1982. It accommodates approximately 85 dealers selling antiques, arts and crafts and collectibles, furniture, collectible glassware, clothing, groceries and more. There is also a selection of new merchandise. There are three more markets in this area, DJs, Itchys, and Sidekick.
DEALER RATES: $140 plus a 6% fee per 100-square-foot space, per month. Reservations are required; monthly rates only are available.
CONTACT: Vince and Joy Barnhart, Fort Collins Flea Market, 6200 S College, Fort Collins CO 80525-4046. Tel: (970) 223-6502.

LAFAYETTE

Lafayette Flea Market

DATES: Daily, year round.
TIMES: 10:00 AM–6:00 PM.
ADMISSION: Free. Parking is free.
LOCATION: 130 E Spaulding, just behind the Conoco gas station at the corner of South Public Rd and Spaulding St.
DESCRIPTION: This market opened April 1, 1990 with 20,000 square feet in a climate-controlled, heated and cooled, former bowling alley. They were ranked 12th out of 50 of the "Biggest and Best" Flea Markets in the U.S. in the March 1994 issue of *Good Housekeeping* magazine. Antique stores are two blocks away. There are 116 dealer spaces, with 90 dealers

specializing in glassware, hobbies, stamps, coins, antique furniture, collectibles, sports cards, secondhand items, jewelry and consignments.
DEALER RATES: $1.50 per square foot per month or $150 per month for a 10' × 10' booth. Reservations are required.
CONTACT: Bill Hopkins, Lafayette Flea Market, 130 E Spaulding, Lafayette CO 80026. Tel: (303) 665-0433.

LONGMONT

Front Range Flea Market

DATES: Daily.
TIMES: 10:00 AM–6:00 PM. Sunday 12:00 PM–5:00 PM.
ADMISSION: Free. Parking is also free.
LOCATION: 1420 Nelson Rd. West off US 287 on Colorado Rt 119.
DESCRIPTION: This growing market opened in 1989 and currently has 50 dealers with room for more. Housed in a 28,000-square-foot building, these dealers sell new merchandise, collectibles, antiques, jewelry, furniture, sports cards, tack—and "a lot of everything." No food is available, but restrooms are on site.
DEALER RATES: $1.65 per square foot plus 10%. Reservations are required as there is a waiting list.
CONTACT: Vicky Andrew or Marj Sater, Front Range Flea Market, 1420 Nelson Rd, Longmont CO 80501. Tel: (303) 776-6605.

PUEBLO

Sunset Flea Market

DATES: Saturday and Sunday, rain or shine.
TIMES: 7:00 AM–5:00 PM.
ADMISSION: Free. Parking is also free.
LOCATION: 2641 North I-25, Exit 104 Eden. Only 35 miles south of Colorado Springs.
DESCRIPTION: Open since 1980, and now at a new location, this indoor/outdoor market hosts between 100 and 175 dealers selling antiques, collectibles, or "whatever you want"—everything and anything. There is unlimited space available to grow. Food is available on the premises.
DEALER RATES: $12 general space, $14 for reserved space. Reservations are not required, first come, first served.
CONTACT: Sunset Flea Market, Sunset Enterprises, 2641 I-25 N, Pueblo CO 81008-9614. Tel: (719) 584-2000 or 583-8039. Fax: (719) 546-2269.

> Remember the horrendous winter storm of October 1997? The one that dropped 50 inches of snow on Colorado at once, closing everything? This market is right on I-25, the Interstate seen around the world as the one closed by the storm. Imagine the skiing! And it's soooo close.

OTHER FLEA MARKETS

We know or have heard about these markets, but have not personally contacted each one, as we have the markets with descriptions. If you plan to visit one of these markets listed below, *please call first* to make sure they are still open. Flea markets do come and go. While they were open when we went to press, they may not be later. We can't be responsible. *Call first!*

Aurora: Colorado Indoor Flea Market, 9605 E Colfax Ave. Tel: 303-367-2790.

Colorado Springs: The Mini Flea, 33 E Fillmore St. Tel: 719-635-5055.

Denver: Federal Indoor Flea Market, 830 Federal Blvd. Tel: 303-534-1778.

Denver: Mississippi Flea Mart, 2915 W Mississippi Ave. Tel: 303-727-9091.

Denver: SOS Indoor Flea Market, 3870 Tennyson St. Tel: 303-458-8555.

Dillon: Bears Den Flea Market, 105 Dillon Mall Ave. Tel: 970-262-1253.

Englewood: Arapahoe Flea Market, 3400 S Platte River Dr. Tel: 303-789-2710.

Englewood: Mini Flea Mart, 3057 S Broadway. Tel: 303-761-5118.

Englewood: Mini Flea Mart, 4596 S Federal Blvd. Tel: 303-797-3086.

Evans: United Flea Market, 922 37th St. Tel: 970-330-4143.

Fort Collins: Itchy's Flea Market, 6132 S College Ave. Tel: 970-226-4150.

Fort Collins: Sidekick Flea Mart, 6024 S College Ave. Tel: 970-226-3210.

Fort Morgan: Odds & Ends Flea Market, 516 W Railroad Ave. Tel: 970-867-4862.

Greeley: Mini Flea Market, 1911 9. Tel: 970-346-9443.

Longmont: Longmont Flea Market, 473 Main St. Tel: 303-772-0968.
Longmont: This N That Flea Market, 624 S Sunset St. Tel: 303-651-1292.
Loveland: Bill's Antiques & Flea Market, 339 E 4th St. Tel: 970-663-4355.
Loveland: Loveland Flea Market, 851 S Lincoln Ave. Tel: 970-669-9972.
Loveland: North Fork Antique Flea Market, 3121 W Eisenhower Blvd. Tel: 970-203-1522.
Loveland: Treasure Cove Indoor Flea Market, 1021 S Lincoln Ave. Tel: 970-669-1355.
Pueblo West: Jun Indoor Flea Market, 728 E 4th St. Tel: 719-545-2902.
Strasburg: Strasburg Flea Market. Tel: 303-622-4652.

CONNECTICUT

CANTON

The Cob-Web

DATES: Every Sunday, May through September.
TIMES: 8:00 AM–whenever.
ADMISSION: Free. Parking is also free.
LOCATION: At the junction of Rts 44 and 202 near Rt 179, about 20 miles west of Hartford. (On Dyer Cemetery Rd.)
DESCRIPTION: This show first opened in 1968 and currently draws up to 50 dealers outdoors. Shoppers may purchase just about anything: antiques, arts and crafts, plants, jewelry, tools, coins, collectibles, furniture and new merchandise. The fare changes weekly. There is always a friendly atmosphere here. There are restaurants, stores, motels and campgrounds nearby. Snack food is available on the premises from a food stand.
DEALER RATES: $18 for an approximately 20' × 20' space or more. Reservations are advised. Space is available. Setup starts at 7:30 AM.
CONTACT: Dolly or Dawn, The Cob-Web, PO Box 954, Canton CT 06019. Tel: (860) 693-2658.

COVENTRY

Coventry Indoor-Outdoor Flea Market

DATES: Every Sunday, year round, except Christmas Sundays.
TIMES: 9:00 AM–4:00 PM.
ADMISSION: Free. Parking is free.
LOCATION: 44 Lake St. Junctions of Rts 31 and 275.
DESCRIPTION: Open since October 1990, this indoor/outdoor market of approximately 80 dealers sells sports cards, comics, antiques and collectibles with dealers specializing in jewelry, tag sale items, paper, linens, glass, coins and books. "We will always have dealers with the latest collectibles, tag sale items, fine antique furniture and just plain junk." In 1993 they opened the Coventry General Store selling Coventry-made products: vinegars, dried flowers, furniture, and Westerwald pottery from Pennsylvania with the Coventry pattern. There is a "great clean snack bar with more than hot dogs" as well as handicapped-accessible, clean restrooms.
DEALER RATES: $12 to $25 depending on size and location. Reservations are requested.

CONTACT: Joseph and Rose Fowler, Coventry Flea Market, 110 Wall St, Coventry CT 06238. Tel: (203) 742-9362. Day of market call: (860) 742-1993.

EAST HARTFORD

Connecticut Comic Book Flea Market

DATES: Sundays, monthly except January.
TIMES: 11:00 AM–5:00 PM.
ADMISSION: $.99 fee. Parking is free.
LOCATION: Elks Hall at 148 Roberts St. Take Exit 58 from I-84, follow SIGNS.
DESCRIPTION: This show started in 1974 and has approximately 30 dealers. It is an indoor market that sells collectibles, antiques, new merchandise, as well as pulp magazines, science fiction, collectibles, gum cards, and movie items, but they specialize in comic books for collectors. Food is served on the premises.
DEALER RATES: $40 for an 8' table. Advance reservations are required.
CONTACT: Harold E Kinney, c/o The Bookies Bookstore, 206 Burnside Ave, E Hartford CT 06108. Tel: (860) 289-1208 in afternoons.

FARMINGTON

Farmington Antiques Weekend

DATES: Second weekend in June and Labor Day Weekend. 1998: June 13–14, September 5–6; 1999: June 12–13, September 4–5; 2000: June 10–11, September 2–3.
TIMES: 10:00 AM–5:00 PM. Early admission 7:00 AM.
ADMISSION: $5 for adults. Parking is free. Early admission fee $20.
LOCATION: At the Farmington Polo Grounds, 10 miles west of Hartford and 3 miles from Exit 39 off I-84.
DESCRIPTION: This national antiques event opened in 1980 and is held both outdoors and under tents. There are around 600 dealers at each show selling antiques, fine art, and collectibles, but this market specializes in antiques from rural America. This claims to be the #l large antiques and better collectibles event in the United States, and it draws approximately 30,000 people per show. All merchandise is guaranteed to be as represented: no new merchandise, no reproductions. Good home-cooked food is available on premises.

DEALER RATES: $275 on the lawns, $350 and up under the tents. Reservations are required well in advance as there is a long waiting list. Write for map and motel list.
CONTACT: Abby or Bob McInnis, Revival Promotions Inc, PO Box 388, Grafton MA 01519. Tel: (508) 839-9735. Week of show call (203) 677-7862.

JEWETT CITY

College Mart Flea Market

DATES: Every Sunday.
TIMES: 9:00 AM–4:00 PM.
ADMISSION: Free. Parking is free.
LOCATION: Wedgewood Drive. Exits 84 and 85 off I-395.
DESCRIPTION: Started in 1982 in the old Slater Textile Mill, this market now hosts 140 vendors indoors and outdoors selling antiques, glassware, clothing, collectibles, toys, crafts, furniture, all types of old and new jewelry, gold, silver, and new merchandise. Food is available on the premises.
DEALER RATES: $12.50 for a half space to $25 for a full space. Reservations are strongly recommended.
CONTACT: Bob Leone, College Mart Flea Market, Wedgewood Dr, Jewett City CT 06351. Tel: (203) 376-3935 or (203) 642-6248.

MANSFIELD

Eastern Connecticut Flea Market

DATES: Sundays, first Sunday in April through Thanksgiving, weather permitting.
TIMES: 8:00 AM–3:00 PM.
ADMISSION: Free. Parking is $1 from 8:00 AM–9:00 AM; $.50 after that.
LOCATION: Mansfield Drive-In Theatre at 228 Stafford Rd. At the junction of Rts 31 and 32.
DESCRIPTION: Operating since 1975, and one of the first markets in Connecticut, this outdoor market's 200-plus dealers sell antiques, clothes, collectibles, new and used books, tools, toys and more. Breakfast and lunch are served at the market, or bring your own. This market is held at a thriving three-screen drive-in theater and its concession is open during the market.

DEALER RATES: $20 for a 14' × 14' space weekly; or $17.50 per week on a monthly basis. Rental tables are $3 a day, if you need one. Reservations are taken on a monthly basis only; not necessary for weekends only.
CONTACT: Michael Jungden, 228 Stafford Rd, Mansfield CT 06250. Tel: (860) 456-2578.

NAUGATUCK

Peddlers Market

DATES: Every Sunday from the beginning of first Sunday in April to the end of November. Weather permitting.
TIMES: Dawn to dusk.
ADMISSION: Free. Parking is $1 per car.
LOCATION: On Rt 63 (New Haven Rd) between Waterbury and New Haven.
DESCRIPTION: This market began operation in 1969 but was taken over by the present owners in 1980. There are anywhere from 75 to 150 dealers at this family-oriented outdoor market. You can find most anything here from antiques and collectibles to new merchandise and fresh produce, including fishing equipment, furniture, and household items. It is located in a beautiful setting not far from the highway. For your convenience, this clean market maintains a lunch wagon and restrooms on the premises.
DEALER RATES: $25 for 20' front per day. Reservations are not required.
CONTACT: Thomas Murray, Gunntown Rd, Naugatuck CT 06770. Tel: (203) 729-6339; or Gerald Garceau, 33 Hazel Ave, Naugatuck CT 06770. Tel: (203) 729-7762.

NEW HAVEN

Boulevard Flea Market

DATES: Saturday and Sunday, year round.
TIMES: 7:00 AM–4:00 PM.
ADMISSION: Free. Parking is free.
LOCATION: 520 Ella T Grasso Blvd. Northbound: I-95, take Exit 44 Kimberly Ave. Bear right off exit, go left at traffic light at ET Grasso Blvd (Rt 10). Market is ¾ mile on the left. Southbound: I-95, Exit 45 Rt 10, bear right down ramp, go straight, market is still 3/4 mile on left.
DESCRIPTION: Opened in 1949, this outdoor market has to be the oldest in Connecticut. Depending on the weather (if it's raining, the market is

open but not overwhelmed) their 100-plus dealers sell about 80% new merchandise including clothes, tapes, produce (in season); and loads of "tag sale" or garage finds. Although not many antiques appear, plenty of collectibles do find their way here. On a good day up to 15,000 customers roam and buy. Several snack carts and vendors feed the famished.
DEALER RATES: Call for reasonable rates for 20' space. There is always space for dealers. Reservations are not required.
CONTACT: Chuck, Boulevard Flea Market, 520 Ella T Grasso Blvd, New Haven CT 06519. Tel: (203) 772-1447.

NEW MILFORD

Elephant's Trunk Flea Market

DATES: Sundays only, April through Sunday before Christmas, except Easter Sunday.
TIMES: 6:00 AM–3:00 PM.
ADMISSION: $1 adults, children 13 and under free. Parking is free and plentiful. No pets allowed!
LOCATION: Route 7. Exit 7 from I-84, 7 miles north of Danbury.
DESCRIPTION: This market started in 1977. The 300-plus dealers break down their sales as approximately 30% antiques and collectibles; 30% general line merchandise; 20% new items: tools and jewelry, etc. and 20% anything and everything else. There are dealers who have been with this market since the beginning and buyers who return the same time every weekend and have, over the years, become friends. There are 55 acres with room for 500 dealer spaces. Food is available on the premises.
DEALER RATES: $25 per 25' × 20' space. All dealers are urged to have a Connecticut Tax number. Reservations are not required.
CONTACT: Contact Greg Baecker by telephone: (203) 355-1448.

NIANTIC

Between the Bridges Antique and Collectibles Flea Market

DATES: Thursday through Tuesday, year round.
TIMES: 10:00 AM–5:00 PM.
ADMISSION: Free. Parking is free.
LOCATION: 65 Pennsylvania Ave. Take Exit 74 off I-95, turn right, 3 miles.

DESCRIPTION: Opened in May 1991, this new market has 60 dealers, and a waiting list, selling just antiques, collectibles and used furniture. No new merchandise or crafts. There is a restaurant next to the market for the hungry.
DEALER RATES: $25 for 65 square feet of space. You don't have to be there to sell. There is a waiting list, so call first.
CONTACT: John and Diane Deer, 65 Pennsylvania Ave, Niantic CT 06357. Tel: (860) 691-0170.

OLD MYSTIC

Old Mystic Antique Flea Market

DATES: Every Sunday, weather permitting.
TIMES: 8:00 AM–5:00 PM.
ADMISSION: Free. Parking is free.
LOCATION: Route 27 in Old Mystic. Across from the southern entrance to I-95, at the Mystic Visitor and Transportation Center.
DESCRIPTION: This market, in business since 1974, has co-op dealers in winter, to 25 dealers in the summer. While the market deals mostly in antiques, there is some new merchandise sold as well, including toys. One dealer specializes in antique Matchbox cars. Mystic Seaport is less than one mile away. Breakfast, lunch and snacks are available on the premises.
DEALER RATES: $25 per Sunday for 14' × 22' space. Reservations are strongly recommended.
CONTACT: Sonny Hendel, 6 Hendel Dr, Old Mystic CT 06372. Tel: (860) 536-0646.

TORRINGTON

Wright's Barn and Flea Market

DATES: Saturday and Sunday, year round. Rain or shine.
TIMES: 10:00 AM–4:30 PM.
ADMISSION: Free. Parking is free.
LOCATION: Wright Road off Rt 4, between Torrington and Goshen. Follow the large signs on Rt 4.
DESCRIPTION: This indoor market opened in 1981 in a huge 10,000-square-foot dairy barn with 40 dealers selling mostly antiques and some collectibles. One dealer has 3,000 old books (not all there at one time, mind you). Most of their dealers are permanent (12 dealers having been there over 15 years) and come from over 20 miles away. There is a snack bar and a fireplace to keep you warm in winter.

DEALER RATES: $20 for 10' × 14' booth, Saturday and Sunday. Reservations are required.
CONTACT: Milly Wright, Wright's Barn, 149 Wright Rd, Torrington CT 06790. Tel: (860) 482-0095.

WALLINGFORD

Redwood Country Flea Market

DATES: Every Saturday and Sunday, and some holidays, year round, weather permitting (even in snow!).
TIMES: 8:00 AM–4:00 PM.
ADMISSION: Free. Parking is also free.
LOCATION: At 170 Hartford Turnpike in Wallingford. Take Exit 13 off I-91, or take Exit 64 off Wilbur Cross Pkwy.
DESCRIPTION: This show began in 1973. There are approximately 75 to 90 dealers at this outdoor market selling almost anything from antiques and collectibles to new merchandise and fresh produce. They do extensive advertising in area papers and trade magazines. The Dubar's have a restaurant on the premises that is well known to the rich and famous whose pictures cover the walls. Walter Dubar, the original founder of this market has retired, leaving his son and grandsons to run this unique place. However, if you can find Walter, he has some wonderful stories to tell! Hi, Walter!
DEALER RATES: Spaces measure 20' × 10', but it's best to call for their reasonable rates as they vary. Reservations are suggested.
CONTACT: Ken Dubar and Steven Hugo, Redwood Country Flea Market, 170 Hartford Tnpk, Wallingford CT 06492. Tel: (203) 269-3500 between 1:00–7:00 PM weekdays or all day Saturday and Sunday.

> They aren't kidding...
> It isn't unheard of to have large snowstorms in Connecticut. Out come the snowplows and the market continues.

WOODBURY

Woodbury Antiques and Flea Market

DATES: Every Saturday, year round, weather permitting.
TIMES: 7:00 AM–2:00 PM.
ADMISSION: Free. Parking is free.
LOCATION: Junction of Rts 6 and 64. Off I-84, take Exit 15, go 3½ miles on Rt 6E to market.

DESCRIPTION: For over 30 years this outdoor market has been considered one of the best antiques markets in Connecticut. Located in a beautiful country setting, their 90 to 180 dealers sell primarily antiques, collectibles, furniture, memorabilia, coins, antique tools, jewelry, books, military items, art and a constantly changing assortment of fascinating items. New merchandise includes tools, jewelry, clothes, household goods, over-the-counter products, plants and new surprises every week. It is described as the "#1 Saturday market in Connecticut" with "great browsing and buying in Woodbury, the Antiques Capital of Connecticut." This market has a strong following because of the quality of the goods sold and its pleasant setting. Food is available on the premises.
DEALER RATES: $30 for a 20' × 20' space. Reservations are not required, but recommended.
CONTACT: Don and Diane Heavens, PO Box 184, Woodbury CT 06798. Tel: (203) 263-2841.

OTHER FLEA MARKETS

We know or have heard about these markets, but have not personally contacted each one, as we have the markets with descriptions. If you plan to visit one of these markets listed below, *please call first* to make sure they are still open. Flea markets do come and go. While they were open when we went to press, they may not be later. We can't be responsible. *Call first!*

Bridgeport: Tumpis Flea Market, 1494 Stratford Ave. Tel: 203-384-0539.
Bristol: This & That Flea Market, 181 Mn RR Tryvl. Tel: 860-584-1324.
Bristol: C P's Flea Market, 331 Park St. Tel: 860-585-8450.
Harwinton: Johnnycake Airport Flea Market, Rt 4. Tel: 860-689-8025.
New Milford: Maplewood Indoor Flea Market, 458 Danbury Rd. Tel: 860-350-0454.
Somersville: Pleasant View Country Flea Market, 452 South Rd. Tel: 860-749-5868.
Thomaston: Seth Thomas Industrial Park Indoor Flea Market, 135 S Main St. Tel: 860-283-4080.
Westbrook: Westbrook Flea Market, 110 Boston Post Rd. Tel: 860-664-1737.
Winsted: Red Barn Antiques & Flea Market, 19 Gay St. Tel: 860-738-2900.

DELAWARE

DOVER

Spence's Auction and Flea Market

DATES: Every Tuesday and Friday, rain or shine.
TIMES: 8:00 AM–11:00 PM.
ADMISSION: Free. Parking is free.
LOCATION: 550 South New St, 2 blocks west of Kent General Hospital.
DESCRIPTION: This indoor/outdoor market first began in 1933. With a variety of shops on site and 200 dealer tables, a shopper can find antiques, collectibles, household and secondhand items. Also on the premises are a farmers market selling cheeses, meats, produce, pizza, ice cream and loads more, as well as a restaurant and restrooms.
DEALER RATES: $15 for a 3-table setup. Reservations are not necessary.
CONTACT: Gregory Spence or Jack Scott, Spence's Auction, 550 S New St, Dover DE 19904-3536. Tel: (302) 734-3441.

LAUREL

Bargain Bill, Shore's Largest Flea Market, Inc

DATES: Every Friday, Saturday and Sunday, rain or shine.
TIMES: Friday 8:00 AM–4:00 PM; Saturday and Sunday 6:00 AM–5:00 PM.
ADMISSION: Free. Free parking is provided.
LOCATION: At the intersection of US 13 Dual and Rt 9 East, 14 miles north of Salisbury. From Washington, DC take Rt 50 West to Rt 404 East, then Rt 13 south.
DESCRIPTION: This indoor/outdoor show began in 1978 and is located just 30 minutes from the Atlantic Ocean and listed as a Delaware tourist attraction. People come from all over the United States to buy from the 200 (in winter) to 500 dealers (in summer) who sell everything from antiques to new merchandise, from collectibles to fresh produce—all tax free! Other items to be found are: large selection of depression glass, electronics, books, airbrush artist, baked goods, records, jewelry, vacuums, new and used clothing and tools, wicker, doors, portable buildings, and groceries among others. They built a unique covered market with skylights to illuminate the merchandise, where vendors can park next to their treasures. When this market first opened, vendors laid their merchandise on the ground. Now they have a 400' air-conditioned/heated indoor market with over 800 tables.

Talk about having everything—in December 1992 they had a wedding here, complete with wedding gown, tuxedo, minister, cake and music. A restaurant serves breakfast and lunch. Overnight camping with electric hook-ups and air-conditioned/heated restrooms with showers are available.
DEALER RATES: $18.75 per 8' × 10' indoor space. $13 per 16' frontage outdoor space, includes two 8' tables. Reservations are not required.
CONTACT: Bill and Leslie Brown, RD 4 Box 547, Laurel DE 19956. Tel: (302) 875-9958 or (302) 875-2478. Email: fleamkt@magpage.com. Website: www.bwci.com/bbfmlg.htm.

Route 13 Outlet Market

DATES: Friday, Saturday and Sunday, year round.
TIMES: Friday and Saturday 9:00 AM–7:00 PM; Sunday 9:00 AM–6:00 PM.
ADMISSION: Free. Parking is also free.
LOCATION: Route 13 at State Rd 462.
DESCRIPTION: Started in 1985, they now have over 100 vendors selling collectibles, as well as items ranging from clothing to jewelry in this 84,000-square-foot building. There are plenty of collectibles. One vendor has loads of new tools that are "priced less than Wal-Mart." Another sells all sorts of electronics: stereos, telephones, car radios and accouterments. Thirty-two vendors sell sportswear and clothing, others jewelry. You can't possibly starve—15 restaurants, including Thai, Chinese, several down-home country, pizza and Italian, and some hot dog purveyors feed the famished. Their huge Amish market and restaurant is one of the big draws of the market selling fresh cheeses, meats, deli and baked goods. Ninety-five percent of the merchandise is new and 80% of the vendors have been with this market from the beginning. Over the last year much of the merchandise has become even more high-end, top quality goods. If an item fails to satisfy, it is quite common to be able to return it to the original vendor.
DEALER RATES: $45 per 12' × 18' space per weekend and up. Reservations are not required.
CONTACT: R J Shingleton, Route 13 Outlet Market, PO Box 32, Laurel DE 19956-0032. Tel: (302) 875-4800. Fax: (302) 875-2640.

NEW CASTLE

New Castle Farmers Market

DATES: Friday, Saturday and Sunday, year round.
TIMES: Friday, Saturday 10:00 AM–10:00 PM; Sunday 10:00 AM–6:00 PM.

ADMISSION: Free. Parking is also free.
LOCATION: Rt 13 and Hares Corner.
DESCRIPTION: Started in 1954, this indoor/outdoor market is really two markets in one. The outside is the flea market restricted to used items only, antiques and collectibles; the inside market is the farmer's market with over 60 merchants. This is said to be one of the premier markets on the East Coast with genuine Pennsylvania Dutch merchants selling outstanding quality beef, pork, poultry, cheeses and homemade baked goods. The produce stands are works of art. Food is available on the premises.
DEALER RATES: Friday $12 per day; Saturday and Sunday $16 per day. First come, first served.
CONTACT: Steven Stein, New Castle Farmers Market, Rt 13 and Hares Corner, New Castle DE 19720. Tel: (302) 328-4102 or fax (302) 328-9525.

OTHER FLEA MARKETS

We know or have heard about these markets, but have not personally contacted each one, as we have the markets with descriptions. If you plan to visit one of these markets listed below, *please call first* to make sure they are still open. Flea markets do come and go. While they were open when we went to press, they may not be later. We can't be responsible. *Call first!*

Bethany Beach: Bethany Flea Market, 759 Garfield Pkwy. Tel: 302-537-5180.
Harrington: B & B Antiques and Flea Market, RR 439. Tel: 302-398-4252.
Selbyville: Helen's Flea Market, 113 Dupont Hwy. Tel: 302-436-2960.
Selbyville: Rag Tag Treasures & Rt 54 Flea Market, RR 54. Tel: 302-436-9948.

DISTRICT OF COLUMBIA

Georgetown Flea Market

DATES: Every Sunday from first Sunday in March to Sunday before Christmas.
TIMES: 9:00 AM–5:00 PM.
ADMISSION: Free. Parking is free.
LOCATION: Parking lot of Rosario Education Center on Wisconsin Ave across from the Safeway, between S and T Sts, NW.
DESCRIPTION: Started in 1971, this outdoor market has become a legend since its inception. Author Larry McMurty (of *Lonesome Dove* fame) based his novel *Cadillac Jack* on this market. The owner, Michael Sussman, describes his market's wares as "good, solid, middle-class stuff," with many a great bargain. His 120-plus *good* exhibitors, many of whom are regulars, sell fine antiques, collectibles, vintage clothing, antique silver, crafts, homemade furniture, and other fine items. Don't worry about food, there are plenty of places to chow down in Georgetown, and a snack bar on site. Mary Randolph Carter, an avid collector, Ralph Lauren ad exec, and author of *American Junk*, loves this market and raids it occasionally. Diane Keaton comes to buy vintage clothing. Restroom facilities are at the north side of the market. If you find Michael at the market say "Hi" and tell him "we still miss the Phoenix," he'll understand.
DEALER RATES: $15–$45 depending on space and if you have your vehicle with you. Reservations are an excellent idea, but Michael will try to squeeze you in if necessary. No reservations will be made by phone. Setup starts at 6:00 AM.
CONTACT: Michael Sussman, 2109 N St NW, Washington DC 20037. Tel/fax: (202) 223-0289.

Someone bought a painting here for $300 that was worth $9,000. Stickley chairs have gone for $15. Marsten Luce started here as a dealer and is now an antiques shop owner. Well-known antiques dealer Guy Bush, who purchased former Supreme Court Justice Abe Fortas' Georgetown home, shops here every Sunday morning.

This market is written up all the time in the "big" rags for being "one of *the* places to be in Washington on weekends."

FLORIDA

APOPKA

Three Star Flea Market

DATES: Every Saturday and Sunday. Rain or shine.
TIMES: Dawn to dusk.
ADMISSION: Free. Free parking is available.
LOCATION: 2930 South Orange Blossom Trail. Hwy 441.
DESCRIPTION: This market began in 1966. About 60 dealers sell their antiques, collectibles, handicrafts, garage sale items and produce from covered stalls outdoors. They are only 18 miles from Disney World. There is a food wagon on the premises.
DEALER RATES: $10.80 per space and parking per day. They provide tables and clothes racks. Reservations are required.
CONTACT: Mary C Markeson, Owner, c/o Three Star Flea Market, 2390 S Orange Blossom Trail, Apopka FL 32703-1870. Tel: (407) 293-2722.

AUBURNDALE

International Market World

DATES: Every Friday, Saturday, and Sunday, rain or shine.
TIMES: 8:00 AM–5:00 PM.
ADMISSION: Free. Free parking is available.
LOCATION: 1052 Hwy 92 West Auburndale. Between Orlando and Tampa, just east of Lakeland.
DESCRIPTION: This market opened in 1981 and currently attracts anywhere from 750 (summer) to 1,000-plus (winter) dealers. A new building was added in 1991 adding another 200 stalls. As one of Florida's largest markets, Market World attracts customers from throughout Central Florida as it is only a short 45-minute drive from either Tampa or Orlando down I-4. There is an endless variety of merchandise from collectibles to new merchandise and fresh produce. Several attractions include a fishing pond, 1909 antique carousel, alligator display, buffalo farm, exotic animal zoo featuring Florida panthers and karaoke to name a few. There is a delightful country atmosphere and an eager-to-please management. There are numerous concessions serving a variety of foods on the premises.
DEALER RATES: $40 per 8' x 10' space weekly; $155 monthly. Reservations are not required. Dealers may start setting up shop at 7:00 AM.

CONTACT: International Market World, 1052 Hwy 92 W, Auburndale FL 33823. Tel: (941) 665-0062. Fax: (941) 666-5726.

BRADENTON

Red Barn Flea Market Plaza

DATES: Entire market Wednesday, Saturday and Sunday; plaza area Tuesday through Sunday.
TIMES: Wednesday, Saturday and Sunday 8:00 AM–4:00 PM; Tuesday, Thursday and Friday 10:00 AM–4:00 PM.
ADMISSION: Free. Parking is free.
LOCATION: 1707 1st St East. Located on US 41 and US 301 at 17th Ave. From I-75 take Exit 42 West on SR 4 to US 41. Take a left on US 41, go approximately 2 miles.
DESCRIPTION: This market opened in May 1981 and the plaza area opened in May 1985. On October 21, 1996, the entire market was destroyed by a devastating fire. It will be reopened by early 1998 with state-of-the-art architecture. Plans include the original 23 retail stores and approximately 500 covered, and 200 uncovered booths with a variety of new and used merchandise including antiques, collectibles, crafts, clothing, produce, meats, coins, cards, garage sale goodies, and furniture. Over 100,000 square feet under roof will shelter a bike shop, tackle store, communications store, beauty store, video games, tool store, art gallery and tons more. They are crammed with variety of goods and services. When the munchies strike, pick from four restaurants and an ice cream stand. Handicapped-accessible restrooms provide relief. This is a popular, clean, high-traffic market located near the Gulf Coast, and it has over 50 peacocks in the trees on the hill.
DEALER RATES: All spaces are approximately 10' x 10'. Inside booths are $25 plus tax per day, outside covered booths $18 plus tax per day, and outside uncovered booths are $20 plus tax per day. There is a 5% discount if paid in advance, monthly. Security patrolled by uniformed off-duty deputies.
CONTACT: Red Barn Rental Office, 1707 1st St E, Bradenton FL 34208. Tel: (941) 747-3794 or 1-800-274-FLEA. Fax: (941) 747-6539. Email: redbarnmkt@aol.com.

The Red Barn has very unique mascots in their beautiful peacocks roaming the grounds. Many customers have their pictures taken with the tame birds. Occasionally, when the market is closed, the peacocks roam the aisles playing "customer" until gently ushered back into their "home" among the giant oaks and oleanders. During these strolls, they can be caught admiring themselves in the glass doors. Among the flock is a rare white peacock.

BROOKSVILLE

Airport Flea Market

DATES: Every Saturday and Sunday, rain or shine.
TIMES: 8:00 AM–3:00 PM.
ADMISSION: Free. Parking is also free.
LOCATION: 17375 Spring Hill Drive. Six miles south of Brooksville, just off US 41.
DESCRIPTION: Now under new management, this show started in 1977. The market accommodates approximately 400 dealers and is held both indoors and outdoors. There are no specialties but rather a large assortment of goods is offered including antiques, fine art, arts and crafts, collectibles, and new merchandise, fresh produce, used household items, and tools. Food concessions serve the starving.
DEALER RATES: $73 for 8' x 12' space indoors, per month; $10 for Saturday, $9 for Sunday or $17 for the weekend for three-table set-up under covered space outdoors, per day. Reservations are required except during the summer.
CONTACT: Judy or Jim Jones, Airport Flea Market, 17375 Spring Hill Dr, Brooksville FL 34609. Tel: (352) 796-0268.

CHIEFLAND

McCormack Flea Market, Inc

DATES: Friday through Sunday, year round. Rain or shine.
TIMES: 7:00 AM–4:00 PM.
ADMISSION: Free. Parking is free.
LOCATION: US Hwy 19 and 98, Alt 27, North. Market located across from ABC Pizza and Best Western Motel.
DESCRIPTION: Since 1983 this indoor flea market has expanded four times on its 23 acres and is in the Suwannee River area, in the center of town, near motels. There are a total of 310 selling spaces, all under one roof, with concrete floors and screens. Water and electricity are available to each booth, as well as RV electricity. There is an RV park close by for the customers. Dealers can park their RV next to their booth or in the park.

Currently the market attracts approximately 55 dealers in the summer and 100 in the winter selling antiques, collectibles, handmade crafts, vegetables, meats, cheeses, dairy products, plants, flowers, nuts, birds and new merchandise among other treats. In addition, there is a small grocery store, bake shop, tools, tape store, leather craft shop, pump sales, RV parts, laundry, cabinet shop and carpet and vinyl store. Three restaurants feed the hungry.
DEALER RATES: $6 per 10' x 10' booth on Friday and $8 on Sunday; $10 on Saturday; $22.50 for three days. Reservations are suggested.
CONTACT: Jack McCormack, McCormack Flea Market Inc, PO Box 1970, Chiefland FL 32644-1970. Tel: (352) 493-1493 or 493-1491.

DAYTONA

Daytona Flea Market

DATES: Friday, Saturday, and Sunday, year round.
TIMES: 8:00 AM–5:00 PM.
ADMISSION: Free. Parking is free.
LOCATION: Southwest corner of I-95 and US 92.
DESCRIPTION: This indoor/outdoor market opened in 1981, just five miles from the "World's Most Famous Beach," attracting 2.5 million visitors. Over 1,000 booths on 40 acres sell antiques, collectibles, home furnishings, clothes, jewelry, used and new merchandise, produce, plants and just about everything imaginable. Two sections of the market are fully air-conditioned. Two sit-down restaurants and nine snack bars provide ample food for the hungry.
DEALER RATES: For a booth with 10' frontage, $15 and up for Saturday and Sunday, $8 on Friday. Ninety percent of this market is under roof. Reservations are suggested, in some cases required.
CONTACT: John Schnebly, Manager, or Janie, Rental Agent, 2987 Bellevue Rd, Daytona Beach FL 32115. Tel: (904) 252-1999.

DELRAY BEACH

Delray Swap Shop

DATES: Always Friday through Sunday. Seasonally Thursdays, December through April.
TIMES: Thursday and Friday 8:00 AM–3:00 PM; Saturday and Sunday 8:00 AM–4:00 PM.
ADMISSION: Free. Parking is free.

LOCATION: 2001 North Federal Hwy. Take I-95 to Atlantic Ave in Delray Beach to North Federal Hwy, north 3 miles to Swap Shop.
DESCRIPTION: This market has been open since 1976 with 430 dealer spaces mostly outdoors. Items for sale are mostly new merchandise including: health and beauty aids, clothing, jewelry, hats, pictures and frames, household goods, and vegetables in season. In November 1993 they opened a special antique section of this market. Several snack bars serve the hungry. Handicapped-accessible restrooms are on site.
DEALER RATES: Friday $5; Saturday and Sunday from $25 to $100 for 11' x 15' spaces. For the antique mall: free Thursday and Friday, $5 Saturday and Sundays. Reservations are required. There is a waitlist for no-shows at $25 for space at the last minute with no guarantees.
CONTACT: Loretta Shaw, Manager, Delray Swap Shop, 2001 N Federal Hwy, Delray FL 33444. Tel: (561) 276-4012. Fax: (561) 276-9019.

FORT LAUDERDALE

Oakland Park Blvd Flea Market

DATES: Every Wednesday through Sunday, year round. Open every day from Thanksgiving to New Years.
TIMES: Thursday through Saturday 10:00 AM–9:00 PM; Wednesday and Sunday 10:00 AM–7:00 PM.
ADMISSION: Free. Parking is plentiful and free.
LOCATION: 1½ miles west of I-95, and ½ mile east of State Rt 7, at 3161 West Oakland Park Blvd.
DESCRIPTION: This popular market has been a landmark in Fort Lauderdale since 1971. "This is the place where the neighborhood shops," as well as Fort Lauderdale's original indoor flea market. Over 200 dealers sell only all-new merchandise although antiques and collectibles can be found. There are many clothing and fine jewelry merchants in this modern, clean and air-conditioned facility. Local residents and tourists alike make frequent visits to this market located near major highways, airports and cruiseports. It is a bit of southern charm that makes this flea market such a success. Handicapped-accessible restrooms, two snack bars and a restaurant serving home-cooked fare add to the amenities.
DEALER RATES: $600 and up per space per month includes utilities, advertising and plenty more. Reservations are required. Currently they are accepting applications for the waiting list.

CONTACT: Leonard Bennis, Manager, Oakland Park Blvd Flea Market Inc, 3161 W Oakland Park Blvd, Ft Lauderdale FL 33311. Tel: (954) 733-4617. Fax: (954) 731-1150.

Swap Shop of Ft. Lauderdale

DATES: Everyday including holidays, year round. Rain or shine.
TIMES: 7:00 AM–5:00 PM.
ADMISSION: Free. Free parking is available. Preferred parking Saturday and Sunday is $1.
LOCATION: 3291 West Sunrise Blvd, between I-95 and the Turnpike.
DESCRIPTION: This well-known show began in 1967. About 2,000 dealers sell both indoors and out on 88 acres of grounds. All sorts of things can be found here—antiques, crafts and collectibles, new and used items, produce, watches, electronics, clothing, plants—you name it! All new merchandise comes with a full guarantee. They say they are "the largest flea market in the Eastern United States." Free circus shows are presented daily, and they feature 17 international restaurants in their air-conditioned 180,000-square-foot entertainment center. At night they have the world's largest 13-screen drive-in showing first-run movies nightly.
DEALER RATES: Call for current rates. Reservations are advised during the winter season.
CONTACT: Reservation Office, c/o Swap Shop, 3501 W Sunrise Blvd, Fort Lauderdale FL 33311. Tel: (954) 791-SWAP (7927). Fax: (954) 792-7962.

FORT MYERS

Fleamasters Fleamarket

DATES: Friday, Saturday and Sunday, year round.
TIMES: 8:00 AM–4:00 PM.
LOCATION: 4135 Dr Martin Luther King, Jr Blvd.
ADMISSION: Free. Parking is free.
DESCRIPTION: Opened in 1985, this completely undercover outdoor market, billed "as the largest market in southwest Florida," hosts an average of 1,200 dealers year round. It is still growing—they added another 200 stalls in 1993. Their dealers sell everything "from fruit to nuts," including antiques, collectibles, clothing, wheelchair rentals to psychic readings. The food courts provide an ample feast from pizza to ice cream, Mexican, Oriental and good-old-USA fast food. In fact, this market is so popular it has become a tourist attraction in its own right.

DEALER RATES: $48–$61, plus tax and license, per 10' x 12' booth for a 3-day weekend, depending on location. Reservations are not required, first-come, first-served. Although dealers can continue to hold the same spot week after week.
CONTACT: Donna Matthews, Fleamasters Fleamarket, 4135 Dr Martin Luther King Jr Blvd, Ft Myers FL 33916. Tel: (941) 334-7001. Fax: (941) 334-2087. Website: www.fleamall.com.

FRONTENAC

Frontenac Flea Market

DATES: Friday, Saturday and Sunday.
TIMES: 8:00 AM–4:00 PM.
LOCATION: 5605 North US Hwy 1, midway between Cocoa and Titusville, right on US 1.
ADMISSION: Free. Parking is free.
DESCRIPTION: In operation over 21 years, this market has an average of 450 dealers selling antiques, collectibles, new and used merchandise, silk flowers, and a farmers market selling fresh fruits and vegetables. One of the several food concessions sells a "famous quarter-pound hot dog." This market is close to the Kennedy Space Center and beaches. They hold an auction every Saturday at 2:00 PM.
DEALER RATES: $18.02 per day for a 10' x 8' space indoors; $13.78 for a 10' x 20' space outdoors. First come, first served.
CONTACT: Ronnie Christian, Frontenac Flea Market, PO Box 10, Sharpes FL 32959-0010. Tel: (407) 631-0241. Fax: (407) 631-0246. Email: ronnie@palmnet.net.

HOMOSASSA SPRINGS

Howard's Flea Market

DATES: Saturday and Sunday, year round.
TIMES: 7:00 AM–3:00 PM.
ADMISSION: Free. Parking is free.
LOCATION: Hwy 19, 3 miles south of Homosassa.
DESCRIPTION: Open since 1969, this market of 700 to 800 dealers occupies 50 acres full of antiques, collectibles, some new merchandise, clothes, typical flea market fare, produce and occasionally dairy products (cheeses), and one aisle devoted to garage sale goodies. A polebarn structure houses many of the dealers while the rest are outdoors. Their many concession

stands are "excellent" the office assures me. This is a family-oriented market with an annual Haunted Hay Ride at Halloween used to raise funds for local children's charities. For Christmas and Easter they hold services. Like their sister market in Webster, they hold Car Shows.
DEALER RATES: Daily including tax: Covered $11.66 per 10' x 12' space with 3 tables. Outside $8.48 per 10' x 10' space, or $11 to $13 per 10' x 30' space depending on location. Reservations are suggested. Although, if you do show up, they will manage to find you a spot, somehow. The office is open for reservations on Thursday and Friday.
CONTACT: Teri Shannon, Howard's Flea Market, 6373 S Suncoast Blvd, Homosassa FL 34446. Tel: (352) 628-4656 or (352) 628-3532.

JACKSONVILLE

Ramona Flea Market

DATES: Saturday and Sunday, year round.
TIMES: 8:00 AM–5:00 PM.
ADMISSION: $.50 per adult. Parking is free.
LOCATION: 7059 Ramona Blvd. From I-295 take I-10 east to first Exit 54 Lane Ave, go south. The first intersection is Ramona Blvd. Turn right. We are 3 blocks down the road on the right.
DESCRIPTION: Started in 1971, this indoor/outdoor market has 600 to 800 dealers (depending on the season) selling crafts, produce, coins, new merchandise, garage sale goodies and furniture. Two snack bars and three restaurants, including beer garden and an ice cream parlor, fill the famished. And yes, handicapped-accessible restrooms are available.
DEALER RATES: $7.52 to $14.91 (includes tax) depending on the location of the 10' x 7' space. They have open or under cover with 2 tables, electricity for inside spaces at $2 per day. The office is open for reservations Wednesday and Thursday from 9:00 AM–5:00 PM and Friday from 9:00 AM–6:00 PM. They recommend reserving space at least 2 weeks in advance. They open for vendors to set up at 6:30 AM.
CONTACT: Rick Waller, General Manager, or Joan Wade, Reservation Manager, 7059 Ramona Blvd, Jacksonville FL 32205. Tel: (904) 786-3532 or 1-800-583-3532 (FLEA). Fax: (904) 783-1661. Email: fleaman@jaxinter.net.

KEY LARGO

Key Largo Warehouse Market

DATES: Saturday and Sunday.
TIMES: 8:00 AM–5:00 PM.
ADMISSION: Free. Free parking is available.
LOCATION: on US Route 1, at Mile Marker 103.5.
DESCRIPTION: This small, selective, but excellent market has 60 dealers selling "everything you could want," with an emphasis on antiques and collectibles. Charlie's vegetables are said to be "the best on the Keys." A sampling of some of their dealers' specialties are baskets, bathing suits, marine and fishing gear, orchids and exotic plants, ceramic goods and bikes. A snack bar serves American dishes to the hungry. This is the only market open all year long on the Keys. They place a high value on "treating our people right."
DEALER RATES: $357 for a front-row 10' x 40' space if you are lucky enough to get one; $210.05 for a second-row 10' x 30' space; and $123.19 for a 10' x 10' space. Reservations are most necessary.
CONTACT: Key Largo Warehouse Market, Key Largo Storage, 103530 Overseas Hwy, Key Largo FL 33037. Tel: (305) 451-0677.

LAKE CITY

Lake City Flea Market

DATES: Every Saturday and Sunday, rain or shine. Closed from mid-October to mid-November for Columbia County Fair.
TIMES: 7:00 AM–4:00 PM.
ADMISSION: Free. Free parking is available.
LOCATION: Columbia County Fairgrounds, 1 mile east of I-75 on US 90 at State Rd 247 (Branford Hwy).
DESCRIPTION: This indoor/outdoor market opened in 1980 and now accommodates approximately 100 to 150 dealers selling everything from antiques and collectibles to new merchandise and fresh produce. There are 1,500 motel rooms available at reasonable rates located within ½ mile of the flea market. Food is served on the premises.
DEALER RATES: $9 per 10' x 10' space indoors, per day; $6 and up per day outdoors. Reservations for space indoors are required and all reservations must be prepaid. No reservations are taken by phone.
CONTACT: Ralph Tiner, Lake City Flea Market, 2640 Montgomery St, Lake City FL 32025. Tel: (904) 752-1999.

LAKELAND

Lakeland Farmer's Market

DATES: Every Thursday through Sunday, rain or shine.
TIMES: 6:00 AM–5:00 PM.
ADMISSION: Free. Free parking is available.
LOCATION: 2701 Swindell Rd. Take I-4 to West Memorial Blvd exit, then go 1 mile. At the intersection of Swindell Rd and West Memorial Blvd at Kathleen High School.
DESCRIPTION: This market started out as a "Curb Market" in the 1930s, moved to its present location in 1971 where local farmers and craftsmen could sell their goods; some of these original sellers still work here. The market now accommodates from 225 to 350 dealers that sell collectibles, arts and crafts, new merchandise, used items, clothing, tools, household necessities, used farm- and work-related items and fresh produce and meats. Thursday and Friday's market is mainly produce and plants. This is a rustic, down-to-earth flea market with a museum, free of charge, on the premises. There are five restaurants and snack bars to choose from.
DEALER RATES: $11 per 10' x 10' space under cover on Saturday and Sunday. Rates in the open field are $6 per 25' x 15' space on Saturday and Sunday; $4 per space uncovered on Friday; Thursday is free. $84 per month. Reservations are advised.
CONTACT: Bill Hudson, 2701 Swindell Rd, Lakeland FL 33805. Tel: (813) 682-4809 or 665-3723.

LAKE WORTH

Lake Worth High School Flea Market

DATES: Saturday and Sunday, year round.
TIMES: Saturday 4:00 AM–3:00 PM, Sunday 3:00 AM–3:00 PM. Really.
ADMISSION: Free. Parking is free.
LOCATION: 1701 Lake Worth Rd at Lake Worth High School parking lot. At I-95 and Lake Worth Rd, under the I-95 overpass next to the Tri-Rail Station. From Florida Turnpike: Exit 93 East 6 miles. From I-95: Exit 6th Ave South, right to "A" St to Lake Worth Rd OR Exit 10th Ave North, left to "A" St, right to Lake Worth Rd.
DESCRIPTION: So how does a high school raise funds for scholarships for needy students and other necessaries? Hold a flea market! Since the mid-'80s this market has contributed more than $1 million dollars to student scholarships. Not bad. In fact the market is so popular it has been

repeatedly written up in Florida papers. Every weekend their 200 dealers spread out across the school parking lot selling wonderful books, antiques, collectibles, produce, new and used merchandise, rugs, luggage, garage sale goodies and discount groceries. This place is the local "weekend mall" for locals.
DEALER RATES: $8 or $10 per spot.
CONTACT: Betty Brown, Lake Worth High School Flea Market, PO Box 6592, Lake Worth FL 33466-6592. Tel: (561) 439-1539. Fax: (561) 533-6334.

MARGATE

Margate Swap Shop

DATES: Saturday, Sunday and Tuesday.
TIMES: 5:00 AM–2:00 PM.
ADMISSION: Free. Parking is $1.
LOCATION: 1000 North State Rd 7 (US 441). West of Pompano Beach; west of Florida Turnpike and I-95 (Atlantic Blvd to Rt 441 then north several blocks).
DESCRIPTION: This family-type indoor/outdoor market opened in 1976 and has grown to 300 to 550 dealers selling collectibles, new and used merchandise and fresh produce. This flea market has one of the largest produce sections around. The Lake Shore Motel is on the property as well. Two snack bars and handicapped-accessible restrooms are on site.
DEALER RATES: $8 per 10' x 20' space. Reservations are suggested.
CONTACT: Manager, Margate Swap Shop, 1000 N State Rd 7, Margate FL 33063. Tel: (954) 971-7927. Fax: (954) 979-3729.

MELBOURNE

Super Flea and Farmers Market

DATES: Friday, Saturday and Sunday.
TIMES: 9:00 AM–4:00 PM.
ADMISSION: Free. Parking is free.
LOCATION: 4835 West Eau Gallie Blvd. At the corner of I-95 and Eau Gallie Blvd, Exit 72.
DESCRIPTION: Opened in 1987, this indoor market of 200–350 dealers sells antiques, collectibles, cars, crafts, produce, coins, cards, garage sale goodies, new merchandise, furniture (new and used), quality 14K and silver jewelry, ruby and gem mining and a huge selection of professional chef

and restaurant supplies. Hungry? Try Italian, Chinese, Mexican, daily specials, great subs, whatever. Get this: the weekend before Thanksgiving Day they hold their Annual Turkey Bowl. People actually bowl frozen turkeys down a bowling lane to win a free turkey, cokes and other prizes. They have been told that their handicapped-accessible restrooms are the cleanest of any flea market by vendors and customers alike.
DEALER RATES: $20 per day for 10' x 8' space; $118 monthly. Storage units of 10' x 15' are available. Reservations are suggested.
CONTACT: Teri Kuscsik, Reservations Manager, Super Flea, 4855 W Eau Gallie Blvd, Melbourne FL 32934. Tel: (407) 242-9124 Thursday through Saturday.

MIAMI

Opa Locka/Hialeah Flea Market

DATES: Daily.
TIMES: 5:00 AM–7:00 PM.
ADMISSION: Free and $1 plus parking.
LOCATION: 12705 NW 42nd Ave. Take I-75 south to Opa Locka exit. I-95 to NW 103st St Exit, west 4 miles to NW 42nd Ave and north 1 mile, market is on both sides. The market is just 15 minutes north of Miami International Airport on Le Jeune Rd (NW 42nd Ave) at 127th St.
DESCRIPTION: Opened in 1985, this indoor/outdoor market boasts 1,000-plus dealers selling collectibles, new merchandise, produce, meats, garage sale goodies, furniture, clothing, you name it. Thirteen restaurants and handicapped-accessible restrooms add to the amenities.
DEALER RATES: $60 and up per 20' x 20' space per week. Reservations are not required.
CONTACT: Scott Miller, Opa Locka/Hialeah Flea Market, 12705 NW 42 Ave, Miami FL 33054. Tel: (305) 688-0500 × 25. Fax: (305) 687-8312.

MIAMI BEACH

"World's Largest" Indoor Flea Market

DATES: For 1998: March 11–15; June 24–28; December 16–20. 1999: Call, but check around the same weekends.
TIMES: Wednesday and Thursday 12:00 PM–10:00 PM; Friday and Saturday 12:00 PM–11:00 PM; Sunday 12:00 PM–8:00 PM.

ADMISSION: $3.50 for adults, $1 for children (6–12 years); or $5 for a five-day unlimited pass. Parking costs $.75 per hour for city meters or $1 per hour for use of the parking lot/garage. Valet parking is also available.
LOCATION: At the Miami Beach Convention Center, 1901 Convention Center Drive. Take I-95 to I-195, then east to Alton Rd; follow signs to Convention Center.
DESCRIPTION: Started in 1979 and celebrating their 62nd phenomenally successful edition of this event. This is a market of over 1,000 booths that has something for everyone. Exhibitors include nationally prominent firms, hundreds of local companies, individual dealers, importers, wholesalers, manufacturers, artists and craftsmen from throughout the United States and overseas. Used merchandise is not permitted, but there is a large selection of antiques, collectibles, and fine art. The *New York Times* reported this event as "a one stop (Christmas) shopping spree." It was voted #1 for "most amazing bargains" by a reader's survey in *South Florida* magazine. There are many special attractions as well as guest lecturers and well-known celebrities. There are continuous broadcasts from the show's "celebrity corner" where a prize machine promotion, operated by the *Miami Herald* newspaper, is a favorite treat for visitors. This market is widely advertised and is known as "the flea market tradition brought to an outrageously exalted level."
DEALER RATES: $550 per 10' x 10' space plus 6½% sales tax. Reservations are required as most shows are sold out before the show date. Larger spaces are available.
CONTACT: IBS Flea Markets Inc, 190 NE 199 St Ste 203, N Miami Beach FL 33179-2918. Call Louis Shelley, Show Director, at (305) 651-9530, Monday–Friday 9:00 AM–5:00 PM. Fax: (305) 652-2568.

How's that again?
Years ago, a dealer brought in and set up a little antique hand-carved wooden circus complete with animals, people, the works. It wasn't long after that an official from the Department of Natural Resources showed up saying someone had lodged a complaint against the market for abusing the lions.

MOUNT DORA

Florida Twin Markets

DATES: Saturday and Sunday, except for the 3-day extravaganzas held the third full Friday through Sunday of November, January and February.
TIMES: Flea market 8:00 AM–4:00 PM; antique market 9:00 AM–5:00 PM. Extravaganza Fridays 10:00 AM–5:00 PM.
ADMISSION: Free on regular dates. Extravaganzas: $10 on Friday, $5 on Saturday, $3 on Sunday. Parking is free.
LOCATION: East of Mt. Dora, 25 miles north of Orlando on new Hwy 441, just past intersection of Hwy 441 over Hwy 46 at the bottom of the hill on the right.
DESCRIPTION: These markets, started in 1983, are sister markets to the highly successful Pennsylvania Renninger's markets. Sitting on 115 acres, they are actually two distinct and separate markets about 900 feet apart. One is devoted to antiques with over 150 dealers, the other is a farmers and flea market with over 500 dealers. However, during Extravaganzas the antique dealers numbers swell to over 1,200. In addition, they have eight Antique Fairs from March through October on the third full Saturday and Sunday. As you can imagine, they sell just about anything and everything at these two markets. Four restaurants and handicapped-accessible restrooms add to the amenities.
DEALER RATES: Flea Market: $13.50 per 10' x 10' space under roof, $7 per 15' x 25' space outside. Extravaganza rates run from $125 and up depending on where the space is. Reservations are required.
CONTACT: Florida Twin Markets, Inc, PO Box 1699, Mt Dora FL 32757-1699. Tel: (904) 383-8393 Antiques, or (904) 383-3141 Flea Market.

NAPLES

Naples Drive-In Flea Market

DATES: Saturday and Sunday, year round; also Fridays October through April.
TIMES: 7:00 AM–3:00 PM.
ADMISSION: Free. Parking is free.
LOCATION: 7700 East Davis Blvd. Off Exit 15 from I-75.
DESCRIPTION: Open since 1975, and under new ownership/management, this outdoor market of 200–350 dealers is half flea market, half farmers market with loads of produce and loads of garage sale goodies. Antiques, collectibles, souvenirs, furniture and new merchandise can be found here.

One big restaurant and handicapped-accessible restrooms add to the amenities.
DEALER RATES: Summer, May through October, $6 or $10 per 10' x 20' space; winter, November through April, $10 or $15 per space. Reservations are first come, first served. Canopies and tables are available from the market.
CONTACT: Jack, Naples Drive-In Flea Market, 7700 E Davis Blvd, Naples FL 33942. Tel: (941) 774-2900.

NORTH FORT MYERS

North Side Drive-In Swap Shop

DATES: Wednesday, Friday through Sunday, weather permitting.
TIMES: 5:00 AM–2:00 PM.
ADMISSION: Free. Free parking is available.
LOCATION: 2521 North Tamiami Trail. On Old Rt 41 N, in the old business district. Off Exit 26 from I-75.
DESCRIPTION: This outdoor market began around 1982. As of August 1995, it is under new management and ownership. Wednesday is their *big* day as it is the only Wednesday market around. It accommodates approximately 250–350 dealers selling antiques, arts and crafts, collectibles, fresh produce, and both new and used merchandise. One snack bar and handicapped-accessible restrooms add to the amenities.
DEALER RATES: Wednesday $9; Friday $3; Saturday and Sunday $6. Reservations are not required. Do reserve for Wednesday—it fills quickly!
CONTACT: Art, North Side Drive-In and Flea Market, 2521 N Tamiami Trail, N Ft Myers FL 33903. Tel: (941) 995-2254.

NORTH FORT PIERCE

Biz-E-Flea Market

DATES: Saturday and Sunday, year round.
TIMES: 7:00 AM–closing (up to 3:00 PM).
ADMISSION: Free. Parking is also free.
LOCATION: 3252 North US 1, 1 mile north of St. Lucie Blvd (Airport Rd) and 11 miles south of Olso Rd, Vero Beach.
DESCRIPTION: This covered outdoor market first opened in 1980. There are anywhere from 50 dealers during the summer to 90 dealers during the winter selling antiques, collectibles, crafts, tools, electronic equipment, carpeting and new and good used merchandise. Fresh vegetables are also

sold. This is a family-style market boasting sidewalks for easy walking. One complete concession with seating and restrooms add to the amenities.
DEALER RATES: For a 10' x 10' space daily: $8 uncovered with 3 tables, no electric; $10 or $12 covered with electric and 3 tables. Weekly and monthly rates are available. Reservations are suggested.
CONTACT: Irma Partridge, 1000 SW 27th Ave Lot 61, Vero Beach FL 32968. Tel: (561) 466-3063.

NORTH MIAMI

North Miami Flea Market

Note: The market owner wasn't sure if it would stay open after 1998, so call before setting out for this one.

DATES: Every Wednesday through Sunday; open daily Thanksgiving through Christmas. Rain or shine.
TIMES: Wednesday and Sunday 10:00 AM–7:00 PM; Thursday through Saturday 10:00 AM–9:00 PM.
ADMISSION: Free. Free parking is available.
LOCATION: 14135 NW Seventh Ave, 1 block west of I-95 off north 135th St (The Blue Building).
DESCRIPTION: This is South Florida's original indoor flea market, and it all began in 1967. More than 200 dealers assemble to sell a variety of goods including antiques as well as new merchandise, fine art, and fresh produce. There is also clothing for the entire family, housewares, electronics, toys—the list goes on. Actually, due to the many fine jewelry dealers in the markets, it is practically a jewelry exchange and flea market all in one! This famous Miami landmark, also referred to as "the Blue Building," is conveniently located to South Florida's major artery, I-95. The indoor market is clean and air-conditioned and features deluxe snack bars, a new ice cream shop and a restaurant.
DEALER RATES: $250 and up (plus tax) for 10' x 15' space, monthly with annual lease preferred. Includes telephone service, advertising, security service, electric and maintenance.
CONTACT: Walton Lee, Market Manager, North Miami Flea Market, 14135 NW 7 Ave, N Miami FL 33168. Tel: (305) 685-7721.

OCALA

Ocala Drive-In Flea Market

DATES: Saturday and Sunday, year round. Rain or shine.
TIMES: 7:00 AM–4:00 PM.
ADMISSION: Free admission and free parking.
LOCATION: 4850 South Pine Ave (South 441-301-27).
DESCRIPTION: Started in 1979, the Ocala Flea Market is located at the only drive-in theater in the county, which is open on Friday, Saturday, and Sunday. Approximately 300 dealers occupy selling space in the summer and 450 in the winter, offering antiques, collectibles, handmade crafts, vegetables, tools, clothes, plants, birds, and new merchandise. There is a pawn shop on the premises. Food is available.
DEALER RATES: $10.50 per day for a 10' x 10' booth under roof; $8 per day for a 10' x 10' booth outside. Reservations are suggested.
CONTACT: Sheri Williams, 4850 S Pine Ave, Ocala FL 34480. Tel: (904) 629-1325.

OKEECHOBEE

The Market Place Flea Market

DATES: Saturday and Sunday, year round.
TIMES: 8:00 AM–4:00 PM.
ADMISSION: Free. Parking is free.
LOCATION: 3600 Hwy 441 South. From I-95: go west on Hwy 710, then west on Hwy 70, then south on Hwy 441. They are approximately 3 miles down the road on the left across from Scotty's.
DESCRIPTION: This family-owned and operated market has been filling the need of "everything and anything" market for the locals as well as the transient workers from this area. Their 550 dealers (in season) sell some antiques and collectibles, tons of fresh produce (just picked) and loads of new merchandise (tends towards the flashy stuff, electronics, jewelry, hair decorations). The entire market is under cover on pavement. There are six snack bars, just in case you can't wait to eat. Local advice: "Bring your fishing gear!" They are located on the north end of Lake Okeechobee.
DEALER RATES: Winter: $22.50 per 10' x 10' space and table per weekend. Summer: $16 per 10' x 10' space and table per weekend. Reservations are strongly recommended, especially in winter as they get full quickly.
CONTACT: The Market Place Flea Market, 3600 Hwy 441 S, Okeechobee FL 34947. Tel: (941) 467-6639 or (941) 467-6803.

OLDSMAR

Oldsmar Flea Market

DATES: Friday, Saturday and Sunday, year round.
TIMES: Friday 10:00 AM–3:00 PM, weekends 9:00 AM–5:00 PM.
ADMISSION: Free admission and free parking available.
LOCATION: 180N Racetrack Rd, at the corner of Hillsboro Ave and Racetrack Rd.
DESCRIPTION: This market began in 1980. About 1,100 dealers sell to the public. Ninety-five percent of them are indoors and offer antiques, collectibles, handmade and craft items, produce, meats, and cheeses. New merchandise is also sold. In addition, there are two bakeries, two nurseries, and even beauticians on the premises. Ten snack bars provide plenty of food and refreshment.
DEALER RATES: Prices vary from $10.70 daily with 1 table and parking, rented on a first come, first served basis. Their office is open Wednesday through Friday 9:00 AM–3:00 PM, and weekends 7:00 AM–4:00 PM. They take reservations only one week in advance.
CONTACT: Oldsmar Flea Market, PO Box 439, Oldsmar FL 34677-0439. Tel: (813) 855-5306 or (813) 855-2587. Fax: (813) 855-1263.

ORLANDO

Colonial Flea Market

DATES: Friday, Saturday and Sunday.
TIMES: 8:00 AM–5:00 PM.
ADMISSION: Free. Parking is free.
LOCATION: 11500 East Colonial Dr. On Hwy 50, 12 miles east of downtown Orlando, 6 miles east of 436 on your map.
DESCRIPTION: Opened in 1991, this indoor/outdoor market hosts from 500 dealers selling antiques, collectibles, crafts, produce, furniture, housewares, new merchandise and a huge selection of used merchandise. Six snack bars take care of the munchies. There are 550 covered and paved spaces and 100 outdoor spaces. They are located close to Disney World, Universal Studios and the Space Center. Located on the premises are a beer garden and five snack bars and restrooms. Activities besides shopping include bingo and raffles.
DEALER RATES: $7–$14 daily for a 7' x 9' space, or $75–$125 monthly. Reservations are suggested.
CONTACT: Mary or Tom Gowenlock, 11500 E Colonial Dr, Orlando FL 32817. Tel: (407) 380-8888.

PALMETTO

Midway Flea Market

DATES: Friday, Saturday and Sunday, year round.
TIMES: 8:00 AM–4:00 PM.
ADMISSION: Free. Parking is free.
LOCATION: 10816 US 41 North. Take Exit 45 from I-75. Market is midway between Tampa and Sarasota, near Sun City.
DESCRIPTION: Since 1987, this indoor/outdoor market's 250 to 450 dealers have been selling antiques, collectibles, produce, coins, cards, new merchandise, clothes, furniture, crafts and garage sale goodies. When the munchies strike pick from two restaurants, two snack bars, a bakery or beer garden. And yes, there are handicapped-accessible restrooms. The outdoor vendors are under cover, so don't worry about any stray rain. This market is busy from October through May. The management maintains an exceptionally clean market and prides itself on its friendliness.
DEALER RATES: $10 and up per 10' x 10' space under cover, or $200 per month per 10' x 10' space indoors monthly. Reservations are necessary for indoors, recommended for outdoors.
CONTACT: Carey, Midway Flea Market, 10816 US 41 N, Palmetto FL 34221. Tel: (941) 723-6000. Fax: (941) 723-9093.

PENSACOLA

T & W Flea Market

DATES: Saturday and Sunday, rain or shine.
TIMES: Dawn to dusk.
ADMISSION: Free. Free parking is available.
LOCATION: 1717 North "T" St, on the west side of Pensacola.
DESCRIPTION: This indoor/outdoor market started in 1979. There are 400 dealers per weekend selling a variety of objects including antiques, fine art, arts and crafts, new merchandise, fresh produce, etc.—it's all here. They have made many improvements in this market including concrete aisles. Four snack bars provide food for the hungry. Handicapped-accessible restrooms complete the amenities.
DEALER RATES: $10 and up. Reservations are required for the more desirable spaces.
CONTACT: Red Cotton, 1717 N T St, Pensacola FL 32505. Tel: (850) 433-4315 or 433-7030.

PLANT CITY

Country Village Flea Market

DATES: Every Wednesday, Saturday, and Sunday, rain or shine.
TIMES: 7:00 AM–2:00 PM.
ADMISSION: Free. Free parking is available.
LOCATION: On corner of State Rd 39 and Sam Allen Rd, 1 mile north of I-4 (Tampa area).
DESCRIPTION: This market began in 1979 and currently ranks among the largest Wednesday markets. It accommodates dealers both indoors and outdoors, selling plenty of used goods. Also available are antiques, collectibles, and fresh produce. Food is served on the premises. Their Wednesday market is so popular that they have turned away dealers for lack of room! There is a wholesale produce market seven days a week from 6:00 AM to whenever.
DEALER RATES: $7 and up for 10' x 24' indoor space. $7 for 24' outdoor space. No reservations are required and there are no advance shopping hours for dealers.
CONTACT: Sylvia Utter, Country Village Flea Market, 3301 Paul Buchman Hwy 39 N, Plant City FL 33565-5051. Tel: (813) 752-4670.

PORT RICHEY

USA Fleamarket

DATES: Friday, Saturday and Sunday.
TIMES: 8:00 AM–4:00 PM.
ADMISSION: Free. Parking is free.
LOCATION: 11721 US Hwy 19, 200 yards south of State Rd 52 on US Hwy 19.
DESCRIPTION: Started in 1980, this market runs from 600 dealers in summer to crammed full in winter. Their dealers sell antiques, collectibles, crafts, produce, jewelry, western wear, records, tapes, hobby supplies, tools, clothing, perfumes, pewter, scrubs, purses, clocks, art, appliances, silk flowers, sneakers, lamps and other new merchandise. There is a Dollar Shop, an automotive shop, a beauty salon, hobby shop, and seven snack bars as well. Look for their humongous electronic sign at the entrance—"You can't miss it!" "One of the best flea markets on the west coast (of Florida)."
DEALER RATES: From $10 and up daily for a 10' x 12' booth. There are weekly and monthly rates available as well as shed rentals. Vendors set up at 7:00 AM, vacate by 5:00 PM.

CONTACT: Marie Bruno, USA Fleamarket, Inc, 11721 US Hwy 19, Port Richey FL 34668. Tel: (813) 868-7418.

ST. AUGUSTINE

St. John's Flea Market

DATES: Saturday and Sunday.
TIMES: 9:00 AM–5:00 PM.
ADMISSION: Free. Parking is also free.
LOCATION: I-95 and State Rd 207, Exit 94.
DESCRIPTION: This market opened in 1985 and has 500 spaces indoors and out with dealers selling "everything"—antiques, collectibles, new and used merchandise, produce, plants, and more. It is all under roof. Located in historic St. Augustine, the country's oldest city and a major tourist attraction. Food is available on the premises as are clean restrooms and RV facilities.
DEALER RATES: $11 per day. Reservations are suggested.
CONTACT: St. John's Flea Market, PO Box 1284, St Augustine FL 32085-1284. Tel: (904) 824-4210. Fax: (904) 824-9287.

SANFORD

Flea World

DATES: Every Friday, Saturday, and Sunday. Rain or shine.
TIMES: 9:00 AM–6:00 PM.
ADMISSION: Free. Free parking is available for 4,000 cars.
LOCATION: On Hwy 17-92, Sanford. From I-4, take Exit 50 east to Hwy 17-92, turn right 1 mile.
DESCRIPTION: This market started on May 20, 1982, with just a 12-acre tract. It has now grown to accommodate 1,700 dealers on 104 acres of land. There is an "all-under-one-roof" building with 1,700 booths and three other air-conditioned buildings. Shoppers really can get it all here from antiques and collectibles to the unusual: a lawyer, an optometrist, a barber and beauty shop, and an exotic pet shop. The Friday market features $5 garage sales free before 9:00 AM. Fifteen fun food stops quell hunger and a Family Fun Park is located next door.
DEALER RATES: $10–$16 per space and up. Reservations are required.
CONTACT: Alice Butcher, Rental Manager, Flea World, Hwy 17-92, Sanford FL 32773. Tel: (407) 330-1792 ext. 224.

STUART

B & A Flea Market

DATES: Saturday and Sunday, rain or shine.
TIMES: 8:00 AM–3:00 PM.
ADMISSION: Free. Parking $1.
LOCATION: South US Hwy 1, just north of Indian St, across from Martin Square Mall.
DESCRIPTION: This market first opened in 1975. It accommodates over 500 dealers both indoors and outdoors who assemble to sell just about everything including antiques, collectibles, fine art, arts and crafts, new merchandise, and everything else imaginable. A farmer's market sells fresh produce. Hot dog carts roam the market and a deli and other concessions quell hunger. Handicapped-accessible restrooms are on site.
DEALER RATES: $14–$24 per daily space. Reservations must be made in person and paid for by 7:00 AM the day of the market.
CONTACT: Mary Sue Davis, Flea Market Manager, B & A Flea Market, 2201 SE Indian St, Stuart FL 34997. Tel: (561) 288-4915. Fax: (561) 288-2140.

TAMPA

Big Top Flea Market

DATES: Saturday and Sunday, year round.
TIMES: 9:00 AM–4:30 PM.
ADMISSION: Free. Parking is free.
LOCATION: Take I-75 south to Fowler Ave (SR 582), Exit 54, heading east. Market is 500 yards east of I-75.
DESCRIPTION: The Big Top Flea Market, opened in October 1990, was built in a unique hub and spoke design so that every booth is well traveled and easily accessible. The market is named after the 27,000-square-foot center core that resembles a huge circus tent. It houses 620 booths with 160,000 square feet of both covered and enclosed spaces. Eventually the Market will have over 1,100 spaces. While there is a wide variety of merchandise including produce, fine jewelry, antiques, collectibles and crafts, this market is keeping the true spirit of a flea market: value, bargains and fun. A full food court and handicapped-accessible restrooms add to the amenities.
DEALER RATES: Winter: $83 to $231 depending on location. Summer rates are discounts off winter rates depending on location. Rates are based

on a 4-week month. Daily and weekend rates are available. Office is open Monday 1:00 PM–4:00 PM, Friday 9:00 AM–4:00 PM.

CONTACT: Big Top Flea Market, 9250 E Fowler Ave, Thonotosassa FL 33592. Tel: (813) 986-4004.

WALDO

Smiley's Pocket Change Flea Market

DATES: Saturday and Sunday.

TIMES: 8:00 AM–5:00 PM.

ADMISSION: Free. Parking is free.

LOCATION: 1½ miles north of Waldo on the west side of US 301.

DESCRIPTION: Started in 1982, this indoor/outdoor market of 100 dealers sells mostly antiques and collectibles. There is some new merchandise, but basically it's all old treasures and goodies. One snack bar and four sets of clean restrooms are on site including one set particularly designed for the handicapped. They also have a special easy-access parking area for the handicapped. An RV park is next door.

DEALER RATES: $11 for a 10' x 10' space and two tables per weekend. Reservations are recommended.

CONTACT: Sylvia Hall, Smiley's Pocket Change Flea Market, PO Box 194, Waldo FL 32694-0194. Tel: (352) 468-1785 or 331-2999 or 375-4152.

Waldo Farmer's and Flea Market

DATES: Every Saturday and Sunday. Rain or shine.

TIMES: 7:30 AM–4:30 PM.

ADMISSION: Free. Free parking available.

LOCATION: Located on Hwy 301 North, north of Waldo.

DESCRIPTION: This Farmer's and Flea Market attracts an average of 750 dealers in the summer and 900 dealers during the winter who sell antiques, collectibles, handmade craft items, vegetables, tools and new merchandise. The market has been running since 1973. There is a huge antique mall here, open every day. The majority of spaces are under cover sheds, however outside space and lock-up stalls are also available. Dealers may stay overnight and no county or city licenses are required. There is a snack bar on the premises and camping nearby. The office is open everyday. "Look for the Big Horse." They describe themselves as a, "Country market with big city crowds. Friendly folks."

DEALER RATES: $7 and up per 10' x 10' space.

CONTACT: Waldo Farmer's and Flea Market, 17805 NE US Hwy 301, Waldo FL 32694. Tel: (352) 468-2255.

WEBSTER

Sumter County Farmer's Market, Inc

DATES: Every Monday year round, except Christmas Day. Rain or shine.
TIMES: 8:00 AM–3:00 PM.
ADMISSION: Free. Free parking is provided on market grounds.
LOCATION: On Hwy 471 in Webster. Accessible from Hwy 50, Hwy 301, or Hwy 98.
DESCRIPTION: This market opened in 1937 and currently attracts between 1,200 (summer) and 2,000 (winter) dealers who sell a range of antiques, collectibles, craft items, new merchandise, and fresh produce, including citrus and flower plants. This market is well known for its selection of antique items and locally grown vegetables. There is a large wholesale area on site as well. Snack food is available on the premises.
DEALER RATES: $9 per 10' x 10' booth, covered with 2 tables; $7 per 12' x 12' booth, open with 2 tables. Cancellations are done by a lottery system at 7:00 AM. All dealers must have city and county licenses, available at office every Monday between 7:30 AM and 9:30 AM for $7 per day or $35 for the year.
CONTACT: Margie Hayes, Office Manager, PO Box 62, Webster FL 33597. Tel: (352) 793-3551.

Webster Westside Flea Market

DATES: Mondays, year round.
TIMES: 5:00 AM until the last dealer leaves, literally.
ADMISSION: Free. Parking is $2.
LOCATION: 516 NW 3rd St. On Hwy 478 at NW 3rd St. On the west side of town.
DESCRIPTION: Considered the oldest flea market in the state, they opened as an outdoor market in 1931. Many of the dealers are under cover although, not really indoors. Also known as "Antique Alley" for their quality antiques and collectibles, this market's 800 or so dealers also sell some new merchandise, produce and whatever. They hold Car Shows the first Sunday of the month, with a three-day Extravaganza in February. They tried an antiques-only show one weekend in 1997 and found it was so successful that they will be doing them in the future. Watch for the advertisements as to the dates. Plenty of concessions dot the market. Howard's Flea Market in Homosassa is their sister market and headquarters.

DEALER RATES: Daily including tax: Covered with 2 tables: $14.98 and 2 tables per 10' x 10' space. Small field: $9.63 per 10' x 10' with 1 table. Big field: $25 per 30' x 15' space, no tables. Reservations are suggested. Although, if you do show up, they will manage to find you a spot, somehow. The office is open for reservations on Thursday and Friday.
CONTACT: Teri Shannon, Howard's Flea Market, 6373 S Suncoast Blvd, Homosassa FL 34446. Tel: (352) 628-4645. For a tape of Webster-only information and their voicemail, call 1-800-832-7396.

WEST PALM BEACH

Beach Drive-In Theatre Swap Shop

DATES: Wednesday, Friday, Saturday, and Sunday.
TIMES: 6:00 AM–2:00 PM.
ADMISSION: Saturday and Sunday $.50 per car.
LOCATION: 1301 Old Dixie Hwy. Between I-95 and US 1.
DESCRIPTION: This outdoor market started in 1965 and attracts 400 dealers selling mostly used and new merchandise and fresh produce. "All kinds of goodies," according to the manager. There is a nice snack bar on premises.
DEALER RATES: Wednesday $3, Friday $4; Saturday and Sunday $7–$10 depending on season (winter higher). Reservations are not required.
CONTACT: Beach Drive-In Theatre Swap Shop, 1301 Old Dixie Hwy, Riviera Beach FL 33404. Tel: (561) 844-5836.

ZEPHYRHILLS

Zephyrhills Flea Market

DATES: Friday, Saturday and Sunday, September through May.
TIMES: 8:00 AM–3:00 PM.
ADMISSION: Free. Parking is free.
LOCATION: 39336 Chancey Rd. Follow Rt 301 to the south side of Zephyrhills, turn east on Chancey Rd. Go about 1½ miles, the market is on the right.
DESCRIPTION: Started in 1991, this indoor/outdoor market has 340 or so spaces with 100 or more dealers depending on who takes up how much room. The outdoor sellers are under roof on concrete paths. They sell antiques, collectibles, baked goods, ceramics, watches, coins, plants, household goods, oldies music and one dealer selling motorized scooters for the

handicapped. Food wagons quell hunger. One aisle is devoted to yard sales only. This market has been noted for its cleanliness and friendly people.
DEALER RATES: Outside: $15 for a proper space, yard sale aisle is $6 per day. Indoors: $150–$175 per month (there are 64 spaces).
CONTACT: Zephyrhills Flea Market, 39336 Chancey Rd, Zephyrhills FL 33540. Tel: (813) 782-1483 or 1-800-932-9674.

OTHER FLEA MARKETS

We know or have heard about these markets, but have not personally contacted each one, as we have the markets with descriptions. If you plan to visit one of these markets listed below, *please call first* to make sure they are still open. Flea markets do come and go. While they were open when we went to press, they may not be later. We can't be responsible. *Call first! Area codes may have changed!*

Bartow: Bartow Outdoor Drive-In Theatre & Flea Market, 1705 US Hwy 17 S. Tel: 941-533-6395.
Big Pine Key: Big Pine Key Flea Market, US Hwy. Tel: 305-872-4103 or 305-872-2025.
Boca Raton: Forty Fifth St Flea Market, 1710 45th St. Tel: 561-863-6424.
Boca Raton: Hallandale Flea Market, 901 S Federal Hwy. Tel: 561-457-6130.
Bradenton: Roma Flea Market, 5715 15th St E. Tel: 941-756-9036.
Bushnell: Bushnell Flea Market, 5845 Cr 313. Tel: 352-793-6515.
Bushnell: Sumter Flea Market, 7368 State Rd 471. Tel: 352-793-3581.
Carrabelle: L & J Flea Market, 606 SE Ave B. Tel: 904-697-4033.
Clearwater: 49er Flea Market, 10525 49th St N. Tel: 813-573-3367.
Cocoa: Jumping Flea Market, 2507 N Cocoa Blvd. Tel: 407-636-9664.
Cocoa: Little Big Flea Shop. Tel: 407-639-3354.
De Funiak Springs: De Funiak Flea Market, E Hwy 90. Tel: 904-892-3668.
Delray Beach: Delray Indoor Flea Market, 5283 W Atlantic Ave. Tel: 561-499-9935.
Ellenton: Enterprise Flea Market, 2408 US Hwy 301 N. Tel: 941-723-9424.
Fort Lauderdale: A-1 Flea Market, 1621 N State Rd 7. Tel: 954-777-2990.

Fruitland Park: North Lake Flea Market Inc, 2557 US Hwy 441/27. Tel: 352-326-9335..

Greensboro: Odom's Flea Market & Shop, Hwy 12. Tel: 904-442-4515.

Gulf Breeze: The Flea Market, 5760 Gulf Breeze Pkwy. Tel: 904-934-1971.

Hallandale: Hollywood Dog Track Flea Market, 831 N Federal Hwy. Tel: 954-454-8666.

Hilliard: Bargain Mart Flea Market & Auction, US 1. Tel: 904-845-2889.

Holiday: Midway Swap Shop Flea Market, 1315 US Hwy 19. Tel: 813-937-3807.

Holly Hill: Squeekie Clean Flea Market & Country Store, 998 N Beach St. Tel: 904-257-2398.

Hollywood: Jake's Flea Market, 6401 Sheridan St. Tel: 954-962-3080.

Homestead: Bargain Town Flea Market, 24400 Packinghouse Rd. Tel: 305-257-4335.

Homestead: Bargain Town Flea Market, 24420 S Dixie Hwy. Tel: 305-258-3923.

Homestead: Florida City Flea Market, 450 NW 6th Ter. Tel: 305-247-2287.

Hudson: Romans Flea Market, 8026 New York Ave. Tel: 813-862-1185.

Indian Harbor Beach: A1A Flea Mart Inc, 765 Pinetree Dr. Tel: 407-777-3380.

Interlachen: Rodriguez Flea Market, 1300 Hwy 20. Tel: 904-684-4969.

Jacksonville: ABC Flea Market, 10135 Beach Blvd. Tel: 904-642-2717.

Jacksonville: Beach Blvd Flea & Farmers Market, 11041 Beach Blvd. Tel: 904-645-5961.

Jacksonville: Blanding Flea Market, 6016 Blanding Blvd. Tel: 904-772-8008.

Jacksonville: Jacksonville Market Place Flea & Farmers Market, 614 Pecan Park Rd. Tel: 904-751-6770.

Jacksonville: Jacksonville Playtime Flea Market, 6300 Blanding Blvd. Tel: 904-771-2300 or 904-771-9939.

Jacksonville: Liberty St Flea Market, 3805 N Liberty St. Tel: 904-634-8824.

Kissimmee: Osceola Flea & Farmers Market Orlando Number, 2801 Erl Brnsn Mm Hwy. Tel: 407-238-1296 or 407-846-2811.

Lake City: Lake City Flea Market, Hwy 247. Tel: 904-752-1999.

Lake Wales: Lake Wales Flea Market, 1250 State Rd 60 W. Tel: 941-676-7701.

Lake Wales: Sunshine Flea Market, 4447 N US Hwy 27. Tel: 941-676-0368.

Lakeland: King Flea Inc, 333 Lake Parker Ave N. Tel: 941-688-9964.

Lauderdale Lakes: Bazaar Flea Market, 3200 W Oakland Park Blvd. Tel: 954-739-2805.

Lawtey: Zephyrhills Auto & Antique Flea Market, 2738 Gall Blvd. Tel: 904-782-0835.

Lecanto: Stokes Flea Market, 5220 W Gulf to Lake Hwy. Tel: 352-746-7200.

Live Oak: Anna V's Flea Market, 230 Howard St. Tel: 904-364-1015.

Lynn Haven: Annie's Flea Market, 716 Ohio Ave. Tel: 904-265-4202.

Mayo: B J's Flea Market, Main St. Tel: 904-294-1924.

Miami: 183rd St Flea Market, 18200 NW 27th Av. Tel: 305-624-1756.

Miami: Flagler Flea Market, 401 NW 38th Ct. Tel: 305-649-3000.

Miami: Golden Glades Flea Market, 1313 NW 167th St. Tel: 305-620-9498 or 305-626-9696.

Miami: Golden Glades Flea Market, Hlh Trl. Tel: 305-826-3532.

Miami: Hallandale Flea Market at Gulfstream Park, 21301 Biscayne Blvd. Tel: 305-931-7223.

Miami: International 54th St Flea Market, 1100 NW 54th St. Tel: 305-758-4822.

Miami: Liberty Flea Market, 7900 NW 27th Ave. Tel: 305-836-9848.

Miami: North Miami Flea Market, 14135 NW 7th Ave. Tel: 305-685-7721.

Miami: Tropicaire Drive-In Flea Market, 9769 S Dixie Hwy. Tel: 305-264-9078.

Miami: US 1 Americas Indoor Flea Market, 18901 S Dixie Hwy. Tel: 305-234-2828.

Miami: We Are One Inc Flea Market, 1313 NW 167th St. Tel: 305-623-7010.

Miami: Worlds Largest Indoor Flea Market, 190 NE 199th St. Tel: 305-651-9530.

Milton: Big Oak Flea Market, 4132 Hwy 90. Tel: 904-995-9181.

Milton: I-10 Flea Market & Antiques, 3524 Garcon Point Rd. Tel: 904-623-6349.

Milton: Junk to Treasures Flea Market. Tel: 904-623-4958.

Milton: Pea Ridge Flea Market, 5186 Hwy 90. Tel: 904-994-8056.

Mount Dora: Golden Triangle Antique & Flea Market, 2751 W Old US Hwy 441. Tel: 352-383-9404.

Naples: Bass & Bass Flea Mart, 230 Industrial Blvd. Tel: 941-643-4424.

Naples: Florida Sports Park Flea Market, 4701 SR 951 S. Tel: 941-774-7979.

Naples: Naples Drive-In Flea Market, Davis Blvd Ext. Tel: 941-774-2900.

Oak Hill: Oak Hill Flea Market, 351 N US Hwy 1, Tel: 904-345-3570.

Odessa: Gunn Hwy Flea Market, 2317 Gunn Hwy. Tel: 813-920-3181.

Okeechobee: Cypress Hut Flea Market, 4701 Hwy 441 SE. Tel: 941-763-5104.

Opa Locka: The Flea Market, 12705 NW 42nd Ave. Tel: 305-688-0500.

Orlando: Colonial Flea Market, 11500 E Colonial Dr. Tel: 407-380-8888.

Orlando: KK Flea Market, 1325 W Washington St. Tel: 407-841-0736.

Orlando: Orlando Flea Market, 5022 S Orange Blossom Trl. Tel: 407-857-0048.

Orlando: Southwestern Flea Market, 4702 W Colonial Dr. Tel: 407-578-9060.

Palmetto: Country Fair Flea Market, 512 10th St E. Tel: 941-722-5633.

Panacea: D & J Flea Market, Hwy 98. Tel: 904-984-5339.

Panama City: 11th St Flea Market, 1517 E 11th St. Tel: 904-872-9290.

Panama City: 15th St Flea Market, 2233 E 15th St. Tel: 904-769-0137.

Panama City Beach: Laguna Flea Market, 19987 Panama City Beach Pkwy. Tel: 904-230-8687.

Pensacola: Apple Flea Market, 1241 W Nine Mile Rd. Tel: 904-857-1800.

Pensacola: B & B Antiques And Flea Market, 3721 W Navy Blvd. Tel: 904-455-3200 or 904-457-8070.

Pensacola: Chicken Nest Flea Market, 1316 N New Warrington Rd. Tel: 904-456-3226.

Pensacola: Doris's Antiques & Flea Market, 1201 N T St. Tel: 904-432-7700.

Perry: The Perry Flea Market, 3609 S Byron Butler Pkwy. Tel: 904-838-1422.

Pinellas: Wagon Wheel Flea Market, 7801 74th St, Park. Tel: 813-544-5319.

Placida: Englewood Flea Market, 2900 Placida Rd. Tel: 941-697-2067.

Port Charlotte: Rainbow Flea Market, 4628 Tamiami Tr. Tel: 941-629-1223.

Port Charlotte: Sun Flea Market Inc, 18505 Paulson Dr. Tel: 941-255-3532.

Saint Petersburg: Mustang Flea Market, 350 1st St N # 7301. Tel: 813-544-3066.

Saint Petersburg: Peddler's Flea Market, 9401 Bay Pines Blvd. Tel: 813-392-2198.

Seffner: Joe & Jackie's Flea Market, 311 Dr Martin Luther King Jr. Tel: 813-689-6318.

Southport: 77 Flea Market, 6515 Hwy 77. Tel: 904-271-9577.

Tallahassee: Noah's Ark Daily Flea Market & Antiques, 3919 Woodville Hwy. Tel: 904-656-2879.

Tallahassee: Tallahassee Flea Market Tallahassee, 200 Capital Cir SW. Tel: 904-877-3811.

Tampa: Basics Flea Market, 11309 N Nebraska Ave. Tel: 813-975-8455.

Tampa: Floriland Flea & Farmers Market, 9309 N Florida Ave. Tel: 813-932-4319.

Tampa: North 301 Flea Market, 11802 US Hwy 301 N. Tel: 813-986-1023.

Tampa: Smith's Flea Mart, 9250 Fowler Ave E. Tel: 813-986-0891.

Tampa: Tampa Flea Market, 802 E Fletcher Ave. Tel: 813-977-7700.

Vernon: Fran's Flea Market, Hwy 79. Tel: 904-535-9400.

Waldo: Trading Flea Market, US Hwy 301 N. Tel: 352-468-2622.

Wauchula: Hilltop Flea & Farmers Market, N Hwy 17. Tel: 941-773-6148.

Webster: In-Door Flea Market, 537 N Market Blvd. Tel: 352-568-7050.

GEORGIA

ACWORTH

Lake Acworth Antique and Flea Market

DATES: Every Saturday and Sunday.
TIMES: 8:00 AM–5:00 PM.
ADMISSION: Free. Parking is free.
LOCATION: 4375 Cobb Parkway NW, approximately 35 miles north of Atlanta and 5 miles west of I-75, off Hwy 92 Exit. Follow Hwy 92 to Cobb, turn right, go approximately 1 mile. Market is on the left.
DESCRIPTION: Started in 1978, this flea market was formerly known as Delight's. It is held indoors, in the open air, and under cover. There are 400 dealers exhibiting antiques, arts and crafts, fresh produce, collectibles, and new merchandise. Located near Allatoona Lake on Lake Acworth, the average daily attendance ranges between 5,000 and 6,000 people. Here you will find something for everyone. Three concession stands feed the famished.
DEALER RATES: $5, $7, and $10 depending upon location and size of space. Reservations are recommended. No vendors license required.
CONTACT: James Little, Lake Acworth Antique and Flea Market, 4375 Cobb Pkwy N, Acworth GA 30102. Tel: (770) 974-5896 (Saturday and Sunday only).

ALBANY

Kitty's Flea Market

DATES: Friday, Saturday and Sunday, year round.
TIMES: 7:00 AM–6:00 PM.
ADMISSION: Free. Parking is also free.
LOCATION: 3331 Sylvester Rd. On US 82, 3 miles north of Albany.
DESCRIPTION: This market opened in 1985 in the middle of a pecan orchard and accommodates 320 regular dealers under roof and another 350 in the open or under shade and adding new tables all the time. "Anything you can think of" is sold here, including produce, furniture, clothes and jewelry. It is described by one regular as real "country, very laid back" and agreeable. This market is doing a booming business. If you love pecans, you can even pick your own! Four concession stands quell the screaming munchies.

DEALER RATES: $5 per table under the shed, $3 outside space. Reservations are required under the shed only. Outside dealers can set up outside with no reservation.
CONTACT: Jim Andrews, Kitty's Flea Market, PO Box 51324, Albany GA 31705. Tel: (912) 432-0007.

ATLANTA

Lakewood Antiques Market

DATES: Second weekend of every month, Friday–Sunday, year round. Extravaganzas held in April for four days and November for five days.
TIMES: Friday 9:00 AM–6:00 PM; Saturday 9:00 AM–6:00 PM; Sunday 10:00 AM–5:00 PM.
ADMISSION: $3. Parking is free. Thursday is early buyers day for $5.
LOCATION: 2000 Lakewood Way. Take I-75-85 South, Exit 88 East and follow the signs.
DESCRIPTION: Since 1969 this market has been hosting from 800 to 1,200 dealers selling at least 75% antiques and collectibles. Their historic buildings are situated on 117 acres of land with a fully-equipped bar and restaurant and dealer camping stops on site. They have added new air-conditioned and heated buildings.
DEALER RATES: $95 per 8' × 10' booth inside space; $70 per 11' × 15' outside space. After advance reservations are filled, then it is first come, first served.
CONTACT: Ed Spivia, PO Box 6826, Atlanta GA 30315. Tel: (404) 622-4488. Day of show contact Diane Kent at above number.

Scott Antique Market Antiques & Collectibles Show

DATES: January 9–11, February 13–15, March 13–15, April 10–12, May 8–10, June 12–14, July 10–12, August 7–9, September 11–13, October 9–11, November 13–15, December 11–13, 1998. Call for 1999 dates.
TIMES: Friday and Saturday 9:00 AM–6:00 PM, Sunday 10:00 AM–5:00 PM.
ADMISSION: $3 per weekend. Parking is free.
LOCATION: Atlanta Exposition Centers, North and South Facilities at 3650 Jonesboro Rd. Take Exit 40 (Jonesboro Rd) off I-285, 3 miles east of Atlanta Airport.
DESCRIPTION: Since 1986 this indoor/outdoor market has 2,400 dealers selling the finest in antique and collectibles only. Exhibitors from all

over the country feature fine antique furniture, jewelry, silver, glassware, textiles, linens, advertising items, military items, paintings, and much more. Four snack bars and one restaurant supply the energy to keep you browsing. Restrooms are on site.

DEALER RATES: Indoors: $95 for a 8' × 10' space; outdoors: $75 for a 10' × 15' open space or 10' × 10' covered space. There is an open field space for $35 for a 15' × 20' space to park and display. Reservations are required.

CONTACT: Scott Antique Market, PO Box 60, Bremen OH 43107-0060. Tel: (614) 569-4112. Fax: (614) 569-7595. During the show call (404) 361-2000.

CHAMBLEE

Atlanta Flea Market

DATES: Every Friday, Saturday, and Sunday, rain or shine.

TIMES: Friday and Saturday 11:00 AM–7:00 PM (may change to 9:00 PM closing), Sunday 12:00 PM–7:00 PM.

ADMISSION: Free. Free parking is available.

LOCATION: 5360 Peachtree Industrial Blvd, 1½ miles inside I-285, off Exit 23A.

DESCRIPTION: This indoor show began in 1974 and is now serving the surrounding, largely Hispanic community. Items sold include: gold, silver, jewelry, western apparel, Hispanic art and music, electronics, books, collectibles, old furniture and furniture reproductions, close-outs, cosmetics, groceries, luggage, plenty of clothing, South and Central American artifacts, toys, kitchen utensils and essentials. This permanent flea market is housed in 80,000 square feet of climate-controlled selling space. There is a Mexican restaurant on the premises.

DEALER RATES: $75-$100 per weekend, one month minimum.

CONTACT: Elias Hatoun, 5360 Peachtree Industrial Blvd, Chamblee GA 30341. Tel: (404) 458-0456.

DECATUR

Kudzu Antique Flea Market

DATES: Friday, Saturday, and Sunday.

TIMES: Friday and Saturday 10:30 AM–5:30 PM; Sunday 12:30 PM–5:30 PM.

ADMISSION: Free. Parking is also free.

LOCATION: 2874 East Ponce de Leon. Off I-285, Exit 31.

DESCRIPTION: This dealer's paradise opened in October 1980. Their 27 dealers, in a 27,000-square-foot barn-like building, sell mostly American antiques, collectibles, and furniture. There is very little new merchandise sold here and what comes in is exceptionally good. No food available on premises.
DEALER RATES: Rarely any vacancies, call for information.
CONTACT: Emily Campbell, 178 Lamont Dr, Decatur GA 30030. Tel: (404) 373-6498 or (404) 378-3909.

EAST POINT

Greenbriar Flea Market

DATES: Thursday through Monday, year round.
TIMES: Monday and Thursday 11:00 PM–8:00 PM; Friday and Saturday 10:00 AM–9:00 PM; Sunday 12:00 PM–7:00 PM.
ADMISSION: Free. Parking is also free.
LOCATION: 2925 Headland Dr. Across from the Greenbriar Mall.
DESCRIPTION: Opened in 1983, this market hosts 136 dealers selling all new merchandise including jewelry, clothes, hats, fragrance, shoes, photos, and endless amounts of more at very reasonable prices. They remodeled the entire market in 1993 adding 10,000 square feet, a few retail stores and a little restaurant to handle all your hunger problems.
DEALER RATES: $225 and up per month. Reservations are suggested especially around the holidays.
CONTACT: Greenbriar Flea Market, 2925 Headland Dr, East Point GA 30344-1908. Tel: (404) 349-3994.

GAINESVILLE

Mule Camp Trade Days
Gainesville Flea Market

DATES: First weekend of each month and preceding Friday, rain or shine.
TIMES: Friday and Saturday 9:00 AM–6:00 PM; Sunday 12:00 noon to 6:00 PM.
ADMISSION: Free. Free parking is available.
LOCATION: Gainesville Fairgrounds, Hwy 13 S, between Atlanta and Helen, Georgia, 50 miles north of Atlanta, Exit 4 off I-985.
DESCRIPTION: Known for its friendliness and courtesy, many of the 75 dealers have been with this flea market since it opened in 1978. Antiques, arts and crafts, collectibles, and new merchandise are exhibited both in-

doors and out. The concession is excellent, serving home-cooked food that includes home-baked cakes and cookies.
DEALER RATES: A 3-day weekend fee of $30 for space measuring 10' × 10', which includes two tables. Reservations are preferred.
CONTACT: Johnny and Barbara Benefield, 3064 Poplar Springs Dr, Gainesville GA 30507-8627. Tel: (770) 536-8068. Day of show call Barbara Benefield at (770) 534-9157.

MACON

Smiley's Flea Market

DATES: Saturday and Sunday.
TIMES: 7:00 AM–5:00 PM.
ADMISSION: Free. Parking is free.
LOCATION: On US 129/GA 247, 4 miles south of Macon.
DESCRIPTION: Opened in 1985, this indoor/outdoor market's several hundred dealers sell everything from "antiques to zebras" and everything in between, new and pre-owned. There are snack bars to satisfy the munchies, and clean handicapped-accessible restrooms. RV parking is available.
DEALER RATES: $5 for 9' × 9' outside space with table in parking lot area, inside the fence with a 10' × 10' space and one table $11 per day. Lock-up buildings are available by the month. Reservations are recommended. Office hours are Thursday and Friday 9:00 AM–5:00 PM; Saturday and Sunday 7:00 AM–5:00 PM.
CONTACT: George or Shirley Kulcsar, 6717 Hawkinsville Rd, Macon GA 31216. Tel: (912) 788-3700.

SAVANNAH

Keller's Flea Market

DATES: Saturday and Sunday, year round.
TIMES: 8:00 AM–6:00 PM.
ADMISSION: Free. Parking is free.
LOCATION: 5901 Ogeechee Rd. From Hwy 95 take 204 Exit south towards Savannah. Take Hwy 17 exit off 204. You can see the signs from Hwy 204.
DESCRIPTION: This outdoor market hosts 300-400 dealers selling antiques, collectibles, garage sale goodies, produce, plants and new merchandise either under cover or in a few spots in the open. Several snack bars and restaurants feed the famished.

DEALER RATES: $12 or $18 depending on where, per day. Setup starts Friday between 8:00 AM–6:00 PM. The office is open the same hours Friday through Sunday. Reservations are not required, first come, first served.
CONTACT: Keller's Flea Market, 5901 Ogeechee Rd, Savannah GA 31419-8905. Tel: (912) 927-4848. Fax: (912) 925-2638.

OTHER FLEA MARKETS

We know or have heard about these markets, but have not personally contacted each one, as we have the markets with descriptions. If you plan to visit one of these markets listed below, *please call first* to make sure they are still open. Flea markets do come and go. While they were open when we went to press, they may not be later. We can't be responsible. *Call first!*

Acworth: Great American Flea Market, 3355-N N Cobb Pkwy. Tel: 770-974-9660.

Albany: Albany Flea Market, 1540 N Washington St. Tel: 912-435-0409.

Alpharetta: A Flea Antique, 222 S Main St. Tel: 770-442-8991.

Alto: Linda's Flea Market & Auction, 3399 Hwy 365. Tel: 706-776-9654.

Americus: Plains Flea Market, Hwy 280 W. Tel: 912-928-5165.

Athens: J & J Flea Market, 11661 Commerce Rd. Tel: 706-613-2410.

Atlanta: Five Points Flea Market, 82 Peachtree St SW. Tel: 404-681-9439.

Atlanta: I Twenty Flea Market, 2425 Gresham Rd SE. Tel: 404-243-6623.

Atlanta: Johnson's Flea Market, 279 Candler Rd SE. Tel: 404-284-7478.

Atlanta: Les Flea Mart, 316 McDonough Blvd SE. Tel: 404-627-2500.

Atlanta: People Flea Market, 2649 Martin Luther King Jr Dr SW. Tel: 404-699-2405.

Atlanta: Richard's Doyle Flea Market, 1404 Dresden Dr NE. Tel: 404-237-3157.

Atlanta: Rowena's Flea Market, 833 Cascade Rd SW. Tel: 404-755-6438.

Atlanta: S & A Flea Market, 1974 Dekalb Ave NE. Tel: 404-371-8977.

Atlanta: Scavenger Hunt Flea Market, 3438 Clairmont Rd NE. Tel: 404-634-4948.

Atlanta: Swan Coach House Flea Office, 3084 Slaton Dr NW. Tel: 404-365-0780.

Atlanta: Westgate Flea Market, 3131 Campbellton Rd SW. Tel: 404-344-0290.

Augusta: A-1 Flea Market, 3404 Deans Bridge Rd. Tel: 706-798-8043.

Augusta: King's Flea Market, 3035 Milledgeville Rd. Tel: 706-738-9555.

Augusta: Pioneer Junction Flea Market, 3217 Milledgeville Rd. Tel: 706-667-0903.

Augusta: South Augusta Flea Market, 1562 Doug Barnard Pkwy. Tel: 706-798-5500.

Bainbridge: Joe's Flea Market, 1329 3rd St. Tel: 912-243-9585.

Bainbridge: Mimi's Mini Flea Market, 603 N Miller Ave. Tel: 912-246-0013.

Blakely: Blakely Flea Market, 556 N Main St. Tel: 912-723-6056.

Bonaire: Bonaire Flea Market, 409 GA Hwy 96. Tel: 912-329-9865.

Bowdon Junction: West Georgia Flea Market, Hwy 27. Tel: 770-832-6551.

Brunswick: Brunswick Flea & Farmers Market, 204 Old Jesup Rd. Tel: 912-267-6787.

Buena Vista: Cotton Gin Antiques & Flea Market, 6th Ave. Tel: 912-649-2350.

Buford: A Flea Antique, 4300 Buford Dr. Tel: 770-932-6833.

Buford: Pendergrass Flea Market, Hwy 129. Tel: 770-945-1900.

Buford: Village Fair Flea Market, Hwy 129 & I-85. Tel: 770-945-1900.

Cairo: Old South Flea Market, 1122 US Hwy 84 E. Tel: 912-377-6537.

Calhoun: Newtown Flea Mkt, 469 Newtown Rd NE. Tel: 706-625-9088.

Canton: M & M Flea Market, 2323 Marietta Hwy. Tel: 770-720-1897.

Cartersville: Brock's Flea Market. Tel: 770-386-4731.

Cartersville: Ruth's Flea Market, 18 Wingfoot Trl. Tel: 770-606-0995.

Cedartown: Cedar Creek Flea Market, 591 West Ave. Tel: 770-748-6916.

Cedartown: R & M Flea Market, 1573 Buchanan Hwy. Tel: 770-748-0467.

Centerville: Snay's Flea Market & Wholesale, 2806 Watson Blvd. Tel: 912-953-7245.

Chamblee: Buford Hwy Flea Market, 5000 Buford Hwy NE. Tel: 770-452-7140.

Chamblee: My Favorite Place Flea Market, 5596 Peachtree Industrial Blvd. Tel: 770-452-8397.

Chamblee: Ultimate Flea Market, 3685 Chamb Dunwoody Rd. Tel: 770-454-0484.

Clarkston: Clarkston Flea Market, 4222 E Ponce De Leon Ave. Tel: 404-292-0059.

Cleveland: 129 Flea Market, Hwy 129 S. Tel: 706-865-5730.

Cochran: Rainbow's End Flea Market, 100 Mendal Ln SW. Tel: 912-934-1221.

College Park: College Park Flea Market, 3763 Main St. Tel: 404-768-2164.

Columbus: Columbus Flea Market, 3850 Victory Dr. Tel: 706-685-1020.

Columbus: Columbus Indoor Flea Market, 3850 Victory Dr. Tel: 706-682-7000.

Commerce: Banks Crossing Flea Market, Ridgeway Rd. Tel: 706-335-6541.

Conyers: J & J Flea Market, 1566 Rockbridge Rd NW. Tel: 770-388-0546.

Conyers: Rockdale Flea Market, 2556 Jeremiah Industrial Way SW. Tel: 770-860-0204.

Cordele: Manhattan Flea Market, 439 Rockhouse Rd E. Tel: 912-273-5527.

Cumming: County Line Antique Flea Market, 14213 Cumming Hwy. Tel: 770-844-0845.

Cumming: Cumming Antique & Flea Market, 337 Dahlonega Rd. Tel: 770-844-7059.

Cumming: Dixie 400 Flea Market, 4750 Settingdown Cir. Tel: 770-889-5895.

Cumming: Heard's Flea Market, 4120 Poplar Pl. Tel: 770-887-6687.

Dahlonega: Seabolt's Flea Market, Hwy 19 N. Tel: 706-864-1007.

Dalton: Big D Flea Market, 3451 Cleveland Rd. Tel: 706-259-3269.

Dalton: North Georgia Farmers & Flea Market, 310 Legion Dr. Tel: 706-278-6369.

Dalton: Walnut Grove Flea Market, 2815 Airport Rd. Tel: 706-278-2277.

Danielsville: All-American Flea Market, Rt 1. Tel: 706-795-5550.

Dawsonville: T & L Flea Market, Public Sq. Tel: 706-265-3566.

Dearing: Vickie Flea Market & Craft Shop, 3147 Augusta Hwy. Tel: 706-597-8078.

Decatur: 285 Flea Market, 4525 Glenwood Rd. Tel: 404-289-4747.

Decatur: Glenwood Flea Mart, 3900 Glenwood Rd. Tel: 404-284-9139.

Decatur: South Dekalb Flea Market, 2023 Candler Rd. Tel: 404-284-2184.

Dillard: Rabun Flea Market, Hwy 441 N. Tel: 706-746-2837.

Dunaire: This-N-That Antique & Flea Market, 8813 Roswell Rd. Tel: 770-640-6110.

East Point: Greenbriar Flea Market Inc, 2925 Headland Dr. Tel: 404-349-3994.

East Point: Mae's Flea Market, 2473 Delowe Dr. Tel: 404-209-0540.

Eastman: Eastman Flea Mart & Antiques, 1107 Herman Ave. Tel: 912-374-7868.

Eatonton: Crystal Palace Flea Market, 1242 Madison Rd. Tel: 706-485-9010.

Elberton: OK Flea Market, 1784 Fortson Dr. Tel: 706-283-7333.

Ellijay: Cartecay Salvage & Flea Market, Hwy 52 E. Tel: 706-635-1026.

Forest Park: South Atlanta Flea Market, 4140 Jonesboro Rd. Tel: 404-363-6694.

Forsyth: High Falls Flea Market, 4917 High Falls Rd. Tel: 912-994-9770.

Gainesville: Gainesville Flea Market, 3600 Atlanta Hwy. Tel: 770-534-9157.

Gainesville: Old Athens Hwy Flea Market, 996 Athens St. Tel: 770-534-4448.

Grantville: Ruins & Relics Flea Market, 5320 S Hwy 29. Tel: 770-583-3032.

Greensboro: Greensboro Flea Market, 1281 E Broad St. Tel: 706-453-9424.

Griffin: Betty's Flea Market, 600 Searcy Ave. Tel: 770-227-2461.

Hampton: Sweetie's Flea Market, Hwy 19-41. Tel: 770-946-4721.

Hartwell: Hartwell Craft Antique & Flea Market, 121 Vickery St. Tel: 706-376-6789.

Hazlehurst: Drucie's Flea Market, 106 Hinson St. Tel: 912-375-9485.

Jefferson: Pendergrass Flea Market, 5641 Hwy 129 N. Tel: 706-693-4466.

Jesup: Back Yonder Flea Market, 3343 Odum Hwy. Tel: 912-588-0143.

Jonesboro: Clayton Flea Market, 281 Upper Riverdale Rd. Tel: 770-994-1225.

Jonesboro: Clayton Flea Market Pager, 281 Upper Riverdale Rd. Tel: 770-907-9893.

Kennesaw: Hwy 41 Flea Market, 3352 N Cobb Pkwy. Tel: 770-975-0100.

Lagrange: Bailey's Flea Market, 1308 Hogansville Rd. Tel: 706-883-7902.

Lagrange: Rockville Flea Market, 2266 Westpoint Rd. Tel: 706-845-0507.

Lake Park: Bargainville Flea Market. Tel: 912-559-0141.

Lawrenceville: Action Point Flea Market, 524 Buford Dr. Tel: 770-995-6781.

Lawrenceville: Dot's Antique Flea Market, 111 E Crogan St. Tel: 770-962-2868.

Lawrenceville: North Metro Antique & Flea Market, 422 E Crogan. Tel: 770-963-6397.

Lawrenceville: Stella's Flea Market, 524 Buford Dr. Tel: 770-963-5943.

Lexington: Willis Flea Market, Hutchinson Rd. Tel: 706-743-8965.

Lithia Springs: Bill's Flea Market, 4085 Bankhead Hwy. Tel: 770-819-9071.

Lithia Springs: Bill's Flea Market, 4205 Bankhead Hwy. Tel: 770-949-1188.

Lithonia: Lithonia Flea Mart, 6933 Main St. Tel: 770-482-5263.

Loganville: Flatcreek Flea Market, 3084 Hwy 78. Tel: 770-466-4223.

Macon: Martin's Unique Flea Market, 3768 Mercer St. Tel: 912-477-4629.

Macon: Ruth's Flea Market, 6230 Hawkinsville Rd. Tel: 912-781-4197.

Martinez: Westside Flea Market, 4497 Columbia Rd. Tel: 706-868-1449.

McDonough: Peachtree Peddlers Flea Market, 155 Mill Rd. Tel: 770-914-2269.

McDonough: The Cornerstone Flea Market, 1161 Jonesboro Rd. Tel: 770-957-8474.

McRae: Helena Hardware & Flea Market, 507 Main St. Tel: 912-868-6672.

Millen: Thompson's Flea Market, 525 Cotton Ave. Tel: 912-982-2401.

Monroe: Monroe Antiques & Flea Market, 1320 W Spring St. Tel: 770-207-6110.

Monroe: Walton County Flea Market, 216 Davis St. Tel: 770-267-9927.

Montezuma: Warehouse Flea Market, 131 Sumter St. Tel: 912-472-8683.

Moreland: M & M Flea Market, 3481 S Hwy 29. Tel: 770-254-1584.

Oglethorpe: Great New York Flea Market, 189 Cloud Springs Rd. Tel: 706-866-2926 or 706-858-0188.

Perry: Arledge Flea Market, 909 Massee Ln. Tel: 912-987-3184.

Perry: Elko Flea Market, 101 Pyles Rd. Tel: 912-988-1016.

Ringgold: Market Place Flea Market, 4031 Cloud Springs Rd. Tel: 706-866-4261.

Roopville: BJ's Flea Market, 185 S Hwy 27. Tel: 770-854-7222.

Rutledge: Bruceville Trading Post Flea Market, 7170 Atlanta Hwy. Tel: 706-557-1800.

Saint Mary's: St Mary's Flea Market, 206 W Gallop St. Tel: 912-882-8106.

Savannah: Charlie Washington Flea Market, 1106 NE 36th St. Tel: 912-231-0920.

Savannah: John's Barn & Flea Market, 103 Sunshine Ave. Tel: 912-238-3532.

Savannah: Pennsylvania Flea Market, 2416 Waters Ave. Tel: 912-236-2365.

Scottdale: Scottdale Flea Market, 3110 E Ponce De Leon Ave. Tel: 404-378-1896.

Smyrna: Windy Hill Flea Market, 1000 Windy Hill Rd SE. Tel: 770-431-9440.

Sparta: Twice Around Flea Market, 219 E Broad St. Tel: 706-444-5793.

Stone Mountain: A Village Flea Market, 791 Main St. Tel: 770-413-6436.

Stone Mountain: HJ's Flea Market, 693 Rays Rd. Tel: 404-297-0240.

Stone Mountain: Stone Mountain Flea Market, 5615 Memorial Dr. Tel: 404-294-8806.

Stone Mountain: Village Flea Market, 791 Main St. Tel: 770-413-6436.

Suwanee: Hilda's Flea Market, 345 Saw Mill Dr. Tel: 770-271-0041.

Swainsboro: Oak Park Flea Market & Collectibles, 3802 Harrington St. Tel: 912-578-3166.

Thomaston: Cecil's Flea Market, 3131 Barnesville Hwy. Tel: 706-647-2258.

Thomasville: Kelly's Flea Market, 210 W Jackson St. Tel: 912-225-9054.

Thomson: Bargain Box Flea Market, 510 Jackson St. Tel: 706-595-4324.

Trenton: Trenton Indoor Flea Market, Hwy 11 S. Tel: 706-657-6115.

Tucker: Acropol Flea Market, 3377 Lawrenceville Hwy. Tel: 770-939-8827.

Valdosta: Five Point Flea Market, 2913 N Ashley St. Tel: 912-259-0024.

Valdosta: Valdosta Flea Market, 407 N St Augustine Rd. Tel: 912-333-0330 or 912-333-9635.

Vienna: Downtown Flea Market. Tel: 912-268-2307.

Warner Robins: Snay's Flea Market, 10127 N Hwy 247. Tel: 912-328-0772.

Waycross: H & H Flea Market, 3880 Brunswick Hwy. Tel: 912-285-4642.

West Point: Hood's Flea Market, 710 3rd Ave. Tel: 706-643-4771.

Winder: Frank's Flea Market. Tel: 770-307-4199.

Winder: Frazier & Jameson Antiques & International Flea, 21 E Athens St. Tel: 770-867-0057.

Woodbine: Eudell's Flea Market, 300 Bedell Ave. Tel: 912-576-3600.

HAWAII

AIEA

Kam Super Swap Meet

DATES: Wednesday, Saturday, Sunday and most holidays, weather permitting.
TIMES: 5:15 AM–3:00 PM.
ADMISSION: Free. Parking is free.
LOCATION: 98-850 Moanalua Rd, across from the Pearlridge Shopping Center.
DESCRIPTION: This outdoor meet started in 1966. There are hundreds of dealers in Polynesian and Hawaiian crafts and collectibles, new items, slightly used items, fresh produce, milk caps, ethnic delicacies and much more. You will also find a varied assortment of clothes and Polynesian-made arts and crafts. Food is available on the premises.
DEALER RATES:
Unreserved Sellers: $9 per stall Saturday and Sunday, $8 Wednesday and weekday holidays.
Reserved Sellers: Monthly reservations are $17 per stall per day of the week, for an entire month (i.e. a month of Sundays, a month of Wednesdays). Holidays are free to reserved sellers. There is also a daily charge for reserved sellers: $7 per Saturday and Sunday, $6 per Wednesday and weekday holiday.
Marketplace Sellers: $65 per stall per day per month (i.e. a month of Sundays, etc.) for Saturdays and Sundays; $55 per stall per day per month for Wednesdays.
CONTACT: Kam Super Swap Meet, Kam Drive-In Theatre, 8 Moanalua Rd, Honolulu HI 96818-3936. Tel: (808) 483-5933 recorded message and instructions or between 7:30 AM–1:30 PM to speak to someone. Fax: (808) 847-9270.

HONOLULU

Aloha Flea Market

DATES: Wednesday, Saturday, Sunday and some holidays. The week before Christmas open every day.
TIMES: 6:00 AM–3:00 PM.
ADMISSION: $.50 per person. Children 12 and under are free. Parking is free.

LOCATION: Aloha Stadium. Right across the street from the Arizona Memorial in Pearl Harbor. Fifteen minutes from Waikiki.
DESCRIPTION: This market opened in 1979 and averages 1,200 vendors selling shirts, antiques, collectibles, diving gear, tools, sporting goods, shoes, new and used merchandise. During the holiday season, the dealer ranks swell to monumental proportions. Rows of shade trees line the market, so it stays cool. Of course, it offers the ideal weather. No flammables are allowed. Food and restrooms are on the premises. This is the largest market in the state of Hawaii and "on a per capita basis, the largest in the US."
DEALER RATES: Wednesday $10-$42.75 per space; Saturday $10.75-$42.75; Sunday $12.75-$42.75 per stall. One of the four stall sizes is 18' × 20'. Reservations are not required.
CONTACT: Aloha Flea Market, 99-500 Salt Lake Blvd, Honolulu HI 96818. Tel: (808) 486-1529.

OTHER FLEA MARKETS

We know or have heard about these markets, but have not personally contacted each one, as we have the markets with descriptions. If you plan to visit one of these markets listed below, *please call first* to make sure they are still open. Flea markets do come and go. While they were open when we went to press, they may not be later. We can't be responsible. *Call first!*

Hilo: Pahoa Village Flea Market, PO Box 10211. Tel: 808-965-0623 or 808-965-8882.
Honolulu: Hawaiian Flea Market, 2330 Kalakaua Ave. 808-926-3963.
Honomu: Akaka Falls Flea Market. Tel: 808-963-6171.
Kailua Kona: Kona Flea Market, Kona Marketplace. 808-329-9296.

IDAHO

BOISE

Spectra's Flea Market

DATES: Saturday and Sunday, usually the second or third week of September through March. Do call, as the dates depend on the availability of the Fairgrounds buildings.
TIMES: Saturday 9:00 AM–6:00 PM.
ADMISSION: $1. Parking is free.
LOCATION: West Idaho Fairgrounds. From Chinden Blvd to the corner of Glenwood and Chinden. Look for the market.
DESCRIPTION: This exceptionally clean indoor market has been around for "15–20" years with 130–180 dealers selling mostly antiques, collectibles, memorabilia, candy, jerky, furniture, Tupper Ware and some new merchandise. There are snack bars and handicapped-accessible restrooms on site as well as special access.
DEALER RATES: $50 per 10' × 10' "in-line" space, $60 for a corner space. Reservations are required.
CONTACT: Sam Jones, Spectra Productions, 4149 W State St, Eagle ID 83616-4439. Tel: (208) 939-6426.

CASCADE

Cascade Flea Market

DATES: Daily if the dealers want to, Memorial Day through Labor Day. But mainly Friday through Sunday.
TIMES: 9:00 AM–6:00 PM.
ADMISSION: Free. Parking is free.
LOCATION: Cascade Airport, Hwy 55. Out of Boise to north on Hwy 55 to Cascade. Watch for all the state flags flying!
DESCRIPTION: Opened in 1992, this small growing market of 25–35 vendors is held outdoors at an airport. They have nice, clean, family-oriented market with vendors selling antiques, collectibles, Indian crafts and jewelry, old license plates and bumper stickers, clothes, music tapes and CDs, and whatever. Most of their vendors return every year, bringing pals along. When the necessaries need, there are handicapped-accessible restrooms on site as well as a snack bar. Located in a tourist's paradise of hunting, fishing, hiking—the usual extraordinary mountain pleasures—this market has plenty of new faces visiting all the time.

DEALER RATES: $25 per 20' × 40' space outside for Friday through Sunday, plus $3 per day electric if needed. $8 per day with electric if the dealer wants to stay all week. Reservations are suggested if you wish to use electric. Thursday is a free day, used for setup. There are RV facilities at the airport for dealers who wish to stay all week, but only if selling during the entire stay.
CONTACT: Jim Larsen, Cascade Flea Market, PO Box 417, Cascade ID 83611. Tel: (208) 382-3049 (Larsen's home) or 382-3600 during the season.

> Note: If a dealer isn't at his or her post—blame the Morell mushrooms. Many dealers have been known to bug-out in search of the delicacies. So, if you see dealers sneaking off—you have an idea where they are going.

KETCHUM–SUN VALLEY
WARM SPRINGS VILLAGE
Antique Peddler's Fair Antique Show

DATES: July 4th weekend and Labor Day weekend, each year; rain or shine.
TIMES: 9:00 AM–7:00 PM.
ADMISSION: Free. Free parking is available.
LOCATION: In Warm Springs Village, Ketchum–Sun Valley. On world-famous Picaboo Street at the base of the ski lift.
DESCRIPTION: This show first opened in 1970 in the heart of Wood River Valley, Ketchum and Sun Valley. It is Idaho's largest antique market with over 125 dealers coming from Maine to California bringing wonderful antiques, Oriental carpets, rare books and fine art. There is always a large selection of furniture, Indian and Oriental collectibles, china, high-end jewelry, loads of silver, and vintage clothes, to name a few. Their Labor Day weekend show is "Wagon Days Celebration" with parades of wagons, rodeo, "shoot-em outs" and plenty to keep everyone busy (including buying awesome goodies).

Because of its extraordinary natural beauty this area has become a summer playground offering guided pack and river trips, hiking, swimming, fantastic fishing and ice shows featuring the champions. These shows attract many famous people including some Hollywood stars who have homes in the area. Food is served on the premises.

DEALER RATES: $165 per 10' × 12' space for all three days. Reservations are required. Bring your own canopy and booth setup or there are a limited number of canopies to rent.
CONTACT: Jan Perkins or Jeffrey, 2902 Breneman St, Boise ID 83703. Tel: (208) 345-0755 or 368-9759.

> Jan wants you to know that "Sun Valley is the first destination ski resort in the country—and had the first chair lifts in the world." (Betcha Mad River Glen in Vermont has the oldest still-running original chair lift in the world... and Heaven help the person who tries to change it!)

OTHER FLEA MARKETS

We know or have heard about these markets, but have not personally contacted each one, as we have the markets with descriptions. If you plan to visit one of these markets listed below, *please call first* to make sure they are still open. Flea markets do come and go. While they were open when we went to press, they may not be later. We can't be responsible. *Call first!*

Caldwell: Main Street Flea Market, 724 Main St. 208-454-3542.
Rexburg: Rexburg Flea Market-Mini Storage, 24 S 1st W. 208-356-7889.
Sagle: Sagle Flea Mart, 5217 Algoma Rd. 208-263-2244.

ILLINOIS

ALSIP

Tri-State Swap O Rama

DATES: Every Saturday and Sunday, rain or shine.
TIMES: 7:00 AM–4:00 PM.
ADMISSION: $.75 per person. Free parking available for 5,500 cars.
LOCATION: 4350 West 129th St. Take I-294 to Cicero Ave (Rt 50) south to 131st, east to Door or Pulaski Rd to 129th west.
DESCRIPTION: The Tri-State Swap O Rama is held both indoors and outdoors. Started in 1979, there are now 700 to 900 dealers selling antiques, fresh produce, meats, collectibles, and new merchandise. In 1997 they added another 1,000 parking spaces and a new wing accommodating 200 more dealers. Food is served on the premises.
DEALER RATES: $20 for space that measures 8' × 12' indoors or $18 per 12' × 24' outdoor booth. Advance reservations are suggested.
CONTACT: Jim Pierski, Swap O Rama, 4600 W Lake St, Melrose Park IL 60160. Tel: (708) 344-7300.

AMBOY

Amboy Happening Flea Market

Note: I couldn't get through to Mr. Edwards in time to update this market listing. I do know that it continues from speaking to another market owner. Keep in mind that the rates may change.

DATES: Third Sundays of February, March, April. First Sundays of May, June, July, October and November. August has two: first and fourth Sundays (the fourth Sunday is a Special Show).
TIMES: 8:00 AM–4:00 PM.
ADMISSION: $1 per person. Free parking with lots of available space.
LOCATION: 4-H Fairgrounds, 1 mile east of Rts 52 and 30 on US 30.
DESCRIPTION: Started in 1965, this market is held both indoors and outdoors. It consists of 72 dealers indoors selling antiques, arts and crafts, collectibles, new merchandise, coins, jewelry, and furniture. Others exhibit outdoors. A full kitchen serves good food on the premises. Occasionally they feature a special guest collector displaying in his or her specialty. However, the guest's goods are not for sale. There are special events scheduled throughout the year. Watch for announcements. Some past events in-

cluded a John Deere Antique Tractors show, English Horse Jumping, and more. The fourth August show is in conjunction with the Amboy Depot Days, the town's celebration of its history as a railroad town. While the flea market is open only on Sunday, the rest of the celebration starts on Friday.
DEALER RATES: $35 for three tables inside; $15 outside. Setup on Saturday and there is security. Reservations are required inside only; first come, first served outside. Free coffee is available to all dealers.
CONTACT: Bill Edwards, Bil-Mor Promotions, PO Box 603, Rock Falls IL 61071-0603. Tel: (815) 626-7601. Day of show call (815) 857-3488.

BELLEVILLE

West Main Flea Market

DATES: Saturday and Sunday, year round.
TIMES: Saturday 10:00 AM–5:00 PM. Sunday 12:00 PM–5:00 PM.
ADMISSION: Free. Parking is free.
LOCATION: 2615 West Main St. Take Hwy 159 into Belleville. Go to the right around Belleville Square and follow the road. This is now West Main St. The market is just across the street from the high school.
DESCRIPTION: A brand-new market having opened in October 1997, they have places for 47 dealers inside and are already full. There are a few places for dealers outside in decent weather and those are used as well. So far, their dealers have been selling antiques, collectibles, some new merchandise and crafts. A couple of vendors sell snacks and lunch foods as concessions. They hold an auction the first Wednesday night of the month.
DEALER RATES: $10 per 7' × 6' booth inside with table and pegboard. First come, first served.
CONTACT: Jack and Beatrice Rehbein, 2615 W Main St, Belleville IL 62226. Tel: (618) 239-6038.

BLOOMINGTON

Third Sunday Market

DATES: Third Sunday, June through November.
TIMES: 8:00 AM–4:00 PM.
ADMISSION: $4.50, children under 13 free. Parking is free. Early-bird Saturday admission: $25 for one, $40 for two people.
LOCATION: Interstate Center at the McLean County Fairgrounds. Take Exit 160B off I-39, or I-74, or I-55.

DESCRIPTION: Started in 1987, this market of 450 dealers sells only antiques and collectibles. There are 275 antiques dealers inside an Expo Center that is 2½ acres under roof, the rest either sell under a polebarn or in the open. There is plenty of food available and handicapped-accessible restrooms. Because Don and Carol are experts on antiques and collectibles themselves, the market is consistent in its quality of goods.
DEALER RATES: Expo Center: $95-$240 per space. Polebarn: $110–$125. Outside: $75-$120. Reservations are suggested.
CONTACT: Don and Carol Raycraft, PO Box 396, Bloomington IL 61761-0369. Tel: (309) 452-7926.

Serendipity

One cold, miserable, market day, an older man approached Don carrying a paper bag and looking quite stunned. Don, noticing his demeanor, asked him what happened. The gentleman explained that he collected tobacco tins. For 40 years he had searched for the elusive yellow one. He had heard about them, read about them, but had never seen one, much less owned one. Tobacco tins come in red, green and the elusive yellow. The yellow ones are rare and worth $1500 according to the gent. And he had plenty of red and green ones. It was that yellow prize that eluded him.

Until that day. He had come into the market on early-bird admission, just to see what was there. As he turned to look at something else—a yellow spot caught his eye.

Yes! His heart pounding, he reached for the prized yellow tin. Quite prepared to lay out $1500 for this gem—he turned the tin over and marked on the bottom was $12.95. *Hunh?*

Trembling, he inquired of the dealer as to how much the dealer *really* wanted.

The dealer took back the tin and turned it over, "$11 bucks."

Sold.

Author's Note

Don and Carol have written 55 books on antiques and collectibles. Have any questions? And yes, some of the book dealers at the market sell their books. Their latest, published by Wallace Homestead, *Price Guide to American Country Antiques,* came out in November 1997.

CHICAGO

Ashland Ave Swap-O-Rama

DATES: Thursday, Saturday and Sunday.
TIMES: Thursday 2:00 PM–9:00 PM; Saturday and Sunday 7:00 AM–4:00 PM.
ADMISSION: $.50 per person; free parking.
LOCATION: 4100 South Ashland Ave. One mile west of I-94, near White Sox Park.
DESCRIPTION: Started in 1990, there are now 800 to 1000 indoor and outdoor dealers exhibiting fresh produce and new and used merchandise. Described as "very ethnic and cosmopolitan," this market now claims to be the largest in the Chicago area. Three restaurants serve the hungry.
DEALER RATES: $19 per 12' × 8' inside space; $16 per 24' × 12' outside space. Reservations are suggested.
CONTACT: Jim Pierski, Swap O Rama, 4600 W Lake St, Melrose Park IL 60160. Tel: (708) 344-7300.

New Maxwell St Market

DATES: Sundays, year round.
TIMES: 7:00 AM–3:00 PM.
ADMISSION: Free. Parking is free where you can find it. Or there is $3 parking on Clinton and 14th Place.
LOCATION: Canal and Roosevelt Sts on Canal between Taylor St and Depot Place.
DESCRIPTION: The New Maxwell St Market is a continuation of the former one started blocks away in the early 1900s. From 350 to 500 dealers sell just about anything you could imagine. However, if you love antiques and fine collectibles, get there especially early and follow or race ahead of the other dealers scarfing up the real treasures. There is plenty of clothing, Mexican and African art and crafts, tons of food including the famous Maxwell St Polish sausages, tools, toys, household necessities—just about anything. There are the appropriate relief facilities dotted around the market, as well as security. Plenty of great music from renowned blues artists adds to the festivities.
DEALER RATES: $10 for a table and table-sized space, if lucky enough to get one. $30 for a selling space with place for a vehicle. *You must have a license before you can sell*. Reservations are mandatory. This is how they are done: The first Thursday of the month the fax line is used only for "alternate" dealers (non-permanent, or those without assigned spaces) to

call in and get put on the Alternate List for the month. When a permanent dealer doesn't take the assigned spot that weekend, then the alternates are called in order. Keeps people from lining up for 12 hours just to get a space. The office is open to get your license Wednesday through Friday 10:00 AM–6:00 PM; Saturday 7:00 AM–1:00 PM; Sunday 5:00 AM–2:00 PM.
CONTACT: Job Menchaca, New Maxwell St Market, 548 W Roosevelt Rd, Chicago IL 60607. Tel: (312) 922-3100. Fax: (312) 922-3169 (also used solely for reservations the first Thursday of the month).

DIXON

Sauk Valley Community College Flea Market

Note: I couldn't get through to Mr. Edwards in time to update this market listing. Do call first before going to this show. And keep in mind that the rates may change.

DATES: Third Sunday in January.
TIMES: 9:00 AM–4:00 PM.
ADMISSION: $1.50, parking is free.
LOCATION: Sauk Valley Community College on Rt 2 between Dixon and Sterling.
DESCRIPTION: Started in 1987 as a fundraiser for the college, this market boasts 75-100 dealers selling primarily antiques, collectibles and more. There are special guests and special collections to view. The proceeds from this market are used to benefit the sports program at the college. The college women run the food concessions as part of the fundraising effort.
DEALER RATES: $45 for a 3-table setup; $65 for 5-table setup. Reservations are required.
CONTACT: Bill Edwards, Bil-Mor Promotions, PO Box 603, Rock Falls IL 91071-0603. Tel: (815) 626-7601.

MELROSE PARK

Melrose Park Swap-O-Rama

DATES: Every Friday, Saturday and Sunday.
TIMES: 7:00 AM–4:00 PM Saturday and Sunday; Fridays 10:00 AM–4:00 PM.
ADMISSION: $.50 per person. Free parking is available for 1,000 cars.
LOCATION: 4600 West Lake St, at corner of Lake St (Rt 20) and Mannheim Rd (Rt 45).

DESCRIPTION: Started in 1975, 450 dealers both indoors and outdoors offer antiques, fine art, arts and crafts, fresh produce, collectibles, and new merchandise. Food is served on the premises.
DEALER RATES: $20 per 12' × 8' space inside, and $13 per 12' × 24' space outside. Reservations are suggested.
CONTACT: Jim Pierski, Swap O Rama, 4600 W Lake St, Melrose Park IL 60160. Tel: (708) 344-7300.

PECATONICA

The "Pec-Thing"

DATES: May 16 & 17 (third Sunday weekend); September 19 & 20.
TIMES: 8:00 AM–5:00 PM.
ADMISSION: $2 per person. Plenty of free parking is available.
LOCATION: Winnebago County Fairgrounds in Pecatonica, 7th and 4th St entrances.
DESCRIPTION: Started in 1980, this market operates both indoors and out. Over 400 dealers sell antiques, collectibles, handmade crafts, new and used items. All food must pass Fair Board approval. Several local homes are listed in the National Registry. Breakfast and lunch are served on the premises by one restaurant and six snack bars.
DEALER RATES: $25 per 10' × 25' space outdoors per weekend; $35 per 16' × 12' open outdoor shed; $50 per 16' × 12' indoor space per weekend. Tables are extra. Reservations are required. Friday setup 9:00 AM–9:00 PM, gates open at 6:00 AM for setup Saturday and Sunday. Also they have some space on a first-come, first-served basis.
CONTACT: Manager, PO Box K, Pecatonica IL 61063. Tel: (815) 239-1641. Day of show call (815) 239-1641.

PEOTONE

Antique Show

DATES: For 1998: January 25, February 22, March 22, April 26, May 24, September 27, October 25, November 29. Generally the last Sunday of each month except June, July and August (no show) and December (depends on Christmas), it's a good idea to check first in 1999. Rain or shine.
TIMES: 7:00 AM–4:00 PM.
ADMISSION: $2 per person. Free parking is available.
LOCATION: Will County Fairgrounds. South of Chicago between Chicago and Kankakee, 1 mile east of I-57.

DESCRIPTION: Started in 1967 and now run by the second generation of Mitchells, this show is held inside an air-conditioned building. Sixty-five dealers display a variety of antiques and collectibles. The market boasts lots of good glassware and primitives. Honey's Catering Service provides excellent meals, and there are handicapped-accessible restrooms. When weather permits, there are outside dealers as well.
DEALER RATES: $60 for four-table booth approximately 15' × 10', $70 for a 5-table booth. Large space outside: $25. Tables are provided for the inside booths and available for rent for the outside booths.
CONTACT: Robert W Mitchell Jr, 823 Center St, Dixon IL 61021. Tel: (815) 284-9216.

Peotone All-Night Flea Market

DATES: Overnight June 20, 1998.
TIMES: 5:00 PM–5:00 AM.
ADMISSION: $3 per person. Free parking is available.
LOCATION: Will County Fairgrounds. South of Chicago between Chicago and Kankakee, 1 mile east of I-57.
DESCRIPTION: Started in 1992, this all-night anything-goes flea market is held inside an air-conditioned building or outside on the grounds. Last year there were 75 dealers selling mostly antiques and collectibles, however this adjunct market to the Antique Show lets anything reasonable sell here. Therefore, the garage sale goodies make great pickings. There is an auction here at 7:00 PM for about two hours. They had up to 4,000 visitors roaming through here during this popular annual event. Honey's Catering Service provides excellent meals, and there are handicapped-accessible restrooms.
DEALER RATES: $65 for 5-table booth inside. Tables are provided. $65 for outside booth, approximately 25' × 25' with tables available to rent. Electricity is available outside.
CONTACT: Robert W Mitchell Jr, 823 Center St, Dixon IL 61021. Tel: (815) 284-9216.

ROCKFORD

Greater Rockford Antique and Flea Market

DATES: Every Saturday and Sunday, rain or shine.
TIMES: 8:00 AM–5:00 PM.
ADMISSION: Free admission and parking.

LOCATION: Alpine/Sandy Hollow Rd at 3913 Sandy Hollow Rd. Take Hwy 20 to Alpine exit, go north to Sandy Hollow, then west 1½ blocks.
DESCRIPTION: Started in 1976 at Alpine Village. At the current location, this market has room for 200 dealers outside and 60 indoors, offering antiques, fresh produce, collectibles (books, records, coins, baseball cards, etc.), and new merchandise. Food is served on the premises.
DEALER RATES: $25 per weekend for space measuring 10' × 12' inside (dealers must furnish own tables). Reservations are required in advance for indoor space only. $10 setup fee outdoors.
CONTACT: Carol A Fritsch, 6350 Canyon Wood Dr, Rockford IL 61109. Tel: (815) 397-6683.

ROSEMONT

Wolff's Flea Market

DATES: Sundays, April through October.
TIMES: 7:00 AM–3:00 PM.
ADMISSION: $1. Parking is free.
LOCATION: Rosemont Horizon. Take I-90 west to Lee St Exit near intersection of I-90 and I-294.
DESCRIPTION: This outdoor summer market started in 1991 and has 350 dealers selling antiques, collectibles, crafts, produce, coins, stamps, cards, garage sale goodies, furniture, and new merchandise. Two snack bars and handicapped-accessible restrooms add to the amenities.
DEALER RATES: $22 per 25' × 18' space. Reservations are not required.
CONTACT: David Wolff, 970 Arkansas, Elk Grove IL 60007. Tel: (847) 524-9590 or (630) 833-7469.

SANDWICH

Sandwich Antiques Market

DATES: Held six times each summer, May through October. Call for exact dates.
TIMES: 8:00 AM–4:00 PM.
ADMISSION: $4 per person. Parking is free.
LOCATION: The Fairgrounds, State Rt 34. From I-88, Sugar Grove Exit to Rt 30 to Hinckley. Follow signs on west side of Hinckley. Just 60 miles west of Chicago.
DESCRIPTION: Started in 1988, this 160-acre shaded indoor-outdoor market attracts 550 dealers selling only top-quality antiques and collectibles.

It is the only market in Illinois where dealers must give a 10-day money-back guarantee that the merchandise is as represented. There is a furniture delivery service available. Food is available on the premises.
DEALER RATES: $100 per 25' × 25' outside booth: $95 per 10' × 10' inside booth. Reservations are required.
CONTACT: Robert C Lawler, Show Manager, Sandwich Antiques Market, 1510 N Hoyne, Chicago IL 60622-1804. Tel: (773) 227-4464. Day of show call: (815) 786-3337.

ST. CHARLES

Kane County Flea Market

DATES: First Sunday of every month and preceding Saturday afternoon. Rain or shine.
TIMES: Saturday 12:30 PM–5:00 PM; Sunday 7:00 AM–4:00 PM.
ADMISSION: $4, children under 12 are free. Free parking is available.
LOCATION: Kane County Fairgrounds (Randall Rd); west side of St. Charles between Rt 64 and Rt 38.
DESCRIPTION: Having started with a humble 35 dealers in 1967, there are currently as many as 1,400 dealers (average 1,200 in summer, 800 in winter) selling antiques, fine art, collectibles, coins, fancy "junque" and the occasional new merchandise. Dealers, shoppers and collectors have come from as far away as Korea and all over the United States to shop here. "If you can't find it at Kane County, it was probably never made." There are four indoor buildings for winter months, and nine indoor buildings and seven sheds for summer months. This market has been listed in *Good Housekeeping* as one of the top 25 markets in the United States. So popular is this market, it prompted a local minister to ask: "Would Jesus skip church to shop at the Kane County Flea Market?" Plenty of good food, served by two restaurants and several snack bars, including country-style breakfast, is served on the premises.
DEALER RATES: Shed space at $105, North Main building $125, Stripe Buildings at $105 per space; $115 per weekend for a 10' × 20' space outdoors (cash only). Advance reservations are required for space under cover only; outside space is first come, first served. Setup Saturday at 9:00 AM. There is a parking lot in back for dealers.
CONTACT: Helen Robinson, Kane County Flea Market Inc, PO Box 549, St. Charles IL 60174-0549. Tel: (630) 377-2252.

STERLING

Antique Show

Note: I couldn't get through to Mr. Edwards in time to update this market listing. Do call first before going to this show. And keep in mind that the rates may change.

DATES: Second weekends in March, July, and October.
TIMES: Saturday 10:00 AM–9:00 PM; Sunday 10:00 AM–5:00 PM.
ADMISSION: Free. Parking is also free.
LOCATION: Inside Northland Mall on Hwy 2, east end of Sterling.
DESCRIPTION: This market started in 1973 with 50 to 55 dealers selling primarily antiques and collectibles and some flea market goods. This is a well-established show that attracts quite a crowd. The food and handicapped-accessible restrooms are the mall's amenities.
DEALER RATES: $65 for 2 days and 3-table booth (tables are furnished) and plug-in for lights in all booths. Reservations are required and pay in advance. $85 for five-table booth.
CONTACT: Bill Edwards, Bil-Mor Promotions, PO Box 603, Rock Falls IL 61071-0603. Tel: (815) 626-7601.

SYCAMORE

Antique, Craft, and Flea Market

DATES: The last full weekend in October.
TIMES: 9:00 AM–5:00 PM.
ADMISSION: $1.50 for adults; $1 senior citizens; students K–12 $.50; under 5 free. Free parking is available.
LOCATION: At the Sycamore High School. Take Rt 23 south through downtown Sycamore to the south edge of town. Turn onto Spartan Trail at stop light on Rt 23.
DESCRIPTION: This indoor craft fair and flea market, started in 1973 and currently consisting of 155 dealer booths, is operated by the Sycamore Music Boosters. It is run in conjunction with Sycamore's Annual Pumpkin Festival, which includes a variety of activities on that weekend such as carved and decorated pumpkins on the Court House lawn (approximately 1,000), 10K race on Sunday, food booths, art fair, a haunted house, and a giant parade Sunday afternoon. Proceeds from all activities associated with the weekend are used to support non-profit organizations in the community. It is estimated that approximately 100,000 people will visit the com-

munity over Pumpkin Festival weekend. This is a juried show which in the past has had wool products, stained glass, handmade dolls, hand-carved wood products and other non-commercial goods produced by artists. There are antiques and collectibles as well as the usual flea market fare. Food is available on the grounds. The Huskie Bus Line will provide transportation between the school and the downtown area for $.50 per person. A "stroller park" is available, with attendants, as strollers are not allowed in the market. Sycamore is only 65 miles northwest of Chicago on Rt 64.
DEALER RATES: $75 for 10' × 12' booth, reservations required.
CONTACT: Sycamore Music Boosters, PO Box 432, Sycamore IL 60178-0432. (Show chairmen change yearly.) Day of show call Beverly Smith at (815) 895-6750.

TOWANDA

Towanda Antique Flea Market

DATES: Every July 4th.
TIMES: 9:00 AM–5:00 PM, rain or shine.
ADMISSION: Free. Free parking is available.
LOCATION: Northwest of Bloomington, Illinois, on I-55. Take Exit 171.
DESCRIPTION: Started in 1968, the show has grown larger every year and currently features 250 dealers outdoors selling antiques, arts and crafts, collectibles, and new merchandise. This market has become known as a buyer's market because of the fair prices. Food is available on the premises. Since this is a July 4th activity, expect the usual festivities and fireworks.
DEALER RATES: $30 per 12' × 12' space. Reservations are required.
CONTACT: Lyle and Mary Merritt, PO Box 97, Towanda IL 61776. Tel: the Merritts at (309) 728-2810 or Linda Potts at (309) 728-2384.

URBANA

CU Last Sunday at the Market

DATES: The last Sunday of every month from September through April. The December/January show is held New Year's Day.
TIMES: 8:00 AM–4:00 PM.
ADMISSION: $2. Parking is free. Free passes can be obtained through local antique shops.
LOCATION: National Guard Armory, corner of Rts 45 and 150 (University and Cunningham Aves).

DESCRIPTION: This market, opened in 1995, sells a "general line" of antiques and collectibles featuring dealers from all over Illinois and Indiana. State-of-the-art barbecue lunches are available.
DEALER RATES: 50% off for first-timers. $50 for a 10' × 15' inside space, $100 for a 10' × 40' inside space. Setup during Saturday evening from 6:00–8:00 PM and Sunday 6:00–8:00 AM. "Reservations are a darn good idea."
CONTACT: Manette Messenger, 1101 S Prairie, Champaign IL 61820. Tel: (217) 355-0852 or fax: (217) 355-8991.

OTHER FLEA MARKETS

We know or have heard about these markets, but have not personally contacted each one, as we have the markets with descriptions. If you plan to visit one of these markets listed below, *please call first* to make sure they are still open. Flea markets do come and go. While they were open when we went to press, they may not be later. We can't be responsible. *Call first!*

Anna: OK Flea Market, 129 W Chestnut St. Tel: 618-833-2999.
Bloomingdale: Jungle Park Flea Market. Tel: 815-597-2951.
Bolingbrook: Montana Charlie's Flea Market. Tel: 630-739-4338.
Chicago: Buyer's Flea Market, 4545 W Division St. Tel: 773-227-1889 or 773-342-4546
Chicago: MP Flea Market, 3937 W Madison St. Tel: 773-722-7386.
Chicago: MP Flea Market, 7 S Pulaski Rd. Tel: 773-826-1020.
Chicago: Nook Flea Market, 604 E 50th. Tel: 773-268-7570.
Chicago: Robinson's Flea Market, 1545 W 47th St. Tel: 773-376-3300.
Chicago: SMW Flea Market, 3850 S Indiana Ave. Tel: 773-624-4172.
Compton: Country Inn Motel Lounge & Flea Market, 1204 SR 251. Tel: 815-497-3203.
East Saint Louis: Fairmont Flea Market, 5410 Collinsville Rd. Tel: 618-271-9885.
Glen Ellyn: World Bazaar Flea Market. Tel: 630-858-6410.
Grafton: Jacob's Flea Market. Tel: 618-786-3689.
Harvey: Halsted South Flea Market, 16900 Halsted St. Tel: 708-333-3300.
Joliet: Derald's Indoor Flea Market, 219 Maple St. Tel: 815-723-0700.
Joliet: Preacher's Flea Market, 804 E Cass St. Tel: 815-726-0858.
Joliet: Save A Buck Flea Market, 379 S Chicago St. Tel: 815-722-4918.

Marengo: Marengo Flea Market, 20023 E Grant Hwy. Tel: 815-568-3532.

Marion: Williamson County Flea Market, 1701 E Main St. Tel: 618-993-6721.

Moline: 5th Ave Flea Market, 1321 5th Ave. 309-764-5109.

Mundelein: Mundelein Square Flea Market Inc, 350 Townline Rd. Tel: 847-566-4750.

Park Forest: Bingo City Flea Market, 200 Norwood Square Dr. Tel: 708-481-1600.

Sheldon: AJ's Flea Market, RR 1. Tel: 815-429-3108.

Tinley Park: I-80 Flea Market, 19100 Oak Pk Ave. Tel: 708-532-8238.

Wheeling: Twin Flea Market & Drive-In, 1010 S Milwaukee Ave. Tel: 847-459-0078.

INDIANA

BROOKVILLE

White Farmers Market

DATES: Every Wednesday, rain or shine.
TIMES: Daylight (really) to noon.
ADMISSION: Free. Free parking is available.
LOCATION: White's Farm on Holland Rd, 3 miles southeast of town on Hwy 52, 30 miles northwest of Cincinnati, Ohio.
DESCRIPTION: A combination flea market and livestock auction, this market was originally started by the present owner's grandfather in 1940. Currently there are between 350 and 400 dealers in summer and between 50 and 75 dealers in the winter selling antiques, arts and crafts, fresh produce and fruits, collectibles and new merchandise on a 160-acre farm. Amish baked goods are offered as well as farm fresh eggs and small animals such as ducks, rabbits and chickens. Don't miss the Chicken Man, he is amazing, as is his flock of creatures. Look for the fellow with a head full of feathers. Next door to the farm one can see and visit the oldest church in Indiana on its original foundation. The market is located in the scenic Whitewater Valley. Indoor setups are located in the farm's original granary and tobacco barns. The buildings have been refurbished in the original antique atmosphere. They had added more storage buildings for inside setups. Special events are held throughout the year.
DEALER RATES: $10 per 20' × 22' space outdoors. Reservations are not necessary for outside space, but are required for inside space. Inside spaces from $10 to $18, depending on size and location.
CONTACT: Dave or Paula White, 6119 Little Cedar Rd, Brookville IN 47012. Tel: (317) 647-3574 (business) or (317) 647-5360 if desperate.

CANAAN

Canaan Fall Festival

DATES: Second weekend in September, rain or shine.
TIMES: Friday and Saturday 9:00 AM–10:00 PM; Sunday 9:00 AM–6:00 PM.
ADMISSION: Free. Free parking is available.
LOCATION: On the Canaan Village Square.
DESCRIPTION: Publicized as an old-fashioned event, this outdoor festival draws a very large crowd to this small village. Approximately 160 dealers sell a range of items from antiques and collectibles to craft items, fresh

produce, and some new merchandise. Highlights include the longest-running annual Pony Express in the United States, plus many games, contests, and stage entertainment. On Saturday the old-fashioned parade starts at 10:30 AM and features floats, bands, horses, a Postal Representative swearing in the Pony Express rider, and other events. The Fire Department's food concession does something special with its fish dish, it's a perennial favorite. The Kremer House Museum with three generations of furnishings was donated to the town in 1980 and is open to the public during this festival.

For those of you who need more exercise they have added the 6K Yellow Britches Valley/Indian Trails Run/Walk. Enjoy!

DEALER RATES: $30 per 20' × 20' space outside for the entire weekend plus $5 for electric.

CONTACT: Gale H Ferris, President, Canaan Restoration Council Inc, 9713 N State Rd 62, Canaan IN 47224. Tel: (812) 839-4770.

Wandering Pets

Years ago, a buffalo got lose from Rising Sun, a town in Ohio County, and wandered across two more counties, and through the Canaan Fall Festival. He didn't seem to be a problem, just visiting, but he really had people wondering. By the time the wanderer got to the Proving Grounds, he was deemed a hazard to population and killed. But the people of Canaan haven't forgotten their buffalo visitor.

CENTERVILLE

Big Bear Flea Market

DATES: Saturday and Sunday, April through October.

TIMES: 8:00 AM–4:00 PM.

ADMISSION: Free. Parking is free.

LOCATION: On I-70 at Centerville, Exit 145 at the southeast corner, 4 miles west of Richmond, Indiana, 45 miles west of Dayton, OH and 62 miles east of Indianapolis.

DESCRIPTION: Opened in July 1993, this market has plenty of space on 17 acres with 60 spaces under canopies. Their dealers sell everything from antiques and collectibles, crafts, new merchandise to secondhand merchandise and produce. A concession stand, convenience store, a complete campground with RV hook-ups and restrooms add to the amenities.

DEALER RATES: $10 a day or $16 for 2 days. Reservations are not required.
CONTACT: Ed or Shelby Newman, 2131 N Centerville Rd, Centerville IN 47330. Tel: (765) 855-3912.

> Ed tells of one lonely dealer who sells ladies jewelry, a "very nice man" who wanted to put up a sign, "Looking for a wife who likes to travel and do Flea Markets." No problem with the Newmans. At last check, he still hadn't found his mate. Ladies, if you're interested, check in with the Newmans. Apparently they do keep an eye on him. Just in case.

FRANKLIN

Grey Goose Collector's Fair

DATES: Second Saturday and Sunday, September through May.
TIMES: 9:00 AM–4:00 PM.
ADMISSION: Free admission and free parking.
LOCATION: At the Johnson County Fairgrounds on Fairgrounds St. Take I-65 south, Exit 90, from Indianapolis to Rt 44 to Franklin. Junction 31 at Fairgrounds.
DESCRIPTION: This indoor show began operation in 1966 and was sold to the present owners in 1994. It is southern Indiana's largest. Although a small market with 44–48 dealers, they carry a variety of strictly antiques and collectibles. This is a very friendly market with good dealers who are willing to go out of their way to help their customers. Concessions and a full kitchen provide food on the premises.
DEALER RATES: $55 for a 12' × 14' area and two tables for both days inside, outside is $15 per day or $25 for the weekend. Reservations are required inside; not required outside.
CONTACT: Doris Hubbell or Vicki Jordal, 753 Hillcrest Dr, Greenwood IN 46142. Tel: (317) 881-5719 (Doris) or Vicki at 888-6783.

FRIENDSHIP

Friendship Flea Market

DATES: Two nine-day shows. 1998: June 13–21; September 12–20. Call for 1999 dates. Generally, starting the second Saturday through the following Sunday a week later.
TIMES: All day and night, really, rain or shine.
ADMISSION: Free admission. Parking is available at $2 per vehicle.

LOCATION: On State Hwy 62, 6 miles west of Dillsboro, Indiana.
DESCRIPTION: Started in 1968, this indoor/outdoor market consists of approximately 500 dealers selling antiques, arts and crafts, fresh produce, collectibles such as guns, knives, and beads, and new merchandise. It is located on the grounds adjoining the National Muzzle Loading Rifle Association. Up to 100,000 people attend this event. Food is served on the premises. In 1984, this market was listed by *Good Housekeeping* magazine as one of the 25 best flea markets in the United States. It is the largest of the four markets within one-half mile of each other. Every night of the market, a campfire is crackling with country music entertainment. They really mean it is open day and night!
DEALER RATES: $150 for nine days per 10' × 10' space indoors or a 20' × 20' space outdoors. Advance reservations are required.
CONTACT: Tom Kerr or Jan Hopkins, 654 Wayskin Dr, Covington KY 41015. Tel: (606) 356-7114. Days of the show call the flea market at (812) 667-5645.

FT. WAYNE

Fort Wayne Flea Market

DATES: Friday, Saturday and Sunday, year round. Rain or shine.
TIMES: Friday 12:00 PM–6:00 PM, Saturday 9:00 AM–7:00 PM, Sunday 9:00 AM–6:00 PM.
ADMISSION: Free. Free parking is available.
LOCATION: Hwys 27 and 33 and South Hanna St.
DESCRIPTION: Opened on August 1, 1990, this already successful market has 153 dealers in an air-conditioned and heated building selling typical flea market fare including: T-shirts, tools, coins and quite a bit of new merchandise. For your convenience, a food concession is on the premises.
DEALER RATES: $45 for 15' × 10' or $65 for 15' × 20' per weekend. Reservations are suggested.
CONTACT: Kap Lee, Fort Wayne Flea Market, 6901 S Hanna St, Ft Wayne IN 46816. Tel: (219) 447-0081 Friday through Monday.

Indiana Flea Market at Ft. Wayne

DATES: 1998 dates: January 9–11, February 20–22, March 27–29, and November 6–8. Call for 1999 dates.
TIMES: Friday 3:00 PM–9:00 PM; Saturday 10:00 AM–7:00 PM; Sunday 11:00 AM–5:00 PM.
ADMISSION: $1. Parking is free.

LOCATION: Allen County War Memorial Coliseum. Corner of Coliseum and Parnell Aves.
DESCRIPTION: This new market started in 1991 with 400 dealers selling antiques, collectibles, and the usual flea market everything. Already it is quite successful. Food is available on the premises.
DEALER RATES: \$75 per 14' × 8' space; \$113 per 21' × 8' space; \$150 per 28' × 8' space. Reservations are required.
CONTACT: Stewart Promotions, 2950 Breckinridge Ln Ste 4A, Louisville KY 40220. Tel: (502) 456-2244 except Tuesday and Friday.

INDIANAPOLIS

Indiana Flea Market

DATES: 1998: January 2–4, 23–25, February 13–15, March 13–15, April 17–19, May 15–17, June 12–14, July 17–19, September 25–27, October 23–25, November 27–29, December 11–13 and New Year's. Three-day show monthly except for August during State Fair. Usually the second weekend each month, depending on availability of the fairgrounds.
TIMES: Friday noon to 7:00 PM; Saturday 10:00 AM–7:00 PM; Sunday 11:00 AM–5:00 PM. New Year's: Friday and Saturday 10:00 AM–7:00 PM; Sunday 11:00 AM–5:00 PM.
ADMISSION: Free. Parking is also free.
LOCATION: Indianapolis State Fairgrounds.
DESCRIPTION: This indoor market opened in 1976 and hosts between 400 to 1,000 dealers depending on the seasons. There are special Antique and Country Craft shows scattered throughout their schedule in addition to the flea markets. Some of these scheduled events fill three buildings! The dealers sell mostly antiques, collectibles and flea market treasures. Food is available on the premises.
DEALER RATES: \$75 (\$85 New Year's) per 14' × 8' space; \$113 (\$128 New Year's) per 21' × 8' space; \$150 (\$170 New Year's) per 28' × 8' space depending on the building the show is housed in. Reservations are required and there is a waiting list.
CONTACT: Stewart Promotions, 2950 Breckinridge Ln Ste 4A, Louisville KY 40220. Tel: (502) 456-2244 (except Tuesday and Friday).

Liberty Bell Flea Market

DATES: Friday through Sunday, year round.
TIMES: Friday 12:00 PM–8:00 PM; Saturday 10:00 AM–7:00 PM; Sunday 10:00 AM–6:00 PM.

ADMISSION: Free. Free parking is available.
LOCATION: 8949 East Washington St (US 40).
DESCRIPTION: This indoor/outdoor show has been operating for 20 years. Over 88 dealers spread over 200 spaces (they like this market!) sell everything and anything from antiques, collectibles, and new merchandise to produce, meats, cheese, and handmade items. There are food concessions on the grounds.
DEALER RATES: $45 per 12' × 14' booth per weekend. No advance reservations required.
CONTACT: Noble Hall, Liberty Bell Flea Market, 8949 E Washington St, Indianapolis IN 46219. Tel: (317) 898-3180.

LAPORTE

Wildwood Park Flea Market

DATES: Saturday and Sunday, April 1st through October.
TIMES: 9:00 AM to whenever.
ADMISSION: Free. Parking is free.
LOCATION: At the junction of I-94—Hwy 20 and Hwy 35, Exit 40A, off I-94.
DESCRIPTION: Opened in 1978, this outdoor summer market, on lovely park-like grounds covered with oak and maple trees, hosts 120 dealers selling basically antiques, collectibles, produce and coins. There is an indoor antique mall on the grounds. A snack bar and handicapped-accessible restrooms are on site.
DEALER RATES: $7 per 20' × 25' space. Reservations are not required.
CONTACT: Wildwood Flea Market, 4938 W US 20 NE, LaPorte IN 46350. Tel: (219) 879-5660. Fax: (219) 879-0297.

LAWRENCEBURG

Tri-State Antique Market

DATES: Always the first Sunday of the month, from May through October.
TIMES: 7:00 AM–3:00 PM.
ADMISSION: $2 per adult. Free parking is available.
LOCATION: On Rt 50, 1 mile west from Exit 16, off I-275.
DESCRIPTION: Started in 1986, this indoor/outdoor market now draws 300 dealers from three surrounding states. The promoter of this show has said that this is where many shop owners come to stock their shelves and

floor space, buying both furniture and small items. "Lots of good treasures." Only antiques and old collectibles are sold. Food is served on the premises.

DEALER RATES: $30 per 25' × 25' outside space paid in advance or $35 at site if available; $30 per 10' × 15' space indoors. Advance reservations are suggested. Early birds are admitted for advance shopping at 5:30 AM.

CONTACT: Bruce Metzger, PO Box 35, Shandon OH 45063-0035. Tel: (513) 738-7256.

Classic Market Tales

In 1989, in Lawrenceburg, there was a "dust devil" during the show. Hypnotized, the vendors and buyers watched this little mini-tornado form at the end of the fairgrounds. Slowly, it moved down the midway street of the market flipping tables, toppling cupboards, lifting cast-iron ware and dropping it through glass showcases, scattering the "smalls" and light-weight merchandise. After traveling about 100 feet, the twister stood still, lifted off the ground and retreated back to the rear of the grounds, leaving choking dust in the air and wreckage marking its route.

Says Bruce Metzger, the promoter of this show: "No one was injured in this occurrence, although some merchandise sustained damage and some was just plain lost. It's a hell of a thing to be remembered for, but people still like to talk about the dust devil at Lawrenceburg."

METAMORA

Canal Days Flea Market

DATES: The first full weekend in October, rain or shine.

TIMES: All day Saturday and Sunday.

ADMISSION: Free. Parking is available at $3 to $5 per vehicle.

LOCATION: From Indianapolis take US 52 east. From Cincinnati go west on I-74 to Exit 169, then west on US 52, and then go 8 miles west of Brookville.

DESCRIPTION: An estimated 175,000 people attend this October weekend initiated as a continuation of the time, in the 1800s, when local farmers would set up along Main St to unload their farm surplus. In 1969 a couple of guys got together and thought they'd restart an old tradition by setting up a few card tables next to the canal. The idea took over and grew. Obviously, its time had come. Currently over 700 dealers set up to sell antiques,

fine art, arts and crafts, collectibles, and a little bit of new merchandise. Metamora is a lovely old town with a canal and canal boat pulled by horses, and there is an old Grist Mill which still operates. There are over 130 shops open May until December, and a passenger train runs on the weekends.
DEALER RATES: From $150 per 10' × 10' space for the three-day weekend and up depending on size space. Reservations are required.
CONTACT: Al and Pat Rogers, PO Box 76, Metamora IN 47030. Tel: (317) 647-2194.

MUNCIE

Greenwalt's Flea Market

DATES: First weekend of every month, September through May, except when September's first weekend falls on Labor Day, then it is the second weekend. They hold a craft fair the following weekend in September.
TIMES: Saturday 9:00 AM–5:00 PM; Sunday 9:00 AM–4:00 PM.
ADMISSION: Free admission and free parking.
LOCATION: At Delaware Fairgrounds–Memorial Building. Take I-69 to Muncie/Frankton Exit 332. Go approximately 7 miles (becomes McGalliard Ave) to Wheeling Ave, then turn south and go 7 blocks to the Fairgrounds.
DESCRIPTION: This indoor market, which opened in 1976, houses approximately 65–70 dealers selling antiques, collectibles, handmade/craft items, toys, jewelry, baseball cards and new merchandise. Food is available on the premises.
DEALER RATES: $35 a weekend for a 10' × 10' booth. Advance reservations are required.
CONTACT: Mary Greenwalt, 604 N Kettner Dr, Muncie IN 47304. Tel: (765) 289-0194.

ROCKVILLE

RocKERRville Flea Market Extravaganza

DATES: October 9–18, 1998. Generally runs from the second Friday in October through the following Sunday. Please check first.
TIMES: 9:00 AM–6:00 PM.
LOCATION: Just 3 miles north of Rockville on US 41.
ADMISSION: Free. Parking is free.
DESCRIPTION: Held at the same time as the Covered Bridge Festival in historic Parke County, this outdoor market hosts approximately 200 deal-

ers selling antiques, crafts, collectibles, and new merchandise. Just for the record, there are 33 covered bridges in the area. There is food available.
DEALER RATES: $125 for the 10-day festival for a 22' × 22' space.
CONTACT: Tom Kerr or Jan Hopkins, RocKERRville, 654 Wayskin Dr, Covington KY 41015. Tel: (606) 356-7114. For reservations call: (765) 498-8988.

SCOTTSBURG

Saw Mill Hill Flea Market

DATES: Wednesday through Sunday, year round.
TIMES: 8:00 AM–5:00 PM.
ADMISSION: Free. Parking is free.
LOCATION: Hwy 56 West. From I-65 take Exit 29 to Hwy 56 W about ½ mile off the Interstate.
DESCRIPTION: Opened in 1990, this indoor/outdoor market hosts 65 dealers inside year round and, weather permitting, lots outside. When the outdoor market is running there is also a food concession. The dealers sell a fair amount of antiques and collectibles, groceries, tools, musical instruments, loads of household goods and whatever comes in. Their motto is: "If we ain't got it, it ain't worth having."
DEALER RATES: $19 per weekend inside, $5 per day outside. Reservations are suggested.
CONTACT: Michael E Davisson, Saw Mill Hill Flea Market, 1621 McClain Ave, Scottsburg IN 47170. Tel: 812-752-3551.

SHIPSHEWANA

Shipshewana Auction and Flea Market

DATES: Every Tuesday and Wednesday, May through October. Rain or shine.
TIMES: Tuesday 7:00 AM–5:00 PM, Wednesday 7:00 AM–3:00 PM, May through October.
ADMISSION: Free. $2 per car parking during June, July and August.
LOCATION: On State Rt 5 on the southern edge of Shipshewana, 160 miles north of Indianapolis, 50 miles east of South Bend and 100 miles south of Grand Rapids.
DESCRIPTION: This show first opened in 1922 and moved to its present location in 1947. It is held both indoors and outdoors and accommodates approximately 800 dealers (fewer in winter) and has room for more. Just

about anything you might want can be found at this market, from antiques and collectibles, to fine art, arts and crafts, to new merchandise, to fresh produce. There is also a Miscellaneous and Antique Auction every Wednesday at 8:00 AM, and a livestock auction at 11:00 AM. The widely-known Horse and Tack Sale is held on Fridays at 9:00 AM and always draws a full house of spectators. One full-service, and three fast-food restaurants, one snack bar and four drink stands take care of any possible hungers.
DEALER RATES: Approximately $36 per 20' × 25' space outdoors, for two days; $45 per 8½' × 10' space indoors, for two days. Reservations are required.
CONTACT: Kevin Lambright, PO Box 185, Shipshewana IN 46565-0185. Tel: (219) 768-4129. Fax: (219) 768-7041.

TERRE HAUTE

Terre Haute Flea Market

DATES: 1998: May 9–10, June 6–7, August 15–16 and September 12–13. Check the same weekends for 1999, but call first.
TIMES: Saturday 8:00 AM–6:00 PM, Sunday 9:00 AM–5:00 PM.
ADMISSION: Free. Parking is free.
LOCATION: Wabash County Fairgrounds.
DESCRIPTION: This market, one of several run by Stewart Promotions in Indiana and Kentucky, has over 200 dealers inside selling about 60% antiques and collectibles and 40% crafts and new items. Generally the collectible dealers prefer to setup under the shed area.
DEALER RATES: $15 daily outside; indoor $55 for a 14' × 8' space; sheds $55 for a 12' × 12' space.
CONTACT: Stewart Promotions, 2950 Breckenridge Ln Ste 4A, Louisville KY 40220. Tel: (502) 456-2244 except Tuesdays and Fridays.

OTHER FLEA MARKETS

We know or have heard about these markets, but have not personally contacted each one, as we have the markets with descriptions. If you plan to visit one of these markets listed below, *please call first* to make sure they are still open. Flea markets do come and go. While they were open when we went to press, they may not be later. We can't be responsible. *Call first!*

Bloomingdale: Jungle Park Flea Market, US Rt 41. Tel: 765-597-2951.
Cloverdale: Antique Mall & Flea Market. Tel: 765-795-4550.
Denver: Chili Flea Market, SR 16 & SR 19. Tel: 765-985-2102.

Evansville: Cain's Flea Market, 322 W Columbia St. Tel: 812-425-0795.

Evansville: Diamond Flea Market, 1250 E Diamond Ave. Tel: 812-464-2675.

Evansville: Evansville Flea Market, 1800 Mesker Park Dr. Tel: 812-422-3532.

Evansville: Giant Flea Market, 2600 S Kentucky Ave. Tel: 812-421-8274.

Evansville: Southlane Flea Market, 2608 S Kentucky Ave. Tel: 812-424-2608.

Fort Wayne: Speedway Mall Flea Market, 217 Marciel Dr. Tel: 219-484-1239.

Fort Wayne: Summit City Flea Market, 6901 Hanna St. Tel: 219-447-0081.

Friendship: Friendship Downtown Flea Market, PO Box 82. Tel: 812-667-5322.

Gary: Central Ave Flea Mart, 2750 Central Ave. Tel: 219-962-5524.

Gary: Dunes Plaza Flea Market, 8000 Melton Rd. Tel: 219-938-6937.

Gary: Market City Flea Market, 4121 Cleveland St. Tel: 219-980-3646.

Gary: Village Flea Market Inc, corner of Cleveland & Ridge. Tel: 219-980-1111.

Gas City: Mick's Flea Market, 212 E Main St. Tel: 765-677-0281.

Greenwood: Greenwood Flea Market, 1601 E Main St. Tel: 317-882-7615.

Greenwood: South Indy Flea Market, 7555 US Hwy 31 S. Tel: 317-885-8900.

Indianapolis East Indy Flea Market, 8101 Pendleton Pike. Tel: 317-898-4322.

Indianapolis: Irvington Flea Market, 6301 E Washington St. Tel: 317-375-1885.

Indianapolis: Town & Country Flea Market, 4435 N Keystone Ave. Tel: 317-545-5608.

Indianapolis: West Washington Flea Market, 6445 W Washington St. Tel: 317-244-0941.

Kendallville: Connie's Corner Flea Market, 1571 S Main St. Tel: 219-347-2564.

Laurel: Pioneer Flea Market, 22211 US Hwy 52. Tel: 765-698-1210.

Marion: Marion Antiques & Flea Market, 3355 W Delphi Pike. Tel: 765-384-5731.

Michigan City: Wildwood Park Community Farm & Flea Market, 4938 W US Hwy 20. Tel: 219-879-5660.

Montgomery: Main St Flea Market. Tel: 812-486-3214.

Muncie: Main St Flea Market, 1710 E Main St. Tel: 765-289-5394.

Nashville: Olde Time Flea Market, SR 46. Tel: 812-988-2346.

Nashville: Westward Ho Flea Market, SR 46. Tel: 812-988-0750.

New Albany: Pine Ridge Flea Market, 3328 Corydon Pike. Tel: 812-941-1111.

North Vernon: Green Meadows Flea Market. Tel: 812-346-9945 or 812-346-1990.

Pennville: Herche Furniture & Flea Market, 170 S Union St. Tel: 219-731-5131.

Portland: Grouch's Flea Market, 973 S Meridian St. Tel: 219-726-8175.

Saint Joe: St Joe Flea Market, 207 Washington. Tel: 219-337-5633.

San Pierre: San Pierre Flea Market, 208 N Fisher St. Tel: 219-828-Tel: 3171.

Scottsburg: Scottsburg Sale Barn & Flea Market, 708 S Main St. Tel: 812-752-6831.

Veedersburg: Steam Corner Flea Market, 2164 S US Hwy 41. Tel: 765-798-5710.

Washington: Hometown Flea Market, 401 E Main St. Tel: 812-257-1043.

IOWA

AMANA COLONIES

Collector's Paradise Flea Market

DATES: Last full weekend in June. For 1998: June 27–28. And another the weekend of October 17–18. Watch for the same weekends in 1999.
TIMES: Saturday 7:00 AM–5:00 PM, Sunday 7:00 AM–4:00 PM.
LOCATION: Amana Colonies Outdoor Convention Facility. At Exit 225 off I-80, 12 miles north. Across from the Visitors Center.
ADMISSION: $1 per day, 12 and under free with an adult. Parking is free.
DESCRIPTION: Opened in 1991, this indoor/outdoor market hosts 200 dealers selling antiques, collectibles, old tools, primitives, coins, furniture, glassware, jewelry, stamps, postcards, baseball cards and new merchandise. If this market is as successful as their What Cheer markets, buyers and sellers are in for a treat. Food is available at the market. Amana Colonies is a top tourist attraction in Iowa. See their companion market at What Cheer three times a year.
DEALER RATES: $30 outside without electric, $35 with electric. Dealer setup starts Friday at 7:00 AM. No reservations taken, first come, first served.
CONTACT: Larry D Nicholson, PO Box 413, What Cheer IA 50268-0413. Tel: (515) 634-2109.

DUBUQUE

Dubuque Flea Market

DATES: Three times yearly, call for dates. Generally Sundays the middle of February, April and October. Do call to check first.
TIMES: 8:00 AM–4:00 PM.
ADMISSION: $1 for 12 and over, 11 and under free. Parking is free.
LOCATION: Dubuque County Fairgrounds, 5 miles west of town on Hwy 20.
DESCRIPTION: This indoor/outdoor market began in 1970. Approximately 100 to 160 dealers sell a variety of antiques, collectibles, art objects, and crafts. Among the local attractions are a dog track and river boats. For your convenience, there is food available on the premises.
DEALER RATES: $14 per 8' space inside including a table; wall space is $16. Reservations are required for inside space.
CONTACT: Jerome F Koppen, 260 Copper Kettle Ln, E Dubuque IL 61025. Tel: (815) 747-7745.

LAKE OKOBOJI AT MILFORD

Treasure Village Flea Market and Antiques Shows

DATES: Memorial Day weekend (Saturday through Monday); July 4th weekend; Labor Day weekend (Saturday through Monday); and first weekend in August (Saturday and Sunday). Call for specific dates as July 4th falls on different days each year.

TIMES: 8:00 AM–6:00 PM.

ADMISSION: Free. Parking is also free.

LOCATION: Treasure Village, 2033 Hwy 86, 3 miles northwest of Milford.

DESCRIPTION: Held outdoors under the trees, this market generally limits its dealers to about 80. They show a variety of toys, coins, collectibles, primitives, antiques, sports cards, crafts, tools, and novelties, among other treasures. To amuse the children there is a children's theatre and for everyone—miniature golf. Hand-dipped ice cream, sandwiches, and the usual concession fare are available. This is a real family affair and social gathering for tourists and the local residents. Lake Okoboji is one of only three "blue-water lakes" in the world, the others are Lake Geneva in Switzerland, and Lake Louise in Canada. It is also the #1 tourist attraction in Iowa.

DEALER RATES: $65 for a 20' × 20' space Memorial Day, Labor Day and July 4th; August first weekend $45. Reservations are required. Prepaid reservations are allowed a discount.

CONTACT: Garth Neisess, Manager, 2033 Hwy 86, Milford IA 51351-7348. Tel: (712) 337-3730.

OTTUMWA

Collector's Fair

DATES: Third full weekend in January, March and October.

TIMES: 9:00 AM–4:00 PM.

ADMISSION: $.50. Parking is free.

LOCATION: Ottumwa Coliseum basement, between Hwys 34 and 63.

DESCRIPTION: This indoor market began in 1970. It attracts approximately 40 dealers selling only antiques and collectibles. Some of the items sold are fine furniture, glassware, cookie jars, collectible coins and stamps, and cards. Food is served on the premises.

DEALER RATES: $14 per 8' table. Reservations are required.

CONTACT: Frosti Chicchelly, 2917 van Buren Dr SW, Cedar Rapids IA 52404. Tel: (319) 396-2654.

SPIRIT LAKE

Annual Antique Show and Flea Market at Vick's Corner

DATES: Memorial Day, July 4th, and Labor Day weekends.

TIMES: 8:00 AM–6:00 PM.

ADMISSION: Free. Parking is also free.

LOCATION: Junction of Hwys 9 and 86 at Vick's Corner.

DESCRIPTION: This market started the Spirit Lake market corner in 1966. Ninety dealers from 10 different states sell antiques, collectibles and primitives. Absolutely no junk is allowed. People plan their vacations around these market days as the dealers who come here are famous throughout the country for the quality of their goods. This is a 10-acre grove area all grassed and kept up like a golf course. Vick's Corner is a general store established in 1930 and a well-known landmark in the area. Food concessions and restrooms are on site.

DEALER RATES: $75 per booth for one show. Reservations are highly recommended.

CONTACT: L W Vick, Vick's Corner, RR Box 9131, Spirit Lake IA 51360 Tel: (712) 336-1912 or (712) 336-1496 or 336-5602.

WHAT CHEER

Collectors Paradise Flea Market

DATES: First full weekends Sundays in May, August, and October. 1998 dates: May 2–3, August 1–2, October 3–4.

TIMES: Saturday 7:00 AM–5:00 PM, Sunday 7:00 AM–4:00 PM.

ADMISSION: $1 per person per day, 12 and under free with adult. Free parking is available.

LOCATION: At the Keokuk County Fairgrounds in What Cheer. Take Exit 201 off I-80 and drive south 20 miles on Hwy 21.

DESCRIPTION: According to local shoppers, Larry Nicholson's Collectors Paradise is well named. Having started this indoor/outdoor market in 1977, Mr. Nicholson has raised dealer attendance up to around 500, with some dealers showing up for setup as early as the Wednesday before the show. Dealers come from all of the Midwest states. This market is one of the major antique and collectible markets in the Midwest. Shoppers, who can number as high as 7,000, are invited on the Saturday preceding the main sale day for the same $1 fee, to get an early chance to browse through the innumerable bargains. Antiques and collectibles of every shape and size are to be found here including glassware, toys, tools, coins, jewelry, stamps, baseball cards, postcards, primitives, furniture, and more. Among the foods served is funnel cake, a favorite among local flea marketeers. Lunch is available.

DEALER RATES: $35 for outside space for the weekend. Reservations are required.

CONTACT: Larry D Nicholson, PO Box 413, What Cheer IA 50268-0413. Tel: (515) 634-2109.

OTHER FLEA MARKETS

We know or have heard about these markets, but have not personally contacted each one, as we have the markets with descriptions. If you plan to visit one of these markets listed below, *please call first* to make sure they are still open. Flea markets do come and go. While they were open when we went to press, they may not be later. We can't be responsible. *Call first!*

Aplington: Luck Marketing Flea Market, 1227 Parrott St. Tel: 319-347-6242.

Council Bluffs: Phillip's Flea Mart & Mexican Imports, 3143 W Broadway. Tel: 712-328-9716.

Des Moines: Donna's Flea Market, 1942 Indianola Ave. Tel: 515-247-9280.

Des Moines: North 2nd Ave Flea Market, 5238 NW 2 Ave. Tel: 515-244-1409.

Des Moines: SE 14th Street Flea Market, 5912 SE 14th St. Tel: 515-285-8761.

Knoxville: Junk & Treasures Flea Market, 2902 E Main St. Tel: 515-842-6827.

Sioux City: Old Towne Antiques & Flea Market, 1024 4th St. Tel: 712-258-3119.

KANSAS

BAXTER SPRINGS

Cowtown Marketplace

DATES: Daily.
TIMES: Monday through Saturday 10:00 AM–6:00 PM; Sunday 1:00 PM–6:00 PM.
ADMISSION: Free. Parking is free.
LOCATION: 1021 Military Ave, on old Rt 66.
DESCRIPTION: Opened under new management in 1995 and located on old Rt 66, this market has over 30 dealers selling antiques, collectibles, war memorabilia, beer signs, primitives, furniture, coins, glassware, pottery, toys, tools, crafts and more. The ratio is about 85% old treasures to newer items, such as cake/baking supplies and crafts. They are housed in one of the oldest buildings in Baxter Springs. Snacks and beverages are available. While this is obviously a "store" market, I've been told it's a great place to get collectibles and thought readers might be interested.
DEALER RATES: $30–$120 per month, 10% commission on sales. Reservations are obviously needed.
CONTACT: Dana Lynch, Cowtown Marketplance, 1021 Military Ave, Baxter Springs KS 66713-1546. Tel: (316) 856-2280.

HUTCHINSON

Mid-America Flea Markets

DATES: First Sunday of each month, October through June.
TIMES: 9:00 AM–4:00 PM.
ADMISSION: $1 per person. Free parking is available.
LOCATION: At the Kansas State Fairgrounds, well marked in Hutchinson.
DESCRIPTION: This indoor market first opened its doors in 1964. Currently there are approximately 200 dealers who specialize in a variety of types of antiques and collectibles, exhibiting miscellaneous items at a wide range of prices. There is food available on the premises.
DEALER RATES: $15 per 10' × 12' space. Reservations are required.
CONTACT: Av Hardesty, Mid-America Flea Markets, PO Box 1585, Hutchinson KS 67504-1585. Tel: (316) 663-5626.

OPOLIS

Opolis Flea Market

Note: Louie Kukovich had serious health problems in 1997, but is expected to be hale and healthy again and working in the market in 1998. Call first to make sure the market is open.

DATES: Most Saturdays, every Sunday, and by chance, year round. Rain or shine.

TIMES: Daylight hours.

ADMISSION: Free, with free parking.

LOCATION: On the Kansas-Missouri State Line; junction of US 171 and 57.

DESCRIPTION: Since 1978 this relatively small flea market has only antiques and collectibles, including miscellaneous Volkswagen autos and parts. All of it collected by two antique fanatics. This collection of treasures is housed in several warehouses and is a haunt of dealers looking to replenish their stocks. They have had other dealers with them in the past, but the whole situation is in flux. Call first. And say, "Hi" to Norma and Lou.

DEALER RATES: Call for availability, as there wasn't any space available as we went to press. But you never know.

CONTACT: Norma Kukovich, Box 42, Opolis KS 66760. Tel: (316) 231-2543.

SPARKS

Sparks Flea Market

DATES: Three shows a year: 1) the first Sunday in May plus the preceding three days for a 4-day show; 2) the second weekend in July, Friday through Sunday for a 3-day show; 3) Labor Day and the preceding four days for a 5-day show.

TIMES: Most dealers open between 7:00–8:00 AM and close up by 6:00 PM.

ADMISSION: Free. Parking is free on 4 acres next to the market as well as around town.

LOCATION: K-7 Hwy and old US 36, now known as Mission Rd. Just 23 miles west of St. Joseph, MO or 19 miles east of Hiawatha, KS on Old US 36 Hwy or 24 miles north Atchison, KS or 11 miles south of White Cloud, KS on K-7 Hwy.

DESCRIPTION: Of this market's 300 dealers, 270 sell antiques. You can count on plenty of quality antiques and collectibles. Started in 1982, this market is on the way to several other markets held the same weekend and together they draw 75,000 people trolling for treasures. As the other markets aren't open on Labor Day itself, this market's dealers (and customers) make out like bandits. Plenty of food is available either at the market or around town, including treats from the Sparks Flea Circus Cafe (formerly the Road Kill Cafe) and Granny's Old Fashioned Lemonade. You can't starve. There are 16 food vendors including the cafe serving Mexican, German, Indian, and barbecue among the myriad choices. It's always nice to hear from Ray. He's full of information and ideas. Stop in, find Ray, and say "Hi" for me!
DEALER RATES: $45 for 20' × 30' outside space or $55 for 10' × 15' inside space for the week. There are larger spaces available. Electricity is $5 a day extra. Table rental is $5 per table for the entire show. Setup starts on Wednesday, Thursday is dealer day. Don't miss it! The Cafe is open to dealers from 6:00 AM–9:00 PM just for you.
CONTACT: Ray Tackett, PO Box 223, Troy KS 66087-0223. Tel: (785) 985-2411 except during market hours when Ray can be reached at the market: (785) 442-5555.

WICHITA

Mid-America Flea Markets

DATES: Irregular dates. Either 2nd to 4th Sunday, September through June. 1998 dates: January 25, February 8, March 29, April 26, May 17, June 28, September 13, October 11, November 22, December 13.
TIMES: 9:00 AM–4:00 PM.
ADMISSION: $1 per person. Free parking is available.
LOCATION: At the Kansas Coliseum, at the intersection of 85th Street and I-135 North, Exit 17.
DESCRIPTION: This indoor market opened in 1978 and accommodates approximately 600 dealers. Visitors come to view the large selection of antiques and collectibles; there is always a wide variety to choose from, at a wide range of prices. For your convenience, food is served on the premises.
DEALER RATES: $15 per 8' × 10' space. Reservations are required.
CONTACT: Av Hardesty, Mid-America Flea Markets, PO Box 1585, Hutchinson KS 67504-1585. Tel: (316) 663-5626. Show date phone: (316) 755-2560.

Village Flea Market

DATES: Every Friday, Saturday, and Sunday, rain or shine.
TIMES: 9:00 AM–5:30 PM.
ADMISSION: Free. Parking is also free.
LOCATION: At 2301 South Meridian.
DESCRIPTION: This indoor/outdoor market first opened in 1974. Their 125 to 150 dealers sell everything from antiques and collectibles to handmade craft items, vegetables, meats, and cheeses. An interesting variety of garage items are also available. For your comfort the building is heated as well as air-conditioned. It is also equipped with a modern security system. Food is available on the premises.
DEALER RATES: \$30 per 10' × 10' booth. Space is rented on a first come, first served basis.
CONTACT: Dale Cooper, 2301 S Meridian, Wichita KS 67213. Tel: (316) 942-8263.

OTHER FLEA MARKETS

We know or have heard about these markets, but have not personally contacted each one, as we have the markets with descriptions. If you plan to visit one of these markets listed below, *please call first* to make sure they are still open. Flea markets do come and go. While they were open when we went to press, they may not be later. We can't be responsible. *Call first!*

Anthony: Anthony Flea Market, 128 W Main St. Tel: 316-842-3490.
Chanute: Proctor's Flea Market, 227 W 7th St. Tel: 316-431-7655.
Coffeyville: B & K Pecans & Nu 2 U Flea Market, 802 E 11th St. Tel: 316-251-6887.
Coffeyville: Country Time Antiques Flea Market, 1613 W 8th St. Tel: 316-251-4968.
Columbus: Columbus Market Mall & Flea Market, 124 S East Ave & 69 Hwy. Tel: 316-429-1489.
Crestline: Sam's Flea Market, PO Box 96. Tel: 316-389-2244.
Dodge City: Happy Trail Flea Market, 317 W Trail St. Tel: 316-227-2168.
Erie: Erie Antiques & Flea Market, 307 S Main St. Tel: 316-244-3467.
Eureka: Country Flea Market With Antique Mall, RR 2 Box 223. Tel: 316-583-5242.
Fort Scott: Old Fort Antiques Collectibles & Flea Market, 3 W Oak St. Tel: 316-223-6880.

Fredonia: Valley Flea Market, RR 4 Box 196. Tel: 316-378-4479.

Galena: Ole Miners Antiques & Flea Market, 610 S Main St. Tel: 316-783-2444.

Garden City: San Juan Flea Market, 902 E Fulton St. Tel: 316-276-6049.

Garnett: Garnett Flea Market, RR 1. Tel: 913-448-3216.

Girard: Girard Flea Market, 117 S Summit St. Tel: 316-724-4291.

Glade: Leydig Greenhouse Flea Market, PO Box 295. Tel: 913-543-2802.

Humboldt: What Chu Want Flea Market, 814 Bridge St. Tel: 316-473-3216.

Independence: Out West Antique & Flea Marketmall, 1625 W Main St. Tel: 316-331-5703.

Iola: Brooklyn Park Flea Market, 1119 East St. Tel: 316-365-5570.

Kansas City: Armourdale Collectibles & Flea Market, 823 Osage Ave. Tel: 913-342-3654.

Kansas City: Merriam Lane Flea Market, 1270 Merriam Ln. Tel: 913-677-0833.

Leavenworth: Anything Stores Variety Flea Market, 200 Seneca St. Tel: 913-651-1100.

Manhattan: City Farmers Flea Market & Surplus Store, 201 S 4th St. Tel: 913-539-8579.

Manhattan: Time Machine Antique Mall Flea Market, 4910 Skyway Dr. Tel: 913-539-4684.

Osawatomie: Old Country Store Flea Market, 510 Main St. Tel: 913-755-6595.

Pittsburg: Camptown Flea Market. Tel: 316-232-2695.

Pittsburg: The Crafty Flea, 708 Main. Tel: 316-232-5050.

Pittsburg: Pittsburg Flea Market, 312 N Elm St. Tel: 316-231-3862.

Salina: 4th Street Mini Mall & Flea Market, 127 S 4th St. Tel: 913-825-4948.

Shawnee Mission: Armourdale Collectibles & Flea Market, 7824 Tomahawk Rd. Tel: 913-648-7146.

Shawnee Mission: Mini Mall Flea Market, 7327 W 80th St. Tel: 913-642-7334.

Topeka: Bob's Flea Market, Tel: 316 SE 29th St. Tel: 913-234-2874.

Topeka: Boyle's Joyland Flea Market, 2700 SE California Ave. Tel: 913-266-5401.

Topeka: Eagle Rock Antique Sales & Flea Market, 3729 SE US Hwy 40. Tel: 913-235-8761.

Topeka: J & J Gifts & Flea Market, 1100 SW 17th St. Tel: 913-235-6538.

Topeka: JL's Specialty Merchandise & Flea Market, 106 SE 8th Ave. Tel: 913-235-6314.

Topeka: Rollaway Flea Market, 2305 SE 11th St. Tel: 913-234-4420.

Welda: Welda Flea Market, 511 Commercial. Tel: 913-448-3367.

White Cloud: White Cloud Flea Market, 103 Main. Tel: 913-595-6683.

Wichita: Mid Town Flea Market, 509 E Harry St. Tel: 316-262-7150.

Wichita: North End Flea Market, 2759 N Broadway St. Tel: 316-838-5801.

Wichita: That's You Flea Market, 1710 E 13th St N. Tel: 316-267-9060.

Wichita: Village Flea Market, 2301 S Meridian Ave. Tel: 316-942-8263.

KENTUCKY

FLEMINGSBURG

Annual Old-Fashioned Court Day

DATES: Second Monday and preceding weekend of October, rain or shine. (Essentially Columbus Day weekend and Monday.)
TIMES: Saturday, sunup to whenever, Sunday at noon until Monday whenever.
ADMISSION: Free. Parking is wherever you find it, some is free, some isn't.
LOCATION: The entire town of Flemingsburg! In the center of town, on Main Street.
DESCRIPTION: Started in 1969 to continue the tradition of the circuit judge plying this trade (trials and hangings), this town turns into a huge market centered in downtown Flemingsburg. From 450 to 600 outside vendors sell everything and anything you can imagine—old, new and otherwise. They do try to have a booth or two of unusual things like games and rides for kids, clogging, and live entertainment. This shebang ends with a good old-fashioned square-dance on Monday night. See also Maysville and Mt. Sterling for the first and third Monday Court Days markets and you too can follow the judge's historical "necktie" circuit. This huge event is *the* fundraiser for the local Rescue Squad who sponsors this market.
DEALER RATES: Setup anytime after 6:00 PM Friday. $75 per 10' × 10' space for three days. Reservations are strongly recommended.
CONTACT: Mr Kim Brewer, Annual Old-Fashioned Court Day, Rt 3 Lot 3 Crestview, Flemingsburg KY 41041-0126. Tel: (606) 849-4797. Email: kimjb@kih.net. Watch for their website in 1998.

GEORGETOWN

Country World Flea Market

DATES: Friday through Sunday, April through November.
TIMES: Friday 7:00 PM–Sunday afternoon, sometime.
ADMISSION: Free. Parking is free.
LOCATION: On US Rt 460 off I-75, Georgetown interchange at Exit 125.
DESCRIPTION: Founded in 1967 in the back of a truck stop, and temporarily closed for 2½ years, this market is back—big time! With up to 250 dealers selling antiques, collectibles, crafts, farm goods, and "everything

in the world." (Even coffins occasionally.) There are food concessions on site.

DEALER RATES: $9 on Saturday, $11 on Sunday for 14' × 30' space. Electric is $2 per day. First come, first served. No reservations needed or taken. (For the record, they raise their rates by $1 every 5 years. It just happened.)

CONTACT: Jack Mitchell, 208 Montgomery Ave, Georgetown KY 40324-1248. Tel: (502) 863-1557.

GREENVILLE

Luke's Town and Country Flea Market

DATES: Monday and Tuesday, year round, weather permitting.

TIMES: 8:00 AM–dark Monday; 6:00 AM–2:00 PM Tuesday.

ADMISSION: Free, with some free parking, $1 parking is available nearby.

LOCATION: Hwy 62 West, 1 mile from Greenville city limits.

DESCRIPTION: This outdoor market has been operating since May 1979. On Monday about 25 to 100 dealers show. Tuesdays are busier, with between 200 and 400 dealers selling antiques, collectibles, crafts, new merchandise, and produce, as well as poultry and livestock. The surrounding area is rustically scenic, with Lake Malone and many other state parks nearby. There is a real family atmosphere here and a large antique display and collection to view (but not for sale) and several antique shops nearby. Food is available on the grounds.

DEALER RATES: $3 and up per 8' × 10' space per day Tuesdays and Monday holiday; $2 on non-holiday Mondays. Reservations are appreciated but not necessary.

CONTACT: Wayne and Judy Rice, Managers, Luke's Town and Country Flea Market, 2006 US Hwy 62 W, Greenville KY 42345. Tel: (502) 338-4920 or (502) 338-6284.

HENDERSON

Ellis Park Flea Market

DATES: May 8–10, June 12–14, September 11–13, October 9–11, 1998. One market a month during May, June, September and October.

TIMES: Friday 1:00 PM–6:00 PM, Saturday 10:00 AM–6:00 PM, Sunday 10:00 AM–5:00 PM.

ADMISSION: Free. Parking is free.

LOCATION: Ellis Park Race Track. Hwy 41 North.

DESCRIPTION: This market has recently been taken over by the race track itself. Their 200 dealers sell many antiques, collectibles, garage sale goodies and new merchandise. While the market is going on, so is the racing! If a real race isn't happening, then a similcast is. Oh, yes, there is betting going on too. A cafeteria serves hot lunches, and snack concessions abound selling hot dogs and other requirements of track visiting. Handicapped-accessible restrooms are also plentiful.
DEALER RATES: $65 for 14' × 8' space, $98 for 21' × 8' space, $130 for 28' × 8' space. Outside $30 the weekend, $15 daily.
CONTACT: Bob Jackson, Ellis Park Office, PO Box 33, Henderson KY 42420-0033. Tel: (502) 826-0608 or 1-800-333-8110.

LEITCHFIELD

Bratcher's Flea Market

DATES: Wednesday and Saturday, year round, weather permitting.
TIMES: Dawn to 2:00 PM.
ADMISSION: Free admission and parking, including overnight before show days.
LOCATION: On Hwy 62, 1 mile east of Leitchfield.
DESCRIPTION: This market opened over 30 years ago and is now run by the granddaughter of the founder. Approximately 150 dealers sell their antiques and collectibles outdoors. Handicrafts, new merchandise, and produce in season are also for sale. This is a well-managed, well-run market. There is a food concession at the market.
DEALER RATES: $7–$8 per 8' × 10' space per day. Reservations for the month are suggested.
CONTACT: Carol Heffley, Bratcher's Flea Market, PO Box 396, Leitchfield KY 42754-0396. Tel: (502) 259-5948.

LEXINGTON

Antique and Flea Market

DATES: January 16–18, March 6–8, June 19–21, August 7–9, November 6–8, 1998. Call for 1999 dates.
TIMES: Friday and Saturday 11:00 AM–7:00 PM; Sunday 11:00 AM–5:00 PM.
ADMISSION: Free. Parking is free.
LOCATION: Lexington Center. Downtown Main and Patterson.

DESCRIPTION: Started in 1980 this market has about 250 dealers selling antiques, collectibles and flea market fare and everything else but food or weapons. This is considered a fine antique market. Food is available on the premises.
DEALER RATES: $75 per 14' × 8' space; $113 per 21' × 8' space; $150 per 28' × 8' space. Reservations are required. Tables available at $8 each inside.
CONTACT: Stewart Promotions, 2950 Breckinridge Ln Ste 4A, Louisville KY 40220. Tel: (502) 456-2244 except Tuesday.

LONDON

Flea Land Flea Market

DATES: Saturday and Sunday, year round.
TIMES: 9:00 AM–5:00 PM. Extended holiday shopping days Thanksgiving through Christmas.
ADMISSION: Free. Parking is free.
LOCATION: Take London Exit 38 off I-75, 2 miles east. Follow the signs.
DESCRIPTION: Opened in 1990, this indoor/outdoor market of 400 dealers sells antiques, collectibles, crafts, produce, coins, cards, garage sales goodies, furniture, gold, jewelry, all sorts of home furnishings, rugs, NASCAR items and new merchandise. Their building is 80,000-square-feet of selling space with one restaurant, a concession stand and handicapped-accessible restrooms—"the largest in the state of Kentucky." They say they are "known as one of the cleanest and best."
DEALER RATES: $38.50 per 10' × 15' space weekly; $43.50 per 10' × 19' space weekly; or $12 per 10' × 10' outside space. Reservations are required.
CONTACT: Brenda Hail, PO Box 862, London KY 40741-0862. Tel: (606) 864-3532.

London Tobacco Warehouse Flea Market

DATES: Friday, Saturday and Sunday, year round.
TIMES: 9:00 AM–5:00 PM.
ADMISSION: Free. Parking is free.
LOCATION: Off the London bypass, watch for the signs.
DESCRIPTION: For 15 years, this market's 80 dealers have been selling antiques, collectibles, garage sale goodies, some new merchandise and produce in season. There are handicapped-accessible restrooms and a concession stand on site.

DEALER RATES: $30 per weekend or $10 per day for a 12' × 16' space. Reservations are an excellent idea as the market is usually full.
CONTACT: Carl Tuttle, London Tobacco Warehouse Flea Market, 420 Tobacco Rd, London KY 40741-1384. Tel: (606) 878-7726.

LOUISVILLE

Derby Park Trader's Circle

DATES: Friday, Saturday and Sunday, year round. Rain or shine.
TIMES: 8:00 AM–6:00 PM.
ADMISSION: Free. Free parking for public.
LOCATION: I-264 to Taylor Blvd North exit. Turn right on Taylor and go 4 stoplights. Turn left on Arcade. At light make a left onto 7th Street Rd and the market is on the right at 2900 7th Street Rd.
DESCRIPTION: Located 7/10 of a mile from Churchill Downs, this indoor, air-conditioned, 100,000-square-foot market with 150 outside booths has been operating since 1985. They have dealers in approximately 400 indoor spaces selling antiques, collectibles, handmade crafts, vegetables, furniture, clothing, knives, guns, toys, carpet, baseball cards and new merchandise. They had an "Outrageous Giveaway Promotion" culminating with the winner driving off in a 1969 Rolls Royce Silver Shadow. Wonder what they'll do next time? Four snack bars provide food on the premises and handicapped-accessible restrooms complete the amenities.
DEALER RATES: $34 per 6' × 20' or 10' × 12' indoor booth for the weekend; $39 per weekend for 18' × 10' booth; $10 per outdoor booth per day or $25 for the weekend. Reservations are first come, first served.
CONTACT: Art Henoch, Derby Park Traders Circle, 2900 7th Street Rd, Louisville KY 40216-4126. Tel: (502) 636-3532 or fax: (502) 634-0094.

Kentucky Flea Market

DATES: 1998: January 30–31, February 1, 28–29, March 1, April 3–5, 24–26, May 22–25, July 2–5, September 4–6, October 2–4, 29–31, December 31 through January 3, 1999. Rain or shine.
TIMES: Friday 12:00 PM–7:00 PM; Saturday 10:00 AM–7:00 PM; Sunday 11:00 AM–5:00 PM. Memorial Day: Friday 12:00 PM–7:00 PM; Saturday 10:00 AM–7:00 PM; Sunday 11:00 AM–6:00 PM, Monday 10:00 AM–5:00 PM. July 4th: Thursday 12:00 PM–7:00 PM, Friday 10:00 AM–7:00 PM; Saturday 10:00 AM–6:00 PM; Sunday 11:00 AM–5:00 PM.
ADMISSION: Free. $2 for parking in 15,000 spaces.

LOCATION: Kentucky Fair and Exposition Center. Junctions of I-264 and 65. Follow the signs.
DESCRIPTION: Started in 1972 and housed in a 250,000-square-foot climate-controlled building, this market consists of 1,000 to 2,000 dealers selling antiques, fine arts, arts and crafts, collectibles, and new merchandise. It is promoted as one of the largest indoor flea markets in the United States, in one of this country's finest facilities. On regular show days the market draws between 30,000 and 50,000 shoppers; on holidays, the crowds can swell to 100,000 or more. Food is served on the premises.
DEALER RATES: $85 ($100–$110 holidays) per 14' × 8' space per show; $128 ($150–$165 holidays) per 21' × 8' space; $170 ($200–$220 holidays) per 28' × 8' space. Larger spaces are available. Higher holiday rates. Reservations are required well in advance.
CONTACT: Stewart Promotions, 2950 Breckinridge Ln Ste 4A, Louisville KY 40220. Tel: (502) 456-2244 (except Tuesday and Friday).

MAYSVILLE

Maysville's Old-Fashioned Court Days

DATES: First weekend in October, rain or shine.
TIMES: 9:00 AM–10:00 PM.
ADMISSION: Free. Parking is also free.
LOCATION: The streets of Market Street and another parking lot nearby and McDonald Parkway.
DESCRIPTION: Started in the horse and buggy days of 1870 when the circuit judge would ride from town to town in Kentucky, then try and hang offenders, this series of Court Days (including Flemingsburg and Mt. Sterling) blossomed from the trading that naturally happened when people were brought together from outlying districts for a common gathering once a year. "If you can't find it on one of those trading days, then it doesn't exist, from jewelry to bent hinges (and bent nails!), even dogs!" Apples, crafts, wooden tool handles, at one time goldfish, sorghum molasses, collectibles, new merchandise, parts of kitchen sinks, furniture and anything. Food is available on the premises and run by local charity and fraternal groups. Country ham and cheese sandwiches are one of the specialties sold in the special food court area. "The best beef and country ham you ever put in your mouth."

Party! Along with the flea market is a rousing festival with bands, shows, contests, carnival, sternwheeler trips on the Ohio River (Maysville lies along the river) and whatever they can do for fun. Not to be missed!
DEALER RATES: $50 each booth up to 3 booths, 4 or more for $25 each. Some electric available. Reservations are a must. Setup begins Friday at 6:00 PM.
CONTACT: Duff Giffen, Maysville Special Events Committee, PO Box 326, Maysville KY 41056-0326. Tel: (606) 564-5186.

Recycling:

A dealer in window and doors went to a local tavern, bought two green bottles of Coke, drank them, and put them on his table. Along came a woman from Dayton, OH and asked the price of the bottles. "$1 each," replied the dealer. Remarking that she hadn't seen the green Coke bottles in ages, she bought them.

Entrepreneur in the Making:

A small boy carrying a bucket of bent nails was stopped by dealer. He asked the boy how much he wanted for the bucket of nails? The child answered, "Thirty-five cents."

"I'll give you twenty-five."

"No, thirty-five." After a bit of this haggling, the child got his thirty-five cents and watched the man go off with the bucket. But then the man put the bucket down on a nearby table and walked off into the crowd. The boy snatched his bucket from the table and went the opposite direction and sold the bucket again.

MT. STERLING

October Court Days

DATES: The weekend of and including the third Monday in October, annually.
TIMES: 6:00 AM Saturday through 12:00 midnight Monday, non-stop.
ADMISSION: Free admission; parking from $5 to $10 per day or wherever you can find it.
LOCATION: The entire town of Mt. Sterling! Take Exit 110 off I-64, 35 miles east of Lexington; or take Exit 113 off I-64, 100 miles west of Ashland, Kentucky.

DESCRIPTION: Mt. Sterling has always been a big trading center. Around 1870 it was traditional for the local county judge to hang convicted offenders on the third Monday in October, which naturally started people trading over the entire weekend. People came from miles away to buy and sell cows, horses, dogs, produce, tools, and other farm goods. This market attracts 2,000 dealers and up to 150,000 shoppers (although another flea marketeer in the know says closer to 200,000 shoppers). Even now, during Court Days, people bring objects of all shapes and sizes for sale or trade—more dogs and other farm animals, guns, axe handles, hammer handles, and antiques of all kinds that defy cataloging. Among the various foods for sale are corn meal and real Kentucky sorghum molasses, which is still made right in this mountain area. See also Flemingsburg and Maysville Court Days and follow the judge's circuit.
DEALER RATES: Average rate is $125 plus $20 for city license per 20' × 20' space for three days. Reservations are required in advance.
CONTACT: October Court Days, Montgomery County Tourism Dept, 51 N Maysville, Mt Sterling KY 40353. Tel: (606) 498-8732.

RICHWOOD

Richwood Flea Market

DATES: Tuesday, Saturday, and Sunday, year round.
TIMES: Saturday and Sunday 9:00 AM–5:00 PM; Tuesday outdoors daybreak to 1:00 PM, weather permitting.
ADMISSION: Free. $1 per car for parking.
LOCATION: 10915 US 25, Richwood exit. I-75 to Exit 175, north on US 25, 15 minutes south of Cincinnati.
DESCRIPTION: Opened in 1980, this market has about 300 indoor and 100 outdoor sellers. The indoor sellers are housed in a former tobacco warehouse over three acres *big*. There are many antiques, collectibles, craft items, sporting goods, tools, guns and knives, shoes, general merchandise as well as farm goods, jewelry, and new merchandise to be found. The Tuesday market is a genuine old-fashioned flea and farmers market with loads of in-season produce and used stuff.

Newly remodeled in 1997, they added two food courts with a big screen television and local entertainment. Their fried chicken is considered the best around and they added a meat smoker and feature fresh pork and chicken barbecue every weekend. Handicapped-accessible restrooms add to the amenities.

DEALER RATES: $70 per 16' × 15' space per weekend, or $40 per 8' × 15' space. Reservations are suggested. $12 for a 3-car parking space outdoors on Tuesday; $25 for weekends.
CONTACT: Mike Stallings, PO Box 153, Florence KY 41022-0153. Tel: (606) 371-5800.

SUWANEE

Country Village Flea Market

DATES: Weekends, year round, rain or shine.
TIMES: 8:00 AM–5:00 PM.
ADMISSION: Free with free parking.
LOCATION: On Hwy 62, 3 miles west of Exit 40 off I-24 and east of Barkley and Kentucky Dams.
DESCRIPTION: There are several indoor and outdoor markets on both sides of the road with approximately 50 vendors. Some of the vendors have been selling here for 20 years. You can find almost anything here such as antiques, glassware, knives, guns, tools, toys, in-season produce, and all kinds of collectibles. This is "a very pleasant shopping experience. One you'll want to tell your friends about."
DEALER RATES: Setup fees vary a little between the different markets, but are approximately $4 per 8' × 10' space.
CONTACT: Tom Strack, 625 SR 810 N, Kuttawa KY 42055. Tel: (502) 388-7824.

OTHER FLEA MARKETS

We know or have heard about these markets, but have not personally contacted each one, as we have the markets with descriptions. If you plan to visit one of these markets listed below, *please call first* to make sure they are still open. Flea markets do come and go. While they were open when we went to press, they may not be later. We can't be responsible. *Call first!*

Ashland: Hillbilly Flea Market Office, Russell Rd. Tel: 606-329-1058.
Barbourville: Cumberland Gap Parkway Flea Market, Cumberland Gap Pkwy. Tel: 606-546-4822 or 606-546-9906.
Burnside: Sundown Flea Market, 5351 S Hwy 27. Tel: 606-561-5584.
Burnside: Trader's Paradise Flea Market, 6320 S Hwy 27. Tel: 606-561-8688.
Butler: Crossroads Flea Market, 2105 Hwy 27. Tel: 606-472-6952.

Calvert City: Loco Flea Market, 4844 US Hwy 62. Tel: 502-395-7762.

Campbellsville: Campbellsville Flea Market, 426 Woodlawn Ave. Tel: 502-575-5444.

Corbin: Corbin Indoor Flea Market, US Hwy 25 W S. Tel: 606-528-3091.

Corbin: Cumberland Parkway Flea Market, 305 W Cumberland Gap Pkwy. Tel: 606-526-9712.

Corydon: Hwy 60 West Flea Market, 12401 US Hwy 60 W. Tel: 502-533-9912.

Coxs Creek: High Grove Antiques & Flea Market, 11 Crenshaw Ln. Tel: 502-349-9239.

Danville: Baker's Flea Market & Antique Barn, 118 E Main St. Tel: 606-236-6968.

Elizabethtown: Bowling Lanes Flea Market, 4547 N Dixie Hwy. Tel: 502-737-5755 or 502-789-0708.

Fountain Run: Lane's Flea Market, Main St. Tel: 502-434-4880.

Fountain Run: Rutherford's Flea Market, Main St. Tel: 502-434-4880.

Fredonia: Old Fredonia School Flea Market, 306 Cassidy Av. Tel: 502-545-9115.

Georgetown: Georgetown Flea Market, 150 Edwards Ave. Tel: 502-868-0858.

Glasgow: Giant Flea Market of Glasgow, 926 Happy Valley Rd. Tel: 502-651-1579.

Greensburg: Summerville Flea Market. Tel: 502-932-3260.

Guthrie: Southern Kentucky Flea Market, 10741 Dixie Beeline Hwy. Tel: 502-483-2166.

Hagerhill: Super Flea Market, 7280 S US Hwy 23. Tel: 606-789-9799.

Harrodsburg: Harrodsburg Flea Market, 1170 Louisville Rd. Tel: 606-734-4686.

Hazard: Hazard Village Flea Market, 210 Dawahare Dr. Tel: 606-439-2529.

Hazel Green: Red River Flea Market & Cabinet Shop. Tel: 606-662-4914 or 606-662-6090.

Hopkinsville: 41 North Flea Market, 2180 Madisonville Rd. Tel: 502-885-9623.

Irvine: Ed's Flea Market, Richmond Rd. Tel: 606-723-7296.

Junction City: TJ's Flea Market, 10 Shelby St. Tel: 606-854-3623.

Kuttawa: Stolz Flea Market, 5586 US Hwy 62 W. Tel: 502-388-5118.

Lexington: Georgetown Flea Market, 150 Edwards Ave. Tel: 606-868-0858.

Lexington: Lexington Flea Market Customer Information. Tel: 606-252-1082.

Lexington: Lexington Flea Market Dealer Information. Tel: 606-252-1076.

Lexington: Mid-State Flea Market & Antiques, 1527 N Limestone St. Tel: 606-255-7419.

London: Finishing Touch Fleamarket Flea World, 235 Barbourville Rd. Tel: 606-878-8661.

London: Flea World Flea Market Inc, 235 Barbourville Rd. Tel: 606-864-3532.

Louisville: Country Fair Flea Market, 3502 7th Street Rd. Tel: 502-368-6186.

Maceo: Hog Heaven Flea Market, 8424 US Hwy 60 E. Tel: 502-264-4420.

Mannsville: Cowboy's Flea Market, 188 Bradfordsville Rd. Tel: 502-789-1881.

Maysville: AA Flea Market, 4196 AA Hwy. Tel: 606-759-5641.

Morehead: Great Flea Market, 530 Fraley Dr. Tel: 606-784-2444.

Mount Sterling: Queen Street Flea Market, 109 S Queen St. Tel: 606-498-8058.

Murray: Gray's Flea Market, 609 S 4th St. Tel: 502-753-7047.

Owensboro: Mac's Cozy Corner Flea Market, 424 W 2nd St. Tel: 502-685-2807.

Owensboro: Melba's Flea Market, 1218 Hall St. Tel: 502-686-7904.

Paducah: Benton Road Trade Fair Flea Market, 3104 Benton Rd.

Paducah: Pirate's Cove Flea Market, 8940 US Hwy 60 W. Tel: 502-744-6873.

Prestonsburg: Storm's Driving Range & Flea Market, 243 Storm Hollow. Tel: 606-889-9902.

Radcliff: Hardin County Indoor Flea Market, Redmar Plaza. Tel: 502-351-0200.

Shepherdsville: Betty Lou's Flea Market, 2385 N Preston Hwy. Tel: 502-543-4175.

Shepherdsville: Rountree's New & Used Furniture & Flea Market, 2385 N Preston Hwy. Tel: 502-543-8700.

Simpsonville: Shelby Co Flea Market, I 64 at Exit 28. Tel: 502-722-8883.

Smithland: Marlene's Antique & Flea Market, 519 E Adair. Tel: 502-928-1161.

Somerset: Flo's Flea Market, 140 Sunset Blvd. Tel: 606-679-6526.

Somerset: Lake Cumberland Flea Market, 95 Super Service Dr. Tel: 606-678-0250.

Stanford: Stanford Drive-In Flea Market, 1645 Kentucky Hwy 78. Tel: 606-365-1317.

Stanton: Industrial Park Flea Market, Hwy 15 W. Tel: 606-663-9297.

Williamsburg: Three Point Flea Market, 2122 S Hwy 25 W. Tel: 606-549-2505.

Winchester: Goff's Corner Flea Market, 12449 Ironworks Rd. Tel: 606-842-3803.

Winchester: Winchester Flea Market, 4400 Revilo Rd. Tel: 606-745-4332.

LOUISIANA

ARCADIA

Bonnie & Clyde Trade Days, Inc

DATES: The weekend before the third Monday of each month, Friday through Sunday.
TIMES: Dawn to dark.
ADMISSION: Free. Parking is $3.
LOCATION: Take Exit 69 off I-20 in Arcadia and go south 3½ miles to market.
DESCRIPTION: Since its opening in September 1990, this show has grown from the original 635 dealers to over 800 dealer spaces. The grounds feature three stocked lakes for free fishing, a restaurant, amphitheater and stage, 100 RV hook-ups and facilities. There are dozens of concessions and dealers selling just about anything and everything. They have added both a washateria and free shower facilities.
DEALER RATES: $35 per 12' × 20' booth. Reservations are suggested.
CONTACT: Bonnie & Clyde Trade Days Inc, PO Box 243, Arcadia LA 71001-0243. Tel: (318) 263-2437.

BATON ROUGE

Deep South Flea Market

DATES: Every Friday, Saturday, and Sunday, rain or shine.
TIMES: 10:00 AM–6:00 PM.
ADMISSION: Free. Parking is also free.
LOCATION: 5905 Florida Blvd.
DESCRIPTION: This indoor market began in 1974. Approximately 275 dealers sell everything from antiques and collectibles, to a variety of crafts and art work, to secondhand merchandise and produce. A restaurant and handicapped-accessible restrooms add to the amenities.
DEALER RATES: $60 per 8' × 10' space, per weekend. Reservations are not required.
CONTACT: Bill Vallery, 5905 Florida Blvd, Baton Rouge LA 70806. Tel: (504) 923-0142 or 923-0333 for a tape.

GREENWOOD/SHREVEPORT

Greenwood Flea Market

DATES: Saturday and Sunday, year round.

TIMES: 10:00 AM–6:00 PM.

ADMISSION: Free. Parking is free.

LOCATION: 9249 Jefferson-Paige Rd. I-20, Exit 5.

DESCRIPTION: This unusual market started in 1982, with 150 dealer spaces inside, 25 railroad boxcars and numerous outside setups. Their dealers sell antiques, collectibles, primitives, baseball cards, glassware, furniture, jewelry and everything old and new. One of the owners saw the railroad boxcars sitting around a Texas siding and decided they would be fun and brought them over to Louisiana. Restrooms and food are available on the premises.

DEALER RATES: $30 per weekend; $110 per month. $110 per railroad car plus electric. $7.50 per day outside. Reservations are required.

CONTACT: Larry Milligan, Greenwood Flea Market, 9249 Jefferson-Paige Rd, Greenwood LA 71033. Tel: (318) 938-7201.

JEFFERSON

Jefferson Flea Market

DATES: Friday through Sunday, year round.

TIMES: 10:00 AM–6:00 PM.

ADMISSION: Free. Parking is free.

LOCATION: 5501 Jefferson Hwy. Three blocks west of Clearview, off the Huey P Long Bridge.

DESCRIPTION: This market, opened in 1978, occupies an old 90,000-square-foot building supply warehouse with 70–75 dealers specializing in antiques, collectibles and awesome old stuff. Very little is new. (Maybe some reproductions? They do make furniture here.) Some of their dealers are nationally known for their expertise. "Chef Tommy" holds court in the snack bar serving the "finest hot dogs in the South." The loading dock area is used by the locals for their garage sale goodies and for transient dealers.

DEALER RATES: Permanent dealers: $200–$250 for an average-sized space. Daily is $15 in the dock area.

CONTACT: Jim and Beverly Russell, Jefferson Flea Market, PO Box 23223, Harahan LA 70183. Tel: (504) 734-0087. Fax: (504) 734-0304.

LACOMBE

190 Trading Post Flea Market

DATES: Every Saturday and Sunday, rain or shine.
TIMES: 9:00 AM–5:00 PM.
ADMISSION: Free. Free parking is available.
LOCATION: On Hwy 190, 4 miles east of Lacombe and 6 miles west of Slidell.
DESCRIPTION: Started in 1958, this indoor/outdoor market is said to be the oldest in Louisiana, having been in continuous operation since that time (not counting the next entry). There are 20 dealers selling antiques, fine art, arts and crafts, fresh produce, collectibles, new merchandise, appliances, and furniture, as well as unusual items such as farm equipment, American-made tools, etc. One can find anything and everything here, even hard-to-find items. Food is available nearby.
DEALER RATES: From $6 to $40 depending upon size of space.
CONTACT: Mary and Harold Fayard, 470 Pine St, Slidell LA 70460. Tel: (504) 882-6442. Day of the market call Mary Fayard at (504) 641-3476.

NEW ORLEANS

French Market Community Flea Market

DATES: Daily.
TIMES: 9:00 AM–5:00 PM.
ADMISSION: Free. Parking is where you find it, or in paid lots.
LOCATION: 1235 N Peters St. Located on the riverfront behind the old US Mint (yes, coins were minted here), between the Mint and Cafe duMont. It is quite the tourist attraction.
DESCRIPTION: This has got to be the great-grandaddy of all flea markets, started in 1791! Located in a historic part of New Orleans, this market (and the adjoining markets that sort of just run together) has around 300 dealers selling just about everything: African clothes and artifacts, antiques, collectibles, quilts, Guatemalan clothes, tie-dye clothing, t-shirts, stainglass, purses, dolls, toys, ceramics, glasses, masks, furniture, stones and rocks, jewelry, plenty of produce, seafood and whatever. Many of the dealers are permanent fixtures, some are seasonal. Try to find Sonny, the Market Director, and say "Hi" for me!
DEALER RATES: Weekdays: $7–$20 a space; weekends: $12–$36 a space, depending on what is available. Spaces are given out by tenure on a

weekly basis. All vendors must have city and state licenses and current photo ID and social security number.
CONTACT: Sonny Davidson, French Market Office, 1235 N Peters St, New Orleans LA 70116. Tel: (504) 596-3420 or fax (504) 596-3427.

OTHER FLEA MARKETS

We know or have heard about these markets, but have not personally contacted each one, as we have the markets with descriptions. If you plan to visit one of these markets listed below, *please call first* to make sure they are still open. Flea markets do come and go. While they were open when we went to press, they may not be later. We can't be responsible. *Call first!*

Alexandria: Cenla Flea Market, 1007 Snow White Dr. Tel: 318-445-9805.
Alexandria: Dantzler's Flea Market, 5416 Masonic Dr. Tel: 318-443-1589.
Baton Rouge: Merchants Landing Flea Market, 9800 Florida Blvd. Tel: 504-925-1664.
Boyce: Crossroad Flea Market, 505 St Clair Rd. Tel: 318-793-5690.
Dequincy: Lost & Found Resale & Flea Market, 102 Estates Frth St #D. Tel: 318-786-3373.
Dubach: Hilly Junction Flea Market, 3171 Hwy 167. Tel: 318-777-3424.
Eunice: Cajun Flea Market, 1051 W Laurel Ave. Tel: 318-457-7274.
Eunice: Eunice Flea Market, 1600 W Laurel Ave. Tel: 318-457-1223.
Ferriday: Linda's Flea Market, 5852 Hwy 84. Tel: 318-757-7187.
Greenwood: Greenwood Flea Market, 9249 Jefferson-Paige Rd. Tel: 318-938-7201.
Gretna: Gretna's Indoor Flea Market, 225 5th St. Tel: 504-367-6362.
Harrisonburg: Harrisonburg Flea Market. Tel: 318-744-5994.
Harvey: The Golden Flea, 3714 Westbank Expy. Tel: 504-340-1888.
Harvey: Rock Bottom Flea Market, 900 Manhattan Blvd. Tel: 504-367-9870.
Houma: Neeny's Flea Market. Tel: 504-857-8888.
Houma: Old Town Flea Market, 1140 Barrow St. Tel: 504-872-5100.
Iowa: Southwest Auction & Flea Market, 15311 Hwy 165. Tel: 318-582-6752.
Kenner: J & J Flea Market, 309 Pollock Pl. Tel: 504-464-0403.
Kinder: Kinder Flea Market, 417 N 8th St. Tel: 318-738-4749.

Labadieville: Trash & Treasures Flea Market, 2707 Hwy 1010. Tel: 504-526-3869.

Lacombe: Midway Flea Market, 31204 Hwy 190. Tel: 504-882-3267.

Lafayette: JD Flea Market, 172 Eraste Landry Rd, Lafayette. Tel: 318-237-0994.

Lafayette: Little Cajun Flea Market, 1304 Louisiana Ave. Tel: 318-235-3506.

Lafayette: Pinhook Flea Market, 3131 W Pinhook Rd. Tel: 318-234-1538.

Lake Arthur: Green Barn Antiques & Flea Market, 807 Third St. Tel: 318-774-3347.

Lake Charles: Bee & Bee Flea Market, 109 Widgeon St. Tel: 318-439-0101.

Lake Charles: Kelly's Flea Market, 332 N Martin Luther King Hwy. Tel: 318-439-0382.

Leesville: Pickering Flea Market, Hwy 171 S. Tel: 318-537-0342.

Many: B & B Flea Market, 848 Texas Hwy. Tel: 318-256-5621.

Marrero: Homestyle Mini Flea Market, 539 Barataria Blvd. Tel: 504-340-6097.

Maurice: Maurice Flea Market, 8701 Maurice Ave. Tel: 318-898-2282.

Metairie: Fancy Flea Market, 4815 Thrush St. Tel: 504-888-8471.

Metairie: Veterans Trading Bazaar & Flea Market, 4032 Veterans Memorial Blvd. Tel: 504-887-2969.

Natalbany: Doug's Flea Market, 15054 Hwy 1064. Tel: 504-345-8277.

Natalbany: Natalbany Flea Market, Hwy 51. Tel: 504-542-7018.

New Iberia: Girouard's Flea Market, 5205 Hwy 90 E. Tel: 318-367-1383.

New Orleans: Algiers Mini Mart Flea Market, 2105 Behrman Hwy. Tel: 504-361-1637.

New Orleans: Canal Furniture & Flea Mart, 4030 Canal St. Tel: 504-488-5516.

New Orleans: Paul's Flea Market, 1834 N Claiborne Ave. Tel: 504-943-5115.

New Orleans: Prince Toys & More Flea Market, 8219 Oak St. Tel: 504-866-8834.

New Orleans: Simpson's Flea Market, 8921 Jefferson Hwy. Tel: 504-737-0263.

New Orleans: Stelly's Trading Post & Flea Market, 8617 Hwy 71. Tel: 504-623-3003.

Opelousas: J & R Flea Market, 1612 W Landry St. Tel: 318-948-4379.
Opelousas: Ma Jik Grocers & Flea Market, 813 Hwy 749. Tel: 318-942-5087.
Opelousas: Twyla's Flea Market & Appliance Shop, 1282 Hwy 749. Tel: 318-942-3060.
Pineville: Lasanre's Woodshop & Flea Market, 2902 Monroe Hwy. Tel: 318-641-1308.
Pineville: 28 E Flea Market & Antiques, 5625 Hwy 28 E. Tel: 318-443-9966.
Ponchatoula: Starky's Flea Market, 630 E Pine St. Tel: 504-386-2648.
Prairieville: Greater Baton Rouge Flea Market, 15545 Airline Hwy. Tel: 504-673-2682.
Rayne: Dupont's Flea Market, 319 S Adams Ave. Tel: 318-334-3036.
Rosepine: A 1 Pawn Shop & Flea Market, 18192 Central Ave. Tel: 318-462-5649.
Scott: Millie & Paw Paw's Gifts & Collectibles Flea Market, 1348 St Mary St. Tel: 318-233-0095.
Shreveport: Dunn's Flea Market. Tel: 318-687-1501.
Shreveport: Dunn Robby & Marabella Flea Mkt, 1854 S Brookwood Dr. Tel: 318-687-1840.
Slidell: PJ's Flea Market & Salvage Company, 1590 Gause Blvd W. Tel: 504-649-5207.
Violet: T & M Flea Market, 5701 E Judge Perez Dr. Tel: 504-682-8296.
Washington: Cajun Antique Flea Market, 400 S Main St. Tel: 318-826-3710.
Winnsboro: Annie's Flea Market, 1750 Hwy 15. Tel: 318-435-9457.

MAINE

BRUNSWICK

Waterfront Flea Market

DATES: Saturday and Sunday, year round.
TIMES: 8:00 AM–5:00 PM.
ADMISSION: Free. Parking is free.
LOCATION: 14 Maine Street. It's the huge four-story brick mill building down by the Androscoggin River Bridge. You really can't miss this one.
DESCRIPTION: Opened in 1996 in a very old 1830s' textile mill, this building houses 70 dealers selling literally everything from antiques and collectibles, cards, books, to produce and new merchandise. Their snack bar is so popular that people come to the snack bar for the food, and then to shop. Next door is a 140-dealer antique mall, a candle factory and outlet store as well as other shops. (Lock up your wallet!)
DEALER RATES: $10 per day for 10' × 10' space including 1 table. Reservations are necessary as there is a waiting list for space.
CONTACT: Arthur Young, Waterfront Flea Market, 14 Maine St, Brunswick ME 04011. Tel: (207) 729-0378. Fax: (207) 725-9500.

FREEPORT

Red Wheel Flea Market

DATES: Saturdays, Sundays, and holidays, from April through October. Rain or shine.
TIMES: 9:00 AM–4:00 PM.
ADMISSION: Free. Free parking is available.
LOCATION: US Rt 1 in Freeport on the south side.
DESCRIPTION: This market is in its 29th year with 120 dealers selling both indoors and out. About 50% of the show is collectibles and used merchandise, the rest is new and/or more modern. Right in town is the Freeport Mall with over 90 new outlet stores (LL Bean included). Food is served from a snack bar serving all home-cooked food. While in Freeport, check out the Blue Onion Restaurant, just down the road from LL Bean's.
DEALER RATES: Outside: $7 per 8' table with parking frontage; $10 on Sunday. Inside: $10 on Saturday, $12 on Sunday. $25 for permanent space per weekend. Reservations are suggested.
CONTACT: Ed Collett, 275 US Rt 1 S, Freeport ME 04032. Tel: (207) 865-6492.

OXFORD

Undercover Antiques & Flea Market

DATES: Daily.
TIMES: 8:00 AM–5:00 PM.
ADMISSION: Free. Parking is also free.
LOCATION: Rt 26. One-half mile north of Oxford Plains Speedway on left. Only 30 minutes from I-95 Gray exit and 45 minutes from Conway.
DESCRIPTION: Under new ownership since June 1997, this market originally opened in 1984. There are 65 dealers inside year round and 20 to 30 and growing outside in summer under awnings selling antiques, collectibles, sports cards, books, "you name it."
DEALER RATES: $5 a day for outside 3-table setup. Inside: $120–$140 a month for a 8' × 10' booth, tables $70 a month and the market does the selling.
CONTACT: Bert Morin, Undercover Flea Market, 960 Main St, Oxford, ME 04270. Tel: (207) 539-4149.

PORTLAND

Portland Expo Flea Market

DATES: Every Sunday except "other scheduled show" Sundays when they can't hold the flea market. Please call to double-check the Sunday in question as they have regular "other" shows scheduled in February (1 show scheduled), March (2), April (4), September (2), October (3).
TIMES: 9:00 AM–4:00 PM.
ADMISSION: Free. Free parking is also available.
LOCATION: Portland Exposition Building, 239 Park Ave. From Maine Turnpike Exit 6A or Exit 7, follow I-295 to Exit 5 Congress Street exit (Maine Rt 22). At the first set of lights, take a left onto St John St, then at the next set of lights take a right onto Park Ave. Expo is on the left.
DESCRIPTION: Started in 1981, this is Maine's largest indoor flea market located in the historic Portland Exposition Building, the second oldest arena in continuous operation in the United States. It is heated, clean, and friendly. There are an average of 150 dealers selling antiques, fine art, arts and crafts, collectibles, new merchandise, and "junque." Full-service concessions provide home-style food on the premises.
DEALER RATES: $20 for regular space and table; $26 for bleacher space (includes table); $32 for corner space (includes 2 tables in "L" formation). Reservations are advised.

CONTACT: Kathy Bouchard, Portland Exposition Building, 239 Park Ave, Portland ME 04102. Tel: (207) 874-8200.

SACO

Cascade Flea Market

DATES: Weekends, May through October. Daily from mid-June through Labor Day.
TIMES: 7:00 AM–5:00 PM. Or as late as the customers hang around.
ADMISSION: Free. Parking is free.
LOCATION: Rt 1. Take Exit 5 off Maine Turnpike. After the toll take Exit 2B, sign will read Rt 1 N, Portland Rd. Take that exit, go approximately 2 miles north on Rt 1. On the right-hand side at the corner of Rt 1 and Cascade Rd.
DESCRIPTION: This outdoor market has been operating since 1979 near Old Orchard Beach and Funtown-Splashtown USA. The dealers numbering anywhere from 100 to 350 (depending on who hogs how much space) sell plenty of antiques, collectibles, crafts, produce and new merchandise. Two snack concessions serve the hungry. Restrooms are on site.
DEALER RATES: Spaces, 15' frontage (with tables): Monday through Friday $8, Saturday $18, Sunday $20. Tables and its little space, each: Monday through Friday $4, Saturday $9, Sunday $10. Reservations are suggested as they are usually full.
CONTACT: Betty O'Donnell, Cascade Flea Market, 885 Portland Rd. Saco ME 04072. Tel: (207) 282-8875. Fax: (207) 883-9033.

TRENTON

Bargain Barn Flea Market

DATES: Saturday, Sunday and holidays, Memorial Day through September, weather permitting.
TIMES: 7:00 AM–5:00 PM.
ADMISSION: Free. Parking is free if you can find a place. Hint: Look behind the building, there is plenty of room there.
LOCATION: Rt 3, between Ellsworth and Bar Harbor, ¼ mile from the bridge entering Acadia National Park and Mt. Desert Island.
DESCRIPTION: Over 20 years old, this market has between 40 and 50 dealers with room for more selling everything from collectibles to new merchandise, expensive collectibles, good old "stuff," to good new stuff, "quite a mixture," including some crafts. Food is available on the premises.

DEALER RATES: $10 per space per day, seasonal rates available. Reservations are suggested.
CONTACT: George Wallace, Bargain Barn Flea Market, RR1 Box 176, Trenton ME 04605-9717. Tel: (207) 667-5022.

WOOLWICH

Montsweag Flea Market

DATES: Wednesday, Saturday and Sunday, May through October. Also, Friday, June through August.
TIMES: 6:30 AM–3:00 PM.
ADMISSION: Free. Free parking is available.
LOCATION: On Rt 1 in Woolwich, 5 miles north of Bath.
DESCRIPTION: The promoter tells us that this market, started in 1977, is rated number one in Maine and number three in New England. It is pictured in the book *Coastal Maine, A State of Maine*. There are about 100 dealers selling antiques, arts and crafts, fresh produce, collectibles, new merchandise, tools, plants and seedlings, early primitives, and fine jewelry. This market mainly deals with antiques and collectibles. The market is held outdoors and there is food served on the premises.
DEALER RATES: $7 and $9 for 3' × 8' tables, depending on market day. Advance reservations are required.
CONTACT: Norma Thompson Scopino, PO Box 252, Woolwich ME 04579. Tel: (207) 443-2809.

OTHER FLEA MARKETS

We know or have heard about these markets, but have not personally contacted each one, as we have the markets with descriptions. If you plan to visit one of these markets listed below, *please call first* to make sure they are still open. Flea markets do come and go. While they were open when we went to press, they may not be later. We can't be responsible. *Call first!*

Bath: Fort Andross Flea Market. Tel: 207-442-0436.
Gardiner: West Gardiner Flea Market Hall, Litch Rd. Tel: 207-724-3952.
Gorham: Gorham Flea Market, 19 State St. Tel: 207-839-3153.
Hampden: Hampden Flea Market & Antiques, 281 Western Ave. Tel: 207-862-3211.
Hollis Center: Gorham Flea Market, RR 35. Tel: 207-929-3676.
Hollis Center: Hide Away Flea Market, River Rd. Tel: 207-929-8320.
North Vassalboro: North Vassalboro Flea Market, Rt 32. Tel: 207-872-9253.
Poland: Evergreen Flea Market, Mechanic Falls Rd. Tel: 207-345-3521.
Portland: Morrill's Corner Flea Market, 33 Allen Ave. Tel: 207-878-0238.

MARYLAND

BALTIMORE

North Point Drive-In Outdoor/Indoor Flea Market

DATES: Every Saturday and Sunday, rain or shine.

TIMES: 7:00 AM–2:00 PM.

ADMISSION: $.25 per person. Parking for 800 cars is free.

LOCATION: 4001 North Point Blvd. Take the Baltimore Beltway 695, off at Exit 41, bear left, go to the McDonald's, they are across the street on the right.

DESCRIPTION: Started in 1971, this indoor/outdoor market runs year round in a 24,000-square-foot building next to a drive-in theater. It is claimed to be the oldest and one of the largest flea markets in the area. On Saturdays 150–200 dealers (300 on Sunday) sell antiques, arts and crafts, fresh produce, collectibles, new merchandise, used items, junk, plants, furniture, etc. One snack bar inside, a hot dog stand outside and handicapped-accessible restrooms add to the amenities.

DEALER RATES: $10 on Saturday inside or out; Sundays $10 inside per table, $15 per space outside. Please call for information. Reservations are helpful.

CONTACT: Dottie Stevens, North Point Drive-In Flea Market, 7721 Old Battlegrove Rd, Baltimore MD 21222. Day of market call at (410) 477-1337.

Patapsco Flea Market

DATES: Saturday and Sunday, rain or shine.

TIMES: 7:00 AM–4:00 PM.

ADMISSION: $.25. Parking is free.

LOCATION: Corner of 1400 West Patapsco Ave and Annapolis Blvd.

DESCRIPTION: Started in 1982 in a former strip mall, this market has 700 dealers indoors and outdoors selling "everything"—antiques, new and used merchandise, collectibles, and more. There are weekly bingo games, a warehouse across the street for dealers, an international food court, bakery, deli, ice cream parlor, carry-out lunch counters, barbecue pit, hot dog stand and more for the hungry.

DEALER RATES: $10 for large outdoor space; $15 and up for table space inside. Reservations are not required. Office hours are 9:00 AM–2:00 PM Thursday and Friday.

CONTACT: Patapsco Flea Market, 1400 W Patapsco Ave, Baltimore MD 21230. Tel: (410) 354-5262. Fax: (410) 354-3876.

BETHESDA

Farmer's Flea Market

DATES: Every Sunday, April through November.
TIMES: 9:00 AM–5:00 PM.
ADMISSION: Free. Free parking is available.
LOCATION: Two miles south of Rt 495 at 7155 Wisconsin Ave in Bethesda (northwest Washington, DC area).
DESCRIPTION: Started in 1974, 50 to 60 outside dealers now sell antiques, collectibles, and furniture. Great sales are available at the Montgomery County Farm Women's Market. Food is served on the premises.
DEALER RATES: $15 per 10' × 20' space. Reservations are not required.
CONTACT: James R Bonfils, PO Box 39034, Washington DC 20016.

COLUMBIA

The Columbia Market

DATES: Every Sunday, March to mid-December. Rain or shine.
TIMES: 9:00 AM–3:00 PM.
ADMISSION: Free. Parking is available and is also free.
LOCATION: Between Baltimore and Washington DC. Off I-95, Exit 41 West to Rt 175, at the mall on the JC Penney's side.
DESCRIPTION: This market first opened in 1972. It is held outdoors but protected from weather, and accommodates up to 300 dealers—200 undercover and 100 in the open. There is a huge variety of antiques, collectibles, and crafts for sale under a double-deck parking lot. Food is available at the mall.
DEALER RATES: $55 per 16' × 16' space undercover, $45 per space unprotected, pre-paid. Call for more rates. Reservations are suggested.
CONTACT: Bellman Promotions Inc, 11959 Philadelphia Rd, Bradshaw MD 21021. Tel: (410) 329-2188, (410) 679-2288, or 24-hour voice mail 1-800-805-7257. Fax: (410) 679-6919. Market number for Sunday only: (410) 997-6050.

EDGEWOOD

Bonnie Brae Flea Market

DATES: Every Sunday, weather permitting.

TIMES: 7:00 AM–until.
ADMISSION: Free. Free parking is available.
LOCATION: 1301 Pulaski Hwy in Edgewood, Harford County, Company grounds. Take Rt 40 (Pulaski Hwy), 20 miles NE of Baltimore, between Joppa and Aberdeen; Exit 74 off I-95.
DESCRIPTION: Opened in 1974, this indoor/outdoor flea market was at one time (during the '50s and '60s) one of the largest truck stops on the East Coast built and operated by the Merritt family. When I-95 was built the traffic left. Now it's coming back. Their dealers are selling antiques, fine art, arts and crafts, Depression glass (many patterns), some Flo-blue and Carnival, oyster cans, dolls, Roseville and other pottery, some furniture, marbles, clocks, record players, and china dishes, collectibles, new merchandise, baseball cards, and much more. The market specializes in Depression and Carnival glass.
DEALER RATES: $10 per 12' × 10' space per day. No advance reservations required.
CONTACT: Juanita Merritt, 1003 Magnolia Rd, Joppa MD 21085. Tel: (410) 679-2210 or (410) 679-6895.

ELDERSBURG

Freedom Lions Club Flea Market & Craft Show

DATES: Annually on the last Saturday of April. For 1998: April 25.
TIMES: 8:00 AM–3:00 PM.
ADMISSION: Free, and parking is free.
LOCATION: In Carroll County, 2 miles south of Eldersburg at the Freedom District Fire Company Carnival Grounds. Only 20 minutes NW of Baltimore and about 8 miles north of I-70.
DESCRIPTION: Limited to 150 quality dealers and 30 indoor crafters, this market is the fundraiser for the Freedom District Lions Club and benefits the Wilmer Eye Institute at Johns Hopkins Hospital. Among the treasures sold are: antiques, collectibles, baseball cards, homemade dolls, tools, to spring flowers. There is a variety of food to please everyone.
DEALER RATES: $15 for a 24' × 24' space outdoors; indoors $25 per table. Reservations are required.
CONTACT: Denton or Janet Boyd, 229 E Nicodemus Rd, Westminster MD 21157. Tel: (410) 857-5362.

INDIAN HEAD

Village Green Flea Market

DATES: Saturdays, April through October, except July 4th. Rain or shine.
TIMES: 7:00 AM–1:00 PM.
ADMISSION: Free. Parking is also free.
LOCATION: On the Village Green. From out of town take Indian Head Hwy South (formerly known as I-210 South) to the very end. Village Green is located on the right just outside the main entrance to the Naval Surface Warfare Center, off Lackey Dr and Pye St.
DESCRIPTION: Started in 1987 by the Town of Indian Head as a way for local residents to hold a flea market and a place to have yard sales, this market usually has about 30–40 dealers and residents selling flea market goods, yard sale items, some new merchandise, wood crafts, and local fresh produce.
DEALER RATES: $6 per space collected on site. Reservations are not required. Local permit required for food sales (excludes produce). Pet sales/ give-aways not permitted.
CONTACT: Town of Indian Head Community Affairs, Attn: Karen L-Williams, 4195 Strauss Ave, Indian Head MD 20640. Tel: (301) 753-6633.

NORTH EAST

North East Auction Galleries and Flea Market

DATES: Every day, rain or shine.
TIMES: 8:00 AM–dusk.
ADMISSION: Free. Ample free parking is provided.
LOCATION: Off I-95, on the corner of Rt 40 and Mechanics Valley Rd.
DESCRIPTION: This market has been in operation since 1973 and currently attracts between 50 dealers in winter and 150 in summer who sell a variety of goods including antiques, collectibles, craft items, new merchandise, auto parts, furniture, household goods, appliances, baseball cards, Oriental rugs and fresh produce. The market is located at the head of the picturesque Chesapeake Bay, in a high-traffic area near state parks, marinas, campgrounds, yacht clubs, and other local attractions. In addition, a consignment auction is held every Tuesday evening and an automobile auction held every Thursday evening. Food is available on the premises.
DEALER RATES: $15 per 8' × 10' table inside; outside tables are $10. Reservations are suggested for inside, outside first come, first served.

CONTACT: Mr R C Burkheimer, North East Auction Galleries, PO Box 551, North East MD 21901-0551. Tel: (800) 233-4169. In Maryland, call (410) 287-5588. Fax: (410) 287-2029.

OCEAN CITY

Antiques and Crafts Flea Market

Note: This market is not being held at the Convention Center anymore, nor run by them as previously. Dot and Jim Robinson are taking it over and moving it. They weren't certain where it would go, but it was such a good market it was left in, as Dot would be able to direct you to it.

DATES: Weekends, starting with Saturday and Sunday in May, then Friday, Saturday and Sunday through first weekend in October.
TIMES: 9:00 AM–5:00 PM.
ADMISSION: Free. Parking is also free.
LOCATION: See above note.
DESCRIPTION: Started in 1970 and operated by the town of Ocean City, this market has up to 41 vendors selling antiques, collectibles, small furniture, baseball cards, coins, crafts, glassware, assorted old treasures, used or old merchandise only. No new merchandise or food is allowed. There are two baseball card shows scheduled by the Center not connected with this flea market and also separate antique shows held in the same building but scheduled by others. This is a resort beach—there is plenty of food around on the boardwalk, from local restaurants and concessions.
DEALER RATES: $40 per day per 20' × 26' space; or $35 per day if staying for two days; $30 per each of three days. A $6 daily sales license is required and issued on site. Reservations are suggested.
CONTACT: Dot or Jim Robinson, Rt 50 & Morris Rd, Pittsville MD 21850. Tel: (410) 835-3687.

RISING SUN

Hunter's Sale Barn, Inc

DATES: Every Monday, rain or shine.
TIMES: 3:00–9:00 PM, auction at 6:00 PM.
ADMISSION: Free. Free parking is available.
LOCATION: Take Exit 93 off I-95, then go north 2½ miles to a dead end, turn right on Rt 276; market is 2½ miles down on the right.

DESCRIPTION: Originally this business was a livestock market. The flea and farmers market started in 1975, and the livestock sales stopped in 1985. This indoor/outdoor market has 120 dealers selling antiques, arts and crafts, fresh produce, collectibles, and new merchandise. This is a family oriented market kept clean and very pleasant. In addition, an auction is also conducted at the market at 6:00 PM selling eggs, produce and general merchandise. Monday night is Sale Barn Auction Night for the county. There is a full restaurant on the premises. This is a well-attended market drawing 300-plus people to the auction alone. As a result of a nasty Easter Sunday fire that burned down their auction house, they have built a new state-of-the-art heated/air-conditioned 17,500 square-foot building to replace the old one.
DEALER RATES: $20 per 4' × 8' space, $40 for a 16' × 16' space. First come, first served.
CONTACT: Norman E Hunter and Carol A or Ronda L Hunter, PO Box 427, Rising Sun MD 21911-0427. Tel: (410) 658-6400. Fax: (410) 658-3864.

OTHER FLEA MARKETS:

We know or have heard about these markets, but have not personally contacted each one, as we have the markets with descriptions. If you plan to visit one of these markets listed below, *please call first* to make sure they are still open. Flea markets do come and go. While they were open when we went to press, they may not be later. We can't be responsible. *Call first!*

Baltimore: Fullerton Flea Market, 7560 Belair Rd. Tel: 410-668-8817.
Baltimore: Hilltop Indoor Flea Market, 4207 Menlo Dr. Tel: 410-358-5870.
Baltimore: North Point Indoor Flea Market, 7721 Old Battle Grove Rd. Tel: 410-477-1337.
Baltimore: Morrie Flea Market, 1925 Frederick Ave. Tel: 410-362-0163.
Baltimore: Mt Vernon Antique Flea Market, 226 W Monument St. Tel: 410-523-6493.
Baltimore: Ritchie Hwy Flea Market, 5724 Ritchie Hwy. Tel: 410-969-3532 or 410-789-2180.
Boonsboro: Boonsboro Antiques & Flea Market, Alt Rt 40. Tel: 301-432-4868.
Boonsboro: Boonsboro Flea Market. Tel: 301-416-2788.

Brunswick: Brunswick Antiques & Flea Market, 600 W Potomac St. Tel: 301-834-5367.

Cambridge: Nancy's Flea Market, 2906 Ocean Gtwy. Tel: 410-228-6220.

District Heights: Pennsylvania Avenue Flea Market, 3300 Walters Ln. Tel: 301-420-2000.

Dundalk: Plaza Flea Market, 2401 N Point Blvd. Tel: 410-285-4504.

Ellicott City: Oella Flea Market, 787 Oella Ave. Tel: 410-461-1535.

Grasonville: Delmarva Flea Market, 300 Drummer Dr. Tel: 410-827-6400.

Hagerstown: First Inner-City Indoor Flea Market, 13617 Pennsylvania Ave. Tel: 301-791-6408.

Havre De Grace: Bonnie Brae Flea Market, 1301 Pulaski Hwy. Tel: 410-679-6895.

Hughesville: Hughesville Bargain Barn & Flea Market, Rt 5 S. Tel: 301-274-9801.

Joppa: Pulaski Flea Market, 12420 Pulaski Hwy. Tel: 410-679-3206.

Marion: Marion Trading Post & Flea Market, Rt 413. Tel: 410-623-2913.

Newburg: Wise Flea Market, 11165 Crain Hwy. Tel: 301-934-4458.

Randallstown: Randallstown Flea Market, 8514 Liberty Rd. Tel: 410-521-7200.

Salisbury: Rt 50 West Flea Market. Tel: 410-543-4189.

Silver Spring: Prevention of Blindness Society Paris Flea Market, 942 Wayne. Tel: 301-585-0331.

Thurmont: Looking Glass Flea Market, 204 N Church St. Tel: 301-271-4481.

MASSACHUSETTS

AUBURN

Auburn Antique and Flea Market, Inc

DATES: Every Sunday indoors and outdoors, year round, rain or shine. April through November, Saturdays outdoors, weather permitting.
TIMES: 7:00 AM–4:00 PM.
ADMISSION: $.50 for adults, children free during winter. Free during summer months.
LOCATION: 773 Southbridge St, Rt 12. From Massachusetts Turnpike take Exit 10, follow Rt 12 south for ½ mile. From I-290 take Exit 8, follow Rt 12 south for ½ mile. From I-395 take Exit 7, follow Rt 12 south ½ mile.
DESCRIPTION: This indoor/outdoor market has been open since 1975. It accommodates approximately 100 dealers indoors and 75 dealers outdoors. Many items such as antiques, arts and crafts, collectibles, new merchandise, and even fresh produce can be found. Many dealers also sell a variety of stamps, coins, and baseball cards. Food is served on the premises.
DEALER RATES: $30 per 9' × 9' space indoors. $15 per space outdoors on Sundays, $10 on Saturdays. Reservations are required for indoor space during the winter season only.
CONTACT: Auburn Antique & Flea Market Inc, 773 Southbridge St, PO Box 33, Auburn MA 01501-0033. Tel: (508) 832-2763.

BRIMFIELD

Crystal Brook Antique Show

DATES: 1998 dates: May 12–16, July 7–11, and September 9–12. Usually the same weekends every year.
TIMES: 6:00 AM–5:00 PM.
ADMISSION: Free. However, they don't have any parking area as they are so small.
LOCATION: On Rt 20. Take the Palmer exit off the Massachusetts Turnpike to Rt 20, then 10 miles east to Brimfield. Or Sturbridge exit on Massachusetts Turnpike, then 10 miles west of Sturbridge on Rt 20.
DESCRIPTION: It is an outdoor market that accommodates approximately 35 dealers. This is considered a relatively small market, but there are many quality antiques and collectibles sold.

DEALER RATES: Call for current rates.
CONTACT: Maureen Ethier, Rt 20, Brimfield MA 01010. Tel: (413) 245-7647.

J & J Promotions Antiques and Collectibles Shows

DATES: In 1998: May 15–16, July 10–11; September 11–12. Rain or shine. Generally, the same Friday and Saturday each year.
TIMES: Friday 6:00 AM–5:00 PM; Saturday 8:00 AM–5:00 PM.
ADMISSION: Friday $5 per person, Saturday $3. $5 parking fee. Oversized vehicles are $8.
LOCATION: From Boston: take Massachusetts Turnpike west to Exit 9 at Sturbridge; follow Rt 20 west to Brimfield for approximately 7 miles to Auction Acres. From New York City: take I-95 north to I-91 north. Go through Hartford to I-84 east to Sturbridge and Rt 20 west for about 6 miles. Or, I-95 north to I-91 through Hartford to Springfield to I-291 east to I-90 (Massachusetts Turnpike) east to Exit 8 at Palmer, go beyond exit booth and turn right at stop light, then left to Rt 20 east for approximately 6 miles.
DESCRIPTION: This outdoor show first opened in 1959. Auction Acres is the home of Gordon Reid's original Antique Market. Now owned by his two daughters, this prestigious property covers 40 acres at the center of Brimfield. Today, antiques and collectibles enthusiasts from all over the world continue to visit this famous market. Dealers and exhibitors alike have year after year relied on the experience and quality in the organization and presentation of these shows of antiques and collectibles. Food is served on the premises.
DEALER RATES: Space size and prices vary. Please call for more information.
CONTACT: Jill Reid Lukesh and Judith Reid Mathieu, J & J Promotions, Auction Acres, PO Box 385, Brimfield MA 01010-0385. Tel: (413) 245-3436 or (978) 597-8155. Email: jnjbrimfld@hey.net

New England Motel Antiques Market, Inc

DATES: 1998 dates: May 13–17, July 8–12, September 9–13.
TIMES: Wednesday opening days 6:00 AM–dusk; other days, 8:00 AM to dusk.
ADMISSION: $5, opening day only. Parking is $5.
LOCATION: Rt 20, Palmer Rd in the center of the Mart.

DESCRIPTION: This show started in 1986 and is said "to have the finest and freshest merchandise in the Brimfield's." About 400 reputable dealers from the United States, Canada and Europe sell quality antiques and collectibles in the center of the Northeast's greatest outdoor show. There is a food court on the premises.
DEALER RATES: $210 for a 20' × 24' booth. Reservations are required. Parking is also available.
CONTACT: Marie Doldoorian, PO Box 186, Sturbridge MA 01566. Tel: (508) 347-2179. Day of show call: (413) 245-3348.

Shelton Antique Shows

DATES: 1998: May 12–17, July 7–12, September 8–13. Brimfield markets are held: the second Tuesday of May through the following Sunday; Tuesday after July 4th through Sunday; Tuesday after Labor Day through Sunday.
TIMES: Daybreak on.
LOCATION: 34 Main St, aka Rt 20 (aka Palmer Rd). Between Exit 9 Sturbridge or Exit 8 Palmer off Massachusetts Turnpike. Exit Sturbridge Rt 86 from Connecticut.
ADMISSION: Free. Parking is $4–$6 a day, overnight parking is $10.
DESCRIPTION: This market started in 1975 and is located on a one mile strip of the largest outdoor antique event in the United States. Approximately 175 dealers sell antiques and collectibles. There are dealer showers, food service and table rentals available. And pets are welcome.
DEALER RATES: From $235 per 20' × 20' booth. Reservations are required. One-day rates offered after opening day.
CONTACT: Lois J Shelton, PO Box 124, Brimfield MA 01010-0124. Tel: (413) 245-3591.

EAST DOUGLAS

Douglas Flea Market, Antiques, and Collectibles

DATES: Saturday, Sunday and some holidays.
TIMES: Saturday 10:00 AM–2:00 PM; Sunday 8:00 AM–4:00 PM.
ADMISSION: Free. Parking is free.
LOCATION: Northeast Main St. From Providence or Worcester: take Rt 146 to Rt 16, Douglas exit, go west 3 miles to flashing light, make sharp right turn. Market is ¼ mile on left.

DESCRIPTION: This indoor/outdoor market is housed in an historic dairy barn on 50 acres. Dealer tables replace the cows and the silo houses the Snack Bar serving all homemade foods including breakfast, snacks and meals, homemade ice cream. Furniture is sold in the hayloft. Other treasures sold include antiques, memorabilia, glassware, antique toys, country goods, cards, and garage sale goodies. Handicapped-accessible restrooms add to the amenities of this unique and friendly market.
DEALER RATES: Outside: $2 per car length, with table $5 = $7. Inside: $10 per week. Reservations are required for inside only.
CONTACT: Marlene Bosma, PO Box 634, E Douglas MA 01516. Tel: (508) 278-6027 or weekends at (508) 476-3298.

GRAFTON

Grafton Flea Market, Inc

DATES: Every Sunday, rain or shine.
TIMES: 6:00 AM–5:00 PM.
ADMISSION: $.50 for an adult, children free. Free parking is available.
LOCATION: On Rt 140 near the Grafton-Upton town line. Take the Massachusetts Turnpike to Rt 495 south, then take Upton Exit 21B to Rt 140.
DESCRIPTION: This show first opened in 1970. There are approximately 200 to 250 dealers attending this market, which is held both indoors and outdoors. A variety of items such as antiques, collectibles, arts and crafts, new merchandise, and fresh produce can be found. There is also a selection of baseball cards, stamps, and coins. There is catered food available on the premises.
DEALER RATES: $20 per space outdoors. $25 per space indoors. Reservations are required for indoor space only.
CONTACT: Harry Peters, PO Box 206, Grafton MA 01519. Tel: (508) 839-2217.

HADLEY

Olde Hadley Flea Market

DATES: Every Sunday from the third Sunday in April through the first Sunday in November, weather permitting.
TIMES: 6:00 AM–5:00 PM.
ADMISSION: Free. Free parking is available.
LOCATION: On Rt 47 South, Lawrence Plain Rd. Take Exit 19 off Rt 91 north. Or, take Exit 20 off Rt 91 south. Follow Rt 9 east to center of Hadley, then 2 miles south on Rt 47.

DESCRIPTION: This show opened in 1980. There are 200-plus dealers selling their goods at this outdoor market. There is everything from antiques and collectibles, from new merchandise to fresh produce sold here including maple sugar, honey and plants. Excellent catered food is available on the premises. This flea market has a beautiful country setting at the foot of the Mount Holyoke Range. Special features of this flea market include antique auto viewing and the Silver Eagle Hot Air Balloon lift-off. There is also the Olde Hadley Museum, Skinner State Park, Mitch's Marina, as well as shopping malls and many fine restaurants nearby.
DEALER RATES: \$18 per 25' × 25' space. Reservations are not required. First come, first served. There are advance shopping hours for dealers starting at 6:00 AM.
CONTACT: Raymond and Marion Szala, 45 Lawrence Plain Rd, Hadley MA 01035. Tel: (413) 586-0352.

HUBBARDSTON

Rietta Ranch Flea Market

DATES: Sundays, April through October. Rain or shine.
TIMES: 6:00 AM–til.
ADMISSION: Free admission and free parking.
LOCATION: On Rt 68.
DESCRIPTION: Opened in 1967, this market attracts 600 dealers who offer antiques, collectibles, handmade/craft items, vegetables, and new merchandise. They offer a full concession with indoor and outdoor dining offering fried dough, hamburgers, hot dogs and they even have a liquor license. Plenty of restrooms and 20 acres of parking make this an easy place to spend the day. They are in the process of restoring a complete antique train with a 1915 steam engine for display.
DEALER RATES: Dealers are charged \$15 for outside space about the size of a large car including one table. \$15 for two tables on the inside. First come, first served or reserve for the season only.
CONTACT: Ronnie and Joyce Levesque, PO Box 35, Hubbardston MA 01452-0035. Tel: (508) 632-0559.

HYANNIS

Hyannis Indoor Flea Market and Antique

DATES: Saturday and Sunday.
TIMES: 10:00 AM–5:00 PM.

ADMISSION: Free. Parking is also free.
LOCATION: 500 Main St. Downtown Hyannis.
DESCRIPTION: Opened in October 1989, this mall–flea market includes vendors and shops. There is a 10,000-square-foot antique co-op, furniture consignments, merchandise mart, collectibles, new merchandise, and "Something for everyone!"
DEALER RATES: Rates vary, around $20–$30 and up. Reservations are required.
CONTACT: Jeff Rose, Hyannis Indoor Flea Market and Antique, 500 Main St, Hyannis, MA 02639. Tel: (508) 790-3412.

MASHPEE

Dick and Ellie's Flea Market

DATES: Saturday and Sunday, April through mid-November. Wednesday through Sunday, end of June through Labor Day.
TIMES: 8:00 AM–4:00 PM.
ADMISSION: Free. Parking is free.
LOCATION: Rt 151 and Rt 28, at the Mashpee Rotary on Cape Cod.
DESCRIPTION: Opened in 1975, this is a popular market on the main route to the far reaches of Cape Cod. From 200 dealers on Saturday to 300 on Sunday sell antiques, collectibles, produce and new merchandise. Sunday's 150 antique dealers are well known for the quality of their goods. Their restaurant serves the world-famous "Four Seas" ice cream, made famous by the Kennedy family. This is a booming area with a new theater complex under construction.
DEALER RATES: $20 per 20' × 20' booth per day (individual tents). There are reserved spaces available, but reservations are not necessary.
CONTACT: Al Wiseman, Dick and Ellie's Flea Market, PO Box 1907, Mashpee MA 02649. Tel: (508) 477-3550.

NORTH QUINCEY

Neponset Flea Market

DATES: Saturday and Sunday.
TIMES: 9:00 AM–5:00 PM.
ADMISSION: Free. Loads of free parking.
LOCATION: 2 Hancock St. From the north: Rt 93 South, Exit 12 to Neponset Circle. 3A South across the bridge, first exit (North Quincy) cross left under bridge, take Frontage Rd to 2 Hancock St. From the south:

Hancock St (3A) North to Neponset Bridge; stay right, go past entrance to bridge to 2 Hancock St.
DESCRIPTION: Open since 1992 this market's 50 dealers sell antiques, collectibles, crafts, produce, coins, stamps, cards, garage sale goodies, furniture, and new merchandise. There are speciality shops including Thrift Groceries and More, freight damaged goods and a pet store; the Serendipity Cafe; and "the largest thrift store in New England (open daily)" on the premises.
DEALER RATES: $39 per 8' × 10' space per weekend.
CONTACT: Flea Market Manager, 2 Hancock St, N Quincy MA 02171. Tel: (617) 472-3558 or (617) 471-8387 or fax: (617) 471-1164.

RAYNHAM

Raynham Flea Mart

DATES: Every Sunday, Monday holidays and Saturdays, Thanksgiving through Christmas.
TIMES: 8:00 AM–6:00 PM.
ADMISSION: $.75. Free parking is available.
LOCATION: At junction of Rt 24 and Rt 44.
DESCRIPTION: This show began in 1974. There are 500 dealers indoors in a 60,000-square-foot one-story building and over 400 dealers outdoors on 10 acres of land. This market screens its dealers to ensure variety and quality of items. These include antiques, arts and crafts, collectibles, jewelry, new merchandise, fresh produce and more. There are six snack bars, a full restaurant and parking for 1,000 cars.
DEALER RATES: Call for rates as they vary according to location and size. Reservations are recommended.
CONTACT: J Mann, Raynham Flea Market, Judson and South St, Raynham MA 02767. Tel: (508) 823-8923.

ROWLEY

Todd's Farm Famous Old-Fashioned Flea Market

DATES: Sundays, April to mid-November.
TIMES: 4:00 AM or 5:00 AM to whenever. Flashlights welcome.
ADMISSION: Free. Parking is free.
LOCATION: Rt 1A. From Boston: take Rt 1 or I-95 north to Rt 133. Then east to Rt 1A, go north 1 mile.

DESCRIPTION: This popular, classic flea market, opened in 1973, has 300-plus dealers selling antiques, collectibles, some produce, furniture, plants, some new merchandise and garage sale goodies. There are eight shops at this location, one snack bar inside and one out. Restrooms are available.
DEALER RATES: $25 per generous 30' × 30' space per day. First come, first served.
CONTACT: Todd's Farm, Rt 1A Main St, Rowley MA 01966. Tel: (508) 948-2217.

WELLFLEET

Wellfleet Drive-In Flea Market

DATES: Every Saturday, Sunday, and holiday Mondays, April through October. Also open every Wednesday and Thursday during July and August. Rain or shine.
TIMES: 8:00 AM–4:00 PM.
ADMISSION: $1 per carload. $2 per carload during Sundays in high season.
LOCATION: On Rt 6 towards Provincetown, on Wellfleet-Eastham line. Once you are on Cape Cod, just follow the road to Provincetown.
DESCRIPTION: This show started about 26 years ago at the Cape Cod National Seashore at Wellfleet. They have 26 acres of family entertainment. Depending upon the season, there can be anywhere from 50 to 250 dealers at this outdoor market. They specialize in antiques, collectibles, local shellfish, furniture and new merchandise. There are also arts and crafts vendors, tarot readers, artists, and anything else that is legal! For your convenience, food is available on the premises. The owners of this market pride themselves on running a very clean market with a very fine reputation.
DEALER RATES: Saturday and Thursday $15 per 18' × 22' space; Wednesday and Sunday $20 for a 18' × 22' space. Reservations are not required.
CONTACT: Eleanor Hazen, Wellfleet Drive-In Flea Market, Box 811 Wellfleet MA 02667-0811. Tel: (508) 349-2520.

OTHER FLEA MARKETS

We know or have heard about these markets, but have not personally contacted each one, as we have the markets with descriptions. If you plan to visit one of these markets listed below, *please call first* to make sure they are still open. Flea markets do come and go. While they were open when we went to press, they may not be later. We can't be responsible. *Call first!*

Boston: The Fenway Flea, 1312 Boylston St. Tel: 617-266-7894.
Brockton: Cary Hill Flea Market, 220 E Ashland St. Tel: 508-583-3100.
Dennis Port: Swan River Flea Market, 19 Main St. Tel: 508-394-2006.
Dracut: The Big Flea, 1 Mill St. Tel: 508-957-4242.
Fall River: Lakeside Flea Market, 275 Martine St. Tel: 508-672-9604.
Fitchburg: Caron's Flea Market, 11 Summer St. Tel: 508-345-5682.
Fitchburg: Dugout Flea Market, 551 Electric Ave. Tel: 508-345-2769.
Hubbardston: Rietta Flea Market, Gardner Rd. Tel: 508-632-0559.
Leominster: Four Seasons Flea Market. Tel: 508-534-3890.
Malden: Malden Flea Market, 42 Ferry St. Tel: 617-324-9113.
Middleboro: Middleboro Flea Market, 15 Spruce St. Tel: 508-946-1900.
New Bedford: Brook St Flea Market, 251 Brook St. Tel: 508-990-7067.
New Bedford: Sunshine Plaza Flea Market, 139 Hathaway Blvd. Tel: 508-999-7209.
North Attleboro: Witschi's Flea Market, 3 Washington St. Tel: 508-699-8482.
Palmer: Tri-Town Flea Market & Snack Bar, 3341 Boston Rd. Tel: Tel: 413-284-0313.
Plainville: Plainville Flea Market Inc, 23 W Bacon St. Tel: 508-695-2638.
Plymouth: Plymouth Flea Market, 377 Court St. Tel: 508-747-2266.
Revere: Revere Flea Market, 565 Squire Rd. Tel: 617-289-7100.
Rowley: Ginny's Flea Market, 31 Main St. Tel: 508-948-2591.
Shelburne Falls: Shelburne Flea Market, 1394 Mohawk Trail. Tel: 413-625-2046.
Shelburne Falls: West County Flea Market & Antiques, 351 Mohawk Trail. Tel: 413-625-8160.
Taunton: Taunton Flea Market, 93 Williams. Tel: 508-880-3800.
Tewksbury: Old N Golden Flea Market, 540 Main St. Tel: 508-640-1198.

Uxbridge: Douglas Flea Market Antiques Collectibles, W Hartford Ave. Tel: 508-278-6027.

Vineyard Haven: Pyewacket's Flea Circus, 135 Beach Rd. Tel: 508-696-7766.

Webster: The Mini Flea, 377 S Main St. Tel: 508-943-7552.

Westborough: Westboro Antique & Flea Market, 161 Milk St. Tel: 508-836-3880.

MICHIGAN

ARMADA

Armada Flea Market

DATES: Tuesday and Sunday, mid-April through October.
TIMES: 6:00 AM–2:00 PM, or total exhaustion, whichever comes first.
ADMISSION: Free. Parking is free.
LOCATION: Ridge Rd. Take M97 (Groesbeck Hwy, aka North Ave) north to Village of Armada. Turn right at the four-way stop, they are approximately 3 miles down the road.
DESCRIPTION: Started in a stockyard in the 1940s, this outdoor market gradually became a flea market in the 1960s. Depending on the weather, they will have up to 300 dealers selling mostly antiques and collectibles, a few crafts, produce in season and some new merchandise. There is a snack bar when the munchies hit.
DEALER RATES: $10 for a single space, $15 for a double space. And no, they don't take reservations. Just come on down!
CONTACT: Armada Flea Market, PO Box 525, Armada MI 48005-0525. Tel: (810) 784-9604.

CENTREVILLE

Centreville Antiques Market

DATES: Held five times each summer. May through August and October. Call for exact dates.
TIMES: 7:00 AM–4:00 PM.
ADMISSION: $4. Handicapped-accessible parking is available.
LOCATION: At St. Joseph's County Fairgrounds on M-86. In the heart of Michigan's Amish area, halfway between Chicago and Detroit, 150 miles from either city.
DESCRIPTION: This show opened in 1973. It is both an indoor and outdoor market that accommodates approximately 650 dealers. This show is limited to antiques, fine art, and select collectibles. There is also plenty of food available on the premises. This show provides a chance to "slip back in time and visit a part of small-town America." One can stroll around the 174 acres on the fairgrounds and recheck the merchandise, or walk to the fence near the viewing stand and watch a driver take a practice run around the track. This show is well thought out and well planned. Although

this is a rather large market, Robert Lawler, the show manager, has done his very best to maintain a cozy, family-like environment.
DEALER RATES: $100 per 25' × 25' space. Inside space for $95 for 10' × 10' space. Reservations are required.
CONTACT: Robert C Lawler, Show Manager, 1510 N Hoyne, Chicago IL 60622-1804. Tel: (773) 227-4464.

FLAT ROCK

Flat Rock Historical Society Antique and Flea Market

DATES: First Sundays in May and October, rain or shine.
TIMES: 8:00 AM–5:00 PM.
ADMISSION: Free. Parking is free.
LOCATION: At the Flat Rock Speedway, 1 mile south of Flat Rock on Telegraph Rd.
DESCRIPTION: This outdoor market opened in 1973 and accommodates about 350 dealers. There are a variety of antiques, arts and crafts, and collectibles. The money from this show is used to support the Flat Rock Historical Society Museum. Food is served on the premises.
DEALER RATES: $25 for a 20' × 20' space. Reservations are not required.
CONTACT: Flat Rock Historical Society, PO Box 337, Flat Rock MI 48134-0337. Tel: (313) 782-5220.

LEXINGTON

Lexington Harbor Bazaar

DATES: Saturday and Sunday.
TIMES: 10:00 AM–6:00 PM.
ADMISSION: Free. Parking is free.
LOCATION: 5590 Main St, 2 blocks south of stop light on US 25 (Main St).
DESCRIPTION: Open since 1987, this indoor market of 50 dealers sells antiques, collectibles, crafts, coins, cards, garage sale goodies, furniture and new merchandise. One snack bar and handicapped-accessible restrooms add to the amenities.
DEALER RATES: $27 per booth. Reservations are not required.
CONTACT: Main Office, Lexington Harbor Bazaar, 5590 Main St, Lexington MI 48450. Tel: (810) 359-5333 from 10:00 AM–5:00 PM daily.

MASON

Superfest Collectors Event

DATES: May 16–17, July 18–19, October 17–18, 1998. Check the same weekends for 1999.
TIMES: Saturday 8:00 AM–6:00 PM, Sunday 9:00 AM–4:00 PM.
ADMISSION: $4, children 12 and under free. Parking is free.
LOCATION: Ingham County Fairgrounds. Off Rt 127, Kipp Rd Exit.
DESCRIPTION: Since 1988, this market of 500-plus dealers has been selling antiques, collectibles, jewelry, vintage clothing, crafts, coins, furniture, cards, stamps and new merchandise. Considered unique with ten different "shows" running at once: auto, antiques, crafts, etc. Snack bars and handicapped-accessible restrooms add to the amenities. This location has 10 houses containing loads of antiques and collectibles forming an old village.
DEALER RATES: $65 for 15' × 20' space. Reservations are recommended.
CONTACT: Jeff Taylor, PO Box 343, Holt MI 48842-0343. Tel: (517) 676-2079. Fax: (517) 676-6615.

MONTAGUE

Hump-T-Dump

DATES: Tuesday through Saturday, May through Labor Day, weather permitting.
TIMES: 10:30 AM–6:00 PM. May and August only, 10:30 AM–5:00 PM.
ADMISSION: Free admission and free parking.
LOCATION: Oceana Dr (Old US 31); 3 miles north of Montague or 2½ miles south of Rothbury on old US 31.
DESCRIPTION: This one-woman flea market opened in 1978 specializing in general used merchandise, arts and crafts, some antiques and collectibles. They have a unique Peddler's Cart to mark their entrance and a large Humpty Dumpty by the building. Candy and soda are available.
DEALER RATES: Not applicable.
CONTACT: Sharon Briggs, 9494 Oceana Dr, Montague MI 49437. Tel: (616) 894-8753.

MT. CLEMENS

Gibraltar Trade Center North

DATES: Friday through Sunday, year round.
TIMES: Friday 12:00 PM–9:00 PM, Saturday 9:00 AM–9:00 PM, Sunday 9:00 AM–6:00 PM.
ADMISSION: $2 a carload.
LOCATION: I-94 to Exit 237 North River Rd, go 1 mile down on right-hand side.
DESCRIPTION: Opened in 1990, this market has 1,200 dealer spaces and 50,000 square feet of selling space indoors. Dealers sell through special shows: Sports Cards, Gun and Knife, Antiques, Home Improvement, Boat & Fishing, Arts and Crafts, etc. Watch for the ads with the listing as to what show is on for the weekend. There is plenty of food available in snack bars and restaurants; and clean, handicapped-accessible restrooms.
DEALER RATES: Starting at $75 for a 12' × 6' space, $85-$120 for 12' × 8' space, $175 for 12' × 10', and $275 for 12' × 16'. Outdoors for a 10' × 8' booth under canopy April through October only: to sell new merchandise spaces are $10 a day; for used items, produce, plants, antiques or collectibles—the space is free.
CONTACT: Gibraltar Trade Center North Inc, 237 N River Rd, Mt Clemens MI 48043. Tel: (810) 465-6440. Fax: (810) 465-0458.

MUSKEGON

Golden Token Flea Market

DATES: Saturdays.
TIMES: 6:00 AM–2:00 PM.
ADMISSION: Free. Parking is also free.
LOCATION: 1300 East Laketon Ave. One block west of US 31 on Laketon Ave.
DESCRIPTION: Started in 1985, this growing market of about 75 dealers fills two rooms selling whatever—from antiques and collectibles to whatever comes in. In summer the market is held outside; it moves inside the first weekend in October. Food, from hot dogs to shrimp dinners is available on the premises.
DEALER RATES: $5-$6 per table. Reservations are not required. Yearly rates are available. There is plenty of room!
CONTACT: Golden Token, 1300 E Laketon Ave, Muskegon MI 49442. Tel: (616) 773-1137 or (616) 722-4646.

Muskegon Flea Market

DATES: Wednesdays, mid-May through mid-October. They are hoping to expand into November, weather permitting.
TIMES: 5:00 AM–3:00 PM.
ADMISSION: Free. Parking is free.
LOCATION: Seaway Dr at Eastern Ave, ½ mile north of downtown Muskegon, take US 31 business North/Seaway Dr to Eastern Ave.
DESCRIPTION: This outdoor market of 300 dealers started in 1965. Antiques, collectibles, produce, cards, garage sale finds, ethnic clothing and music as well as new merchandise is sold. Two snack bars and handicapped-accessible restrooms add to the amenities.
DEALER RATES: $7 per 10' × 15' covered space; $6 per 10' × 30' asphalt space; $5 per 10' × 40' field space. Overflow area is available if usual space is filled. Reservations are required.
CONTACT: Cheri Burdick, Manager, c/o City of Muskegon, 933 Terrace St, Muskegon MI 49443. Tel: (616) 722-3251.

Select Auditorium Flea Market

DATES: Saturday, year round.
TIMES: 6:00 AM–2:00 PM.
ADMISSION: Free. Parking is free.
LOCATION: 1445 East Laketon Ave. At US 31 and Laketon Exit, easy-on-and-off crossway.
DESCRIPTION: Opened in 1975, this indoor/outdoor market of 75–100 dealers sells antiques, collectibles, crafts, coins, stamps, cards, garage sale finds, some furniture, new merchandise and bingo supplies. They hold bingo games after the market. One snack bar and handicapped-accessible restrooms add to the amenities. The market is held outdoors in summer, indoors in winter.
DEALER RATES: $6 for 2 parking spaces outdoors, or $7 per 4' × 8' table inside. Reservations are required for inside only.
CONTACT: Terry Durham, Select Auditorium, 1445 E Laketon Ave, Muskegon MI 49442. Tel: (616) 726-5707.

PAW PAW

Reits Flea Market

DATES: Saturdays, Sundays, and summer holidays, from April through October. Rain or shine.
TIMES: 8:00 AM–4:00 PM.
ADMISSION: Free. Free parking is available.
LOCATION: Five miles west of Paw Paw on Red Arrow Hwy, Exit 56 off I-94.
DESCRIPTION: This indoor/outdoor market opened in 1965 and currently accommodates approximately 550 dealers. There are many garage sale items along with antiques, toys, tools, household items, jewelry, collectibles, art, and much more. This is a clean and well-managed family market with events all summer long including a wine feast. Food is available on the premises as well as handicapped-accessible restrooms.
DEALER RATES: $10 per 22' × 20' space per day outdoors. $9 per space indoors. Reservations are not required. New dealers welcome.
CONTACT: Bob Hixenbaugh and Dene Broadwater, 45146 Red Arrow Hwy, Paw Paw MI 49079. Tel: (616) 657-3428.

ROMULUS

Green Lawn Grove Flea Market

DATES: Saturday and Sunday, and holiday Fridays and Mondays.
TIMES: 7:00 AM–4:00 PM.
ADMISSION: Free. Parking is also free.
LOCATION: 16447 Middlebelt Rd, between Pennsylvania and Eureka St, 5 miles south of the airport.
DESCRIPTION: Since 1973 this market has 200 dealers in summer and 80 in winter, selling everything "from soup to nuts" including novelties, some antiques and collectibles, baseball cards, crafts, produce and new merchandise. Two kitchens and two restrooms are available on the premises.
DEALER RATES: Reserved space is $15, unreserved is $14 for a 4' × 10' space. Reservations are required.
CONTACT: Jane Pai, Green Lawn Grove Flea Market, 16447 Middlebelt Road, Romulus MI 48174-3121. Tel: (313) 941-6930 or (313) 941-9733. Email: janepai@aadi.com.

TAYLOR

Gibraltar Trade Center

DATES: Friday through Sunday, year round.

TIMES: Friday 10:00 PM–9:00 PM, Saturday 9:00 AM–9:00 PM, Sunday 9:00 AM–6:00 PM.

ADMISSION: $2 a carload.

LOCATION: I-75 and Eureka Rd (Exit 36).

DESCRIPTION: Opened in 1980, this market has 1,200 dealer spaces and 50,000 square feet of selling space indoors. Dealers sell through special shows: Sports Cards, Gun and Knife, Antiques, Home Improvement, Boat & Fishing, Arts and Crafts, etc. Watch for the ads with the listing as to what show is on for the weekend. There is plenty of food available in snack bars and restaurants, and clean, handicapped-accessible restrooms.

DEALER RATES: Starting at $75 for a 12' x 6' space, $85-$120 for 12' x 8' space, $175 for 12' x 10', and $275 for 12' x 16'. Outdoors for a 10' x 8' booth under canopy April through October only: to sell new merchandise spaces are $10 a day; for used items, produce, plants, antiques or collectibles—the space is free.

CONTACT: Gibraltar Trade Center Inc, 15525 Racho Rd, Taylor MI 48180-5213. Tel: (313) 287-2000. Fax: (313) 287-8330.

WARREN

Country Fair Flea Market

DATES: Every Friday, Saturday, and Sunday, year round.

TIMES: Friday 4:00 PM–9:00 PM, Saturday and Sunday 10:00 AM–6:00 PM.

ADMISSION: Free. Parking is also free.

LOCATION: 20900 Dequindre Blvd, 2 blocks north of Eight Mile Rd.

DESCRIPTION: This indoor show began in 1978 and currently has about 300 dealers exhibiting antiques, collectibles, produce, crafts, new merchandise, 14K gold and silver jewelry, leather, Amish furniture, Hush-Puppy shoes (very popular), and brass items. One snack bar and handicapped-accessible restrooms add to the amenities. Watch for their special shows coming in 1998 (Gun, Knife, Barbie and Toys, and more). They expanded their sports collection. About 50% of the market is antiques housed in Antique Village. Their dealers take great pride in their merchandise. Watch for their sister market opening in Ypsilanti in 1999.

DEALER RATES: $53 per 5' × 10' space per weekend or $105 for a double-size space. Reservations are suggested.
CONTACT: Mike and Katie Holland, Owners, or Terry Bingham, Country Fair Flea Market, 20900 Dequindre, Warren MI 48091. Tel: (810) 757-3740 or 757-3741.

WATERFORD

Dixieland Antique Flea Market

DATES: Friday, Saturday, and Sunday.
TIMES: Friday 4:00 PM–9:00 PM; Saturday and Sunday 10:00 AM–6:00 PM.
ADMISSION: Free. Parking is also free.
LOCATION: On corner of Dixie Hwy and Telegraph Rd.
DESCRIPTION: It is nice to discover a market that hangs on to local color. Garland Brown is one of the fixtures of Dixieland, do look for him and say "Hi." Since 1975 and under its present ownership since 1986 this market has over 200 dealers selling antiques, collectibles, new and used merchandise, and a food court. It has been described as being like a giant outdoor garage sale in summer. Four restaurants across the back of the market create a small food court.
DEALER RATES: $45 and up. Reservations are not required.
CONTACT: Dixieland Flea Market, 2045 Dixie Hwy, Waterford MI 48328. Tel: (248) 338-3220.

OTHER FLEA MARKETS

We know or have heard about these markets, but have not personally contacted each one, as we have the markets with descriptions. If you plan to visit one of these markets listed below, *please call first* to make sure they are still open. Flea markets do come and go. While they were open when we went to press, they may not be later. We can't be responsible. *Call first!*

Cheboygan: Treasure Hunt Flea Market & Antiques, 405 Duncan Ave. Tel: 616-627-6080.
Clinton Township: Arrow Trade Flea Market, 19100 15 Mile Rd. Tel: 810-791-7270.
Columbiaville: Columbiaville Flea Market, 4654 Water. Tel: 810-793-4942.
Detroit: American Flea Market, 11500 E 8 Mile Rd. Tel: 313-371-2130.
Detroit: Bargain Flea Market, 12712 E 8 Mile Rd. Tel: 313-371-1415.
Detroit: Central Flea Market, 3700 Central St. Tel: 313-849-2232.

Detroit: Metro Flea Market, 6408 W Vernor Hwy. Tel: 313-841-4890.

Detroit: Rosaiah's Flea Market, 11400 Kelly Rd. Tel: 313-839-4321.

Fort Gratiot: Wurzel Flea Market, 4189 Keewahdin Rd. Tel: 810-385-4283.

Grand Rapids: Belt Line Flea Market, 1400 28th St SW. Tel: 616-532-6301.

Grayling: Ernie's Flea Market, M 72 West. Tel: 517-348-5695.

Harrison: Parkview Flea Market & Campgrounds, 3033 N Clare Ave. Tel: 517-539-3507.

Holland: Unique Flea Market, 5139 N 144th Ave. Tel: 616-399-1982.

Howell: Family Flea Market, 6070 E Gd Riv. Tel: 517-546-8270.

Lake City: Lake City Flea Market, 518 E Union Lcky. Tel: 616-839-3206.

Lansing: Jolly Rd Flea Market, 933 W Jolly Rd. Tel: 517-393-1913.

Mount Pleasant: North Winn Flea Market & Auction Barn, 3368 W Walton Rd. Tel: 517-866-2710.

Munising: Country Tyme Antique Flea Market, H 58. Tel: 906-387-5112.

Newaygo: Newaygo Flea Market, 8576 Mason Dr. Tel: 616-652-2114.

Plainwell: Plainwell Flea Market, 585 10th St. Tel: 616-685-5443.

Portland: Portland Flea Market, 143 Kent St. Tel: 517-647-4484.

Potterville: Main Street Flea Market, 112 E Main. Tel: 517-645-2062.

Ravenna: Sullivan Flea Market & Auction, 11851 Heights Ravenna Rd. Tel: 616-853-2435.

Rogers Heights: Rogers Heights Flea Market, 11 Mile Rd & Northland Dr. Tel: 616-592-3132.

St Johns: Beck's Flea Market, N US 27 Hwy.

Sand Lake: Sand Lake Flea Market, 17990 Northland. Tel: 616-636-4280 or 616-636-4772.

Saugatuck: Jordan's Flea Market, 64th. Tel: 616-857-4481.

Trufant: Trufant Auction & Flea Market, 303 N C St. Tel: 616-984-2168.

Utica: Red Barn, 47326 Dequindre. Tel: 810-680-1615.

Warren: Michigan's Flea Market, 24100 Groesbeck Hwy. Tel: 810-771-3535.

Warren: Tri-County Flea Market, 14401 Frazho Rd. Tel: 810-774-2320.

Warren: Van Dyke Flea Market, 23524 Van Dyke Ave. Tel: 810-757-5883.

MINNESOTA

DETROIT LAKES

Shady Hollow Flea Market

DATES: Sundays from Memorial Day to the Sunday after Labor Day. Three-day shows Saturday through Monday on Memorial Day and Labor Day weekends. Two-day show (Saturday and Sunday) weekend of We-Fest, the first weekend in August, and a two-day show near July 4.

TIMES: 7:00 AM–5:00 PM.

ADMISSION: Free. Parking is free.

LOCATION: On Highway 59, 5 miles south of Detroit Lakes.

DESCRIPTION: Started in 1968, this outdoor market averages 75–100 dealers selling antiques, collectibles, furniture, garage sale stuff, junk, crafts, produce, cards, coins and whatever else. Eighteen cabins are rented for an entire season by dealers. Several lunch wagons serve the market.

DEALER RATES: $15 and up, depending on size. Reservations are not required.

CONTACT: Ardis Hanson or Monte Jones, Shady Hollow Flea Market, 1760 East Shore Dr, Detroit Lakes MN 56501. Tel: (218) 847-9488 (the Hansons) or 847-5706 (the Jones).

Talk about success!

Several years ago a one-shot-a-year vendor called early in the season to request her special, coveted shady spot for Labor Day Sunday. She arrived early with a loaded truck and set up.

Around 8:00 AM she came to the market managers asking for her money back, as she had sold out and was leaving!

DULUTH

27th Annual Studebaker Drivers Club Swap Meet Flea Market and Classic Car Show

DATES: Annually, the second Sunday in August. Rain or shine.

TIMES: 8:00 AM–4:00 PM.

ADMISSION: $2 per person, children under 12 and seniors (65 and older) free. $2 parking per car.

LOCATION: Lake Superior College, 2101 Trinity Rd, 2 miles south of Miller Hill Mall.
DESCRIPTION: This show opened in 1972. Both an indoor and outdoor market, it accommodates anywhere from 35 spaces inside to 200 spaces outside. You can buy anything from antiques and collectibles to junk, coins, gifts, crafts, glass, hobbies and new merchandise. Many old and restored antique cars are on display for the Car Show (200 cars). There are also old car parts for all makes and models on sale. Food is served on the premises. There is a car corral with usually 50 cars for sale.
DEALER RATES: $10 per 10' × 20' space outdoors; $10 per 10' × 10' space indoors. Reservations are recommended. There are advance shopping hours for dealers on the Saturday before the show.
CONTACT: North Land Wheels Chapter, PO Box 1004, Duluth MN 55810-1004. Tel: (218) 722-8533.

MONTICELLO

Orchard Fun Market

DATES: Every Saturday and Sunday, rain or shine.
TIMES: 9:00 AM–5:00 PM.
ADMISSION: Free. Acres of free parking are provided.
LOCATION: On Orchard Road. Take Rt 75, 3 miles west from the stoplight in downtown Monticello, then turn at Orchard Rd and go approximately ¼ mile.
DESCRIPTION: This indoor/outdoor market began around 1972 and currently attracts between 250 and 500 dealers per market day, depending on the season; the facilities include 250 tables inside and 400 outside. The fare at this market includes antiques, collectibles, and used household items, as well as new merchandise and fresh produce. Other attractions include a beer garden and live entertainment on two stages, bumper boat rides, and "slick-rack racers" for the kids. Chicken dinners, bratwurst, hot dogs, funnel cakes, corn dogs and more are served on the premises.
DEALER RATES: $10 per 8' table per day. Reservations are not accepted. First come, first served.
CONTACT: Orchard Fun Market, 1479 127 St NW, Monticello MN 55362. Tel: (612) 295-2121.

ORONOCO

Downtown Oronoco Gold Rush, Inc

DATES: Third Saturday and Sunday in August. Rain or shine.
TIMES: Sunup to sundown.
ADMISSION: Free. Parking is also free. The town provides free outlying parking with bus transportation into town. Parking costs you in town.
LOCATION: The entire downtown Oronoco!
DESCRIPTION: Started in 1972, the entire town participates in this weekend-long flea market. The main street is closed off to traffic and over 1,500 dealers setup selling antiques, collectibles, flea market goodies, crafts, unfound and re-found treasures; as one organizer says "If they don't have it here in those two days, you can't find it!" Some residents sell right out of their garages. Over 40,000 people come through here each day. The money raised is used to help the City of Oronoco finance their First Response system, the fire department, planting new trees, fixing the community center, fireworks for July 4th and whatever else is needed. Ample food is available.
DEALER RATES: $55 per 15' × 15' space for the weekend. Reservations are required. Many spaces are reserved well in advance.
CONTACT: Oronoco Gold Rush, PO Box 266, Oronoco MN 55960-0266. Tel: (507) 367-4405, the City Clerk's Office. Fax: (507) 367-4982.

WABASHA

Wabasha Indoor/Outdoor Flea Market

DATES: Saturday and Sunday, year round.
TIMES: 9:00 AM–5:00 PM.
ADMISSION: Free. Parking is also free.
LOCATION: Hwy 61 and Industrial Court.
DESCRIPTION: Since 1988, this market of 120 tables has been selling new and used merchandise, carpet, furniture, antiques, and collectibles. Coinciding with the arrival of the Mississippi Queen Riverboat, usually in September, the town celebrates Riverboat Days with a parade as well as a huge celebration. Food is available on the premises.
DEALER RATES: $9 per table. Reservations are required.
CONTACT: Doc Carlson, Wabasha Indoor/Outdoor Flea Market, PO Box 230, Wabasha MN 55981-0230. Tel: (612) 565-4767.

OTHER FLEA MARKETS

We know or have heard about these markets, but have not personally contacted each one, as we have the markets with descriptions. If you plan to visit one of these markets listed below, *please call first* to make sure they are still open. Flea markets do come and go. While they were open when we went to press, they may not be later. We can't be responsible. *Call first!*

Hinckley: Hinckley Flea Market. Tel: 320-384-9911.
Marshall: KMHL Flea Market & Radio Auction, 1414 E College Dr. Tel: 507-532-9626.
Park Rapids: Country Flea Market, Hwy 34 E. Tel: 218-732-5570.
Prior Lake: Priordale Flea Market, Priordale Mall, 16760 Toronto Ave SE. Tel: 612-447-8024.

MISSISSIPPI

AMORY

Bigbee Waterway Trade Days

Note: Trying to contact anyone connected to this market is nigh on impossible; however, they are said to be there and they are listed on an Internet site as open. Check first!

DATES: The weekend before and including the first Monday of the month.

TIMES: Daylight hours, whatever they are.

ADMISSION: Free. Parking is free.

LOCATION: Three miles north of Amory on Hwy 371. Only ½ mile from the Ten Tom Waterway.

DESCRIPTION: Opened in July 1991, this market attracts about 100 dealers selling the usual flea market fare: antiques, collectibles, crafts, new merchandise, coins, stamps, cards and whatever. There are two concession stands on the grounds selling ice cream, plate lunches, snacks, nachos, funnel cakes, etc. Restrooms and showers are available. There's fishing on the waterway nearby, just in case you need something extra to do.

DEALER RATES: $15 for a 20' × 20' space. Reservations are recommended. They have sheds and full hook-ups.

CONTACT: Bigbee Waterway Trade Days, 30211 Hwy 371, Amory MS 38821-7807. Tel: (601) 256-1226.

> It is said that a picture and frame were sold for $5 at an auction near here. The new owner took the picture and frame to another auction and sold it for $115 and thought he did real well! The savvy New York buyer took it back to New York and reportedly sold it for over $50,000. So there.

BAY SAINT LOUIS

Hancock County Humane Society Flea Market

DATES: Tuesday through Saturday.

TIMES: 10:00 AM–3:00 PM.

ADMISSION: Free. Parking is free.

LOCATION: 1005 Hwy 90 at Hwy 90 and Drinkwater St.

DESCRIPTION: This admittedly tiny market exists solely to raise money for the local humane society to help pay for their programs and to protect

and feed animals. You never know what will be donated. Recently they sold some "gorgeous 19th-century chairs" for a very good price. Along with the antiques (lots of these) they sell collectibles, appliances, clothes, furniture, and literally whatever else comes in. Dealers take note: if you are passing through, do stop in—just in case.
DEALER RATES: All items are donated. Have anything to drop off?
CONTACT: Lorraine Taylor, Hancock County Humane Society Flea Market, PO Box 2273, Bay St Louis MS 39521-2273. Tel: 601-467-7686.

JACKSON

Fairgrounds Antique Flea Market

DATES: Saturday and Sunday, year round.
TIMES: Saturday 8:00 AM–5:00 PM; Sunday 10:00 AM–5:00 PM.
ADMISSION: $1 per person. Free parking.
LOCATION: Take High Street exit off I-55 to 890 Mississippi St at the State Fairgrounds. In the big "steel building."
DESCRIPTION: This indoor flea market is in its eleventh year and has over 200 dealers in antiques, collectibles, handicrafts, produce, and new merchandise. There are also some primitives and books. This is a very well-rounded flea market. A complete concession provides food on the premises. Camper hook-ups are available.
DEALER RATES: $35 for a wall booth, $45 for an aisle booth, $4 each for tables. Reservations are required one week in advance only.
CONTACT: Frank Barnett, Fairgrounds Antique Flea Market, PO Box 23579, Jackson MS 39225. Tel: (601) 353-5327.

RIPLEY

First Monday Flea Market

DATES: First Monday and preceding Saturday and Sunday of each month, but primarily on Saturday and Sunday.
TIMES: Dawn to dusk.
ADMISSION: Free. $1.50 parking fee.
LOCATION: On Hwy 15, 65 miles from Memphis and 45 miles from Tupelo.
DESCRIPTION: This outdoor market has operated under present management since the mid-1970s, although local sources claim to be able to trace it back to first Mondays as early as 1893, ranking it among the nation's most venerable. Presently accommodating an average of 700 dealers, there

is everything from antiques, collectibles, fresh produce, and new merchandise to a variety of crafts and reproduction oak furniture available. Food is served on the premises.
DEALER RATES: $25 for a 18' × 18' booth. Reservations are suggested.
CONTACT: Ripley First Monday Trade Days, 10590 Hwy 15 S, Ripley MS 38663. Tel: 1-800-4-RIPLEY Monday through Friday, (601) 837-4051. Fax: (601) 837-7080.

TUPELO

Tupelo's Gigantic Flea Market

DATES: Friday, Saturday and Sunday, the second full weekend of the month, except February and August.
TIMES: Friday evening 6:00 PM–9:00 PM, Saturday 9:00 AM–7:00 PM, Sunday 10:00 AM–5:00 PM.
ADMISSION: Free. Parking is free.
LOCATION: Tupelo Furniture Market Buildings at 1301 Coley Rd.
DESCRIPTION: This maybe-seven-year-old market hosts over 800 dealers selling "everything" (they all say that, and usually mean it). From antiques, collectibles, new merchandise, from high-end to low-end, it's all here, housed in two large buildings with outside spaces as well. Concessions stands feed the famished.
DEALER RATES: $65 for the full 3-day weekend. Spaces are 9' × 11'. Reservations are preferred.
CONTACT: Debbie Griffin or Sheila Smith, Tupelo's Gigantic Flea Market, 1301 Coley Rd, Tupelo MS 38801. Tel: (601) 842-4442. Fax: (601) 844-3665.

OTHER FLEA MARKETS

We know or have heard about these markets, but have not personally contacted each one, as we have the markets with descriptions. If you plan to visit one of these markets listed below, *please call first* to make sure they are still open. Flea markets do come and go. While they were open when we went to press, they may not be later. We can't be responsible. *Call first!*

Amory: 41 Flea Market, 30025 Hwy 278 W. Tel: (601) 256-9354.
Biloxi: Bargain Barn Flea Market, 1787 Pass Rd. Tel: (601) 374-9585.
Biloxi: Bargain City Flea Market, 1737 Pass Rd. Tel: (601) 435-3355.

Brookhaven: Brookhaven Flea Market, 118 E Monticello St. Tel: (601) 835-1987.

Brookhaven: M & M Flea Market, 704 SE E Wallace Blvd. Tel: (601) 757-6880.

Canton: Canton Flea Market Inc, 3332 N Liberty St. Tel: (601) 859-8055.

Centreville: Centreville Trade Days Flea Market, 1152 Old Hwy 33. Tel: (601) 645-6548.

Clinton: Clinton Flea Market, 941 Hwy 80 E. Tel: (601) 924-0095.

Columbus: Island Road Flea Market, 370 Island Rd. Tel: (601) 328-4484.

Corinth: Corinth Flea Market Cafe, 1224 Hwy 72 E. Tel: (601) 287-5304 or (601) 287-9110.

Gautier: Deep South Antiques & Flea Market, 3813 Hwy 90. Tel: (601) 497-9401.

Greenville: Florida Flea Market, 609 Washington Ave. Tel: (601) 335-8596.

Gulfport: Jun-Co Flea Market, 4005 Arkansas Ave. Tel: (601) 865-9744.

Hattiesburg: Dealer Choice Flea Market, 5691 US Hwy 49. Tel: (601) 584-9400.

Iuka: Hill Top Antique & Flea Market, 803 Quitman. Tel: (601) 423-9153.

Jackson: Victoria Enterprise Jones Center Flea Market, 3064 Hwy 80 E. Tel: (601) 939-9930.

Kosciusko: C & C Auction & Flea Market, 410 Hwy 12 E. Tel: (601) 289-6747.

Lucedale: Tri-County Flea Market, Hwy 98 E. Tel: (601) 947-9699.

Macon: Lindley's Flea Market, 105 W Adams St. Tel: (601) 726-9923.

McComb: Howe St Flea Market, 610 Howe St. Tel: (601) 249-1007.

McComb: McComb Flea Market Inc, 131 N Front St. Tel: (601) 249-0290.

Mendenhall: Mendenhall Flea Market, Old Hwy 49 N. Tel: (601) 847-5005.

Meridian: Allen's Flea Market, 2516 Street C. Tel: (601) 482-4002.

Meridian: Carol's Flea Market, 2604 State Blvd. Tel: (601) 693-0760.

Moss Point: Big G Flea Market, 4228 Old Saracennia Rd. Tel: (601) 474-1920.

Natchez: Hwy 61 N Flea Market & Produce, 105 Shadyside St. Tel: (601) 446-9695.

Natchez: White Apple Flea Market, 1032 Hwy 61 S. Tel: (601) 445-0103.

New Albany: New Albany Flea Market, 514 Bankhead St W. Tel: (601) 534-0370.

Ocean Springs: Fountain Bleau Flea Market, 6515 Hwy 90. Tel: (601) 875-7936.

Pascagoula: Jackson County Flea Market, 2519 Telephone Rd. Tel: (601) 762-9994.

Picayune: McNeil Flea Market, 2 Cemetery Rd. Tel: (601) 798-0350.

Sandersville: Books & More Flea Market. Tel: (601) 426-6913.

Saucier: S & S Flea Market, 23519 Central Dr. Tel: (601) 832-2609.

Shannon: Shannon Flea Market, 241 Old Hwy 45. Tel: (601) 767-9050.

Tupelo: Skyline Auction & Flea Market, Hwy 78 E. Tel: (601) 680-4559.

Vicksburg: 61 South Flea Market, Hwy 61 S. Tel: (601) 638-7550.

Vicksburg: Catfish Town Flea Market, 745 Hwy 61 Bypass S. Tel: (601) 629-9637.

Woodville: 61 South Flea Market, 211 US Hwy 61 N. Tel: (601) 888-6999.

MISSOURI

JOPLIN

Gingerbread House Antique Mall and Flea Market

Note: For you antique dealers, I know this is more a "store" than a flea market, but it is full of antiques and collectibles and recommended by Norma Kukovick in Opolis, Kansas. So, say "Hi" to Nellie for me, she's delightful.

DATES: Daily.

TIMES: 9:00 AM–6:00 PM.

ADMISSION: Free. Parking is free.

LOCATION: Intersection of I-44 and South 43 Hwy on North Outer Rd. Across from the Petro Truck Stop. Take Exit 4 off I-44 to North Outer Rd.

DESCRIPTION: Opened in February 1995, this market of 85–90 dealers sells antiques and collectibles and includes dealers with NASCAR, Hot Wheels, and PEZ among other collectibles. They stress friendly service and will go out of their way to help you find something. Food and drinks are available.

DEALER RATES: $1 per square foot of space. Reservations are necessary.

CONTACT: Nellie, Gingerbread House, PO Box 3466, Joplin MO 64803. Tel: (417) 623-6690.

Joplin Flea Market

DATES: Every Saturday and Sunday, year round. Rain or shine.

TIMES: 8:00 AM–5:00 PM.

ADMISSION: Free admission and free parking.

LOCATION: 1200 block of Virginia Ave in the Old City Market; 1 block east of 12th and Main Sts.

DESCRIPTION: This indoor/outdoor show is in its 16th year. It comprises 200 dealers selling all kinds of curios and antiques. There are crafts, collectibles, new and used merchandise, produce, meats and cheeses, primitives, stamps and coins, tools, jewelry, clothing, postcards, and the list goes on. An entire city block, indoors, of flea market space has grown behind this market with new heating units to keep the dealers warm year round. They added another shed with roof in 1996. For your convenience, a snack bar keeps the hunger away.

DEALER RATES: Call for reasonable rates on 10' × 18' space per day outside with parking space by booth or 9' × 20' space inside. There are open butler sheds with asphalt paving, and open space for dealers with their own canopies. Free storage for the following week is provided for inside dealers with advance payment. Reservations are suggested.
CONTACT: Laverne Miller, c/o Joplin Flea Market, 2572 Markwardt Ave, Joplin MO 64801. Tel: (417) 623-3743 or (417) 623-6328.

A Tad of History
This market was built in the 1930s for the City of Joplin by the WPA to house their produce market. It was the largest watermelon distribution center in the entire United States with trucks parked all around it awaiting their turn. Laverne Miller purchased the property from the city in 1977 to open the area's first flea market. She has since bought up much of the property around here to enlarge her flea market, upgrading the area in the process.

KANSAS CITY

Jeff William's Flea Market

DATES: One or two Sundays each month. (Dates vary; please write for latest schedule.)
TIMES: 8:00 AM–4:00 PM.
ADMISSION: $2. Free parking is available.
LOCATION: Governor's Building (Kemper Arena Complex), 1800 Genessee. Go west on 12th St and follow signs to Kemper Arena in downtown Kansas City.
DESCRIPTION: This show opened in 1973. It is an indoor market that accommodates over 500 dealers. Along with a large variety of antiques, collectibles, arts and crafts, and new merchandise, they sell lots of nostalgia and memorabilia. Because this monthly flea market has recently moved to a larger facility, it no longer takes two years to rent a space! This show is definitely worth calling for more information about dates. Food is served on the premises.
DEALER RATES: $35 per 10' × 10' space, $70 for a 10' × 20' space. Reservations are required.
CONTACT: Jeff Williams Productions, PO Box 543, Blue Springs MO 64013. Tel: (816) 228-5811.

PEVELY

The Big Pevely Flea Market

DATES: Every Saturday and Sunday, year round, rain or shine.
TIMES: 7:00 AM–5:00 PM.
ADMISSION: Free admission and free parking.
LOCATION: Take I-55 south from St. Louis to Pevely/Hillsborough Hwy Z Exit to Hwy 61/67, then go ¼ mile to market on the right-hand side.
DESCRIPTION: This indoor/outdoor market opened in 1969 in an old drive-in theater. Over the years they have added two buildings housing about 200 dealers each. Altogether their 500 to 600 dealers sell antiques, collectibles, crafts, furniture, cards, clothing, garage sale goodies, vegetables, and new merchandise. A snack bar serves the hungry. There is a special place outdoors for the "garage sale" vendors. One of the buildings is now a Flea Market Mall open daily where the market sells for the vendors. Just in case, there is an ATM machine on site.
DEALER RATES: Outside $10 a day. Inside: $15 a single space, $37 for a corner double space. Reservations are required indoors. Outdoor space can be reserved, or is allocated on a first come, first served basis. At the Mall: call for rates; the market does the selling.
CONTACT: Ken Smith or Lee Douglas, The Big Pevely Flea Market, PO Box 300, Pevely MO 63070-0300. Tel: (314) 479-5400.

SIKESTON

Tradewinds Flea Market

DATES: Every Friday through Sunday, rain or shine.
TIMES: All day.
ADMISSION: Free. Free parking is available.
LOCATION: 875 West Malone. Sikeston is 150 miles south of St. Louis, 150 miles north of North Memphis.
DESCRIPTION: This indoor/outdoor market opened in 1974 and now accommodates approximately 300 dealers. There is everything here from antiques and collectibles to arts and crafts to new merchandise. Tools, toys, fresh produce, as well as chickens, turkeys, guinea pigs, and rabbits are available. The Tradewinds Restaurant is in the middle of the market. This market has been growing steadily since it began as more and more dealers are coming from all over the United States to sell their goods.

DEALER RATES: $7 per 14' × 14' space, per day; Sundays only $5 per space. If you rent for Friday and Saturday ($14), Sunday is free. Reservations are first-come, first served.
CONTACT: Tradewinds Flea Market, 875 W Malone, Sikeston MO 63801. Call the Tradewinds Restaurant at (573) 471-3965 or 471-8419.

SPRINGFIELD

I-44 Swap Meet

DATES: Saturday and Sunday, March through December, rain or shine.
TIMES: Daylight to dark.
ADMISSION: $1 per car admission and parking.
LOCATION: 2908 North Neergard across from the Zenith TV plant. 2600 block of East Kearney and Neergard, ½ mile north on Neergard.
DESCRIPTION: "Sooner or later it's out there, if you want it." Started in 1984, this swap meet has from 200 to 300 dealers selling everything! It is on 40 acres right along I-44. Live bands and 5 snack bars liven things up. Free camping on Friday and weekends.
DEALER RATES: For a 30' × 20' space: $6 on Saturday; $8 Sundays. First come, first served.
CONTACT: Butch Koonce or Bob, 2743 W Kearney, Springfield MO 65803. Tel: (417) 866-7493 or (417) 864-4340 or (417) 864-6508.

Old PO Flea Market

DATES: Monday through Saturday.
TIMES: 10:00 AM–5:00 PM.
ADMISSION: Free. Parking is free.
LOCATION: 304 W Commercial St in the old Post Office building.
DESCRIPTION: Opened in an old post office building (hence the name), this 11-year-old market has been under new management since November 1996. There are 32 dealers in primarily antiques, collectibles, old books, linens, furniture, old paper, or, as Dan says, "stuff from 50¢ to $750." There is a big turnover in merchandise as it sells so fast and new goods are always coming in. Another dealer's buying paradise. No food, unless you are a termite.
DEALER RATES: $30 per month for a "table section" with shelves, $65 per month for a 8' × 10' booth. There is a large furniture room if you need it. Reservations are a good idea.
CONTACT: Dan, Old PO Flea Market, 304 W Commercial St, Springfield MO 65803-2666. Tel: (417) 865-8444.

It is said that somewhere in northwest Missouri is a state highway that becomes a 39-mile long flea market. If you pass through it, just stop and set up. Or buy.

OTHER FLEA MARKETS

We know or have heard about these markets, but have not personally contacted each one, as we have the markets with descriptions. If you plan to visit one of these markets listed below, *please call first* to make sure they are still open. Flea markets do come and go. While they were open when we went to press, they may not be later. We can't be responsible. *Call first!*

Anderson: Anderson Main St Flea Market. Tel: 417-845-6941.
Anderson: Hwy 59 Flea Market. Tel: 417-845-6811.
Asbury: Asbury Flea Market, Rt 1 101 E Main. Tel: 417-642-5724.
Asbury: State-Line Trade Center & Flea Market, PO Box 62. Tel: 417-642-5850.
Aurora: Houn Dawg Flea Market, 16 W Olive St. Tel: 417-678-4555.
Aurora: Madison Place Flea Market & Antiques, 330 S Aurora. Tel: 417-678-6307.
Aurora: Shorty's Flea Market, 25 W Locust St. Tel: 417-678-7554.
Barnhart: Barnhart Flea Market, 6850 Hwy 61 67. Tel: 314-464-5503.
Barnhart: Kohler City Flea Market, 7045 US Hwy 61 67. Tel: 314-464-2322.
Bernie: Downtown Flea Market, 107 E Main Ave. Tel: 573-293-4183.
Bertrand: Bertrand Flea Market, 412 Hwy 62 W. Tel: 573-683-6345.
Bolivar: Downtown Flea Market, 110 W Jackson St. Tel: 417-777-2288.
Bolivar: Hidden Treasures Flea Market, 3100 S Morrisville Rd. Tel: 417-326-4499.
Bolivar: Super Flea Market, 2869 W Broadway St. Tel: 417-326-6360.
Bourbon: Seller's Flea Market. Tel: 573-732-4106.
Bowling Green: 3-G Flea Market, North Business Hwy 61. Tel: 573-324-2929.
Branson: Branson Heights Flea Market, 1139 W 76 Country Blvd. Tel: 417-335-3165.
Branson: Cadwell's Downtown Flea Market, 114 Main St. Tel: 417-334-5051.

Branson: Crossroads Flea Market. Tel: 417-334-3220.

Branson: Finders Keepers Flea Market, 204 N Commercial St. Tel: 417-334-3248.

Branson: The Flea Bag Flea Market, 106 E Main St. Tel: 417-334-5242.

Branson: Fugitt's Trout Inn & Flea Market, Hwy 165. Tel: 417-337-8337.

Branson: Stacy's Flea Market, 2855 W 76 Country Blvd. Tel: 417-339-3573.

Brookline Station: Parakeet Flea Market, 5759 W US Hwy 60. Tel: 417-866-0785.

Buckner: Buckner Flea Market, 300 N Hudson St. Tel: 816-249-6588.

Buffalo: Polly's Flea Market Mall, N Hwy 65 & W Main. Tel: 417-345-5949.

Butler: 3 Mile Junction Flea Market, RR 4 Box 203-A. Tel: 417-679-6016 or 816-679-6016.

Cabool: Cabool Flea Market, 731 Roberts. Tel: 417-962-4258.

Camdenton: DB's Flea Market. Tel: 573-346-7515.

Camdenton: Greenview Auction & Flea Market. Tel: 573-873-0635.

Cape Girardeau: Doris Flea Market, 631 Good Hope St. Tel: 573-651-1665.

Carl Junction: Carl Junction Flea Market, 118 S Main St. Tel: 417-649-7131.

Carthage: Carthage Rt 66 Antique Mall & Flea Market, 1221 Oak St. Tel: 417-359-7240

Cassville: Deole Garage Antique Mall & Flea Market, Hwy 112. Tel: 417-847-5919.

Cassville: E & E Flea Market, RR 1. Tel: 417-847-5301.

Cassville: Highway 112 Flea Market, Hwy 112. Tel: 417-847-5778.

Cassville: Hilltop Flea Market. Tel: 417-847-3029.

Centertown: From the Heart Antiques & Flea Market, 1217 Monroe St. Tel: 573-584-9707.

Centralia: Classic Collectors Flea Market, 106 N Allen St. Tel: 573-682-5000.

Chaffee: E & B Flea Market, Hwy 77. Tel: 573-887-3700.

Clark: Vanhook's Antiques & Things Flea Market, 300 Main. Tel: 573-641-5038.

Climax Springs: L & M Flea Market, Hwy 7. Tel: 573-347-4211.

Clinton: C & J Flea Market & Antiques, 256 NW 131st Rd. Tel: 816-885-5558.

Clinton: Emporium Flea Mall, 126 N Washington St. Tel: 816-885-9285.

Clinton: K-Sarah Salon & Flea Market, 203 N Washington St. Tel: 816-885-9277.

Clinton: Tightwad Treasures Flea Market, 1093 S 7th St. Tel: 816-477-3630.

Clinton: Wagon Wheel Antique Mall & Flea Market, RR 2. Tel: 816-885-2733.

Columbia: Itchys Stop & Scratch Flea Market & Antiques, 1907 N Providence Rd. Tel: 573-443-8275.

Columbia: Little Itchy's Stop & Scratch Flea Market, 5170 N Oakland Gravel Rd. Tel: 573-886-8500.

Columbia: Paris Rd Flea Market, 1729 Paris Rd. Tel: 573-499-9920.

Crane: Another Darn Flea Market, 208 N Main. Tel: 417-723-5404.

Crane: Country Treasures Antiques & Flea Market, 209 Maud St. Tel: 417-723-5270.

Crane: Crane Creek Flea Market & Gifts, 223 Main. Tel: 417-723-5415.

Crocker: Bear Ridge Flea Market, 17984 Hwy 17. Tel: 573-736-5858.

Curryville: R & E Furniture & Flea Market. Tel: 573-324-5354.

De Soto: Redfield's Flea Market, 502 S Main St. Tel: 314-586-3456.

Dexter: Dexter Flea Market, 1570 W Business US Hwy 60. Tel: 573-624-6157.

Dexter: Old Timers Flea Market, Hwy 60 W. Tel: 573-624-8288.

Diamond: Diamond Flea Market. Tel: 417-325-6402.

Doniphan: Ripley County Flea Market, RR 1. Tel: 573-996-4573.

Eagle Rock: Ozark Family Antique Flea Mart Northside. Tel: 417-271-4705.

Eagle Rock: The Red Barn Flea Market. Tel: 417-271-4522.

Eldon: Al's 54 Flea Market & Boat Storage. Tel: 573-392-7113.

Eldon: Homeless Jewels Flea Market, 206 E 2nd St. Tel: 573-392-4541.

Eugene: Second Time Around Flea Market, RR 1. Tel: 573-498-6286.

Fair Grove: Old Mill Antique & Flea Market, Marin St. Tel: 417-759-2040.

Falcon: Falcon Flea Market, RR 1. Tel: 417-453-6250.

Farmington: Fairground Flea Market, Hwy 67. Tel: 573-756-1691.

Fredericktown: M & M Flea Market, Hwy O. Tel: 573-783-8474.

Fulton: Lumpy's Flea Market, 2990 N Bluff St. Tel: 573-642-7998.

Gladstone: KC Flea Market, 4141 N Oak Trfy. Tel: 816-452-1998.

Goodman: Ole Yeller Barn Flea Market, Hwy 71 North. Tel: 417-364-7227.

Granby: Granby Flea Market, Hwy 60. Tel: 417-472-3532.

Greenville: County Seat Flea Market. Tel: 573-224-3156.

Halltown: Dogwood Village & Flea Market, I-44 & Exit 58. Tel: 417-491-4838.

Harrisonville: Peddlers Flea Market, 1104-A S Commercial St. Tel: 816-884-4048.

Hazelwood: North County Flea Market & Auction House, 8780 Pershall Rd. Tel: 314-524-2405.

Hermitage: Hermitage Flea Market, W Hwy 54. Tel: 417-745-2200.

Hermitage: L & V's Klassi Flea Market, Hwy 54. Tel: 417-745-2314.

Highlandville: Eagles Nest Flea Market, 6922 US Hwy 160 S. Tel: 417-443-7710.

Holt: Days Past Flea Mall, I-35 Exit 33. Tel: 816-264-3115.

Houston: Echo Flea Market, Hwy 17 N. Tel: 417-967-2456.

Houston: Little Rock House Flea Market. Tel: 417-967-2488.

Imperial: Beck's Flea Market, 1595 Miller Rd. Tel: 314-464-4664.

Jefferson City: Andrew's Antiques Flea Market, 2615 Missouri Blvd. Tel: 573-659-5199.

Jefferson City: Van's Flea Market, 4931 Business 50 W. Tel: 573-761-4622.

Joplin: Connie's Antiques, Collectibles & Flea Market, 3421 N Rangeline Rd. Tel: 417-781-2602.

Joplin: Rusty Nail Flea Market, 3004 Silver Creek Rd. Tel: 417-624-7157.

Kansas City: Granny's Flea Mart, 9628 E 40 Hwy. Tel: 816-353-5046.

Kansas City: Midtown Flea Market, 3308 Troost Ave. Tel: 816-561-4777.

Kansas City: Old Westport Flea Market & Bar & Grill, 817 Westport Rd. Tel: 816-931-1986.

Kansas City: Troost 33 Flea Market, 3301 Troost Ave. Tel: 816-531-4516.

Kansas City: Waldo Flea Market, 224 W 75th St. Tel: 816-363-9938.

Kansas City: Westport Flea Market & Bar & Grill, 817 Westport Rd. Tel: 816-931-1986.

Kennett: Times Past Flea Market, 713 1st St. Tel: 573-888-4224..

Kimberling City: Joe Bald Flea Market, Joe Bald Rd. Tel: 417-739-5519.

Kirksville: Ron's Flea Market, 512 E Elson. Tel: 816-665-2502.

Kirksville: Square Deal Antique Mall & Flea Market, N Hwy 63. Tel: 816-665-1686.

Kirksville: Windmill Krafts & Flea Market, U S Hwy 63. Tel: 816-665-0100.

Lake Ozark: Fiesta Flea Market, Hwy 54. Tel: 573-302-0288.

Lake Ozark: Osage Beach Flea Market. Tel: 573-348-5454.

Lake Ozark: Village Flea Market, Poverty Flts. Tel: 573-348-5616.

Lamar: Oakton Flea Market. Tel: 417-682-3217.

Lamar: Treasure Seekers Antiques & Flea Market, 1015 Gulf St. Tel: 417-682-2900.

Laquey: Rt 66 Flea Market. Tel: 573-765-5323.

Laurie: Sam's Flea Mart, Hwy 5. Tel: 573-374-4101.

Lebanon: Annie's Flea Market, 204 W 2nd St. Tel: 417-532-2413.

Lockwood: The Crafty Flea, 708 Main. Tel: 417-232-5050.

Lowry City: J & L Flea Market, S Hwy 13. Tel: 417-644-2929.

Macon: Colonel Flea Market, 312 S Missouri St. Tel: 816-385-2497.

Macon: Huggy Bears Flea Market, 903 Hwy 63 S. Tel: 816-385-1333.

Macon: Wilcox Country Opry & Flea Market, Hwy 63 S. Tel: 816-385-2304.

Malden: Ronnie's Flea Market, PO Box 2. Tel: 573-276-3365.

Malden: This N That Flea Market, 132 S Madison St. Tel: 573-276-2166.

Mount Vernon: Doc's Pawn & Flea Market, Business Loop I-44. Tel: 417-466-4043.

Mountain View: East Side Flea Market, 220 W 1st St. Tel: 417-934-6997.

Mountain View: Mountain View Flea Market, 50 E 7th. Tel: 417-934-5505.

Mountain View: Renegar Flea Market & Used Furniture. Tel: 417-934-9051.

Neosho: South Elwood Flea Market, Rt 5. Tel: 417-451-5140.

Neosho: Vern's Flea Market, Alt Hwy 71. Tel: 417-451-9565.

Nevada: Nevada Flea Market. Tel: 417-667-7738.

Newburg: I-44 Flea Market. Tel: 573-762-3532.

New Madrid: New Madrid Flea Market, 420 Virginia Ave. Tel: 573-748-5947.

Nixa: Red Barn Flea Market, Hwy 14. Tel: 417-725-3338.

Novinger: Boon's Flea Market. Tel: 816-488-5581.

Oak Grove: Oak Grove Flea Market, 1120 N Broadway St. Tel: 816-625-8885.

Oak Grove: Oak Grove Flea Market, 1120 S Broadway St. Tel: 816-690-8885.

Oak Grove: Yesterday Treasures Flea Market, 1221 N Broadway St. Tel: 816-690-6265.

Osceola: Wisner's Flea Market & Antiques, Hwy 13 S. Tel: 417-646-8555.

Overland: Bel-Ridge Flea Market, 8943 Natura Bridge. Tel: 314-426-7848.

Ozark: Country Junction Flea Market, 205 E South St. Tel: 417-581-8116.

Ozark: Ozark Flea Market, S Town Ctr. Tel: 417-581-8544.

Ozark: Riverview Plaza Flea Mart, Riverview Plz. Tel: 417-581-3080.

Park Hills: Jose's Flea Market, 217 W Main St. Tel: 573-431-7002.

Park Hills: Rick's Flea Market, 211 W Main St. Tel: 573-431-9677.

Pineville: Pineville Flea Market. Tel: 417-223-7473.

Poplar Bluff: 5th St Flea Market, 1712 Missouri Ave. Tel: 573-686-5852.

Poplar Bluff: Jordan's Lake Rd Flea Market, County Rd 556. Tel: 573-686-4542.

Poplar Bluff: Memory Lane Antique Mall & Flea Market, Hwy 67 S. Tel: 573-785-7552.

Poplar Bluff: Mid-America Flea Market, 510 Henderson Ave. Tel: 573-785-8935.

Poplar Bluff: Southtown Trade Fair & Flea Market, Hwy 67 S. Tel: 573-785-9864.

Poplar Bluff: Westwood-A Flea Market, Hwy 67 N. Tel: 573-686-3184.

Potosi: Washington County Auction & Flea Market. Tel: 573-438-7191.

Republic: West County Flea Market, 336 N US Hwy 60. Tel: 417-732-8415.

Rockaway Beach: Malloy's Treasure Trove Flea Market, 2796 Beach Blvd. Tel: 417-561-4232.

Rocky Comfort: Rocky Comfort Flea Market, PO Box 65. Tel: 417-652-3681.

Rolla: Jenny's Antiques & Flea Market, 612 Lanning Ln. Tel: 573-364-7911.

Rutledge: Colony Flea Market. Tel: 816-434-5504.

Saint Elizabeth: Schell Trading Co & Flea Market. Tel: 573-493-2502.

Saint Louis: Frison Indoor Flea Market Inc, 7025 St Charles Rock Rd. Tel: 314-727-0460 or 314-727-4479.

Salem: Nina's Antique & Flea Market, Hwy 72 N. Tel: 573-729-2958.

Seligman: Hwy 37 Flea Market, Hwy 37. Tel: 417-662-3890.

Seligman: Tom's Flea Market, Hwy 37. Tel: 417-662-3205.

Seymour: Duck Pond Antiques & Flea Market, Old Hwy 60. Tel: 417-935-4027.

Springfield: Attic Flea Market, 1451 E Pythian St. Tel: 417-272-3072.

Springfield: Charlie's Flea Market, 718 S Scenic Ave. Tel: 417-865-5711.

Springfield: Classic Flea Market, 1701 S Campbell Ave. Tel: 417-863-7770.

Springfield: Country Corner Flea Market, 351 N Boonville Ave. Tel: 417-862-1597.

Springfield: Discount Flea Market, 819 W Commercial St. Tel: 417-873-9803.

Springfield: Downtowner Flea Market, 507 N Boonville Ave. Tel: 417-866-6259.

Springfield: Ferguson Flea Market, Rt 2. Tel: 417-863-6699.

Springfield: Kountry Korner Flea Market, 1917 W Atlantic St. Tel: 417-865-9510.

Springfield: Old Spring Flea Market, Main St. Tel: 417-272-3173.

Springfield: Park Central Flea Market, 429 N Boonville Ave. Tel: 417-831-7516.

Springfield: Scenic Hill Flea Market, 605 S Scenic Ave. Tel: 417-865-1800.

Springfield: S TD Storage & Flea Market, 1820 E Trafficway St. Tel: 417-831-6367.

Springfield: S TD Storage & Flea Market, 651 S Kansas. Tel: 417-831-6331.

Springfield: Viking Storage & Flea Market, 628 W Chase St. Tel: 417-869-7075.

Stockton: G & G Antique Flea Market, 800 South St. Tel: 417-276-4419.

Sullivan: Attic Flea Market, 24 Taylor St. Tel: 573-468-5800.

Sullivan: Missouri Ave Flea Market, 619 Missouri Ave. Tel: 573-468-4304.

Summersville: Little T Auction & Flea Market, Hwy 17. Tel: 417-932-6613.

Sweet Springs: B & N Brickstreet Flea Market, 315 A S Miller. Tel: 816-335-6551.

Tuscumbia: WW Flea Market. Tel: 573-369-0044.

Union: Mason Dixon Line Flea Market, I-44 & 50. Tel: 314-583-2014.

Van Buren: Riverways Flea Market. Tel: 573-323-8628.

Walnut Grove: Cat's Eye Flea Market. Tel: 417-788-2939.

Wappapello: American Way Flea Market, RR 1. Tel: 573-222-8432.

Wappapello: York Village Flea Market, PO Box 50. Tel: 573-297-3226.

Warrenton: West End Flea Market, 548 Progress Pkwy. Tel: 314-456-4641.

Warsaw: Knight's Flea Market, 325 E Main St. Tel: 816-438-7313.

Warsaw: Riverside Flea Market, 303 Seminary. Tel: 816-438-6512.

Warsaw: Wagon Master Flea Market, HC 66. Tel: 816-438-2639.

Wellsville: The Flea Market, 101 N 1st St. Tel: 573-684-3223.

West Plains: Donlo's Flea Mart, Hwy 160. Tel: 417-256-7586.

West Plains: Grandpa's Flea Mart, W 160 Hwy. Tel: 417-257-1472.

West Plains: Jefferson St Flea Market, 310 Jefferson Ave. Tel: 417-256-4788.

West Plains: Old Time Flea Market Mall, 601 Washington Ave. Tel: 417-256-3322.

Wheatland: Memories & More Flea Market, RR 2. Tel: 417-282-5707.

Willow Springs: Ozark Peddler Flea Market, 120 E Main St #122. Tel: 417-469-2746.

Willow Springs: Pomona Flea Market & Dealer Auction. Tel: 417-469-4602.

Winona: Stein's Flea Market, 200 Ash. Tel: 573-325-8271.

MONTANA

GREAT FALLS

Great Falls Farmer's Market

DATES: Every Saturday and Wednesday, from the first Saturday in June through the first Saturday in October.
TIMES: Wednesday 4:30 AM–6:00 PM; Saturday 8:00 AM–12:00 PM.
ADMISSION: Free. Ample free parking is available.
LOCATION: At the Civic Center.
DESCRIPTION: This outdoor market hosts about 75 dealers and has been running for 17 years. This traditional farmer's market also features local crafts alongside the traditional meat, dairy, produce and baked goods of local farmers. There is food served on the premises. They have about 2,500 visitors per day.
DEALER RATES: $2 minimum or 10% commission up to $30 maximum per 8' × 10' space. Show up and sell.
CONTACT: Michael Winters, Great Falls Farmer's Market, 2405 6th St NW, Great Falls MT 59401. Tel: (406) 761-3881.

OTHER FLEA MARKETS

We know or have heard about this market, but have not personally contacted it, as we have the markets with descriptions. If you plan to visit the market listed below, *please call first* to make sure they are still open. Flea markets do come and go. While they were open when we went to press, they may not be later. We can't be responsible. *Call first!*

Laurel: Blue Bell Antiques & Flea Market, 210 E Main St. Tel: 406-628-2002.

NEBRASKA

BROWNVILLE

Spring Flea Market/Fall Flea Market

DATES: Spring: Memorial Day weekend, Friday through Monday. Fall: Last full weekend in September, Saturday and Sunday.
TIMES: 8:00 AM–5:00 PM.
ADMISSION: Free. Parking is free.
LOCATION: Main Street. From I-29, exit for Hwy 136, 5 miles to Brownville. Only 70 miles south of Omaha, 80 miles from Topeka or Kansas City. Brownville is next to the Missouri River.
DESCRIPTION: Started in 1957 as a fundraiser for the Town of Brownville to preserve its heritage, this market increases the town population of 148 to 10,000 on market days. Their 260 dealers sell mostly antiques, collectibles, attic finds, some crafts and new merchandise. Several food concessions aid and abet the hungry. Restrooms are available.
DEALER RATES: $30 for 22' × 15' space for each event. Reservations are recommended.
CONTACT: The Head Flea, Brownville Historical Society, PO Box 1, Brownville NE 68321-0001. Tel: (402) 825-6001 or 825-4751 (Zac Vice, current Head Flea).

Brownville, the oldest town in Nebraska (founded in 1854) and located on the Missouri River, was a starting point for immigrants on the Oregon Trail. Wagons would gather, up to 176 at a time, to await a leader to take them out west. In its heyday, 30 packet boats a day would unload their supplies for the wagon trains and later the Denver Gold Rushers in their quests for new lands and riches. The population would grow to 5,000 until the wagons left, then it shrank until the next train formed.

Most of the town is registered on the National Historic Register and was recently included as one of 25 towns in a book on Historic Towns in America. An excursion boat still operates from spring until mid-summer. To top all this off, think of Brownville along with "sister cities" San Francisco and Rome—all are built on seven hills.

LINCOLN

Pershing Auditorium Flea Market

DATES: Saturday and Sunday. Held monthly, dates vary.
TIMES: 10:00 AM–5:00 PM.
ADMISSION: $.75 per person, children under 12 free. $1–$2 parking fee at various commercial garages or metered parking on the street.
LOCATION: Pershing Auditorium, lower level. 226 Centennial Mall South, at 15th and N in downtown Lincoln, 2 blocks north of state capitol.
DESCRIPTION: This show opened in 1978 and has grown from a small market of 25 booths to one of full capacity accommodating 80 dealers from a five-state area. It is an indoor market selling antiques, collectibles and new merchandise. Food is served on the premises.
DEALER RATES: $45 per 8' × 13' space; $62 per 8' × 21' space; $80 per 8' × 29' space. Rates include both Saturday and Sunday. Reservations are required. Rates include 8' tables and folding chairs.
CONTACT: Derek Andersen, PO Box 81126, Lincoln NE 68508-1126. Tel: (402) 441-8744. Website: www.interlinc.ci.lincoln.ne.us. Email: andersen@inetnebr.com.

YORK

Lions Club Antique and Flea Market

DATES: April 5, 1998. Watch for 1999 around the same time—usually before Easter.
TIMES: 9:00 AM–5:00 PM.
ADMISSION: Free. Parking is free.
LOCATION: York City Auditorium at the corner of 6th and Nebraska.
DESCRIPTION: For 16 years this market has been the main fundraiser of the York Lions Club. Their 65 dealers sell all types of goods, from standard flea market fare to loads of antiques and collectibles and some crafts.
DEALER RATES: $32–$35 for upstairs level and $20–$22 for downstairs level. There is an elevator to get downstairs and the Lions Club members are there to help load and unload the treasures. Reservations are most necessary.
CONTACT: Gene Mulinix, York Lions Club Flea Market, 137 S Michigan, York NB 68467. Tel: (402) 362-3593 (Gene's home) or (402) 362-4040 (business).

OTHER FLEA MARKETS

We know or have heard about these markets, but have not personally contacted each one, as we have the markets with descriptions. If you plan to visit one of these markets listed below, *please call first* to make sure they are still open. Flea markets do come and go. While they were open when we went to press, they may not be later. We can't be responsible. *Call first!*

Lincoln: Cornhusker Mall Antiques & Flea Market, 2120 Cornhusker Hwy. Tel: 402-438-5122.

Lincoln: Indian Village Flea Market Emporium, 3235 S 13th St. Tel: 402-423-5380.

Minden: Minden Flea Market & Antiques, 515 N Minden Ave. Tel: 308-832-0844.

North Platte: Antique Mini Mall & Flea Market, 507 N Jeffers St. Tel: 308-534-8476.

North Platte: RJ Flea Market, RR 1. Tel: 308-534-0138.

Omaha: Blue Ribbon Flea Market & Antique Mall, 6606 Grover St. Tel: 402-397-6811.

Schuyler: Schuyler Flea Market, 218 E 12th St. Tel: 402-352-3164.

Scottsbluff: Scottsbluff Flea Market, 624 W 20th St. Tel: 308-632-1933.

Walthill: Nottelman Flea Market. Tel: 402-846-9150.

York: I-80-81 Antiques & Flea Market, 1120 S Lincoln Ave. Tel: 402-362-1975.

NEVADA

LAS VEGAS

Fantastic Indoor Swap Meet

DATES: Friday, Saturday and Sunday, year round. Also open daily from December 15 to Christmas.
TIMES: 10:00 AM–6:00 PM.
ADMISSION: $1. Parking is free on 15 acres.
LOCATION: 1717 South Decatur at Oakey Blvd.
DESCRIPTION: Opened in 1990, this huge market (3½ acres under one roof) has 350 dealers in 600 booths selling all new merchandise, crafts, "the most wonderful things" from satellite dishes to more usual fare. There are four restaurants selling a variety of ethnic fare, ice cream, popcorn, hot dogs and food.
DEALER RATES: From $350 and up for 4 weeks. Advance reservations are required as there is a two-week waiting period to get a city license. All sellers must have a state tax permit. Office hours: Thursday 8:30 AM–5:00 PM.
CONTACT: Berny Krebs, Fantastic Indoor Swap Meet, 1717 S Decatur, Las Vegas NV 89102. Tel: (702) 877-0087 or fax: (702) 877-3102.

NORTH LAS VEGAS

Broadacres Open-Air Swap Meet

DATES: Friday, Saturday, and Sunday, year round, rain or shine.
TIMES: 6:30 AM to whenever.
ADMISSION: $.50 on Friday, otherwise $1 per person weekends, children under 12 free.
LOCATION: 2960 Las Vegas Blvd, Las Vegas Blvd North at Pecos. Four miles north of the Union Plaza Hotel on Las Vegas Blvd North.
DESCRIPTION: Opened in November 1977, this outdoor market is in its 21st year of business. Their 700 dealers in the summer attract 18,000 buyers weekly, and 1,000 dealers attract 25,000 buyers during the winter months. Antiques, collectibles, tools, toys, crafts, produce, and new merchandise are available. There are plenty of shade trees and, when necessary, clean restrooms.
DEALER RATES: The charge for a booth measuring 15' × 30' is $15 on Saturday and Sunday and $8 on Friday. Advance reservations are suggested at least three weeks in advance. Make your reservations during business

hours. They have 700 reserved spaces and only 300 daily unreserved spaces. Office hours: Friday 6:30 AM–12:30 PM, weekends 6:30 AM–2:00 PM.
CONTACT: Jake Bowman, Broadacres Open-Air Swap Meet, PO Box 3059, N Las Vegas NV 89030-3059. Tel: (702) 642-3777.

SPARKS

El Rancho Flea Market

DATES: Saturdays and Sundays, year round, weather permitting.
TIMES: Summer from 6:00 AM–4:30 PM: winter from 6:00 AM–whenever.
ADMISSION: $.50 per person; children under 12 free, includes parking.
LOCATION: 555 El Rancho Dr at the El Rancho Drive-In Theater. Off I-80 at the "B" St exit, go east 2 blocks on Prater then 2 blocks north on El Rancho Dr, turn left on G St. If you are on El Rancho Dr, you can't miss them, they are next to Paradise Park.
DESCRIPTION: Located in Sparks, well known for gambling casinos, near Lake Tahoe. Twin city to Reno. Opened in 1978, this outdoor flea market attracts 200–250 dealers selling antiques, collectibles, fresh produce, new merchandise, and garage sale items. There are plenty of food carts roaming the market, a beer garden (they do card you) and handicapped-accessible restrooms.
DEALER RATES: $16 for booths measuring 10' × 30'; there are other sizes, call for rates. Reservations are not required; first come, first served. Although some space is reserved until 8:00 AM.
CONTACT: Lance Edwards, El Rancho Swap, 555 El Rancho Dr, Sparks NV 89431. Tel: (702) 331-3227. Fax: (702) 359-2833.

OTHER FLEA MARKETS

We know or have heard about these markets, but have not personally contacted each one, as we have the markets with descriptions. If you plan to visit one of these markets listed below, *please call first* to make sure they are still open. Flea markets do come and go. While they were open when we went to press, they may not be later. We can't be responsible. *Call first!*

Fernley: Fernley Flea Mart, 825 Mesa Dr. Tel: 702-575-4445.
Sun Valley: Pack Rat Flea Market, 5520 Sun Valley Blvd. Tel: 702-674-6179.

NEW HAMPSHIRE

DERRY

Grand View Flea Market

DATES: Saturday and Sunday, year round. Rain or shine.
TIMES: Saturday 9:00 AM–3:00 PM, Sunday 7:00 AM–4:00 PM.
ADMISSION: Sunday only: $.50 for adults; children under 12 free.
LOCATION: At the Junction of Rt 28 and Bypass 28 South.
DESCRIPTION: This show, established more than 30 years ago, is one of northern New England's first and finest. In the center of the market is a pond with a 30-foot-tall Indian totem pole. It also has a strange collection of statuary including two very large elephants, a bear, and several genies purchased from a old amusement park. Two hundred to 400 dealers work indoors and out, selling all sorts of antiques, collectibles, crystals, books, novelties, jewelry, gifts, appliances, fabric and lace, new and used furniture, handmades, and new items. A new addition was added in the fall of 1990 increasing the indoor market by 60 spaces, then another 24,000 square feet was added in 1993. This is an interesting market always trying new things—like magic shows to amuse the children. Chinese and American food is available on the premises. A golf range is next door.
DEALER RATES: $25 per 12' x 8' space indoors per day including 3 tables Sundays, Saturdays are $10; $20 per "large car length" space outdoors per day. Tables are available for rental at $1.50 per day. Reservations are not required.
CONTACT: Kathi Taylor, 34 S Main St, Derry NH 03086. Tel: (603) 432-2326.

HOLLIS

Hollis Country Store and Flea Market

DATES: Every Sunday, first Sunday of April through the second Sunday of November; plus Memorial Day and Labor Day.
TIMES: 7:00 AM–dusk.
ADMISSION: Free. $1 parking fee.
LOCATION: On Silver Lake Rd (Rt 122). Take Exit 7W off Rt 3 (in Nashua) to 101A west. Go 8 miles, then turn left onto Rt 122S. Market is 2½ miles on the right.

DESCRIPTION: Opened in 1965, this outdoor market now attracts over 250 dealers selling antiques and collectibles as well as new merchandise and fresh produce. This is a well-attended, busy market, attracting dealers and customers from all over New England and as far away as California. They have an excellent reputation for quality goods at reasonable prices. Food is served on the premises.
DEALER RATES: $16 per 15' x 20' space. Reservations are preferred.
CONTACT: Gil and Alice Prieto, 436 Silver Lake Rd, Hollis NH 03049. Tel: (603) 465-7813.

This'll Get'em Department:
A woman brought in a trailer with a shed on it loaded with over $10,000 worth of power tools—and sold it all for $10. She was divorcing her husband.

LEBANON

Colonial Antiques & Flea Market

DATES: Daily indoors, Sundays outdoors, weather permitting.
TIMES: 9:00 AM–5:00 PM. However, Sundays during the dark months the whole market opens at 8:00 AM; and during the light months they open at 6:00 AM.
ADMISSION: Free. Parking is free.
LOCATION: Rt 12A at Exit 20 off I-89.
DESCRIPTION: Opened in 1976 and under new management since mid-June 1995, this market's over 90 dealers sell antiques, collectibles, estate jewelry, furniture, old books, old clothes, dolls, old tools, postcards, stamps, fine glassware, paintings, bottles, crafts and much more. Many of their dealers are recognized authorities in their field. There are "loads of fine treasures, a bargain hunters paradise," with fine smalls and rare prints among other found prizes. This market strives for the finest quality available. They have a reputation as the "first and oldest and funnest market in New England."
DEALER RATES: $27.50 for about 7' x 10' space weekly inside. Outdoors is $12 for 2 parking spaces. Reservations are mandatory for inside as there is a waiting list. No reservations for the outside space.
CONTACT: Andy Anderson, Colonial Plaza Antiques and Flea Market, Route 12A, West Lebanon NH 03784. Tel: (603) 298-7712 or 298-8132.

Okay, I Believe That Department:

A woman came in looking for a Christmas present for her doctor husband and "hit" on a 1820 anatomy book published in Edinburgh, Scotland. She leafed through the pages with their copper-plate pictures and found a handsome adult male skeleton. Obviously intrigued she asked, "Who is this?" The dealer, without hesitation, replied, "George Washington." That didn't faze her. Then she happened upon another skeleton picture of an infant. "Who's this?" she asked. Again, without a blink, the dealer replied, "George Washington—as an infant."

She didn't buy the book.

MEREDITH

Burlwood Antique Center

DATES: Daily, May 1–October 31.
TIMES: 10:00 AM–5:00 PM.
ADMISSION: Free. Free parking is available.
LOCATION: On Rt 3. From I-93, take Exit 23, then go east on Rt 104, 9 miles to Rt 3, then turn right to get to Burlwood Antique Center.
DESCRIPTION: This indoor market opened in 1983 and currently accommodates over 170 dealers. There is a variety of antiques and collectibles sold and an entire floor of furniture. Fine art is also available. Because they are open only six months a year, all the merchandise is fresh each year.
DEALER RATES: $100 per 5' x 3' x 8' space per month. Reservations are required.
CONTACT: Thomas and Nancy Lindsey, 106 Daniel Webster Hwy, Meredith NH 03253. Tel: (603) 279-6387.

OTHER FLEA MARKETS

We know or have heard about these markets, but have not personally contacted each one, as we have the markets with descriptions. If you plan to visit one of these markets listed below, *please call first* to make sure they are still open. Flea markets do come and go. While they were open when we went to press, they may not be later. We can't be responsible. *Call first!*

Claremont: The Weekly Flea. Tel: 603-542-5904.
Contoocook: Davisville Barn Sale & Flea Market, Rt 103. Tel: 603-746-4000.
Hollis: Brad & Donna's Super Duper Flea Market, 447 Silver Lake Rd. Tel: 603-465-7677.
Laconia: Lakes Region Flea Market & Antiques Exchange, 38 Pearl St. Tel: 603-524-2441.
Nashua: Londonderry Gardens Flea Market & Crafts, 300 Main St. Tel: 603-880-9935.
Pelham: Pelham Flea Market, Bridge St. Tel: 603-635-1033.
Pittsfield: Jim's Flea Market, Dover Rd. Tel: 603-798-5603.
Salem: Salem NH Flea Market Inc, 1820 Hampshire Rd. Tel: 603-893-8888.

NEW JERSEY

ABSECON HIGHLANDS

L'Erario's Flea Market

DATES: Every Saturday and Sunday, weather permitting.
TIMES: 7:00 AM–whenever.
ADMISSION: Free. Free parking is available.
LOCATION: At intersection of Jim Leeds Rd and Pitney Rd, Absecon-Highlands Rt 561. Only minutes from Atlantic City.
DESCRIPTION: This outdoor market began in 1968 and currently accommodates approximately 50 to 80 dealers selling anything from antiques, arts and crafts, and collectibles to new and used merchandise. There are three snack bars and restaurants on the premises.
DEALER RATES: $15 Saturdays; $18 Sundays per 10' × 20' space plus vehicle. Reservations are not required. Bring your own table.
CONTACT: L'Erario's, PO Box 572, Absecon NJ 08201-0572. Tel: (609) 652-0540.

BELVIDERE

Five Acres

DATES: Every Saturday and Sunday, year round and holidays.
TIMES: 8:00 AM until everyone is gone.
ADMISSION: Free. Parking is also free.
LOCATION: On Rt 80, take Exit 12 south to Rt 46, go east 1,500 feet. Market is on right.
DESCRIPTION: This outdoor flea market opened in 1965. There are between 75 and 100 dealers selling anything from antiques and collectibles to arts, crafts and new merchandise. Fresh produce is also available. There are clean restrooms, a game room and a bar on premises. They are planning to open a small antiques mall in 1998.
DEALER RATES: $15 per 10' × 20' space on Sunday, $10 on Saturday. Reservations are not required. If interested in selling in the new antique building, contact Totsy.
CONTACT: Totsy Phillips, PO Box 295, Belvidere NJ 07823-0295. Tel: (908) 475-2572.

BERLIN

Berlin Farmers Market

DATES: Thursday, Friday, Saturday and Sunday, rain or shine.
TIMES: 8:00 AM–4:00 PM outside flea market, Saturday and Sunday only, weather permitting. Farmer's Market Thursday-Friday 11:00 AM–9:30 PM; Saturday 10:00 AM–9:30 PM; Sunday 10:00 AM–6:00 PM inside.
ADMISSION: Free. Free parking is available.
LOCATION: 41 Clementon Rd. Just off Rt 30, Rt 73 or Rt 42 about 40 minutes from either Atlantic City or Philadelphia.
DESCRIPTION: This market started in 1930 as a livestock auction. Today it is located on about 60 acres of land. These spacious accommodations house the outdoor flea market and parking lot. The indoor shopping market is in a building a ¼ mile long. Between their indoor and outdoor market, on any given weekend there are anywhere from 700 to 800 dealers. The types of merchandise to be found are unlimited: from antiques to new merchandise, from quality new and used furniture, from arts and crafts to fresh produce. Seen and sold: clothing of all kinds, gold stuff, toys, tools, hardware, health & beauty aids, furniture, sports cards, video games and tapes, etc. Once a customer brought in a house on a trailer—and sold it! There are two snack bars and three other food vendors inside, and eight food vendors outside. This flea market is proudly owned and operated by the third generation of the Giberson family.
DEALER RATES: For flea market vendors: $20 per 12' × 30' booth–for strictly used merchandise for 2 days ($15 for one day); $35 per 12' × 30' booth for all new merchandise. Reservations are suggested. Office is open Thursday and Friday.
CONTACT: Stan Giberson, Jr or Ron Smith, 41 Clementon Rd, Berlin NJ 08009. Tel: (609) 767-1284.

CLIFTON

Boys' and Girls' Club of Clifton Flea Market

DATES: Third Sunday of every month year round; additionally there are other shows throughout the year. Call for more information on those.
TIMES: 8:00 AM–4:00 PM.
ADMISSION: Free admission and free parking available.
LOCATION: 802 Clifton Ave at the Boys' and Girls' Club.
DESCRIPTION: This annual indoor event has been taking place for 25 years with 85 to 100 dealers selling antiques, collectibles, new merchan-

dise, and craft items. This show is used as a fundraiser for the 1,500 children who use the Club. One snack bar and handicapped-accessible restrooms add to the amenities.
DEALER RATES: $20 for the first 8' × 4' table, $10 each additional table. Reservations are required.
CONTACT: Joe and Arlene Jiuliani, 46 Potomac Ave, Paterson NJ 07503-1604. Tel/fax: (201) 977-8134.

COLUMBUS

Columbus Farmer's Market

DATES: Every Thursday, Friday, Saturday and Sunday, rain or shine.
TIMES: Inside hours: Thursday and Saturday 8:00 AM–8:00 PM; Friday 10:00 AM–8:00 PM; Sunday 8:00 AM–5:00 PM. Outside hours: Thursday, Saturday and Sunday, dawn to whenever!
ADMISSION: Free. Free parking is available.
LOCATION: On Rt 206, 5 miles south of Exit 7 off the New Jersey Turnpike.
DESCRIPTION: This outdoor market began in 1929. This indoor/outdoor market accommodates from 400 dealers in winter to 1,700 dealers in summer, selling antiques and collectibles as well as new merchandise and fresh produce. There are 70 permanent stores including seven restaurants, monogramming, shoe repair, sewing machine repair, a Chinese food shop and all types of specialty shops. Food is served on the premises.
DEALER RATES: Thursday $30 per 12' × 30' space; Saturday $10; Sunday $30 per 12' × 30' booth—new items, $15 per 12' × 30' booth—used items. Reservations are not required; spaces are assigned by the management.
CONTACT: Columbus Farmers Market, 2919 Rt 206 S, Columbus NJ 08022-0322. Tel: (609) 267-0400.

DORCHESTER

Campbell's Flea Market

DATES: Saturday and Sunday, March through December, rain or shine.
TIMES: 7:00 AM–5:00 PM.
ADMISSION: Free. Parking is also free.
LOCATION: Three miles south on Rt 47 from Rt 55.
DESCRIPTION: This market opened in 1961 on six acres of century-old trees providing plenty of shade. Route 47 is the major highway to the beaches

making this a terrific spot to attract buyers. Sixty dealers inside and 80 outside sell antiques and crafts to attic treasures, collectibles, glassware, aluminum, and flea market fare. This is a market where social time among dealers and customers is common. Rare finds are still out here. Food is available on the premises. A Texaco station, ice cream parlor and deli are next door.
DEALER RATES: $10 per table inside; outside $10. Reservations are not required.
CONTACT: Terri Campbell, PO Box 131, Dorchester NJ 08316. Tel: (609) 785-2222.

EDISON

New Dover United Methodist Church Flea Market

DATES: Every Tuesday, mid-March through December. Rain or shine.
TIMES: 7:00 AM–1:00 PM.
ADMISSION: Free. Free parking is available.
LOCATION: 687 New Dover Rd. Take Exit 131 on Garden State Parkway, bear right, go to first light (Wood Ave), turn right, go to second light (New Dover Rd), finally, turn left.
DESCRIPTION: This indoor/outdoor market began in 1971. Since that time it has grown to accommodate approximately 60 dealers during summer months. Many items such as collectibles, new merchandise, and fresh produce can be purchased. This market is a fundraiser for the church. There are two security guards on the premises. Restrooms are available. The church kitchen, run by volunteers, sells hot homemade food.
DEALER RATES: $20 per table, bring your own table; tables on the inside and front parking lot are rented on monthly basis only. Reservations are required for monthly.
CONTACT: New Dover United Methodist Church, 687 New Dover Rd, Edison NJ 08820. Tel: (908) 381-7904.

ENGLISHTOWN

Englishtown Auction Sales Flea Market

DATES: Saturday and Sunday, year round; also open Good Friday, Labor Day, Columbus Day and Friday after Thanksgiving.
TIMES: Saturday 7:00 AM–4:00 PM; Sundays and holidays 9:00 AM–4:00 PM.
ADMISSION: Free, with free parking available.

LOCATION: 90 Wilson Ave; New Jersey Turnpike Exit 9; access from Rt 18 S and Rt 527 S.
DESCRIPTION: Since 1929 this market has been known as "shopping at its best for the entire family." This combination indoor/outdoor show is held in five buildings and on 40 acres of outside dealer space. Their hundreds of dealers sell antiques and collectibles, jewelry, hubcaps, clothing, housewares, furniture, as well as new merchandise. Food items are restricted, but three food courts and an air-conditioned tavern as well as handicapped-accessible restrooms add to the amenities.
DEALER RATES: Spaces start at $5 a day. Monthly reservations are suggested.
CONTACT: Manager, Englishtown Auction Sales, 90 Wilson Ave, Englishtown NJ 07726. Tel: (732) 446-9644. Fax: (732) 446-1220. Email: englishtwn@aol.com. Website: www.englishtownauction.com.

FLEMINGTON

The Flemington Fair Flea Market

DATES: Every Wednesday, April through November. Rain or shine.
TIMES: 6:00 AM–4:00 PM.
ADMISSION: Free. Free parking is available.
LOCATION: On Hwy 31, 22 miles north of Trenton; 18 miles north of New Hope, Pennsylvania; 30 miles southeast of eastern Pennsylvania; 45 miles west of New York City.
DESCRIPTION: Started in 1980, this market now accommodates anywhere from 75 to 120 dealers outdoors as well as 16 indoor shops. Although the majority of vendors sell antiques and collectibles, fine art, arts and crafts, new merchandise, plants, clothing, fresh produce and everything under the sun can be found. Besides the many things you can buy here, there are events for children including an Easter contest and a costume contest. The town of Flemington has hundreds of outlet stores. Situated in the beautiful, historic country setting of the Flemington Fairgrounds, this can be a fun day for the entire family!
DEALER RATES: $6 per 8' × 20' space outdoors; $500 per season per 10' × 12' indoor shop which includes 10' × 30' outdoors. Reservations are required for indoor space only. Vendors set up at 6:00 AM on Wednesday.
CONTACT: Melissa L Yerkes, 25 Kuhl Rd, Flemington NJ 08822. Tel: (908) 782-7326 after 5:00 PM. Day of show call main office at (908) 782-2413.

GILLETTE

Meyersville Grange Antique Flea Mart

DATES: Every Sunday, October through April.

TIMES: 8:00 AM–2:00 PM.

ADMISSION: Free. Free parking is available.

LOCATION: On Meyersville Rd, between Rt 78 and Rt 24, in the heart of the Great Swamp Wildlife Preserve, in southeast Morris County.

DESCRIPTION: This market started in 1970 in the Grange building, which was built in the early 1900s in the middle of a swamp. Approximately 35 dealers specialize in antiques, collectibles and handmade craft items. Free coffee is served to all customers, and vendors can get free doughnuts while they set up. From 10:00 AM–2:00 PM, hot dogs, homemade soup, and pastries are served.

DEALER RATES: $15–$25 per 8' table, per day. Reservations are required and can be made any evening after 6:00 PM.

CONTACT: Danny Goldstein, PO Box 238, Fanwood NJ 07023-0238. Tel: (908) 654-3089. Day of show call (908) 647-9727.

JEFFERSON

Jefferson Township Fire Company #2 Flea Market

DATES: Saturday from April through October.

TIMES: 6:30 AM to whenever.

ADMISSION: Free. Parking is free.

LOCATION: Rt 15 South, across from the Pathmark. Take I-80 West to Exit 34B (Rt 15 North), go down 3 traffic lights. Go down Pathmark ramp and cut across through Pathmark.

DESCRIPTION: Opened seven or eight years ago as a fundraiser for the Fire Department, this market of 30–50 dealers sells antiques, collectibles, crafts, produce in season, trading cards, t-shirts and sweats, whatever comes in. The Fire Department runs the food concession.

DEALER RATES: $15 for a "oh, car-sized-wide" space daily, $60 monthly, or $338 for a full season. Reservations are suggested and appreciated.

CONTACT: Jefferson Township Fire Company, PO Box 5, Lake Hopatcong NJ 07849-0005. Tel: (201) 663-5810.

LAMBERTVILLE

Golden Nugget Antique Flea Market

DATES: Every Wednesday, Saturday and Sunday outdoors, year round. Indoor shops are open on weekends. Rain or shine.

TIMES: Outdoors: 6:30 AM–5:00 PM; indoors 8:30 AM–4:00 PM.

ADMISSION: Free. Parking is $1 on Sundays, otherwise free.

LOCATION: Rt 29, 2 miles south of Lambertville, 5 miles north of Exit 1 on I-95.

DESCRIPTION: This indoor/outdoor market began its operation in 1960 and currently accommodates 43 indoor shops and 200 tables outdoors. The main building offers 15,000 square feet of space and is air-conditioned for use year round. Dealers offer antiques and collectibles such as furniture, glassware and porcelain, craft items, and new merchandise. Friday evenings, weather permitting, they hold tailgate auctions. Food is served on the premises. This market is located within a few miles of several historic sites: Washington Crossing, New Hope-Lahaska and Lambertville.

DEALER RATES: $5 for a 8' × 3' table on Wednesday, $12 on Saturday, $20 on Sunday. Reservations are required for Sunday, recommended for Saturday. Please reserve in person.

CONTACT: Tony Rizzello, Manager, Golden Nugget Antique Flea Market, 1850 River Rd, Lambertville NJ 08530. Tel: (609) 397-0811.

> In September 1997, Dan Rather for *CBS Eye on America* filmed a segment on a falcon figurine sold at the market in 1990. Unusual about the falcon, it had the initials "WB" on the bottom. The purchaser believes it is the figurine used as a prop in the Humphrey Bogart film *Maltese Falcon* filmed by Warner Bros. If true, then the falcon, purchased for $8, has been estimated to be worth $400,000. Oh, what a return on investment!

Lambertville Antique Flea Market, Inc

DATES: Outdoors: every Wednesday, Saturday and Sunday, rain or shine. Indoors: Wednesday through Sunday.

TIMES: Outdoors: 6:00 AM–4:00 PM. Indoors: Wednesday through Friday 10:00 AM–4:00 PM, weekends 8:00 AM–4:00 PM.

ADMISSION: Free. Free parking is available.

LOCATION: On Rt 29, 1½ miles south of Lambertville, along the Delaware River.

DESCRIPTION: Opened in 1967, this is both an indoor and outdoor market with a pavilion covering for 56 of its spaces outside. In total, there are close to 150 dealers who attend selling strictly antiques and collectibles. Although they do not specialize in one type of item, there is a wonderful assortment of items on display. This market was listed in *Good Housekeeping* as one of the 25 best antique markets in the United States. Indoors there are 68 showcases of antiques, and three buildings with five individual dealers selling only antiques and collectibles. The country kitchen serves homemade specials and handicapped-accessible restrooms add to the amenities.
DEALER RATES: Wednesdays $10 for a two-table space under the pavilion, or $6 for a 2-table setup outside. Sundays $46 for a two-table space under the pavilion and $38 outside; Saturday $30 under the pavilion; $24 outside. Reservations for Sunday and Saturday pavilion area are required.
CONTACT: Heidi and Tom Cekoric, 1864 River Rd, Lambertville NJ 08530. Tel: (609) 397-0456.

MANAHAWKIN

Manahawkin Flea Mart

DATES: Friday, Saturday, and Sunday, year round.
TIMES: 9:00 AM–5:00 PM.
ADMISSION: Free. Parking is also free.
LOCATION: 657 East Bay Avenue, off Rt 9. Take Garden State Parkway to Exit 63 Manahawkin Exit. Follow signs to Manahawkin Business District, Bay Ave. Mart is on the righthand side of the road.
DESCRIPTION: This good year-round show started in 1977 and hosts 100 outdoor and 45 indoor dealers, featuring antiques, collectibles, produce, meats, new merchandise, and stained glass items. One snack bar and handicapped-accessible restrooms add to the amenities. They are located within two miles of Long Beach Island on the Atlantic Ocean, a popular tourist spot.
DEALER RATES: $20 per 22' × 19' space per day outdoors; $160 monthly. Inside rates vary. Reservations are not required outdoors, but are for indoors.
CONTACT: Warren Petrucci, Manahawkin Flea Mart, PO Box 885, Manahawkin NJ 08050-0885. Tel: (609) 597-1017.

NESHANIC STATION

Neshanic Flea Market

DATES: Every Sunday, March through December, rain or shine.
TIMES: 6:00 AM–5:00 PM.
ADMISSION: Free. $.50 parking donation to the Neshanic Volunteer Fire Company.
LOCATION: Midway between Somerville and Flemington, off Hwy 202.
DESCRIPTION: This outdoor market opened in 1970 and currently draws approximately 100 dealers. Some of the types of items you can find include antiques and collectibles, fine art, and arts and crafts, as well as new merchandise and fresh produce. There is a snack bar on the premises. This friendly market is family owned and operated, and is located in a beautiful historic village.
DEALER RATES: $12 per two 4' × 8' spaces, BYOT (bring your own table). Reservations are not required.
CONTACT: Mary and Jack Weiss, 100 Elm St, Neshanic Station NJ 08853. Tel: (908) 369-3660.

NEW EGYPT

New Egypt Auction and Farmers Market

DATES: Every Wednesday and Sunday, year round.
TIMES: 7:00 AM–2:00 PM. (Some vendors leave after noon.)
ADMISSION: Free. Free parking is available.
LOCATION: On Rt 537 between Rts 528 and 539. Take Exit 7 or 7A off the New Jersey Turnpike. Six miles west of Great Adventure/Six Flags Amusement Park.
DESCRIPTION: This indoor/outdoor "flea market village" has been in existence since 1959. There are approximately 100 dealers and 60 buildings (six antique shops) buying and selling antiques, collectibles, arts and crafts, and new and used clothing, tools, hardware, coins, books, furniture, metals recycling, and lots of other used items and oddities. This market is located near campsites, an amusement park and in the heart of New Jersey race horse country. An outstanding used book and collectible paper store is nearby. Food is served on the premises.
DEALER RATES: $6 per 5' × 12' space on Wednesday; $7 per space on Sunday. Prices include parking space. Reservations are not required.
CONTACT: Les Heller, New Egypt Flea Market, 933 Rt 537, Cream Ridge NJ 08514. Tel: (609) 758-2082.

NORTH CAPE MAY

Victoria Commons Flea Market

DATES: Last Saturday in September.
TIMES: 9:00 AM–3:00 PM.
ADMISSION: Free. Parking is free.
LOCATION: Intersection of Bayshore and Townbank Rds. About ¼ mile from the ferry. Take Garden State Parkway south to the end; follow signs to the Cape May-Lewes Ferry. Turn right at the Acme Shopping Center (Bayshore Rd). Go to Townbank Rd (second light) and make a right. Turn right onto our driveway.
DESCRIPTION: This annual flea market is a basic tailgate market of 50 dealers held on the grounds of the Victoria Commons Retirement Community parking lot. Food and restrooms are on premises.
DEALER RATES: $18 for one parking space, $30 for two. Reservations are recommended.
CONTACT: Nadia Promotions Inc, PO Box 156, Flourtown PA 19031-0156. Tel: (215) 643-1396. Fax: (215) 654-0896. In NJ call: (609) 898-0677.

PALMYRA

Tacony-Palmyra Swap N' Shop Flea Market

DATES: Every Saturday, Sunday, and selected holidays, rain or shine, year round.
TIMES: 6:00 AM–3:00 PM.
ADMISSION: Free. Free parking is available.
LOCATION: On Rt 73. From New Jersey follow Rt 73 to Tacony-Palmyra Bridge. From Pennsylvania take I-95 exit and follow signs to Tacony-Palmyra Bridge.
DESCRIPTION: This outdoor market has been open since 1972. There are, on an average, 400 dealers that sell a wide range of objects, including antiques, fine art, collectibles, and arts and crafts, along with new merchandise and fresh produce. Food is served on the premises.
DEALER RATES: $20 per 18' × 18' space Saturday and select holidays; $25 on Sunday. Reservations are not required. Dealers must have a valid NJ license. There is a reserved line, if interested call.
CONTACT: Lauresia Phillips, PO Box 64, Palmyra NJ 08065-0064. Tel: (609) 829-3001. Day of show call the general line at (609) 829-3000.

RAHWAY

Rahway Italian-American Club Flea Market

DATES: Wednesday and Friday, year round.

TIMES: 7:00 AM–3:00 PM.

ADMISSION: Free. Parking is also free.

LOCATION: 530 New Brunswick Ave. Corner of Inman and New Brunswick Aves.

DESCRIPTION: This market has been held for 20 years, featuring up to 75 dealers both indoors and out selling antiques, collectibles, crafts, designer clothes, baseball cards, jewelry and new merchandise. A snack bar featuring homemade food serves the hungry.

DEALER RATES: Start at $15 per 12' booth. Reservations are suggested.

CONTACT: Bob, Rahway Italian-American Club Flea Market, 530 New Brunswick Ave, Rahway NJ 07065-2929. Day of show call (908) 574-3840 (the club number).

RANCOCAS WOODS

William Spencer's Antique Show

DATES: Second Sunday of the month, March through December. Rain date the following Sunday.

TIMES: 9:00 AM–4:00 PM.

ADMISSION: Free. Free parking is available.

LOCATION: On Creek Rd, 1 mile from the Rancocas Woods exit off I-295.

DESCRIPTION: This very popular market first opened in 1950. There are over 150 dealers attending this outdoor market set in a beautiful, wooded area. They specialize in antiques and collectibles, and they also have a craft show on the fourth Saturday of every month from March through November. Antique show items include jewelry, glass, vintage clothing, furniture, etc. Craft show items include handicrafts, quilted gifts, handmade toys, etc. They were written up in the *New York Times* in 1993 and people are still coming because of the recommendation. Food is served on the premises.

DEALER RATES: They request that you call for more information as there are too many variations on size and show to list here.

CONTACT: Orin Houser, c/o William Spencer, 118 Creek Rd, Rancocas Woods NJ 08054. Tel: (609) 235-1830.

During the winter of 1996/97 some locals decided that they had had enough of the traffic and noise of this still growing market. When a Zoning Board meeting was held to decide the market's fate, the attendance at the meeting was close to unanimous in favor of continuing the market with slight modifications as to parking and location of stands and how early the vendors can set up. It seems that many local merchants profit from the market's crowds, keeping the area alive and healthy.

VINELAND

U-Sell Flea Market

DATES: Friday, Saturday and Sunday, year round.
TIMES: 6:00 AM–5:00 PM.
ADMISSION: Free. Parking is free.
LOCATION: 2896 South Delsea Dr. From Philadelphia go south on SR 55 to Sherman Ave exit. Turn left, proceed 2 miles to SR 47 Delsea Dr. Turn right, market is 300 feet down on the right.
DESCRIPTION: Opened in 1974, this market hosts up to 350 dealers under steel canopies on a 15-acre blacktop. Some antiques and collectibles, clothing, toys, tools, sports cards, fresh produce, "you name it" are sold here. Three food courts dispense breakfast and lunch.
DEALER RATES: $12 Friday, $17 Saturday and Sunday for a 10' × 26' space and one 8' × 4' table. Reservations are not required.
CONTACT: Tim, U-Sell Flea Market, 2896 S Delsea Dr, S Vineland NJ 08360-2016. Tel/fax: (609) 691-1222.

WARREN

Washington Valley Fire Company Flea Market

DATES: Every Sunday, Easter to Christmas, weather permitting.
TIMES: 7:30 AM–4:00 PM.
ADMISSION: Free. Free parking is available, although a $1 donation is much appreciated.
LOCATION: 140 Washington Valley Rd. Go north from Greenbrook 1½ miles from Rt 22 west on Warrenville Rd to first traffic light, turn left, go 1 mile.
DESCRIPTION: Formed in 1971, this outdoor market's 150 to 200 dealers sell antiques and collectibles as well as new merchandise. All this is

done by and for the volunteers of the Washington Valley Fire Company so that they can provide their own fire-fighting equipment. Food is served on the premises.
DEALER RATES: $15 per 10' × 11' space, including a 3' × 10' table. Reservations are not required. Monthly rates are 25% less.
CONTACT: Jerome Boschen, 12 Washington Valley Rd, Warren NJ 07059. Tel: (908) 469-2443 or 469-1571.

WOODSTOWN
Cowtown Bawl, Inc

DATES: Every Tuesday and Saturday, rain or shine, year round.
TIMES: 8:00 AM–4:00 PM.
ADMISSION: Free. Free parking is available.
LOCATION: On Rt 40. From South Delaware Memorial Bridge, take Atlantic City exit to Rt 40 and go 5 miles to Cowtown. From North 295, take Exit 4 onto Rt 48, go east 5 miles until joining Rt 40. Market is 2 miles on right.
DESCRIPTION: This market opened in 1926 in the center of Woodstown and moved to this location in 1940 as they had outgrown their original spot. Nearly 700 dealers sell anything from antiques, arts and crafts, and collectibles to fresh produce, meats, cheeses and new merchandise. This market is held both indoors and outdoors. Plenty of concession stands and handicapped-accessible restrooms add to the amenities. They draw anywhere from 15,000 to 40,000 people a day. Election day is very popular here. Maybe it has something to do with the livestock market on Tuesdays. They sell cattle, the occasional buffalo or as the boss says, "If it walks in here, we'll sell it!" During the summers, there is a professional rodeo every Saturday night.
DEALER RATES: $15–$35 per space. Reservations are not required.
CONTACT: Robert Becker, Manager, Cowtown Bawl Inc, 780 Rt 40, Pilesgrove NJ 08098. Tel: (609) 769-3000.

> This market grew from the traditional Colonial markets held in New Jersey, officially and legally, on Tuesdays. The current owner, Grant Harris, is the fourth generation of his family to own and run it. Which, of course, explains the popularity of Tuesdays at the Cowtown Bawl!

OTHER FLEA MARKETS

We know or have heard about these markets, but have not personally contacted each one, as we have the markets with descriptions. If you plan to visit one of these markets listed below, *please call first* to make sure they are still open. Flea markets do come and go. While they were open when we went to press, they may not be later. We can't be responsible. *Call first!*

Asbury Park: Asbury Casino Antiques & Flea Market, Boardwalk & Ocean Ave. Tel: 908-988-8585.

Atlantic City: Sand Flea Market, Sovereign Ave & Boardwalk. Tel: 609-449-9415.

Bayonne: St Vincent's Flea Market, 28 W 47th St. Tel: 201-823-3032.

Bridgeton: Bank St Indoor Flea Market, 515 Bank St. Tel: 609-451-9848.

Cherry Hill: Garden State Park Flea Market, St Hwy N 70 & Crnl. Tel: 609-665-8558.

Chester: Chester Lions Club Flea Market administration, 9 Delwood Rd. Tel: 908-879-4408.

Clementon: Rt 30 Flea Market, 260 White Horse Pike. Tel: 609-784-6544.

Elmer: Circle 40 Flea Market, 770 US Hwy No 40. Tel: 609-358-8183.

Lakewood: Rt 70 Flea Market & Consumers Outlet, 117 Hwy 70. Tel: 908-370-1837.

Pleasantville: Pleasantville Flea Market, 306 S Main St. Tel: 609-383-9833.

Roselle: Mini Flea Mart, 409 E 2nd Ave. Tel: 908-245-7524.

Rutherford: Meadowlands Flea Market, 50 State Hwy No 20 E. Tel: 201-935-5474.

Wayne: Wayne Flea Market, 1244 State Rt 23. Tel: 201-694-1024.

Williamstown: Collingwood Auction & Flea Market, 1350 State Hwy No 33, Tel: 908-938-7941 or 908-938-4425 or 908-938-5833.

NEW MEXICO

ALBUQUERQUE

Indoor Mercado

DATES: Friday, Saturday and Sunday, year round.

TIMES: Friday 12:00 PM–6:00 PM; weekends 10:00 AM–6:00 PM.

ADMISSION: $.50. Parking is free.

LOCATION: 2035 12th St and I-40.

DESCRIPTION: This market opened in September 1991 and has 190 to 200 dealers selling mostly new merchandise, some antiques and collectibles, loads of southwestern arts and crafts and jewelry, ceramics, tools, toys, new clothes, books, art and the "usual fare." There are two food courts, just in case.

DEALER RATES: $220 to $290 for a 10' × 10' space for 4 weeks depending on length of reservation. Reservations must be made at least 2 weeks in advance. There is some first-come, first-served space.

CONTACT: Alan and Linda Weir, Indoor Mercado, 2035 12 St, Albuquerque NM 87104. Tel: (505) 243-8111. Fax: (505) 243-8419.

New Mexico Open-Air Flea Market

DATES: Saturday and Sunday, except for September during State Fair.

TIMES: 6:00 AM–5:00 PM.

ADMISSION: Free. $2 parking fee.

LOCATION: New Mexico State Fairgrounds at Louisiana and Central Sts, Northeast.

DESCRIPTION: This market opened in 1979 and currently has between 100–1,000 dealers, depending on the weather, selling everything: antiques, collectibles, arts and crafts, new merchandise—everything! Probably the largest market in New Mexico. Known for a jewelry row with exhibitors with one section of Native American arts and crafts to another section of commercial manufacturers. Race track racing next door occasionally coincides with the market. Excellent food from American to Mexican is available on the premises.

DEALER RATES: $10 per space. Reservations are not required.

CONTACT: Julie Leahy, New Mexico Open-Air Flea Market, PO Box 8546, Albuquerque NM 87198-8546. Tel: (505) 265-1791. Fax (505) 266-7784.

FARMINGTON

Farmington Flea Market

DATES: Every Friday through Sunday, rain or shine.

TIMES: 6:00 AM–8:00 PM during summer; 7:00 AM–7:00 PM during winter.

ADMISSION: Free. Free parking is available.

LOCATION: On Hwy 550, halfway between Farmington and Aztec, at 7701 E Main St.

DESCRIPTION: This outdoor market opened in 1970 and currently accommodates up to 300 dealers during peak season. Among the articles available are antiques and collectibles, fine art, crafts, household items, furniture, new merchandise, and fresh produce. A notable feature of this market is that it also offers animals such as horses, goats, pigs, dogs, and cats. One food concession building and handicapped-accessible restrooms add to the amenities.

DEALER RATES: $4 per 12' × 26' space Friday and Sunday; $8 per space on Saturday. Reservations are required March through August only. Self-contained trailers may stay on the grounds Friday through Sunday night for no additional fee. Food is served on the premises.

CONTACT: Cathey Wright, Owner, 4301 Holiday Dr, Farmington NM 87402. Tel: (505) 325-3129.

LAS CRUCES

Big Daddy's Market Place, Inc

DATES: Saturday and Sunday, year round.

TIMES: 6:30 AM–4:00 PM.

ADMISSION: Free. Parking is also free.

LOCATION: 7320 North Main (Hwy 70 East).

DESCRIPTION: Since 1981 there have been between 200 to 400 dealers selling antiques, collectibles, new and used merchandise, anything and everything. A convenience store and laundromat are on premises. To satisfy the munchies, there are two Mexican and one international restaurant on the premises.

DEALER RATES: $8 per space under giant metal sheds, outside $6 per space. They supply the tables. Reservations are not required. They do take reservations on Fridays from 8:00 AM–5:00 PM. Motorhomes may stay overnight Friday and Saturday for $5 a night including hook-up.

CONTACT: Manager, Big Daddy's Market Place Inc, PO Box 1954, Las Cruces NM 88004-1954. Tel: (505) 382-9404 or 382-1055.

ROSWELL

Daltons Trading Post

DATES: Every Saturday and Sunday, year round.
TIMES: 7:00 AM–5:00 PM.
ADMISSION: Free. Free parking is available.
LOCATION: 2200 South Sunset at Poe.
DESCRIPTION: This show, started in 1980 and now under new ownership, has 50 to 60 dealers inside a 11,000-square-foot building or outdoors on five acres under cover or in the open air. Antiques, collectibles, tools, quality used furniture, lawn equipment, crafts, and new merchandise are featured, but jewelry, clothing and accessories, Native American art, and traditional craft items are also to be found. A cafe is on the premises as are handicapped-accessible restrooms. The new ownership has been upgrading the market extensively, making all but a couple of smaller buildings ADA accessible. Say "Hi" to Daryel for me!
DEALER RATES: $5 per 10' × 20' space per day (BYOT—bring your own table) or $5 per day for a table and its space. Reservations for best locations are required in advance. Accepts Visa and MC. There is an RV park with full hook-ups for dealers.
CONTACT: Daryel P Kann and Tommy L Blair, Owners, BK Enterprises, The Trade Village, 2200 S Sunset, Roswell NM 88201. Tel: (505) 622-7410. Fax: (505) 622-7557.

Now, a little historical bunch of notes—

The main building here was originally a cement company that furnished the concrete for the silos at Walker AFB near here.

As to the real fun stuff:

Yes, this is the famous (infamous?) Roswell NM where the alleged UFOs landed on July 4, 1947. Find Daryel and ask him about this.

OTHER FLEA MARKETS

We know or have heard about these markets, but have not personally contacted each one, as we have the markets with descriptions. If you plan to visit one of these markets listed below, *please call first* to make sure they are still open. Flea markets do come and go. While they were open when we went to press, they may not be later. We can't be responsible. *Call first!*

Albuquerque: Indoor Flea Market Things Etc, 1138 San Mateo Blvd SE. Tel: 505-268-1717.
Albuquerque: Star Flea Market, 543 Coors Blvd NW. Tel: 505-831-3106.
Bosque Farms: B & J Flea Market, 1775 Blvd A. Tel: 505-869-6995.
Clovis: La Pulga Flea Market, 1421 Mabry Dr. Tel: 505-769-8414.
Gallup: Downtown Flea Mart, 115 W Coal Ave. Tel: 505-863-3975.

NEW YORK

BOUCKVILLE

Bouckville Antique Pavilion

DATES: Every Sunday, from the last Sunday of April through the last Sunday of October. Special shows: June Two-Day Show (second weekend in June with antique cars), August Five-Day Show (third weekend in August).

TIMES: 7:00 AM–4:00 PM.

ADMISSION: Free. Parking is also free.

LOCATION: On Rt 20, in the center of Bouckville, 100 miles west of Albany, 35 miles east of Syracuse, 25 miles west of Utica.

DESCRIPTION: This market started in 1984 is located "in the heart of antique country." There are 41 shops as well as 6 multi-dealer co-ops included in this show. Close to 200 dealers specialize in antiques and collectibles including furniture, glass, toys, jewelry, paintings, baseball cards, lamps, military items, coins, dishes, dolls, and tools. During the August show there will be around 2,000 dealers in town for this one show. Whether you are shopping outdoors or under cover, all booths are conveniently protected from the mud if it rains. In 1995, the new owner acquired more land next door making more room for dealers. The June market is a Pre-WWII Antique Car Show. When you need a break from shopping, food is available on the premises.

DEALER RATES: $15 for 20' × 25' space outdoors; $20 for 12' × 12' space plus 12' × 20' space for vehicle. Reservations are advised.

CONTACT: Steve and Lynda Bono, Rt 20, Bouckville NY 13310. Tel: (315) 893-7483.

CALLICOON

Callicoon Flea Market

DATES: Weekends June through December; also Monday, Thursday and Friday during July and August.

TIMES: Saturdays 9:00 AM–5:00 PM; other days 10:00 AM–3:00 PM.

ADMISSION: Free. Parking is also free.

LOCATION: Main St, Rt 17B West from Monticello, New York. Or Rt 97 from Port Jervis or Hancock, New York.

DESCRIPTION: This market began in 1980 in the historical town of Callicoon in sight of the Delaware River. It is privately run with a variety

of interesting collectibles, antiques, crafts, lighting fixtures, depression and carnival glass, some new merchandise, furniture, and the occasional railroad and jewelry collectibles. The owner tries to have a bit of something for everyone. Many of the original buildings in town are wonderful examples of 1800s' architecture. There is camping and canoeing nearby, as well as local bed and breakfast inns.
DEALER RATES: Not applicable.
CONTACT: Carol Kay, Callicoon Flea Market, PO Box 278, Callicoon NY 12723. Tel: (914) 887-5411. Call for seasonal hours.

CHEEKTOWAGA

Super Flea and Farmer's Market

DATES: Every Saturday and Sunday, rain or shine.
TIMES: 9:00 AM–6:00 PM.
ADMISSION: Free. Parking is free.
LOCATION: Off New York State Thruway, Exit 52 East, at 2500 Walden Ave.
DESCRIPTION: Begun in 1975, this is the largest indoor and outdoor flea market in western New York, with 300 dealers outside in the summer and another 200 inside year round. Offered are a wide range of antiques, collectibles, crafts, new merchandise, as well as fresh produce, meats, and dairy products. The Super Flea and Farmer's Market boasts four fast-food restaurants on the premises.
DEALER RATES: \$20 per 7½' × 6' booth inside, \$30 for a 8' × 8' booth inside per day; \$15 per 11' × 22' booth outside per day. Space is available on a first come, first served basis.
CONTACT: Ronald A Wagner, General Manager, 2500 Walden Ave, Cheektowaga NY 14225. Tel: (716) 685-2902.

CLARENCE

Antique World and Marketplace

DATES: Every Sunday, year round.
TIMES: 8:00 AM–4:00 PM.
ADMISSION: Free. \$1 parking from May through October; free the rest of the time.
LOCATION: 10995 Main St, 15 miles east of Buffalo and 40 miles west of Rochester on Main St (Rt 5).

DESCRIPTION: There are approximately 350 dealers in winter and 650 dealers in summer displaying their merchandise. The three buildings on the premises help to separate the various sale items. One building is exclusively for antiques and collectibles (this building went co-op in 1998), one specializes in dealers selling "flea market" merchandise, and the other building also serves as an exhibition center. There is an enormous variety of items with everything from antiques and collectibles to new merchandise, meats, and cheeses for sale. They hold Great American Garage Sales the first Sunday of each month from June through September. Special shows are scheduled during the year including: Guitars in May, Paper Show in June, Collectible Dolls and Bears in July, Toys in September, Country Harvest antique and crafts in October, a twice yearly EXPO featuring 600 of the finest Antique and Collectible dealers from 22 states and Canada. There are admission charges for these special shows. There are five restaurants and handicapped-accessible restrooms scattered around the market.
DEALER RATES: Flea market rates are $15 per 21' × 20' space outdoors; $20–$30 per 9' × 9' booth indoors. Reservations are not required outside; are required for inside space.
CONTACT: Katy Toth, Antique World, 10995 Main St, Clarence NY 14031. Tel: (716) 759-8483. Fax: (716) 759-6167.

FISHKILL

Flea Market at Dutchess Stadium

DATES: Sundays, from the last Sunday in April through the last in October.
TIMES: 8:00 AM–3:00 PM.
ADMISSION: Free. Parking is free.
LOCATION: Rt 9D at Dutchess Stadium. From NY: Take I-87 (NY Thruway) to Exit 17. Take I-84 east to Exit 11. At the end of the exit ramp turn left at the light. Go 1 mile to stadium on the right. From CT: I-84 West into NY to Exit 11. Follow directions.
DESCRIPTION: This new market, started in 1997, is held on the blacktop of the stadium parking lot. There are 250 booths and vendors selling both new and previously owned merchandise—so far the merchandise has been a mix of antiques, collectibles, clothes, garage sale goodies, as well as the standard new items. Concessions and handicapped-accessible restrooms are readily available.

DEALER RATES: $22.50 per day and up. Reservations are not required, but nice.
CONTACT: Alan Finchley, 515 Boston Post Rd, Port Chester NY 10573. Tel: (914) 939-1800.

LEVITTOWN

Tri-County Flea Market

DATES: Thursday through Sunday.
TIMES: Thursday and Friday 12:00 PM–9:00 PM; Saturday and Sunday 10:00 AM–6:00 PM.
ADMISSION: Free. Parking is also free.
LOCATION: 3041 Hempstead Turnpike.
DESCRIPTION: Opened in 1981, this indoor market has 400 dealers selling literally everything. All new merchandise and collectibles including shoes, leather, toys, plants, jewelry, flags, and all sorts of clothing. You could furnish your house and clothe a family from the merchandise sold here. There is one floor of just jewelry, another at mezzanine level has a collectible card show and a huge wicker furniture display. They have 55,000 square feet of display area loaded with just furniture. A food court provides food to starving patrons. For all merchandise purchased here, there is a seven-day money-back guarantee, except on special orders.
DEALER RATES: $800 to $900 for a very large space for 16 working days (about one month). Reservations are required.
CONTACT: Barbara Eve, Tri-County Flea Market, 3041 Hempstead Tpke, Levittown NY 11756. Tel: (516) 579-4500. Fax (516) 579-6715.

MAYBROOK

Maybrook Flea Market

DATES: Sundays, year round, except holidays like Easter.
TIMES: 8:00 AM–4:00 PM.
ADMISSION: Free. $.75 per vehicle.
LOCATION: Rt 208, 2 miles south of I-84, Exit 5. At the drive-in theater.
DESCRIPTION: For over 20 years this market has been hosting from 100 dealers in winter to 500 dealers in summer selling antiques, collectibles, garage sale treasures, new merchandise or what the owner describes as "gems to junk." There is a snack bar on premises as well as clean restrooms. This is the site of a drive-in theater that operated in 1997 and may continue

to do so. Which leads to funny moments at 2:30 AM when the dealers want to come in to set up and there are still theater patrons occupied...
DEALER RATES: Must have NY State license to sell. The 1997 rates are $30 for a liberal 18' × 18' space outdoors, $26 for 6' × 10' inside space.
CONTACT: Nick Perilli, Maybrook Flea Market, Rt 208, Maybrook NY 12543. Tel: (914) 427-2715.

MONTICELLO

Alan Finchley's Flea Market at Monticello Raceway

DATES: Memorial Day through Labor Day: Saturday, Sunday and holidays.
TIMES: 9:00 AM–5:00 PM.
ADMISSION: Free admission and free parking for 1,000 cars.
LOCATION: Rt 17B at Quickway (Rt 17), Exit 104.
DESCRIPTION: Established in 1976, this market is New York State's original new merchandise-only flea market. Located in the heart of the Catskills near the world-famous Concord Hotel. From Memorial Day to the end of June, this market is essentially a small local affair with 20 vendors. From July 4th through Labor Day, this market explodes to accommodate the huge influx of summer tourists and residents. Sundays and holidays feature live harness racing while the market is operating making for some extra excitement. Up to 80 dealers from all over the country offer recognizable savings on famous-maker brand-name fashions and accessories, as well as a fascinating variety of novelties, toys and jewelry. All new and unused. Food carts and handicapped-accessible restrooms add to the amenities.
DEALER RATES: All selling spaces accommodate vendor's vehicle. Rates from $25 per vendor during May and June. From July through Labor Day weekend $35 and up. All vendors must have NY State Sales Certificate. Dealers may sign up by the week or season and receive a discount. Non-reserved daily vendors need no reservation or phone call. Simply line up at the sign near the vendor setup that reads: "Daily vendors line up here." Management will be at the site at 8:00 AM to rent the space. At least 20 non-reserved spaces are set aside each market day.
CONTACT: Alan Finchley, 42 Ohio Ave, Long Beach NY 11561. Tel: (914) 796-1000.

MORRIS

Twenty-Second Annual Antiques, Collectibles and Toys Show and Sale

Note: This market will be changed from this weekend to another. But at press time the new date was uncertain. As it is such a good market, we're leaving it in with this caveat: Please call first before making plans.

DATES: Annually on Labor Day Saturday.

TIMES: 8:30 AM–4:00 PM.

ADMISSION: $3 per person. Parking is free.

LOCATION: At the Otsego County Fairgrounds on Rt 23, 20 miles from their old site in Norwich.

DESCRIPTION: This market started in 1976 in Norwich (moved in 1994 to this site) and has grown to host approximately 300 to 350 dealers both outside and under covered spaces. This show expanded by adding a Toy Show in a new building on the grounds in 1990. It has been a real "crowd pleaser" and compliments the rest of the show with antique and collectible toys. They exhibit all types of merchandise from furniture to small collectibles and accessories, such as quilts and art glass. Specialized dealers with high standards make it a quality and growing antique and collectibles show. Special historical exhibits are a feature at the show. A food stand and handicapped-accessible restrooms are on the premises.

DEALER RATES: $40 for 10' × 12' covered space, includes electricity. $35 for 20' × 30' space outside. Toy space is per table. Reservations are required.

CONTACT: Arleta Miller, RD 2 Manley Rd, Norwich NY 13815. Tel: (607) 336-4184.

NEW YORK CITY

The Annex Antiques Fair and Flea Market

DATES: Every Saturday and Sunday, year round. Rain or shine.

TIMES: 9:00 AM–5:00 PM.

ADMISSION: $1 for antique market. Flea market is free. Ample parking is available, but not free.

LOCATION: Ave of the Americas, between 24th and 27th Sts in Manhattan.

DESCRIPTION: This show began over 30 years ago and is claimed to be the longest running outdoor show in the metropolitan area. The market

accommodates 600 to 700 dealers who come from all over the United States, Canada, and Europe to sell an amazing variety of merchandise including antique jewelry, vintage clothing, bronzes, Art Deco, porcelain, and rugs. There are five outdoor selling areas and a new indoor selling area—The Garage—that holds 150 dealers. Restaurants are nearby.
DEALER RATES: Saturday: $95 per 10' × 14' booth; $60 per 5' × 14' booth. Sunday: Antique Fair $125 per 10' × 14' booth; $80 per 5' × 14' booth; Flea Market $100 per 9' × 12' booth; $70 per 4½ × 12' booth. The Garage is $125 for a 9' × 12' space for the weekend. Reservations are preferred. Office hours are Tuesday through Friday 12:00 PM–5:00 PM.
CONTACT: Michael, Annex Antique Fair, PO Box 7010, New York NY 10116-4627. Tel: Michael (212) 243-5343 or for The Garage (212) 647-0707; fax: (212) 463-7099. Day of show call (212) 243-7922.

GreenFlea at IS 144

DATES: Every Sunday, year round. Rain or shine.
TIMES: 10:00 AM–4:00 PM.
ADMISSION: Free. Parking space is not provided. Garages are available nearby at standard city rates.
LOCATION: Columbus Ave at 77th St. Across the street from the Museum of Natural History.
DESCRIPTION: This show first opened in 1980 as a benefit for the school. Over 350 dealers attend this market, selling their merchandise both indoors and outdoors. This market is known for its quality antiques, fine art, arts and crafts (many special orders and made-to-orders by metalworkers, wood carvers, and the like), vintage clothing and jewelry, and collectibles. Of special interest are the smoked meats, cheeses, and fresh flowers that are available from their farmers market, an extension of the famous GreenMarket at Union Square. Proceeds are used directly for the benefit of the children, with over $300,000 given to the school each year. This market is unique as one of the first of its kind in the country whose purpose is education and support of the public school system. It is now a community event with a following of many thousands of people attending every Sunday. Beverly Sills, the famous opera diva, said this is one of her favorite places to visit.
DEALER RATES: $22 up to $130 for space depending on size. Reservations are required in advance.
CONTACT: GreenFlea Inc, 162 W 72nd St, New York NY 10023-3300. Tel: (212) 721-0900. Day of show call: (212) 734-3578.

GreenFlea at PS 183

DATES: Every Saturday, year round. Rain or shine.

TIMES: 6:00 AM–6:00 PM.

ADMISSION: Free. Parking space is not provided. Garages are available nearby at standard city rates.

LOCATION: 419 East 66th; or 67th St between First and York Aves.

DESCRIPTION: This show first opened on August 12, 1979 as the PS 183 Antique Flea and Farmer's Market. It is now under new management. Over 150 dealers attend this market selling their merchandise both indoors and outdoors. One may purchase quality antiques, fine art, arts and crafts, and collectibles; of special interest are the smoked meats, cheeses, and fresh flowers that are available from farmers in the tri-state area. Proceeds are used directly for the benefit of the children, with over $150,000 given to the school each year. This market is unique as one of the first of its kind in the country whose purpose is education and support of the public school system. It is now a community event with a following of 3,000-5,000 people attending every Saturday.

DEALER RATES: $22 up to $130 for space depending on size. Reservations are required in advance.

CONTACT: GreenFlea Inc, 162 W 72nd St, New York NY 10023-3300. Tel: (212) 721-0900. Day of show call: (212) 734-3578.

The New Yorkville Antiques and Flea Market

Dates: Saturday, year round.

Times: 6:00 AM–5:00 PM.

Admission: Free. Parking is where you can find it.

Location: Jan Hus Church, 351 E 74th St between 1st and 2nd Ave in the upper Eastside.

Description: Under new management, this market is patterned after a quaint and cozy English-style antiques and collectibles market. Over 40 dealers sell antiques, collectibles, jewelry (from Georgian and Victorian eras, fine estate, to retro costume), textiles, laces, vintage clothing, pottery, china, silver, furniture and more. This is a great family place with plenty of home-made foods.

Dealer Rates: $50 per table. Reservations are suggested.

Contact: Bob DiTroia, 98-30 67th Ave, Forest Hills NY 11374. Tel: (718) 897-5992. Fax: (718) 997-8192.

The Showplace

DATES: Saturday and Sunday, year round. An antiques gallery is open daily on the second floor only.

TIMES: 8:30 AM–5:30 PM. Upstairs antique gallery weekdays 10:00 AM–6:00 PM.

ADMISSION: Free. On weekends, parking around the market is available on the streets.

LOCATION: 40 West 25th Street, between Sixth Ave and Broadway.

DESCRIPTION: This hugely successful market opened January 23, 1993, and moved to larger quarters. Their 135 dealers on two floors with 31,000 square feet of selling space specialize in antiques and collectibles only. In addition, The Antique Gallery has 32 dealers selling daily on the top floor. They were featured in the *New York Times* two months after their opening when they were the hot topic during the famous 1993 blizzard. If it's old it's probably here: furniture, lamps, jewelry, paintings, silver, toys, clothing, timepieces, books, comics, whatever. They do plenty of advertising and as a result the market draws in buyers by the thousands each weekend. Lines form here early every weekend before opening with people looking for the as-yet-unfound bargains. And they have been found here. An espresso bar offers sandwiches, coffee and teas, and excellent light foods.

DEALER RATES: \$200 for a 8' × 10' space, \$250 for a 10' × 12' space for the weekend. Reservations are required.

CONTACT: Amos Balaish, The Showplace, 40 W 25 St, New York, NY 10001. Tel: (212) 633-6063. Fax: (212) 633-6064.

> So popular is this antique emporium that not only are commercials frequently filmed here, but location shots from the movie *The Mirror Has Two Faces* were filmed here too.

Soho Antiques Fair, Collectibles and Crafts

DATES: Saturday and Sunday, year round.

TIMES: 9:00 AM–5:00 PM.

ADMISSION: Free. Parking? Take a bus (#6 on Broadway) or subway (Spring St and Canal St stations Lexington Ave, Broadway, 6th Ave, 7th Ave lines.) If you must drive, there are garages and some on-street parking.

LOCATION: At the corner of Broadway and Grand St in Soho.

DESCRIPTION: This well-known and popular market is a "must do" weekend event in New York. Up to 100 dealers sell the best antiques, memorabilia and collectibles outdoors. It has been written up as the "best flea market in downtown Manhattan" by the *NY Press* in 1992. Right in the middle of the downtown art scene in Soho and next door to Chinatown and Little Italy, they boast a variety of ethnic diversity in their wares. They draw as many as 10,000 shoppers on any weekend day. Plenty of neighborhood restaurants are nearby.

DEALER RATES: For a 8' × 12' space $70; 12' × 12' space $90; 20' × 20' space $120. Reservations are a good idea.

CONTACT: Soho Antiques Fair & Collectibles, PO Box 337, Garden City NY 11530. Tel: (212) 682-2000 or fax: (516) 742-4424.

NORWICH

33rd Annual Antique Auto Show and Flea Market

DATES: Annually, the Saturday and Sunday of Memorial Day. For 1998: May 23–24.

TIMES: 8:00 AM–5:00 PM.

ADMISSION: $3 daily. Shuttle buses run from city parking lots to the site. There is no on-site parking, it's already full of antique cars and dealers. There is parking in the school adjacent to the fairgrounds.

LOCATION: Chenango County Fair Grounds, East Main St.

DESCRIPTION: This market is a car buff's dream with proud owners and dealers showing and selling antique cars (Sunday), car parts, muscle cars (Saturday), show cars—and then the regular antique flea market, crafts, and auctions. There were over 700 antique cars on display in 1995, and over 300 muscle cars. They hold two auctions on site: the Car Auction and then the "2+2" Auction, nicknamed the Poor Man's Auction. At the 2+2, the buyer and seller each pay the auctioneer $2 as a fee. All sorts of odds and ends are sold during this auction including "cheap" cars. Naturally, the fabulous cars are sold during the Car Auction. In 1997, they added a military display, and while the Reserves brought in a tank, they'll probably stick to smaller jeeps and trucks for the future (it costs too much to move a tank!).

DEALER RATES: Reserved before May 15: for 20' × 30' outdoor space or 10' × 12' inside space $40, after May 15 it is $45. Car parts dealers for 20' × 30' space $25 (before May 15)/$35 (after May 15); crafts space $40/ $45, car sales 10' × 30' space $25 anytime. If you want to sell here, be savvy, register *early*, as in 1996, they were filled before May 15.

CONTACT: Ray Hart, PO Box 168, Norwich NY 13815-0168. Tel: (607) 334-4044.

PORT CHESTER

Empire State Flea Market Mall

DATES: Friday, Saturday and Sunday, year round. Thanksgiving through New Year's Eve (closed Christmas Day), daily with extended hours.

TIMES: Friday 12:00 PM–8:00 PM; Saturday, Sunday 10:00 AM–6:00 PM.

ADMISSION: Free. Parking is also free.

LOCATION: Caldor Shopping Center at 515 Boston Post Rd (US 1) at intersection of I-95 and I-287. From NYC and south: I-95 north to Exit 21. Bear right on exit ramp to US 1, immediate right into Caldor Shopping Center. From the Tappanzee Bridge take I-287 E to Exit 11, left ¼ mile. Enter right into Caldor.

DESCRIPTION: This market started in 1976 and is New York State's original year-round indoor flea market mall. A vast majority of the merchandise offered by the 150 vendors is famous-label quality at obvious savings. Featured are over 100 new merchandise vendors and Westchester County's only fine jewelry exchange. Handicapped-accessible parking and entrances. One level, climate-controlled shopping.

DEALER RATES: Space is sold on a monthly basis only. A typical booth (10' × 7') rents for $500 per month ($35 per day). A security deposit of one month is required. All vendors must have or acquire a NY State Sales Tax Certificate.

CONTACT: Alan Finchley, 515 Boston Post Rd, Port Chester NY 10573. Tel: (914) 939-1800.

QUEENS

Aqueduct Flea Market

DATES: Saturday and Sunday, May through October; Tuesday, April through Christmas. Call, because they have been known to add Monday to their open days.

TIMES: 7:30 AM–4:00 PM.

ADMISSION: $2 per car load. $.50 per walk-in.

LOCATION: Take Belt Pkwy to Exit 18B Lefferts Blvd, go north to Rockaway Blvd, then a left to 108th St.

DESCRIPTION: This outdoor market first opened in 1974. There is a wide variety of merchandise to choose from including hardware, electronics, clothing, jewelry, household items, linens and leather to shoes and sneakers. Everything from antiques and collectibles to new merchandise

and fresh vegetables can be found. They boast of friendly merchants and customers from all over the world. There are all types of prepared foods available when you need a break from shopping.
DEALER RATES: $45 and up per 12' × 24' booth depending on location. Monthly rates available. Reservations are suggested.
CONTACT: Aqueduct Flea Market, 257 Hempstead Tpke, Elmont NY 11003-1539. Tel: (516) 775-8774 Wednesday 10:00 AM to 2:00 PM.

RHINEBECK

Rhinebeck Antiques Fair

DATES: Two shows annually on the Saturday and Sunday of Memorial Day weekend in May and Columbus Day weekend in October.
TIMES: Saturday 10:00 AM–5:00 PM. Sunday 11:00 AM–5:00 PM.
ADMISSION: $6. Parking is free.
LOCATION: Indoors on the Dutchess County Fairgrounds, on Rt 9 at northern edge of Rhinebeck. From New York Thruway, take Exit 19 to Rhinecliff Bridge, cross bridge and continue 1 mile to Rt 9G, then south 1 mile to Rt 9, and then south to fairgrounds.
DESCRIPTION: 1998 marks the 22nd year of this antiques fair. This indoor market attracts approximately 190 dealers exhibiting a wide variety of quality antiques at a variety of prices. Food is served on the premises.
DEALER RATES: $350 per space (1996 rates, as Jimi wouldn't give us the current rates). Reservations are required.
CONTACT: Jimi Barton, PO Box 310, Red Hook NY 12571-0310. Tel: (914) 758-6186. Show days call (914) 876-3644.

SCHENECTADY

White House Flea Market

DATES: Wednesday through Sunday, rain or shine.
TIMES: 9:00 AM–5:00 PM; Thursday 9:00 AM–9:00 PM.
ADMISSION: Free. Free parking is also available.
LOCATION: 952 State St.
DESCRIPTION: This indoor market has been held every weekend since 1985. Approximately 40 dealers gather here to sell antiques, collectibles, handmade craft items, furniture, books, records and toys, as well as new merchandise. This is the area's largest indoor year-round market and an excellent place for dealers to find great treasures.

DEALER RATES: Average $27 per week. Advance reservations are required. Permanent dealers usually fill this market.
CONTACT: Rudy or Jeanette Fecketter, 952 State St, Schenectady NY 12307. Tel: (518) 346-7851.

SPRING VALLEY

Spring Valley Flea Market

DATES: Friday, Saturday and Sunday, year round. December, seven days a week.
TIMES: Friday 3:00 PM–9:00 PM; Saturday 10:00 AM–8:00 PM; Sunday 10:00 AM–6:00 PM. Call for December hours.
ADMISSION: Free. Parking is also free.
LOCATION: New York State Thruway (87) to Exit 14, 1 mile west on Rt 59.
DESCRIPTION: This indoor market has been in operation since 1981. They feature professional vendors year round selling top quality merchandise at discount prices. Market is located in an excellent high-volume area and is considered one of the "world's largest" indoor markets. Their 500 dealers sell a wide variety of new merchandise. Food is available on the premises.
DEALER RATES: $105 per week for an 8' × 8' booth; $200 per week for an 8' × 16' booth. Reservations are suggested.
CONTACT: Al Bonadonna, Spring Valley Flea Market, 175 E Central Ave, Spring Valley NY 10977. Tel: (914) 356-1171.

STATEN ISLAND

Antiques, Arts and Crafts Market

DATES: Three shows per year. First Sunday in June; Sunday after Labor Day in September; first Sunday in October. Rain dates: the following Sundays.
TIMES: 10:00 AM–5:00 PM.
ADMISSION: $1. Parking is free.
LOCATION: At the Staten Island Historical Society, Historic Richmond Town, 441 Clarke Ave. From Verrazano Narrows Bridge, follow New Jersey West Rt to Richmond Rd/Clove Rd Exit; proceed to the second light and turn left onto Richmond Rd; about 5 miles ahead turn left onto St. Patrick's Place, and finally turn right on Clarke Ave. From St. George, take bus #74.

DESCRIPTION: This show has been in existence since 1970. It is an outdoor market that accommodates approximately 140 dealers from Staten Island, Manhattan, Brooklyn, Long Island, New Jersey, Pennsylvania, and Connecticut. They sell antiques, collectibles, stamps, coins, old photographs, books, baseball cards, oil and watercolor paintings, plants, handmade crafts, and much more. Hot dogs, soda, donuts and coffee are available for hungry shoppers. This show attracts crowds of over 3,000 visitors. For an additional fee visitors will also have the opportunity to see the exhibit buildings and museum.
DEALER RATES: $35 per 10' × 19' space. Reservations are required.
CONTACT: Historic Richmond Town, 441 Clarke Ave, Staten Island NY 10306. Tel: (718) 351-1611 × 280.

Flea Market at Rodeo Field

(tenative name)

Note: This market, formerly the Roosevelt Raceway Flea Market, has just moved to this new location. At press time, the admission and rates were still being decided.

DATES: Every Sunday from April through December, rain or shine.
TIMES: 9:00 AM–5:00 PM.
ADMISSION: Call for information.
LOCATION: Rodeo Field.
DESCRIPTION: Formerly the Roosevelt Raceway Flea Market, this flea market began as an antique show over 20 years ago out at the Roosevelt Raceway and moved here in 1998. It was originally held in the horse paddock and grew to occupy 12 acres outdoors and the entire grandstand building. As they outgrew their space they had to move. Almost anything can be purchased from at least 2,000 dealers. New merchandise includes anything from fur, jewelry, and sporting goods to computers, tools, and coat hangers. There is also a variety of antiques and collectibles for sale. Food is available on the premises.
DEALER RATES: Call for the new rates.
CONTACT: Carol De Santo, Plain and Fancy Shows of Westbury, PO Box 978, Westbury NY 11590-0978. Tel: (516) 222-1530. Fax: (516) 745-5706.

Yankee Peddler Day

DATES: First Sunday in May. Rain date is third Sunday in May.
TIMES: 10:00 AM–5:00 PM.
ADMISSION: $1. Parking is free.
LOCATION: At the Staten Island Historical Society, Historic Richmond Town, 441 Clarke Ave. From Verrazano Narrows Bridge, follow New Jersey West Rt to Richmond Road/Clove Rd exit; proceed to the second light and turn left onto Richmond Rd, about 5 miles ahead turn left onto St. Patrick's Place, and finally, turn right on Clarke Ave. From St. George, take bus #74.
DESCRIPTION: This outdoor market began in 1968. It hosts over 150 dealers from New York, New Jersey, Connecticut, and Pennsylvania who sell antiques, arts and crafts, silver, glass, furniture, jewelry and collectibles. The Women's Auxiliary at the Staten Island Historical Society is responsible for this fundraising event. This is claimed to be the first large outdoor flea market on the Island. This show is always well attended by dealers and buyers alike. Food is served on the premises.
DEALER RATES: $35 per 10' × 19' space. Reservations are required.
CONTACT: Historic Richmond Town, 441 Clarke Ave, Staten Island NY 10306. Tel: (718) 351-1611.

STORMVILLE

Stormville Airport Antique Show and Flea Market

DATES: Held annually on the last Sunday of May (Memorial weekend), first Sundays of July (July 4th weekend), August, September (Labor Day weekend), the second Sunday in October (Columbus weekend) and their Christmas show the first Sunday in November. Rain or shine.
TIMES: Dawn to dusk.
ADMISSION: Free. Parking is free.
LOCATION: At the Airport. On Rt 216 in Stormville.
DESCRIPTION: This massive outdoor market began in 1970. Over 700 dealers attend their shows. A variety of purchases can be made including antiques, arts and crafts, and collectibles. Shopping for new merchandise and fresh produce can also be accomplished at this market. Food is served on the premises.
DEALER RATES: $60 prepaid per 20' × 20' space or $75 at the gate. Reservations are suggested. Advance shopping hours for dealers begin at

6:00 AM on the Saturday before the show. (I'm told by friends who visited here that the goodies go *real* fast early on Saturday. Step lively!)
CONTACT: Pat Carnahan, PO Box 125, Stormville NY 12582-0125. Tel: (914) 221-6561.

WALTON

Walton Riverside Open-Air Market

DATES: Saturdays, Memorial Day through October.
TIMES: 8:00 AM–4:00 PM.
ADMISSION: Free. Parking is free.
LOCATION: Bridge St in downtown Walton. From NY I-88 (from Albany) take the exit for Rt 28 at Oneonta, follow Rt 28 to Rt 357, turn right on Rt 357, go through the village of Franklin, turn left to Walton. The market is one block off Main St.
DESCRIPTION: This outdoor market is run by the Chamber of Commerce and features from 20 to 50 dealers selling most anything: garage sale goodies, antiques, collectibles, produce in season and crafts. This started as a farmer's market and graduated to include flea market fare as well. This place is wild during their County Fair in mid-August.
DEALER RATES: $10 per space. Reservations are suggested.
CONTACT: Chamber of Commerce, 1 Liberty St, Walton NY 13856-1111. Tel: (607) 865-6656 or 1-800-639-4296.

YONKERS

Yonkers Raceway Market

DATES: Sundays, last Sunday in March through the Sunday before Christmas.
TIMES: 9:00 AM–4:00 PM.
ADMISSION: $2 per car.
LOCATION: Yonkers Racetrack. Cross the George Washington Bridge, take the Major Deegan Expressway to New York Thruway Exit 2, right there. From the other direction, from the New York Thruway take Exit 4 (Central Ave) to the racetrack.
DESCRIPTION: This outdoor market's 400 dealers sell mostly new merchandise. Although when there are enough dealers (40 or more) in antiques and collectibles, one corner will be put aside for their wares exclusively. There are loads of different foods available: bratwurst, fish and chips, pizza,

sausages, and lots more on traveling food trucks and snack bars. Naturally, there are clean restrooms for your convenience.

DEALER RATES: $40 for a 9' × 28' space with reservations; $50 without reservations.

CONTACT: Marty McGrath, Yonkers Raceway Market Inc, Yonkers Raceway, Yonkers NY 10704. Tel: (914) 963-3898 or 968-4200 x 216. Fax: (914) 968-1121.

OTHER FLEA MARKETS

We know or have heard about these markets, but have not personally contacted each one, as we have the markets with descriptions. If you plan to visit one of these markets listed below, *please call first* to make sure they are still open. Flea markets do come and go. While they were open when we went to press, they may not be later. We can't be responsible. *Call first!*

Avon: East Avon Flea Market, 1520 E Avon Rochester Rd. Tel: 716-226-8320.

Belfast: Belfast Flea Market, Rts 305 & 19. Tel: 716-365-9989.

Bridgeport: South Shore Flea Market, Rt 31. Tel: 315-633-9766.

Brooklyn: Diana's Flea Market, 379 Rockaway Pkwy. Tel: 718-385-1388.

Brooklyn: Goldstein Mark Mall Flea Market, 51 Lee Ave. Tel: 718-388-7005.

Brooklyn: Margarita's Flea Market, 1231 Surf Ave. Tel: 718-946-5188.

Buffalo: Thomas Flea Market, 1526 Genesee St. Tel: 716-896-1910.

De Kalb Junction: Deb's Antique Flea Market, 2910 Cty Rt 17. Tel: 315-347-3393.

Elmira Heights: Elmira Heights Mini Flea Market, 207 E 14th St. Tel: 607-733-6790.

Farmington: Flea Market at Ontario Square, 1740 Rochester Rd. Tel: 716-398-3997.

Flushing: 5 Corners Flea Market Inc, 71 20 Cypress Hills. Tel: 718-456-2290.

Flushing: Mini Flea Market, 84 18 Astoria Blvd. Tel: 718-476-1247.

Fredonia: Fredonia Flea Market, Rt 60. Tel: 716-679-9848.

Hudson: PJ's Flea Market, 348½ Warren St. Tel: 518-828-2271.

Jamaica: Jamaica Flea Market Corp, 92 61 165. Tel: 718-298-5858.

Jeffersonville: Jeffersonville Flea Market & Auctions, Main. Tel: 914-

482-3810.

Long Island City: Astoria Square Flea Market, 22 08 Astoria Blvd. Tel: 718-545-3935.

Lowman: Lowman Flea Market, Rt 17. Tel: 607-734-3670.

Margaretville: RK's Flea Market, RR 28. Tel: 914-586-1854.

Massena: Something Old Something New Flea Market, 17 Main St. Tel: 315-764-5433.

New York: Christopher St Flea Market, 122 Christopher St. Tel: 212-924-6118.

New York: Columbus Ave Flea Market, 162 W 72nd St. Tel: 212-721-0900.

Newburgh: Laura's Flea Market, 99 S William St. Tel: 914-561-2938.

Niagara Falls: Betty's Flea Market, 3015 Hyde Park Blvd. Tel: 716-285-5279.

Niagara Falls: Terry's Flea Market, 739 #19. Tel: 716-284-2009.

Orangeburg: All Star Flea Market, 9 Helanie Ct. Tel: 914-359-5131.

Plattsburgh: Ralph's Flea Market, 1 Healey Ave. Tel: 518-561-4801.

Plattsburgh: South End Flea Market, 133 Sharron Ave. Tel: 518-561-6926.

Pottersville: Dick's Flea Market, Rt 9. Tel: 518-494-4931.

Rochester: Northgate Antique & Flea Market, 3800 Dewey Ave. Tel: 716-621-1380.

Rochester: Red Rovers Flea Market, 3319 Lake Ave. Tel: 716-663-6123.

Rochester: Westgate Flea Market, 1940 Chili Ave. Tel: 716-426-5508.

Saugerties: The Fancy Flea, 50 Market St. Tel: 914-246-9391.

Sayville: Attia's Flea Market, 5750 Sunrise Hwy. Tel: 516-244-5755.

Schoharie: Cater's Flea Markets, Grand. Tel: 518-295-8057.

Spring Valley: Spring Valley Flea Market, Rt 59. Tel: 914-356-1100.

Springwater: Springwater Flea Market, Mill St. Tel: 716-669-2646.

Staten Island: Four Bridges Flea Market, 680 Arthur Kill Rd. Tel: 718-356-5112.

Warnerville: I-88 Flea Market Antiques & Auction Center, Rt 7. Tel: 518-234-3386.

Yonkers: AAA Flea Market, 52 Main St. Tel: 914-423-9235.

NORTH CAROLINA

ALBEMARLE

Albemarle Flea Market

DATES: Friday, Saturday and Sunday, year round.
TIMES: Friday and Saturday 9:00 AM–9:45 PM, Sunday 10:00 AM–8:30 PM.
ADMISSION: Free. Parking is free.
LOCATION: Stony Gap Rd. Take Hwy 52 south from Albemarle, at the former skating rink. Between Hwys 52 and 2427.
DESCRIPTION: Located in a former dance hall and skating rink, this market houses 50 dealers year round selling treasured antiques to yard sale stuff including collectibles, old beer signs and advertisements, depression glass, leather, tools, new merchandise, Avon, army surplus and crafts. It is said that Fats Domino performed on their stage during the dance hall years. Restrooms and a snack bar are on site.
DEALER RATES: $22 for space along the wall with peg boards, $14 for non-wall space. Reservations are required, as there is a waiting list.
CONTACT: Lyman Jones, Albemarle Flea Market, 1100 NC Hwy 109S, Mt Gilead NC 27306. Tel: (704) 982-5022.

ASHEVILLE

Dreamland Flea Market

DATES: Every Wednesday, Friday, Saturday, and Sunday.
TIMES: 7:00 AM–4:30 PM.
ADMISSION: Free. Free parking is available.
LOCATION: Off I-240 at Tunnel Rd Exit.
DESCRIPTION: This market began operation in 1971 and currently attracts approximately 350 dealers selling antiques, collectibles, garage sale goodies, attic treasures, craft items, fresh produce, and some new merchandise. Two snack bars, a convenience store and handicapped-accessible restrooms add to the amenities. I'm told that "we have the best chicken in town." This market is near all major shopping in Asheville, the Blue Ridge Parkway, and Biltmore House.
DEALER RATES: Wednesdays: $4 per day for a 20' open space, first come, first served; Friday $5 for open space, $8 for space with shed and table; weekends $8 open space, $11 for shed and table space. Reservations are required for Friday through Sunday spaces.

CONTACT: Dusty Pless, PO Box 5936, Asheville NC 28813. Tel: (704) 255-7777 or (704) 254-7309.

> They used to have a part-time deputy sheriff on site just to keep things in order while Dusty and his staff worked inside their office. One day an excited man burst into the office to announce that one of the dealers had brought a lion! Dusty and his partner decided to check this out. After three walks through the market they still hadn't seen this lion. Then Dusty noticed a school bus taking up three to four spaces with something rather lion-like next to one wheel. Upon closer inspection it proved to be a young male, about 100 pounds, just growing his mane and fortunately on a very short chain. "The deputy pitched a fit!" The dealer put the lion in the school bus for the duration of the market and was never seen again.
>
> It was here that someone bought a WWII artillery shell, took it home, fiddled around with it—and found $400 stashed in the base. You never know what you'll find.

CHARLOTTE

Cook's Plaza-Charlotte

DATES: Friday, Saturday and Sunday.
TIMES: Friday 10:00 AM–6:00 PM, Saturday 8:00 AM–5:00 PM, Sunday 9:00 AM–5:00 PM.
ADMISSION: Free. Parking is free.
LOCATION: Statesville Rd, Hwy 21, across from the Metrolina Expo (see next listing).
DESCRIPTION: Opened in March 1996, this market has 900 dealer spaces for vendors to sell literally "everything," from antiques and collectibles to loads of new merchandise and garage sale goodies. Snack bars, food vendors, a restaurant and handicapped-accessible restrooms add to the amenities. There are sister markets, Plaza I & II, in Winston-Salem.
DEALER RATES: $50 per 10' × 10' space per three-day weekend. Reservations are a required.
CONTACT: Cook's Plaza, 7335 Statesville Rd, Charlotte NC 28269. Tel: (704) 598-4464.

Metrolina Expo

DATES: First and third full weekend based on the first Saturday of the month (Friday, Saturday and Sunday).
TIMES: Friday and Saturday 8:00 AM–5:00 PM, Sunday 9:00 AM–5:00 PM.
ADMISSION: Yes, there is a charge, but they want you to call 1-800-824-3770 or (704) 596-4643.
LOCATION: 7100 Statesville Rd (Hwy 21).
DESCRIPTION: This market, started in 1971, has grown from 800 to 2,000 exhibitors. The first weekend is devoted to selling antiques and antique collectibles only. The third weekend includes antiques, collectibles, handmade and craft items, new merchandise, clothing, and jewelry—just about anything and everything. Food is available.
DEALER RATES: Their reasonable rates vary according to location and size of space. Reservations are required. Contact Metrolina Expo for the latest information.
CONTACT: Aileen Lisk, Metrolina Expo, PO Box 26652, Charlotte NC 28226-6652. Tel: (704) 596-4643 or 1-800-824-3770.

DEEP GAP

Wildcat Flea Market

DATES: Friday through Sunday, May through October.
TIMES: Friday 9:00 AM–5:00 PM; Saturday and Sunday 8:00 AM–6:00 PM. Auction every Saturday at 6:00 PM.
ADMISSION: Free. Parking is free.
LOCATION: 8156 US Hwy 421 south, 7 miles east of Boone.
DESCRIPTION: High in the Blue Ridge Mountains, along the Blue Ridge Pkwy, this family-run flea market has been in business since 1972. From 70-80 dealers sell antiques, collectibles, crafts, old and new glassware including depression, old and new gold jewelry, novelties, tools, hardware, new merchandise, coins, cards, furniture, computers and electronics and whatever. From 3,000-5,000 buyers show up at this market every weekend. There is an auction every Saturday night at 6:00 PM, year round. Antique auctions are held as needed on Tuesdays. There is a restaurant on premises serving full breakfast, lunch and dinner. Restrooms are on site. Located in the rafters of the main building is a “Hanging Museum” said to make the most diehard collector “envious.”
DEALER RATES: Outside rates $5 a day for a shed (except free on Friday). Inside and more permanent space available from $60 per month, please

call for more information. Reservations are required as most space is reserved for the season.

CONTACT: Elaine, Jack or Kevin Richardson, PO Box 163, Deep Gap NC 28607. Tel: (828) 264-7757.

A piece of depression glass was purchased here for $5 and later resold for $240.

Historical note: The original market was built in 1972, and as they were putting the finishing touches on the roof—it collapsed! The builders had to rebuild the entire building again. Obviously, it stayed up this time. They've used it for 22 years.

International folk recording artist "Doc" Watson makes his home in Deep Gap and can occasionally be found inside the main building "pickin" with his childhood friend and local dealer, Denver Cheek.

FLETCHER

Smiley's Flea Market and Antique Mall

DATES: This market is open every Friday, Saturday, and Sunday, year round. Antique mall is open daily.

TIMES: 7:00 AM–5:00 PM. Antique mall is open 10:00 AM–5:00 PM.

ADMISSION: Free with over 10 acres of free parking.

LOCATION: Halfway between Asheville and Hendersonville on Rt 25. Take Exit 13 off I-26; then travel north ½ mile on Rt 25.

DESCRIPTION: This indoor/outdoor market began in 1984. The market provides over 11,000 square feet of space in the antique mall and over ½ mile of covered selling space (500 spaces) in the flea market. It attracts an average of more than 250 dealers. A large variety of items can be found including antiques, collectibles, handicrafts, fresh produce, and some new merchandise. This place is known as the "Baseball Card Capital of Western North Carolina." Two snack bars serve the hungry. RV parking available.

DEALER RATES: $11 per 10' × 10' space per day inside the flea market area with two tables. Outside space is $7 for first table, $5 for each additional. 10' × 25' lockable units are available at $149 per month. $115 per 10' × 12' space per month in the antique mall. Reservations are not required outside.

CONTACT: Wade McAbee, Smiley's Flea Market and Antique Mall, PO Box 458, Fletcher NC 28732-0458. (704) 684-3532 or Polly Hickling at the antique mall 684-3515.

FOREST CITY

74 By-Pass Flea Market

DATES: Friday, Saturday and Sundays, year round.
TIMES: 7:00 AM–5:00 PM.
ADMISSION: Free. Parking is also free.
LOCATION: 180 Frontage Rd. Eight miles east of Rutherfordton and 15 miles west of Shelby, exit Alexander-Forest City off 74 Bypass.
DESCRIPTION: This indoor/outdoor market opened in 1986 and hosts up to 240 dealers in summer and 100 in winter. They sell antiques, ball cards, racing cards, collectibles, electronics, groceries and fresh produce, cheeses, baked goods, clothing, leather goods, tools, jewelry and new merchandise. Two snack bars and handicapped-accessible restrooms add to the amenities.
DEALER RATES: $7 per 10' × 10' inside booth; $6 outside under shed; $3 in the open. Reservations are suggested.
CONTACT: Gary Hardin, 74 By-Pass Flea Market, 180 Frontage Rd, Forest City NC 28034. Tel: (704) 245-7863 anytime.

GREENSBORO

"Super Flea" Flea Market

DATES: 1998: January 24–25, March 14–15, April 18–19, May 16–17, June 13–14, July 11–12, August 15–16, September 12–13, October 10–11, November 14–15, December 12–13. Usually scheduled for the second weekend every month. But call to make sure.
TIMES: Saturday 8:00 AM–5:00 PM; Sunday 10:00 AM–5:00 PM.
ADMISSION: $1.50 per person. $3 for parking.
LOCATION: Greensboro Coliseum Complex, Exhibit Hall. 1921 West Lee St. Follow signs posted in town.
DESCRIPTION: This very successful indoor market recently attracted as many as 10,000 shoppers on a weekend, with 500 dealers selling various types of antiques and collectibles, along with arts and crafts and some new merchandise. Food is served on the premises.
DEALER RATES: $70 per 8' × 10' space. Reservations are required in advance.

CONTACT: Smith-Tomlinson Co, PO Box 16122, Greensboro NC 27416. Tel: (910) 373-8515. Email: info@superflea.com.

HICKORY

Hickory Livestock and Flea Market

DATES: Every Thursday.
TIMES: All day, starting at 5:00 AM.
ADMISSION: Free. Parking is $.50 per vehicle.
LOCATION: On Sweetwater Rd, 100 yards north of the junction of Hwy 64 and Rt 70. You can see it from the stop.
DESCRIPTION: "There's no better Thursday market. Come one, come all and get the bargains while they're here." This outdoor market, which began in 1962 and is probably the oldest in the area, has grown to include approximately 300 dealers selling a selection of antiques and collectibles, craft items, and some new merchandise. There is also a livestock auction selling everything from cattle to birds, chickens and rabbits at 1:30 PM every week except during the weeks of Thanksgiving, Christmas, and July 4th. "When you mix animals and cowboys there's never a dull moment," says Mr. Hahn of the auctions within a flea market. The Stockyard Cafe serves such special meals that people come from all over to eat here, market or not. The cafe also operates a "mobile dealer food cart" taking food to the dealers in their spaces so the dealers don't have to leave their merchandise and miss a sale. What a great idea!
DEALER RATES: $7 per 12' space on pavement. Reservations are not required.
CONTACT: George E Hahn (father or son), Hickory Livestock & Flea Market, 1958 Kool Park Rd NE, Hickory NC 28601-9260. Tel: (704) 256-5772 (home) or (704) 324-7354 (market).

Springs Road Flea Market

DATES: Saturday and Sundays, year round.
TIMES: 8:00 AM–4:00 PM.
ADMISSION: Free. Parking is free.
LOCATION: 3451 Springs Rd.
DESCRIPTION: This market opened in the Springs Road Drive-In Theater in 1981. From 200 to 300 dealers sell anything and everything imaginable including antiques, arts and crafts, collectibles and new merchandise. There is a heated building 500' long for indoor sales which has proved so

popular they added 2 outdoor sheds. Two concessions provide food to the hungry.
DEALER RATES: $5 per day for a 20' × 20' outdoor space (2 car parking spaces), $7 under a shed with 2 tables, and $8 per day for a 12' × 12' space inside, if available (there is a waiting list). Monthly and yearly rates are available. Reservations are a good idea for the shed spaces, first-come, first-served for the outside.
CONTACT: Jim, Springs Road Flea Market, 3451 Springs Rd, Hickory NC 28601. Tel: (704) 256-7669.

LEXINGTON

Davidson Cooperative Farmer's Market and Flea Market

DATES: Tuesday and Wednesday, year round. Rain or shine.
TIMES: Early (say daybreak?) until everyone drops (usually after dark). Really!
ADMISSION: Free. Parking is free.
LOCATION: 64 Westside Dr.
DESCRIPTION: Since the 1930s this market has been running a livestock and flea market. The flea market has around 400 vendors selling antiques, collectibles, new merchandise, garage sale goodies, lots of produce, clothes, tools and whatever comes in. Wednesday mornings they hold a "Junk Sale Auction" at 9:00 AM. For a 20% commission they sell the stuff you don't want to! There is a cafe with appropriate restrooms on site.
DEALER RATES: $6 per space. Reservations not required.
CONTACT: Davidson Farmers Cooperative Inc Office & Sales, PO Box 926, Lexington NC 27292-3402. Tel: (910) 248-2173. Contact Dan York the day of the markets to reserve at (910) 248-5208.

Farmer's Market and Flea Market

Note: We know these guys are still in business. It's the trying to get a hold of them that is difficult. And their phone keeps getting disconnected. But—they are there!

DATES: Every Monday, Tuesday and Wednesday of the year, rain or shine.
TIMES: Monday 3:00 PM–9:00 PM (wholesale only); Tuesday 6:30 AM–2:00 PM (wholesale and retail); Wednesday 8:00 AM–12:00 PM (retail only).
ADMISSION: Free. Free parking is available.
LOCATION: On Old Hwy 64 W, ¾ mile off of the I-85 business loop.

DESCRIPTION: This outdoor market has been in business since 1973 and is run by brothers Tim and Jim Fritts. It attracts 300 to 500 dealers selling a full range of antiques and collectibles, as well as new merchandise, farm produce, and tag sale items. Tim handles the retail end of the market.

There is also a wholesale market that operates on Mondays and Tuesdays at this same location. They have over 250 wholesale vendors selling all new merchandise: new clothing, novelties, toys, jewelry, crafts and other assorted goodies. "Wholesale Alley" is not open to the general public and requires a state Sales Tax ID to be able to enter the area. Jim handles the wholesale market. The Wholesale Alley has been a real success story here.

DEALER RATES: $15 for a 10' × 10' sheltered booth to $10 per 12' × 16' outside space per day. Wholesale Alley rates are $200 per quarter for a sheltered space. Reservations are suggested.

CONTACT: Tim and Jim Fritts, Owners, 224 Berrier Ave, Lexington NC 27292. Tel: (910) 246-2157. Jim handles the Wholesale Alley and Tim handles the rest of the flea market.

> Tim bought an empty grenade shell for his young son from an army surplus dealer. Unknown to his mother, Tim's son took it to his kindergarten Show and Tell at school, wrapped in a bag. When his teacher opened the bag, she naturally freaked. "Cleaned the whole school out," says Tim. The sheriff's department was called, and, of course, Tim and his wife were summoned. The janitor, fearing for his life I'm sure, carefully took the grenade out to the middle of the playing field and guarded it there. The cops arrived and did their thing. Of course, Tim's son was terribly upset that the officials were taking his favorite toy. Tim duly arrived, went to the field, and pocketed the harmless casing. But not before catching a severe lecture from the deputy and the school principal.

MORGANTOWN

Jamestown Flea and Farmers Market

DATES: Saturday and Sunday, year round. Rain or shine.

TIMES: 7:00 AM–5:00 PM.

ADMISSION: Free admission and free parking.

LOCATION: Jamestown Rd. One half mile off I-40 at Exit 100.

DESCRIPTION: This flea market, which attracts 300–400 dealers year round, has been held since 1983. Dealers sell antiques, collectibles, handmade crafts, vegetables, and new merchandise. There are clean restrooms, spacious parking, storage, showers, and security available. Seasonally, up to five restaurants and several snack bars take care of hunger problems (and boost the calorie count).
DEALER RATES: $60 for a 10' × 10' booth for 4 weeks; advance reservations are very nice, but not always necessary. But especially during holiday seasons.
CONTACT: Pete Patton, Manager, Jamestown Flea Market, PO Drawer 764, Morgantown NC 28655-0764. Tel: (704) 584-4038.

> They once had a skunk walk through the market that decided it really didn't want to be there. "It disrupted the equilibrium of quite a few, but did no harm."

RALEIGH

North Carolina State Fairgrounds Flea Market

DATES: Every Saturday and Sunday, except the month of October during State Fair.
TIMES: 9:00 AM–5:00 PM.
ADMISSION: Free. Parking is also free.
LOCATION: North Carolina State Fairgrounds at the intersection of Hillsborough St and Blue Ridge Rd. Take I-40 to Wade Ave, Exit 289 or 290, Rt 54 east to Hillsborough St.
DESCRIPTION: They must be doing something right as they have 500 dealers inside and out in a total of 200,000 square feet of selling space. They particularly welcome antiques and have been known for the quality and quantity of their selection. Among the items sought after by loyal customers are the quality antiques, collectibles, craft items, fresh produce and a huge variety of new merchandise and services (framing, jewelry and bike repairs and more). The 1853 Grill serves up, I'm promised, the best homemade chicken and dumplings, as well as plenty of other homemade soups and sandwiches and awesome Italian pizza. There are outside food vendors, an indoor snack bar and handicapped-accessible restrooms. The park-like fairgrounds boast benches and quiet places. For the kids, the pet dealers have plenty of animals to pet and love.

DEALER RATES: $13 per 10' × 20' outside space, including vehicle. There is a waiting list for inside space. Inside space is by the square foot. Outside space is first come, first served.
CONTACT: Joan Long, Fairgrounds Flea Market, 1025 Blue Ridge Rd, Raleigh NC 27713. Tel: (919) 829-3533.

SALISBURY

Webb Road Flea Market

DATES: Saturday and Sunday, year round. Rain or shine.
TIMES: 8:00 AM–5:00 PM.
ADMISSION: Free admission and free parking.
LOCATION: Six miles south of Salisbury on I-85 at Webb Rd, Exit 70. Just 30 miles north of Charlotte.
DESCRIPTION: This flea market was started in 1985 and attracts 300 to 400 dealers. They sell antiques, collectibles, handmade crafts, vegetables, and new merchandise, coins, specializing in jewelry, furniture, glass, tools, auto accessories, books and just about anything. Most of the merchandise is new. Food is available on site. There are clean handicapped-accessible restrooms, spacious parking, storage, and 24-hour security.
DEALER RATES: $60 per 10' × 10' booth for four weeks inside. Advance reservations are suggested inside. Outside rates: $6 for open 10' × 10' space, $7 for sheltered space.
CONTACT: John Nash, Manager, Webb Road Flea Market, 905 Webb Rd, Salisbury NC 28146-8536. Tel: (704) 857-6660.

WINSTON-SALEM

Cook's Plaza

DATES: Saturday and Sunday.
TIMES: Saturday 8:00 AM–5:00 PM; Sunday 9:00 AM–5:00 PM.
ADMISSION: Free. Parking is free.
LOCATION: 5721 University Pkwy. At Hwy 52 North and University Pkwy.
DESCRIPTION: Open since 1990, this market of approximately 400–450 dealers sells literally "everything," from antiques, crafts and collectibles to loads of new merchandise and garage sale goodies. Snack bars, food vendors and handicapped-accessible restrooms add to the amenities. There is a sister market Plaza II as well as a market in Charlotte.
DEALER RATES: $34 per 10' × 10' space per weekend. Reservations are a must as there is a waiting list.

CONTACT: Cook's Plaza, 5721 University Pkwy, Winston-Salem NC 27105. Tel: (910) 661-0610.

Cook's Plaza II

DATES: Saturday and Sunday.
TIMES: Saturday 8:00 AM–5:00 PM; Sunday 9:00 AM–5:00 PM.
ADMISSION: Free. Parking is free.
LOCATION: 4263 North Patterson Ave.
DESCRIPTION: Open since 1991 (the other one got full), this market of approximately 100–125 dealers sells literally "everything," from antiques and collectibles to loads of new merchandise and garage sale goodies. Snack bars, food vendors and handicapped-accessible restrooms add to the amenities. There is a sister market Plaza I as well as a market in Charlotte.
DEALER RATES: $25 per 10' × 10' space per weekend. Reservations are a must as there is a waiting list here too.
CONTACT: Cook's Plaza, 5721 University Pkwy, Winston-Salem NC 27105. Tel: (910) 661-0610 or (910) 661-0999.

OTHER FLEA MARKETS

We know or have heard about these markets, but have not personally contacted each one, as we have the markets with descriptions. If you plan to visit one of these markets listed below, *please call first* to make sure they are still open. Flea markets do come and go. While they were open when we went to press, they may not be later. We can't be responsible. *Call first!*

Ahoskie: Ahoskie Flea Market, 960 Academy St N. Tel: 919-209-0040.
Ahoskie: Daniel's Projects Inc Flea Market, 301 Main St E. Tel: 919-209-9144.
Ahoskie: Sue's Company Flea Market, 960 Academy St N. Tel: 919-209-0009.
Albemarle: Albemarle Flea Market, 40818 Stony Gap Rd. Tel: 704-982-5022.
Albemarle: Hoot's Flea Market, 1311 Salisbury Ave. Tel: 704-982-9193.
Alliance: Down Home Flea Market, Hookerland Shopping Ctr. Tel: 919-745-5891.
Anderson: Anderson Flea & Farmers Market, Hwy 62 & Baynes Rd. Tel: 910-421-9300.
Angier: Bailey's New & Used Flea Market, 104 E Depot St. Tel: 919-639-6792.

Asheboro: Cedar Creek Flea Mall, 3297 Old Cedar Falls Rd. Tel: 910-625-1521.

Asheville: Bargain Barn Antiques & Flea Market, 905 Riverside Dr. Tel: 704-251-5396

Beaufort: Beaufort Flea Market, 131 Turner St. Tel: 919-728-2325.

Brevard: Lady Bee's Flea Market, New Hendersonville Hwy. Tel: 704-883-4337.

Bryson City: Mile Post 64 Flea Market, 103 Depot St. Tel: 704-488-9629.

Burlington: West Webb Flea Market, 2419 W Webb Ave. Tel: 910-584-5014.

Cameron: US 1 Flea Market, US Hwy 1. Tel: 910-245-4420.

Castalia: Perry School Alumni Flea Market, RFD 6. Tel: 919-853-6681.

Charlotte: D & M Flea Market, 5700 Wilkinson Blvd. Tel: 704-394-8100.

Cherokee: Gateway Flea Market, Hwy 441. Tel: 704-497-9664.

Climax: Old Feed Mill Flea Market & Auction, 3704 Security Mills Rd. Tel: 910-676-1003.

Clinton: Sampson County Flea Market, 400 Smithfield Rd. Tel: 910-592-7425.

Creswell: Creswell Flea Market, 105 E Main St. Tel: 919-797-4183.

Dallas: I-85 321 Flea Market, US 321 Hwy. Tel: 704-922-1416.

Durham: Poppa Joe's Flea Market, 207 E Club Blvd. Tel: 919-220-0901.

Eden: Eden Flea Market, 122 N Van Buren Rd. Tel: 910-627-9440.

Elizabethtown: Bladen Flea Market, 404 Ben St. Tel: 910-862-5563.

Elm City: Antique World Auction & Mini Mall Flea Market, 4723 Elm City Rd S. Tel: 919-236-3198.

Elm City: JC Enterprises Flea Market, 507 Church St E. Tel: 919-236-3868.

Farmville: Farmville Flea Market, Horne Ave. Tel: 919-753-3662.

Fayetteville: Basics Flea Market, 3315 Bragg Blvd. Tel: 910-868-3100.

Fayetteville: Hope Mills Rd Flea Market, 2419 Hope Mills Rd. Tel: 910-425-8053.

Forest City: Melton's Odds & Ends Little Flea Market, 1586 Old Caroleen Rd. Tel: 704-245-2425.

Franklinton: B & W Flea Market, 11 S Main St. Tel: 919-494-6900.

Fuquay Varina: Fuquay Flea Market, 6109 NC Hwy 55. Tel: 919-552-4143.

Gastonia: I-85 Flea Market. Tel: 704-867-2317.

Gastonia: Stateline Flea Market, 134 Anne Neely Dr. Tel: 704-861-8874.

Gibsonville: S & L Flea Market, 64 Brown Rd. Tel: 910-584-1614.

Goldsboro: Artis Flea Market, 117 W Walnut St. Tel: 919-736-8590.

Goldsboro: Downtown Flea Market & Auction, 217 N Center St. Tel: 919-734-0641.

Goldsboro: Goldsboro Flea Market Office, 2102 Wayne Memorial. Tel: 919-736-4422 or 919-735-6505 or 919-736-3131.

Goldsboro: Hwy 70 East Flea Market, 5201 US Hwy 70 E. Tel: 919-778-5311.

Goldsboro: Olde Antiques & Flea Market, 5552 US Hwy 70 E. Tel: 919-778-4004.

Goldsboro: Wayne County Flea Market, 2793 US Hwy 117 S. Tel: 919-731-2854.

Graham: Graham Flea Market, 614 W Elm St. Tel: 910-227-0505.

Greensboro: Super Flea Flea Market. Tel: 910-373-8515.

Hamlet: 381 Flea Market, Grace Chapel Church Rd. Tel: 910-582-3891.

Hamptonville: Martin Monroe Flea Market, 3134 US Hwy 421. Tel: 910-468-2376.

Hamptonville: Vintage Village Flea Market, 2832 US Hwy 421. Tel: 910-468-8616.

Havelock: A & W Enterprises Flea Market, 460 Bade Rd. Tel: 919-447-3250.

Havelock: Plaza Trade Center Flea Market, 1317 E Main St. Tel: 919-447-0314.

Hayesville: Dan's Flea Market. Tel: 704-389-9725.

Henderson: Harris Flea Market, 1001 Warrenton Rd. Tel: 919-438-5816.

Henderson: Randy's Flea Mart, 1651 Vicksboro Rd. Tel: 919-492-8062.

Hertford: Dail's Flea Market, 405 W Grubb St. Tel: 919-426-4060.

Hickory: Thunderbird Drive-In Theatre & Flea Market, 3451 Springs Rd NE. Tel: 704-256-7669.

High Point: Westchester Flea Market, 2200 Westchester Dr. Tel: 910-884-5063.

Jacksonville: Triangle Flea Market, 531 Richlands Hwy. Tel: 910-346-5333.

Kannapolis: Koco's Flea Mall, 485 S Cannon Blvd. Tel: 704-938-Tel: 9100.

Kill Devil Hills: Indoor Flea Market, 306 W Lake Dr. Tel: 919-441-8830.

Kinston: Bargain Barn Flea Market, 3654 NC Hwy 58 S. Tel: 919-527-3378.

Kinston: Dean Flea Market, RFD 7. Tel: 919-939-1591.

Lexington: North Myrtle Beach Flea Market, 1008 Hwy 17. Tel: 910-249-4701.

Lexington: US Flea & Farmers Market, 999 7 Oak Dr. Tel: 910-853-8449.

Louisburg: Franklin Sales Flea Market, 105 W Nash St. Tel: 919-496-3548.

Louisburg: West River Road Flea Market & Sewing Shop, RR 7. Tel: 919-496-1737.

Lumberton: Country Flea Market, 1102 Kite Rd. Tel: 910-738-2823.

Lumberton: Lumberton Flea Market, 3651 Lackey St. Tel: 910-738-4519.

Lumberton: Robeson Flea Market, 3551 Fayetteville Rd. Tel: 910-618-1026.

Lumberton: T & A Flea Market, US 74 Hwy. Tel: 910-739-1885.

Lumberton: Traders Station Flea Market, NC 41 Hwy. Tel: 910-618-0004.

Manson: Manson Road Flea Market & Produce Flea Market, RR 1. Tel: 919-456-4905.

Monroe: JB Flea Market, 3603 Plyler Mill Rd. Tel: 704-764-9523.

Monroe: Sweet Union Flea Market, 4420 W Hwy 74. Tel: 704-283-7985.

Morehead City: Dot's Place Flea Market, 1113 Arendell St. Tel: 919-808-3068.

Morehead City: Trash & Treasures II Flea Market, Hwy 70 W. Tel: 919-240-0005.

Morganton: Morganton Flea & Farmers Market, 315 Enola Rd. Tel: 704-438-9575.

Mount Airy: 52 Flea Market, Hwy 52. Tel: 910-786-2321.

Mount Airy: Greyhound Flea Market, 2134 W Pine St. Tel: 910-789-0417.

Mount Airy: Mayberry Flea Market, 1275 US Hwy 52 N. Tel: 910-789-0920.

Mount Olive: George S Holmes Flea Market, E NC 55 Hwy. Tel: 919-658-5637.

Mount Olive: Southern Wayne Flea Market, US 117 Hwy. Tel: 919-658-8228.

Murfreesboro: Inside Outside Flea Market, 904 W Main St. Tel: 919-398-8198.

New Bern: Cabbage Rose Flea Market, 2403 Trent Rd. Tel: 919-635-1235.

New Bern: Poor Charlie's Flea Market & Antiques, 210 Hancock St. Tel: 919-633-4841.

Newport: Morehead Flea Mall, Hwy 70 W. Tel: 919-223-4117.

North Wilkesboro: CJ's Flea Market, Hwy 268 E. Tel: 910-667-6877.

Ocean Isle Beach: Connie's Flea Market, 6690 Ocean Hwy W. Tel: 910-579-4222.

Ocean Isle Beach: Ray's Flea Market, 6690 Ocean Hwy W. Tel: 910-579-4222.

Otto: Otto Country Music Hall Flea Market & Auction, 2390 Georgia Hwy. Tel: 704-369-2704.

Oxford: Oxford Flea Market, Oak Plaza Mall. Tel: 919-603-1994.

Pittsboro: Super Duper Flea Market & Antiques, 304 East St. Tel: 919-542-1080.

Raleigh: Raleigh Flea Market Mall, 1924 Capital Blvd. Tel: 919-839-0038.

Raleigh: Watson's Flea Market, 1436 Rock Quarry Rd. Tel: 919-832-6232.

Reidsville: Reidsville Flea Mall, 1624 Freeway Dr. Tel: 910-349-4811.

Riegelwood: Rhonda's World of Antiques & Flea Market, 1355 Old Stage Rd. Tel: 910-655-4006.

Rocky Mount: The Pack House Flea Market, Hwy 64 E. Tel: 919-446-6910.

Rocky Point: Stallings Flea Market. Tel: 910-675-3023.

Rolesville: Rolesville Flea Market, 105 W Young St. Tel: 919-556-3226.

Rural Hall: Lewis Hand Car Wash & Flea Market, 7906 Broad St. Tel: 910-969-4733.

Rutherfordton: Breeze Lane Trading Post & Flea Market, 898 Coney Island Rd. Tel: 704-287-5411.

Sanford: Kendale Plaza Flea Market, 2726 Industrial Dr. Tel: 919-774-3807.

Sanford: Main Street Flea Mall, 2335 S Horner Blvd. Tel: 919-708-5409.

Sanford: Sanford Flea Market, 405-A Wicker St. Tel: 919-776-7041.

Siler City: Crump New & Used Flea Market, 1202 E 11th St. Tel: 919-742-5687.

Smithfield: Traders Flea Market, 1505 US 70 Bus Hwy W. Tel: 919-989-6026.

South Mills: South Mills Flea Market, 105 Main St. Tel: 919-771-8016.

Southport: Dosher Hospital Volunteers Flea Market, 380 Long Beach Rd. Tel: 910-457-5620.

Spring Lake: 210 Flea Market, 4115 NC Hwy 210 N. Tel: 910-960-8112.

Statesville: Signal Hill Flea Market, 120 Signal Hill Dr. Tel: 704-878-0820.

Sugar Grove: 105 Flea Market, 105 Hwy. Tel: 704-963-7230.

Supply: Bridgeside Flea Market, 3506 Holden Beach Rd SW. Tel: 910-842-2080.

Sylva: Four-Forty-One Flea Market. Tel: 704-586-6768.

Sylva: Uncle Bill's Flea Market, Barkers Cr. Tel: 704-586-9613.

Tabor City: Plunder Shop Flea Market, 104 S Main St. Tel: 910-653-5139.

Tarboro: H & H Flea Market, Hwy 33. Tel: 919-823-4618.

Tarboro: Pridgen's Flea Market, RR 3. Tel: 919-641-9813.

Taylorsville: Taylorsville Fairground Flea Market, 170 Fairgrounds Rd. Tel: 704-635-0058.

Thomasville: Eleven Acre Flea Market, 825 Julian Ave. Tel: 910-472-0244.

Vanceboro: Vance Mill Flea Market, 206 1st Ave. Tel: 919-244-2800.

Vass: Vass Flea Mall & Auction Inc, 341 US Hwy 1 N. Tel: 910-245-1042.

Wallace: Consignment Warehouse Flea Market, 1201 N Norwood St. Tel: 910-285-8343.

Wallace: Wallace Flea Market, Hwy 117 N. Tel: 910-285-3642.

Washington: Main Street Flea Mall, 219 W Main St. Tel: 919-975-8993.

Washington: Poor Man's Flea Market, Hwy 264 E. Tel: 919-975-9956.

Waynesville: Ragmill Flea Market & Antiques, 108 Allens Creek Rd. Tel: 704-452-5900.

Wilkesboro: Autrey's Flea Market, 4641 W US Hwy 421. Tel: 910-973-4470 or 910-973-5010.

Wilmington: Mighty Flea Flea Market, 1510 S 3rd St. Tel: 910-763-0610.

Wilmington: Star Way Flea Market, 2346 Carolina Beach Rd. Tel: 910-763-5520.

Wilson: Jeffrey's Flea Market, 207 Moss St W. Tel: 919-242-5242.

Wilson: Mildred's Flea Market, 3122 US Hwy 301 S. Tel: 919-237-2729.

Wilson: Nichol's Big Flea Flea Market, 1817 US Hwy 301 S. Tel: 919-234-2008.

Wilson: The Wilson Flea Market, 569 Ward Blvd. Tel: 919-243-7762.

Winston Salem: King Plaza Flea Market, 3025 Waughtown St. Tel: 910-785-9184.

Winston Salem: Schley Community Flea Market, 3301 NC 57. Tel: 910-732-6702.

Winterville: Winterville Flea Market, 116 W Main St. Tel: 919-756-1726.

Yadkinville: Yadkin Flea Market, Hwy 421. Tel: 910-679-3360.

Yanceyville: Hwy 86 Flea Market, 3233 NC Hwy 86 N. Tel: 910-694-5915.

Zebulon: Bullock's Mini Storage & Flea Market, 722 W Gannon Ave. Tel: 919-269-6070.

NORTH DAKOTA

MANDAN

Dakota Midwest Flea Market and Antique Show

DATES: First weekend of every month, except January.
TIMES: Saturday 9:00 AM–5:00 PM; Sunday 10:00 AM–4:00 PM.
ADMISSION: $1 per person age 10 and older. Free parking.
LOCATION: At the Mandan Community Center, 901 Division St. Take Exit 152 off I-94, then travel south on 6th Ave northwest to Division St. Signs are posted.
DESCRIPTION: This show has operated indoors since 1984 and currently attracts an average of 80 dealers who sell a wide range of items including antiques and collectibles and fine art works. One snack bar and handicapped-accessible restrooms add to the amenities. The market is close to historic Fort Abraham Lincoln, which was once the home of General Custer and has been restored as a national landmark.
DEALER RATES: $10 per 8' × 4' table per day. There are special rates for more tables. Reservations are required.
CONTACT: Barb and Bruce Skogen, 107 Esteven Dr, Bismarck ND 58501. Tel: (701) 223-6185. Day of show call the Community Center at (701) 667-3260.

MINOT

Magic City Flea Market

DATES: Second Saturday and Sunday of every month, February through December.
TIMES: 9:00 AM–4:00 PM.
ADMISSION: $1 per person. Free parking is available.
LOCATION: On State Fairgrounds. Well marked in downtown Minot.
DESCRIPTION: This indoor market first opened in 1967 and currently accommodates an average of 75 dealers. There is a variety of antiques, collectibles, and crafts available at this market. This is an old-fashioned flea market with plenty of treasures dragged out of local attics and basements. Lots of old primitives, crockery and some Victorian treasures are still to be found. Food is served on the premises.
DEALER RATES: $22 per 8' × 10' space per weekend, includes table and chairs. Reservations are required.

CONTACT: Richard Timboe, Manager, PO Box 1672, Minot ND 58701. Tel: (701) 852-1289 at home or at the antique shop (701) 838-1150.

Drat!

When a former salesman died his family came across loads of his old samples: pipes, combs, sunglasses, condoms, razors and other "stuff" from his cases. Stuff that was sold to the likes of cigar shops, billiard halls and barbershops. Three truckloads of this still-in-original-packaging stuff was taken to the local dump. Some was left on the side of the road for anyone to help themselves. Eventually, some of this 1940s' treasure made it to the flea market.

Another customer bought an old roll-top desk and took it home. Stashed away by one of its former owners: $17,000.

OHIO

BEACH CITY

Shady Rest Flea Market

DATES: Every Sunday, from the last Sunday in April through the second Sunday in October.
TIMES: Dawn to dusk.
ADMISSION: Free. The ample parking is free. But no dogs or other pets are allowed on the grounds. Please!
LOCATION: Rts 250 and 93.
DESCRIPTION: Held under the trees, this old-fashion outdoor market, started in the late 1960s, now averages about 75–100 dealers and offers a range of miscellaneous items including produce, collectibles, new merchandise, and handmade crafts. This is the oldest flea market in Tuscarawas County. In 1997 they considerably updated their facilities. Food and toilet facilities are available. The owner of the market, Mike, is 94 years young and still helps out at the market on Sundays. Stop in and say "Hi, Mike!"
DEALER RATES: $7 per day per dealer. Advance reservations not required.
CONTACT: Mike Vukich or Mildred Dinger Miller, 1762 Johnstown Rd NE, Dover OH 44622. Tel: (330) 343-9508.

BLOOMFIELD

Bloomfield Flea & Farm Market

DATES: Every Thursday, year round. Rain or shine.
TIMES: 7:00 AM–3:00 PM.
ADMISSION: Free. Parking is free.
LOCATION: One-half mile west of North Bloomfield on Rt 87.
DESCRIPTION: Now under new ownership, this market claims to have been in business since 1943, making it one of the oldest markets in the state of Ohio. They are located in the heart of Amish country attracting Amish dealers as well as buyers. There is a buggy parking area away from the car parking. It draws 150–300 dealers who sell both indoors (100) and outdoors (up to 200). Among the offerings are two meat markets (fresh and smoked), cheese deli, fresh farm products, Amish baker, tools, bulk spices, candles, canned goods, socks, candy, potpourri, collectibles, lots of garage sale goodies, as well as crafts, new goods and antiques. Food concessions

(three to five) and toilet facilities are available. Next door in the cattle barn they hold auctions.

DEALER RATES: $8 per 10' × 12' stall outside; inside, when available, $8 to $10. Reservations are required for some stalls.

CONTACT: Jo or Bill Herman, PO Box 51, Kinsman OH 44428-0051. Tel: (330) 876-7233. Day of market call (216) 685-9791.

COLUMBIANA

Theron's Country Flea Market

DATES: Every Sunday, year round.

TIMES: 9:00 AM–5:00 PM.

ADMISSION: Free. Ample free parking.

LOCATION: 1641 Columbiana-Lisbon Rd (County Rd 440), Old State Rt 164. One mile south of downtown Columbiana, just off I-11.

DESCRIPTION: This market has been around since the mid-1960s and operates both indoors and outdoors. More than 60 dealers sell a variety of items including real antiques, furniture, collectibles, homemade pastries, jewelry, glassware, etc. An annual feast is held in October. Auctions are held every Saturday night at 6:00 PM. Jolinda's Restaurant features home-cooking, open daily 6:30 AM–8:00 PM, Saturday 6:30 AM–10:00 PM, closed on Mondays. Restrooms are available inside.

DEALER RATES: $5 outdoor setups for transients. Shops $40-$160. Waiting list for shops.

CONTACT: Joann or Linda, Theron's, 1641 Columbiana-Lisbon Rd, Columbiana OH 44408. Tel: (330) 482-4327.

COLUMBUS

Amos Indoor Flea Market

DATES: Fridays through Sundays, year round.

TIMES: 10:00 AM–7:00 PM.

ADMISSION: Free. Free parking nearby.

LOCATION: 3454 Cleveland Ave at Innis Rd. Take I-71 north to Webber Rd; east on Webber Rd to Cleveland Ave; north about 1 mile on Cleveland Ave.

DESCRIPTION: This indoor market has been open since 1980; its dealers, which number approximately 250, sell general flea market merchandise as well as new goods. Food and toilet facilities are available on the premises.

DEALER RATES: $16.50 for a 9' × 8' space per day, $33 per weekend. Advance reservations are suggested.
CONTACT: Doug Hott and Paul Gwilym, Rainbow Enterprises, 865 King Ave, Columbus OH 43212. Tel: (614) 291-3133. For information call Paul at the market: (614) 262-0045.

Livingston Court Indoor Flea Market

DATES: Friday, Saturday, and Sunday, year round.
TIMES: 10:00 AM–7:00 PM.
ADMISSION: Free. Parking is also free.
LOCATION: 3575 East Livingston Ave. Just west of Courtright Rd.
DESCRIPTION: Opened in 1988, this market has about 300 dealers selling antiques, collectibles, arts and crafts, flea market fare and new merchandise. Two snack bars and handicapped-accessible restrooms add to the amenities.
DEALER RATES: Starting at $15 per day or $30 per weekend. Reservations are preferred.
CONTACT: Bill Marcum, Rainbow Enterprises, 865 King Ave, Columbus OH 43212. Tel: (614) 291-3133. Day of show call Bill Marcum at: (614) 231-7726.

Scott Antique Market

DATES: January 24–25, February 21–22, March 28–29, April 25–26, May 30–31, June 27–28, November 28–29, December 19–20, 1998. Watch for about the same weekends in 1999.
TIMES: Saturday 9:00 AM–6:00 PM, Sunday 10:00 AM–5:00 PM.
ADMISSION: Free. Parking is $3.
LOCATION: Ohio Exposition Center (formerly Ohio State Fairgrounds). Off I-71, Exit at 17th Ave to the fairgrounds.
DESCRIPTION: This market opened in 1989 with over 1,200 dealers (over 1,600 in November) selling exclusively antiques and collectibles. Considered "a treasure hunter's paradise" their dealers sell antique furniture, jewelry, silver, glassware, textiles, linens, advertising items, military items, paintings and more. There are four snack bars and one restaurant to perk up the weary shopper. Handicapped restrooms are also available.
DEALER RATES: $83 for a 10' × 10' space in the Multi-Purpose and Celeste buildings.

CONTACT: Scott Antique Markets, PO Box 60, Bremen OH 43107-0060. Tel: (614) 569-4112. Fax: (614) 569-7595. During the show call (614) 296-4484.

South Drive-In Theatre Flea Market

DATES: Every Wednesday, Saturday, and Sunday, April through October.
TIMES: 7:00 AM–2:00 PM.
ADMISSION: $.50 per carload includes parking.
LOCATION: 3050 South High St. Take I-71 south to Frank Rd; east on Frank Rd to High St; south on High St about 1 mile.
DESCRIPTION: In business since 1975, this market averages 350 dealers, outdoors only. Crafts, fresh produce, and new merchandise complement general flea market fare. Food and restrooms are available.
DEALER RATES: $5 for a 20' × 20' space, Saturdays and Sundays; $1 on Wednesdays. Reservations not required.
CONTACT: Doug Hott, Rainbow Enterprises, 865 King Ave, Columbus OH 43212. Tel: (614) 291-3133 or 491-6771.

Westland Indoor Flea Market

DATES: Friday through Sunday.
TIMES: 10:00 AM–7:00 PM.
ADMISSION: Free. Parking is free.
LOCATION: 4170 West Broad St at Georgesville Rd.
DESCRIPTION: This newer market has 400 spaces for dealers selling everything from antiques and collectibles to newer merchandise. It is a sister market to three others in the Columbus area covering north, east, south and this one the west side. Two snack bars and handicapped-accessible restrooms add to the amenities.
DEALER RATES: $5 per space per day outdoors. Indoor $17 per day, $33 per weekend. Reservations not recommended.
CONTACT: Doug Hott, Rainbow Enterprises, 865 King Ave, Columbus OH 43212. Tel: (614) 291-3133 or 272-5678.

DAYTON

Paris Flea Market

DATES: Sunday, mid-April through mid-November.
TIMES: 7:00 AM–4:00 PM.
ADMISSION: $.75 per car.

LOCATION: 6201 North Dixie Dr. Take Needmore Exit off I-75.
DESCRIPTION: There are 60 to 250 dealers in this outdoor market, a fixture here since 1966. There are plenty of antiques for sale, as well as collectibles, arts and crafts, produce in season, and new merchandise. The Air Force Museum is three miles down the Rd. Dayton is the home of the Wright Brothers. Food is served on the premises.
DEALER RATES: $10 per 19' × 25' area. Reservations are not required, first come, first served.
CONTACT: Gary Castle, 6201 N Dixie Dr, Dayton OH 45414. Tel: (937) 890-5513 or (937) 223-0222.

DELAWARE

Kingman Drive-In Theatre Outdoor Flea Market

DATES: Every Sunday, April through October.
TIMES: 10:00 AM–2:00 PM.
ADMISSION: $.50 per carload, includes parking.
LOCATION: On Rt 23 North at Cheshire Rd, 1 mile south of Delaware and 8 miles north of I-270.
DESCRIPTION: This outdoor market began in 1982 and currently attracts about 275 dealers selling a variety of collectibles, as well as fresh produce, handmade goods, and new merchandise. Food and restrooms are available.
DEALER RATES: $6 per 20' × 20' space. No advance reservations are required.
CONTACT: Dale Zinn, Rainbow Theatres, 865 King Ave, Columbus OH 43212. Tel: (614) 548-4227 or (614) 291-3133.

FREMONT

Fremont Flea Market

Note: This market was taken over by the Fairgrounds from the previous owners. It is said to still be running.

DATES: Year round: Second weekend of every month, rain or shine. Winter: Also fourth weekends.
TIMES: Saturday 10:00 AM–5:00 PM, Sunday 10:00 AM–4:00 PM.
ADMISSION: Free. Free parking is available.
LOCATION: 821 Rawson Ave. At the Fremont Fairgrounds, 4 miles south of Exit 6 off the Ohio Turnpike.

DESCRIPTION: This began in 1976 and currently operates both indoors and outdoors. It attracts approximately 100 (winter) to 250 (summer) dealers who show up to sell antiques and collectibles, as well as crafts, tools, fresh produce when in season, and some new merchandise. Three snack bars serve the famished. Dirt track car races are held during the market in the summer.
DEALER RATES: $13 for a 10' × 10' space indoors; $12 for a 20' × 10' space outdoors. Reservations are required for inside space; not for outside space.
CONTACT: Fremont Flea Market, Fremont Fairgrounds, 821 Rawson Ave, Fremont OH 43420.

HARTVILLE

Hartville Flea Market

DATES: Every Monday and Thursday, year round. Rain or shine.
TIMES: 7:00 AM–5:00 PM.
ADMISSION: Free. Parking available, $1 per car.
LOCATION: 788 Edison St NW; Take Rt 77 to Exit 118 (Rt 241) to Rt 619 East. Go east on Rt 619, 6 miles to market.
DESCRIPTION: This market began in 1947 as a livestock auction; it currently draws up to 1,200 dealers during the summertime (Mondays tend to draw the largest crowds) and 200 in the winter. Indoor and outdoor selling spaces offer a place to find all sorts of antiques and collectibles, as well as local farm goods, craft items, and new merchandise. Food is available at the Hartville Kitchen; restrooms are also available on the premises.
DEALER RATES: $7–$8 per 12' × 30' space depending on location. Advance reservations are suggested.
CONTACT: Mr Marion O Coblentz, 788 Edison St NW, Hartville OH 44632. Tel: (330) 877-9860.

JOHNSTOWN

Johnstown Lions Memorial Day Flea Market

DATES: Every Memorial Day, rain or shine.
TIMES: 6:30 AM–5:00 PM.
ADMISSION: Free. Free parking is available.
LOCATION: On the public square in Johnstown, at the intersection of Rts 62 and 37.

DESCRIPTION: This annual outdoor market has been in operation since 1972 and is now the occasion for 50 or more sellers to show up to offer their collectibles, crafts, and sometimes new merchandise. Food is served on the square on the day of the market. This market is sponsored by the Johnstown Lions Club to raise money for eyeglasses or eye health care for the needy. Some of the dealers have been here since the market began. This tiny town attracts over 3,500 to this event.
DEALER RATES: $15 per 10' × 24' space. Reservations are required.
CONTACT: Dick Scovell, PO Box 428, Johnstown OH 43031-0428. Tel: (614) 967-1279.

LIMA

Lima Antique Show and Flea Market

DATES: First full weekend, Saturday and Sunday, every month except February, June, July, August, and September.
TIMES: 9:00 AM–5:00 PM.
ADMISSION: $1 per person; children under 12 enter free. Free parking available.
LOCATION: At the Allen County Fairgrounds.
DESCRIPTION: This indoor market opened in 1976. Antiques and collectibles, new merchandise, and crafts are available from over 50 dealers. One snack bar and handicapped-accessible restrooms add to the amenities.
DEALER RATES: $35 per 10½' × 13' space per weekend; $55 per 20' × 10½' space per weekend. Advance reservations are required. Tables are available at $5 each per weekend.
CONTACT: Aubrey Martin, Manager, 716 S Main St, Lima OH 45804. Tel: (419) 228-1050, Monday through Friday, weekends and evenings (419) 339-7013.

MONROE

Turtle Creek Flea Market

DATES: Saturday and Sunday, year round, also Memorial Day and Labor Day, rain or shine.
TIMES: 9:00 AM–5:00 PM.
ADMISSION: Free. Free parking is available.
LOCATION: Just off I-75, Exit 29. Go west on Rt 63, right on Garver Rd. You can see the market from the highway.

DESCRIPTION: This flea market opened in 1992. It is held both indoors and outdoors and accommodates approximately 500 dealers during the summer and 300 dealers during the winter. From 7,000 to 11,000 people per weekend come here to shop. Items found here include antiques, collectibles, craft items, as well as fresh produce and dairy products. There are a number of food concessions dotted around the market and handicapped-accessible restrooms on site.
DEALER RATES: Inside: $35 to $45 for smaller 10' × 13' booths. Outside space: uncovered $11 per 10' × 12' space on the gravel, or $15 per 10' × 14' covered space per day. Reservations are required for indoor space, while outside space is given out on a first come, first served basis.
CONTACT: Darren Foster, 320 Garver Rd, Monroe OH 45050. Tel: (513) 539-4497 or the main office (937) 223-0222.

PROCTORVILLE

Proctorville Flea Market

DATES: Friday through Sunday.
TIMES: 8:00 AM–5:00 PM.
ADMISSION: Free. Parking is free.
LOCATION: Near the Huntington East End Bridge, 2 blocks off Rt 7. Follow the signs.
DESCRIPTION: Open since February 1991, this market is readily accessible to the many travelers going through three states: West Virginia, Kentucky and Ohio. It has 185 inside dealer spaces and 60 outdoor spaces. Dealers sell antiques, collectibles, produce, coins, stamps, books, ceramics, crafts and supplies, carpeting, tapes and records, electronics, new and used clothing, tools, lots of new merchandise, garage sale goodies and more. There is a restaurant with clean restrooms on site.
DEALER RATES: $20 for a 10' × 14½' space for the weekend or $10 per day inside; $3 a day outside for a 16' × 26' space. Reservations are suggested for inside, outside is first come, first served.
CONTACT: Todd Riley, Proctorville Flea Market, 187 Township Rd 1280, Proctorville OH 45669. Tel: (614) 886-7606.

> The story is told here of the dish marked for "40" purchased for $40. The seller thought she did really well as she had marked it for 40 *cents*, not $40. The pleased buyer later told the seller that it was actually a rare dish worth $250!

ROGERS

Rogers Community Auction and Open-Air Market

DATES: Every Friday, rain or shine.
TIMES: 7:30 AM on, there isn't really a closing time.
ADMISSION: Free, with plenty of free parking.
LOCATION: On SR 154, 8 miles east of Lisbon.
DESCRIPTION: This market and auction has been operating on this site since 1955. It is mostly outdoors, with about 300 indoor traders. The 1,200 dealers sell antiques, collectibles, crafts, vegetables, fruit, meats and cheeses, as well as new merchandise. On mid-summer peak weekends as many as 30,000 shoppers and browsers show up. There is a state park campgrounds nearby, and they have their own small restaurant serving homemade food, several good stands around the market and handicapped-accessible restrooms. The auction starts at 6:00 PM auctioning eggs, produce, miscellaneous items, and poultry.
DEALER RATES: $13–$14 per 15' × 30' setup space per day. Reservations are required. However, if there is a vacant space available due to a cancellation, then it's first come, first served.
CONTACT: Manager, Open-Air Market, 5640 Raley Rd, New Waterford OH 44445. Tel: (330) 227-3233.

ROSS

Stricker's Grove Flea Market

DATES: Every Thursday, year round. Except Thanksgiving and Christmas.
TIMES: 8:00 AM–1:00 PM.
ADMISSION: Free. Free parking is available on 25 acres.
LOCATION: On Rt 128, 1 mile south of Ross, near Cincinnati.
DESCRIPTION: This indoor/outdoor market began July 1977 and hosts 50 to 100 dealers. There are 100 spaces under roof. Among the merchandise for sale are mostly antiques and interesting collectibles, crafts, and fresh produce. In the winter the market is held in a heated hall, in the summer it is held outdoors under covered pavilions, on the grounds of a privately owned amusement park. There is a snack concession open during the market.
DEALER RATES: $11 for two tables (furnished) and setup space per day. Reservations are required for indoor selling in winter; first come, first served in summer.

CONTACT: Gladys Jordan, 9468 Reading Rd, Cincinnati OH 45215-3420. Tel: (513) 733-5885.

SOUTH AMHERST

Jamie's Flea Market

DATES: Every Wednesday and Saturday, year round. Rain or shine.
TIMES: 8:00 AM–4:00 PM.
ADMISSION: Free. Free parking.
LOCATION: On Rt 113, ½ mile west of Rt 58, 30 miles west of Cleveland.
DESCRIPTION: This market, opened around 1970, has 200 permanent dealers indoors and an average of 400 transient dealers outdoors. All types of goods are available here, both new and used, including books, tools, crystal, china, silver, glassware, jewelry, coins, stamps, handmade goods, baseball cards, floral displays, greenhouse plants and garden supplies, candles, Hummels and Goebbels collector plates, Amish crafts, clocks, lamps, music boxes, clothes, etc. One shopper even reported seeing a kitchen sink here ($50)! Claimed to be the largest and the oldest in Northeast Ohio, average daily attendance has been put at 6,000 in the summer and 2,500 in the winter. An annual Christmas special is held on the first Sunday in December from 10:00 AM–4:00 PM. Fresh farm produce featuring German, Amish and American specialties are conveniently located for the hungry shopper. More variety of foods is available including bread, health food stands, candy and nuts. Food concessions and restrooms add to the amenities.
DEALER RATES: $24–$26 per 10' × 12' space indoors, $10 per 10' × 15' space per day outdoors. There is a waiting list for indoors; outdoors first come, first served.
CONTACT: Jamie's Flea Market, PO Box 183, Amherst OH 44001-0183. Day of show call Ralph or Lolita Mock at: (330) 986-4402.

SPRINGFIELD

Springfield Antique Show & Flea Market

DATES: Saturday and Sunday, usually the third weekend of every month except July. June and August are Saturday only. May and September shows are three-day Extravaganzas—Friday through Sunday. Call for specific dates.

TIMES: Saturday 8:00 AM–5:00 PM, Sunday 9:00 AM–4:00 PM, and Extravaganza Fridays 12:00 PM–6:00 PM. June and August Saturday only 8:00 AM–5:00 PM.
LOCATION: Clark County Fairgrounds, next to Exit 59 off I-70.
ADMISSION: $2. Extravaganzas $3. Parking is free.
DESCRIPTION: Started in 1971, this market attracts 1,500 dealers in summer and 600 indoors in winter selling quality antiques, collectibles, handmade craft items, dairy products and new merchandise. Several snack bars and handicapped-accessible restrooms add to the amenities.
DEALER RATES: Reserved asphalt spaces 15' × 20' are $30 per weekend; grass spaces 14' × 30' are $45 per weekend. First come, first served spaces $20 per day. Extravaganza rates: asphalt $45, grass $60 per weekend. For other building and long-term rates call. Reservations are required.
CONTACT: R Bruce Knight, Manager, PO Box 2429, Springfield OH 45501-2429. Tel: (937) 325-0053.

TIFFIN

Tiffin Flea Market

DATES: Two shows May and October; one weekend each month, June through September. Call for exact dates.
TIMES: 9:00 AM–4:00 PM.
ADMISSION: Free. Plenty of free parking.
LOCATION: Seneca County Fairgrounds, Hopewell Ave. Take State Rt 53 to Euclid Ave, then turn west; or, take State Rt E18 to Wendy's, then turn right; or, take State Rt 224 and turn east at Wolohan's.
DESCRIPTION: Started in 1977 and sponsored by the Seneca County Jr Fair Foundation, this market operates from May through October with an average of over 200 dealers selling all types of antiques and collectibles, as well as fresh produce, handmade crafts, tools, clothing, and new merchandise. Proceeds go to promoting the welfare of the Seneca County Jr Fair and its activities. Overnight camping is available on the site for $5 per vehicle. Food concessions and handicapped-accessible restrooms add to the amenities. Sunday shows feature a dinner or barbecue put on by various organizations. July and August Sunday shows have Car and Truck Shows.
DEALER RATES: $8 per day for a 10' × 10' space inside; $8 per day for a 15' × 15' space outside. Reservations are required for inside space only.

Tables are available for a rental fee of $4 per table for two days; tables must be reserved in advance. Showers are available for campers.
CONTACT: Mr and Mrs Don Ziegler, 6627 S TR 173, Bloomville OH 44818. Tel: (419) 983-5084.

URBANA

Urbana Antiques and Flea Market

DATES: Saturday and Sunday, first full weekend monthly. Not in August because of the Fair.
TIMES: 9:00 AM–5:00 PM. Winter hours are 9:00 AM–4:00 PM.
ADMISSION: $.50 adults, children free. Free parking is available.
LOCATION: Champaign County Fairgrounds, Park Ave.
DESCRIPTION: This very successful indoor/outdoor market, started in 1971, has a bit of everything available from over 150 indoor dealers alone. Weather permitting, from 100 to 200 dealers sell outside. There are antiques and collectibles, handicrafts and new merchandise, vegetables, meats, and cheeses. Refreshments and food are available on the premises. This is a growing market, full of very good antiques and collectibles. There are three heated buildings full of dealers year round. One of the buildings is air-conditioned for summer.
DEALER RATES: $22 and up for a three 8' table setup per weekend. Reservations are required for inside sellers. This market is more than willing to work with their dealers.
CONTACT: Elizabeth and Steve Goddard, 934 Amherst Dr, Urbana OH 43078. Tel: (937) 653-6013 or (937) 788-2058.

WILMINGTON

Caesar Creek

DATES: Saturday and Sunday, year round, also Memorial Day and Labor Day, rain or shine.
TIMES: 9:00 AM–5:00 PM.
ADMISSION: $.35 per person. Free parking is available.
LOCATION: 7763 State Rt 73 at I-71, Exit 45. Five miles east of Caesar Creek Lake State Park on Rt 73. Conveniently located only 19 miles south of Kings Island Amusement Park on I-71.
DESCRIPTION: This flea market first opened in 1979. It is held both indoors and outdoors and accommodates approximately 600 dealers during the summer and 400 dealers during the winter. From 10,000 to 14,000

people per weekend come here to shop. Items found here include antiques, collectibles, craft items, as well as fresh produce, dairy products, and meats. There are seven restaurants serving a variety of foods on the premises and handicapped-accessible restrooms.

DEALER RATES: Inside: $46 to $54 for smaller 10' × 12' booths; $130 per 20' × 25' booth per weekend. Outside space: uncovered $12, sheltered $16. Reservations are required for indoor space, while outside space is given out on a first come, first served basis.

CONTACT: Louis Levin, Caesar Creek Flea Market, 7763 SR 73, Wilmington OH 45177. Tel: (937) 382-1669 or (937) 223-0222.

OTHER FLEA MARKETS

We know or have heard about these markets, but have not personally contacted each one, as we have the markets with descriptions. If you plan to visit one of these markets listed below, *please call first* to make sure they are still open. Flea markets do come and go. While they were open when we went to press, they may not be later. We can't be responsible. *Call first!*

Akron: Fifth Ave Flea Market, 33 5th St SE. Tel: 330-753-5530.

Akron: Barberton Antique Mall & Flea Market, 135 Snyder Ave. Tel: 330-848-1549.

Alliance: Carnation Craft & Flea Market, 2025 W State St. Tel: 330-823-1898.

Amherst: Johnnie's Flea Market, 46585 Telegraph Rd. Tel: 216-986-5681.

Ashtabula: Bargain Mart Flea Market, 3729 Jefferson Rd. Tel: 216-992-9060.

Ashtabula: Tannery Hill Flea Market, 3908 Tannery Hill. Tel: 216-998-6211.

Barnesville: East Main Flea Market, 511 E Main St. Tel: 614-425-4310.

Bridgeport: Chapter Square Flea Market, 68210 Belmont Ave. Tel: 614-635-0090.

Canton: Al's Flea Market & Swap Shop, 3655 Dueber Ave SW. Tel: 330-484-4014.

Carroll: Dumontville Flea Market, 980 Ginder Rd NW. Tel: 614-756-4457.

Chesapeake: Chesapeake Flea Market, Old Rt 52. Tel: 614-867-6355.

Cincinnati: Brusman's St Bernard Flea Market, 4813 Vine St. Tel: 513-641-3000.

Cincinnati: Ferguson Hills Flea Market, 2310 Ferguson Rd. Tel: 513-451-1270.

Cincinnati: Peddlers Flea Market, 4343 Kellogg Ave. Tel: 513-871-3700.

Cincinnati: Rink's Outlet Store & Flea Market, 9651 Hamilton Ave. Tel: 513-521-7465.

Cincinnati: Vick's Flea Mart, 4156 Hamilton Ave. Tel: 513-541-5084.

Cincinnati: Village Flea Market, 2100 Losantiville Ave. Tel: 513-351-3151.

Cleveland: Broadway Flea Market, 7640 Broadway Ave. Tel: 216-341-0007.

Cleveland: Cedar Thrift & Flea Market, 8600 Cedar Ave. Tel: 216-229-1735.

Cleveland: Clark Flea Market, 5109 Clark Ave. Tel: 216-631-5091.

Cleveland: Cloverleaf Flea Market & Trading Center, 7525 Granger Rd. Tel: 216-524-3020.

Cleveland: Kinney Flea Market, 12512 Superior Ave. Tel: 216-231-7227.

Cleveland: Sal's Flea Market, 4101 E 131st St. Tel: 216-921-5199.

Cleveland: Variety Flea Market, 4031 E 71st St. Tel: 216-429-0223.

Cleveland: Variety Flea Market, 15301 Waterloo Rd. Tel: 216-692-3532.

Columbiana: Theron's Country Flea Market, 1641 State Rt 164. Tel: 330-482-4327.

Columbus: Amos Indoor Flea Market, 3454 Cleveland Ave. Tel: 614-262-0044.

Columbus: D & E Flea Market, 1359 W Broad St. Tel: 614-272-1330.

Columbus: Giant Indoor Flea Market Westland Flea Market, 3575 Cleveland Ave. Tel: 614-262-0044 or 614-231-7726.

Columbus: Giant Indoor Flea Market Westland Flea Market, 4170 W Broad St. Tel: 614-272-5678.

Columbus: Harvey's Best Little Flea Market & Gift Shop, 2697 Sullivant Ave. Tel: 614-272-0182.

Columbus: Livingston Court Flea Market, 3575 E Livingston Ave. Tel: 614-231-7726.

Columbus: Westland Flea Market, 4170 W Broad St. Tel: 614-272-5678.

Damascus: The James Gang Flea Market, 14628 Alliance Salem Rd. Tel: 330-537-4411.

Dayton: Brandt Pike Flea Market, 6123 Brandt Pike. Tel: 937-236-0028.

Dayton: Dad's Furniture & Flea Market, 5499 W 3rd St. Tel: 937-262-8208.

Dayton: Dayton Flea Market, 1001 Shiloh Springs Rd. Tel: 937-276-6931.

Dayton: Forest Park Flea Market, 4444 N Main St. Tel: 937-274-3983.

Dayton: Miracle Ln Flea Market, 2110 Miracle Ln. Tel: 937-274-1476.

Dayton: Traffic Circle Flea Market, 3700 Keats Dr. Tel: 937-277-1224.

Delaware: 36 & 37 Flea Market Collectibles & Furniture, 4059 State Rt 37 E. Tel: 614-363-6446.

Dover: Dover Flea Market, 120 N Tuscarawas Ave. Tel: 330-364-3959.

Eastlake: Indoor Flea Market, 33180 Vine St. Tel: 216-946-9726.

Edgerton: Edgerton Flea Market, 228 N Crane St. Tel: 419-298-3491.

Elyria: Hadis Flea Market, 38871 Center Ridge Rd. Tel: 216-327-0977.

Franklin: Schomy's Flea Market, 100 Schomy Dr. Tel: 513-746-0389.

Hartville: Byler's Flea Market, 900 Edison St NW. Tel: 330-877-6433.

Hartville: Hartville Flea Market, 788 Edison St NW. Tel: 330-877-9860.

Hubbard: Hubbard Liberty Flea Market, 5959 W Liberty St. Tel: 330-534-9855.

Lima: Shawnee Flea Market, 3945 S Dixie Hwy. Tel: 419-991-5544.

Madison: Madison Flea Market, 1963 Hubbard Rd. Tel: 216-428-2631.

Marion: Marion Flea Market, 1238 Linn Hipsher Rd. Tel: 614-383-9027.

Miamisburg: Davis Flea Mart, 48 S Main St. Tel: 937-859-4748.

Midland: Starlite Drive-In Theatre & Flea Market, 2255 Ohio Pike. Tel: 513-734-4033 or 513-734-4001.

Millersburg: Holmes County Amish Flea Market, 3149 State Rt 39. Tel: 330-893-2836.

Monroe: Turtle Creek Flea Market, 320 Garver Rd. Tel: 513-539-4497.

Morristown: Mediterranean Beautiful View Flea Market, 38200 National Rd. Tel: 614-782-1628.

Navarre: Navarre Indoor Flea Market, 2 Main St N. Tel: 330-879-0252.

Newark: 11th St Flea Market, 50 N 11th St. Tel: 614-349-9179.

Newark: Community Flea Market, 34 Waterworks Rd. Tel: 614-366-7656.

Newark: East End Flea Market, 1001 E Main St. Tel: 614-349-0532.

Newark: Yellow Barn Antiques & Collectibles Flea Market, 142 Union St. Tel: 614-522-0087.

North Bloomfield: Bloomfield Flea Market Inc, 2211 Kinsman Rd NW. Tel: 216-685-9791.

North Jackson: Dourm's Flea Market & Auction, 53 N Salem Warren Rd. Tel: 330-538-0620.

Northwood: Craig's Flea Market, 4211 Woodville Rd. Tel: 419-698-8847.

Norwich: Big Rock Flea Market, 5705 East Pike. Tel: 614-872-4120.

Oberlin: East Oberlin Flea Market, 43433 Oberlin Elyria Rd. Tel: 216-774-4312.

Painesville: Painesville Flea Market, 1301 Mentor Ave. Tel: 216-352-7373.

Pataskala: Red Barn Flea Market & Auto Sales, 10501 Columbus Expressway Park. Tel: 614-927-2276 or 614-927-1234.

Perry: Perry Flea Market, 4650 N Ridge Rd. Tel: 216-259-2404.

Piqua: Piqua Flea Market, 8225 Looney Rd. Tel: 937-773-4131 or Tel: 937-778-2299.

Proctorville: Proctorville Flea Market, N Jones. Tel: 614-886-7606 or Tel: 614-886-9500.

Saint Marys: Grand Lake Flea Market, 1533 Celina Rd. Tel: 419-394-1684.

Shelby: Paul & Thelma's Flea Market, 175 N Gamble St. Tel: 419-342-3623.

Springfield: Springfield Antique Show & Flea Market, 4401 S Charleston Pike. Tel: 937-325-0053.

Strasburg: Garver's Flea Market. Tel: 330-878-5664.

Tiffin: Tiffin Flea Market, 100 Hopewell Ave. Tel: 419-447-9613.

Toledo: Mom & Pop's Flea Market, 4340 S Detroit Ave. Tel: 419-382-4155.

Uhrichsville: Dryden's Flea Market & Furniture Mart, 109 N Water St. Tel: 614-922-3799.

Vandalia: D & S Antique & Flea Market, 7140 N Dixie Dr. Tel: 937-890-2184.

Vandalia: Paris Flea Market, 6201 N Dixie Dr. Tel: 937-890-5513.

Warren: Warren Flea Market, 428 Main Ave SW. Tel: 330-399-8298.

West Jefferson: West 40 Flea Market, 4280 US Hwy 40. Tel: 614-879-5801.

Westerville: 3 C Flea Market, 6930 Chandler Dr. Tel: 614-882-5076.

Wooster: Wayne County Flea Market & Auction, 5730 Cleveland Rd. Tel: 330-345-1600.

Xenia: Heartland Flea Market & Bingo, 457 Dayton Ave. Tel: 937-372-6699.

Youngstown: Austintown Flea Market, 5370 Clarkins Dr. Tel: 330-799-1325.

Youngstown: Four Seasons Flea Market, 3000 McCartney Rd. Tel: 330-744-5050.

Youngstown: Uptown Flea Market, 2720 Market St. Tel: 330-782-2871.

OKLAHOMA

DEL CITY

Cherokee Flea Market & Swap Meet

DATES: Daily, year round.
TIMES: 7:00 AM–5:00 PM.
ADMISSION: Free. Parking is also free.
LOCATION: 3101 SE 15th St, corner of SE 15th and Bryant.
DESCRIPTION: Said to be one of the oldest flea markets in Oklahoma, and at the same location for 28 years, this market has over 40 dealers selling everything from antiques and collectibles, to garage sale loads, attic finds, furniture, produce, new, used and old merchandise, VCRs, TVs, and whatever. A snack bar on premises serves breakfast, lunch and other treats. They invite you to drop in to watch the domino games in the Domino Room of the snack bar.
DEALER RATES: $5 per outside table setup; building space starts at $45 and up per space. Reservations are not required. No peddler's license required as they are considered their own 8-block county.
CONTACT: KO, Jose or Lee, 3101 SE 15 St, Del City OK 73115. Tel: (405) 677-4056.

OKLAHOMA CITY

AMC Flea Market Mall

DATES: Saturday and Sunday, year round.
TIMES: 9:00 AM–6:00 PM.
ADMISSION: Free. Free parking is available.
LOCATION: 1001 North Pennsylvania St.
DESCRIPTION: This indoor/outdoor market started in 1988 and has 600 booth spaces with dealers selling antiques, collectibles, baseball cards, coins, stamps, office supplies and furniture, new furniture, Indian art, garage sale treasures, 14K gold jewelry, and new merchandise among other things. Housed in a 135,000-square-foot building, with about 50 dealers spaces outside, this is probably the largest flea market in Oklahoma. Four concession stands selling German, Chinese, and American foods as well as handicapped-accessible restrooms add to the amenities.
DEALER RATES: $44 per weekend; $158 per month. Reservations are not required. Daily rates also available: $7 per day outside.

CONTACT: Nick Adams, AMC Flea Market Mall, 1001 N Pennsylvania St, Oklahoma City OK 73107. Tel: (405) 232-5061.

Mary's Ole Time Swap Meet

DATES: Every Saturday and Sunday, year round. Rain or shine.
TIMES: Dawn to dusk.
ADMISSION: Free admission and parking.
LOCATION: Northeast corner of 23rd St and Midwest Blvd.
DESCRIPTION: This market started in 1963. There are 300 dealers selling both indoors and out. Lots of antiques, collectibles, primitives, and Western curios complement an assortment of handmade items, produce, as well as new merchandise. One cafe and two concession stands provide eatables, handicapped-accessible restrooms provide relief. There is a Dodge City western town as part of the market where they hold music shows. It has a saloon, authentic old wagons and a jail among other buildings (of course, if the kids get rowdy…).
DEALER RATES: $5 and up for 12' × 20' booths, plus electric. No advance reservations are required.
CONTACT: Dennis Sizemore, 7905 NE 23 St, Oklahoma City OK 73141-1430. Tel: (405) 427-0051.

Old Paris Flea Market

DATES: Every Saturday and Sunday, year round. Rain or shine.
TIMES: 9:00 AM–6:00 PM.
ADMISSION: Free admission and parking.
LOCATION: 1111 South Eastern Rd; access from I-40 and I-35.
DESCRIPTION: This indoor/outdoor show started January 3, 1976 and hosts 400-plus dealers selling everything from antiques, crafts, and collectibles to produce, meats, cheeses, and new merchandise. Close to a KOA campground and near the Baseball Hall of Fame. Four snack bars and handicapped-accessible restrooms add to the amenities.
DEALER RATES: $26.50 per 8' × 15' booth indoors per selling day. $12.50 for 10' × 20' outdoor space daily. Reservations are required by the Monday before the weekend requested. Monthly rate discounts available.
CONTACT: Norma Wise, Old Paris Flea Market, 1111 S Eastern Rd, Oklahoma City OK 73129. Tel: (405) 670-2611 or 670-2612.

OOLOGAH

Oologah Flea Market

DATES: Thursday through Sunday, year round. Flea market outside in the summers.
TIMES: 9:00 AM–5:00 PM.
ADMISSION: Free. Parking is free.
LOCATION: 505 S Hwy 169, 30 miles north of Tulsa.
DESCRIPTION: Although admittedly small and off the beaten path, due to a new highway, this market sells antiques, collectibles, garage sale finds, books, jewelry and "mostly small stuff." The owner regularly attends auctions and fills his market with treasures. There is a half-acre lot outside where dealers show up and sell in warm weather. Oologah is the birthplace of Will Rogers, whose home is 5 miles down the road. While there isn't any food served at the market itself, there is a pizza parlor and a donut shop nearby. Try this town's markets, they might be worth the detour.
DEALER RATES: $2 for an outside space. Reservations are not required.
CONTACT: Richard Plute, 505 S Hwy 169, Oologah OK 74053. Tel: (918) 443-2568.

TULSA

The Great American Flea Market and Antique Mall

DATES: Friday, Saturday and Sunday, year round.
TIMES: 10:00 AM–6:00 PM.
ADMISSION: Free. Parking is also free.
LOCATION: 9206-9244 East Admiral Place.
DESCRIPTION: Opened in 1989, this market holds 500 dealers inside and up to 100 outside selling antiques, collectibles, glassware, jewelry, baseball cards, garage sale stuff, and more "from A to Z." There is an electronic message board with advertising messages for dealers! A cafe provides meals. There is a mall section adjacent to this market open daily and a produce market on site.
DEALER RATES: Reasonable rates vary according to location, size and length of rental. Reservations are suggested.
CONTACT: The Great American Flea Market, 9212 E Admiral Pl, Tulsa OK 74115. Tel: (918) 834-6363.

The Tulsa Flea Market

DATES: Saturday, closed during the fair and some holiday weekends.
TIMES: 8:00 AM–5:00 PM.
ADMISSION: Free. Parking is free.
LOCATION: Tulsa Fairgrounds at 21st and Yale.
DESCRIPTION: This indoor air-conditioned/heated market has been operated by the same family for 25 years. From 235 booths, their dealers sell antiques, primitives and antique collectibles. Very little crafts or new merchandise. This is a dealer's paradise and people come from all over the country to buy here. One snack bar and handicapped-accessible restrooms add to the amenities. Described by a lot of dealers as "the best one."
DEALER RATES: $25 per space regardless of size, deposit required. Spaces are approximately 10' × 12' or larger. Table and chairs are available for rental. Reservations are requested.
CONTACT: Tulsa Flea Market, PO Box 4511, Tulsa OK 74159. Tel: (918) 744-1386. Office hours: Wednesday through Friday, 8:00 AM–12:00 PM, Saturday 8:00 AM–5:00 PM.

OTHER FLEA MARKETS

We know or have heard about these markets, but have not personally contacted each one, as we have the markets with descriptions. If you plan to visit one of these markets listed below, *please call first* to make sure they are still open. Flea markets do come and go. While they were open when we went to press, they may not be later. We can't be responsible. *Call first!*

Adair: Sixty Nine Flea Market, Hwy 69 S. Tel: 918-785-2903.
Claremore: Claremore Flea Market, 1620 W Dupont St. Tel: 918-341-1365 .
Claremore: Hoover's Flea Market, 714 W Will Rogers Blvd. Tel: 918-341-7878.
Eagletown: Lasch's Flea Market. Tel: 405-835-7443.
Edmond: Buchanan's Antique Flea Market. Tel: 405-330-1330.
Enid: Enid Flea Market, 1821 S Van Buren St. Tel: 405-237-5352.
Eufaula: Pack Rat's Flea Market, 6 miles E of Efl Hwy 9 E. Tel: 918-452-3595.
Fairland: Fran's Flea Market, 110 N Main St. Tel: 918-676-3400.
Gore: Shady Deals Flea Market. Tel: 918-489-5345.
Grove: Ned's Antique & Flea Market, 3638 Hwy 59 N. Tel: 918-786-4409.

Grove: Odds & Ends Flea Market, 5527 Hwy 59 N. Tel: 918-786-7403.
Idabel: American Legion Flea Market, 16 & Indian St. Tel: 405-286-9418.
Jay: Eucha Flea Market. Tel: 918-253-8460.
Jay: Karin's Flea Market. Tel: 918-253-8338.
Jay: R U Kiddin Flea Market. Tel: 918-253-8220.
Jones: General Store Flea Market, 204 E Main St. Tel: 405-399-3532.
Lawton: Flea City Flea Market, 1025 SW Sheridan Rd. Tel: 405-353-9381.
Lawton: Lawton Flea Market, 3701 SW 11th St. Tel: 405-355-1292.
Mead: Mead Flea Market. Tel: 405-924-7242.
Mead: Wayne's World Too Flea Market. Tel: 405-924-4540.
Muskogee: Ben's Flea Market. Tel: 918-683-3773.
Muskogee: Good Stuff Flea Market, Hwy 69. Tel: 918-682-9226.
Muskogee: McClain's Flea Market, 1300 S 32nd St W. Tel: 918-687-6957.
Oklahoma City: Hidden Treasure Flea Market, 1024 SE 44th St. Tel: 405-677-8333.
Okmulgee: KC's Flea Mart, 1303 N Wood Dr. Tel: 918-756-2715.
Pauls Valley: Swap Shop Inside Flea Market, 215 W McClure Ave. Tel: 405-238-5065.
Ponca City: Fran's Flea Market City, 2216 N 14th St. Tel: 405-762-6501.
Sapulpa: Sapulpa Flea Market, 802 W Dewey Ave. Tel: 918-224-4802.
Shawnee: Ole Shawnee Town Flea Market, 1 W Main St. Tel: 405-273-5044.
Tahlequah: Shady Acres Flea Market, E of City. Tel: 918-456-2256.
Tulsa: Admiral Flea Market, 9401 E Admiral Pl. Tel: 918-834-9259.
Tulsa: Jim's Knife Shop & Flea Market, 9244 E Admiral Pl. Tel: 918-838-2693.
Tulsa: Treasure Island Flea Market, 7626 Charles Page Blvd. Tel: 918-241-9809.
Tulsa: 21st St Flea Market, 11666 E 21st St. Tel: 918-437-6513.
Tulsa: Van L's Flea Market, 5308 E Admiral Pl. Tel: 918-832-1124.
Turpin: K/O Flea Market. Tel: 405-778-3339.
Wagoner: Main St Flea Market, 108 S Main St. Tel: 918-485-5496.
Wagoner: Wagoner Furniture & Flea Market, 127 S Main St. Tel: 918-485-9098.
Wilson: Pioneer Trade Center Flea Market, Hwy 70. Tel: 405-668-3302.

OREGON

EUGENE

Picc-A-Dilly Flea Market

DATES: Sunday shows throughout the year, generally two per month excluding July and August. Call or write for 1998–99 dates.
TIMES: 10:00 AM–4:00 PM.
ADMISSION: $1.50 per adult; children under 10, enter free.
LOCATION: Lane County Fairgrounds, 796 West 13th (8 blocks west of city center).
DESCRIPTION: Claiming to be "Oregon's First Giant Flea Market," this indoor show has been going strong since February 1970 and draws 300 to 550 dealers and 1,000 to 4,000 customers depending on the season, making it one of the largest flea markets in the area. Among the items available are antiques and collectibles, handmade crafts, sports cards, coins, clocks, records, Indian artifacts, plants, gold, silver, toys, new merchandise, and fresh produce when in season. Hot and cold lunches are available.
DEALER RATES: $15 per 8' x 2½' table and cloth and 1 chair provided. Reservations are recommended. Setup time begins at 8:00 AM on day of show.
CONTACT: Picc-A-Dilly, PO Box 2364, Eugene OR 97402-2364. Tel: (503) 683-5589. Phone open one week prior to each market or leave message.

HILLSBORO

Banner Flea Market

DATES: Fridays, Saturdays, and Sundays.
TIMES: 12:00 PM–5:30 PM.
ADMISSION: Free. Free parking.
LOCATION: 4871 SE Tualatin Valley Hwy, next to Banner Furniture.
DESCRIPTION: This indoor/outdoor market is said to be the oldest in Washington County. Between 25 and 30 dealers sell all types of antiques, collectibles, tools, jewelry and regular flea market fare. Coffee and snacks are available on the premises, restrooms are next door.
DEALER RATES: $15 per table per weekend (three days), $5 daily. Reservations are not required.
CONTACT: Betty Hansen, Banner Flea Market, 4871 SE Tualatin Valley Hwy, Hillsboro OR 97123. Tel: (503) 640-6755 and ask for Betty.

PORTLAND

"America's Largest" Antique and Collectible Sale

DATES: 1998 dates: March 7–8, July 11–12, October 24–25. Call for 1999 dates.

TIMES: Saturday 8:00 AM–7:00 PM; Sunday 9:00 AM–5:00 PM.

ADMISSION: $5 per person, kids under 12 free, 12–17 $2. Parking is available (4,000 spaces) for $4 per vehicle.

LOCATION: Multnomah County Expo Center. Take Exit 306B off I-5.

DESCRIPTION: This series of shows, which began operation in October 1981, is certainly one of the largest in the country, filling 1,300 dealer booths in March and October, and an additional 500 in July, in an impressive 240,000 square feet of indoor selling space devoted exclusively to antiques and collectibles. It is held three times each year in March, July, and October and is so successful that the promoter runs similar events in Tacoma and San Francisco. Three snack bars and handicapped-accessible restrooms add to the amenities.

DEALER RATES: $140 per 10' x 10' booth. Reservations are required well in advance of shows, as they are sold out for the next 4 years in March and October. There is a lottery system to sell remaining spaces for the July show only.

CONTACT: Christine or Chuck Palmer, Palmer/Wirfs Associates, 4001 NE Halsey, Portland OR 97232. Tel: (503) 282-0877. Fax: (503) 282-2953.

"America's Largest" Antique & Collectible Sale

DATES: November 21–22, 1998.

TIMES: Saturday 8:00 AM–7:00 PM, Sunday 9:00 AM–5:00 PM.

ADMISSION: $5, kids under 12 are free. Parking is $4.

LOCATION: Oregon Convention Center.

DESCRIPTION: This is the ninth show at this facility which began operation in 1990. The Oregon Convention Center is one of the nicest in the country, and filling 800-plus booths you will find an excellent assortment of antiques and collectibles. Food is available on the premises.

DEALER RATES: $140 for a 10' x 10' booth. Reservations are required.

CONTACT: Chuck Palmer, Palmer/Wirfs & Associates, 4001 NE Halsey, Portland OR 97232. Tel: (503) 282-0877. Fax: (503) 282-2953.

"America's Largest" Christmas Bazaar

DATES: November 27–29, December 4–6, 1998. Generally the same weekends every year.
TIMES: Friday and Saturday 10:00 AM–8:00 PM, Sunday 10:00 AM–6:00 PM.
ADMISSION: $5 per person, $2.50 under 17, free under 12. Parking available (4,000 spaces) at $4 per vehicle. Friday December 5, admission is 2 cans of donated food for the Oregon Food Bank, or $5.
LOCATION: Multnomah County Expo Center. Take Exit 306B off I-5.
DESCRIPTION: This annual indoor 6-day show began in 1983 and currently draws around 1,000 dealers selling mostly craft items, gifts, with some new merchandise and some antiques and collectibles. The show draws over 40,000 shoppers buying stocking stuffers and gifts for the holidays. Food and restrooms are available on the premises.
DEALER RATES: $310 per 10' x 10' space for crafters, with one 8' table and 500 watts electricity per 6-day show. Reservations are required.
CONTACT: Christine Palmer, Palmer/Wirfs and Associates, 4001 NE Halsey, Portland OR 97219. Tel: (503) 282-0967 or fax: (503) 282-2953.

Catlin Gabel Rummage Sale

DATES: Annually, first weekend in November.
TIMES: All day.
ADMISSION: Free. Parking is available at $3 per vehicle.
LOCATION: Multnomah County Exposition Center. Off I-5, near Jantzen Beach.
DESCRIPTION: This indoor 60,000-square-foot "rummage sale" has been held annually since 1943 by the Catlin Gabel School, and certainly ranks among the largest markets of its type in the state of Oregon, with an average of over 6,000 shoppers attending. Material is donated locally and ranges from antiques and collectibles to books, hardware, furniture and even some new merchandise. In 1998, they sold three used cars! In the past, they've sold a beer truck and a horse—a most unusual sale. This place is considered a treasure trove of goodies. Imagine, it takes 22 semi-trucks to deliver the goods to the Expo Center. Food is served on the premises.
DEALER RATES: All merchandise is donated. No independent dealers are admitted.
CONTACT: Catlin Gabel School, 8825 SW Barnes Rd, Portland OR 97225. Tel: (503) 297-1894.

Sandy Barr's Flea Market

DATES: Saturday and Sunday, year round.
TIMES: 8:00 AM–5:00 PM.
ADMISSION: $1; seniors and children $.50. Parking is free.
LOCATION: 1419 NE Lombard Pl. Right next to Columbia Blvd, between Columbia and Lombard.
DESCRIPTION: Opened in March 1969, this market moved in 1997 to its present location. There are up to 750 dealers selling everything: antiques, collectibles, office equipment, bulk food, shampoo, electronics, jewelry, dog clothes—you name it! A mini-mall sells very special antiques and collectibles including dolls, glass, and other treasures. Several restaurants serve Chinese, Mexican and American foods. "Probably the most congenial flea market in the world."
DEALER RATES: Tables are $5 Saturday, $10 on Sunday. Reservations are required for Sunday only.
CONTACT: Sandy Barr's Flea Market, 1419 NE Lombard Pl, Portland OR 97211. Tel: (503) 283-6993 or 283-9565 (use this for reservations).

SALEM

Salem Collectors Market

DATES: Generally two shows per month except July and August. Call for dates.
TIMES: 9:30 AM–3:30 PM.
ADMISSION: $1 per adult $.50 per senior; children under age 12 are admitted free with an adult. $8 "Early Shoppers" admission fee allows shoppers to enter between 4:00 PM–7:00 PM the evening before the show and 7:00 AM–9:00 AM day of show.
LOCATION: Oregon State Fairgrounds, 2770 17th Street, corner of Silverton Road. Take the Market Street exit off I-5, then west on Market to 17th, then north to Fairgrounds.
DESCRIPTION: This show has been in business since 1972 under the same family management (the Haley's daughter is now running these events), and currently averages 500 tables of merchandise per show. Shows generally feature antiques, collectibles, and craft items; specialty shows include "Sounds of Nostalgia," featuring old-time phonographs and records (first show in February); glassware shows in April and October; clock and watch sale, first show in May; "Paper Caper" show featuring advertising memorabilia and other Americana, first show in September; and a toy and doll

show, first show in November. This is considered the largest continuous twice-monthly antique and collectibles market in the Northwest. Food is served on the premises.
DEALER RATES: $13 per 8' x 2½' table. Reservations are required.
CONTACT: Karen Haley Huston, PO Box 20805, Salem OR 97307-0805. Tel: (503) 393-1261. Fax: (503) 463-1167.

SUMPTER

Sumpter Valley Country Fair

DATES: Always the weekends of Memorial Day and Labor Day Saturday through Monday, and July 4th weekend, usually Friday through Sunday.
TIMES: 8:00 AM–5:00 PM.
ADMISSION: Free. Free parking is also available.
LOCATION: 365 SE Ash St. When entering town from Hwy 7, take first right and go 3 blocks to SVCA parking lot.
DESCRIPTION: Started in 1971 at the Black Market Antique Shop, when the owners retired they asked the Sumpter Valley Community Association to take over the market and keep it alive. This flea market is one of the ways in which Sumpter is being turned into "the Liveliest Ghost Town in Oregon." Originally held in downtown Sumpter, by 1986 the event grew so large much of the market moved to the SVCA grounds. The event, which takes place in a town of 170 people, features 300–400 dealers in antiques, collectibles, handcrafts and new merchandise. Fresh produce and food are also available. While in town, visitors can also ride the restored portion of the Sumpter Valley Railway, a steam–operated narrow-gauge railroad. Usually visitors enjoy an old-time fiddlers show. Says the director, "you never know who you will run into here. Neighbors from far away towns have found each other here."
DEALER RATES: $2 per foot with minimum space of 12'. Reservations are required.
CONTACT: Leland or Nancy Myers, SVCA, PO Box 213, Sumpter OR 97877-0213. Tel: (541) 894-2264.

WALDPORT

SeaMarket

DATES: Daily.
TIMES: Weekends: 9:00 AM–5:00 PM. Weekdays: 11:00 AM–5:00 PM.
ADMISSION: Free. Parking is free.

LOCATION: Hwy 101 at 260 SW Arrow. Literally right on the highway.
DESCRIPTION: Opened in the winter of 1994, this admittedly little indoor/outdoor market houses 30 dealers inside and as many as want to set up outside. The inside dealers are generally there all the time selling antiques, collectibles, "junk," just about everything, according to Pauline. The garage sale goodies come in mostly during the warmer weather outside. As this market is located right on a major tourist highway running along the Pacific coast, not only do the tourists stop for the market, but the views are "stunningly gorgeous." What an enticement! There are food vendors on the grounds.
DEALER RATES: $80 monthly inside. Outside: $5 per day during the week, $10 per day weekends. Reservations are a good idea if you want inside space as there is a waitlist. Otherwise, set up outside!
CONTACT: Pauline Gates, 2240 Crestline Dr, Waldport OR 97394. Tel: (541) 563-6436. Email: pgates@server.fbo.com.

OTHER FLEA MARKETS

We know or have heard about these markets, but have not personally contacted each one, as we have the markets with descriptions. If you plan to visit one of these markets listed below, *please call first* to make sure they are still open. Flea markets do come and go. While they were open when we went to press, they may not be later. We can't be responsible. *Call first!*

Brookings: Harbor Indoor Outdoor Flea Market, 99070 W Freeman Ln. Tel: 541-469-6411.
Clackamas: Damascus Bargain Fair & Flea Mart. Tel: 503-658-7535.
Cloverdale: Red Barn Flea Mart, 33920 Hwy 101 S. Tel: 503-392-3973.
Coquille: Coquille Flea Market. Tel: 541-396-7785.
Grants Pass: Mr X's Swap Shop & Flea Market, 1580 NE 7th St. Tel: 541-474-2481.
Lincoln City: Stuffy's Flea Market, 1320 NW 13th St. Tel: 541-994-7711.
McMinnville: Real Deal Flea Market & Thrift Store. Tel: 503-435-1148.
Phoenix: A-1, 3558 S Pacific Hwy. Tel: 541-535-6505.
Portland: Jack's Parkrose Flea Market, 10643 NE Sandy Blvd. Tel: 503-252-6709.
Portland: King's Swap Meet, 6728 NE Martin Luther King Blvd. Tel: 503-289-0773.

Portland: Number 1 Flea Markets, 17420 SE Division St. Tel: 503-761-4646.

Portland: Portland Swap Meet, 12750 SW Pacific Hwy Ste 112. Tel: 503-684-3391.

Roseburg: Mona's Treasures & Flea Market, 2110 NE Stephens St. Tel: 541-672-6648.

Salem: The Bazaar Flea Market, 4675 Portland Rd NE. Tel: 503-393-6626.

Salem: Salem Flea Market. Tel: 503-393-1261.

Silverton: The Littlest Flea, Beverly Dolan. Tel: 503-873-6714.

Sweet Home: Cash Deals Flea Market, 1937 Main St. Tel: 541-367-6273.

PENNSYLVANIA

ADAMSTOWN

Renninger's #1 Antique Market

DATES: Every Sunday, year round.
TIMES: 7:30 AM–4:00 PM.
ADMISSION: Free. Free parking is available.
LOCATION: On Rt 272, 1 mile north of Exit 21 on the Pennsylvania Turnpike, between Adamstown and Denver in Lancaster County.
DESCRIPTION: This indoor and outdoor market has operated since 1967 and houses up to 500 dealers in a huge, indoor building. They deal in fine antiques and all types of collectibles. No crafts or new merchandise are permitted. In fair weather, outdoor dealers number from 200 to 400. Stands are in a grove and lot behind the main market building.
DEALER RATES: $15 per day all Sundays except five special dates, when the fee is somewhat higher. Reservations for indoor stands, if available, are required. No reservations are needed for the outdoor section. Apply at the market office.
CONTACT: Renninger's Promotions, 27 Bensinger Dr, Schuylkill Haven PA 17972. Tel: (717) 385-0104, Monday through Thursday; Friday through Sunday (717) 336-2177.

Stoudt's Black Angus Antique Mall

DATES: Every Sunday, year round. Rain or shine.
TIMES: 8:00 AM–5:00 PM.
LOCATION: Rt 272, 1 mile north of Pennsylvania Turnpike, Exit 21.
ADMISSION: Free. Plenty of free parking is available.
DESCRIPTION: Over 29 years old, this Sunday market is part of a huge complex including Stoudt's Black Angus Restaurant, brewery, brewery hall and the Stoudtburg Village. They hold a Beer Fest every weekend during August and every Sunday in October. Polka weekend is Labor Day weekend! Only antiques and collectibles are sold at the Antiques Mall by 400 permanent indoor dealers year round and another 200 dealers set up in four outdoor pavilions in the summer. One source tells me that the Black Angus Restaurant serves the best steak dinner he has ever eaten and this man travels extensively! They built a Bavarian-style German village, called Stoudtsburg, with homes, an antique co-op, five antique stores. The down-

stairs of each unit is a shop the owners live above on the second and third floor—like European villages.

DEALER RATES: Contact Carl Barto for rates. Reservations are required.

CONTACT: Carl Barto, Manager, Stoudt's Black Angus, PO Box 880, Rt 272, Adamstown PA 19501-0880. Tel: (717) 484-4385. Or call Carl directly at (717) 569-3536.

BENSALEM

Farmers Market at Philadelphia Park

DATES: Every Friday, March through December.

TIMES: 8:00 AM–3:00 PM.

ADMISSION: Free. Parking is free.

LOCATION: On Street Rd, 3 miles from I-95, or just off Exit 28 of the Pennsylvania Turnpike.

DESCRIPTION: Opened in 1982, this outdoor market accommodates 700 dealers selling antiques, collectibles, new merchandise and produce.

DEALER RATES: $25 per day for a 12' × 30' space. $80 per month for a reserved space. Reservations are suggested.

CONTACT: Flea World Inc, PO Box 387, Vorhees NJ 08043-0387. Tel: (609) 795-8393.

CHADDS FORD

Pennsbury-Chaddsford Antique Mall

DATES: Upper Section open daily except Tuesday and Wednesday; lower level weekends only, year round.

TIMES: 10:00 AM–5:00 PM.

ADMISSION: Free. Free parking.

LOCATION: On Rt 1, between Brandywine River Museum and Longwood Gardens.

DESCRIPTION: Located in a two-level building in historic Brandywine Valley near the Brandywine River Museum, this indoor market has 100 regular dealers selling a range of antiques and collectibles, primitives, from stamps and coins to militaria to silver, jewelry, period furniture, and Oriental rugs. Food is served on the premises.

DEALER RATES: Downstairs rates start from $135 to $250 for spaces ranging from 10' × 12' to 24' × 12' per month. Upstairs rates are from $250 to $525 per month. There is a waiting list for dealers. Display cases are also available for rental for $100 a month.

CONTACT: Alfred Delduco, Owner, or Stan Salinski, Manager, 31 S High St, W Chester PA 19382. Tel: (610) 692-6311. Or Mary Dickinson, Upper Level Manager, Pennsbury-Chadds Ford Antique Mall, 640 E Baltimore Pk, Chadds Ford PA 19317. Mall numbers are (610) 388-1620 upper level; (610) 388-6536 for lower level.

COLLEGEVILLE

Power House Antique and Flea Market

DATES: Every Sunday.
TIMES: 9:00 AM–5:00 PM.
ADMISSION: Free. Free parking available.
LOCATION: On Rt 29 North. From Philadelphia: take Rt 422 west to Collegeville, then north on Rt 29. From Reading: take Rt 422 east to Collegeville, then north on Rt 29.
DESCRIPTION: This indoor market has been functioning since 1970 in an old power house and currently holds approximately 50 dealers who sell many antique items, a range of collectibles including coins, baseball cards, books, and jewelry, as well as new merchandise and crafts. Food is not served on the premises, but restrooms are available.
DEALER RATES: $15 for a 9' × 12' space. Reservations are required, and rates for larger spaces are available on request.
CONTACT: Janet McDonnell, 45 First Ave, Collegeville PA 19426. Tel: (610) 489-7388.

DENVER

Barr's Antique World

DATES: Every Saturday and Sunday, rain or shine.
TIMES: Saturday 10:00 AM–5:00 PM; Sunday 8:00 AM–5:00 PM.
ADMISSION: Free. Free parking.
LOCATION: Take Exit 21 off the Pennsylvania Turnpike, take Toll Booth Service Rd to Rt 272 North (¼ mile).
DESCRIPTION: This indoor/outdoor market has operated since 1979 and currently attracts around 150 sellers offering a range of items including antiques, Country French furniture and accessories, furniture, paintings, Oriental art, cigar labels, clocks, glassware, stamps, primitives, jewelry, quilts, tools, toy trains, postcards, and political memorabilia, as well as crafts. An auction room occupies the rear of the building with regular Monday sales. For items viewed on weekends, you can leave a 25% deposit as

an absentee bid. There are special sale dates throughout the year. Food and clean restrooms are available.

DEALER RATES: Outdoor space is unreserved; inside space also available. Call for rates and reservations.

CONTACT: Col Bervin L Barr, 2152 N Reading Rd, Denver PA 17517. Tel: (717) 336-2861.

DOWNINGTOWN

Downingtown Marketplace

DATES: Friday through Sunday, year round.

TIMES: Market: Friday 11:00 AM–10 PM; Saturday 10:00 AM–10:00 PM; Sunday 10:00 AM–6:00 PM. Flea Market: Saturday and Sunday 8:00 AM–5:00 PM.

ADMISSION: Free. Free parking on premises.

LOCATION: On Business Rt 30 (Lancaster Ave). Take Exit 23 off the Pennsylvania Turnpike, head south on Rt 100 to Rt 30, then go west on Business Rt 30 (market will be on right side).

DESCRIPTION: Over 45 years old, the Downingtown Marketplace is more than just a flea market. Over 30 front stores facing Lancaster Avenue have additional hours during the week. Inside the Main Market are over 150 unique stores including produce, baked goods, crafts, clothing, jewelry, furniture, antiques, collectibles and food to satisfy everyone. Plus a 13,000-square-foot Expo Center with family-oriented events year round. Toilet facilities are available on the premises. At more than four football fields long, this is one of the larger markets in the state. The flea market has both dedicated indoor and outdoor areas. Toilet facilities are available on the premises.

DEALER RATES: $15 per 12' × 12' space outdoors, per day. Dealer reservations are not required outside. Inside is by license at $65 a week for a 9' × 13' space up to 3,000 square feet. Setup for outside space starts at 6:00 AM.

CONTACT: For indoor flea market reservations call Joe Piatowski (215) 362-8812. For Market space or Expo Center reservations call K Altman (610) 518-5100, fax (610) 518-5106. Downingtown Marketplace, 955 E Lancaster Ave, Downingtown PA 19335.

Talk about recycling!
In 1953, when a ship-building company canceled a steel order (the ship wasn't to be built), Daniel Tabas of Acorn Iron used the steel to build Downingtown Marketplace.

EDINBURG

Michaelangelo's

DATES: Sunday, year round.
TIMES: 7:00 AM–4:00 PM.
ADMISSION: Free. Parking is free.
LOCATION: On State Rt 422, 5 miles west of New Castle.
DESCRIPTION: This indoor/outdoor market, started in 1971, boasts 200–300 dealers offering antiques, handmades, musical greeting cards, floral arrangements, collectibles, cards, gifts, produce, meats, cheese, and new and used merchandise. Food is always available at the ground's concessions, restaurant, and smorgasbord.
DEALER RATES: $7 and up for a 14' × 16' space outside; $10 and up for an 8' table plus space indoors. Reservations are not required outdoors, but are required for indoor selling.
CONTACT: Michael Carbone, Michaelangelo's, RD 1 Box 211, Edinburg PA 16116. Tel: (412) 654-0382 or 656-8915.

EPHRATA

Green Dragon Farmers Market and Auction

DATES: Every Friday, rain or shine.
TIMES: 9:00 AM–10:00 PM.
ADMISSION: Free. Thirty acres of free parking.
LOCATION: 955 North State St, 1 mile north of Ephrata; ¼ mile off Rt 272. Look for the dragon.
DESCRIPTION: Green Dragon began in 1932 and now has over 400 merchants weekly, including 250 local growers and craftsmen. Meats, fish, poultry, cheeses, and sweets are among the fresh produce available, and all types of antiques and collectibles may be found at the market. The auction offers a range of products from dry goods to small animals. A real down-home country affair for the whole family. Food is served in five restaurants and seven snack bars; restroom facilities are available.

DEALER RATES: $25 per 20' × 20' space. Advance reservations are required.

CONTACT: Larry L Loose, Manager, The Green Dragon, 955 N State St, Ephrata PA 17522. Tel: (717) 738-1117.

FAYETTEVILLE

Fayetteville Antique Mall

DATES: Daily.

TIMES: 9:00 AM–5:00 PM.

ADMISSION: Free. Parking is also free.

LOCATION: I-81, Exit 6 on Rt 30, 18 miles west of Gettysburg, or 4 miles east of Chambersburg.

DESCRIPTION: This market, located in four buildings, has 280 dealers selling mostly antiques, collectibles, castiron, depression glass, books, toys, dolls, china, tools, postcards, primitives, furniture, and more! A snack bar operates daily. Outside setups are available. There are six to eight smaller buildings rented by individuals selling even more items.

DEALER RATES: Call for more information.

CONTACT: L L Dymond Jr, Fayetteville Antique Mall, 3653 Lincoln Way E, Fayetteville PA 17222. Tel: (717) 352-8485 or 352-2525.

GILBERTSVILLE

Gilbertsville Firehouse Indoor Flea Market

DATES: 1998: January 11, February 8, March 8, November 29 and December 13. Try the same weekends for the following years, second Sundays in January, February, March and December; last Sunday in November.

TIMES: 8:00 AM–2:00 PM. Dealers set up after 7:30 AM, the public is welcome to join in.

ADMISSION: Free. Parking is also free.

LOCATION: Rt 73, east of Rt 100 and west of Rt 663.

DESCRIPTION: Started in 1990, this indoor market's 50 to 75 dealers (from 100 tables) sell antiques, collectibles, handmade and craft items and some new merchandise. This market started in 1989. Food sold at the market helps fund the Gilbertsville Firehouse. There is a restaurant on premises as well. Restrooms are handicapped accessible.

DEALER RATES: $20 per space. Reservations are required.

CONTACT: Nadia Promotions Inc, PO Box 156, Flourtown PA 19031-0156. Tel: (215) 643-1396. Fax: (215) 654-0896.

Zern's Farmer's Market and Auction

DATES: Every Friday and Saturday, year round, rain or shine.
TIMES: Friday 2:00 PM–10:00 PM; Saturday 11:00 AM–10:00 PM.
ADMISSION: Free. Free parking for 5,000 cars is available.
LOCATION: On Rt 73, 1 mile east of Boyertown.
DESCRIPTION: First opened in 1922 this market is one of the oldest and largest continuous farmers markets in the country. There are five auctions on Friday and Saturday. Their 400 dealers, both indoors and out, sell a vast variety of antiques, collectibles, Amish crafts, and all types of produce, meats and cheeses, seafood, baked goods, poultry, plants, yard sculptures, new and vintage clothing, new and used books, musical instruments, and whatever. You could probably furnish a house and clothe your family from the markets and auctions here; from hearing aids and glasses to kitchens, from hats to shoes. There is a livestock auction weekly. Located in the heart of "Amish Country," this market is self-billed as the "World's Largest Dutch Treat." It was once voted "Best of Philly" by *Philadelphia Magazine*. There are food concessions on the premises.

Watch for the festivals, auctions and specials: car shows, auto auctions, Planter's Peanut, Elvis Week (impersonators and contests), Nancy's Attic Christmas display with antique ornaments for display and sale, plant auctions... the list is amazing!
DEALER RATES: $25 per 8' × 10' outside space for Friday and Saturday. Reservations are required.
CONTACT: Zern's, Rt 73, Gilbertsville PA 19525. Tel: (610) 367-2899 for reservations.

GREENSBURG

Greengate Flea Market

DATES: Sundays: April through October outdoors; winter indoors.
TIMES: Outdoors 7:00 AM–3:00 PM. Indoors 8:00 AM–3:00 PM.
ADMISSION: Free. Parking is free.
LOCATION: Rt 30 west of Greensburg, on the upper parking lot next to the Greengate Mall. From the turnpike take Exit 7 (Irwin), go east to market. Winter: basement of the old JC Penney store at the mall.
DESCRIPTION: Moved from Latrobe in 1991, this outdoor market has grown with their new space. They can accommodate 150 dealers and have come close in their first year. Their dealers sell antiques, collectibles, crafts, produce, household goods, garage sale finds, coins, stamps, loads of base-

ball cards, baked goods, furniture, new merchandise, whatever. I am assured that the snack concession serves the "best hot sausage sandwich in Pennsylvania." People drive from all over just to have a sandwich! Found among the Tupperware and stuff brought in: a hanging salt in blue spongeware (very rare item), and two beautiful handmade quilts. Watch for the opening of the new indoor market in the basement of the old JC Penney store where 70 dealers will operate for the winter until the outdoor market starts again.

DEALER RATES: Outdoors: $15 for a 21' × 16' space, $9 for a 11' × 16' space. Spaces always available on Sunday mornings. Indoors: $16–$25 with varied sizes available. Dealers supply their own tables.

CONTACT: Carol J Craig, 214 Kenneth St, Greensburg PA 15601. Tel: (412) 837-6881 evenings.

HAZEN

Warsaw Township Volunteer Fire Company Flea Market

DATES: First Sunday of the month, May through October.

TIMES: Daybreak to around 4:00 PM, depending on weather.

ADMISSION: Free. $2 to park.

LOCATION: On Rt 28, ½ mile north of Hazen. Take I-80 to Exit 14, then north 6 miles on Rt 28. Located in northwest Pennsylvania near Brookville, Brockway and Dubois. Only 80 miles from the Ohio stateline.

DESCRIPTION: This extremely successful outdoor market began in the early 1970s as a fundraiser for the fire house. They average 450 dealers selling a variety of antiques and collectibles, as well as farm produce and some new items. This is truly a great place to find treasures. A violin went for $2,000. One customer was seen walking around with a boa constrictor around her neck. It is quite common for out-of-state dealers to fly to this area several times during the year, stock up on antiques, store them, then return later with a truck to collect their booty. Because of the success of this market, area motels and hotels have expanded to accommodate the influx of traffic. On the day of the flea market, the entire area becomes a giant yard sale. If you are a true-blue hunter of treasures and bargains, come in on Saturday when the dealers start setting up and start hunting. Food and toilet facilities are available.

DEALER RATES: $15 for 18' × 24' space outdoors. Call for reservation information. Dealers get discounts at local area hotels and motels. Just ask. All dealers must have a Pennsylvania sales tax number.

CONTACT: Warsaw Township Volunteer Fire Co, RD5 Box 146, Brookville PA 15825. Call the Fire Hall at (814) 328-2528 or Clyde at (814) 328-2536.

Be specific—

An out-of-state dealer asked the price of a butter churn and butter maker dish. "Two-fifty each." Thinking that $250 each was a bit steep, he continued browsing. The next buyer admired the pair and asked the price. "Five bucks for the pair." They were sold on the spot.

Later the dealer told Clyde that he really would have paid $250 each for the items, they were more than worth it.

Get smart!

One woman held up a dish she was selling and asked fellow dealers what they thought it was worth, as she had it marked for $10. The others consulted and said it was a very good, expensive dish. The dealer promptly raised the price to $50. No one bought it—yet. When she checked into the matter with experts, she found the dish was worth $1,200!

HULMEVILLE

Old Mill Flea Market

DATES: Thursday through Sunday, year round. Rain or shine.
TIMES: Thursday and Friday 6:00 PM–9:00 PM; Saturday 12:00 PM–9:00 PM; Sunday 12:00 PM–5:00 PM.
ADMISSION: Free. Free parking is available.
LOCATION: Intersection of Hulmeville Rd/Bellevue and Trenton Aves; 2 miles from Exit 28 on the Pennsylvania Turnpike (US Rt 1); 2 miles from I-95 (US Rt 1) exit for Penndel/Langhorne (used to be Exit 26).
DESCRIPTION: This small, year-round indoor market started in 1971 in a large, 1880's historic Bucks County grist mill. The market draws several hundred shoppers each weekend. A full range of antiques and collectibles is available, including dolls, books, china, textiles, jewelry, furniture, glassware, advertising, breweriana, photographica, pottery, etc. This place is a "haunt" for dealers and collectors, more so than for the general public (who hasn't caught on—yet), as the management buys out house contents and estates. No food is available on the premises. Restrooms are provided.

DEALER RATES: Currently there is no space available.
CONTACT: Kathy Loeffler, PO Box 7069, Penndel PA 19047-7069. Tel: (215) 757-1777.

KUTZTOWN

Renninger's #2 Antique Market

DATES: Every Saturday, year round. Rain or shine. Extravaganzas in April, June, and September.
TIMES: 8:30 AM–4:00 PM. Pennsylvania Dutch Farmer's market is open every Friday 12:00 PM–8:00 PM.
ADMISSION: Free. There is an admission charge for Extravaganzas. Free parking is provided.
LOCATION: 740 Nobel St, 1 mile south from the center of town. Midway between Allentown and Reading on Rt 222.
DESCRIPTION: This indoor/outdoor market has been in operation since 1955 and now ranks among the most popular markets in the Northeast. The market attracts approximately 300 dealers during regular weekends, and up to 1,500 during the Extravaganzas. A wide range of antiques and collectibles is featured along with craft items, new merchandise, and fresh foods including smoked and fresh meats, poultry, seafood, and baked goods. For the Extravaganzas, dealers are said to arrive from as many as 42 different states, as well as from Canada and Europe. There is no flea market on Extravaganza days.
DEALER RATES: $10 per 10' × 25' outdoor pavilion space per day, $8 for special outdoor section, during normal sale days. Call for rates for Extravaganzas. Reservations are required.
CONTACT: Renninger's Promotions, 27 Bensinger Dr, Schuylkill Haven PA 17972. Tel: (717) 385-0104 Monday through Thursday; Friday and Saturday call (610) 683-6848.

LEEPER

Leeper Flea Market

DATES: Saturday and Sunday, from mid-April to mid-October.
TIMES: Dawn to dusk.
ADMISSION: Free. Parking is free.
LOCATION: At the intersection of Rts 66 and 36, 14 miles north on Rt 66 from Clarion, near Cooks Forest National Recreation Area.

DESCRIPTION: Open for over 22 years, this lively outdoor market averages 60–100 dealers (with 170 available spaces) selling just about everything. Antiques, garage sale goodies, crafts, new and used hunting and fishing supplies are among the treasures mentioned by an enthusiastic shopper who sent in this listing of her favorite market. Fresh baked goods are sold by Amish vendors on Saturdays. Fresh produce, mini-donuts, and authentic buffalo burgers are some of the vast variety of foods sold here. They are located near Cooks Forest Recreational Area and the Allegheny National Forest with plenty of camps and weekend getaways around them. On the holiday weeks of Memorial Day, July 4th, and Labor Day, this market stays open for the entire week and is loaded to capacity with dealers.
DEALER RATES: $5 per day for 20' × 20' space. First come, first served. Find Don, the owner, at the Red & White Market located on the upper corner of the market area, daily until 4:00 PM.
CONTACT: Don or Helen, Leeper Red & White Market, PO Box 150, Leeper PA 16233. Tel: (814) 744-8811.

> This market is surrounded by woods. The dumpsters are kept at the lower end of the market away from the crowds. Every fall, black bears come out of the woods to check out the tossed-in goodies. Labor Day 1996 saw a packed market—of shoppers—when the bears decided to pay a visit. "What an audience they had!"

LEESPORT

Leesport Farmers Market

DATES: The flea market is every Wednesday and the first and third Sunday of each month from April through the first Sunday in December; the farmer's market is held every Wednesday, year round.
TIMES: Wednesday flea market from 7:00 AM–close; first and third Sunday 7:00 AM–3:00 PM; farmer's market from 9:00 AM–8:00 PM.
ADMISSION: Free admission and free parking.
LOCATION: One block east off Rt 61; 8 miles north of Reading.
DESCRIPTION: This family-run market has been operating since 1947 and currently has over 600 dealers spaces both indoors and out. The complete farmer's market, with a livestock auction on Wednesday, is comple-

mented by the collectibles, jewelry, clothing, crafts and new merchandise available at the flea market. Many items are supplied by neighboring Pennsylvania Dutch merchants. Food is available on the market grounds.
DEALER RATES: \$10 per 12' × 35' unsheltered space, no tables; \$10 per 10' × 10' space with 8' table. Some spaces are reserved for the season. Otherwise, first come, first served.
CONTACT: Daniel "Woody" Weist, PO Box B, Leesport PA 19533. Tel: (610) 926-1307.

LEOLA

Meadowbrook Market, Inc

DATES: Fridays and Saturdays.
TIMES: Friday 8:00 AM–7:00 PM; Saturday 8:00 AM–5:00 PM.
ADMISSION: Free. Free parking is provided.
LOCATION: 345 West Main St; 4 miles east of Lancaster on Rt 23.
DESCRIPTION: This indoor market has been in operation since 1970 and currently draws approximately 196 dealers selling all types of items including antiques, collectibles, foods, furniture, spices, sheepskins, handmade goods, most anything and new merchandise. The market is air-conditioned in summertime, and shopping carts are provided for added convenience. A new addition was added in 1991 creating more space indoors. This is a big complex that includes three restaurants "outside"; one Chinese, one Italian, one serving Barbecue ribs, and one "inside" the market. In addition, there are six snack bars scattered throughout the complex. Tour buses regularly come from Texas making a yearly pilgrimage, as well as Canada, California and all over the East Coast. Recently they added a Lancaster County Convention Center. Restrooms are available.
DEALER RATES: \$5 to \$10 per booth for outside flea market, no tables supplied. Advance reservations are required.
CONTACT: Frank or Joe Suraci, Meadowbrook Market, 345 W Main St, Leola PA 17540. Tel: (717) 656-2226.

MARSHALLS CREEK

Pocono Bazaar

DATES: Every Saturday and Sunday (except Christmas and New Year's Day if they fall on a weekend), and major holidays (President's Day, Memorial Day, July 4th, Labor Day and Thanksgiving Friday).
TIMES: 9:00 AM–5:00 PM.

ADMISSION: Free. Ample free parking is available.
LOCATION: On US Rt 209. Take Exit 52 off I-80 (1 mile west of the Delaware Water Gap Toll Bridge), then drive 5 miles north on US Rt 209.
DESCRIPTION: Located in the Pocono Mountains and started in 1983, this rapidly expanding indoor/outdoor complex currently supports 50 indoor dealers, 140 more under outdoor pavilions, and about 400 more located in an outdoor paved lot. The indoor market is known as the Pocono Bazaar, and the outdoor arrangements trade in a variety of collectibles, crafts, produce, and new merchandise. Food is available at a food court area with a picnic pavilion. Clean, modern restrooms are onsite.
DEALER RATES: Antique/garage sale outdoor booths (no new merchandise) $10/day. $25 and up for spaces depending on size and location. No reservations are required. Pennsylvania Sales Tax number required for vendors selling taxable items. Not required for one-time garage sale vendors or non-taxable items (like clothing).
CONTACT: Kevin Hoffman, PO Box 248, Marshalls Creek PA 18335-0248. Tel: (717) 223-8640. Email: office@poconofleamarket.com.

MECHANICSBURG

Silver Spring Flea Market

DATES: Every Sunday of the year, rain or shine.
TIMES: 6:00 AM–3:00 PM.
ADMISSION: Parking and admission are free.
LOCATION: 6416 Carlisle Pike, 7 miles west of Harrisburg on US Rt 11.
DESCRIPTION: This flea market, founded in 1969, is the largest in the area, with 700 to 1,000 indoor and outdoor dealers attracting thousands of visitors each Sunday. Here you'll find antiques, collectibles, crafts, farm goods, and new merchandise. "You can find anything at this market." Ten restaurants and snack bars quell any screaming munchies.
DEALER RATES: $12 per 10' × 10' outside space per day; $45 per 3' × 8' table monthly rental cost. First come, first served. There are some reserved outside spaces.
CONTACT: Alan Kreitzer, Silver Spring Flea Market, 6416 Carlisle Pk, Mechanicsburg PA 17055-2393. Tel: (717) 766-7215. Day of market call Anna Smith: (717) 766-9027.

MENGES MILLS
Colonial Valley

DATES: Every Sunday.
TIMES: 8:30 AM–4:30 PM. Special events last longer.
ADMISSION: Free. Free parking is available.
LOCATION: Colonial Valley Road. Off Rt 116, 10 minutes west of York and 10 minutes east of Hanover.
DESCRIPTION: This market grew from a little flea market into a resort. It has 140 dealers indoors and more outdoors, covering over 140 acres. Antiques, collectibles and craft items, and new merchandise are offered. In addition to regular Sunday hours, four three-day shows are held each year, and other special attractions. There are all sorts of races, rodeos and events including Civil War re-enactments, Indian pow-wow, western shows, donkey baseball, horse shows, trail rides, rock concerts, antique car show and street ride show. There is even a haunted house at Halloween. At Christmas, they really light up the whole town with 100,000 lights and have a variety of carriage and sleigh rides! They now have one building devoted to Christmas year round with animated scenes and characters among other goodies. They have a real camel (Bosco), elk, llamas, a miniature horse (22" high), and a petting zoo loaded with an interesting variety of animals. Auctions are held occasionally. Bus tours frequently stop here. "Good country food" and restrooms are available.
DEALER RATES: $10 per table inside; $8 outside. Reservations are required for inside spaces.
CONTACT: Judy Phillips or Herb Sterner, Owners, or Betty Staines, Manager, Colonial Valley Resorts, Box 3561 Colonial Valley Rd, Menges Mills PA 17362. Day of show call (717) 225-4811.

Historical Notes:

This is the site of one of the oldest working post offices. Former President Richard Nixon grew up around here and was at the post office when he got the call to go to China, the first sitting president to do so.

They have over 60 Tennessee walking horses here. Many are trained for police departments all over the country.

MIDDLETOWN

Saturday's Market

DATES: Every Saturday, rain or shine.
TIMES: Inside 8:00 AM–6:00 PM, but shop early! Outside 5:30 AM until ?
ADMISSION: Free. Ample free parking is available.
LOCATION: 3751 East Harrisburg Pike, just off Rt 283, on Rt 230 between Middletown and Elizabethtown, Pennsylvania. Only minutes from Hershey Park and Amish country.
DESCRIPTION: This indoor/outdoor market opened in 1984 and claims to be the "largest indoor market in Pennsylvania" and home for 300-plus dealers indoors and hundreds outdoors. Items sold include antiques, arts and crafts and collectibles. New merchandise is also available. At the farmer's market there is always a large supply of fresh produce, bakery snacks, meats, a deli, candies, sodas, along with the delicacies of 16 other eateries on the premises. They are totally air-conditioned.
DEALER RATES: $43 per month for a 10' space inside. Outside special: two spaces for $18. Consult management, reservations are sometimes required.
CONTACT: Rod Rose, 3751 E Harrisburg Pk, Middletown PA 17057. Tel: (717) 944-2555.

MORGANTOWN

Clock Tower Plaza Flea Market

DATES: Outside flea market: Friday and Saturday, April through December, rain or shine. Inside flea market: year round, Wednesday through Sunday.
TIMES: Outside: 7:00 AM until exhaustion. Inside: 10:00 AM–4:00 PM.
ADMISSION: Free, with free parking available.
LOCATION: At the junction of Rt 23 and Rt 10 in mid-Morgantown.
DESCRIPTION: This market started in 1968 as The Market Place at Morgantown and changed its name in 1997 when the retail stores went independent. The flea market is held indoors year round, and outdoor market only during the warmer months with dealers selling antiques, collectibles, craft items, and new merchandise. Many of the dealers specialize in antiques and collectibles. Two restaurants, several concession stands and handicapped-accessible restrooms add to the amenities.

DEALER RATES: $8 and $10 per 10' × 20' space outside. First come, first served for the outside flea market. Inside rates to be determined, but quite reasonable.
CONTACT: Guy, Clock Tower Plaza Flea Market, 2846-10A Main St, Morgantown PA 19543. Tel: (610) 286-0611.

NEW HOPE

New Hope Country Market

DATES: Tuesday through Sunday, year round, weather permitting.
TIMES: 7:00 AM–5:00 PM.
ADMISSION: Free, with free parking.
LOCATION: On Rt 202, ½ mile south of town and at the intersection of Rt 179.
DESCRIPTION: This outdoor market (formerly Country Host) was formed in 1970 and is now under new management. Their 30–70 dealers sell primarily antiques and collectibles including books, new and vintage clothing, coins, stamps, crafts, fine art, new and used furniture, jewelry and silver, pottery, porcelain, toys, new and used merchandise. They are located in beautiful Bucks County in "antique" country in the "center of Lambertville, NJ and Lahaska, PA" with buyers from New York City and Philadelphia. There is a diner open during market hours next door and handicapped-accessible restrooms.
DEALER RATES: $10 per space with two large tables weekdays, $20 on Saturday; $25 on Sunday. Reservations helpful.
CONTACT: Manager, New Hope Country Market, 463 York Rd Rte 202, New Hope PA 18938. Tel: (215) 862-3111. Fax: (215) 862-9107.

Rice's Sale and Country Market

DATES: Every Tuesday, rain or shine.
TIMES: 6:30 AM–2:00 PM.
ADMISSION: Free. Paid parking is available for $1.
LOCATION: 6326 Green Hill Rd, between Aquetong and Mechanicsville Rds, off Rt 263.
DESCRIPTION: This market is said to have started in 1857 selling cattle and farm goods, ranking it among the very oldest existing flea markets in the state of Pennsylvania (or in the USA for that matter). There are currently over 1,200 spaces each week at this indoor/outdoor event, selling "everything from A to Z" including antiques, collectibles, and fine art to

new merchandise and fresh produce, meats and baked goods and zucchini. Plenty of snack bars and concession stands feed the hungry, paved walkways and handicapped-accessible restrooms add to the amenities.
DEALER RATES: $25 per 8' × 3' table weekly; $100 monthly.
CONTACT: Chuck, 6326 Green Hill Rd, New Hope PA 18938. Tel: (215) 297-5993.

NEWRY

Leighty's 29-Acre Indoor/Outdoor Flea Market

DATES: Saturday and Sunday, year round.
TIMES: 7:00 AM–5:00 PM.
ADMISSION: Free, with ample free parking.
LOCATION: On old Rt 220 (I-99), take Roaring Spring Exit, turn left at the light, go 1 mile. Market is 7 miles south of Altoona.
DESCRIPTION: This show began 17 years ago and has from 60 dealers in the winter to 350 in the summer exhibiting antiques, collectibles, handmades, and new merchandise, as well as an assortment of yard sale items. Food vendors and a concession are on the property. This is a large, clean, well-managed market for the area and is located near the famous "horseshoe curve." They also have a large farmer's market across the street. There is a new sports shop in a 80,000-square-foot building, a golf range and miniature golf—just for fun.
DEALER RATES: $10 and up per 11' × 28' outdoor sales space. Indoor spaces vary in size and price. Reservations are suggested but not necessary. For walk-ins, the earlier you come the better the location for you.
CONTACT: Roger Azzarello, Leighty's Flea Market, PO Box 307, Newry PA 16665-0307. Daily information call (814) 695-5151. Weekends at the market call (814) 695-7520.

PHILADELPHIA

Philadelphia International Antique Toy Convention

DATES: January 11, 1998. Annually, generally the second Sunday in January.
TIMES: 10:00 AM–4:00 PM.
ADMISSION: $5 for adults; children free, accompanied by adult; $1 for senior citizens. Parking is free.
LOCATION: Radisson Inn Hotel and Convention Center, northeast Philadelphia (Trevose). Rt 1, ½ mile south on Pennsylvania Turnpike Exit 28.

DESCRIPTION: For 20 years this show has specialized in antique and collectible toys, dolls, and related items. This market is host to over 200 dealers from all over the US, Europe, and Japan. Food is served on the premises.
DEALER RATES: \$60 per 6' × 30' table. Reservations are required. There are advance shopping hours for dealers from 8:00 AM–10:00 AM.
CONTACT: Bob Bostoff, 331 Cochran Plc, Valley Stream NY 11581. Tel: (516) 791-4858.

Quaker City Flea Market

DATES: Every Saturday and Sunday, rain or shine.
TIMES: 8:00 AM–4:00 PM.
ADMISSION: Free. Free parking nearby.
LOCATION: Tacony and Comly Sts, 3 blocks south of the Tacony-Palmyra Bridge.
DESCRIPTION: This market began operation in 1972 and currently attracts between 150 and 175 dealers on indoor and outdoor spaces, selling a variety of items including antiques, collectibles, handmade crafts, fresh produce, and new and used merchandise. Food and restrooms are available.
DEALER RATES: Between \$20-\$25 for an outside space; \$50 and up for inside space. Reservations are required in advance for indoors. First come, first served outdoors.
CONTACT: Jim or Joan Aiello, Quaker City Flea Market, 5001 Comly St, Philadelphia PA 19135. Tel: (215) 744-2022 or fax: (214) 535-0395.

Wildwood Peddler's Fair

DATES: Every Sunday, year round. Rain or shine.
TIMES: 6:00 AM–4:00 PM.
ADMISSION: Free. Parking on premises is available at \$1 per vehicle; free parking is also available nearby.
LOCATION: 2330 Wildwood Rd. From Pittsburgh: take Rt 8 to Wildwood Rd towards North Park (Yellow Belt).
DESCRIPTION: This indoor/outdoor market has operated year round since 1972 on the site of the Old Wildwood Coal Mine. The mine closed in the 1960s. It currently draws between 350 and 500 dealers, depending on the time of year. A wide variety of antiques to collectibles to new merchandise is offered here. They have grown substantially, having added five new rooms

to the one-acre building, making a total of 300 indoor spaces, currently filled to capacity. Additional restrooms and another complete concession stand were added with the addition, making a total of two complete kitchens offering everything from homemade chili to cotton candy and candy apples. There is a festive family atmosphere at this market.
DEALER RATES: $12 per 14' × 22' space outside; starting at $18 per 8' × 12' space inside. Reservations are not required for outdoor space.
CONTACT: Vince Rutledge, President, Peddler's Fair Inc, 2330 Wildwood Rd, Wildwood PA 15091. Tel: (412) 487-2200.

QUAKERTOWN

Quakertown Flea and Farmer's Market

DATES: Friday, Saturday, and Sunday all year round. Rain or shine.
TIMES: Friday and Saturday 9:00 AM–9:00 PM; Sunday 10:00 AM–5:00 PM.
ADMISSION: Free. Ample free parking is provided.
LOCATION: 201 Station Rd, ¼ mile south of Quakertown.
DESCRIPTION: Originally established as a farmer's market in 1932, this indoor/outdoor market has been in operation as a flea market since 1970. They have a 150,000-square-foot building housing permanent vendors selling plenty of hard goods, soft goods and other items. There are three more "barns" for flea market goods as well as plenty of outside space attracting over 500 dealers. This market covers the gamut of antiques and collectibles, crafts, and new merchandise, as well as the traditional farmer's market fare. "Everything you can eat, wear or use!" They have 12 restaurants, two discount grocery stores, five butcher/delis, three bakeries and four produce markets. Yes, they have food! They hold special events throughout the year with special seasonal events.
DEALER RATES: $10 per 16' space outdoors per day with tables, first come, first served; $45 per 120 square foot space indoors for three days. Reservations are required for indoor selling space only. Office hours are Wednesday, Thursday and Sunday 8:30 AM–5:00 PM, Friday and Saturday 8:30 AM–9:00 PM.
CONTACT: John Chism, Manager, 201 Station Rd, Quakertown PA 18951. Tel: (215) 536-4115.

> This market used to hold auctions of livestock in the barns now housing the flea markets. One regular, Tex, attends this market with his cow. Once, he stopped a president from passing, blocking the road with himself and his companion.

WAYNESBORO

27th Annual Antiques and Collectibles Market

DATES: Annually, second Saturday in June.
TIMES: 7:30 AM–4:00 PM.
ADMISSION: Free. Free parking is available.
LOCATION: On Main St (Rt 16) in downtown Waynesboro, located in Franklin County, just 2 miles from the Mason-Dixon Line or 4.8 miles from I-84.
DESCRIPTION: This outdoor market began in 1971 and currently attracts over 35–40 antique dealers from five states, some of whom are said to have attended annually since the market's beginning. This market specializes in antiques and collectibles of varying types. Food is served on the premises.
DEALER RATES: $30 per 22' space along sidewalks. Reservations are required in advance.
CONTACT: Greater Waynesboro Chamber of Commerce, 323 E Main St, Waynesboro PA 17268. Tel: (717) 762-7123.

WEST MIFFLIN

Woodland Flea Market

DATES: Weekends, rain or shine. Also Memorial Day, July 4th, and Labor Day.
TIMES: 6:00 AM–2:00 PM.
ADMISSION: Free. Parking is $1 per car on Sundays and holidays.
LOCATION: 526 Thompson Run Rd, 1 mile from the Allegheny County Airport, 1½ miles from Kennywood Park and just 7 miles from downtown Pittsburgh.
DESCRIPTION: This indoor/outdoor market has been operating since 1962. It currently attracts between 250 to 500 sellers, and between 10,000 and 15,000 buyers. Antiques, collectibles, handmade and craft items, fresh produce, new merchandise and other items are sold. Food and clean restrooms are available on the premises.
DEALER RATES: Outdoors $10 per 10' × 23' space or 2 spaces for $15; indoors $10 per 8' × 3' table or 2 tables for $15; and garage rentals 10' × 25' at $100 per month. Reservations are required for indoor and garage rentals.
CONTACT: Bob Kranack, Woodland Flea Market, 526 Thompson Run Rd, West Mifflin PA 15122. Tel: (412) 462-4370. Fax: (412) 462-4334.

OTHER FLEA MARKETS

We know or have heard about these markets, but have not personally contacted each one, as we have the markets with descriptions. If you plan to visit one of these markets listed below, *please call first* to make sure they are still open. Flea markets do come and go. While they were open when we went to press, they may not be later. We can't be responsible. *Call first!*

Allentown: Franklin Street Flea Market, 415 N 15th St. Tel: 610-439-1117.

Barto: Jake's Flea Market, 1380 Rt 100. Tel: 610-845-7091.

Beaver Falls: Indoor Flea Market, 1410 7th Ave. Tel: 412-847-9650.

Beaver Falls: Spotlight 88 Flea Market, Mercer Rd. Tel: 412-847-9396.

Biglerville: Midway Antique & Collectables Flea Market, 4583 Chambersburg Rd. Tel: 717-334-5592.

Burnt Cabins: Burnt Cabins Antique & Flea Market, HC 75. Tel: 717-987-3441.

Carbondale: Circle Drive-In Theatre & Flea Market, 12 Salem Ave. Tel: 717-876-1400.

Carlisle: Barrick's Flea Market Barn, 1554 Holly Pike. Tel: 717-245-9303.

Carlisle: Lee's Flea Market, 1446 Holly Pike. Tel: 717-245-0677.

Claysville: Claysville's Big Flea Market, Rt 40. Tel: 412-228-5670.

Cochranville: Carriage Barn Exchange Flea Market. Tel: 610-593-6161.

Concordville: Red Barn Flea Market, 990 Baltimore Pke. Tel: 610-459-5677.

East Stroudsburg: The Little Flea, 766 Milford Rd. Tel: 717-424-2456.

Evans City: Evans City Flea Mart. Tel: 412-538-3695.

Evans City: Pioneer Flea Market, 121 Hawk Dr. Tel: 412-789-9236.

Fort Loudon: M & M Antiques & Flea Market, 13324 Main St. Tel: 717-369-3997.

Gilbertsville: Countyline Flea Market, Rt 100 & Cty Ln Rd. Tel: 610-369-1504.

Homestead: West Homestead Flea Market, 411 W 8th Ave. Tel: 412-461-8472.

Johnstown: West End Flea Market, 79 Fairfield Ave. Tel: 814-536-1512.

Kulpsville: Kulpsville Flea Market, 1375 Forty Foot Rd. Tel: 215-361-7910.

Lansdowne: Clements Flea Market, Baltimore Pk & 4th. Tel: 610-259-4222.

Lewisburg: Rt 15 Flea Market, Rt 15. Tel: 717-568-8080 or 717-523-9952.

Lilly: Charley's Indoor Flea Market, 409 North St. Tel: 814-886-8690.

Lucinda: Midway Auction & Flea Market, Rt 66. Tel: 814-226-6697.

Lykens: Lykens Valley Flea Market. Tel: 717-453-7474.

Mansfield: Mansfield Flea Market, 763 S Main St. Tel: 717-662-3624.

Mars: Spot Light 88 Flea Market, Lctn Rt 65 & 588 Bvr. Tel: 412-538-4055.

Marshalls Creek: R & J Flea World, RR 209. Tel: 717-223-0737.

Mechanicsburg: Silver Spring Antique & Flea Market, 6416 Carlisle Pike. Tel: 717-766-9027.

Middletown: Saturdays Farmers & Flea Market, 3751 E Harrisburg Pike. Tel: 717-944-2555.

Millersburg: Red's Flea Market, 522 Center St. Tel: 717-692-4974.

Mount Pocono: Pocono Beehive Flea Market, RR 611. Tel: 717-839-8521.

Nanty Glo: Nanty Glo Flea Market, 1498 Shoemaker St. Tel: 814-749-6357.

New Castle: Esposito Auction & Flea Market, Rt 422 East Rd 6. Tel: 412-924-9775.

North Versailles: Warehouse Flea Mart, 1707 Lincoln Hwy. Tel: 412-823-4748.

Olyphant: Circle Drive-In Theatre & Flea Market, Scrn Carbondale Hwy. Tel: 717-489-5731.

Paxinos: Paxinos Flea & Farmers Market, S R 61. Tel: 717-648-6232.

Philadelphia: Big T Flea Market, 2600 E Tioga St. Tel: 215-291-0280.

Philadelphia: Bridesburg Flea Market, 4700 James St. Tel: 215-743-0405.

Philipsburg: TJ Wilson's Flea Market, 22 N Front St. Tel: 814-342-7120.

Pulaski: Pulaski Auction & Flea Market. Tel: 412-654-4012.

Red Lion: Lion Farm & Flea Market, 141 W Broadway. Tel: 717-246-2601.

Richfield: Graybill's Flea Market, RR 1. Tel: 717-694-9191.

Royersford: Limerick Flea Market. Tel: 610-489-3338.

Saylorsburg: Blue Ridge Flea Market. Tel: 717-992-8044.

Seneca: Peddlers Village Flea Market. Tel: 814-677-4245.

Sybertsville: Hal's Antique Flea Market. Tel: 717-788-1275.
Temple: Hartman's Flea Market, 4927 Commerce. Tel: 610-921-0816.
Waynesburg: Shirley's Flea Market, RR 21. Tel: 412-627-5390.
Wernersville: Oly's Antiques Collectibles & Flea Market, 6881 Penn Ave. Tel: 610-693-6502.
Wind Gap: Wind Gap Flea Market. Tel: 610-863-8534.
York: H & R Basement Flea Market, 4235 N Susquehanna Trl. Tel: 717-266-0843.

RHODE ISLAND

CHARLESTOWN

General Stanton Inn

DATES: Saturdays, Sundays and Monday holidays, April through November, weather permitting. There will be a Giant Yard Sale by one dealer on the second Saturday in September.
TIMES: Saturdays 7:00 AM–3:00 PM, Sundays and holiday Mondays 7:00 AM–4:00 PM.
ADMISSION: Free. Parking is $1.
LOCATION: 4115A Old Post Rd between Rts 1A and 1. From New York: I-95 North, Exit 92 (Rt 2) 3 miles to Rt 78, 4 miles to Rt 1, go north 12 miles to Charlestown. From Boston: I-95 south, Exit 9 to Rt 1, South Charlestown Beach Exit. They are 35 miles south of Providence and 40 miles northeast of New London, Connecticut.
DESCRIPTION: There is space for 200 dealers (but one visitor stated that only 40–50 were there at his visit) at this outdoor market, started in 1967. It is located on the property of The General Stanton Inn, one of America's oldest inns. There is everything from antiques and collectibles to handmade crafts, vegetables and new merchandise at this market. There is one restaurant and one snack bar on the premises. They are also conveniently located between Mystic and Newport, so there is plenty to do in the area. They are planning a Christmas in July event. Watch for it.

One of their dealers found a $450,000 painting and another person found a $55,000 picture here. You never know!
DEALER RATES: $25 for a 15' × 20' space, $35 for an end spot. Reservations are required. Canopies are available for $10 extra. There is security ($10 extra) for dealers who wish to leave their goods over Saturday night.
CONTACTS: Janice Falcone, General Stanton Inn, Rt 1A Box 222, Charlestown RI 02813. Tel: (401) 364-8888 or fax: (401) 364-3333.

EAST GREENWICH

Rocky Hill Flea Market

DATES: Every Sunday, April through November.
TIMES: 5:00 AM–4:00 PM.
ADMISSION: Free. Parking is $1.
LOCATION: 1408 Division Rd, corner of Division Rd and Rt 2. Take Exit 8A off I-95.

DESCRIPTION: This market has been around since 1960 and now attracts approximately 400 dealers and sometimes more, with virtually all types of merchandise available, including crafts, collectibles, fresh produce, and new merchandise. Food is available on the premises.
DEALER RATES: \$17 per 20' × 25' space, corner spaces go for \$22, smaller spaces are available for \$12. Advance reservations are not required.
CONTACT: Gary Hamilton, 1408 Division Rd, East Greenwich RI 02818. Tel: (401) 884-4114.

PROVIDENCE

Big Top Flea Market

DATES: Saturday and Sunday.
TIMES: 9:00 AM–5:00 PM.
ADMISSION: Saturday free, Sunday \$.50. Parking is free.
LOCATION: 120 Manton Ave. Just one block from Rt 6, towards Olneyville.
DESCRIPTION: Opened in 1976 in a historic 1800s' mill building, this market of 100–150 dealers sells antiques, collectibles, garage sale goodies, produce, used general merchandise, new merchandise, crafts and fresh lobsters! There is other food on the premises, served by a snack bar.
DEALER RATES: \$25 per 8' x 10' booth per weekend. Reservations are suggested.
CONTACT: Sully or Howard, Big Top Flea Market, 120 Manton Ave. Providence RI 02909. Tel: 401-274-0060.

TIVERTON

Route 177 Flea Market

DATES: Saturday, Sunday, and holidays, year round.
TIMES: Saturday 9:00 AM–4:00 PM; Sunday and holidays 8:00 AM–5:00 PM.
ADMISSION: Free admission and free parking.
LOCATION: 1560 Bulgar Marsh Rd.
DESCRIPTION: Opened in April 1966, this indoor/outdoor flea market has been in business for over 30 years. It isn't a big market anymore. Described by one visitor as "10–15 dealers in old wooden sheds. Only one outside dealer selling produce in the shade."
DEALER RATES: \$15 for outside space measuring 15' × 10'; \$10 for inside space measuring 10' × 5'. Advance reservations are not required; first come, first served.

CONTACT: Thomas G Ouellette, 8 Campion Ave, Tiverton RI 02878. Tel: (401) 624-9354 or 625-5954.

Tom has this story to offer:

Twenty-five or so years ago, his brother-in-law, Louie, an avid outdoorsman, was building his home. He asked Tom if he ever saw a pair of snowshoes to let him know. He wanted to put them on the wall over his new basement bar. The next day the first dealer into the market opened her trunk and there was a pair a snowshoes. A quick call brought Louie to the market immediately to buy the snowshoes for $15.

That was the one and only time Tom has ever seen a pair of snowshoes.

WOONSOCKET

Woonsocket Flea Market

DATES: Saturday and Sunday, year round, rain or shine.
TIMES: 9:00 AM–5:00 PM.
ADMISSION: Free. Parking is free.
LOCATION: 6 Davidson Ave. Corner of Rt 122 (Hamlet Ave) and Davidson Ave.
DESCRIPTION: Since 1989, this indoor market of 250 spaces (but not necessarily dealers) has offered a wide variety of new and used merchandise, antiques, collectibles, sport cards, coins, stamps, dolls, a full-line grocery department and anything else that wanders in. Freshly made home-cooked food is served in a large snack bar. All vendors accept Visa and MasterCard. Handicapped-accessible restrooms are also on site.
DEALER RATES: $25 per weekend for a 8' × 10' space. Reservations are not required.
CONTACT: Ron Wilkinson, Woonsocket Flea Market, 6 Davidson Ave, Woonsocket RI 02895-4802. Tel: (401) 762-3101.

OTHER FLEA MARKETS

We have heard about this market, but have not personally contacted it, as we have the markets with descriptions. If you plan to visit this market, *please call first* to make sure it is still open.

West Greenwich: Exit 5B Flea Market, 849 Victory Hwy. Tel: 401-397-9111.

SOUTH CAROLINA

ANDERSON/BELTON

Anderson Jockey Lot and Farmer's Market

DATES: Saturday and Sunday, rain or shine.

TIMES: Saturday 7:00 AM–6:00 PM; Sunday 9:00 AM–6:00 PM.

ADMISSION: Free. Parking is free.

LOCATION: Hwy 29 between Greenville and Anderson, 10 miles from Anderson.

DESCRIPTION: Opened in 1974, this huge market hosts between 1,500 and 2,000-plus dealers selling everything, quite literally. To prove their point, their crowds average 40–60,000! "If we don't have it, you don't need it." Just some of the items sold are: antiques, collectibles, tons of produce, clothing, comics, cleaning supplies, pantyhose, pharmaceuticals, office supplies, cologne, stamps, coins, garage sale goodies and other new merchandise. There are "lots of restaurants and snack bars" and clean restrooms on site.

Just as an aside, they have an Anderson exchange telephone at the front of the market, a Williamston exchange telephone at the back of the market and a Belton address. That's what you get for operating at the junction of three separate entities.

DEALER RATES: Inside: $10 for one day with a wooden table. Outside, pick a vacant, non-reserved space, one of the owners will tap you for $6 for the space and one concrete table for each day. Reservations are required for inside space only. Those spaces can be hard to get. You must reserve in person.

CONTACT: Anderson Jockey Lot and Farmer's Market, 4530 Hwy 29 N, Belton SC 29627. Tel: (864) 224-2027. Fax: (864) 231-6927.

CHARLESTON

Lowcountry Flea Market and Collectibles Show

DATES: Third Saturday and Sunday of each month, year round, except November, the second weekend. Call for specific dates.

TIMES: Saturday 9:00 AM–6:00 PM, Sunday 10:00 AM–5:00 PM.

ADMISSION: $2 per person, kids free.

LOCATION: At Gaillard Auditorium, 77 Calhoun St, in Charleston, near Meeting St and Calhoun St.

DESCRIPTION: This show has been operating since 1973 in the historic downtown area. Over 50 dealers offer antiques, collectibles, estate merchandise and handcrafts from indoor stalls. This is mostly an antiques and collectibles show. For your convenience food is available on the premises.
DEALER RATES: $85 per 10' × 10' booth per weekend. Reservations are required in advance.
CONTACT: Mr and Mrs Nelson Garrett, 513 Pelzer Dr, Mount Pleasant SC 29464. Tel: (803) 884-7204.

COLUMBIA

Barnyard Flea Market

DATES: Friday, Saturday and Sunday, rain or shine.
TIMES: 8:00 AM–6:00 PM and later in summer.
ADMISSION: Free. Paved parking is also free.
LOCATION: Between Lexington and Columbia on Hwy 1. Just 2.3 miles from Exit 58 off I-20; 3 miles from Exit 111A of I-26.
DESCRIPTION: Built as a new market in April 1988, this collection of 12 red-tin-roofed buildings houses 552 spaces for dealers. The number of dealers varies by how many spaces each dealer will rent. They are usually full. The buildings are lit inside and out allowing late evening shopping in summertime. There are 75–100 dealer tables outside without cover. Four restaurants including a brand-new barbecue restaurant take care of hungry shoppers. Among the fares sold are antiques, collectibles, boiled peanuts, car stereos, t-shirts, sunglasses, hardware, fishing supplies, used appliances, fashion jewelry, handbags, clothes—new and used, "and the usual generic flea market stuff." Also notable are air-conditioned restrooms and the Barnyard RV park next door. Their sister market is located in Fort Mill.
DEALER RATES: $10 per day for 4' × 8' tables undercover in a 10' × 10' space; $5 for 4' × 8' tables outside. Reservations are suggested as they do fill up fast.
CONTACT: Manager, Barnyard Flea Market, 4414 Augusta Rd, Lexington SC 29072. Tel: 1-800-628-7496 or (803) 957-6570.

EDMUND

Smiley's Flea Market

DATES: Thursday, Friday, Saturday and Sunday.
TIMES: 7:00 AM–5:00 PM.
ADMISSION: Free. Parking is free.

LOCATION: From Columbia, take Hwy 302 south (9 miles south of the airport). From Lexington, off I-20, Exit 55 take Hwy 6 south to Edmund. Only 7 miles north of Pelion on Hwy 302.
DESCRIPTION: Opened in November 1996, this is another of Smiley's successful flea markets dotting the South. There are over 500 outside spaces, most with tables and many more under cover. Considering that many dealers take several spaces (and at these prices who wouldn't?) they generally have over 100 dealers outside and 40–60 inside selling almost everything imaginable including lots of garage sale goodies. Several times a year they will hold a special antique "show" with their antique dealers having a special section to themselves. The first time they tried this it was a raving success. Watch for more to come. There is a new RV campground in the back with special deals for dealers who wish to stay.
DEALER RATES: Outside: $5 per table, or 3 for $10. Inside: $7 per space, 2 spaces for $10; $9 for a corner space and if you add another space, then it's $9+$7=$16 for 2 spaces. Reservations are suggested only for special shows (i.e. the antique specials) and for holidays inside only.
CONTACT: Marcia Manginelli or Gloria Sinclair, Asst. Manager, Smiley's Flea Market, 5910 Edmund Hwy, Lexington SC 29073. Tel: (803) 955-9111 or evenings and non-market days call Marcia at home at (803) 955-9590. Fax: (803) 955-3311.

FLORENCE

Florence Flea Market

DATES: Saturday and Sunday, year round, rain or shine.
TIMES: 7:00 AM–6:00 PM.
ADMISSION: Free. Parking is free.
LOCATION: Corner of Rts 327 and 76 at 301 North. Exit 170 off I-95, go south 5 miles.
DESCRIPTION: Open since 1980, this indoor/outdoor market of 400 dealers sells crafts, produce, new merchandise and garage sale goodies. Two snack bars and restrooms add to the amenities.
DEALER RATES: $8 per 10' × 10' yard space, $10 per 10' × 10' open shed space, $12 per 10' × 10' space in the main building. Reservations are recommended. Office is open Friday for rentals.
CONTACT: Florence Flea Market, 4001 E Palmetto St, Florence SC 29506-4205. Tel: (803) 667-9585.

FORT MILL

Flea Market at Pineville

DATES: Friday, Saturday and Sunday, rain or shine.

TIMES: Friday 8:00 AM–4:00 PM, Saturday 7:00 AM–5:00 PM, Sunday 8:00 AM–5:00 PM.

ADMISSION: Free. Parking is free.

LOCATION: 3674 Hwy 51. Exit 90 (Carowinds Exit) off I-77.

DESCRIPTION: Built as a new market in June 1995, this collection of red-tin-roofed buildings houses over 350 spaces for dealers. The number of dealers varies by how many spaces each dealer will rent. The buildings are lit inside and out allowing late evening shopping in summertime. There are dealer tables outside without cover. Three restaurants including a deli, pizza place and canteen take care of hungry shoppers. Among the fares sold are antiques, collectible, t-shirts, sunglasses, hardware, fishing supplies, used appliances, fashion jewelry, handbags, clothes-new and used, "and the usual generic flea market stuff." Handicapped-accessible restrooms add to the amenities. Their sister market is located in Columbia.

DEALER RATES: $12 per day for a 10' × 10' space inside. $5 outside for a table per day. Friday is ½ price. Reservations are required. Permanent warehouse facilities available. Office hours are also Monday 9:00 AM–12:00 PM and Thursday 8:00 AM–4:00 PM.

CONTACT: Manager, Flea Market at Pineville, 3674 Hwy 51, Ft Mill SC 29715. Tel: (803) 548-1817 or 1-800-527-4117.

GREENVILLE

Fairgrounds Flea Market

DATES: Saturday and Sunday, rain or shine.

TIMES: Saturday 5:00 AM–5:00 PM, Sunday 6:00 AM–5:00 PM.

ADMISSION: Free. Parking is also free.

LOCATION: 2600 White Horse Rd. From I-85 South, take the White Horse Rd Exit (Exit 44), turn right, go 1 mile to market.

DESCRIPTION: This market, opened in March 1990, hosts 600 to 800 dealers selling everything: some antiques and collectibles, lots of crafts and produce, garage sale goodies, some new merchandise, racing material, tools, pantyhose (is there a run on these in SC?), windows and siding, and lots of cards. Pets are sold here, from the occasional goat to chickens, rabbits, dogs and cats. Home-cooking and the usual snack bar fare feed the famished. There are plenty of restrooms, inside and out, just in case.

DEALER RATES: $8 under the shed, $6 for a 10' × 10' space and table outdoors, $9 inside. Reservations are required for all but a few outside spaces set aside for first come, first served.
CONTACT: Marvin Kelly or Monika Baker, Fairgrounds Flea Market, 2600 White Horse Rd, Greenville SC 29605. Tel: (864) 295-1183.

LADSON

Coastal Carolina Flea Market

DATES: Every Saturday and Sunday, rain or shine.
TIMES: 8:00 AM–5:00 PM.
ADMISSION: Free. Free parking is available on 15 acres.
LOCATION: At the junction of College Park Rd and Hwy 78. Take I-26 to Exit 203 (College Park Rd); or take Hwy 78. Flea market is next door to the local fairgrounds.
DESCRIPTION: This indoor/outdoor market started in June 1981, and now has over 500 indoor booths and 300 outside spaces available. It usually draws 400 to 450 dealers selling a full range of antiques and collectibles such as tools, jewelry, furniture, old and new clothing, baby items, pets, and pet supplies, birds, as well as fresh produce, garage sale items and new merchandise. There are often local airbrush artists on hand for portraits. Computer portraits are also a draw. Their new air-conditioned/heated 100-seat restaurant, "Weekends" at the Flea Market, serves the starving shoppers.
DEALER RATES: $10 per 10' × 10' space per day inside. $6 per table outside. Reservations required for inside space; first come, first served outside.
CONTACT: Michael W Masterson, Coastal Carolina Flea Market Inc, PO Box 510, Ladson SC 29456-0510. Tel: (803) 797-0540.

NORTH CHARLESTON

All New Palmetto State Flea Market

DATES: Saturday and Sunday, year round. Rain or shine.
TIMES: 9:00 AM–5:00 PM.
ADMISSION: Free. Parking is also free.
LOCATION: Just off Ashley-Phosphate Rd on Rivers Ave.
DESCRIPTION: This market, opened in 1988, has 300 dealers selling everything that you can ever think of: antiques, collectibles, a carpet outlet,

new and used furniture, and typical flea market fare. They have 30 outside covered spaces. There is a full concession on premises.
DEALER RATES: $10 per day 10' × 10' per space with 8' table inside. Outside spaces go for $10 a space with 3 tables on a first-come, first-served basis. Reservations are strongly advised. There is security at the market.
CONTACT: All New Palmetto State Flea Market, 7225 Rivers Ave, N Charleston SC 29406. Tel: (803) 553-8030.

SPRINGFIELD

Springfield Flea Market

DATES: Saturday and Monday, rain or shine.
TIMES: Saturday and Monday 5:00 AM until afternoon, generally around 2:00 PM. There is no set opening or closing times, however, most people work during these times.
ADMISSION: Free. Free parking is available nearby.
LOCATION: At the intersection of Rts 3 and 4, approximately 1 mile east of Springfield.
DESCRIPTION: This market evolved from an auction held at a livestock market and has been running as a flea market since 1958. The farmers would often bring along farming tools and "whatever" to auction off as well. Soon, the auctioneer, Oscar Cooper, decided it was time the farmers sold their own stuff and sent them off to the "yard" adjacent to the Stockyard. At first, it was slow going with only ten "dealers," but in the mid-'70s this market blossomed turning sleepy Springfield into a lively town one day a week. The market moved to its current 35-acre location in 1983. It now accommodates between 750 and 1,000 dealers inside and outside, selling a varied selection of antiques and collectibles, fresh farm goods, and some new merchandise. According to its current owner, Oscar's son Henry, while there are many regular dealers, the "first-timers" cleaning out their houses generally bring in a wonderful variety of merchandise. Food is served by a concession stand and a convenience store is on the premises. Clean restrooms are available, and law enforcement officers patrol the grounds. It is said that many people come so early they must use flashlights to find their way to the bargains and treasures.
DEALER RATES: $5 for an open 12' × 12' space with table outdoors; $7 per 10' × 10' shed space with table. Advance reservations are not required.
CONTACT: Henry Cooper, Owner and Manager, PO Box 74, Springfield SC 29146-0074. Tel: (803) 258-3192.

WEST COLUMBIA

US #1 Metro Flea Market

DATES: Friday, Saturday, and Sunday, rain or shine. Wednesday wholesale market only.

TIMES: Friday 8:00 AM–6:00 PM; Saturday 7:00 AM–6:00 PM; Sunday 9:00 AM–6:00 PM; Wednesday 7:00 AM–12:00 PM.

ADMISSION: Free. Free parking is available.

LOCATION: 3500 Augusta Rd, on US Hwy 1. From I-26, take US Hwy 1 south to Lexington (Exit 111A South), approximately 1½ miles; from I-20, take US Hwy 1 (Exit 58) to West Columbia, 4½ miles. Only 5 miles from the state capitol.

DESCRIPTION: This show began in March 1980 and currently draws 600 dealers inside (in permanent stalls) and outside, peddling antiques, collectibles, crafts, fresh farm produce, and some new merchandise. They are the oldest and "most popular" market in the Columbia area drawing between 5,000–15,000 per weekend depending on weather. There is even a vendor selling medical supplies—one wheelchair went for $2.95! This place is garage-sale heaven! Full of surprises. Food is available on the premises. Wednesday is open for a special wholesalers market only, open from 7:00 AM–12:00 PM.

DEALER RATES: Fridays are free—no reservations required; Saturday and Sunday $12 per day for covered stalls and $8 per open outdoor stalls. Wednesday wholesale rate is $25 per day or $60 by the month. Advance reservations are recommended for Saturday and Sunday at least a week to two weeks in advance.

CONTACT: Richard Hook, US#1 Metro Flea Market, PO Box 1457, Lexington SC 29071-1457. Tel: (803) 796-9294.

OTHER FLEA MARKETS

We know or have heard about these markets, but have not personally contacted each one, as we have the markets with descriptions. If you plan to visit one of these markets listed below, *please call first* to make sure they are still open. Flea markets do come and go. While they were open when we went to press, they may not be later. We can't be responsible. *Call first!*

Aiken: The Market Place Flea Market, 2745 Old Camp Long Rd. Tel: 803-643-8175.

Anderson: Cricket's Flea Market, 502 Sayre St. Tel: 864-226-0012.

Anderson: Milltown Flea Market, 2324 S Main St. Tel: 864-225-7548.

Beaufort: Laurel Bay Flea Market, 922 La Chere St. Tel: 803-521-9794.

Bowman: The Bowman Flea Market, S Main St. Tel: 803-829-2442.

Chesterfield: Chesterfield Flea Market & Auction House, 1006 West Blvd. Tel: 803-623-3999.

Cleveland: Cleveland Flea Market, 4129 Geer Hwy. Tel: 864-836-4734.

Columbia: Thieves Antique Flea Market, 502 Gadsden St. Tel: 803-254-4997.

Conway: Carolina's Best Hudson's Surfside Flea Market. Tel: 803-650-9458.

Conway: Smith's Flea Market, Hwy 701 S. Tel: 803-397-6437.

Ehrhardt: Ehrhardt Flea Market, Main St. Tel: 803-267-4203.

Fort Mill: Carousel Flea Market, 3333 Hwy 51 N. Tel: 803-547-7734.

Gaffney: Hwy 18 Flea Market, 905 Shelby Hwy. Tel: 864-488-1712.

Greenwood: Greenwood Flea Market & Jockey Lot, 123 Dixie Dr. Tel: 864-223-3045.

Greenwood: Greenwood Trading Post & Flea Market Inc, 1428 S Main St. Tel: 864-229-3791.

Greer: Tab's Flea Market, 1301 E Wade Hampton Blvd. Tel: 864-877-7209.

Hilton Head Island: Gullah Flea Market, 103 William Hilton Pkwy. Tel: 803-681-7374.

Islandton: Antique Barn & Flea Market, RR 1. Tel: 803-866-2874.

Lancaster: 903 Flea Market, 2142 Flat Creek Rd. Tel: 803-286-9480.

Lexington: Archer's Collectibles Barnyard Flea Market, 4414 Augusta Rd. Tel: 803-951-7230.

Manning: Marie's Flea Market, 304 S Mill St. Tel: 803-435-4926.

McCormick: EJ's Flea Market & Discount Store, Hwy 28 S. Tel: 864-465-2300.

Myrtle Beach: Conway East Flea Market, 1080 Hwy 501. Tel: 803-347-1414.

Myrtle Beach: Hudson's Surfside Flea Market, 1040 Hwy 17 S. Tel: 803-238-0372.

Myrtle Beach: Myrtle Beach Flea Market, 3820 S Kings Hwy. Tel: 803-477-1550.

North Augusta: Belvedere Flea Market, 101 Belvedere Clearwater Rd. Tel: 803-279-0841.

North Myrtle Beach: North Myrtle Beach Flea Market, Hwy 17. Tel: 803-249-4701.

Pageland: Pearl St Furniture Outlet & Flea Market, 117 N Pearl St. Tel: 803-672-6600.

Pickens: Pickens County Flea Market, 1427 Walhalla Hwy. Tel: 864-878-9646.

Rock Hill: Lottie's Flea Emporium, 1264 Curtis St. Tel: 803-329-1180.

Rock Hill: Shirley's Flea Market, 1024 Saluda St. Tel: 803-366-1014.

Ruby: Jewel City Flea Market. Tel: 803-634-6290.

Saint Matthews: St Matthew's Flea Market, 151 Bridge St. Tel: 803-874-4327.

Santee: Santee Flea Market, 7655 Five Chop Rd. Tel: 803-854-3485.

Scranton: Caulder Flea Market, RR 2. Tel: 803-389-7190.

Spartanburg: Spartanburg Flea Market, 8010 Asheville Hwy. Tel: 864-578-9026.

Sumter: Sumter County Flea Market, Hwy 378. Tel: 803-495-2281.

Travelers Rest: Foothills Flea Market, 1131 N Hwy 25. Tel: 864-834-2021.

Trenton: Margie's Flea Market, Hwy 191. Tel: 803-275-3142.

Walhalla: WGOG Radio Station Flea Market, 2058 Westminster Hwy. Tel: 864-638-6810.

Walterboro: Walterboro Flea Market Inc, 415 Sniders Hwy. Tel: 803-538-2266.

Westminster: Traders Junction Flea Market, 4265 S Hwy 11. Tel: 864-638-0100.

York: I-77 Flea Market, 2697 Cherry Rd. Tel: 803-329-5114.

SOUTH DAKOTA

MADISON

Memory Lane Flea Market

DATES: The weekend before Labor Day, the last Friday, Saturday and Sunday in August.
TIMES: 9:00 AM–dusk.
ADMISSION: Free. Parking is free.
LOCATION: Madison bypass curve, south of Pizza Ranch or west of Prostrollo's Auto Mall.
DESCRIPTION: Started in 1995 as a revolt against "greedy market-charging" this venture has 27 dealers selling mostly classic antiques, rummage sale junque, collectibles, crafts and a bit of new merchandise. Although small to start with, there are 25,000 visitors attracted to this area as there are other events, including a "threshing bee," going on. And you can't get into town without passing the market, and the response of the dealers was "well satisfied." There are food vendors on site as well as plenty of food in the surrounding area.
DEALER RATES: $45 plus electricity for 50' × 20' space. Reservations are suggested. A chain-link fence surrounds the grounds for security for dealers who wish to leave their goods overnight.
CONTACT: Cheryl and Doc Howard, Box 385, Howard SD 57349. Best time to call is between 9:00 PM and 2:00 AM—really! Tel: (605) 772-5376.

RAPID CITY

Black Hills Flea Market

DATES: Saturday, Sundays and national holidays if on Friday or Monday, May through September. Rain checks given for days completely rained out outdoors.
TIMES: 7:00 AM–dusk, both days.
ADMISSION: Free. Plenty of easy parking is available.
LOCATION: 5500 Mount Rushmore Rd. Take Exit 57 off I-90 on US 16W south of Rapid City limits.
DESCRIPTION: This indoor/outdoor market, which began operation in 1973, is located on the main highway to Mount Rushmore and therefore has high exposure to the many thousands of tourists who visit this national memorial annually. A lovely panoramic view of the Black Hills is among

the many attractions of this market. There are currently an average of 150 dealers on hand selling antiques and collectibles, and there is a special arts and crafts section featuring locally made handicrafts. Some new merchandise is available, and among the food for sale is fresh produce when in season. This market operates on the concept that "Flea Markets Are Fun!" and has invited the public to "Come out, enjoy the outdoors, and fly your kites" with them.

DEALER RATES: $10 per inside table (arts and crafts) per day; $10 per outside tailgate; $12 to $15 for an indoor booth. Tables are furnished. Eight-foot tables are available outside for $2 rental per day. Reservations are recommended for indoor booths.

CONTACT: Deborah Cooley, 909 Francis, Rapid City SD 57701. Tel: (605) 348-1981 or (605) 343-6477.

Sioux Falls Flea Market

DATES: Saturday and Sunday, first weekend of every month. No shows in June, July or August.

TIMES: Saturday 9:00 AM–5:00 PM; Sunday 11:00 AM–4:00 PM.

ADMISSION: $1 per person. Ample free parking.

LOCATION: Expo Building at 12th and Fairgrounds.

DESCRIPTION: This indoor market first opened in 1970. There are 250 dealers selling antiques, collectibles, arts and crafts items, as well as new merchandise. At least 70% of the items shown are antiques. The crowds keep growing every weekend and have more than doubled in size in this good, clean, smoke-free atmosphere. Handicapped access throughout the market is very easy as this is a large well-lit building with wide aisles. Food is available on the premises.

DEALER RATES: $25 per 8' table and space per weekend; $80 for 4 tables. Advance reservations are required as there is a waiting list.

CONTACT: Ed and Bonnie Benson, PO Box 236, Sioux Falls SD 57101-0236. Tel: (605) 334-1312.

OTHER FLEA MARKETS

We know or have heard about these markets, but have not personally contacted each one, as we have the markets with descriptions. If you plan to visit one of these markets listed below, *please call first* to make sure they are still open. Flea markets do come and go. While they were open when we went to press, they may not be later. We can't be responsible. *Call first!*

Black Hawk: Black Hawk Flea Market, 5805 N Hwy 79. Tel: 605-787-6402.

Madison: Four Seasons Flea Market, 225 N Egan Ave. Tel: 605-256-6696.

Rapid City: Trade Winds Second Hand & Flea Market, 1208 E North St. Tel: 605-342-7286.

Sioux Falls: Cliff Avenue Flea Market, 3515 N Cliff Ave. Tel: 605-338-8975.

TENNESSEE

CROSSVILLE

Crossville Flea Market

DATES: Saturday and Sunday, and Monday holidays, and the Friday after Thanksgiving.
TIMES: 7:00 AM–4:00 PM.
ADMISSION: Free. Parking is free.
LOCATION: Hwy 70 North, mid-way between Knoxville and Nashville. Take I-40, Exit 317 towards Crossville, turn right at second traffic light. Right at the next traffic light. Market is about 1½ miles down the road on the right.
DESCRIPTION: A flea market in the original sense, operating under covered sheds, this market has been running since 1970. Depending on the season, there are 200 to 400 dealers selling antiques, collectibles, furniture, dogs, coins, cats, cards, chickens, garage sale goodies, livestock, new merchandise, crafts, produce, nursery stock, stamps, and whatever else shows up. Because of the nature of this market, much of the merchandise is old and/or used. Think unfound treasures. There are four snack bars and a restaurant as well as handicapped-accessible parking and restrooms. Members of the Tennessee Flea Market Association.
DEALER RATES: Saturday: $6 for a 10' × 12' open space; $8 for a 12' × 14' covered space. Sunday and holidays: $4 for a 10' × 12' open space; $5 for a 12' × 14' covered space. Electricity is extra. Reservations are suggested.
CONTACT: Mary Gunter or Lois Wilbanks, PO Box 3037, Crossville TN 38557-3037. Tel: (615) 484-9970 or (615) 456-9674.

JACKSON

Friendly Frank's Flea Market

DATES: First weekend of every month, except September, from Friday night through Sunday.
TIMES: Saturday and Sunday, 9:00 AM–6:00 PM and Friday evenings 6:00 PM–9:00 PM.
ADMISSION: Free. Parking is free.
LOCATION: Hwy 45 South.
DESCRIPTION: Opened in 1983, this indoor/outdoor market's 200–plus dealers sell antiques, collectibles, coins, stamps, cards, furniture, garage

sale clean-outs, new merchandise and crafts. Two snack bars serve to quell the munchies. There are clean handicapped-accessible restrooms on site.
DEALER RATES: $55 for the weekend for a 9' × 10' space. Reservations are required.
CONTACT: Peggy Mullikin, PO Box 328, Cordova TN 38088-0328. Tel: (901) 755-6561.

KNOXVILLE

Esau's Antique and Collectible Market

DATES: Saturday and Sunday, third weekend of each month, except September when it is held the fourth weekend and December when held the second weekend. October and April dates are huge 3-day extravaganzas.
TIMES: 9:00 AM–5:00 PM.
ADMISSION: $3 per person for regular markets, $4 for extravaganzas. Thirty acres of free parking is provided.
LOCATION: Take the Rutledge Pike Exit 392 off I-40 East.
DESCRIPTION: This indoor market has run since 1975 and now includes 300 dealers selling a range of antiques and collectibles, craft items, and new articles. (Antiques and collectibles account for about 70% of the merchandise.) Food is available on the premises. Members of the Tennessee Flea Market Association.
DEALER RATES: $60 per 9' × 10' space per weekend, plus City and County Business License fee.
CONTACT: Cindy Crabtree, Esau Inc, PO Box 50096, Knoxville TN 37950-0096. Tel: (423) 588-1233 or 1-800-588-ESAU (3728).

KODAK

Great Smokies Craft Fair/Flea Market

DATES: Friday, Saturday and Sunday, year round.
TIMES: Weekdays 10:00 AM–6:00 PM; Saturday and Sunday 9:00 AM–6:00 PM.
ADMISSION: Free. Parking is also free.
LOCATION: 220 Dumplin Valley Rd West. Off I-40, Exit 407, turn onto Dumplin Valley Rd, about ¼ mile down the road. Just 16 miles from Gatlinburg and 12 miles from Dollywood.
DESCRIPTION: Ideally situated on 25 acres next to the interstate, this very successful market opened on August 3, 1990. The dealers are housed in a 230-space air-conditioned building, with unlimited outdoor space. They

have a special section of wonderful antiques and collectibles, including player pianos! The dealers are noted for their friendliness, courtesy and helpfulness. They are more than willing to help each other and their customers out. There is a tremendous variety of superb crafts as well as manufacturer-direct booths. There is a food court selling homemade pizzas and corn bread, soup beans, gourmet burgers and regular burgers, hot dogs, daily specials. A video arcade keeps the kids busy. The market is kept spotlessly clean. They welcome RVs, tour buses, and tractor-trailers. Ninety percent of their dealers are permanent, 80% have been here since they opened. Definitely a family market including vendors with kid's stuff. They choose their vendors to meet the wants and desires of all of their customers. The management strives to be the best market in the business and was chosen as one of the top 10 markets in the state by the Tennessee Flea Market Association. Nearby are 15,000 motels and hotel rooms and plenty of restaurants around the area. Over 71,000 cars go by this market each day! Members of the Tennessee Flea Market Association.

DEALER RATES: Winter: $55 per weekend, Friday through Sunday. Outside open spaces $8 a day, covered sheds $10 a day. Tables $2 a day. Summer rates can vary, but within this scale. Reservations are required because of a long waiting list.

CONTACT: Evelyn Ogle, Great Smokies Craft Fair and Flea Market, 220 Dumplin Valley Rd W, Kodak TN 37764. Tel: (423) 932-FLEA (932-3532). Fax: (432) 932-3534.

LEBANON

Parkland Flea Market

DATES: Every Saturday and Sunday, March 1 through December 15.

TIMES: 7:00 AM–dark.

ADMISSION: Free. Ample free parking is provided.

LOCATION: Across the street from the entrance to Cedars of Lebanon State Park. From I-40 take Exit 238, go 6 miles south. Between Lebanon and Murfreesboro on Hwy 231.

DESCRIPTION: This indoor/outdoor market has operated since 1977 near the center of the state of Tennessee. It has enjoyed steady growth with a "great group of family-type dealers where 90% of the 300 are regulars." They are housed in a complex of seven buildings on 10 acres of land, with another 40 acres available for further expansion. Large and small items, both new and used, can be found including boats, trailers, vans, and trucks,

as well as the traditional flea market fare. Free weekend camping is available for dealers, and food is available at the site. Another attraction nearby is the Grand Olde Opry and Opryland only 30 miles away. Members of the Tennessee Flea Market Association.
DEALER RATES: $10 for 12' × 12' space under shed; $7 per 15' × 15' outside space. Reservations are strongly suggested.
CONTACT: Gwynn or Nancy Lanius, 403 Cambridge, Lebanon TN 37087-4207. Tel:(615) 449-6050.

LOUISVILLE

Green Acres Flea Market

DATES: Saturday and Sunday, rain or shine.
TIMES: 6:30 AM–4:30 PM.
ADMISSION: Free. Plenty of free parking is available. Space is also available for vehicles such as motor homes and trailers.
LOCATION: On Alcoa Hwy 129 between Knoxville and the Knoxville Airport.
DESCRIPTION: Located on 13 acres at the foothills of the Great Smoky Mountains, this indoor/outdoor show has been in operation since 1976. It draws an average of 772 dealers in 400 available spaces outdoors and over 300 indoors selling miscellaneous antiques and collectibles, gold, furniture old and new, can be found, as well as new items and farm goods. There is a large restaurant and large breakfast bar on the premises selling yogurt, cotton candy, pork skins and corndogs. Members of the Tennessee Flea Market Association.
DEALER RATES: $10 per space, approximately 20' × 20'. Reservations are suggested. Dealers can come on Friday and stay overnight.
CONTACT: Green Acres Flea Market, 908 Hillside Dr, Louisville TN 37777. Tel: (423) 681-4433 or fax: (423) 681-1091.

MEMPHIS

Memphis Flea Market

DATES: Third weekend of each month, rain or shine.
TIMES: 8:00 AM–6:00 PM.
ADMISSION: Free. Parking is free.
LOCATION: Memphis Fairgrounds at Central and East Pkwy at 955 Early Maxwell Blvd.

DESCRIPTION: Opened in 1969, this indoor/outdoor market of 900 to 1,200 dealers sells anything from antiques, collectibles, crafts, produce, housewares, clothing to new merchandise. A snack bar and handicapped-accessible restrooms are on premises.
DEALER RATES: \$70–\$75 for a 10' × 10' inside space per weekend, \$40–\$50 for a 10' × 12' outside space for the weekend. Reservations are suggested.
CONTACT: Mike Hardage, Memphis Flea Market, 955 Early Maxwell Blvd, Memphis TN 38104. Tel: (901) 276-3532. Fax: (901) 276-0701.

Mid-South Flea Market

DATES: Every third weekend. Rain or shine.
TIMES: 9:00 AM–5:00 PM.
ADMISSION: Free. Free parking is available.
LOCATION: Mid-South Fairgrounds, mid-town Memphis. Follow signs throughout the city.
DESCRIPTION: This indoor/outdoor market has operated since 1971 and has grown from the original 19 dealers to its present size, encompassing an average of 200 dealers indoors. Antiques, collectibles, and arts and crafts, as well as a smorgasbord of practical merchandise for the home are offered. This market is known to local people and the trade as the Coleman-Simmons Market, after the names of its operators. Food is served on the premises.
DEALER RATES: \$55 per 8' × 10' booth inside, \$35 outside. Tables are available at \$6 each and chairs at \$2 each. Reservations and booth rent are required in advance.
CONTACT: Coleman-Simmons Promotions, PO Box 40776, Memphis, TN 38174. Call Sam or Nancy at (901) 725-0633 or 725-0052.

NASHVILLE

The Flea Market at the Nashville Fairgrounds

DATES: Weekend of the fourth Saturday of every month except December. One week earlier in December. Rain or shine.
TIMES: Saturday 6:00 AM–6:00 PM; Sunday 7:00 AM–5:00 PM.
ADMISSION: Free. Free parking is available for 6,000 cars.
LOCATION: Tennessee State Fairgrounds, at Wedgewood and Nolensville Rd. Easy access from Nashville and middle Tennessee via I-65, I-440, and I-24.

DESCRIPTION: The Flea Market at the Nashville Fairgrounds was established in 1969 and is now run by the Tennessee State Fair. The popular indoor/outdoor market has, on average, about 2,000 booths per month, with the April, May, and October markets being the largest shows of the year. The market contains a large section of antiques and collectible items. Also sold are handmade craft items and some new merchandise. There are a variety of delicious foods available. Member of the Tennessee Flea Market Association.
DEALER RATES: $60 for 10' × 10' outside shed space or 12' × 15' parking lot space; $75 for a 10' × 10' inside booth. Reservations and prepayment are required.
CONTACT: Mary Snider, Manager, Nashville Fairgrounds Flea Market, PO Box 40208, Nashville TN 37204. Tel: (615) 862-5016. Office is open Monday through Friday 8:00 AM–4:30 PM and during show hours.

SWEETWATER

Fleas Unlimited

DATES: Saturday and Sunday, rain or shine.
TIMES: 8:00 AM–5:00 PM.
ADMISSION: Free. Parking is also free.
LOCATION: Directly off I-75 at Exit 60. Between Knoxville and Chattanooga.
DESCRIPTION: Opened in December of 1989, this indoor/outdoor market is housed in a 160,000-square-foot building. It attracts 500 dealers inside and there are another 50 spaces outdoors. There is a bit of everything here including plenty of cards, coins, stamps, garage sale finds and some new merchandise. They have an in-house deli, camping facilities with bath house, and a restaurant/candy factory! Members of the Tennessee Flea Market Association.
DEALER RATES: Main building: $22 per day per space or $17 a day if paid monthly. North and South buildings: $20 per day per space or $15 per day if paid monthly. Outside spaces $15 per day. Reservations are recommended.
CONTACT: Rhonda or Whittney, Fleas Unlimited, 121 Cty Rd 308, Sweetwater TN 37874. Tel: (423) 337-3532.

TELFORD (JONESBOROUGH)

Jonesborough Flea Market

DATES: Sunday, year round.
TIMES: 6:00 AM–4:00 PM.
ADMISSION: Free. Parking is free.
LOCATION: Five miles west of Jonesborough on State Hwy 11.
DESCRIPTION: This outdoor market boasts 200 dealers in summer and 50 in winter selling antiques, collectibles, crafts, produce, coins, stamps, cards, garage sale finds, furniture and new merchandise. Two snack bars and handicapped-accessible restrooms add to the amenities.
DEALER RATES: $7 per 12' × 20' space per day, or $6.50 per day if paid by the month. Reservations are not required.
CONTACT: John Crawford or Alan Shelton, PO Box 413, Jonesborough TN 37659-0413. Tel: (615) 753-4241 or 753-4115 or 753-4999.

OTHER FLEA MARKETS

We know or have heard about these markets, but have not personally contacted each one, as we have the markets with descriptions. If you plan to visit one of these markets listed below, *please call first* to make sure they are still open. Flea markets do come and go. While they were open when we went to press, they may not be later. We can't be responsible. *Call first!*

Arrington: Triune Flea Market, 7960 Nolensville Rd. Tel: 615-395-7140.

Baxter: Baxter Flea Market Inc, 6051 Flea Market Rd. Tel: 615-858-5152.

Benton: Hiwassee Flea Market, Hwy 411. Tel: 423-338-9573.

Bluff City: Tri-City Flea Market, 4571 Hwy 11 E # E. Tel: 423-538-0584.

Bristol: More For Less Flea Market, 714 State St. Tel: 423-652-9825.

Bulls Gap: Nor-A-Lee Flea Market, 1076 Idell Rd. Tel: 423-235-0449.

Camden: Medlin's Flea Market, 131 Robertson St. Tel: 901-584-1852.

Chattanooga: East Ridge Flea Market, 6725 Ringgold Rd. Tel: 423-894-3960.

Chattanooga: 23rd Street Indoor Flea Market, 2210 E 21st St. Tel: 423-624-7017.

Clarksville: ABC Flea World, 1114 Crossland Ave. Tel: 615-645-6378.

Clarksville: Betty's Flea Market, 152 Kraft St. Tel: 615-648-9201.

Clarksville: Carol's Flea Market, 1690 Wilma Rudolph Blvd. Tel: 615-552-1952.
Clarksville: Dean Drive Flea Market, 135 Dean Dr. Tel: 615-553-0562.
Clarksville: Dover Road Flea Market, 852 Dover Rd. Tel: 615-551-7704.
Clarksville: Gate One Flea Market, Fort Campbell Blvd. Tel: 615-431-3907.
Clarksville: Mart Flea Market, 1400 Dover Rd. Tel: 615-503-8224.
Clarksville: Queen City Flea Market, 1156 Fort Campbell Blvd. Tel: 615-648-4174.
Covington: A & B Flea Market, 1024 US Hwy 51 N. Tel: 901-476-4525.
Covington: Westside Flea Market, 3392 Hwy 59 W. Tel: 901-476-8995.
Crossville: Crossville Flea Market Dixons, Hwy 70 N. Tel: 615-484-9970.
Crump: Hill Top Flea Market, 3465 US Hwy 64. Tel: 901-632-0626.
Dyersburg: Dyersburg Flea Market, 2450 Lake Rd. Tel: 901-286-6739.
Elizabethton: Street's Flea Market, 1207 19E Bypass. Tel: 423-543-7515.
Englewood: Englewood Flea Market, 122 N Amhust Pl. Tel: 423-887-7389.
Erin: Febby's Flea Market, Arlington Dr. Tel: 615-289-3561.
Fairview: Fairview Flea Market, 328 Blvd E. Tel: 615-799-0509.
Gallatin: Amfor Gifts & Flea Market, 1470 Southwater Ave. Tel: 615-230-9982.
Gallaway: Galloway Trading Post & Flea Market, 914 Hwy 70. Tel: 901-867-7549.
Harriman: I-40 Flea Market, 1225 S Roane St. Tel: 423-882-1008.
Hendersonville: Hendersonville Indoor Flea Market, 235 E Main St. Tel: 615-264-3900.
Hohenwald: Jim's Flea Market, 115 N Park St. Tel: 615-796-5303.
Hohenwald: Natchez Trader Flea Market, 259 Topsy Rd. Tel: 615-796-5623.
Johnson City: Friendly Flea Market, 1121 N Roan St. Tel: 423-928-2300.
Johnson City: US Flea Market Mall, 3501 Bristol Hwy. Tel: 423-854-4860.
Knoxville: Dockery's Flea Market, 1301 Maryville Pike. Tel: 423-573-8755.

Knoxville: Unusual Corner Flea Market, 4301 Asheville Hwy. Tel: 423-521-0079.

Lebanon: Gracie T's Flea Market, 1022 Murfreesboro Rd. Tel: 615-444-5177.

Lebanon: Lebanon Flea Market Parkland & Restaurant, 4994 Murfreesboro Rd. Tel: 615-449-6050.

Lebanon: Parkland Flea Market, 4994 Murfreesboro Rd. Tel: 615-449-6050.

Louisville: Green Acres Flea Market, 908 Hillside Dr. Tel: 423-681-4433 or 970-7824.

Madisonville: Pioneer Auction & Flea Market, 6314 Hwy 411. Tel: 423-442-7118.

Maryville: Hillbilly Flea Market, 4504 E Lamar Alexander Pkwy. Tel: 423-983-2410.

Memphis: A & A Flea Market, 1436 Airways Blvd. Tel: 901-324-4208 or 324-3988.

Memphis: Airways Mini Flea Market, 1426 Airways Blvd. Tel: 901-323-5505.

Memphis: Cotton's Flea & Salvage Market, 6075 N Hwy 51. Tel: 901-357-7224.

Memphis: CD Flea Market, 3340 Millington Rd. Tel: 901-358-4092.

Memphis: Fairgrounds Flea Market, 1999 Madison Ave. Tel: 901-725-0052.

Memphis: Frayser Flea Market, 3238 Millington Rd. Tel: 901-353-3532.

Memphis: Friendly Frank's Flea Market. Tel: 901-755-6561.

Memphis: Lamar Flea Market, 2851 Lamar Ave. Tel: 901-745-0612.

Memphis: Lucille's Flea Market, 2574 Lamar Ave. Tel: 901-745-1305.

Memphis: Ma & Pa's Flea Market, 1531 Cherry Rd., Tel: 901-744-6905.

Memphis: Mark Flea Market, 2371 Frayser Blvd. Tel: 901-353-4944.

Memphis: Midtown Flea Market, 2018 Court Ave. Tel: 901-726-9059.

Memphis: Second Time Around Flea Market, 942 S Cooper St. Tel: 901-725-1257.

Millington: Flying O Flea Market, 8580 US Hwy 51 N. Tel: 901-873-4111.

Morristown: Big P Produce & Flea Market, 5430 W Andrew Johnson Hwy. Tel: 423-586-1706.

Mount Juliet: Mt Juliet Flea Market & Antiques, 11804 Lebanon Rd. Tel: 615-758-5305.

Mount Juliet: PJ's Flea Market, 11520 Lebanon Rd. Tel: 615-754-6232.

Mount Juliet: Rawlings Flea Market, 13338 Lebanon Rd. Tel: 615-754-7457.

Nashville: Curtis Flea Market, 7102 Charlotte Pike. Tel: 615-356-0079.

Nashville: Giant Flea Market, 2917 Nolensville Rd. Tel: 615-333-8196.

Nashville: Madison Flea Market, 1210 Gallatin Rd. Tel: 615-868-2388.

Nashville: Sullivan's Flea Market, 3501 Charlotte Pike. Tel: 615-385-3254.

Parsons: Tennessee River Flea Market at Perryville, 545 Pentecostal Campground Rd. Tel: 901-847-9383.

Powell: Clinton Hwy Flea Market, 7622 Clinton Hwy. Tel: 423-947-4232.

Sparta: Cherry Creek Flea Market, RR1. Tel: 615-738-3440.

Spring Hill: Spring Hill Flea Market, 1220 School St. Tel: 615-486-2745.

Summertown: Summertown Flea Market, 101 Hwy 20. Tel: 615-964-4345.

Tazewell: Gile's Flea Market, Hwy 25 E. Tel: 423-626-8983.

Tennessee Ridge: Tennessee Ridge Flea Market, Hwy 147. Tel: 615-721-3434.

Union City: Giant Flea Market of Union City, 701 Reelfoot Blvd. Tel: 901-885-2377.

Wartrace: Squez A Buck Flea Market, 2807 Hwy 41A S. Tel: 615-857-4027.

Waverly: Daniel D Auction & Flea Market, Hwy 13 S. Tel: 615-296-9022.

Waverly: Dot's Country Flea Market, Hwy 13 S. Tel: 615-296-9022.

Waverly: Mister C's Flea Market, 115 Waverly Plz. Tel: 615-296-2865.

White Bluff: White Bluff Flea Market, 4221 Hwy 70 E. Tel: 615-797-5686.

Whiteville: B & G Flea Market, 315 Hwy 100 W. Tel: 901-254-8321.

Winchester: Winchester Flea Market, 312 Old Cowan Rd. Tel: 615-967-5866.

TEXAS

ALAMO

All Valley Flea Market

DATES: Saturday and Sunday, rain or shine.
TIMES: 4:30 AM to dark.
ADMISSION: $.50 a carload, or $.25 per walk-in.
LOCATION: Intersection of Cesar Chavez (formerly Morningside) Rd and Expressway 83.
DESCRIPTION: Started in 1969 after a visit to another successful market elsewhere gave Mr. Bruns the idea, he opened his first of four markets in Pharr. Also the first in Valley area. When a highway was built through the market, they moved to Alamo. Now there are around 800 dealers presenting "everything!" And 20,000 to 30,000 buyers coming through every weekend buying everything including antiques, collectibles, used items, some new merchandise. Food concessions and handicapped-accessible restrooms add to the amenities. There are 40 trailer hook-ups available.
DEALER RATES: Saturdays $4.50 for all the tables and space you need; Sundays $8 for a 11' x 18' space. Reservations are strongly suggested.
CONTACT: David Villegas or Dulce Ruiz, All Valley Flea Markets, 501 North Bridge St Ste 528, Hidalgo TX 78557. Tel: (956) 781-1911.

AMARILLO

T-Anchor Flea Market

DATES: Every Saturday and Sunday, year round. Rain or shine.
TIMES: 9:00 AM–5:00 PM.
ADMISSION: Free. Free parking is available.
LOCATION: 1401 Ross St, off I-40.
DESCRIPTION: This indoor market began in 1978. Their 175 vendors in 365 spaces from all over the country sell antiques, collectibles, crafts, produce, and new merchandise. During summer months vendors rent space outdoors. Produce vendors are furnished with a permit. One snack bar and handicapped-accessible restrooms add to the amenities.
DEALER RATES: $8 per day outside and $10–$12 inside. Reasonable daily rates for 10' x 10' and 10' x 30' outside spaces. Reservations are not required, except during the Christmas season.
CONTACT: HD and Claudia Blyth, PO Box 31182, Amarillo TX 79120. Tel: (806) 373-0430.

AUSTIN

Austin Country Flea Market

DATES: Saturday and Sunday, year round. Rain or shine.
TIMES: 10:00 AM–6:00 PM.
ADMISSION: $1 per car.
LOCATION: 9500 Hwy 290 East.
DESCRIPTION: This is central Texas' largest flea market, with over 500 selling spaces. Their dealers sell antiques, collectibles, crafts, vegetables, and new merchandise. Open every weekend, it offers good food, family fun, and big bargains. The entire market is covered.
DEALER RATES: $35 per 10' x 8' booth (20' dealer parking directly behind each space if desired, or dealer's vehicle may be moved to an authorized area and parking space can be used as additional selling area). One display table is provided. RV electricity is available in limited areas. Gates are open to dealers at 7:00 AM; gates close 10:00 PM. Advance reservations required.
CONTACT: Buz Cook, Austin Country, 9500 Hwy 290 E, Austin TX 78724. Tel: (512) 928-2795.

BONHAM

Bonham Trade Days

DATES: Thursday through Sunday the weekend after the first Monday, year round.
TIMES: 7:00 AM–5:00 PM, mostly daylight to dusk.
ADMISSION: Free. Parking is free.
LOCATION: Fort Inglish Park. At the intersection of Hwy 56 and Hwys 121 and 82 bypass.
DESCRIPTION: Sponsored by the Kiwanis, this 26-year-old outdoor market follows the Monday Trade Days tradition. There are 300 dealers selling antiques, collectibles, garage sale goodies, produce and new merchandise—"just everything." Plenty of food vendors satisfy the hungry.
DEALER RATES: $10 per 20' x 30' space per weekend. First come, first served.
CONTACT: Jo, Bonham Trade Days, Rt 4 Box 358, Bonham TX 75418. Tel: (903) 583-2367.

BOWIE

Second Monday Trade Days

DATES: Friday through Sunday before the second Monday of each month.
TIMES: 7:00 AM–dark.
ADMISSION: Free. Parking is free.
LOCATION: Rodeo grounds on East Wise St. Business Hwy 287 and Hwy 81. Going north from Hwy 287, take the US 81 Waurika exit.
DESCRIPTION: Another Monday Court Day market! That judge, he did get around. Now in its second hundred years (started in 1890), this venerable market has approximately 300 dealers (in 470 spots) selling antiques, collectibles, livestock, crafts and whatever comes in. This is the Northern Texas place to be on second Monday. They can easily boast they have 5,000–10,000 visitors each month. In addition to their current restrooms with showers for dealers, they are upgrading their facilities to be ADA compliant.
DEALER RATES: $20-$25 per space, electric is $4 extra per day, per connection. Reservations are required.
CONTACT: Clyde Johnson, Bowie City of Grounds Maintenance Dept, 304 Pecan St, Bowie TX 76230. Tel: (817) 872-1680.

> As you have read above, this market started as a typical livestock trading center with mules, work horses and other stock traded. Herds would come through there so traders could trade. Medicine shows, novelty hawkers and peddlers would ply their "trades"—providing the entertainment. After WWI, commodities were added to the collection of goods.

BUFFALO GAP

Buffalo Gap Flea Market

DATES: Friday, Saturday, and Sunday, third Saturday of each month from February through December (weather permitting in December).
TIMES: 7:00 AM–10:00 PM.
ADMISSION: Free. Parking is available nearby.
LOCATION: In Buffalo Gap, 10 miles south of Abilene on Hwy 89.
DESCRIPTION: This outdoor market began in 1974, and currently draws around 150 dealers selling a wide range of antique, collectibles, fresh produce, crafts, and new merchandise. They have well-lit night shopping on Saturday night "under the stars and trees." This market is described by its

owner as the "prettiest market in the west." Food and toilet facilities are available.

DEALER RATES: $14 per 12' x 18' space for a three-day weekend, plus electricity at $3 per day, if needed. All electric wiring has been updated. Reservations are required at least one week in advance as they have had to turn away dealers before. A $2 city permit is required to sell.

CONTACT: John & Peggy Brolls, PO Box 575, Buffalo Gap TX 79508-0575. Tel: (915) 572-3327.

CANTON

First Monday Trade Days

DATES: Begins on Friday before the first Monday of each month, and runs Friday through Sunday and Monday holidays. Rain or shine.

TIMES: 7:00 AM–dark.

ADMISSION: Free. Parking is available for $3 per vehicle. RV spaces are available with advance reservations.

LOCATION: Two blocks north of downtown square. Easy access on Hwy 19, Hwy 64 and FM Rd 859. From I-20, Exit 526, 2 miles south on left.

DESCRIPTION: This is surely one of the most popular and well-known flea markets in the country, if not the world. Originating in 1876 as the town's court day, people at that time began to take care of their trading and purchasing of animals, produce, etc., while waiting for the judge. In 1965, the city of Canton acquired a three-acre plot of land two blocks north of the Court House which is now the Historic District. The dealers selling animals can be found four blocks east of the Court House on the property known as Curry's Trade Grounds or Dog Grounds. Since 1965, the number of available lots has grown from 150 to well over 4,000. They now have covered pavilions and an indoor civic center. The heated/air-conditioned civic center is 34,000 square feet with a food concession and handicapped-accessible restrooms. From here all the best antique and collectible dealers sell. First Monday Trade Days began advertising its unique market in 1974, and since then has appeared on NBC's "Today Show," the front page of *The Wall St Journal*, in *National Geographic*, *Smithsonian* and in several other local and national media. All kinds of antiques, collectibles, new merchandise, handmade crafts, and food are available. Restrooms with showers are provided.

DEALER RATES: $50 for each lot. Dealer spaces are approximately 12' x 20'. Dealers who reserve in advance may renew for following sale. Unreserved lots are also available. Covered space is limited and ranges from $100-$175.

CONTACT: City of Canton, PO Box 245, Canton TX 75103. Tel: (903) 567-6556.

CHANNELVIEW

White Elephant, Inc

DATES: Every Saturday and Sunday, rain or shine.

TIMES: 7:30 AM–5:30 PM.

ADMISSION: Free. $1 a car.

LOCATION: 15662 I-10 east. Take the Sheldon-Channelview exit; the market is on the Service Rd off I-10.

DESCRIPTION: Between 350 and 375 dealers show up each week for this indoor/outdoor market, which has been in operation since 1971. Articles for sale include antiques, collectibles, garage sale items such as tools, furniture, and jewelry, as well as some new items and fresh produce. Food and toilet facilities are available on the premises.

DEALER RATES: $13–$17 per space depending on location. Reservations not required.

CONTACT: Ruth McDaniel, PO Box 209, Channelview TX 77530-0209. Tel: (281) 452-9022.

GARLAND

Vikon Village Flea Market

DATES: Saturdays and Sundays, year round. Also the Friday after Thanksgiving and some extra dates in December. For 1998: December 22–24.

TIMES: 10:00 AM–7:00 PM.

ADMISSION: Free. Free parking for up to 750 cars is available nearby.

LOCATION: 2918 South Jupiter. Near the corner of Kingsley and Jupiter, 2 blocks north of Rt 635.

DESCRIPTION: This indoor market began in 1975 and averages around 350 booths with 175 dealers selling such items as books, baseball cards, coins, jewelry, furniture, clothing, and plants, as well as new merchandise. One snack bar and handicapped-accessible restrooms add to the amenities.

DEALER RATES: Lease available at $140 and up per month (minimum one month). Reservations are required. Call for information Thursdays from 10:00 AM–5:00 PM or Fridays 10:00 AM–6:00 PM.

CONTACT: Vikon Village Flea Market, 2918 S Jupiter, Garland TX 75041. Tel: (972) 271-0565.

GRAND PRAIRIE

Traders Village

DATES: Every Saturday and Sunday year round. Rain or shine.
TIMES: 8:00 AM–dusk.
ADMISSION: Free. Parking for over 7,000 cars is available at $2 per vehicle. Handicapped parking is available.
LOCATION: 2602 Mayfield Rd in Grand Prairie. In the heart of the Dallas/Fort Worth area, 5 miles south of Six Flags Over Texas Theme Park off Hwy 360. Or, take Hwy 360 north one mile off I-20.
DESCRIPTION: Traders Village is a 106-acre complex which opened in November 1973. Since that date, over 55 million people have visited this market, roughly 2.5 million a year. The market currently attracts between 1,500 and 1,600 dealers who set up on open, covered, and enclosed spaces. Crowds average 35,000–75,000 per weekend. Special events include a chili cook-off (April), Cajun Fest(May), an antique auto swap meet (June), Antique Tractor and Farm Implement Show (July), an authentic Indian powwow (September), a barbecue cook-off (October), and more throughout the year. Most of the special events are open to the public for free. Traders Village runs its own food and beverage department, with over 30 stands selling everything from Spanish specialties to pizza by the slice, from chicken-fried steak to funnel cakes. Produce vendors and bulk-food dealers are also on hand. Other features include kiddie rides, an arcade, stroller and wheelchair rentals, shaded rest areas, two ATM machines and a first-aid room. There is also a sister market in Houston.
DEALER RATES: $20 per 14' x 25' open lot per day. $25 per covered space per day. Reservations are required for two-day rentals only.
CONTACT: Ron Simmons, President and General Manager, c/o Traders Village, 2602 Mayfield Rd, Grand Prairie TX 75051. Tel: (972) 647-2331.

> Traders Village is a continuing extension of the trading that went on between various Indian tribes over the centuries. An historical marker, dedicated in 1980, marks the site of the million acre "Cross Timbers" area where Shoshoni, rooted out by Apaches, in turn chased out by Comanches, traded until white man showed up in 17th and 18th centuries. In the 1840s, white settlers stayed, leading to the Battle of Village Creek on May 24, 1841, marking the end of the Indian domination of the area.

HOUSTON

Traders Village

DATES: Every Saturday and Sunday, year round. Rain or shine.

TIMES: 8:00 AM–dusk.

ADMISSION: Free. Parking for over 4,000 cars is available at $2 per vehicle. Handicapped parking is available.

LOCATION: 7979 North Eldridge Rd. Off Northwest Freeway (Hwy 290), Eldridge Exit, 3/10 mile south.

DESCRIPTION: Traders Village is a 100-acre complex which opened in May 1989. Up to one million people visit a year. The market currently attracts over 600 dealers who set up on covered and enclosed spaces selling imports, antiques, collectibles, crafts, produce, garage sale merchandise, pets, clothes, furniture, auto parts, flowers and plants, electronics and lots more. Crowds average 10,000-15,000 a weekend. Special events include a chili and barbecue cook-offs in January-chili on Saturday and barbecue on Sunday, an antique auto swap meet (March), an authentic Indian pow-wow (May), an Oktoberfest celebration, and more throughout the year. Most of the special events are open to the public. Traders Village runs its own food and beverage department, with over 30 stands selling everything from Spanish specialties to pizza by the slice, from chicken-fried steak to funnel cakes. Produce vendors and bulk-food dealers are also on hand. Other features include kiddie rides, an arcade, stroller and wheelchair rentals, shaded rest areas, an ATM machine, and a first-aid room. There is also a sister market in Grand Prairie.

DEALER RATES: $20 per day, or $41 for the weekend reserved. Reservations are required for two-day rentals only.

CONTACT: Dayton Denton, Traders Village—Houston, 7979 N Eldridge Rd, Houston TX 77041. Tel: (281) 890-5500.

Trading Fair II

DATES: Every Friday, Saturday, and Sunday. Rain or shine.

TIMES: 10:00 AM–6:00 PM.

ADMISSION: Free. Parking $1.

LOCATION: 5515 South Loop East. Midway between the Astrodome and the Galveston Freeway on Loop 610. Use the Crestmont exit either way.

DESCRIPTION: This indoor market started in 1974 and currently draws over 400 dealers selling a wide range of antiques and collectibles, as well

as craft items. They are possibly the largest indoor market in the Houston area. Their two floors—60,000 square-feet each with an additional 30,000-square-foot annex in the back—houses 300 dealers downstairs on a weekly basis. The owner says, "I can drive my Cadillac in an easy circle on the second floor, and the wheelie skaters love the tile floor." They fill that second floor with cat shows, antique-collectible shows, Indian pow-wows, and whatever. Their selection of sale items is described as "some of everything, a lot of some things." Two restaurants and one snack bar take care of hunger problems, handicapped-accessible restrooms provide relief. They do plenty of advertising as well as everything they can to gain the notice, goodwill, and support of the buying public.
DEALER RATES: $200 for a 10' x 10' space and up to $1,000 per month for much larger spaces. Dealer reservations are suggested.
CONTACT: Trading Fair II, 5515 S Loop E, Houston TX 77033. Tel: (713) 731-1111.

LUBBOCK

National Flea Market

DATES: Every Wednesday through Sunday, except Thanksgiving and Christmas week.
TIMES: Wednesday and Friday 9:00 AM–5:00 PM, Saturday and Sunday 9:00 AM–6:00 PM.
ADMISSION: Free. Parking is also free.
LOCATION: 1808 Clovis Rd. One half block west of Ave Q.
DESCRIPTION: This market first opened in 1982. It is both an indoor and outdoor market attracting from 100 to 150 dealers selling everything from antiques and collectibles to crafts and vegetables. New merchandise including clothing, tools and electronics are also available. For your convenience, a snack bar and concession stand are on the premises. The original barn for weekend dealers burned down. They have rebuilt it housing 105 spaces inside with heating, air conditioning and lovely clean handicapped-accessible restrooms.
DEALER RATES: There are two buildings and outdoor space available: weekly rates in the main building start at $43 and up for a 10' x 10' booth depending on location; rates in the other building, which usually houses the weekend dealer, vary from $20–$50, while space varies from 10' x 10' to 10' x 20'. Storage sheds that can be sold from are $45 per week or $175 a month.

CONTACT: Debie Grant, National Flea Market, 1808 Clovis Rd, Lubbock TX 79415. Tel: (806) 744-4979.

MCALLEN-MISSION

All Valley First Sunday Flea Market

DATES: First Sunday of every month.
TIMES: 8:00 AM–5:00 PM.
ADMISSION: $.50. Parking is free.
LOCATION: Villa Real Convention Building. Bentsen Rd, between McAllen and Mission on Expressway 83.
DESCRIPTION: This market first opened in 1976 as one of four markets in the Valley area. The other markets are in McAllen, Mercedes and Alamo. This one attracts quantities of tourists to the 285 dealers and their wares. Mostly antiques and collectibles are shown here. One snack bar and handicapped-accessible restrooms add to the amenities.
DEALER RATES: $8.50 per table per day. Reservations are a must!
CONTACT: David Villegas or Dulce Ruiz, All Valley Flea Markets, 501 North Bridge St Ste 528, Hidalgo TX 78557. Tel: (956) 781-1911.

MCKINNEY

Third Monday Trade Days

DATES: Saturday and Sunday preceding the third Monday each month. (It doesn't always fall on the third weekend.)
TIMES: 9:00 AM–4:00 PM. The deal is: all dealers must be open during these times. However, other than these hours, they can be open earlier or later. Earlier is the rule.
ADMISSION: Free. $2 parking.
LOCATION: 4550 W University Dr. Hwy 380, 2 miles west of US 75.
DESCRIPTION: Another fantastic court day market started when that circuit judge came around and did his job on Mondays (see Kentucky's markets). There are six in Texas—see Canton and Weatherford for First Monday markets, Bowie and Bonham for Second Monday markets and Whitewright for a Fourth Monday market. Although there are 700 spaces here, usually all spaces are filled with at least 500 dealers (some use more space than others). This is a great place to find antiques, collectibles, crafts, produce, animals and new merchandise. There are plenty of food vendors, you won't starve.

DEALER RATES: $35 and up for open air, $125 in a building per space per weekend. Reservations are necessary.
CONTACT: Darrell Lewis, Third Monday Trade Days, 4550 W University Dr, McKinney TX 75070. Tel: (972) 562-5466 or 542-7174.

MERCEDES

Mercedes Flea Market

DATES: Saturday and Sunday, year round.
TIMES: 4:30 AM to dusk.
ADMISSION: $.25. Parking is free.
LOCATION: Mile 2 West and Expressway 83.
DESCRIPTION: Opened in 1973 as the second of the All Valley Flea Markets and now owned by Mr. Kim, this market attracts over 600 vendors selling predominately antiques and collectibles, as well as fresh produce, used and some new merchandise. From 10,000 to 12,000 local people come here each weekend. Thirteen concession stands provide a cure for the munchies.
DEALER RATES: Saturdays $2 outdoors in sun; $6 under shelter per space; Sundays $6 in sun and $6.50 in shade. Monthly reservations are strongly suggested. Daily, just show up.
CONTACT: Tack Kim, Mercedes Flea Market, 501 North Bridge St Ste 528, Hidalgo TX 78557. Tel: (956) 565-2751 market. Or (956) 781-1911 during the week.

PEARLAND

Cole's Antique Village and Flea Market

DATES: Every Saturday and Sunday, rain or shine.
TIMES: 6:30 AM–6:00 PM.
ADMISSION: Free. $1 for parking.
LOCATION: 1014-1022 N Main St, 4 miles south of the Hobby Airport on Telephone Rd (Hwy 35).
DESCRIPTION: This indoor/outdoor market started in 1969 and currently draws approximately 700 dealers selling a range of antiques and collectibles such as furniture, tools, and glassware; fresh produce and plants, crafts and new items are also sold. Food is available on the premises. They added 50 more new covered tables outside in 1997. The antique co-op is open everyday but Wednesday, as is the office.

DEALER RATES: $40 per 10' x 10' space indoors per weekend; $45 per outdoor covered space per weekend. Reservations can be made for these spaces Fridays from 8:00 AM–5:00 PM.
CONTACT: Cole's Antique Village and Flea Market, 1014 N Main St, Pearland TX 77581-2208. Tel: (281) 485-2277.

SAN ANTONIO

Austin Hwy Flea Market and Trade Center

Note: This market will be under new ownership in 1998, but the contract states that they have to remain the same for at least the first six months of operation. And Ed will be keeping an eye on them.

DATES: Friday, Saturday and Sunday, year round. Rain or shine.
TIMES: 7:00 AM–dark.
ADMISSION: Free admission and free parking for 1,000 cars.
LOCATION: Located between Broadway and Harry Wurzbach on Austin Hwy. Take Interstate Loop 410 to either Broadway or Harry Wurzbach and follow south to Austin Hwy. Conveniently located 4 miles from downtown and the historic Alamo, 2 miles from San Antonio International Airport, 1 mile from Fort Sam Houston, and 5 miles from Randolph Air Force Base.
DESCRIPTION: Started in 1976, this market attracts 200 dealers selling antiques, collectibles, crafts, vegetables, and junque including Mexican imports, books, new and estate jewelry, bicycles, lawn equipment, new and vintage clothing, and plants. New merchandise is discouraged and not found here. One snack bar and handicapped-accessible restrooms add to the amenities.
DEALER RATES: Inside spaces vary depending on size; the charge for outside space is $19 for a 10' x 20' covered booth for three days. Reservations are preferred.
CONTACT: Austin Hwy Flea Market, 1428 Austin Hwy, San Antonio TX 78209-4338. Tel: (210) 828-1488 or (210) 828-9188.

Eisenhauer Road Flea Market

DATES: Every day, rain or shine.
TIMES: Weekends 9:00 AM–7:00 PM; weekdays 12:00 PM–7:00 PM.
ADMISSION: Free. Ample free parking is available.
LOCATION: 3903 Eisenhauer Rd.

DESCRIPTION: This market, started in 1979, operates 90% indoors in an air-conditioned space with over 200 steady dealers plus transients. A variety of antiques and collectibles is sold, along with crafts and new merchandise. Food is served at three snack bars on the premises.
DEALER RATES: $5 per 8' table per day. Reservations are suggested.
CONTACT: Harry Weiss or Mrs Pat Walker, 3903 Eisenhauer Rd, San Antonio TX 78218. Tel: (210) 653-7592. Fax: (210) 657-1692.

Mission Open-Air Market

DATES: Tuesday through Sunday.
TIMES: 6:30 AM–4:00 PM.
ADMISSION: $.50 a walk-in or $1 a carload.
LOCATION: 207 West Chavaneaux Rd. Between I-35 and 37, Moursund Blvd Exit inside Loop 410 West.
DESCRIPTION: Started in 1985, this outdoor "real flea market" consists of 1,500 dealers under covered areas selling 90% used merchandise. They claim to be the "largest outdoor market in South Texas." Some of the items sold include antiques, collectibles, produce, garage sale goodies, furniture, and some new merchandise. When hunger hits, try the snack bar. There are handicapped-accessible restrooms on site. Watch for Swap-O the Clown as he greets visitors during the market. For a touch of excitement, they hold drawings and do cash giveaways every day. During Christmas and Thanksgiving holiday season, the prizes are turkeys or hams. This is *not* a dull place.
DEALER RATES: Tuesday, Thursday and Saturday $10 per 15' x 15' space, $15 on Wednesday and Saturday, $18 on Sunday. Reservations are not required.
CONTACT: Mission Open-Air Market, 207 W Chavaneaux Rd, San Antonio TX 78221. Tel: (210) 923-8131 (information), 921-1569 (administration) and fax: (210) 923-8004.

Northwest Flea Market

DATES: Saturday morning to Sunday evening.
TIMES: Saturday morning to Sunday evening.
ADMISSION: Free. Parking is free.
LOCATION: 3600 Fredericksburg Rd. Off Loop 410 on north side of town. Go south toward the city 1½ miles to the Northwest Center on Fredericksburg Rd. The market is behind the mall.

DESCRIPTION: Open since 1973, this market of approximately 150 dealers sells antiques, collectibles, crafts, produce, coins, stamps, cards, garage sale goodies, furniture and new merchandise. "It has not been disputed that this is the first indoor flea market to set up in a modern air-conditioned building for the sole purpose of running a flea market, with permanent tables, storage and lock-up rooms. I have a dealer, Mr. and Mrs. Linderman, who have rented their tables and left them set up for 22 years straight!" says Mr. Markwell.
DEALER RATES: Outdoors: $14 per day for 20' x 20' space, table provided for $2 (first come, first served). Inside: $14 per day with 8' table. Rooms starting at $197 per month. Reservations are suggested one week in advance.
CONTACT: James C Markwell, Northwest Flea Market, 3600 Fredericksburg Rd, San Antonio TX 78201. Tel: (210) 736-6655.

SCHERTZ

Bussey's Flea Market

DATES: Saturday and Sunday, year round.
TIMES: 7:00 AM to dusk.
ADMISSION: Free. $1 per car.
LOCATION: 18738 IH-35 North.
DESCRIPTION: This outdoor show began in 1979. There are 513 dealer spaces, with most of them filled on the weekends. Anything from antiques and collectibles to very little new merchandise, and craft items are available—"anything that's legal." Generally 90% used, 10% new merchandise. Plenty of garage sale items. There are many Mexican imports and a variety of curios as well. Food is available on the premises with seven fantastic snack bars and plenty of hamburgers, hot dogs among other delights (like a sausage on a stick), breakfast tacos and special hand-me-down recipes. This is a family-operated market.
DEALER RATES: $10–$12 on Saturday, $15–$20 on Sunday per space. Rates may go up in April, but then again, they may not. No reservations needed.
CONTACT: Harold Smith, General Partner, Bussey's Flea Market, 18738 IH-35 N, San Antonio TX 78154. Tel: (210) 651-6830. Fax: (830) 609-0800, yes the area code is different, but correct.

Tear Your Hair Out

A woman, cleaning out her attic, brought in a crystal punch bowl and cup set and put them out for $25. She was offered $15 by professional dealer and refused it, another dealer offered her $20 which started a screaming match between the two dealers. Eventually one dealer won and 20 minutes later the victor sold the set for a 900% profit.

WHITEWRIGHT

Whitewright Trade Days

DATES: The weekend before the fourth Monday of every month starting the preceding Friday through Sunday (technically Saturday and Sunday, but some dealers persist in setting up on Thursday and Friday!).
TIMES: All day Friday through early afternoon Sunday, generally 6:00-7:00 AM until they drop late in the day.
ADMISSION: Free. Parking is free.
LOCATION: American Legion grounds on Sears St. From Hwy 69, turn right at the Y onto Grant St, then turn right on Sears.
DESCRIPTION: This 20-plus-year-old market is another of the judge's famous stops. About 150-plus dealers set up selling antiques, collectibles, and all manner of items. There are 300 dealer spaces, so drop on down! This market is the fundraiser for the American Legion. Do stop in at Caraway's Exxon and shout a "Hi" to Jim and Odell!
DEALER RATES: $5 per space. Reservations are nice.
CONTACT: Odell Caraway, Whitewright Trade Days, c/o Caraway Exxon, Box 566, Whitewright TX 75491. Tel: (903) 364-2994.

WICHITA FALLS

Holliday Street Flea Market

DATES: Every Saturday and Sunday, year round.
TIMES: 7:00 AM–dark.
ADMISSION: Free, with free parking available.
LOCATION: 2820 Holliday St. Near Hwys 281 and 287 on Holliday Rd near Holliday Creek.
DESCRIPTION: This market, formerly "Wichita Falls Flea Market and Trade Center" runs both indoors and out. Under the same ownership as before, it began in 1966 and currently hosts 200 to 250 dealers. The prop-

erty was originally an amusement park, swimming pool and trailer park before becoming a flea market. There are antiques, collectibles, and crafts for sale, alongside produce and new merchandise. In addition, there are Mexican imports, musical instruments, saddles, boots, clothes—new and used—t-shirts, furniture, appliances and tack offered. There are 12 acres of selling space (as the city took 5 acres for flood control), including individual buildings with inside lock-ups. There are food concessions on the premises.
DEALER RATES: $7 per 12' x 30' space uncovered; $10 per 12' x 12' covered shed per day; $85 to $125 per lock-up stall indoors per month. Reservations are required for indoor spaces and covered sheds.
CONTACT: Jim and Vivian Parish, Owners, 2820 Holliday St, Wichita Falls TX 76301. Tel: (817) 767-1712 or 767-9038.

> They tell of a dealer couple from Maine who visited several times—selling lobster and bear traps, a bit unusual for Texas!

WINNIE

Old Time Trade Days Flea Market

DATES: The weekend following the first Monday, year round.
TIMES: Daylight to dusk.
ADMISSION: Free. Parking is $2 a carload. Tour buses are free.
LOCATION: I-10, Exit 829 at Winnie. When you get off the Interstate you are there. Between Beaumont and Houston.
DESCRIPTION: Formerly a part of Larry's Antique Mall and Flea Market in Beaumont, this market opened in 1992, taking the major part of the flea market with it. Housed in permanent shops, covered pavilions, or outdoors, it hosts 500 to 1,000 dealers specializing in antiques, collectibles and crafts. The crafters have their own space showing their wares from the Ozarks to the south Texas coast. Decorators come from all over the country to find those "special somethings" to furnish their jobs. There is a special designated place for garage sales and everyone is invited to use it. With the publicity from the move from Beaumont, this market put the town of Winnie on the Texas map. So much so that all the major fast-food companies have space there including McDonald's, Burger King, Taco Bell, and plenty more. There are clean restrooms available. Very quickly this market has become "family" to some as well as a capsule history of Texas in that they have already had at least one wedding, a two-foot flood, tornados, hurri-

canes—"some real hair-raisers," says Mrs. Tinkle, one of the owners. "But our customers are loyal, our vendors are loyal, and somehow the market just keeps growing."
DEALER RATES: $30 and up depending on location and size: outdoors, covered pavilion, indoors, shop; 20' x 20' to 20' x 50'. Reservations are recommended.
CONTACT: Larry and Justine Tinkle, 7135 Concord Rd, Beaumont TX 77708. Tel: (409) 892-4000 or (409) 296-3300.

Well, they had a "big top tent," but that "is somewhere blowing in the wind," according to Justine Tinkle.

OTHER FLEA MARKETS

We know or have heard about these markets, but have not personally contacted each one, as we have the markets with descriptions. If you plan to visit one of these markets listed below, *please call first to make sure they are still open.* Flea markets do come and go. While they were open when we went to press, they may not be later. We can't be responsible. *Call first!*

Abilene: The Crossing Indoor Flea Market, 1505 S 14th St. Tel: 915-672-5325.
Abilene: Elmdale Flea Market, 5423 S 1st St. Tel: 915-673-8623.
Abilene: Old Abilene Town Flea Market, 3300 E US Hwy 80. Tel: 915-675-6588.
Abilene: Red Rooster Collectibles & Flea Market, 1901 S Treadaway Blvd. Tel: 915-673-4635.
Alief: Trade City Flea Market, 9901 Wilcrest Dr. Tel: 281-983-3888.
Alpine: Second Saturday Flea Market, 205 W Murphy St. Tel: 915-837-2241.
Alvarado: All-American Texas Flea Markets. Tel: 817-783-5468.
Alvarado: Johnston's Flea Market, S IH 35 W. Tel: 817-783-8803.
Alvin: PJ's Resale & Flea Market, 304 N Gordon St. Tel: 281-331-2647.
Amarillo: Old ICX Flea Market, 513 Ross St. Tel: 806-373-3215.
Aransas Pass: Shrimp Capital Btq & Flea Market. Tel: 512-758-5812.
Arthur City: Arthur City Flea Market. Tel: 903-732-4576.
Athens: West 31 Flea Market, Hwy 31 W. Tel: 903-675-8578.
Austin: Austin Country Flea Market, 9500 E Hwy 290. Tel: 512-928-4711.

Austin: Oakhill Flea Market, 5526 W Hwy 290. Tel: 512-892-0402.
Balcones: IM Flea Market, I H 10 W. Tel: 210-755-9190.
Bastrop: Wyldwood Flea Market, Hwy 71 W. Tel: 512-321-3280.
Beaumont: Antique Mall & Flea Market, 7135 Concord Rd. Tel: 409-892-4000.
Beaumont: King Mart Flea Market, 2655 S 11th St. Tel: 409-842-5401.
Beeville: Bush Country Flea Market. Tel: 512-358-9111.
Beeville: FM 351 Flea Market, Hwy 351. Tel: 512-358-7368.
Beeville: The Mall Flea Market. Tel: 512-358-9938.
Belton: Bell County Flea Market, George Wilson Rd. Tel: 817-939-6411.
Belton: Centroplex Flea Market, 200 Whitsett St. Tel: 817-939-5242.
Bertram: Traders Paradise Flea Market, 163 Vaughn. Tel: 512-355-2141.
Blanco: Blanco Flea Market, 419 Pecan. Tel: 210-833-2204.
Bridge City: Gulf Coast Flea Market, 3140 Texas Ave. Tel: 409-735-5377.
Brownsville: Mini Flea Market, 102 E Elizabeth St. Tel: 210-548-2076.
Brownsville: Seventy Seven Flea Market, 5955 N Expressway. Tel: 210-350-9425.
Bryan: Jockey Lot & Flea Market of Bryan, College Station Hwy 6 S. Tel: 409-690-6353.
Cameron: Cameron Flea Market & Antiques, 1901 W 4th St. Tel: 817-697-2315.
Cameron: Chris & Wayne's S Flea Market, 3802 N Travis Ave. Tel: 817-697-4167.
Canyon: Fat Man's Flea Market. Tel: 806-655-8914.
Cleburne: Cleburne Flea Market, 1300 E Henderson St. Tel: 817-645-9099.
Cleveland: Frontier Flea Market, 18431 Hwy 105. Tel: 281-592-Tel: 2101.
Clute: Acme Flea Market, 508 S Main St. Tel: 281-265-3766.
Columbus: Southern National Swap Meet, FM 949. Tel: 409-732-6447
Comfort: Hwy 87 Flea Market, Hwy 87 N. Tel: 210-995-2998.
Copperas Cove: A Flea Market, 105 W Ave D. Tel: 817-547-5335.
Corpus Christi: Bell County Flea Market, George Wilson Rd. Tel: 512-939-6411.
Corpus Christi: Casa Linda Flea Market II, 1551 Baldwin Blvd. Tel: 512-884-2264.

Corpus Christi: Corpus Christi Flea Market, 2833 S Padre Island Dr. Tel: 512-854-4943.

Corpus Christi: Irene's Antique Flea Market, 10135 Leopard St. Tel: 512-241-9221.

Corsicana: Northside Flea Market, 708 S 7th St. Tel: 903-872-7170.

Crowley: Crowley Flea Market, 120 S Tarrant St. Tel: 817-297-6111.

Dallas: Southwest Swap Meet. Tel: 214-320-9989.

Decatur: Renegades Trading Post & Flea Market, RR 5 Box 302. Tel: 817-627-2611.

Del Rio: Sal's Flea Market, Spur 239. Tel: 210-775-9588.

Dickinson: Morgan Flea Market, 2802 Hwy 3. Tel: 281-337-1290.

Donna: Don Wes Flea Market, Victoria Rd & Hwy 83. Tel: 210-464-3502.

Donna: Valverde Flea Market, Bsns 83 & Vlvrd Rd. Tel: 210-464-8169.

Eagle Pass: Speedy's Flea Market, N Hwy 277. Tel: 210-773-9783.

Edinburg: 281 Flea Market Inc, N Hwy 281. Tel: 210-380-2616.

Edinburg: Trading Post Flea Market, FM 1426. Tel: 210-787-9824.

El Paso: Bronco Swap Meet, 8408 Alameda Ave. Tel: 915-858-5555.

El Paso: Fox Plaza Swap Meet, 5511 Alameda Ave. Tel: 915-532-2444.

El Paso: Mini Flea Market, 6006 Doniphan Dr. Tel: 915-833-1787.

Fort Stockton: C & C Flea Market & Antiques, 614 W Dickinson Blvd. Tel: 915-336-6329.

Fort Worth: Big Country Flea Market, 900 University Dr. Tel: 817-626-4731.

Fort Worth: Crowley Rd Flea Market, 5701 Crowley Rd. Tel: 817-568-2976 or Tel: 817-568-0674.

Fort Worth: Henderson Flea Market, 1000 N Henderson St. Tel: 817-877-3021.

Fort Worth: Little Flea Market, 1100 S Ayers Ave. Tel: 817-534-1601.

Fort Worth: Shoppers Thrifty Village Flea Market, 3720 E Lancaster Ave. Tel: 817-531-2020.

Galveston: Galveston Flea Market, 5902 Broadway St. Tel: 409-744-4445.

Granbury: Four Seasons Flea Market, 4310 E Hwy 377. Tel: 817-573-1046.

Granbury: Four Seasons II Flea Market, 4334 E Hwy 377. Tel: 817-279-6888.

Granbury: Granbury Flea Market. Tel: 817-579-9663.

Granbury: Old Time Flea Market, 5830 E Hwy 377. Tel: 817-326-6611.

Greenville: Treasure Chest Flea Market, 3624 Sockwell Blvd. Tel: 903-455-6811.

Hallettsville: The Family Resort Flea Market, FM Rd 957. Tel: 512-798-5028.

Harlingen: Harlingen Flea Mart, 4300 S Expressway 83. Tel: 210-423-4535.

Hereford: Chaves Flea Market, 225 Main St. Tel: 806-364-4834.

Highlands: Little Big Flea Market, 108 S Main St. Tel: 281-426-5424.

Houston: Airline Flea Market, 8801 Airline Dr. Tel: 281-445-0126.

Houston: Best Flea Market, 8503 Mesa Dr, Houston. Tel: 713-633-2521 or 713-633-0443.

Houston: Cheng's Flea Market, 10802 Airline Dr. Tel: 281-445-5269.

Houston: East Mart Flea Market, 6059 South Loop E. Tel: 713-641-3591.

Houston: Festival Flea Market, 7938 Long Point Rd. Tel: 713-827-1331.

Houston: Fiesta Flea Mart, 6800 Gulf Fwy. Tel: 713-645-4821.

Houston: 45 Flea Market Inc, 630 W Little York Rd. Tel: 281-445-4566.

Houston: Houston Flea Market Inc, 6116 Southwest Fwy. Tel: 713-782-0391.

Houston: King's Flea Market, 5100 Griggs Rd. Tel: 713-747-9234.

Houston: M & A Flea Market, 8555 Gulf Fwy. Tel: 713-944-4757.

Houston: Magnolia Flea Market, 7555 Harrisburg Blvd. Tel: 713-926-9758.

Houston: The Mini Flea Market, 2150 Wirt Rd. Tel: 713-680-2002.

Houston: New Flea Market, 8315 Long Point Rd. Tel: 713-722-7122.

Houston: North Shepherd Flea Market, 4412 N Shepherd Dr. Tel: 713-697-0111.

Houston: Riches Flea Market, 9820 Gulf Fwy. Tel: 713-944-4390.

Houston: Sin Ta Flea Market, 8813 Airline Dr. Tel: 281-931-8519.

Houston: Sunny Flea Market, 8705 Airline Dr. Tel: 281-445-1981 or Tel: 281-447-8729.

Houston: SW Indoor Flea Market, 6116 Windswept Ln. Tel: 713-266-2785.

Houston: Westheimer Flea Market, 1735 Westheimer Rd. Tel: 713-520-6665.

Humble: Humble Flea Market, 2803 FM 1960 Rd E. Tel: 281-446-5151.

Hurst: Antique Flea The Local Line, 431 W Bedford Euless Rd. Tel: 817-285-8946 or 817-268-6044.

Irving: Irving Flea Market, 635 S Belt Line Rd. Tel: 972-986-2508.

Jasper: Southeast Texas Antique Mall & Flea Market, 2034 S Wheeler St. Tel: 409-384-7078.

Kaufman: Kaufman County Flea Market, Hwy 175. Tel: 972-932-7555.

Kemp: Cedar Village Flea Market, Hwy 85. Tel: 903-432-4333.

Kemp: Seven Points Flea Market, Hwy 334 W. Tel: 903-432-4554.

Kerrville: Martin Flea Market. Tel: 210-257-8332.

Killeen: MJ's Flea Market, 514 N 10th St. Tel: 817-554-5150.

Killeen: Omas Flea Market, 5505 State Hwy 195. Tel: 817-634-3836.

Kingsville: Kingsville Flea Market, 2420 E King Ave. Tel: 512-516-0013.

Kyle: Kyle Flea Market, 1119 N Old Hwy 81. Tel: 512-262-2351.

Laredo: Border Town Flea Market, Hwy 359. Tel: 210-726-1186.

Leander: Drake's Place The Little Flea Market, 18649 FM 1431. Tel: 512-267-2727.

Lindale: Country Gameroom & Flea Market, Hwy 69 N. Tel: 903-882-8344.

Livingston: 146 Flea Markets, Hwy 146. Tel: 409-327-0112.

Livingston: 190 West Flea Market. Tel: 409-967-4317.

Livingston: Boyd Flea Market, W 190. Tel: 409-967-0547.

Lubbock: Cotton's Flea Market, 302 N Ave U. Tel: 806-762-1289.

Lubbock: Inner City Flea Market, 2302 Texas Ave. Tel: 806-744-3190.

Lubbock: Interstate Flea Market, 3424 I-27. Tel: 806-765-7003.

Lubbock: Susie's Place Flea Market, 1123 Grinnell St. Tel: 806-740-0262.

Lubbock: Universal Flea Market, 122 St & S University. Tel: 806-748-1277.

Lufkin: East Texas Flea Market, Hwy 59 S. Tel: 409-639-6011.

Lufkin: Rickel Mini Storage & Flea Market, Hwy 59 S. Tel: 409-632-3030.

Lufkin: Rickel Mini Storage & Flea Market, Hwy 69 S. Tel: 409-824-3333.

Malakoff: Malakoff Flea Market, Hwy 198 N. Tel: 903-489-2908.

Malakoff: Red Barn Crafts & Flea Market, 319 S Terry St. Tel: 903-489-0090.

Maud: Benne Flea Market, 124 Main. Tel: 903-585-2392.

Mercedes: Red Barn Flea Market & Mobile Home Park, 2½ Mile Rd. Tel: 210-565-6566.
Mercedes: Mercedes Flea Market Inc, Mi 2 W & Expressway. Tel: 210-565-2751.
Mesquite: Five Points Flea Market, 2651 S Belt Line Rd. Tel: 972-329-2130.
Mesquite: Metroplex Flea Service, 4136 Arborcrest Dr. Tel: 972-557-0091 or Tel: 972-557-0090.
Midland: Rainbow Flea Market & Trade Center, 1503 W Industrial Ave. Tel: 915-570-4408.
Midland: 2900 W Front Flea Market Inc, 2900 W Front St. Tel: 915-570-1156.
Milam: Texas Louisiana Flea Market, Hwy 21 W. Tel: 409-625-3386.
Mineral Wells: Mineral Wells Flea Market, 301 Gorgas St. Tel: 817-325-Tel: 9153.
Mount Calm: Centex Flea Market, RR 1. Tel: 817-993-1044.
Nacogdoches: Nacogdoches Flea Market, 5900 North St. Tel: 409-564-3611.
Nacogdoches: Twin Cities Flea Market, S Hwy 59. Tel: 409-560-4366.
New Braunfels: Schumansville Flea Market, Fm 725. Tel: 210-625-0993.
Odessa: Callahan's Flea Market, 7570 Sprague Rd. Tel: 915-362-6978.
Odessa: County Rd Flea Market, 6410 N County Rd W. Tel: 915-368-4305.
Odessa: Henry's Flea Market, 7715 Andrews Hwy. Tel: 915-366-8189.
Odessa: VFW Flea Market, 110 E 62nd St. Tel: 915-367-1530.
Odessa: West Texas Flea Market, 4607 Rasco Ave. Tel: 915-367-5760.
Onalaska: Onalaska Flea Market, Hwy 190. Tel: 409-646-5480.
Orange: Hwy 62 Flea Market, 4402 Hwy 62 N. Tel: 409-886-1158.
Orange: Maurceville Flea Market, Hwy 12. Tel: 409-745-4534.
Paris: Gene's Flea Market, 2810 NE Loop 286. Tel: 903-785-1851.
Pipe Creek: Pipe Creek Flea Market, Hwy 16. Tel: 210-535-4615.
Port Lavaca: Fox Flea Market, 809 N US Hwy 35 Bypass. Tel: 512-552-5169.
Port Neches: Old Towne Flea Market, 1216 Port Neches Ave. Tel: 409-721-9690.
Ranger: Ranger Family Flea Mart, 500 W Loop 254. Tel: 817-647-3999.
Robstown: The Red Barn Flea Market, FM Rd 892. Tel: 512-387-5253.

Rosenberg: Best Flea Market, 4020 Ave H. Tel: 281-342-1444.

Saint Jo: Saint Jo Flea Market, 209 S Broad St. Tel: 817-995-2232.

San Angelo: All Seasons Antique Mall & Flea Markets, 6253 Brodnax Ln. Tel: 915-651-9470.

San Angelo: Mini Flea Market, 1618 N Chadbourne St. Tel: 915-659-0674.

San Antonio: Austin Hwy Flea Market, 1428 Austin Hwy. Tel: 210-828-1488 or Tel: 210-828-9188.

San Antonio: Bargain City Flea Market, 1331 Bandera Rd. Tel: 210-432-5142.

San Antonio: Coliseum Flea Market, S IH 35. Tel: 210-225-5612.

San Antonio: Gibson's Flea Market, 1331 Bandera Rd. Tel: 210-432-5142.

San Antonio: International Flea Market, 1419 Commercial Ave. Tel: 210-924-9311.

San Antonio: Marbach Plaza Flea Market, 7014 Marbach Rd. Tel: 210-674-5030.

San Antonio: Mission Flea Market, 410 Moursund Blvd. Tel: 210-921-1569.

San Antonio: Northwest Flea Market, 3600 Fredericksburg Rd. Tel: 210-736-6655.

San Antonio: Optica Flea Mart, 12280 State Hwy 16 S. Tel: 210-628-1999.

San Antonio: Paloma Market Square & Flea Market, 2931 Roosevelt Ave. Tel: 210-927-2662.

San Antonio: San Antonio Flea Market, 1428 Austin Hwy. Tel: 210-828-1498.

San Antonio: Southton Flea Market, 14050 Southton Rd. Tel: 210-633-2220.

San Antonio: WW White Flea Market, 1265 S WW White Rd. Tel: 210-333-7711.

Santa Fe: Mary's Flea Market, 10135 Hwy 6. Tel: 409-925-4165.

Seagoville: Rising Star Flea Market & Craft Mall, 3113 N Hwy 175. Tel: 972-557-4955.

Shiro: Shiro Flea Market. Tel: 409-874-2749.

Sinton: Sinton St Flea Market, 200 W Sinton St. Tel: 512-364-5020.

Skidmore: Rebecca's Flea Market, Hwy 181. Tel: 512-287-3831.

Spicewood: Spicewood Flea Market. Tel: 210-693-2199.

Stephenville: Chicken House Flea Market, Dublin Hwy. Tel: 817-968-0888.

Sweetwater: Havner's Flea Market, 515 Loop 170. Tel: 915-235-0399.

Texarkana: Eylau Flea Market, 4112 S Lake Dr. Tel: 903-832-7964.

Texarkana: Great American Flea Market, 2615 New Boston Rd. Tel: 903-793-7700.

Texarkana: 67 Flea Market, 5605 W 7th St. Tel: 903-838-4663.

Texas City: Eddie Flea Markets, 702 Texas Ave. Tel: 409-943-4771.

Texas City: Texas City Flea Market, 621 7th Ave N. Tel: 409-948-9708.

Tyler: Armory Flea Market, 2114 W Front St. Tel: 903-593-0870.

Tyler: Canton Flea Market, 290 E. Tel: 903-567-6556.

Tyler: Claude Flea Market, 19231 Hwy 155 S. Tel: 903-825-0053.

Tyler: Downtown Flea Market, 302 E Locust St. Tel: 903-592-7123.

Tyler: Vine St Flea Market, 1414 S Vine Ave. Tel: 903-593-1883.

Victoria: R & R Flea Market, 1408 SW Moody St. Tel: 512-574-7049.

Victoria: Traders Ranch Flea Market, Hwy 185. Tel: 512-578-3317.

Victoria: Victoria Flea Market Inc, 1402 E Mockingbird Ln. Tel: 512-576-5924.

Waco: Bargain Mart Flea Market, 1000 S New Rd. Tel: 817-752-2235.

Waco: Prices Unlimited Flea Market, 2728 La Salle Ave. Tel: 817-662-6619.

Waco: Treasure City Flea Market, 2112 La Salle Ave. Tel: 817-752-5632.

Waskom: Waskom Flea Market J, 110 E Texas Ave. Tel: 903-687-4167.

Waxahachie: Waxahachie Flea Market, 2004 Howard Rd. Tel: 972-937-4277.

Wharton: Lees Flea Market, 622 E Milam St. Tel: 409-532-0777.

Whitesboro: 82 Flea Market. Tel: 903-564-5348.

Whitney: Hwy 1713 Flea Market, Hwy 1713. Tel: 817-694-2128.

Wichita Falls: Holliday St Flea Market, 2820 Holliday Rd. Tel: 817-767-3571 or 817-767-1712.

Winnsboro: Hwy 11 Flea Market, 220 10th Ave N. Tel: 903-365-9904.

UTAH

PARK CITY

Park City Ski Resort Center Antique Show and Sale

DATES: Friday, Saturday and Sundays in July. Call to confirm dates.
TIMES: 9:00 AM–7:00 PM.
ADMISSION: Free. Parking is free.
LOCATION: On the ice rink at the base of the alpine slide.
DESCRIPTION: Started in 1991, this antique and collectible market is located in one of the finest summer resorts in the nation. Their 85 dealers specialize in antiques and collectibles, good pine furniture (Mormon and otherwise), Indian artifacts, western memorabilia, jewelry, toys and dolls, Oriental carpets and other treasures. Five restaurants are on the premises. "Park City has more art galleries per capita than any other city." As this is an international resort, people from all over the world shop here.
DEALER RATES: $165 for a 10' × 12' booth. Reservations are required. Bring your own canopy and set up or rent one of theirs (if available).
CONTACT: Jan or Jeffrey Perkins, 2902 Breneman St, Boise ID 83703. Tel: (208) 345-0755 or 368-9759.

SALT LAKE CITY

Antique Collectors' Fair

DATES: 1998: April 18–19; June 27–28; August 14–15; October 3–4.
TIMES: Saturday 10:00 AM–6:00 PM; Sunday 10:00 AM–5:00 PM.
ADMISSION: $4, $3 with ad from local newspaper (in the classified section). Early bird admission for Saturday 9:00 AM–10:00 AM: $10.
LOCATION: Salt Palace Convention Center, in the heart of downtown Salt Lake City, 150 South West Temple (1 block from Temple Square).
DESCRIPTION: Limited to antiques and collectibles only, this market opened in 1986 and hosts 70 to 100 dealers during its four shows per year. Savvy shoppers and other dealers come from all over the west to restock their own inventory buying jewelry, vintage clothing, glassware, a huge variety of oak furniture, primitives, kitchenware, Mormon pine, prints, dolls, postcards, books, old tools, cowboy items, toys and more. Plenty of hotels, motels, and restaurants surround the Center. This is the only market of its type between Denver and the West Coast. Food is available on the premises.

DEALER RATES: $150 for a 10' × 13' booth; 10% additional for a wall or aisle end position. Setup Friday 10:00 AM–7:00 PM. Security is provided by the Salt Palace. RV parking within 3 miles of site.
CONTACT: James Reece Antique Promotion, PO Box 510432, Salt Lake City UT 84151. Tel: (801) 532-3401. Fax: (801) 364-1898.

Redwood Swap Meet

DATES: Every Saturday and Sunday.
TIMES: Winters 9:00 AM–3:00 PM; summers 8:00 AM–4:00 PM.
LOCATION: 3600 South Redwood Rd. Take I-15 to 3300 South. Go west to 1700 West. Go south to Redwood Swap Meet.
ADMISSION: $.50 per person. Parking is free.
DESCRIPTION: This indoor/outdoor market started in 1972 and currently draws approximately 170 dealers in winter and up to 700 dealers in summer. The merchandise available includes antiques, collectibles, tools, electronics, hundreds of garage sales and new merchandise. Fresh farm goods and craft items are also available. Food is served on the premises. Showers and overnight parking are available on premises.
DEALER RATES: $12 per dealer on Saturday; $15 and up per space on Sunday. Reservations are suggested.
CONTACT: Redwood Swap Meet, 3688 S Redwood Rd, West Valley UT 84119. Tel: (801) 973-6060.

OTHER FLEA MARKETS

We know or have heard about these markets, but have not personally contacted each one, as we have the markets with descriptions. If you plan to visit one of these markets listed below, *please call first* to make sure they are still open. Flea markets do come and go. While they were open when we went to press, they may not be later. We can't be responsible. *Call first!*

Ogden: The Mini Flea Market, 128 7th St. Tel: 801-399-2304.
Saint George: Tanner's Flea Markets. Tel: 801-628-3532.

VERMONT

CHARLOTTE

Charlotte Flea Market

DATES: Saturday and Sunday, April through mid-October, weather permitting.
TIMES: 8:00 AM–5:00 PM or later.
ADMISSION: Free. Parking is free.
LOCATION: Rt 7, just south of the Wildflower Farm, 10 miles south of Burlington. About 5 miles south of the Shelburne Museum.
DESCRIPTION: Located next door to the Wildflower Farm and just south of the Shelburne Museum (the second largest tourist attraction in Vermont) this market enjoys the crowds driving scenic Rt 7. One of the oldest (opened in 1970) in Vermont, this market attracts an average of 40 dealers selling literally everything: old tools, books, clothing, garage sale items, paper, jewelry, crafts, glass and bottles, used and antique furniture, "stuff," new merchandise, whatever. A snack bar serves the hungry. This place really is a local flea market in every good sense of the word.
DEALER RATES: For a three-table setup, tables included: $10 a day. Reservations are not required.
CONTACT: Larry Lavalette, PO Box 415, Shelburne VT 05482-0415. Tel: (802) 425-2844.

CHELSEA

Chelsea Flea Market

DATES: Second Saturday of July.
TIMES: 10:00 AM–4:00 PM.
ADMISSION: Free. Parking is free.
LOCATION: On the North and South Common of Chelsea, on Rt 110, south of Barre.
DESCRIPTION: Started in 1971 by the Ladies Service Guild of a local church, this show has grown to include 125 vendors from all over New England. Over 3,000 visitors choose from antiques, collectibles, and whatever. The Fish and Game Department runs the famous chicken barbecue (a special Vermont treat); hot dogs and sodas are sold by the Ladies Service Guild. The Chelsea Library holds their annual Book Sale at the Town Hall during this show. Chelsea is another of Vermont's beautiful towns stretched along the back roads. Definitely worth the trip.

DEALER RATES: $20 per space. Call for reservations as there is a long waiting list.
CONTACT: Lynda Watson, Flea Market Coordinator, PO Box 94 Main St, Chelsea VT 05038-0094. Tel: (802) 685-3161.

CRAFTSBURY COMMON

Craftsbury Antique and Unique Festival

DATES: Second Saturday in July, come heck or high water!
TIMES: 10:00 AM–4:00 PM.
ADMISSION: Free. Parking is free.
LOCATION: On Craftsbury Common itself. From the south: take Rt 100 heading north through Morrisville to Rt 15 east to Rt 14 north, follow the signs to Craftsbury, then Craftsbury Common. From the north: Rt 14 south from Newport and follow the signs.
DESCRIPTION: Set in the picturesque village of Craftsbury Common, this special market, started in 1970, helps raise funds for the Vermont Children's Aid Society. The dealers specialize in antiques, collectibles and unique crafts including stuffed animals, jewelry, handmade wooden clocks and other treasures. Sterling College is next door and the local sports center is home to some wild mountain bike races. Food is provided by local bakers. The Anderson sisters bring in 15 to 20 home-baked pies and there are lines backed up to buy their mouth-watering specialties before they ever get there! This is considered a "four-plunger day" by the two directors of the Festival. You'd better ask either Judy and Alice about this one. Relief facilities are available, for real now.
DEALER RATES: $50 for a 16' frontage and ample space behind. Reservations are a must and should be in by sometime in January as the invitations to sell are sent in February.
CONTACT: Judith Reiss, VCAS, PO Box 127, Winooski VT 05404-0127. Tel: (802) 655-0006.

MANCHESTER CENTER

Manchester Flea Market

DATES: Every Saturday and Sunday, May through October. Rain or shine.
TIMES: 9:00 AM–5:00 PM.
LOCATION: Junction of Rts 11 and 30. Take Bromley Mountain Rd 3 miles from the center of Manchester.
ADMISSION: Free. Free parking is available.

DESCRIPTION: This outdoor show has operated since 1970 in the heart of the Green Mountains and ski country. Stratton, Magic and Bromley ski areas surround Manchester. It currently attracts 35 to 40 dealers of primarily antiques, with collectibles, crafts, with some farm goods also available. There is an exhibit of antique farm machinery here, and this is also the location of a locally well-known Saturday auction. Robert Todd Lincoln's historic home Hildene is nearby and open to the public. Wessners Surplus Store resides here, too. One snack bar and restrooms add to the amenities.
DEALER RATES: $15 per 20' × 15' space. Advance reservations are suggested.
CONTACT: Albert H Wessner, RR1 Box 1960, Manchester Center VT 05255. Tel: (802) 362-1631.

NEWFANE

The Original Newfane Flea Market

DATES: Every Sunday, May through October. Rain or shine.
TIMES: 7:00 AM–5:00 PM.
ADMISSION: Free. Ample free parking is available.
LOCATION: On Rt 30, 1 mile north of downtown Newfane.
DESCRIPTION: This outdoor market has been around since 1963 and is claimed to be the oldest and largest in Vermont. It is well known throughout the state, attracting between 150 and 200 dealers who come from near and far to exhibit such diverse items as antiques, collectibles, craft items, new merchandise, and fresh produce—in a word: "Everything." Three food concessions and an ice cream stand satisfy any hunger pangs you may suffer.
DEALER RATES: $20 per space. No reservations period! Dealers may camp free Saturday nights.
CONTACT: Earl Morse, PO Box 5, Newfane VT 05345-0005. Tel: (802) 365-7685.

SOUTH HERO

South Hero Flea Market

DATES: Saturday and Sunday and holidays, Memorial Day weekend through the end of September.
TIMES: 8:00 AM–4:00 PM.
ADMISSION: Free. Parking is free.

LOCATION: US Rt 2 in the Champlain Islands, with easy access from Burlington off I-89 Exit 16 or from New York State.
DESCRIPTION: This indoor/outdoor market of up to 50 vendors sells a variety of items. According to Helena, "If you can't find it here, you don't need it." Getting to this market is a treat as the drive through the islands is quietly gorgeous—especially towards the end of September.
DEALER RATES: For 30' × 30' space outside: $7 per day. $1 per round table and $2 for a long. Inside units at $100 per month. Some covered areas $10 per day with electricity. Reservations are not required.
CONTACT: Helena Wilder, 595 Rt 2, S Hero VT 05486. Tel: (802) 372-4769. Or contact Charles Langlois, 21 Curtis Ave, Burlington VT 05401. Tel: (802) 864-5091.

WAITSFIELD

Mad River Green Farmer's Market

DATES: Saturday, from last weekend in May through first weekend in October.
TIMES: 9:30 AM–1:30 PM.
ADMISSION: Free. Parking is free.
LOCATION: Mad River Green Shopping Center, Rt 100.
DESCRIPTION: Started in 1992 as a way for local farmers to sell their rich produce, this outdoor market attracts a chair caner, craftspeople, flowers and herbs, fresh organic produce, cookie mixes, new clothing, baked goods, relishes, jams and jellies, maple syrup, hand-crafted furniture and other Vermont-produced goods. A live band of local musicians (different every week) plays during the market in a gazebo constructed for that purpose. There are plenty of home-grown and organic foods as well as homemade snacks available on the green. It is at the far end of a small shopping center which includes a Green Mountain Coffee Roasters coffee shop, a restaurant, hardware store and other businesses. This is quite a tourist attraction in a four-season resort area with three ski areas, golf, horseback riding (and Icelandic pony rides), and soaring among other activities. Labor Day weekend the Valley Players hold their Annual 2-day Craft Fair with over 100 Vermont crafters selling high quality goods.
DEALER RATES: $10 per market day for 12' × 14' space. No walk-ins permitted. Reservations are required.
CONTACT: Burg von Trapp, PO Box 269, Waitsfield VT 05673-0269. Tel: (802) 496-5856.

Local History Lesson:

Waitsfield is located just about in the middle of Vermont. When the founding fathers decided to build a state capital, they reckoned where the middle of the state was—Waitsfield (so they were wrong by 6 miles). They asked Waitsfield's founding father if they could build their capital in this picturesque valley. Henry Wait's reply, "Not in my backyard!" Montpelier was built about 20 miles east on the Winooski River, which is considerably larger than the Mad River that meanders through Waitsfield into the Winooski.

Charles Kuralt did an article on his 10 favorite roads in the United States. This section of Rt 100, from Granville through Waitsfield, was #7 on the list.

Mad River Green Flea Market

DATES: Sundays, from last weekend in May through first weekend in October.
TIMES: 9:30 AM–1:30 PM.
ADMISSION: Free. Parking is free.
LOCATION: Behind the All-Seasons and Gargoyle Shops (look for the large statues out front) and across from The Den, Rt 100. Just north of the corner of Rts 100 and 17.
DESCRIPTION: Starting in 1998 as a way for locals to hold their own flea market, it is the sister market to the above Farmer's Market. There are many antique dealers in the Valley who are expected to take advantage of this market as well as the many locals who now travel to the Waterbury market.
DEALER RATES: $10 per market day for 12' × 14' space. Reservations are suggested.
CONTACT: Burg von Trapp, PO Box 269, Waitsfield VT 05673-0269. Tel: (802) 496-5856 or 496-4274.

WATERBURY

Waterbury Flea Market

Note: I know this one operates; I pass it frequently. It's just hard to track down the owner so the rates may be a bit low. However, if you wish to set up, do so, they'll find you.

DATES: Saturday, Sunday, and holidays, weather permitting, May through October.

TIMES: Daybreak to exhaustion. Usually 6:00 AM to 6:00 PM, but things slow down in the afternoon.

ADMISSION: Free. Parking is free.

LOCATION: Rt 2, just north of Waterbury. Exit 10 West off I-89.

DESCRIPTION: Opened in 1979, this outdoor market attracts anyone and everyone with up to 100 vendors selling everything from classic antiques, attic treasures, ancient books and old magazines, new merchandise, jewelry, tools—new and very old, furniture, yard-sale and house clean-outs, collectibles and "stuff." It's the locals clearing house. Great finds! A snack concession with delicious hot dogs sates hungry appetites. Then again, there is Ben & Jerry's Ice Cream and the Cider Mill around the corner and down Rt 100.

DEALER RATES: $7 Saturday, $9 Sunday for a 20' × 25' space. Dealers may camp over the weekend for free and setup on Friday. No dogs, please.

CONTACT: Waterbury Flea Market, PO Box 178, Waterbury, VT 05676.

Winter Indoor Flea Markets

DATES: Sundays, January 18, February 1, 22, and March 15, 1998. They run markets from October through March or April depending on Armory schedule. Call for 1999 schedule.

TIMES: 9:00 AM–3:00 PM.

ADMISSION: $1. Parking is free.

LOCATION: Waterbury Armory, Take Exit 10 West off I-89 towards Waterbury, at the T-intersection, turn left, then left again. Follow the signs to the Armory.

DESCRIPTION: These popular shows are used as fundraisers for a variety of local non-profit organizations (Red Cross, library programs, and more). At least 30 dealers come to sell their antiques, collectibles, attic finds, garage sale clean-outs, crafts, trinkets, and what-have-yous to eager patrons. A food concession and restrooms are available on the premises.

DEALER RATES: $25 a table. Reservations are required.

CONTACT: Willis & Willis, PO Box 182, Waterbury Center VT 05677-0182. Tel: (802) 244-5519.

WATERBURY CENTER

Stowe Road Flea Market

DATES: Saturday and Sundays, June through October's fall foliage season. Weather permitting.
TIMES: 9:00 AM–5:00 PM. Could be early and later depending on weather, light and dealer inclination.
ADMISSION: Free. Parking is free.
LOCATION: Rt 100. Only 3.2 miles from I-89, Exit 10 Waterbury/Stowe on the road to Stowe. Not even 3 miles north of Ben & Jerry's Ice Cream Factory.
DESCRIPTION: This market, opened in 1992, has the unique distinction of being surrounded by some of Vermont's biggest attractions: Ben & Jerry's Ice Cream Factory (the largest tourist attraction in the state), the Cold Hollow Cider Mill across the street, and the resort town of Stowe just north on scenic Rt 100. They host anywhere from 20 to 50 dealers selling antiques, collectibles, Vermont crafts, glass, furniture, garage sale goodies and whatever turns up. New merchandise is rare and discouraged. If you are hungry, try B&J's or the cider mill. Enjoy!
DEALER RATES: $8 for a 25' × 20' space per day, or $15 for the weekend. Reservations are not required. Tents are available by advance reservation.
CONTACT: Sir Richard's Antiques, PO Box 10, Waterbury Center VT 05677-0010. Tel: Marie at (802) 244-8817 or Barb at (802) 244-8879.

WILMINGTON

Wilmington Outdoor Antique and Flea Market

DATES: Saturday, Sunday and holiday Mondays, from the weekend before Memorial Day through the weekend after Columbus Day.
TIMES: No specific times, really. Say dawn on.
ADMISSION: Free. Parking is free.
LOCATION: Junction of Rts 9 and 100.
DESCRIPTION: Since 1982 this market has been located on a choice 10-acre lot at the junction of two heavily traveled scenic roads through Vermont. They do a lot of advertising and draw crowds. Their dealers sell

antiques, collectibles, garage sale items, all manner of stuff. Food is available from a concession stand.

DEALER RATES: $15 per space. Reservations are not required.

CONTACT: Peter and Sally Gore, PO Box 22, Wilmington VT 05363-0022. Tel: (802) 464-3345.

Sign on the Millbrook Store at Willoughby Lake:
FLEE MARKET
INSIDE

OTHER FLEA MARKETS

This market is really a one-man shop, but probably worth investigating for the treasures.

Vergennes: Bub's Barn Flea Market, 16 New Haven Rd. Tel: 802-877-2839.

If you are on an antique scouring of Vermont, don't miss the markets scattered along Rt 5 along the Connecticut River. They are everywhere!

VIRGINIA

ALTAVISTA

First Saturday Trade Lot

DATES: First Saturday of each month and the preceding Friday, year round.
TIMES: Friday 12:00 PM until 4:00 PM on Saturday.
ADMISSION: Free. Parking is also free.
LOCATION: On Seventh St, 1 block off Business Hwy 29, between Lynchburg and Danville.
DESCRIPTION: This outdoor market first opened in 1911 and is one of the oldest flea markets in the East. There are more than 200 dealers selling mostly antiques, collectibles, crafts, new and secondhand merchandise, as well as some produce. There is also food available on the premises. Don't miss the hot dogs. I am assured they are terrific! The Altavista High School Band Boosters now run this show and man the concession stand to help pay their expenses. Uncle Billy's Day (the first Saturday weekend in June, including the preceding Friday) is a town-wide celebration that lasts three days centered around the Trade Lot. Uncle Billy started the Trade Lot by trading animals at the turn of the century. Fireworks, entertainment and more are featured on this weekend.
DEALER RATES: \$10 per 9' × 20' space for the weekend. Six month reservations are \$8 per weekend paid in advance. Uncle Billy's Day space is \$25 a space unless already reserved for six months. Reservations are strongly suggested, or else. Town permits are required and sold there for \$1.50 a year. No telephone reservations are accepted.
CONTACT: Altavista Band Boosters, PO Box 333, Altavista VA 24517-0333. Tel: (804) 369-5001 (Town Hall).

CHANTILLY

DC Big Flea

DATES: For 1998: January 10–11, July 18–19, August 15–16. Call for 1999 dates.
TIMES: Saturday 10:00 AM–6:00 PM, Sunday 11:00 AM–5:00 PM.
ADMISSION: \$3; children under 12 free. Parking is free.
LOCATION: Chantilly Convention Center.
DESCRIPTION: This show has over 500 dealers from 20 states in one huge building. This will be their first year here, having moved the show

from another Virginia location. Their dealers sell primarily antiques and collectibles, occasionally crafts, and some new merchandise. The other shows are held in Virginia Beach, Richmond and Salem. Food concessions and handicapped-accessible restrooms add to the amenities.
DEALER RATES: $80 single space, $160 double space. Reservations are required. This facility does charge $65 for electrical hook up.
CONTACT: D'Amore Promotions, 544 Central Dr Ste 106, Virginia Beach VA 23454-5227. Tel: (757) 431-9500. Fax: (757) 498-4700.

CHRISTIANBURG

A-1 Flea Market and Antique Emporium

DATES: Saturday and Sunday.
TIMES: 8:00 AM–5:00 PM.
ADMISSION: Free. Parking is also free.
LOCATION: 940 Radford St. Rt 11.
DESCRIPTION: Open since 1982, this market houses 20 permanent dealers selling everything including guns, knives, antiques, dolls, tools, vintage glassware (Fenton, Cambridge, Heisey, Fostoria—loads of these treasures), custom-made clothing, sports (race and ball) cards, comics and much more. A snack bar serves the hungry. Every weekend and Thursday nights they hold remote-control car races both on paved and off-road track!
DEALER RATES: $115 per month for a 12' × 24' space. Reservations are required.
CONTACT: Kathryn Minnick, 940 Radford St, Christiansburg VA 24073. Tel: (540) 382-9811.

FREDERICKSBURG

Manor Mart Flea Market

DATES: Saturday and Sunday, year round.
TIMES: 7:00 AM–dusk.
ADMISSION: Free; parking is also free.
LOCATION: US Hwy 1, just south of Fredericksburg.
DESCRIPTION: An indoor/outdoor flea market established in 1983, the Manor Mart offers antiques, collectibles, handicrafts, and new merchandise, as well as fresh produce. It is located near historic Fredericksburg, scene of much Civil War fighting and near other historic battlefields. Food is available on the premises; motels and campgrounds are nearby.

DEALER RATES: $10 per 16' × 10' booth (indoors and out). Reservations are not required.
CONTACT: Nick or Jeannie Dommisse, Manor Mart Flea Market, 9040 Jeff Davis Hwy, Fredericksburg VA 22407. Tel: (540) 898-4685.

HILLSVILLE

VFW Labor Day Gun Show and Flea Market

DATES: Friday through Monday, Labor Day weekend. Rain or shine.
TIMES: 8:00 AM–6:00 PM.
LOCATION: At the VFW. Complex. On US Rt 58-221 West (Galax Rd), 1 mile east of I-77.
ADMISSION: $1 per person; children under 12 admitted free. $3 a day. $10 a day for RVs.
DESCRIPTION: This market is one of the granddaddys of markets! The population of the town of Hillsville expands five-fold during this annual event sponsored by the Grover King Post 1115 Veterans of Foreign Wars. The show has been held each year since 1967, and in 1986 it brought over 250,000 shoppers despite rain and cold weather according to local police records. There are 2,400 spaces (they added 650 new spaces in 1997), but how many dealers depends on how many spaces a dealer nabs. Usually 950–1,500 dealers set up selling a variety of items that goes beyond fire arms and militaria to encompass all types of antiques and collectibles including coins, jewelry, glassware, tools, toys, and other Americana. For the 1986 show, visitors registered from 40 different states plus four foreign countries, and attendance is growing each year. Food is served on the premises.
DEALER RATES: $55 per 9' × 20' space, for four days. Dealer reservations are required. Advance shopping hours for dealers are held Thursday afternoon before the show.
CONTACT: Joseph G Semones, VFW Flea Market, 2421 Airport Rd, Hillsville VA 24343-8185. Tel: (540) 728-7188.

OAK GROVE

Red Barn Flea Market

DATES: Friday through Sunday. "Absolute" auctions held on the first and third Saturdays. No buyers premium.
TIMES: Winter: Friday and Sunday 12:00 PM–4:00 PM, Saturday 9:00 AM–4:00 PM, 12:00 PM–4:00 PM; Summer: Friday and Sunday 12:00 PM–5:00 PM, Saturdays 9:00 AM–5:00 PM.

ADMISSION: Free. Parking is also free.
LOCATION: Westmoreland County, 36 miles east of Fredericksburg on State Rt 3. On left of road, look for the big red barn.
DESCRIPTION: This market started in August 1989 as an addition to an auction house, which started originally as a huge horse barn—"the size of a football field." Crammed with 38-plus dealers inside and growing, selling antiques, baby booties to house trailers, collectibles, glassware, toys, books, TVS, appliances, "everything." The snack stand is now run by Jack and Mildred, say "Hi." Carolyn loves old books and collects them, if you have any old books or stories, stop and chat. This is a friendly, old-fashioned country market the way flea markets used to be.
DEALER RATES: $35 per month inside. $7.50 a day for outside table space. Reservations are suggested as they have a waiting list.
CONTACT: Curtis and Carolyn Bartmess, 330 Circle Ln, Colonial Beach VA 22443. Tel: (804) 224-1119.

PETERSBURG

South Side Station Market Place

DATES: Daily.
TIMES: Weekdays 10:00 AM–5:00 PM. Weekends 8:30 AM–5:00 PM.
ADMISSION: Free. Parking is free.
LOCATION: 5 River St, off I-95 Exit 52 to Washington St, follow Historic Olde Towne Petersburg signs to Visitor's Center. They are located just behind the farmer's market.
DESCRIPTION: Opened in 1993, this indoor/outdoor market's dealers sell antiques, collectibles, crafts, produce, cards, garage sale goodies, furniture, new merchandise, fabric, Old Mansion coffee, teas and spices, ceramics, fine jewelry, toys and clothing. One coffee shop and handicapped-accessible restrooms add to the amenities.
DEALER RATES: Building 1: $.75 per square foot. Building 2: $150 per 13' × 16' space. First come, first served.
CONTACT: Gibbons Sloan or Emily, PO Box 2820, Petersburg VA 23804-2820. Tel: (804) 733-5050 or fax: (804) 733-0667.

RICHMOND

American Heritage Antique Jubilee

DATES: For 1998: October 23–25. Rain or shine.
TIMES: Saturday 10:00 PM–5:00 PM; Sunday 12:00 PM–5:00 PM.

ADMISSION: Friday $20 (Early Buyers Pass for 3 days); Saturday and Sunday $5 per day. Parking is free.
LOCATION: Richmond State Fairgrounds at Strawberry Hill, 600 E Laburnum Ave.
DESCRIPTION: An annual, multidimensional show featuring indoor and outdoor spaces. Over 1,000 dealers come from 35 states. This is an antique and collectible show only with entertainment and specialty food vendors. Handicapped-accessible restrooms add to the amenities.
DEALER RATES: $110 per heated space. $70 for unheated space, $70 per outdoor space. Tents are available for outdoor vendors at affordable rates. Reservations and prepayment are required.
CONTACT: D'Amore Promotions, 544 Central Dr Ste 106, Virginia Beach VA 23454-5227. Tel: (757) 431-9500. Fax: (757) 498-4700.

Bellwood Flea Market

DATES: Saturday and Sunday, year round. Weather permitting.
TIMES: 5:30 AM–4:30 PM.
ADMISSION: $1 per person. Free parking.
LOCATION: 9201 Jefferson Davis Hwy. Exit 64 off I-95 and Willis Rd, south of Richmond.
DESCRIPTION: This market has been run since 1969 outdoors. Between 150 and 400 dealers offer antiques, collectibles, handmades, produce, meats, musical instruments, auto parts, appliances, real estate, furniture, clothing and new merchandise, as well as tools and curios. A large air-conditioned food concession opens early and remains open all day. There are still reminders of the fierce Civil War battle fought on the Bellwood property as people are occasionally finding minie-balls and some trench-works are still visible.
DEALER RATES: $12 per 20' × 20' space. First come, first served.
CONTACT: Alvin Kline, c/o Bellwood Flea Market, 9201 Jeff Davis Hwy, Richmond VA 23237. Tel: (804) 275-1187 or 1-800-793-0707.

The Big Flea Market at the Richmond State Fairgrounds

DATES: For 1998: January 3–4, 31, February 1, March 7–8, April 4–5, May 30–31, July 4–5, August 1–2, September 5–6, November 28–29.
TIMES: Saturday 10:00 AM–5:00 PM; Sunday 12:00 PM–5:00 PM.
ADMISSION: $2; children under 12 free. Parking is free.
LOCATION: Richmond State Fairgrounds at Strawberry Hill, 600 E Laburnum Ave.

DESCRIPTION: Part of a series of shows started in 1977, this show has between 300 to 600 spaces filled with dealers from 15 states. They sell primarily antiques and collectibles and some new merchandise. This market is considered the largest antique flea market in the Mid-Atlantic region. Food concessions and handicapped-accessible restrooms add to the amenities.
DEALER RATES: $75 per space per show. $140 for two spaces per show. Reservations are required.
CONTACT: D'Amore Promotions, 544 Central Dr Ste 106, Virginia Beach VA 23454-5227. Tel: (757) 431-9500. Fax: (757) 498-4700.

ROANOKE

Happy's Flea Market

DATES: Tuesday through Sunday, year round.
TIMES: Tuesday through Friday 8:00 AM–5:00 PM; Saturday and Sunday 6:30 AM–5:30 PM.
ADMISSION: Free. Parking is free.
LOCATION: 5411 Williamson Rd NW (Rt 11). Hershberger Rd Exit off Rt 581.
DESCRIPTION: Obviously successful, this market has been open since 1978. There are 150 inside dealers, another 300 outside, with 100 of those spaces permanently reserved. The dealers sell an endless variety of everything: antiques, batteries, collectibles, used and new merchandise, and much more. A restaurant is on the premises as well as handicapped-accessible restrooms. There are outlet stores as part of the scene.
DEALER RATES: $9 Saturday and Sunday; $2 Tuesday; $5 Wednesday through Friday. Monthly and yearly rates available. First come, first served.
CONTACT: Bob Meyer, Manager, Happy's Flea Market, 5411 Williamson Rd, Roanoke VA 24012. Tel: (703) 563-4473/4.

SALEM

Roanoke Valley Antique and Collectible Expo

DATES: 1998: January 24–25.
TIMES: Saturday 10:00 AM–5:00 PM; Sunday 12:00 PM–5:00 PM.
ADMISSION: $3; children under 12 are free.
LOCATION: Salem Civic Center. Take I-81, Exit 141, signs to the Civic Center.

DESCRIPTION: Though this show started in 1986, it is part of a series of shows held in Virginia. The other shows are in Richmond, Virginia Beach, and Hampton. Here over 80 dealers sell strictly antiques and collectibles. Food concessions and handicapped-accessible restrooms add to the amenities.

DEALER RATES: $80 single space; $160 for a double space. Reservations and deposits are required.

CONTACT: D'Amore Promotions, 544 Central Dr Ste 106, Virginia Beach VA 23454-5227. Tel: (757) 431-9500. Fax: (757) 498-4700.

VIRGINIA BEACH

Virginia Beach Antique and Collectible Expo

DATES: May 22–24 and August 28–30, 1998.

TIMES: Friday 7:00 PM–10:00 PM; Saturday 10:00 AM–7:00 PM, Sunday 12:00 PM–5:00 PM.

ADMISSION: $2; children under 12 are free. Free parking.

LOCATION: Virginia Beach Pavilion Convention Center. Take Rt 64 to the end Rt 44. Follow the signs.

DESCRIPTION: For 17 years this show has been attracting up to 300 dealers from 15 states selling only antiques and collectibles, plus assorted crafts and new merchandise. This show is considered one of Virginia's largest antiques and collectibles shows and is part of a series of shows held in Richmond, Hampton, DC and Salem. Food concessions and handicapped-accessible restrooms add to the amenities.

DEALER RATES: $75 per single space; $140 per double space per show. Reservations and deposits are required. Dealer space sells out fast.

CONTACT: D'Amore Promotions, 544 Central Dr Ste 106, Virginia Beach VA 23454. Tel: (757) 431-9500. Fax: (757) 498-4700.

OTHER FLEA MARKETS

We know or have heard about these markets, but have not personally contacted each one, as we have the markets with descriptions. If you plan to visit one of these markets listed below, *please call first* to make sure they are still open. Flea markets do come and go. While they were open when we went to press, they may not be later. We can't be responsible. *Call first!*

Abingdon: Banner Star Flea Market, 550 Russell Rd NW. Tel: 540-628-2937.

Aldie: The Great Aldie Flea Market, 39359 John Mosby Hwy. Tel: 703-327-4452.

Bassett: Billy's Flea Market, RR 57. Tel: 540-629-4114.

Boones Mill: Buckboard Flea Market, Rt. Tel: 540-334-2403.

Bridgewater: Mossy Creek Flea Market, 205 S Main St. Tel: 540-828-3924.

Bristol: Campbell Flea Market Mall, 14364 Lee Hwy. Tel: 540-669-1480.

Calverton: Jean's Midway Hall Flea Market. Tel: 540-788-9905.

Capeville: Capeville Flea Market, Rt 13. Tel: 757-331-4930.

Chesapeake: South Norfolk Flea Market, 1707 Park Ave. Tel: 757-543-1940.

Chester: Chester Flea Market & Antique Center. Tel: 804-768-7679.

Christiansburg: A-1 Flea Market & Antique Emporium, 940 Radford St. Tel: 540-382-9811.

Colonial Beach: Red Barn Flea Market Auction, Hwy 3. Tel: 540-224-2939.

Franklin: A-Z Flea Market, 618 South St. Tel: 757-562-3955.

Front Royal: Front Royal Flea Market, 490 N Commerce Ave. Tel: 540-636-9729.

Gloucester: Hall Greene & Riley Flea Market, Hwy 17. Tel: 804-693-9173.

Gordonsville: Gordonsville Antique & Flea Market, Rts 15 & 33. Tel: 540-832-7376.

Gretna: Gretna Flea Market, N Main. Tel: 804-656-6902.

Gretna: Younger's Flea Market. Tel: 804-656-3175.

Hampton: The Big Flea Market, Hampton Coliseum. Tel: 757-826-4674.

Haymarket: Park's Flea Market, 14221 Lee Hwy. Tel: 703-754-4087.

Kilmarnock: Noah's Ark Flea Market, 21 N Main St. Tel: 804-435-6716.

King George: B & S Flea Market, 10312 Indiantown Rd. Tel: 540-775-3968.

La Crosse: Toone's Variety Shop & Flea Market, Hwy 58 E. Tel: 804-Tel: 757-7665.

Luray: Luray Flea Market, Hwy 211 E. Tel: 540-743-7374.

Manassas: Manassas Flea Market, 9608 Grant Ave. Tel: 703-330-1197.

Martinsville: Broad St Flea Market, 226 Broad St. Tel: 540-632-9873.

Mechanicsville: Frances's Flea Market, 6702 Chamberlayne Rd. Tel: 804-730-1230.

Mechanicsville: The Mechanicsville Flea Market & Trade Center, 8238 Mechanicsville Tpke. Tel: 804-746-4248.

Norfolk: Azalea Flea Market, 3450 Azalea Garden Rd. Tel: 757-853-5877.

Norfolk: Big Top Flea Market, 7600 Sewells Point Rd. Tel: 757-480-3122.

Norfolk: The Flea Market of Norfolk, 3416 N Military Hwy. Tel: 757-857-7824.

Petersburg: Poor Richard's Antiques & Flea Market, 16701 Jefferson Davis Hwy. Tel: 804-526-6013.

Petersburg: South Side Station Flea Market, 7 River St. Tel: 804-733-5050.

Portsmouth: J & L Flea Market, 3709 Victory Blvd. Tel: 757-485-3013.

Portsmouth: L & L Flea Market & Auction House, 930 High St. Tel: 757-397-0672.

Pound: Mountain Traders Flea Market, 10115 Orby Cantrell Hwy. Tel: 540-796-9276.

Richmond: Antique Center & Flea Market, 449 E Belt Blvd. Tel: 804-231-6261.

Richmond: Azalea Flea Market, 5209 Wilkinson Rd. Tel: 804-329-8853.

Richmond: The Best Flea Market, 5400 Midlothian Tpke. Tel: 804-232-8828.

Richmond: Gene's Flea Mart & Appliances, 5512 Lakeside Ave. Tel: 804-262-1817.

Richmond: Larry's Flea Mart, 4104 Williamsburg Rd. Tel: 804-236-9378.

Richmond: The Little Flea Market, 3901 Hull St Rd. Tel: 804-231-2716.

Richmond: Plaza Swap Meet & Flea Market, 4730 N Southside Plaza St. Tel: 804-231-9999.

Richmond: Richmond Antique Center & Flea Market, 449 E Belt Blvd. Tel: 804-231-6261.

Richmond: Ross Super Flea Grocery, 5501 Midlothian Tpke. Tel: 804-230-6119.

Richmond: Super Flea Mart, 5501 Midlothian Tpke. Tel: 804-231-6687.

Richmond: USA Flea Market & Mini Mall, 6031 Nine Mile Rd. Tel: 804-328-5642.

Roanoke: Melrose Flea Market & Antique Mall, 4215 Melrose Ave NW. Tel: 540-362-2201.

Rocky Mount: A-1 Flea Market, Rt 220 N. Tel: 540-334-2323.

Rustburg: Big B Flea Market, RR 1. Tel: 804-821-1326.

Smithfield: Smithfield Flea Market & Antiques, 120 N Church St. Tel: 757-357-0417.

South Boston: 58 Flea Market, Hwy 58 W. Tel: 804-753-1637.

South Boston: Riverside Flea Market. Tel: 804-575-6816.

Suffolk: Bank's Flea Market, 2108 Holland Rd. Tel: 757-539-5438.

Temperanceville: Shore Flea Market, 12085 Lankford Hwy. Tel: 757-824-3300.

Verona: Verona Flea Market, RR 11. Tel: 540-248-3532.

Virginia Beach: The Big Flea Market, 544 Central Dr. Tel: 757-431-9500.

Virginia Beach: Bill's Flea Market. Tel: 757-340-0233.

Warsaw: Warsaw Flea Market, 401 B Main St. Tel: 804-333-4062.

Weber City: Janie's Flea Market, 408 Hwy 23. Tel: 540-386-2530.

West Point: West Point Flea Market Inc, 3180 King William Ave. Tel: 804-843-3878.

Winchester: Valley Ave Flea Market & Consignment, 1000 Valley Ave. Tel: 540-722-6768.

Wytheville: A-1 Auction & Flea Market, 2190 W Ridge Rd. Tel: 540-228-2901.

Wytheville: Ideal Flea Market & Crafts, 1035 N 4th St. Tel: 540-223-1938.

WASHINGTON

EVERETT

Puget Park Swap-O-Rama

DATES: Saturday and Sunday, April through October. Weather permitting.
TIMES: 9:00 AM–4:00 PM.
ADMISSION: $1 per person. Free parking is provided.
LOCATION: 13020 Meridian Ave South. The 128th St exit off I-5.
DESCRIPTION: Started in 1975, this market currently attracts up to 250 dealers who set up to sell a wide range of objects including antiques, collectibles, fine art, handicrafts, fresh produce, and some new merchandise. A snack bar feeds the famished. This area is near the marina where the whale-watching boats take off for trips through the spectacular San Juan Islands. Not to be missed.
DEALER RATES: $12 for a 20' × 20' space per day; $16 for a 20' × 25' space with electricity. Advance reservations are advised and can be made in person Fridays from 12:00 PM–5:00 PM or during market hours.
CONTACT: Dan Sutton, Puget Park Swap-O-Rama, 13020 Meridian Ave S, Everett WA 98204. Tel: (425) 337-1435 (market) or call Mike Lancaster at the head office (425) 455-8151. Fax: (425) 455-8165.

PROSSER

Prosser Harvest Festival

DATES: Friday through Sunday, the third weekend of September. For 1998: September 25–26.
TIMES: 10:00 AM–5:00 PM or later.
LOCATION: At the corner of 6th and Meade in downtown Prosser. Mostly downtown Prosser.
ADMISSION: Free. Free parking is available nearby.
DESCRIPTION: This outdoor market started in 1972 and is held in conjunction with the annual Great Prosser Balloon Rally. This is the annual Harvest Festival (formerly known as the Prosser Flea Market) that includes the entire town of Prosser. There are sidewalk sales, farmer's market stands and vendors everywhere. It currently attracts a lot of outside dealers selling a large variety of antiques and collectibles, unbelievable arts and crafts "to die for," fresh herbs, new merchandise, and loads of

freshly harvested produce. Food is available on the premises. There is entertainment for the children. The balloons go up early Saturday and Sunday morning and Saturday night they light the balloons up in a spectacular "night glow" display.

DEALER RATES: $15 per dealer for the whole shebang. Reservations are required.

CONTACT: Shirley Yeary, Prosser Chamber of Commerce Harvest Festival Chairman, 1230 Bennett Ave, Prosser WA 99350. Tel: (509) 786-3177 or 1-800-408-1517.

TACOMA

"America's Largest" Antique and Collectible Sale

DATES: February 14–15, June 6–7, and September 12–13, 1998.

TIMES: Saturday 8:00 AM–7:00 PM; Sunday 9:00 AM–5:00 PM.

LOCATION: Tacoma Dome, Tacoma Dome Exit off I-5.

ADMISSION: $5, kids under 12 are free, kids 12–17 are $2. Parking is handled by the Tacoma Dome and costs $4 to $5.

DESCRIPTION: The first Tacoma Dome market was held June 1989. This market and its more than 785 booths deal only in high quality antiques and collectibles. Food is available on the premises.

DEALER RATES: $140 per 10' × 10' booth, $280 per 10'x 20' booth, $275 for 10' × 30' booth. Reservations are mandatory.

CONTACT: Chuck or Christine Palmer, Palmer/Wirfs & Associates, 4001 NE Halsey, Portland OR 97232. Tel: (503) 282-0877 or fax: (503) 282-2953.

OTHER FLEA MARKETS

We know or have heard about these markets, but have not personally contacted each one, as we have the markets with descriptions. If you plan to visit one of these markets listed below, *please call first* to make sure they are still open. Flea markets do come and go. While they were open when we went to press, they may not be later. We can't be responsible. *Call first!*

Blaine: King's Flea Market & General Store, 2078 Peace Portal Dr. Tel: 360-332-8278.

Burlington: Skagit Valley Flea & Farmers Market, 973 S Burlington Blvd. Tel: 360-757-2443.

Kent: Midway Pacific Flea Market, 24050 Pacific Hwy S. Tel: 206-878-2536.

Pasco: Pasco Flea Market, Pasco Kahlotus Hwy. Tel: 509-547-5035.

Seattle: Seattle Flea Republic, 1512 NE 65th St. Tel: 206-523-5740.

Seattle: Seattle Indoor Swap Meet, 14802 Pacific Hwy S. Tel: 206-243-8347.

Shelton: Blue Willow Flea Market, 1817 Olympic Hwy N. Tel: 360-427-0616.

Shelton: Jackson's Flea Market. Tel: 360-426-7282.

Tacoma: Star Lite Swap & Shop, 8327 S Tacoma Way. Tel: 206-588-8090.

WEST VIRGINIA

BLUEFIELD

City of Bluefield Parking Facilities Flea Market

DATES: Every Saturday, March through November.
TIMES: 6:00 AM–2:00 PM.
ADMISSION: Free. Metered parking is available.
LOCATION: On Princeton Ave, at the junction of Rts 19 and 460, in the heart of Bluefield.
DESCRIPTION: This indoor market began in 1981 and now draws approximately 175 dealers selling a wide range of items including antiques and collectibles, crafts, fresh produce, and new merchandise. Shopping can begin as early as 5:30 AM as people hurry to catch the best bargains. Two snack bars serve the hungry.
DEALER RATES: $5 per 14' × 20' space. First come, first served or some reserved.
CONTACT: Sharon Leffel, City of Bluefield, Parking Commission, 514 Scott St, Bluefield WV 24701. Tel: (304) 327-8031.

FAYETTEVILLE

Bridge Day

DATES: Third Saturday in October (by state law!).
TIMES: 10:00 AM–4:00 PM.
ADMISSION: Free. Parking along roadway and in Fayetteville.
LOCATION: New River Gorge Bridge, US 19 between Fayetteville and Lansing.
DESCRIPTION: Remember the TV ad where a "Jimmy" car was shoved over the side of a bridge attached to a bungee cord? This is the bridge: the longest single arch bridge in the world, the second highest in the United States at 876 feet. Bridge Day is the celebration of the building of this bridge. One day a year the police close off the northbound lanes of this four-lane bridge and all traffic is narrowed down to the two remaining lanes. Tourists come from all over to watch the goings on. Last year 42 vendors set up along the north end of the 3,030-foot-long bridge and the rest (total averages 200 vendors) on the south end, selling or performing West Virginia crafts, food, produce, tourism, gospel singing—whatever! Over 100,000 people invade the bridge on foot to participate. Parachutists

fling themselves off the bridge trying to land on the "landing pad." Some don't make it onto the dry parts and have to be fished out of the water. The dealers must meet and get organized starting at 6:30 AM and then line up in their assigned order of booth number. At the appointed moment, they charge the bridge to their space, set up and sell like mad until 3:00 PM when the state police come by to tell them it's time to pack up. They must be off the bridge by 4:00 PM, otherwise they will be run over.
DEALER RATES: Out-of-state dealer rates: $110 before August 1, $200 for a 25' space after August 1. Reservations are mandatory.
CONTACT: Debra Laird, Executive Director, Bridge Day, 310 Oyler Ave, Oak Hill WV 25901. Tel: 1-800-927-0263.

> A couple married on the bridge during one Bridge Day, then "took the plunge" parachuting down the gorge. That year they had about 210,000 visitors!

> Ace Whitewater runs rafting trips with a special on Bridge Day. They stop under the bridge, serve a gourmet meal and watch, from safe river banks, the shenanigans of parachutists and bungee jumpers—plunging into space.

HARPERS FERRY

Harpers Ferry Flea Market

DATES: Saturday and Sunday, Monday holidays.
TIMES: Dawn to dusk.
ADMISSION: Free. Parking is also free.
LOCATION: On Dual Hwy 340, about 1 mile from Harpers Ferry Historical Park. Only 60 miles from Washington, DC and Baltimore.
DESCRIPTION: Started in 1983, this market hosts an average of 200-plus dealers selling antiques, collectibles, yard sale treasures, crafts, home-made treasures—a veritable variety of goodies. This is definitely a family market! Funnel cakes, fries and hot dogs, as well as breakfast are sold at the snack bar. Visitors come from all over the East Coast but mainly from Baltimore and Washington, DC. Harpers Ferry is located where the Potomac and Shenandoah Rivers converge, where James Brown led his famous raid, with plenty of interesting outdoor activities (hiking, biking, etc.) as well as

a National Park, the C & O Canal and a historical museum. It is truly a beautiful area to visit.
DEALER RATES: $11 per day per space. Reservations are not required. First come, first served.
CONTACT: Harpers Ferry Flea Market, 904 Oregon Trail, Harpers Ferry WV 25425. Tel: Ron at (304) 725-4141 or Dan (304) 725-0092.

MARTINSBURG

I-81 Flea Market

DATES: Friday, Saturday and Sunday, weather permitting, year round.
TIMES: 8:00 AM–6:00 PM.
ADMISSION: Free. Parking is free.
LOCATION: Off Exit 20, off I-81, Spring Mills area.
DESCRIPTION: Opened in 1989, this outdoor market has up to 140 outside dealers selling antiques, collectibles, crafts and new merchandise. Their building, housing the inside dealers and farmer's market, burned down on September 3, 1995, but the outside dealers have kept the market alive. Concessions include ice cream, fries, and standard snack bar fare.
DEALER RATES: Outside: $5 Friday, $11 Saturday and Sunday per space. Reservations are recommended to check on the market's status.
CONTACT: Betty Kline, I-81 Flea Market, Rt 2 Box 230, Martinsburg WV 25401. Tel: (304) 274-3387.

MILTON

Milton Flea Market

DATES: Friday, Saturday and Sunday.
TIMES: Friday 8:00 AM–4:00 PM, weekends 8:00 AM–5:00 PM.
ADMISSION: Free. Parking is free.
LOCATION: Take Exit 28 (Milton WV) off I-64, turn north to junction US 60, turn east ¼ mile. You can't miss it.
DESCRIPTION: Open since 1989, this indoor/outdoor market has 500 dealers inside and spaces for 100 outside (number of dealers depends on the weather!) selling "really old antiques," collectibles, crafts, tools, new and used clothing, musical instruments, baseball cards, books (you can trade in the ones you've read), trains, toys, comic books, *fudge*, woodwork, and a variety of other goods. One restaurant and two snack bars deal with the hunger not quelled by the *fudge*. There are restrooms (handicapped accessible) on the premises. In 1993 they added roofs to the out-

side spaces as well as 60 new vendor spaces. The local Chamber of Commerce recommended this market and said it was one of the biggest around.
DEALER RATES: $28 and up for the weekend indoors (there is a waiting list) for a 10' × 14' space; $7 and up for 10' wide and whatever deep outside space (depends on the location of the space). First come, first served. Reservations are okay.
CONTACT: Boyd & Betty Meadows, PO Box 549, Milton WV 25541-0549. Tel: (304) 743-9862 or 743-1123.

OTHER FLEA MARKETS

We know or have heard about these markets, but have not personally contacted each one, as we have the markets with descriptions. If you plan to visit one of these markets listed below, *please call first* to make sure they are still open. Flea markets do come and go. While they were open when we went to press, they may not be later. We can't be responsible. *Call first!*

Bunker Hill: Bunker Hill Flea Market. Tel: 304-229-7629.
Charleston: Bill's Flea Market, 2559 Sissonville Dr. Tel: 304-344-4337.
Charleston: Capitol Flea Market, 24 Meadowbrook Shopping Plz. Tel: 304-342-1626 or 304-346-5270.
Charleston: Rt 21 Flea Market, 2388 Sissonville Dr. Tel: 304-345-4603.
Elkins: Elkins Flea Market, Crystal Springs. Tel: 304-636-5823.
Fairmont: Baxter Volunteer Fire Department Flea Market, Auburn & Belt St. Tel: 304-366-7201.
Falling Waters: I-81 Flea Market Inc, 1721 Robin Ln. Tel: 304-274-3387.
Glenville: Trash or Treasure Flea Market, 103 S Court St. Tel: 304-462-4621.
Hedgesville: Nine W Flea Market. Tel: 304-754-7467.
Kermit: Corner Flea Market, Rt 52 Eastgate Mall. Tel: 304-393-3643.
Milton: Milton Flea Market, 1215 E US Rt 60. Tel: 304-743-1123.
Moorefield: Tony's Flea Market, 231 S Main St. Tel: 304-538-7680.
Morgantown: Indoor Flea & Antique Market, 1389 University Ave. Tel: 304-292-9230.
Morgantown: Walnut St Indoor Flea Market, 218 Walnut St. 26505-5402, Tel: 304-292-9278.
Petersburg: Auction House Flea Market, 122 S Main St. Tel: 304-257-4554.
Ripley: Fort Ripley Flea Market, Ripley Shopping Ctr. Tel: 304-372-3532.
Ripley: Ripley Flea Market, Rt 33. Tel: 304-372-4366.
Shinnston: The Sunset Flea Market, Rt 19. Tel: 304-592-0405.
Yawkey: Midge's Flea Market, RR 3. Tel: 304-524-7639.

WISCONSIN

ADAMS

Adams Flea Market

DATES: Every Saturday and Sunday, May through October; also open Memorial Day, July 4th, and Labor Day.

TIMES: 5:00 AM–4:00 PM.

ADMISSION: Free. Free parking available.

LOCATION: 556 South Main St, by the railroad tracks in Adams.

DESCRIPTION: This market has been operating since 1980 and growing each year. There are 44 permanent indoor dealers and 100 outdoors, with 15 acres of grounds on which to expand. This is a country market with plenty of trees, grass, wildflowers, birds and small animals around to awe the newcomers. There's a bit of everything here, from antiques, collectibles, and handcrafted items, to farm produce and a good mix of old and new merchandise. One dealer deals with sports cards, another is one of the largest suppliers of canopies around. For your convenience, there is a lunch wagon on the premises. A note: no dogs are allowed on the grounds, please leave them in your car if you bring them.

DEALER RATES: $7 per day with one table provided free; $14 for two tables and there's space for a three-table "U" setup if you have extra tables. No advance reservations are taken. No overnight camping.

CONTACT: Ms Irene Steffen, 2151 Hwy 13, Adams WI 53910. Tel: (608) 339-3192. Day of show call (608) 339-9223.

CALEDONIA

7 Mile Fair/Market Square

DATES: Saturday and Sunday, year round.

TIMES: April through October 7:00 AM–5:00 PM; November through March 9:00 AM–5:00 PM.

ADMISSION: $1.25 for adults, senior citizens $1. Children under 12 free with parents. Free parking is provided.

LOCATION: 2720 West 7 Mile Rd. At the intersection of I-94 and 7 Mile Rd, Exit at 7 Mile Rd. It is 15 miles south of Milwaukee and 25 miles north of the Illinois-Wisconsin state line.

DESCRIPTION: This indoor/outdoor market began in 1961, added a 45,000-square-foot building in 1989, and another 60,000-square-foot build-

ing in 1994. There are now approximately 1,000 dealers in summer and 250 in winter marketing a wide variety of antiques, crafts, collectibles, and new merchandise. The outdoor farmer's market sells fresh vegetables, fruits and flowers. Permanent food concessions and handicapped-accessible restrooms are on the premises.
DEALER RATES: $25 per 12' × 24' space per weekend outside, first come, first served; $50–$80 per 8' × 10' booth inside per weekend, reservations required. Office hours are Monday through Friday 8:00 AM–4:00 PM.
CONTACT: Scott T Niles, 7 Mile Fair Inc, PO Box 7, Caledonia WI 53108-0007. Tel: (414) 835-2177.

CEDARBURG

Maxwell Street Days

DATES: Four shows a year. Always the last Sunday in May and July, Labor Day Monday, first Sunday in October. Rain or shine.
TIMES: 6:00 AM to between 2:00–3:30 PM. (Sorry, no more flashlight hours.)
ADMISSION: Free. Parking $2 on the Park grounds.
LOCATION: Firemen's Park. 796 N Washington Ave. Follow the cars (or pedestrians) and if you find an empty parking space—*grab it!*
DESCRIPTION: This is an all-volunteer non-paid firemen-run market and the main fundraiser for the Cedarburg Fire Department. (The American Legion gets the parking money as their fundraiser.) Opened in the 1960s, it is one of the largest markets in the Midwest. There are 1,150 spaces for dealers. Representative of what is sold includes: lots of antiques and collectibles (no animals, firearms or fireworks), junk, flea market goodies, fresh produce, garage sales, a signmaker, a construction company selling gazebos, and a siding company plying their trade. Some spaces have been property settlements in divorce cases! The firemen handle all the food concessions, including specialties like bratwurst, sauerkraut, pizza (okay, this is the local Booster Club's effort), health food, ice cream, and the usual fare.
DEALER RATES: $30 and up per space per event. Reservations are absolutely necessary. Their waiting list reached 500! Keep trying, it is worth the wait. They do have a postcard drawing for vacant spaces. Send your name, address and phone to the address below. Or call the number and follow instructions on the tape message.
CONTACT: Cedarburg Firemen's Park, PO Box 344, Cedarburg WI 53012-0344. Tel: (414) 377-8412.

EAGLE RIVER

ERRA Flea Market

DATES: Sunday of Labor Day weekend.
TIMES: 8:00 AM–4:00 PM.
ADMISSION: $1. Parking is free.
LOCATION: Eagle River Recreation Arena. One mile east of Eagle River on Rt 70.
DESCRIPTION: Started in 1989 to celebrate the last weekend of the summer season, this market of 100-plus vendors sells antiques, collectibles, new merchandise, junk, tools, crafts and whatever. This area is a summer resort attracting thousands of visitors from all over the country. They close out the season having a field day checking out and buying new "finds." Food is available on the premises.
DEALER RATES: $29.50 per space. Reservations are suggested.
CONTACT: Zurko's Midwest Promotions, 211 W Green Bay St, Shawano WI 54166. Call Eileen Potasnik or Bob Zurko at (715) 526-9769. Fax: (715) 524-5675.

HATFIELD

Giant Flea Market and Crafts at Thunderbird Village

DATES: Memorial Day weekend; July 4th weekend; August 8–9 (second weekend); Labor Day weekend. The holiday weekends are all three days.
TIMES: Sunup to sundown.
ADMISSION: Free. Parking is free.
LOCATION: Thunderbird Village behind the Museum in downtown Hatfield. Just 12 miles NE of Black River Falls on County Trunk E or 6 miles SE of Merrillan on County Trunk K.
DESCRIPTION: For more than 30 years the Thunderbird Museum has held this market for approximately 180 dealers on the grounds of their museum. Amid towering pines, shoppers can browse through loads of antiques, collectibles, crafts, in-season produce, garage sale goodies and some new merchandise. The Thunderbird Eatery, Brenda's Fry Bread and several other food concessions satisfy the hunger pangs. Restrooms add to the amenities. This market is in a summer resort area next to Lake Arbutus with plenty of camping, restaurants and an Indian casino nearby.
DEALER RATES: $10 and up depending on lot size (depends on the number of trees on the space and vehicle size), maximum 25' long. Electricity is available at $2 per day. Reservations are requested.

CONTACT: Bob and Ellen Flood, Thunderbird Museum, Hatfield N9517 Thunderbird Ln, Merrillan WI 54754-8033. Tel: summer (715) 333-5841; winter (909) 735-3171.

HAYWARD

Hayward Fame Flea Market

DATES: Every Tuesday and Wednesday during June, July and August. They have four special events: Memorial and Labor Day weekends, Log Rolling weekend; and the weekend before July 4th and July 4th itself. Call for dates.

TIMES: 7:30 AM–4:00 PM.

ADMISSION: Free admission and free parking.

LOCATION: Junction of Hwy 27 South and Hwy B.

DESCRIPTION: This outdoor flea market, started in 1978, is located across from the National Fishing Hall of Fame. It attracts between 70 and 80 dealers in the summer who sell antiques, collectibles, crafts, and new and used merchandise. A world log rolling contest is held two blocks down the street from this market. Food is available and there are handicapped-accessible restrooms.

DEALER RATES: $8 per 12' × 25' booth. Reservations are suggested.

CONTACT: Jan Thiry, Rt 10 Box 195, Hayward WI 54843. Tel: (715) 634-4794.

KENOSHA

Kenosha Flea Market

DATES: Friday, Saturday and Sunday, year round.

TIMES: Friday 10:00 AM–5:00 PM; Saturday and Sunday 9:00 AM–5:00 PM; Christmas season hours are longer.

ADMISSION: Free. Parking is also free.

LOCATION: 5535 22nd Avenue.

DESCRIPTION: Started in 1985 this small, but solid, market has 40 vendors selling some antiques, collectibles, handmade decorated dolls and clothing, fresh produce, new appliances, more new merchandise, jewelry, household goods, electronics, and more. The variety of items changes as dealers leave and are replaced with different dealers and merchandise.

DEALER RATES: $20 and up depending on booth, location and size. Reservations are required, as they are currently full.

CONTACT: Beth or Don Goll, 5535 22nd Ave, Kenosha WI 53140. Tel: (414) 658-3532.

LADYSMITH

Van Wey's Community Auction and Flea Market

DATES: April 20-something through last weekend in October, plus two-day holiday markets. Now held on either Saturday or Sunday, two or three times a month. Do call or write for the dates.

TIMES: 6:30 AM to sun-down.

ADMISSION: Free. $.50 per vehicle parking.

LOCATION: On Hwy 8, 4½ miles west of Ladysmith.

DESCRIPTION: Now run by the third generation of the same family, this outdoor market began as a small community consignment auction on April 20, 1926, and had operated until 1996 on the fifth and twentieth of summer months, as these are the farmers' paydays from the local creamery. When the paydays changed, the market did too. Now the market is held on weekends, by popular demand. The flea market originally developed beside the auction and now has grown to attract nearly 200 dealers at peak season, along with thousands of shoppers from all over the country. As far as the range of items available, the managers have commented boldly that, "If you don't find it here you don't need it." Aside from the standard flea market fare, antiques, collectibles, auto parts, farm machinery, used clothing, and fresh farm products are available, along with miscellaneous and new merchandise. An auction starts at 10:00 AM on market days. A lunch stand and restrooms are available.

DEALER RATES: $8 or $10 per 14' × 20' space. Reservations are not required.

CONTACT: Mark and Judy Van Wey, W10139 Van Wey Ln, Ladysmith WI 54848. Tel: (715) 532-6044. Send a self-addressed stamped envelope for a schedule card of dates.

MILWAUKEE

Rummage-O-Rama

DATES: The schedule generally follows these weekends depending on holidays: January 1st weekend, February 1st and 3rd, March 3rd, April 2nd, May 3rd, September 2nd, October 1st and 3rd, November 3rd, December 1st and 3rd. For 1998: January 3–4, 31–February 1, 21–22, March 14–15, April 18–19, May 16–17, September 12–13, October 3–4, 17–18, November 7–8, 21–22, December 5–6, 19–20. Call for 1999 dates.

TIMES: 10:00 AM–5:00 PM.

ADMISSION: $1.50–$1.75; seniors $1–$1.25; children 12–16 $.50; under 12 is free. Parking is free.
LOCATION: State Fair Park Grounds in Milwaukee. Off I-94, Exit 306.
DESCRIPTION: Started in 1973, classified as the "largest indoor show in the Midwest" and rated "one of the top ten in the USA," this market has 450–750 dealers selling antiques, collectibles, flea market treasures, new clothes, rummage goods, crafts, oak furniture, reproduction furniture, and a bit of everything including a kitchen sink. The dealers must stand behind their products, with a refund or replacement for new goods sold. This is such a family market/local affair that events are planned around these market dates, including weddings! Early birds come and line up their purses and bags to hold their places in line while they go chat and catch up on local gossip. An excellent biergarten restaurant serves luscious meals including sauerkraut and sausages, as well as booths selling home-made sausages and cheeses and low-cholesterol cookies. "Candid Camera" made an appearance here in September 1992 for one of their shows.
DEALER RATES: $63–$75 for a 10' × 10' space per weekend. Reservations are required.
CONTACT: Rummage-O-Rama, 18445 Weest Coffee Rd, New Berlin WI 53146. Tel: (414) 521-2111.

There's a lesson here somewhere—

One dealer has discovered and purchased, inexpensively from this market, plenty of paintings that he has turned around and sold for over $10,000 each.

OCONTO

Copperfest 98

7th Annual Flea Market

DATES: The second Saturday in June. Same weekend in 1999.
TIMES: 8:00 AM–4:00 PM.
ADMISSION: Free. Parking is free.
LOCATION: Watch for the signs, turn east on Main St at the stop and go lights, 1 block off Main.
DESCRIPTION: This market of about 40 dealers is part of the annual Copperfest celebrated by the entire town of Oconto. Put on by the Business Association and Jaycees with a parade, flea market, and the grand festival which runs from late Thursday through Sunday evening. The town is on

Green Bay on the shores of Lake Superior. Watch for the decorated-with-lights boats in the Venetian Boat Parade on the water after dark. Over 12,000 people view the ground parade through downtown Oconto. Occasionally, the local Native Americans sell their own traditional foods and artifacts as dealers. There's a craft show as part of this festival. A country music pick-off is sponsored by a local tavern. Dealers sell handmade goods, antiques, collectibles and garage sale stuff.
DEALER RATES: $15 for a 20' × 20' space. Reservations are required. This rate will be confirmed by the market managers by market time.
CONTACT: Ed or Marlene Zahn, 110 Brazeau Ave, Oconto WI 54153 or Oconto Area Chamber of Commerce, PO Box 174, Oconto WI 54153-0174. Tel: (920) 834-2255.

> In 1963 Indian burial grounds were found nearby. Money was needed to preserve this treasure. So the City of Oconto decided to hold a festival to raise funds for this preservation work. The Copperfest has been a tradition since 1982.

SHAWANO

Shawano County Fairgrounds Flea Market

DATES: Every Sunday, April through October, except Labor Day weekend (when they hold their Eagle River ERRA market).
TIMES: Dawn-4:00 PM.
ADMISSION: $1 per person Sunday. Free parking (200 spaces).
LOCATION: Shawano County Fairgrounds. On Hwy 29, a 30-minute drive west of Green Bay.
DESCRIPTION: This outdoor market has been around since 1972 and attracts over 200-plus dealers as well as thousands of tourists seeking bargains on such items as folk art, advertising items, antiques, tools, produce, gift items, fresh produce, etc. Special events include a "Super-Special" Memorial Day sale, a "Special Chicken Picnic" in mid-July, a July 4th "Big Bang" annual sale, stock car races every Saturday evening, three Indian casinos and many other attractions. Campgrounds and hotels are available nearby, and there are lots of food sellers, including popcorn and barbecue. Toilets are available.
DEALER RATES: $21.50 for a 20' × 15' space. Reservations are not required.

CONTACT: Zurko's Midwest Promotions, 211 W Green Bay St, Shawano WI 54166. Call Eileen Potasnik or Bob Zurko at (715) 526-9769. Fax: (715) 524-5675.

ST. CROIX FALLS

Pea Pickin' Flea Mart

DATES: Saturday and Sunday and holidays, starting the third weekend in April through third weekend in October.
TIMES: 6:00 AM–5:00 PM.
ADMISSION: Free. Free parking is provided.
LOCATION: On Hwy 8, 5 miles east of St. Croix Falls near the junction of Rt 35N.
DESCRIPTION: This indoor/outdoor market has been in business since 1968 selling a "good variety of things" including new and used merchandise, fresh produce, and "sophisticated junque." Dealers and shoppers come from all over, and camping space is provided for those who want to come on Friday afternoon and spend the night. There is plenty of food available, including a taco stand and snack bar with mini doughnuts and popcorn. Toilet facilities are available.
DEALER RATES: $8 per day. Reservations are suggested.
CONTACT: Steve and Judy Hansen, 1938 Little Blake Ln, Luck WI 54853. Tel: (715) 857-5479 or 483-9460.

WAUTOMA

Wautoma Flea Market

DATES: Saturday and Sunday, mid-April through October; Sundays, October through early November; weather permitting.
TIMES: Saturday 7:00 AM–dusk; Sunday 6:00 AM–dusk.
ADMISSION: Free admission and free parking.
LOCATION: Junction of Hwys 21 and 73, 1 mile east of Wautoma.
DESCRIPTION: Since 1978 this outdoor flea market has been located in "the Christmas Tree Capital of the World." Enjoying a reputation as a friendly market, it attracts approximately 20 dealers on Saturday and 50 on Sunday offering antiques, collectibles, handmade crafts, vegetables, new merchandise, furniture, and rummage items. Food is available. Historic Waushara County boasts an abundance of outdoor recreation facilities, including 96 lakes, 151 miles of trout streams, fine restaurants, a challenging 18-hole golf course open to the public, and a historical museum.

DEALER RATES: $8 for a booth measuring 22 feet. Space is allocated on a first come, first served basis.
CONTACT: Milton F Sommer, Rt 4 Box 42, Wautoma WI 54982. Tel: (414) 787-2300.

OTHER FLEA MARKETS

We know or have heard about these markets, but have not personally contacted each one, as we have the markets with descriptions. If you plan to visit one of these markets listed below, *please call first* to make sure they are still open. Flea markets do come and go. While they were open when we went to press, they may not be later. We can't be responsible. *Call first!*

Cable: Corner Flea Market. Tel: 715-798-3471.
Chippewa Falls: Jerry's Flea Market, 2375 Joles Ave. Tel: 715-726-0460.
Fort Atkinson: Frank's Flea Market, 28 S Water St W. Tel: 414-568-1111.
Janesville: Janesville Flea Market, 3030 S Cty Tk. Tel: 608-755-9830.
Janesville: Red Carpet Flea Market, 3663 N Hackbarth Rd. Tel: 608-756-9878.
Kenosha: Kenosha Flea Market, 5535 22nd Ave. Tel: 414-658-3532.
Merrill: Nancy's Mini Flea Mart, 813 E 1st St. Tel: 715-536-9165.
Superior: Superior Flea Market, 1007 Tower Ave. Tel: 715-392-6661.
Wild Rose: Wild Rose Flea Market & Craft Fair, 350 Cty Rd G & H. Tel: 414-622-4949.

WYOMING

CASPER

Antique Show and Sale

DATES: The first full weekend in June and October.
TIMES: Saturday 10:00 AM–5:00 PM; Sunday 10:00 AM–4:00 PM.
ADMISSION: $1.25 per person. Free parking is provided.
LOCATION: Central Wyoming Fairgrounds. Take CY Ave (Hwy 220) from downtown Casper.
DESCRIPTION: This indoor show began in 1971 and currently draws a select 40 dealers selling only antiques and collectibles. Run by a non-profit organization, The Casper Antique and Collectors Club, which donates to Wyoming museums and other charities, this show is said to be among the largest in the state. Food is served on the grounds.
DEALER RATES: $25 per 8' table, 4-table minimum. Reservations are required. There is a long waiting list.
CONTACT: Casper Antique and Collectors Club Inc, c/o Bruce Smith, 1625 S Kenwood, Casper WY 82601-4049. Tel: (307) 234-6663.

Casper Flea Market

DATES: March, August and November. Call for dates.
TIMES: Saturday 10:00 AM–5:00 PM; Sunday 10:00 AM–4:00 PM.
ADMISSION: $.50. Parking is free.
LOCATION: Central Wyoming Fairgrounds. Take CY Ave (Hwy 220) from downtown Casper.
DESCRIPTION: Started in 1974, this indoor flea market is sponsored by the Casper Antique and Collectors Club, a non-profit organization. Forty-five dealers gather to trade in antiques, collectibles and miscellaneous items.
DEALER RATES: $20 per 8' table. Reservations are required.
CONTACT: Casper Antique and Collectors Club Inc, c/o Bruce Smith, 1625 S Kenwood, Casper WY 82601-4049. Tel: (307) 234-6663.

CHEYENNE

The Bargain Barn

DATES: Daily.
TIMES: Monday through Saturday 10:00 AM–6:00 PM; Sunday 12:00 PM–5:00 PM.
ADMISSION: Free. Free parking is also available.

LOCATION: 2112 Snyder Ave.
DESCRIPTION: This small indoor shop of 35 dealers started in 1987 offering antiques, collectibles, new merchandise, as well as tools, costume jewelry, books, records and used furniture. "Frontier Days, the World's Largest Outdoor Rodeo" is held in Cheyenne the last full week in July.
DEALER RATES: $120 per 9' x 10' booth per month, $110 per 9' × 9' space plus 5% of dealer sales.
CONTACT: Bill M Lucas, 2112 Snyder Ave, Cheyenne WY 82001. Tel: (307) 635-2844.

JACKSON HOLE

Mangy Moose Antique Show and Sale

DATES: Annually, the second weekend in July. Rain or shine. Call for specific dates. They have added another show, Arts and Antiques at the Mangy Moose, the third weekend in August.
TIMES: 9:00 AM–7:00 PM.
ADMISSION: Free. Free parking is available.
LOCATION: In Teton Village, behind the Mangy Moose Restaurant at the base of the gondola to the Tetons.
DESCRIPTION: This outdoor show opened in 1985 and is considered Wyoming's biggest and best antique show. It currently accommodates approximately 95 dealers and is growing fast. This show specializes in fine antiques; dealers display furniture, carpets, jewelry, dolls, accessories, china, silver, Indian items, vintage clothes, books, and much more. All of this is sponsored by the Mangy Moose Restaurant. Food is served on the premises. Jackson Hole, in the heart of the Tetons, offers gondola rides to the top, horseback riding, white water trips, and "the greatest golf in the US."
DEALER RATES: $165 per 10' × 12' space, for all three days. Reservations are required. Bring your own canopy and set up or there are a limited number of canopies for rent.
CONTACT: Jan Perkins or Jeffrey, 2902 Breneman St, Boise ID 83703. Tel: (208) 345-0755 or 368-9759. Day of show call (307) 733-4913.

OTHER FLEA MARKETS

We know or have heard about these markets, but have not personally contacted each one, as we have the markets with descriptions. If you plan to visit one of these markets listed below, *please call first* to make sure they are still open. Flea markets do come and go. While they were open when we went to press, they may not be later. We can't be responsible. *Call first!*

Cheyenne: Avenues Flea Market & Auction Inc, 315-1 E 7th Ave #2. Tel: 307-635-5600.

Cheyenne: Downtown Flea Market, 312 W 17th St. Tel: 307-638-3751.

Cheyenne: Frontier Flea Market, 1515 Carey Ave. Tel: 307-634-4004.

Cheyenne: Rent A Space Flea Market, 715 S Greeley Hwy. Tel: 307-635-6025.

Cheyenne: Tee Pee Flea Market, 3208 S Greeley Hwy. Tel: 307-778-8312.

Laramie: Golden Flea Gallery, 725 Skyline Rd. Tel: Tel: 307-745-7055.

Canada and International Markets

CANADA

BRITISH COLUMBIA

CLEARBROOKE

Abbottsford Flea Market

DATES: Sunday.
TIMES: 5:00 AM–4:00 PM.
LOCATION: Exhibition Park
CONTACT: Tel: (604) 859-7540.

SURREY

HiWay 10 Flea Market

DATES: Saturday and Sunday.
TIMES: 9:00 AM–5:00 PM.
ADMISSION: Free. Parking is free.
LOCATION: 17790 56th Ave Hwy 10.
DESCRIPTION: This market of 300 tables has dealers selling everything including antiques, collectibles, crafts, coins, cards, toys, clothing and new merchandise.
CONTACT: Larry Williams, HiWay 10 Flea Market, 17790 56 Ave. Hwy 10, Surrey, British Columbia V3S 1E2. Tel and Fax: (604) 594-3808.

Surrey Public Market

DATES: Daily.
TIMES: 9:30 AM–6:00 PM.
ADMISSION: Free. Parking is free.
LOCATION: 6388 King George Hwy. At the corner of King George Hwy and 64th.
DESCRIPTION: This lively indoor market of 150 tables, and quite a few other markets (fish, meat, crafts, books and tobacco) is generally full of dealers selling antiques, collectibles, new merchandise and just about everything else. Two restaurants feed the famished. And the views are quite scenic. Try your lunch out on the balcony, accompanied by the sound of rushing water as the river meanders by under the forest canopy.
DEALER RATES: $9.50 per space on weekends, $4.50 weekdays.
CONTACT: Surrey Public Market, 6388 King George Hwy, Surrey BC V3X 1E9. Tel: (604) 596-8899.

ONTARIO

BARRIE

The 400 Market, Inc

DATES: Saturday and Sunday.
TIMES: 9:00 AM–5:00 PM.
LOCATION: Exit 85 Innisfil Beach Road, Hwy 400.
DESCRIPTION: This market of 300 dealers, as per others, sells just about everything including antiques, collectibles and new merchandise.
CONTACT: Tel: (705) 436-1010.

BROCKVILLE

The Market

DATES: Saturday and Sunday.
TIMES: 9:00 AM–4:00 PM.
ADMISSION: Free. Parking is free.
LOCATION: 175 King St West.
DESCRIPTION: This market of 10 vendors specializes in antique and collectibles. It is obviously a tiny but thriving local market. If you stop by, find and say "Hi" to Anna!
DEALER RATES: $25 per space.

Traders Post Flea Market

DATES: Saturday and Sunday.
TIMES: 9:00 AM–4:00 PM.
ADMISSION: Free. Parking is free.
LOCATION: 14 Courthouse Ave.
DESCRIPTION: This market of 10 vendors specializes in antiques and collectibles. Another thriving local market—Anna comes here, too.
DEALER RATES: $25 per space.

> Occasionally, a local gent feels lonely. His cure? He puts out a sign reading, "John's Flea Market." Within minutes, someone is bound to stop to chat. If you see the sign—stop and say, "Hi!"

MISSISSAUGA

Fantastic Flea Market

DATES: Saturday and Sunday.
TIMES: 10:00 AM–5:00 PM.
ADMISSION: Free. Parking is free.
LOCATION: Dixie Mall, QEW and Dixie Rd.
DESCRIPTION: This market of 100 dealers is strictly a flea market in every sense of the word. They sell plenty of old goodies as well as new merchandise. Its sister market is in North York.
CONTACT: Fantastic Flea Market, 1250 S Service Rd, Mississauga, Ontario O5E 1V4, Canada. Tel: (905) 274-9403.

NORTH YORK

Fantastic Flea Market

DATES: Saturday and Sunday for the flea market.
TIMES: 10:00 AM–6:00 PM for the flea market, every day but Monday 10:00 AM–8:00 PM as a regular retail outlet.
ADMISSION: Free. Parking is free.
LOCATION: 2375 Steels Ave West.
DESCRIPTION: On weekends, they open up folding doors and turn the place into a huge flea market with up to 150 dealers selling just about everything you can imagine. During the week they are the Steels West Marketplace.
CONTACT: Fantastic Flea Market, 2375 Steels Ave W. North York, Ontario M3J 3A8. Tel: (416) 650-1090.

STOUFFVILLE

Stouffville Country Flea Market

DATES: Saturday and Sunday.
TIMES: Saturday 8:00 AM–4:00 PM, Sunday 9:00 AM–5:00 PM.
ADMISSION: Free. Parking is free.
LOCATION: 12555 Tenth Line North (Hwy 47 N).
DESCRIPTION: This is a flea market in every sense of the word with 300 to 400 dealers selling loads of stuff. Last year they opened a new building housing a food court and food vendors including a butcher, baker, deli, fresh fruit, and other goodies. I'm told the lasagna is superb.
DEALER RATES: From $40 per day. Reservations are required.

CONTACT: Stouffville Country Flea Market, 12555 Tenth Line North (Hwy 47 N), Stouffville, Ontario L4A 7Z6. Tel: (905) 640-3813.

TORONTO

Dr Flea's Hwy 27 & Albion Flea Market

DATES: Saturday and Sunday.
TIMES: 10:00 AM–5:00 PM.
ADMISSION: Free. Parking is free.
LOCATION: From Toronto—take Hwy 401 to Dixon Rd. Exit (near the airport) to Hwy 27 N. From there it is about a 10–15 minute drive. It would be hard to miss with its 35-foot-tall flea on the top of the building.
DESCRIPTION: This market of 400 vendors sells everything including antiques, collectibles and new merchandise.
DEALER RATES: $375 per month and up.
CONTACT: Dr Flea's Hwy 27 & Albion Flea Market, 8 Westmore Dr, Rexdale, Toronto, Ontario. Tel: (416) 745-FLEA (3532). Fax: (416) 745-7193. Email: drflea@idirect.com.

QUÉBEC

BROMONT

Marché aux Puces de Bromont

DATES: First Sunday of May through second Sunday of November.
TIMES: 9:00 AM–5:00 PM.
ADMISSION: Free. Parking is free.
LOCATION: Motorway 10 at Bromont.
DESCRIPTION: This indoor market's 350 dealers sell crafts, produce, garage sale finds, furniture, coins, stamps, cards, and new merchandise. Nearby: factory outlets, chocolate museum, vineyards.

MONTREAL

Super Mercado

DATES: Thursday through Sunday, year round.
TIMES: 9:00 AM–5:00 PM.
ADMISSION: Free.
LOCATION: Brossard, just south of Montreal.
DESCRIPTION: This is the "hot" place to shop around Montreal— which means it is very crowded. While they don't sell antiques, per se, they do sell just about anything else.

SAINT EUSTACHE

Marché aux Puces de Saint Eustache

DATES: Thursday through Sunday.
TIMES: 9:00 AM–5:00 PM.
ADMISSION: Free. Parking is free.
LOCATION: Road 640 West. Just north of Montreal, 3 miles before Saint Eustache.
DESCRIPTION: This year-round indoor/outdoor market's dealers sell antiques, collectibles, crafts, produce, garage sale finds, furniture, new merchandise, stamps, coins, and cards among other things. This is one of the biggest markets around and apparently crammed full of customers on Sundays. So beat the crowd and go another day.

INTERNATIONAL

A note about European markets in the big cities: Generally everyone just walks about the market—no admission fees—and in the cities, take the subway and save yourself a lot of aggravation.

In Paris, the market seems to run all daylight hours depending on whether you are visiting shops or wandering among the street vendors.

In England, all the markets I have personally visited or my friends have checked and visited lasted through the mornings only. Most of the fun and excitement was gone after lunch, although there may be a few stragglers.

In the provincal markets, Saturdays are the day—usually a farmer's market in season, like in the small town of Jonquières in Provence with the woman selling homemade goat's cheese out of the back end of a small pickup truck, or the occasional roving market like the one we happened upon in northern Germany.

I haven't put any times and admission information in with the listings, therefore, unless it was pertinent.

FRANCE

PARIS

Marché aux Puces

DATES: Saturday through Monday, year round.
TIMES: Daylight and then some; just get there.
LOCATION: Outside the Porte de Clignancourt Metro station (Line 4—Porte D'Orleans to Porte de Clignancourt). Just about due north at the edge of Paris.
DESCRIPTION: This market, started last century when people gathered to sell old clothes, is an institution. Visitors used to eat french fries and dance the polka. In the twenties, masterpiece paintings were found by chance here and made the market famous. Nowadays, it's practically its own village. You can find "anything you want, or don't want, or could ever dream about." You can find the most fabulous antiques and collectibles to the standard flea market t-shirts, bracelets, and whatnots. From food to junque. Vendors are all over the place—on the sidewalks, in shops, filling the streets, wherever. It's a treat. The atmosphere is electric, pulsing, bright, lively, and loud. Hold onto the kids and be prepared to use your elbows.

ENGLAND

LONDON

Bermondsey Market
(aka New Caledonia Market)

DATES: Sundays.
TIMES: 5:00 AM–6:00 AM for the serious dealings, but open all day.
LOCATION: Walk over Tower Bridge (heading south) to the crossroad (past the vinegar factory), turn right and you are there.
DESCRIPTION: This is *the* market in London. The serious antique deals are made here. Just be there very early. If you happen to watch *Lovejoy* on A&E, you'll understand. He mentions this market. It is also the one market where "unauthorized" goods get "legally" traded, according to my source.

Brick Lane Market

DATES: Sundays, year round, 9:00 AM–2:00 PM.
LOCATION: Shoreditch tube station, in the East End.
DESCRIPTION: Described as "straight out of Dickens," "with the best curry in town" by a London friend of mine, although he also describes the area as "Jack-the-Ripper-type." Everything here is second- to fourth-hand, at least.

Camden Lock Market

DATES: Sundays, year round.
LOCATION: Camden Town tube station (Northern Line).
DESCRIPTION: This is the current trendy market selling antiques, clothes, and jewelry. It is getting more popular every year. Traffic can get tricky especially during excellent weather. Take the tube.

Camden Passage (or Walk) Market

DATES: Sundays, year round.
LOCATION: Outside the Angel tube station, turn right, then turn right again.
DESCRIPTION: This outdoor market is mostly shops selling antiques. But they are excellent antiques.

Petticoat Lane

DATES: Sundays, year round.
TIMES: Early to noon, after that the excitement is gone.

LOCATION: Middlesex Street in East End of London. Take the tube to Liverpool Street (take the road facing the station and the road will take you directly to the market), Aldgate or Aldgate East and follow the noise and crowd.
DESCRIPTION: All around the area, vendors are in a garage, on the streets, in shops, wherever. Hold on to anything of yours that you value. Better yet, don't take anything of value with you. This is a granddaddy of markets. Full of new merchandise, used stuff, clothing of all sorts, dishes (you have to see the way the vendors display and demonstrate their wares to believe it—spinning, tossing, balancing—it's a performance!), electronics, the usual flea stuff, literally whatever. Called Petticoat Lane because petticoats were made here a very long time ago.

In the '70s when I was in London, there was a brass band made up of older gents (doing this to raise money for charity) who would play and entertain here. On Wednesdays they entertained us as we boarded the tube for work from the Earl's Court Station. Their band leader would recognize me from Wednesdays and always dance a little jig and wave to say "Hi." I have him immortalized on film.

Portobello Road

DATES: Saturdays, year round for the big market, daily for the shops.
TIMES: Morning is best.
LOCATION: West End of London. Take the tube to Notting Hill Gate.
DESCRIPTION: This was the classic antique and collectible market of London. If you ever saw the movie *Bedknobs and Broomsticks*, this is where the "market" part was filmed. Saturdays is the open air market, otherwise the shops are open normal hours. Now it's rather "old hat."

RUSSIA

MOSCOW

Ismailovsky Park Market

DATES: Saturday and Sunday.
TIMES: All day.
LOCATION: Ismailovsky Park in northeast Moscow. Take the blue Metro line to Ismailovsky Park station. Get out and follow the long lines ambling towards the market.

DESCRIPTION: Another mega market with hundreds and hundreds of vendors at the market, and more poorer vendors lining the way there. All selling everything including nesting dolls, toys, art, Russian everything, wooden spoons and bowls, pins, amber, traditional clothing, linen among others. Advice: take a Russian-speaking friend if you wish to haggle. And don't attempt to take any ancient religious icons with you, they can't leave the country. From an American who frequents this market, it is worth the trip to Moscow for all the sights, smells and sounds.

A Russian friend gave this sage advice "from a Russian reality" for shopping in big Russian flea markets:

1. Never, ever flash any wads of money around. There are people watching foreigners, waiting for them to do this. When they find a mark—a quick push and the money disappears. It is better to stash small amounts in different pockets. Otherwise, as our friend says, "You'll reach for your key and all that's left will be dust and Moscow air."
2. Don't eat the food in these markets—it isn't always cooked thoroughly. The resulting food poisoning can be a serious problem.
3. If not buying souvenirs keep this in mind: "People do not sell things because they are tired of seeing them, they sell them because something is really wrong with their things. So, keep your eyes open and double-check every thing you buy."

RUSSIAN FAR EAST—MAGADAN

Street Market of Magadan

DATES: Saturday and Sunday.
TIMES: Daylight.
LOCATION: 1,000 west of Anchorage, Alaska.
DESCRIPTION: This market of maybe 40-50 dealers is the equivalent of the Super Bowl in Magadan. This is the place to shop. Although, originally it was illegal to hold this market, the police patronized it too. Dealers sell clothing, hardware, and stuff you'd expect to find in a supermarket. Much of the wares come from China and Japan. Americans are welcome.

SPAIN
MADRID

Coin and Stamp Market

DATES: Sundays.
TIMES: Mornings.
LOCATION: Plaza Major (the main Plaza of Madrid).
DESCRIPTION: If you are looking for any type of coin or stamp, this is the place to come. The columns surrounding the plaza are filled with dealers who have hundreds or more items on display. The collection blows the mind.

Rastro

DATES: Every Sunday, forever.
TIMES: Early morning until around 2:00 PM when the place empties.
LOCATION: The Rastro secton of Madrid, on the main road to Toledo.
DESCRIPTION: This monster market has easily thousands of dealers and even more thousands of shoppers spread over miles of main and side roads, up and down the hilly road. It is quite a sight.

CAYMAN ISLANDS

In the Cayman Islands, British West Indies, an unofficial national sport—known locally as Garage Sailing—is trolling the "Leaving the Island Sales." You can snag some real bargains. My friends picked up a $70 dive mask for $5. Start out Saturday morning and cruise through George Town, South Sound, and West Bay or grab a copy of the *Caymanian Compass* and check the listings for lawn sales. Trouble is, getting the goodies back home. Which is why the stuff is being sold in the first place!

HOW TO BE INCLUDED IN THIS DIRECTORY

If you own or operate a flea market and would like to have your market considered for inclusion in the next edition of *The Official® Directory to U.S. Flea Markets*, either write us a letter requesting a questionnaire form or send complete information corresponding to the format currently employed in this directory. Market listings must be complete in order to be considered for publication. For a full explanation of the acceptable format for market listings, refer to the section entitled "How to Use This Book."

Address all mail to:

House of Collectibles
Editorial Department
201 East 50th St
New York NY 10022